PHILIP'S

STRE...S
New...ne
Tyne & Wear

CW00409318

www.philips-maps.co.uk
First published in 2002 by
Philip's, a division of
Octopus Publishing Group Ltd
www.octopusbooks.co.uk
2-4 Heron Quays, London E14 4JP
An Hachette UK Company
www.hachettelivre.co.uk

Third edition 2009
First impression 2009
TWNCA

978-0-540-09297-0 (pocket)

© Philip's 2009

Ordnance Survey®

This product includes mapping data licensed from Ordnance Survey® with the permission of the Controller of Her Majesty's Stationery Office. © Crown copyright 2009. All rights reserved. Licence number 100011710.

Speed camera data provided by **PocketGPSWorld.com Ltd**

Post Office is a trade mark of Post Office Ltd in the UK and other countries.

Printed by Toppan, China

Contents

II   Mobile safety cameras

III   **Key to map symbols**

IV   **Key to map pages**

VI   **Route planning**

VIII   Major administrative and Postcode boundaries

1   **Street maps** at 2⅔ inches to 1 mile

98   **Street maps** of Newcastle upon Tyne and Sunderland at 5⅓ inches to 1 mile

104   **Index** of towns, villages, streets, hospitals, industrial estates, railway stations, schools, shopping centres, universities and places of interest

Digital Data

The exceptionally high-quality mapping found in this atlas is available as digital data in TIFF format, which is easily convertible to other bitmapped (raster) image formats.

The index is also available in digital form as a standard database table. It contains all the details found in the printed index together with the National Grid reference for the map square in which each entry is named.

For further information and to discuss your requirements, please contact victoria.dawbarn@philips-maps.co.uk

Mobile safety cameras

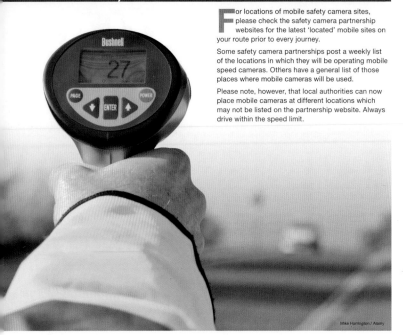

Mike Harrington / Alamy

For locations of mobile safety camera sites, please check the safety camera partnership websites for the latest 'located' mobile sites on your route prior to every journey.

Some safety camera partnerships post a weekly list of the locations in which they will be operating mobile speed cameras. Others have a general list of those places where mobile cameras will be used.

Please note, however, that local authorities can now place mobile cameras at different locations which may not be listed on the partnership website. Always drive within the speed limit.

Useful websites

Northumbria Safer Roads Initiative
www.safespeedforlife.co.uk

Durham Constabulary
www.durham.police.uk/durhamc/central_deps/operations/scu.php

Further information
www.dvla.gov.uk
www.thinkroadsafety.gov.uk
www.dft.gov.uk
www.road-safe.org

Key to map symbols

(22)	Motorway with junction number
	Primary route – dual/single carriageway
	A road – dual/single carriageway
	B road – dual/single carriageway
	Minor road – dual/single carriageway
	Other minor road – dual/single carriageway
	Road under construction
	Tunnel, covered road
(30) (30)	Speed cameras – single, multiple
	Rural track, private road or narrow road in urban area
	Gate or obstruction to traffic – restrictions may not apply at all times or to all vehicles
	Path, bridleway, byway open to all traffic, restricted byway
	Pedestrianised area
BS22	Postcode boundaries
	County or unitary authority boundaries
	Railway with station
	Tunnel
	Railway under construction
	Metro station
	Private railway station
	Miniature railway
	Tramway, tramway under construction
	Tram stop, tram stop under construction
	Bus, coach station

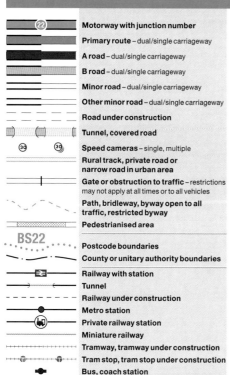

◆	Ambulance station
◆	Coastguard station
◆	Fire station
◆	Police station
✚	Accident and Emergency entrance to hospital
Ⓗ	Hospital
+	Place of worship
🖬	Information centre – open all year
Ⓟ	Shopping centre, parking
P&R	Park and Ride, Post Office
⚑	Camping site, caravan site
▶	Golf course, picnic site
Church ROMAN FORT	Non-Roman antiquity, Roman antiquity
Univ	Important buildings, schools, colleges, universities and hospitals
	Woods, built-up area
River Medway	Water name
	River, weir
	Stream
	Canal, lock, tunnel
	Water
	Tidal water

58 87 246

Adjoining page indicators and overlap bands – the colour of the arrow and band indicates the scale of the adjoining or overlapping page (see scales below)

The dark grey border on the inside edge of some pages indicates that the mapping does not continue onto the adjacent page

The small numbers around the edges of the maps identify the 1-kilometre National Grid lines

Abbreviations

Acad	Academy	Meml	Memorial
Allot Gdns	Allotments	Mon	Monument
Cemy	Cemetery	Mus	Museum
C Ctr	Civic centre	Obsy	Observatory
CH	Club house	Pal	Royal palace
Coll	College	PH	Public house
Crem	Crematorium	Recn Gd	Recreation ground
Ent	Enterprise		
Ex H	Exhibition hall	Resr	Reservoir
Ind Est	Industrial Estate	Ret Pk	Retail park
IRB Sta	Inshore rescue boat station	Sch	School
		Sh Ctr	Shopping centre
Inst	Institute	TH	Town hall / house
Ct	Law court	Trad Est	Trading estate
L Ctr	Leisure centre	Univ	University
LC	Level crossing	W Twr	Water tower
Liby	Library	Wks	Works
Mkt	Market	YH	Youth hostel

Enlarged maps only

	Railway or bus station building
	Place of interest
	Parkland

The map scale on the pages numbered in blue is 2⅔ inches to 1 mile
4.2 cm to 1 km • 1:23 810

0	¼ mile	½ mile	¾ mile	1 mile
0	250m	500m	750m	1km

The map scale on the pages numbered in red is 5⅓ inches to 1 mile
8.4 cm to 1 km • 1:11 900

0	220yds	440yds	660yds	½ mile
0	125m	250m	375m	500m

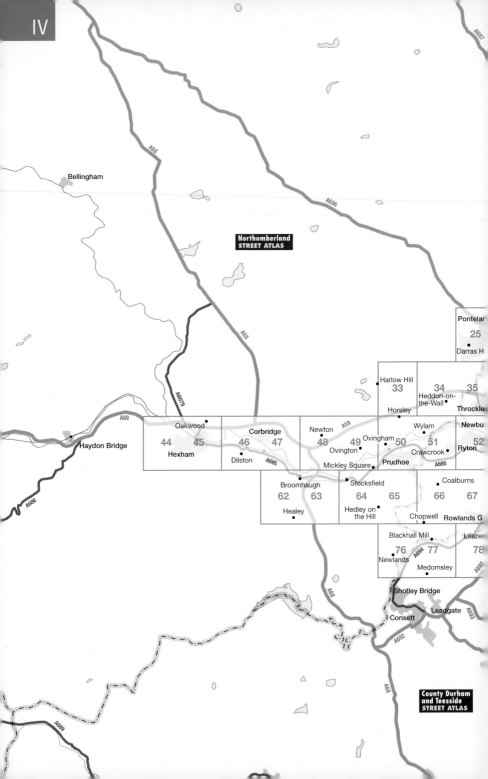

Bellingham

A68

A696

Northumberland
STREET ATLAS

A68

A6079

A69

Oakwood

Haydon Bridge

Harlow Hill
33

34
Heddon-on-
the-Wall

35

Throckle

Pontelar
25
Darras H

Horsley

Corbridge

44 **45**
Hexham

46 **47**

Dilston   A695

Newton

A59

48

Ovingham

Ovington

49

Wylam

50

Crawcrook

51

Newbu

52

Ryton

Mickley Square

Prudhoe

A695

Broomhaugh

62 **63**

Healey

Stocksfield

64 **65**

Hedley on
the Hill

Coalburns

66 **67**

Chopwell   Rowlands G

Blackhall Mill

76 **77**

Newlands

A694

Medomsley

78

Leazes

A692

A697

Shotley Bridge

Consett

Leadgate

A692

A68

A693

A69

County Durham
and Teesside
STREET ATLAS

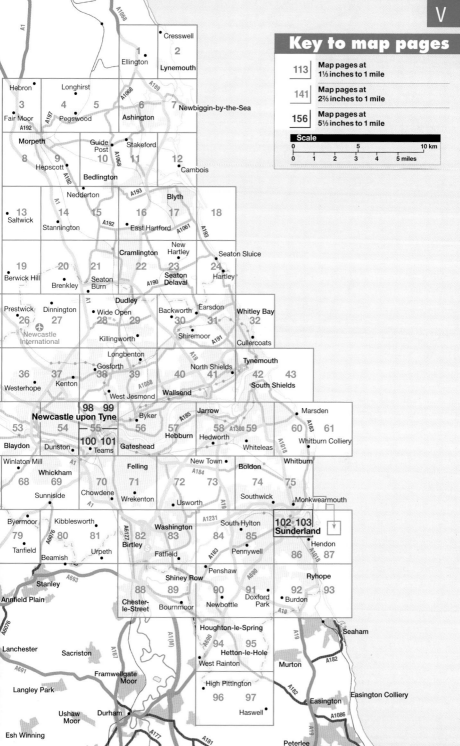

Key to map pages

113	Map pages at 1⅓ inches to 1 mile
141	Map pages at 2⅗ inches to 1 mile
156	Map pages at 5⅓ inches to 1 mile

Scale

0   5   10 km

0   1   2   3   4   5 miles

Cresswell
1 Ellington
2 Lynemouth

Hebron
3 Fair Moor
Longhirst
4 Pegswood
5
6 Ashington
7 Newbiggin-by-the-Sea

Morpeth
8 Hepscott
9
Guide Post
10
Stakeford
11
Bedlington
12 Cambois

Nedderton
13 Saltwick
14 Stannington
15
Blyth
16 East Hartford
17
18

Cramlington
New Hartley
19 Berwick Hill
20 Brenkley
21 Seaton Burn
22
23 Seaton Delaval
24 Hartley
Seaton Sluice

Dudley
Prestwick Dinnington
26
27
Newcastle International
28 Wide Open
29 Killingworth
Backworth Earsdon
30 Shiremoor
31
32 Whitley Bay
Cullercoats

Longbenton
Gosforth
36 Westerhope
37 Kenton
38
39
West Jesmond
North Shields
40 Wallsend
41
Tynemouth
42
43 South Shields

Newcastle upon Tyne
98 99
53 Blaydon
54 Dunston
55
100 101 Teams
56 Byker
57 Hebburn
Jarrow
58 Hedworth
A1300 59 Whiteleas
Marsden
60
61 Whitburn Colliery

Winlaton Mill
Whickham
68 Sunniside
69 Chowdene
70 Wrekenton
71
Felling
72 Usworth
73
New Town
74 Southwick
Boldon
75
Whitburn

Byermoor
79 Tanfield
Kibblesworth
80 Beamish
81 Urpeth
82 Birtley
83 Fatfield
Washington
84
South Hylton
85 Pennywell
102 103 Sunderland
86
87 Hendon

Stanley
Annfield Plain
88 Chester-le-Street
89 Bournmoor
Shiney Row
90 Newbottle
Penshaw
91 Burdon
Doxford Park
92
93 Ryhope

Lanchester
Sacriston
Houghton-le-Spring
94 West Rainton
95 Hetton-le-Hole
Seaham
Murton

Framwellgate Moor
Langley Park
High Pittington
96
97 Haswell
Easington
Easington Colliery

Ushaw Moor
Durham
Esh Winning
Peterlee

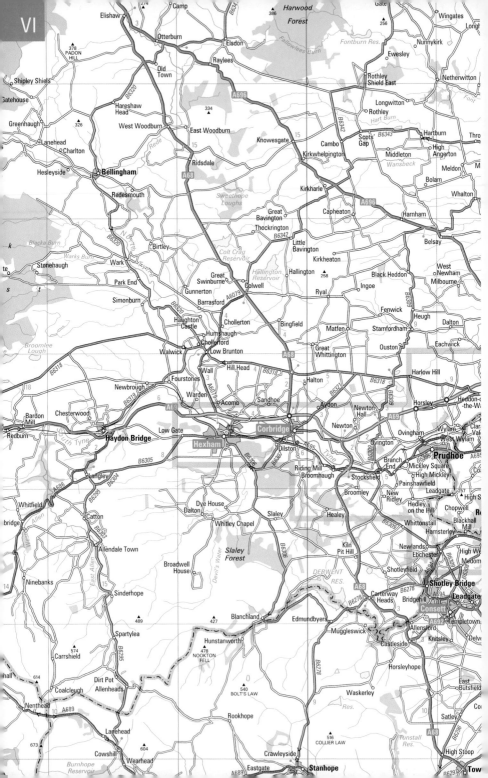

Major administrative and Postcode boundaries

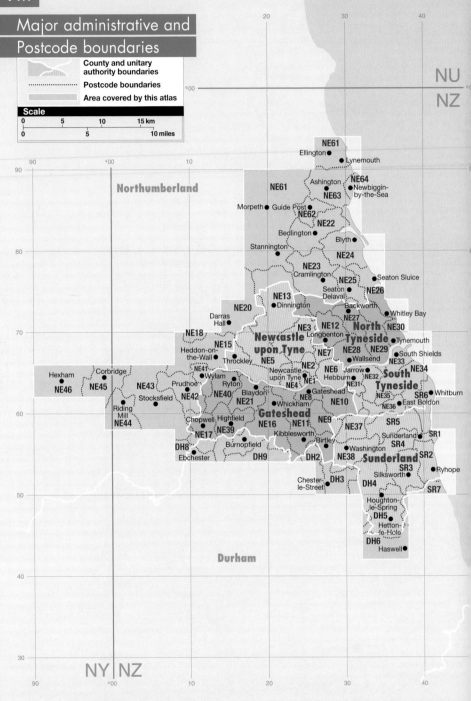

County and unitary authority boundaries
Postcode boundaries
Area covered by this atlas

Scale
0   5   10   15 km
0   5   10 miles

NU
NZ

Northumberland

NE61
Ellington Lynemouth

NE61
Ashington NE64
Newbiggin-by-the-Sea
NE63
Morpeth Guide Post
NE62
NE22
Bedlington
Blyth
NE24
Stannington
NE23
Cramlington NE25
Seaton Sluice
Seaton Delaval NE26
NE13
Dinnington Backworth
Darras Hall NE20 NE27
Whitley Bay
NE18 NE3 NE12 North NE30
Newcastle Longbenton Tyneside
upon Tyne NE7 NE28 NE29 Tynemouth
Heddon-on-the-Wall NE15 Wallsend South Shields
Throckley NE5 NE6 NE33
NE41 NE2 Jarrow NE34
Hexham Corbridge Wylam Newcastle Hebburn South
NE46 NE45 Ryton upon Tyne NE1 NE31 Tyneside
NE43 Prudhoe NE4 NE32 Whitburn
Stocksfield NE42 NE40 Blaydon NE8 NE35 SR6
Riding NE21 Whickham Gateshead East Boldon
Mill NE44 Chopwell Highfield Gateshead NE10 NE36
NE16 NE11 NE9 SR5
NE17 NE39 Kibblesworth NE37 Sunderland SR1
DH8 Burnopfield Birtley SR4
Ebchester DH9 Washington SR2
DH2 NE38 Sunderland SR3
Chester-le-Street DH3 Silksworth Ryhope
DH4 SR7
Houghton-le-Spring
DH5
Hetton-le-Hole
DH6
Haswell

Durham

NY NZ

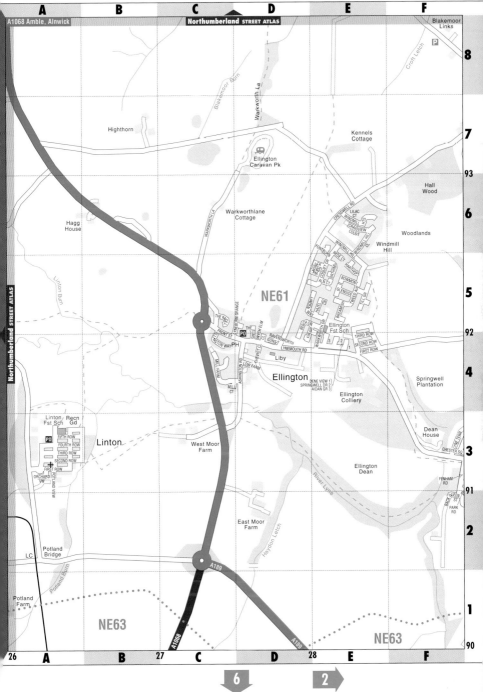

A1068 Amble, Alnwick

Blakemoor Links

Croft Letch

8

93

Highthorn

Kennels Cottage

7

Hall Wood

Warkworth La

Blakemoor Burn

Ellington Caravan Pk

6

Woodlands

Warkworthlane Cottage

WARKWORTH LA

Windmill Hill

Hagg House

NE61

CRESSWELL RD

LILAC
WINDMILL

CRAIGVIEW
COURT

POWBURN

WINDMILL HILL

WINDMILL CT

HAILTHORPE

5

Linton Burn

BOXMOOR

GLENSIDE

92

THE MDT

ASHINGTON GRANGE

THE SNOD
OCK ELM

RAVENSWORTH GONS

Ellington Fst Sch

THIRD ROW

SECOND ROW

FIRST ROW

FRONT ST

PH

DALTON WAY

MILL PKWY

LOW FARM

CHENTLCL

ASHINGTON RD

LYNEMOUTH RD

Liby

Ellington

4

MILL CT

West Moor Farm

DENE VIEW 1
SPRINGWELL DR 2
AIDAN GR 3

Ellington Colliery

Springwell Plantation

Dean House

CHESTER SQ

TYNE TERR

Linton
Fst Sch

Recn Gd

FIFTH ROW
FOURTH ROW
THIRD ROW
SECOND ROW

Linton

River Lyne

Ellington Dean

3

FENHAM RD

91

FIRST ROW

ORCHARD VW

MEA DW

East Moor Farm

Haydon Letch

BACK
QUEEN ST
PARK RD

2

Potland Bridge

LC

A189

A1068

A189

1

Potland Farm

Potland Burn

NE63

NE63

90

26   27   28

A B C D E F

Northumberland STREET ATLAS

A   **B**   **C**   **D**   **E**   **F**

8

7   Cresswell

ST BARTHOLOMEWS
SOUTH SIDE
Sea Lodge

93

6

Snab Point

5

NE61

92

CRESSWELL HOME FARM COTTS
Cresswell Home Farm

4

Chugdon Wood

Bewick Drift

River Lyne

JUBILEE COTTS
CHESTER SQ
CORONATION COTTS
RIVER VIEW
DUNLIN
EDEN TERR
Lynemouth Fst Sch
DALTON AVE
HARLEY TERR
ALBION TERR
GUILDFORD SQ
HENLEY SQ
JERSEY SQ
CHURCH SQ
PO
Lynemouth
MARKET SQ
Liby
QUEEN ST
MATLOCK SQ 1
NEVILLE SQ 2
Sewage Works
Lyne Hill

3

91

2

PARK VIEW

Cemy

Lyne Sands
Power Station

1

NE63

Works

90

29   **A**   **B**   30   **C**   **D**   31   **E**   **F**

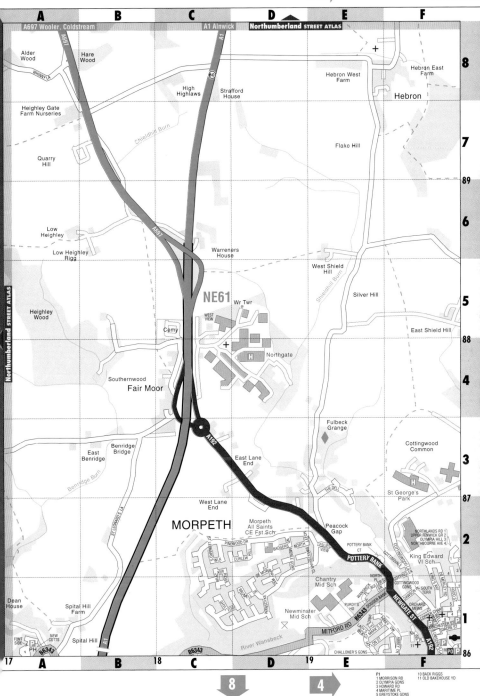

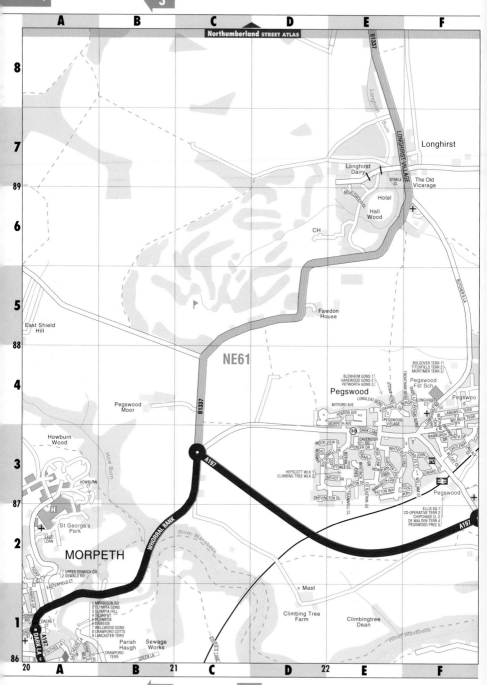

B1337

8

7   Longhirst

Longhirst
Dairy   STABLE   The Old
89   CL   Vicarage

MICKLEWOOD   Hotel
Hall
6   CH   Wood

BUTCHERS LA

5   Fawden
House

East Shield
Hill
88   NE61

BOLSOVER TERR 1
TITCHFIELD TERR 2
MORTIMER TERR 3
BLENHEIM GDNS 1
4   HAREWOOD GDNS 2   Pegswood
PETWORTH GDNS 3   Fst Sch

B1337   Pegswood   LONGLEAT GDNS   Longhirst   Pegswoo
MITFORD AVE   CT

Pegswood   KIRKHABLE CL   LANGWELL TERR
Moor   HEBRON AVE   WELBECK DR
MORPETH AVE   PEGSWOOD
Howburn   VILLAGE
Wood   DARK LANE   BAMBURGH
MOOR VIEW CL   CAVENDISH   DR   CASTLE
HOWBURN   SQ   SPENCER DR   WHITE   DR
CT   JOHN   PO
3   HEPSCOTT WLK 1   CHEVIOT GR   EDWARD ST
CLIMBING TREE WLK 2   STANTON DR
STONE   Pegswood
87   CHEVINGTON CL   TRANWELL CL   WILLIAMS ST
H   ELLIS SQ 1
CO-OPERATIVE TERR 2
St George's   CHIPCHASE CL 3
Park   WHORRAL BANK   DE WALDEN TERR 4
2 EAST   PEGSWOOD PREC 5
LOAN   River Wansbeck   A197

MORPETH
1 UPPER FENWICK GR
2 OSWALD RD   Mast
1 MORRISON RD
2 OLYMPIA GDNS
3 OLYMPIA HILL   Climbing Tree
EASTERFIELD CT   4 SILVA ST   Farm   Climbingtree
5 BURNSIDE   Dean
1   6 DAMSIDE
7 WELLWOOD GDNS
8 CRAWFORD COTTS   River Wansbeck
9 LANCASTER TERR
A197
DARK LA   Parish   Sewage
Haugh   Works
86 CRAWFORD
TERR   GREEN LA

20   A   B   21   C   D   22   E   F

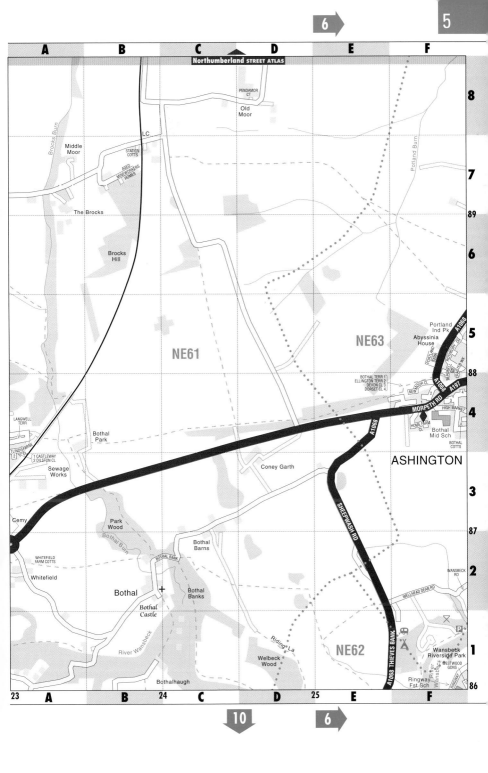

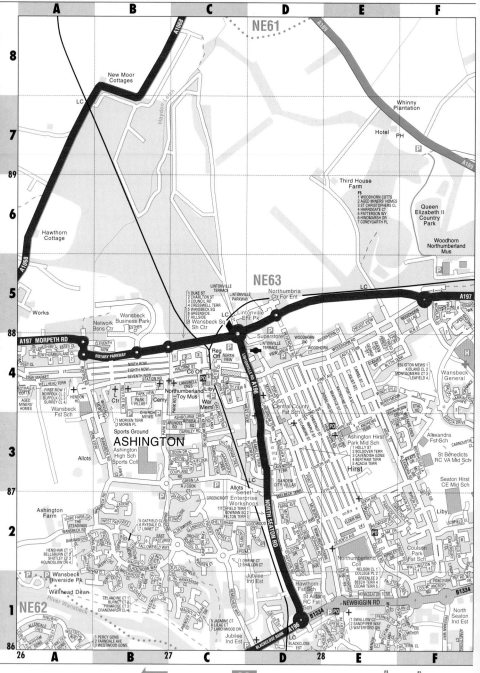

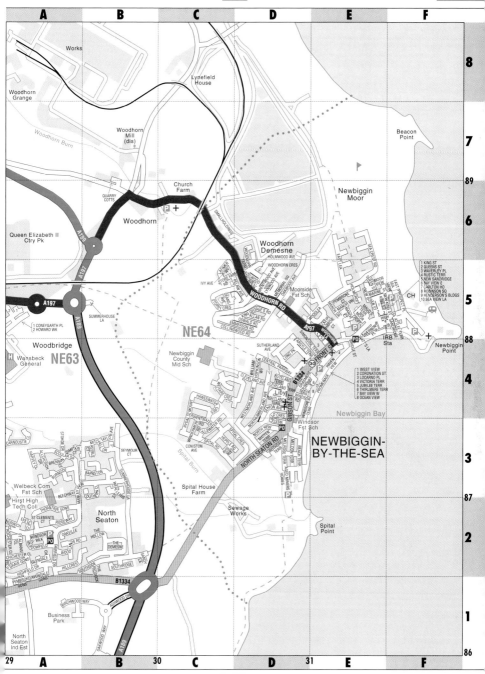

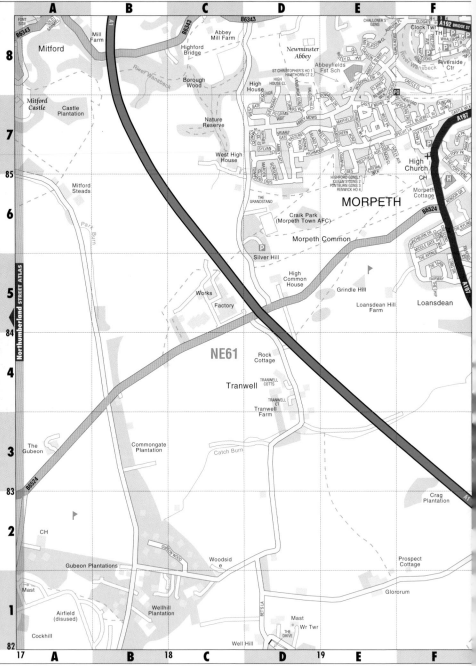

3

Northumberland STREET ATLAS

MORPETH

NE61

Mitford

Mitford Castle

Castle Plantation

Mitford Steads

Mill Farm

Abbey Mill Farm

Highford Bridge

Borough Wood

Nature Reserve

West High House

Newminster Abbey

Abbeyfields Fst Sch

High House

High Church

Morpeth Cottage

THE GRANDSTAND

Craik Park (Morpeth Town AFC)

Morpeth Common

Silver Hill

High Common House

Grindle Hill

Loansdean Hill Farm

Loansdean

Works

Factory

Rock Cottage

Tranwell

TRANWELL COTTS

TRANWELL CT

Tranwell Farm

The Gubeon

Commongate Plantation

Catch Burn

Crag Plantation

CH

Gubeon Plantations

Woodside

Prospect Cottage

Mast

Airfield (disused)

Wellhill Plantation

Cockhill

Mast

Wr Twr

THE DRIVE

Well Hill

Glororum

River Wansbeck

Park Burn

FONT SIDE

Clock Twr

Riverside Ctr

River Wansbeck

13

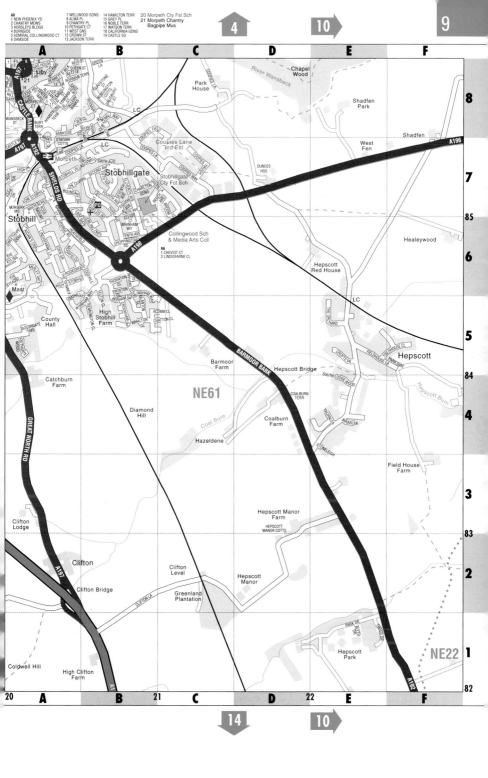

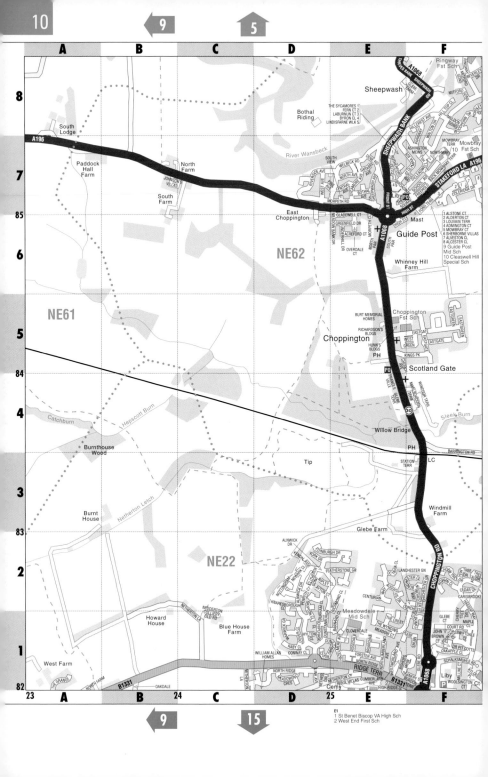

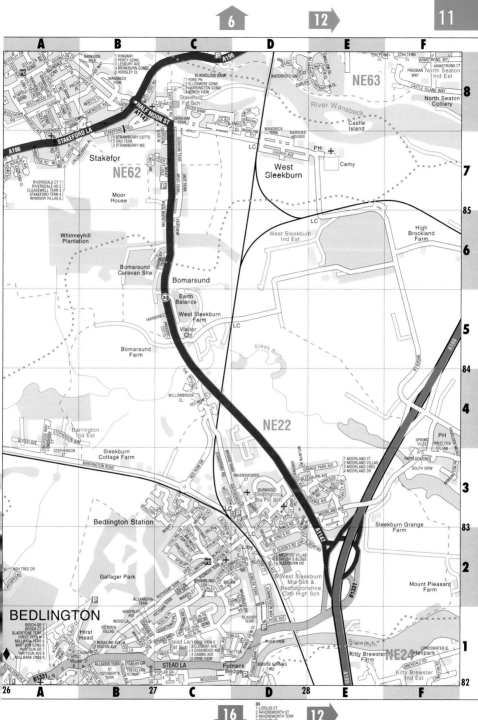

D3
1 LIDDLES CT
2 RAVENSWORTH ST
3 RAVENSWORTH TERR
4 STATION ST
5 WHITLEY TERR
6 MOORLAND COTTS
7 NORTH VIEW
8 EAST VIEW
9 THOMPSON ST

NE63

Ind Est
ARMSTRONG WAY

CASTLE ISLAND WY
WANSBECK ST
LINKS VIEW
SEA VIEW

8

Sandy Bay
Caravan Park

River Wansbeck

7

Works

85

Sewage
Works

6

LC

SOUTH VIEW
NORTH VIEW
WEMBLEY GDNS
WEMBLEY TERR

THE PADDOCKS
WEST LYNN
THE BUCK
LITLEY CT

PADDOCK
ME

Sleekburn
Bsns Ctr

NE24

Cambois

5

Cow Gut

Refuse
Tip

84

Cambois
Fst Sch

LC

4

NE22

NORTHFIELD RD
WILSON AVE
SANDFORD
WATERFORD

1 UNITY TERR
2 RIDLEY TERR
3 AGED MINERS HOMES

East
Sleekburn

HARBOUR
VIEW

SELBOURNE TERR

3

Sleek Burn

WEST BRIDGE

83

2

Factory
Point

River Blyth

Jetties

North
Beach

WEST BRIDGE ST

NE24

Cowpen
New Town

BLYTH

PORTLAND ST 1
THOMPSON ST 2
BALFOUR ST 3
GRIEVE ST 4

1

Mast

Sewage
Works

Kitty Brewster
Ind Est

GRASMERE WAY
CONISTON RD
THIRLMERE WY

COWLEY RD
SPENCER RD
SPENCER CT

1 BUTTERMERE WAY
2 BEECHER ST

TA Ctr

CRAWFORD'S ROW

MALVERN ST
CRESTED ST
LIME ST
WILLOW ST

North
Blyth

5 ARGYLE ST
6 THE CLOSE
7 THOMPSON ST
8 ARGYLE MEWS
9 GOSCHEN ST

82

A193

COWPEN RD

HODGSON'S RD

B1329

B1329

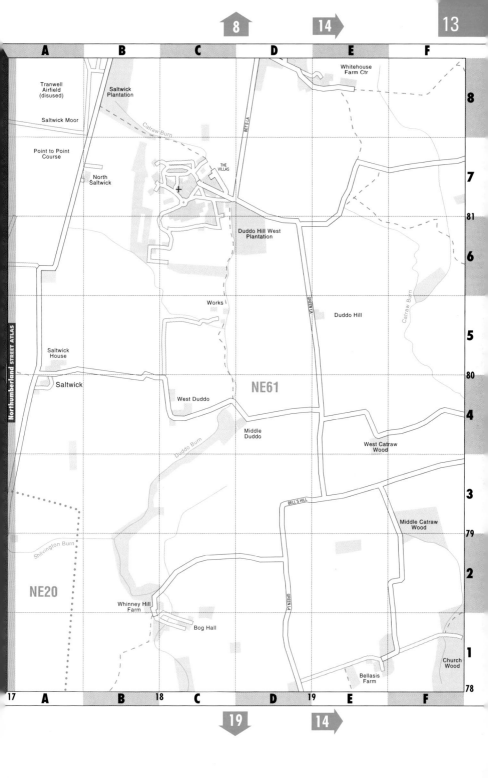

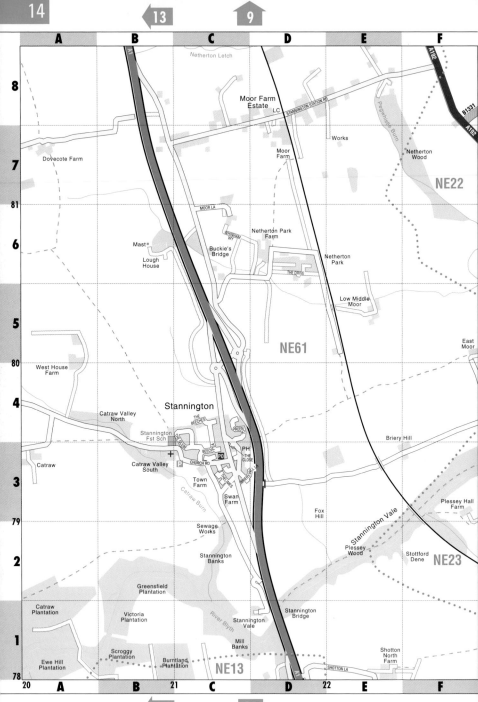

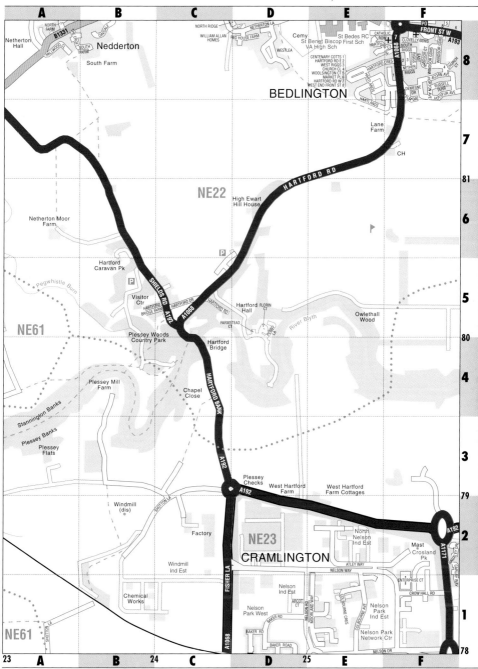

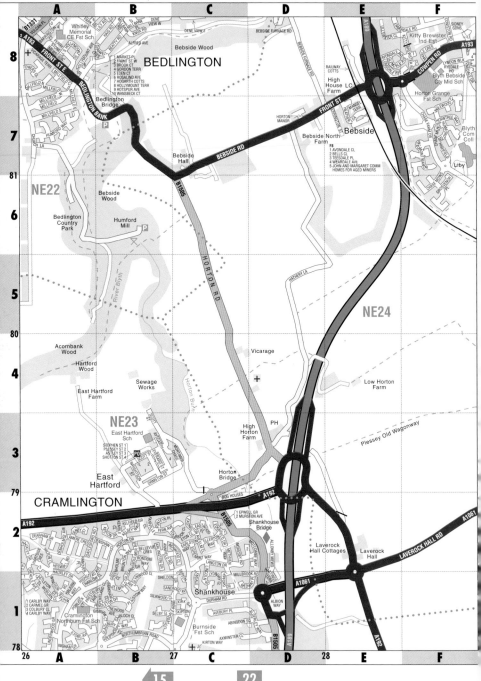

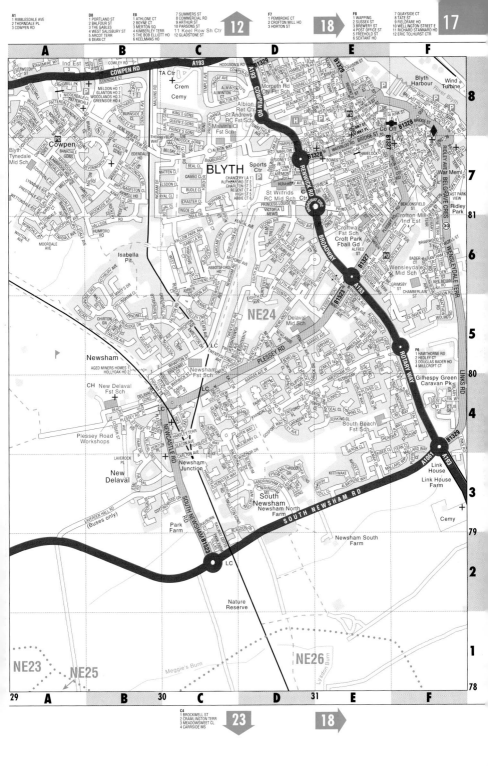

A1
1 RIBBLESDALE AVE
2 THORNDALE PL
3 COWPEN RD

D8
1 PORTLAND ST
2 BALFOUR ST
3 THE GABLES
4 WEST SALISBURY ST
5 ARCOT TERR
6 DEAN CT

E8
1 ATHLONE CT
2 BOYNE CT
3 MERTON SQ
4 KIMBERLEY TERR
5 THE BOB ELLIOTT HO
6 KEELMANS HO

7 SUMMERS ST
8 COMMERCIAL RD
9 ARTHUR ST
10 PARSONS ST
11 Keel Row Sh Ctr
12 GLADSTONE ST

F7
1 PEMBROKE CT
2 CROFTON MILL HO
3 HORTON ST

F8
1 WAPPING
2 SUSSEX ST
3 BREWERY ST
4 POST OFFICE ST
5 FREEHOLD ST
6 SEXTANT HO

7 QUAYSIDE CT
8 TATE ST
9 FIELDFARE HO
10 WELLINGTON STREET E
11 RICHARD STANNARD HO
12 ERIC TOLHURST CTR

17

12

18

	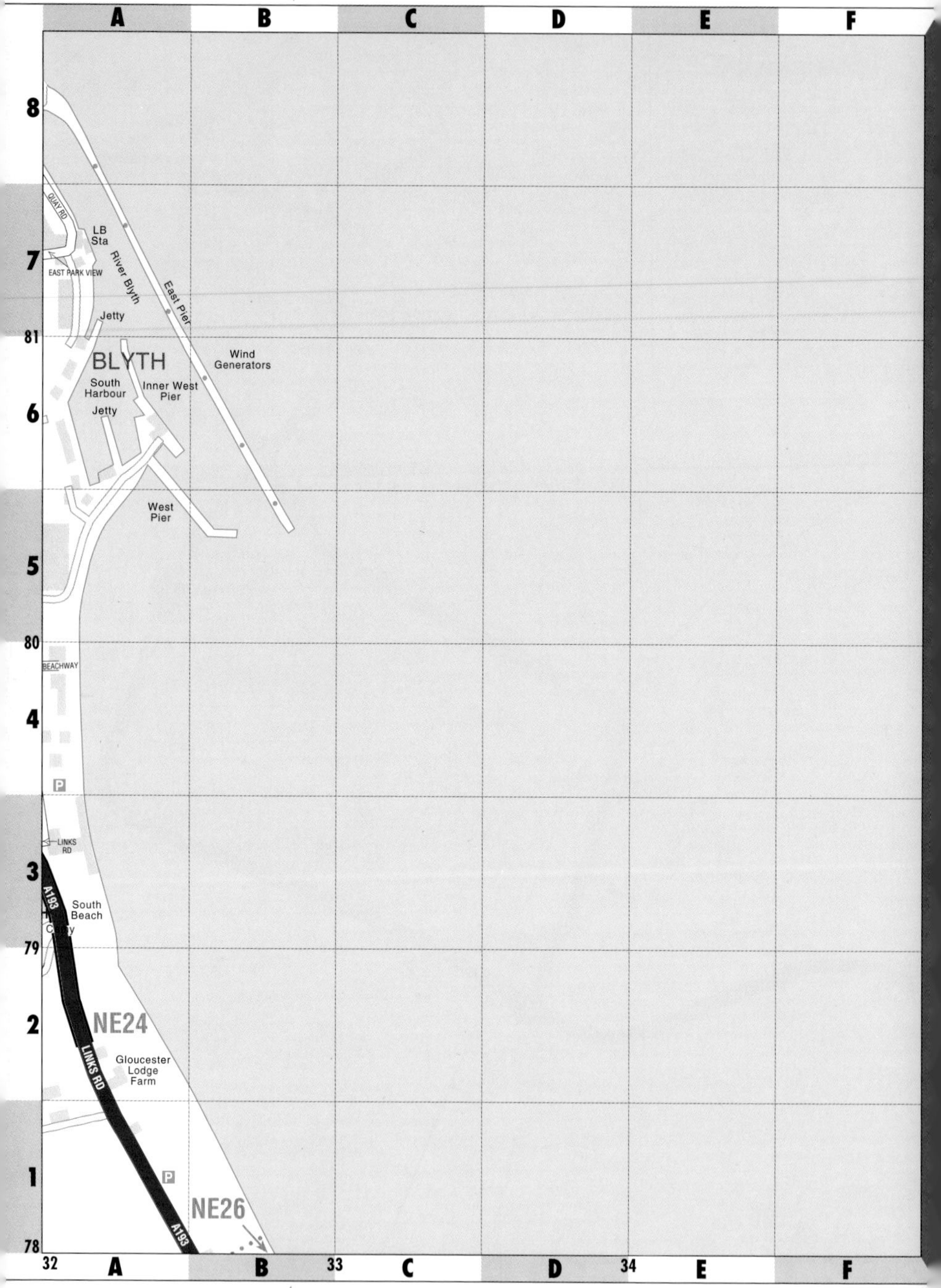 A	B	C	D	E	F

8

QUAY RD

LB
Sta

7 River Blyth

EAST PARK VIEW

East Pier

Jetty

81

BLYTH

Wind
Generators

South
Harbour

Inner West
Pier

6

Jetty

West
Pier

5

80

BEACHWAY

P

LINKS
RD

3

A193

South
Beach
Caravay

79

2

NE24

LINKS RD

Gloucester
Lodge
Farm

1

P

NE26

A193

78

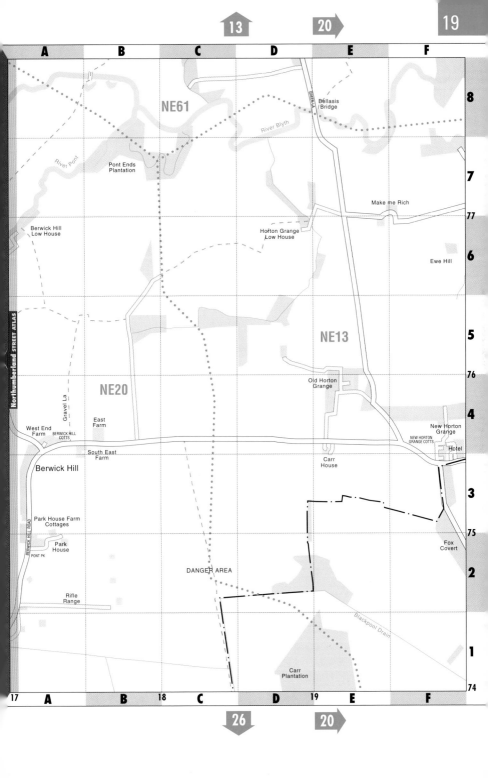

A B C D E F

8

NE61

Bellasis / Bridge

River Blyth

River Pont

Pont Ends Plantation

7

Make me Rich

77

Berwick Hill Low House

Horton Grange Low House

6

Ewe Hill

NE13

5

Old Horton Grange

76

Gravel La

NE20

East Farm

4

West End Farm

BERWICK HILL COTTS

New Horton Grange

NEW HORTON GRANGE COTTS

Hotel

South East Farm

Carr House

Berwick Hill

3

Park House Farm Cottages

75

Fox Covert

BERWICK HILL ROAD

Park House

PONT PK

DANGER AREA

2

Rifle Range

Blackpool Drain

1

74

17 A B 18 C D 19 E F

Carr Plantation

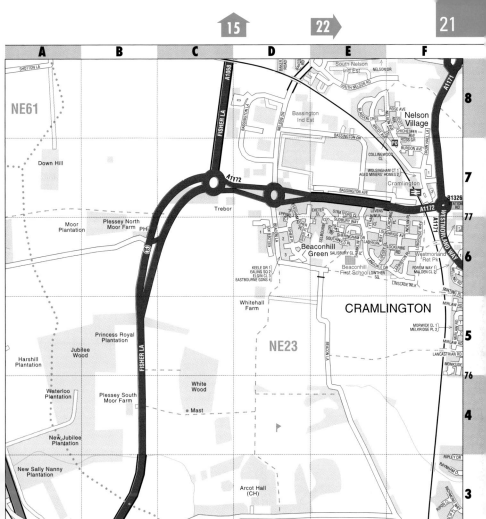

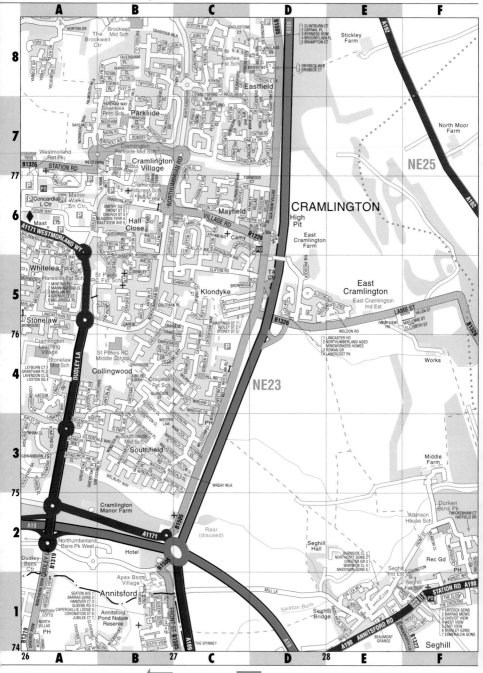

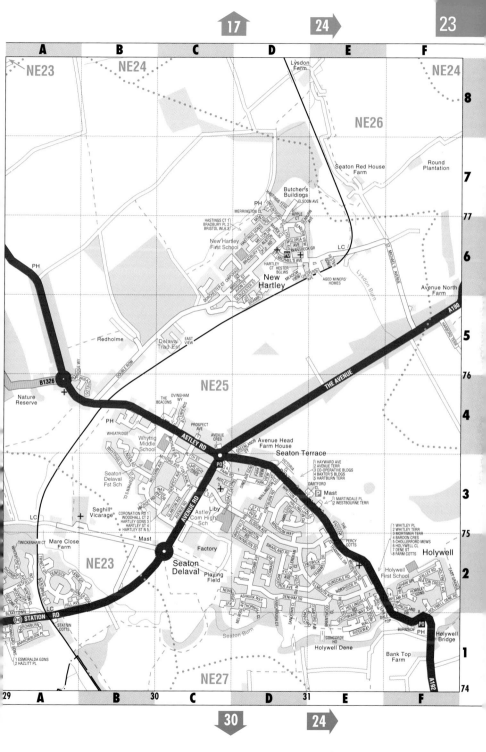

23
18

NE24

A193

Mile Hill

P

Hartley Links

LINKS RD

SEAFIELD MS
Seaton Sluice
Mid Sch

ASTLEY
VILLAS

Blyth to Seaton
Sluice Dunes
Nature Reserve

CONWAY DR

SKELTON DR

BENFIELD GR

DENWAY GR

PH

30

FRANKLIN AVE

MARDEN
AVE

NAYLOR PL

DERWENT RD

FOUNTAIN HEAD BANK

FOUNTAIN
HEAD
BANK

P

The Sumps

Rocky
Island

Sandy
Island

PH

8

Lookout Farm

THE AVENUE

HALL GDNS

GREENRIGG

A190

A190

LINKS RD

FOUNTAIN HEAD BANK

CRESSWELL AVE

PARK RD

THE LINKS

OCHILTREE

PH

WESTFIELD DR

POST OFFICE

The Links

Seaton
Lodge

77

7

6

Seaton Delaval
Hall

+

Seaton Village Farm

Mausoleum

Seaton Lodge
Farm

Holywell Dene

Seaton Sluice

Collywell Bay

Liby

COLLYWELL CT

A193

BERESFORD RD

Crag Point

5

76

NE26

Obelisk
Plantation

Obelisk

Starlight
Castle

MILLFIELD
CT

Seaton
Sluice
South
Fst Sch

MELTON CRES

GRANGE RD

GERHAM RD

St Mary's
WYND

Fort
House

Cvn Pk

P

EAST END

THE
STEADINGS

4

WEST END

Hartley

Masts

3

Hartley West
Farm

B1325

Dark
Plantation

75

Holywell Dene
Nature Reserve

Seaton Burn

HARTLEY LA

BLYTH RD

2

NE25

Crow Hall
Farm

P

1

WHITLEY
BAY

Cemy

+

GERRARD RD

CRANEGLORTH RD

GARSON E RD

WESTLEY CL

ASTLEY

WESTLEY AVE

BORSEDENE RD

THE LINKS

A193

P

HASTINGS

74

Brier Dene
Farm

B1325

32   A   33   B   C   34   D   E   F

23
31

St Mary's
Lighthouse
Visitor Ctr

St Mary's or
Bait Island

Causeway

P

St Mary's Island
Nature Reserve

P

2

75

1

F   35   G

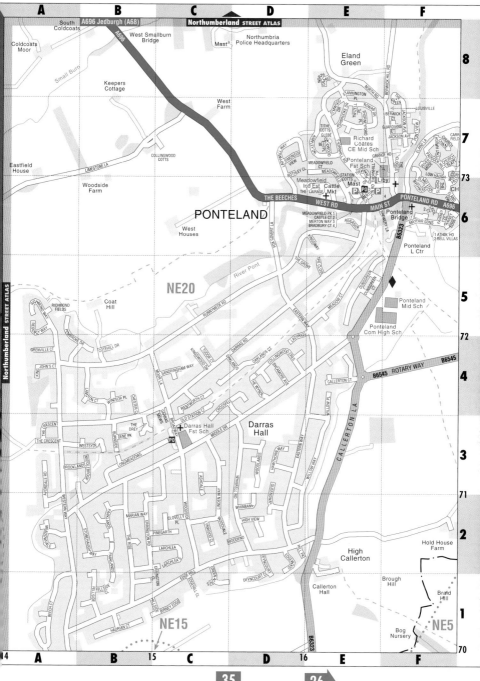

Northumberland STREET ATLAS

PONTELAND

NE20

NE15

NE5

Darras Hall

High Callerton

Eland Green

Northumbria Police Headquarters

South Coldcoats

A696 Jedburgh (A68)

West Smallburn Bridge

Coldcoats Moor

Small Burn

Keepers Cottage

West Farm

Eastfield House

Woodside Farm

Collingwood Cotts

West Houses

Richard Coates CE Mid Sch

Ponteland Fst Sch

Meadowfield Ind Est

Cattle Mkt

Louisville

Ponteland Bridge

Ponteland L Ctr

Ponteland Mid Sch

Ponteland Com High Sch

Coat Hill

Richmond Fields

Darras Hall Fst Sch

Callerton Hall

Hold House Farm

Brough Hill

Braid Hill

Bog Nursery

WEST RD   WEST RD   MAIN ST   PONTELAND RD A696

B6323

B6545 ROTARY WAY   B6545

THE BEECHES

8

7

73

6

5

72

4

3

71

2

1

70

A   B   C   D   E   F

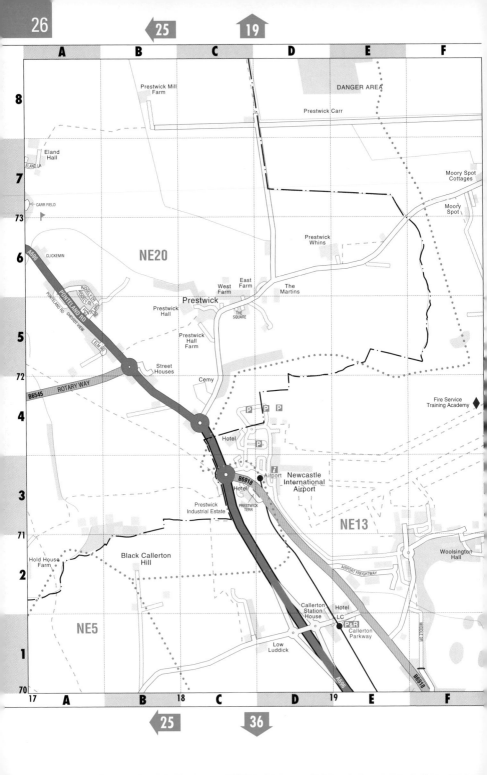

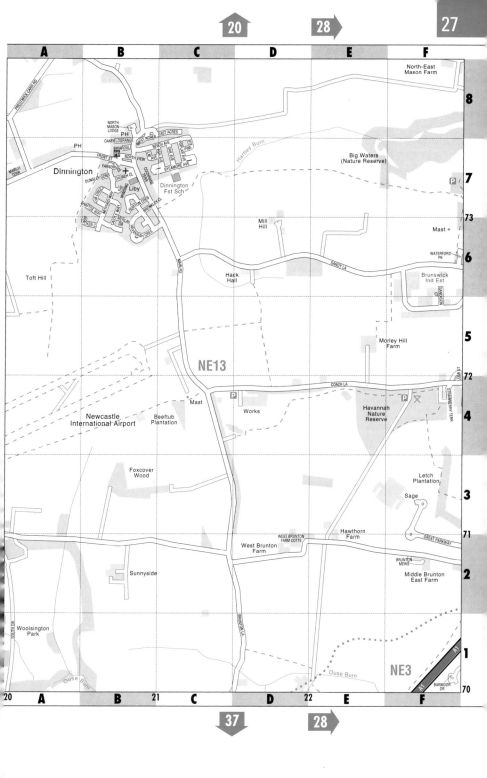

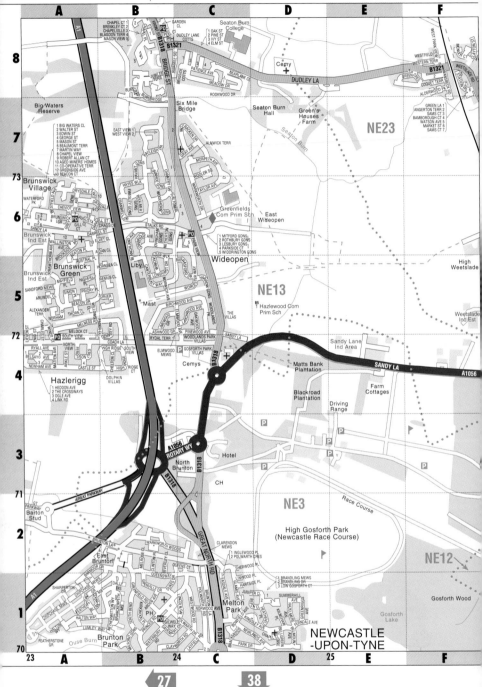

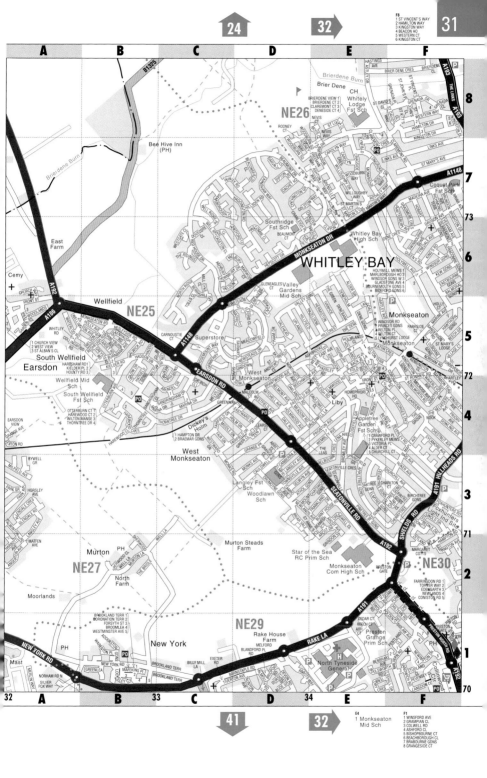

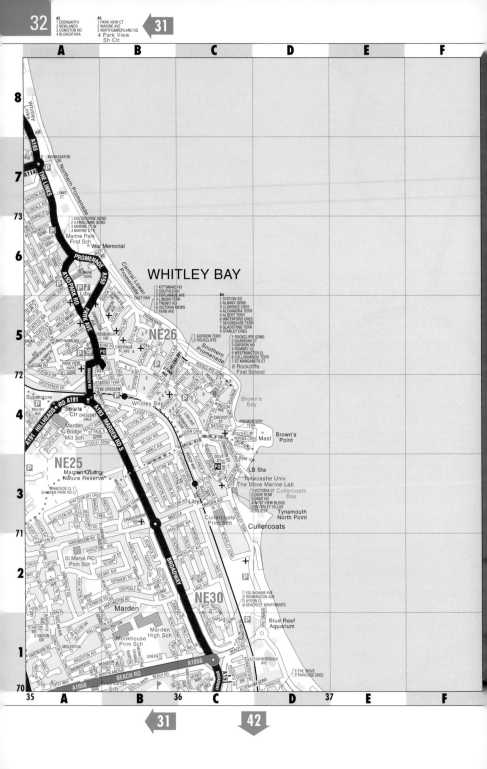

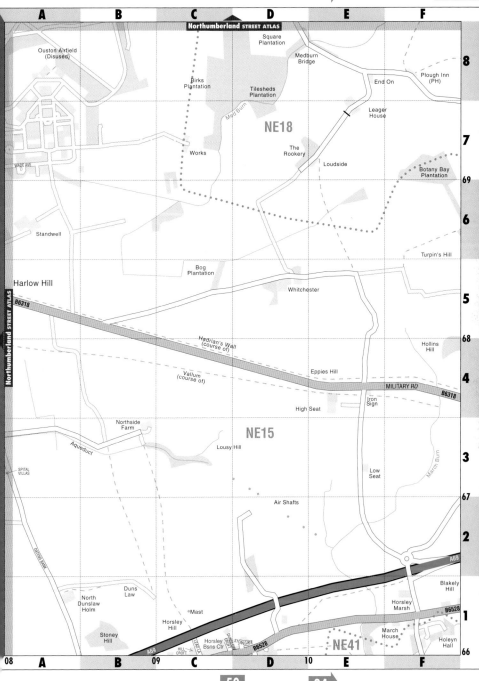

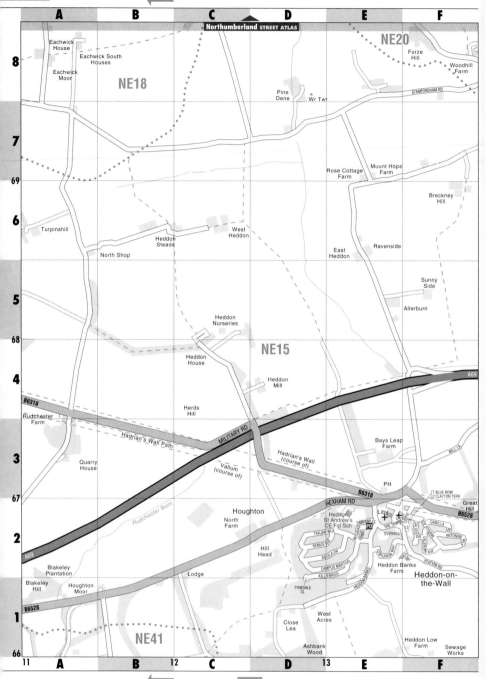

NE20

Eachwick
House

Eachwick South
Houses

Eachwick
Moor

NE18

Furze
Hill

Woodhill
Farm

STAMFORDHAM RD

Pine
Dene

Wr Twr

Turpinshill

Heddon
Steads

North Shop

West
Heddon

Rose Cottage
Farm

Mount Hope
Farm

Breckney
Hill

East
Heddon

Ravenside

Sunny
Side

Heddon
Nurseries

Allerburn

NE15

Heddon
House

Heddon
Mill

A69

B6318

Rudchester
Farm

Hadrian's Wall Path

MILITARY RD

Herds
Hill

Hadrian's Wall
(course of)

Bays Leap
Farm

MILL LN

Quarry
House

Vallum
(course of)

PH

B6318

1 BLUE ROW
2 CLAYTON TERR

Great
Hill

B6528

Rudchester Burn

Houghton

North
Farm

HEXHAM RD

Heddon
St Andrew's
CE Fst Sch

TABERNA CL

Lib

THE TOWNE GATE

PO

CAMILLA

ANTONINE

A69

Blakeley
Plantation

Hill
Head

TRAJAN WLK

REMUS DR

AQUILA DR

OVERHILL

CLAYTON

VALLUM CT

CALVUS DR

VALERIAN AVE

STATION RD

Heddon Banks
Farm

Heddon-on-
the-Wall

Blakeley
Hill

Houghton
Moor

Lodge

CAMPUS MARTIUS

KILLIEBRIGS

TYNEDALE
CL

HEDDON BANKS

B6528

NE41

Close
Lea

West
Acres

Ashbank
Wood

Heddon Low
Farm

Sewage
Works

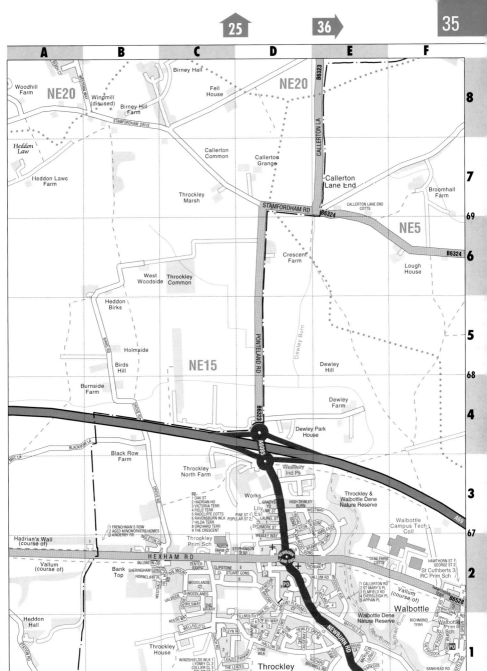

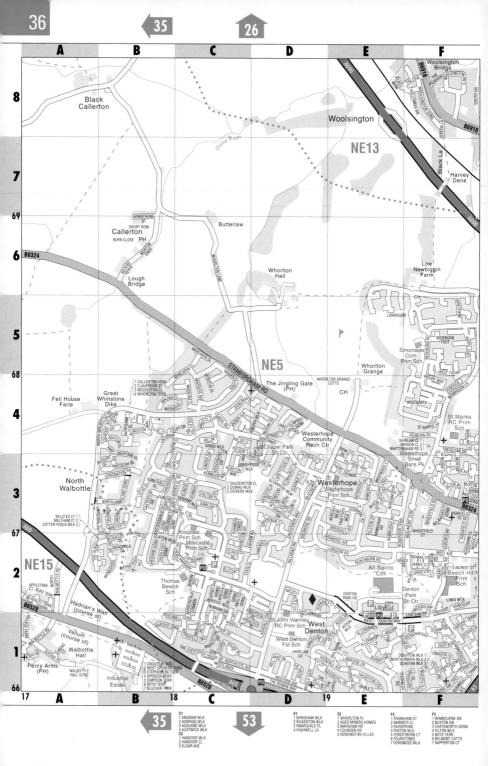

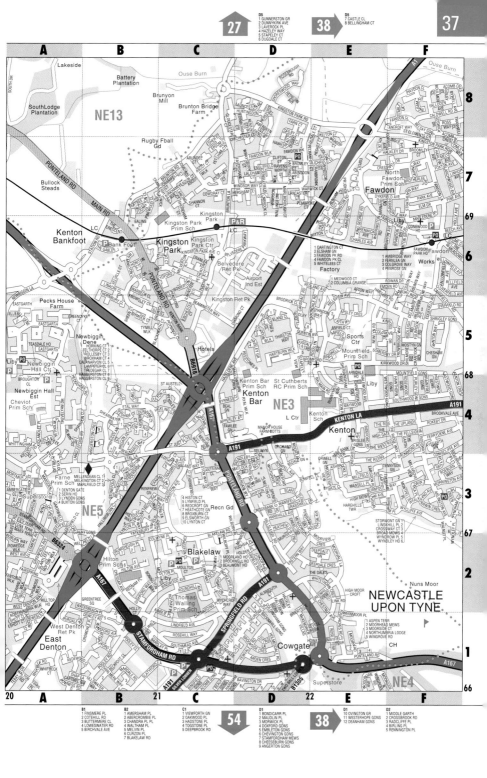

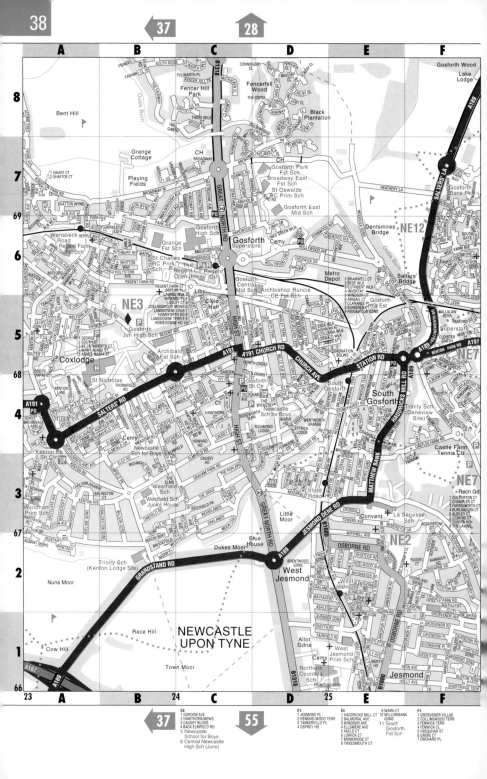

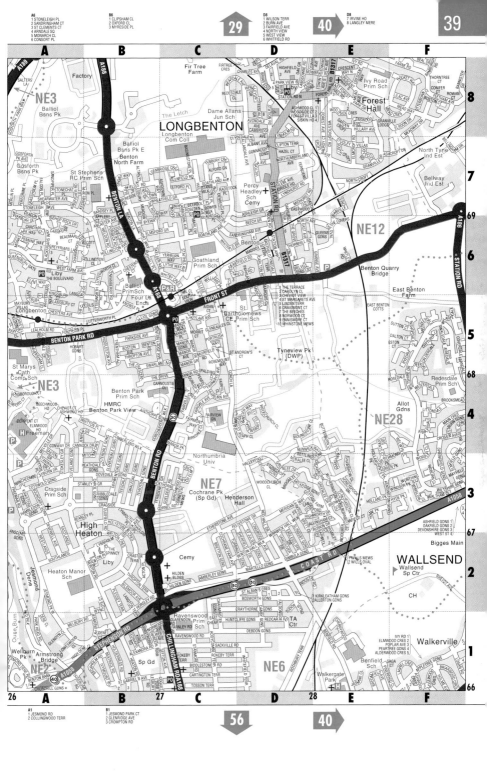

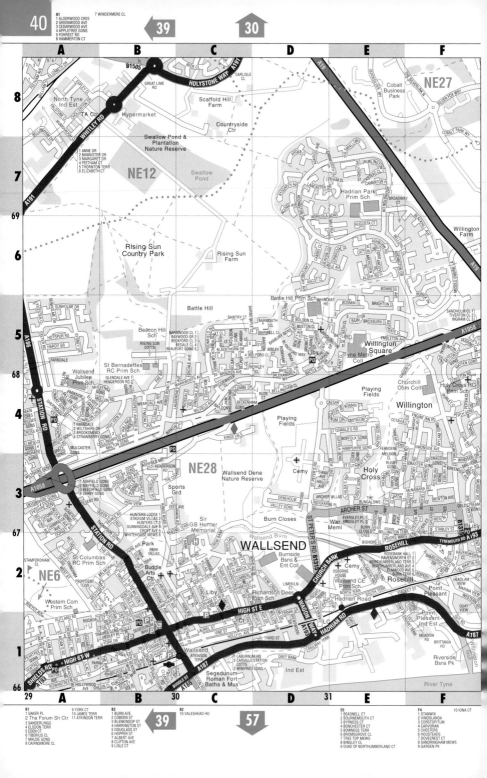

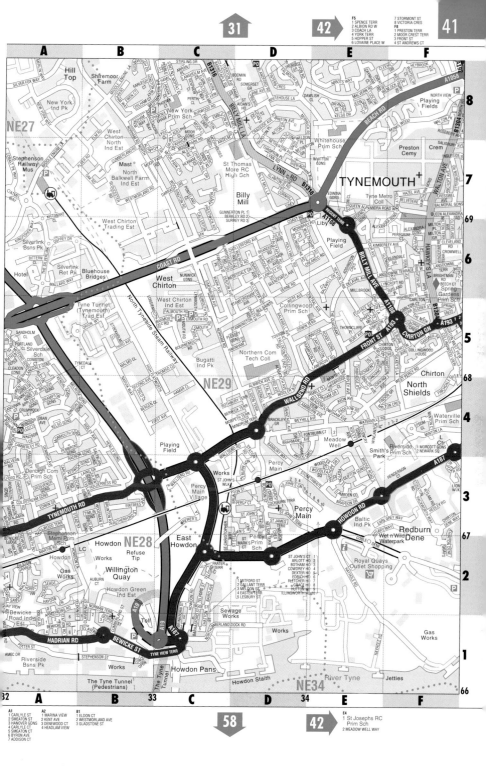

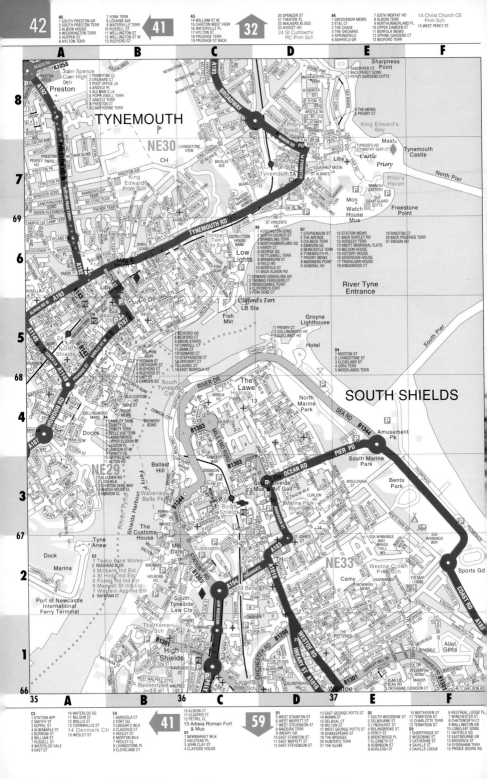

A B C D E F

8
7
69
6
5
68
4
3
67
2
1
66

North Pier

South Pier

PROMENADE
P
PH
Trow Point

NE33
Trow Lea

1 BIDEFORD GDNS
2 CHEVIOT RD
3 NORHAM AVE N
4 SHELDON RD
5 SOUTHFIELD RD

Frenchman's
Bay

NE34
Frenchman's
Lea

COAST RD
A183
BAMBURGH AVE
GARTH CRES

A B 39 C D 40 E F

A6079 Bellingham (B6320)

A69 Carlisle

Coastley Burnfoot Farm

Burnfoot Wood

West Boat

Westwood House

Kingshaw Haugh

Alnmouth Terr

Old Bridge End

River Tyne

A69

A6079

B6531

Highwood Farm

Cemy

LC

CH

High Wood

The Shaws Farm

Cobbler's Hall

EILANSGATE HO 1
MILLFIELD GDNS 2
QUATRE BRAS 3
MILLFIELD CT 4
WESTBOURNE GR 5
PORTLAND TERR 6
LEAZES CRES 7
HIGH BURSWELL 8
BURNLAND TERR 9
LEAZES TERR 10
WESTFIELD CL 11
LEAZES TERR 12

ST ACCA'S CT

BOWMAN DRIVE

BROADWAY

Highside

DUKES RD

THE CROFT

LEAZES LA

WEST QUARTER

Shaws La

Plain Trees Farm

Low Gate

Summerrods West Farm

Leazes

HIGH REINS 1
REINS CT 2

BEECH HILL

ALEXANDRA CRES

Alexandra Terr

TYNEDALE TERR

WHETSTONE GN

MAIDENS CROFT

Queen Elizabeth High Sch

ALLENDALE RD

B6305

NE46

SHAWS LA

Summerrods

St Josephs RC Mid Sch

Woodley Field Farm

B6305

Cockshaw Burn

Summerrods Dean

CANON SAVAGE DR

High House Farm

HIGHFORD LA

HIGHBORO WAY

BISHOPTON WAY

CONNISCLIFFE

NURSERY GRANGE

Breckon Hill

HIGHBORO LANE

ASH CL

ELM CL

THE OAKS

Blossom Hill

DICKSON DR

BIRCH CL

Highford

CAUSEY HILL WAY

HEXHAM

Nichols Dean

Low Yarridge

Barn End

CHARLTON CL

West Plantation

Benson's Fell

Green Hill

High Yarridge

Plover Hill

Rot Sike

Hexham Race Course

A5		7 COCKSHAW CT	14 GLOVERS PL	4 ORCHARD TERR
1 PEARSON'S TERR		8 GIBSON PL	15 STEPHENSON HO	5 ABBEY CT
2 MILLFIELD TERR		9 COCKSHAW TERR	16 GILESGATE CT	6 CHISHOLM PL
3 WESTBOURNE GR		10 TANNERS ROW	**B5**	7 ST MARY'S WYND
4 FENWICK GR		11 HOLY ISLAND	1 CHURCH ROW	8 ST MARY'S CHARE
5 KINGSGATE		12 ALEXANDER PL	2 MARKET PL	9 The Moot Hall Gall
6 DUNWOODIE TERR		13 GILES PL	3 PUDDING MEWS	

46 ▶   **45**

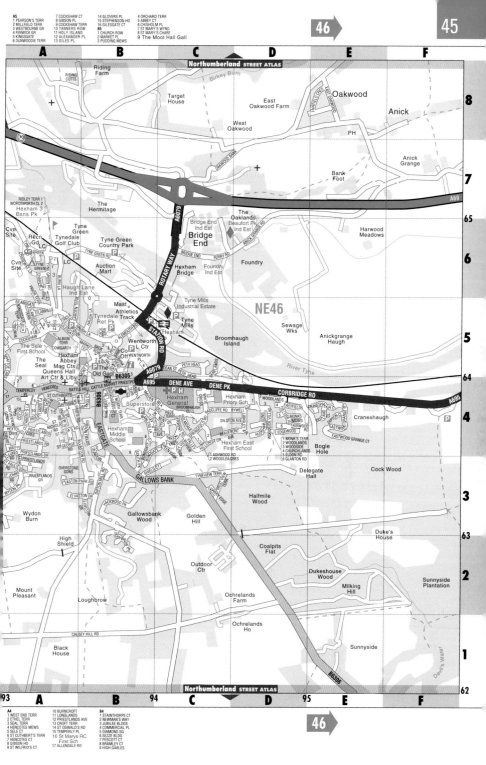

A4	10 BURNCROFT	B4
1 WEST END TERR	11 LONGLANDS	1 STAINTHORPE CT
2 ETHEL TERR	12 PRIESTLANDS AVE	2 NEWMAN'S WAY
3 SEAL TERR	13 CROFT TERR	3 JUBILEE BLDGS
4 HENCOTES MEWS	14 ST OSWALD'S RD	4 COMMERCIAL PL
5 SELE CT	15 TEMPERLY PL	5 DIAMOND SQ
6 ST CUTHBERT'S MEWS	16 St Marys RC	6 SEZZE BLDG
7 HENCOTES CT	First Sch	7 PESCOTT CT
8 GIBSON HO	17 ALLENDALE RD	8 BRAMLEY CT
9 ST WILFRID'S CT		9 HIGH GARLES

A68 Jedburgh

A   B   C   D   E   F

8
Beaufront Castle Flats
Beaufront Castle
The Park
Knoll Hill
Hampstead House
A68

CORCHESTER LA

7
A69
Beaufront Red House
Red House Plantation
Cor Burn
B6529
Corbridge Mid Sch
THE RIGGS

65
Prior Thorns
Redhouse Burn
Redhouse Haughs
Corchester Twrs
STAGSHAW RD
LEAZES RD
CHERRY EST
AVENUE

6
NE46
River Tyne
Corbridge Roman Site
CORCHESTER TERR 1
CORCHESTER AVE 2
TRINITY CT 3
COOKSON CL 4
COOPERS CL 5
MANOR COTTS 6
ROMAN WAY
ST HELEN'S LA
TRINITY TERR
PRIOR TERR
WEST TERR
ORCHARD VIEW
WELL BANK
MIDDLE ST
FRONT ST
MARKET PL
ST MARY'S CHARE
PRINCES ST
TDY
MAIN
PO

5
Widehaugh Nursery
Wide Haugh
Dilston Haughs
TYNEDALE MEWS
B6521
B6529
Corbridge Bridge

64
Sam's Island
LC
A695
Cemy
STATION RD

4
Dilston Plains
Dilston Park
DILSTON HAUGH COTTS
B6321
LC
Corbridge
TINKLER'S BANK
Corbridge Ye

3
Dilston South Park
Bowlingally Hill
Dilston Haugh Farm
Dilston Mill
Dilston
NE45
Scurl Hill
The Scrogs
A695
B6307

63
Dilston Park
East Haugh
Dilston Hall
Dilston West Cotts
High Town
West Fell
LADYCUTTERS LA
Roecliff Lodge

2
Park Wood
Devil's Water
Birchside Wood
Snokoehill Plantation
Snokoe Hill

1
West Haugh
Birchy Sike
Swallowship Wood
Birchy Wood
Quarry Cottage Belt
Temperley Grange Farm

62
Swallowship Hill
B6307

96   A   97   B   C   98   D   E   F

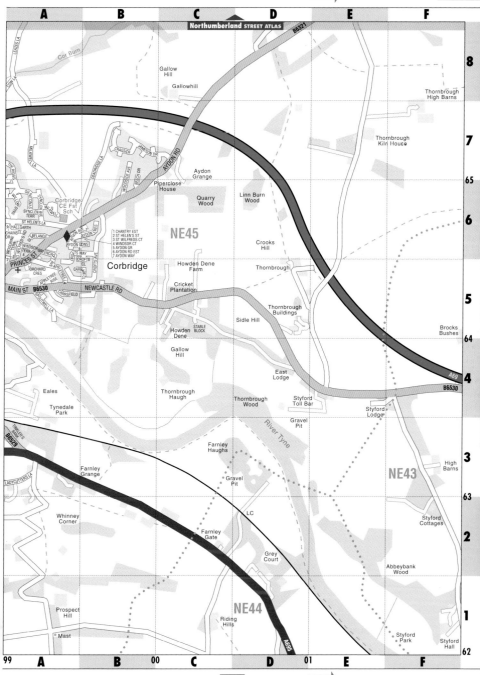

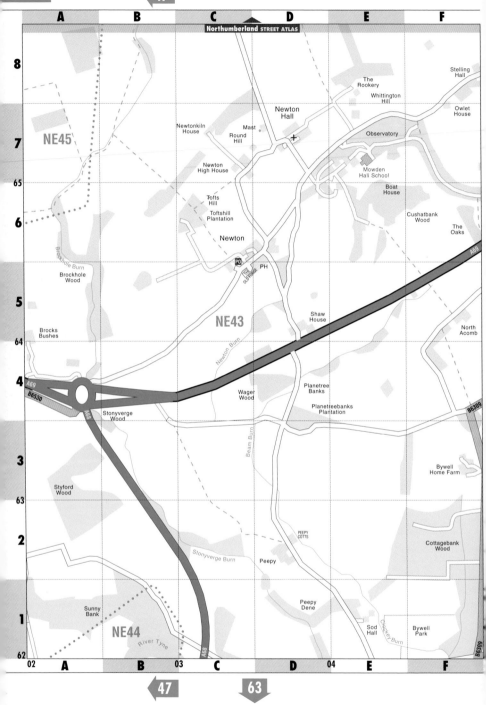

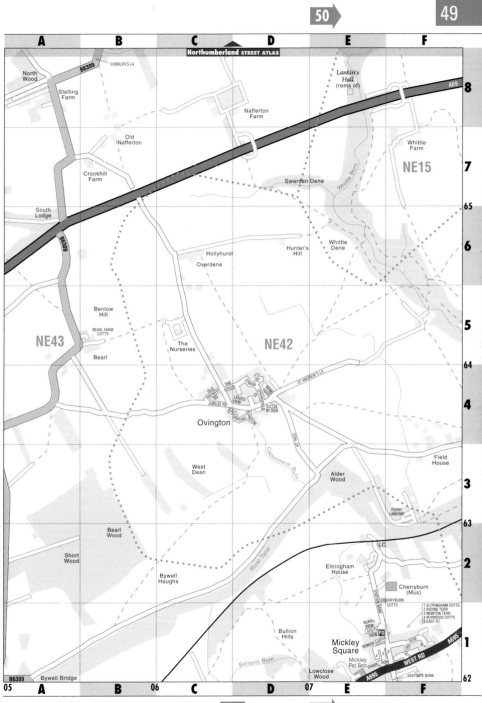

Northumberland STREET ATLAS

A   B   C   D   E   F

North Wood
Stelling Farm
COBBLER'S LA
B6309
Old Nafferton
Nafferton Farm
Lankin's Hall (rems of)
A69
8
Whittle Farm
Crookhill Farm
NE15
7
Swarden Dene
Whittle Burn
65
South Lodge
B6309
Hollyhurst
Overdene
Hunter's Hill
Whittle Dene
6
Benlow Hill
NE42
5
BEARL FARM COTTS
The Nurseries
NE43
Bearl
64
OLD BREWERY SQ
THE GREEN
FIRS
ST ANDREW'S LA
SPRING CL
LEAZES VIEW
CAUSEY FIELD
COAL LA
LITTLE BLDGS
4
JUBILEE RD
BLACKSMITHS BANK
RAMSEY NOOK
Ovington
West Dean
Cockermere Burn
Alder Wood
Field House
3
FERRY LANDING
63
Bearl Wood
River Tyne
LC
2
Eltringham House
Cherryburn (Mus)
Short Wood
Bywell Haughs
CHERRYBURN COTTS
1 ELTRINGHAM COTTS
2 RIDING TERR
3 NEWTON TERR
4 BURNSIDE COTTS
5 EAST ST
STATION BANK
NORTH VIEW
SOUTH VIEW
PO
Bullion Hills
Mickley Square
DENE
CHAPEL ROW
A695
1
BEWICK DRIVE
Mickley Fst Sch
Lowclose Wood
WEST RD
A695
EASTGATE BANK
B6309
Bywell Bridge
62

05   A   B   06   C   D   07   E   F

A B C D E F

Fellside House

A69

B6528

A69 B6528

LEAD LA

B6528

PO PH

SOUTH EAST FARM

Horsley
1 CROWN & ANCHOR COTTS
2 CROFT TERR
3 CASTLE VIEW

Burn Cottage

OATENS BANK

High Barns Farm

WATER LANE

CHERRY TREE GDNS

SOUTH LEA

NE15

Water Works

How Dene

Howdene Burn

8

Pike Hill

NE41

7

Nelson's Hill

DALLINGTON LA

HORSLEY WOOD COTTS

Holly Hill

Gallow Hill

65

Horsley Wood

Horsley Bank

Howdene Bridge

6

Mount Huly

Duke's Dene

Kitty's Burn

Tynewood

The Hermitage

Hagg Farm

The Park

Hagg Bank

5

Ovingham

Cemy

PIPER RD

DENE CL

WELBURN CL

PIPER RD

WINDSOR CRES

WHEATLANDS

CASTLE VIEW

River Tyne

The Spetchells

Park Burn

HAGG BANK COTTS 1
RAILWAY COTTS 2

64

CROFT HO

CROFT VIEW

THE TERR

THE HILL

Ovingham Bridge

Sewage Works

Works

Low Prudhoe Ind Est

Low Prudhoe

Depot

DUKES WAY

DUKES EARLS CT

REGENTS DR

Low Prudhoe Ind Est

A695

4

RIVER VIEW

Prudhoe

PO

LC

NE42

PRINCESS WAY

Castlefields Wood Nature Reserve

Orchard Hill

MILL VIEW

PRINCESS CT

Ind Est

Broom House Farm

NORTHUMBERLAND VIEW

WEST WYLAM VIEW

BELLS LONNEN

VICTORIA GR

SCHOOL ROW

EASTWOOD VILLAS

West Wylam

BROOMHOUSE RD

HORSLEY RD

Eltringham

HIGHFIELD TERR 1
WOODBURN TERR 2
DENE TERR 3
NORTH VIEW TERR 4
PROSPECT TERR 5
WEST VIEW 8

NORTH BURN

Ovingham CE Fst Sch

Ovingham Mid Sch

Tyne Riverside Country Pk

Prudhoe Castle

A30

STATION RD

CASTLE VIEW

CASTLE FIELDS

THE FORGE

ST OSWALDS

TILLEY CROSS

Adderlane Fst Sch

THE MANORS

THE ADDERLANE RD

ADDERLANE RD

PARKWOOD AVE

COLDWELL RD

WOODHEAD RD

EASTWOOD RD

CH

3

CASTLE VIEW

CASTLE CL

KEPWEL BANK TOP

KEPWELL RD

CHERRY RD

DAIRY GR

HOLLY GR

CASTLE RD

CHENER RD

RIVER VIEW

CRANLEIGH GR

TYNE VIEW

UMFRAVILLE DENE

BROOMHILL RD

BIVERFIELD RD

PO

63

Castle Fst Sch

BIRCH CL

LABURNUM AVE

MAPLE CL

ROWAN DR

LANGLEY RD

WESTGREEN AVE

BEECH GR

Front St

Liby

OAKDALE

P

HOLDAKE

Waterworld

P

OAKWELL TERR

STONYFLAT BANK

STANCLEY

CLIFFORD

PRIESTCLOSE COTTS

B6395

PCALES CRES

PRIESTCLOSE

WOODSIDE

2

Beaumont Wood

CRANBROOK

BEAUMONT TERR

ELTRINGHAM RD

WEST RD

Prudhoe West Fst Sch

St Matthews RC Fst Sch

Highfields Mid Sch

MEECH GR

SWALWELL

HAVEN

FAIR VIEW

KINGSTON

P

OAKFIELD RD

MOORFIELD RD

HIGHFIELD

ORCHARD

GRANGE TERR

PRIESTCLOSE RD

OAKLANDS PL

REDWELL RD

CAMERON RD

DRAWBACK

PADDOCK RD

PADDOCK WOOD

WOODSIDE

CHEVIOT VIEW

Cemy

Football & Sp Ctr

SOUTH GRANGE TERR

HOMEDALE

VALLEY RD

Priestclose Wood Nature Reserve

B6395

A695

Broom Wood

LARRISTON 1
AGED MINERS COTTS 2
WHITEBURN 3
EDGEWELL AVE 4
OTTERCOPS 5
TENNYSON CT 6

GREENER RD

EDGEWELL HOUSE RD

BROOM WOOD CT

HIGHFIELD LA

Cemy

Cemy

LOCOMOTIVE CT 1
GORDON TERR 2
WIGLEY ST 3
VICTORIA TERR 4
ST MATHEWS LA 5
ST THOMAS MEWS 6
ST THOMAS CL 7
PHOBE GRANGE BOTTS 8
HOMEDALE TERR 9
DRAWBACK CL 10

Prudhoe Com High Sch

MOOR GRANGE

MOOR RD

NOOKLANDS

Cemy

Stanley Burn

1

NE43

PRUDHOE

62

08 A B 09 C D 10 E F

D3
1 THE WAGGONWAY
2 THE HAUGHS
3 SPETCHELLS
4 HEATHER LEA LA
5 FARM WELL PL
6 BROOMHOUSE FARM CT

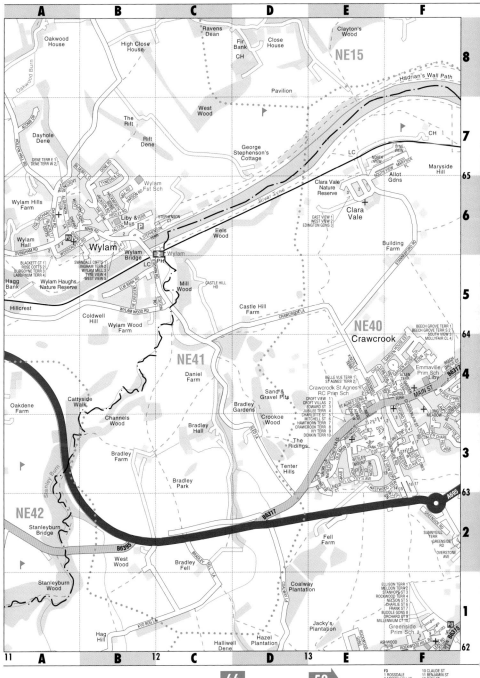

NE15

Clayton's Wood

Ravens Dean

Oakwood House

High Close House

Fir Bank
CH

Close House

Pavilion

Hadrian's Wall Path

CH

The Rift

West Wood

Dayhole Dene

Rift Dene

George Stephenson's Cottage

LC

TYNE VIEW
NORTH VIEW
MARYSIDE PL

Maryside Hill

DENE TERR E 1
DENE TERR W 2

Clara Vale Nature Reserve

EAST VIEW 1
WEST VIEW 2
EDINGTON GDNS 3

Clara Vale

Wylam Hills Farm

Liby & Terr Mus

STEPHENSON CT

STEPHENSON TERR

Eels Wood

Building Farm

Wylam Hall

Wylam

MAIN RD

Wylam Bridge

Wylam

SWINDALE COTTS
INGHAM TERR 2
WYLAM MILL 3
TYNE VIEW 4
WEST VIEW 5

LC
PH

Mill Wood

CASTLE HILL HO

BLACKETT CT 1
ROSE COTTS 2
BURGOYNE TERR 3
LABURNUM TERR 4

Hagg Bank

Wylam Haughs Nature Reserve

Castle Hill Farm

CRAWCROOK LA

NE40

BEECH GROVE TERR 1
BEECH GROVE TERR S 2
SOUTH VIEW 3
MOLLYFAIR CL 4

Hillcrest

Coldwell Hill

Wylam Wood Farm

WYLAM WOOD RD

Crawcrook

NE41

Daniel Farm

Sand & Gravel Pits

Crawcrook St Agnes RC Prim Sch

BELLE VUE TERR 1
ST AGNES' TERR 2

Emmaville Prim Sch

Emmaville Prim Sch Liby

MAIN ST

Oakdene Farm

Cattyside Walk

Channels Wood

Bradley Gardens

Crookoe Wood

CROFT TERR 1
CROFT VILLAS 2
EDWARD ST 3
JUBILEE TERR 4
CHARLOTTE ST 5
MITCHELL ST 6
HAWTHORN TERR 7
CRAWCROOK TERR 8
IVY TERR 9
DONKIN TERR 10

LONG MEADOW

Bradley Hall

The Ridings

Bradley Farm

Tenter Hills

NE42

Bradley Park

A695

Stanleyburn Bridge

B6395

West Wood

Bradley Fell

Fell Farm

SUNNYGILL TERR

GREENSIDE RD

OVERSTONE AVE

Stanleyburn Wood

B6317

Coalway Plantation

ELLISON TERR 1
MELDON TERR 2
STANHOPE ST 3
ROCKWOOD TERR 4
NESTON ST 5
CHARL'E ST 6
FRANK ST 7
BUDDLE GDNS 8
ORCHARD ST 9
MILLENNIUM CT 10

Hag Hill

KYO BOG LA

Halliwell Dene

Hazel Plantation

Jacky's Plantation

Greenside Prim Sch

PO

ASHWOOD TERR

ROCKWOOD HILL RD

F3
1 ROSSDALE
2 MORGY HILL W
3 MORGY HILL E
4 CLIFFORD GDNS
5 GEORGE ST
6 LLOYD ST
7 EMMA VIEW
8 DAVID TERR
9 CATHERINE VIEW
10 CLAUDE ST
11 BENJAMIN ST
12 DICK ST
13 SCOTT'S AVE
14 BRADLEY VIEW
15 FELL VIEW W
16 FELL VIEW
17 MOUNT VIEW

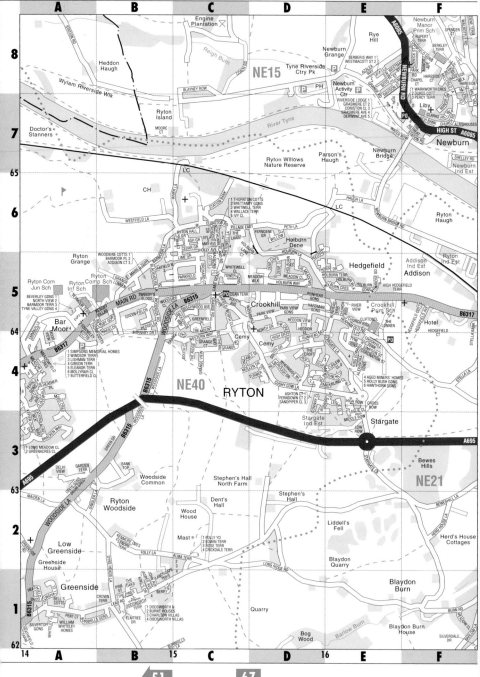

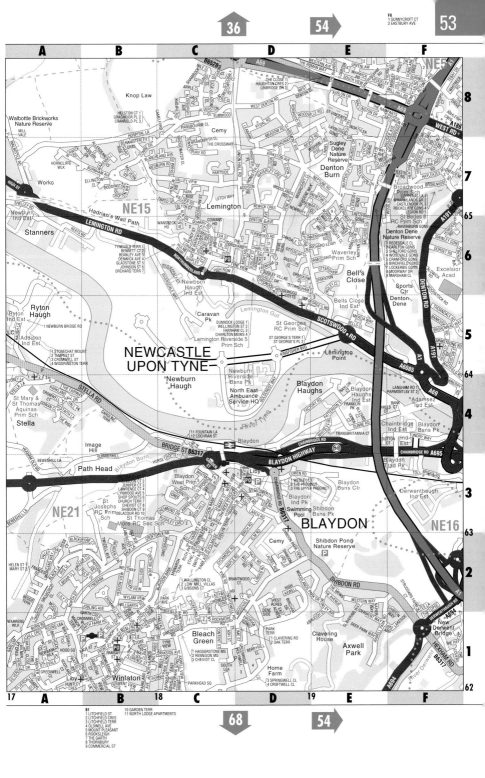

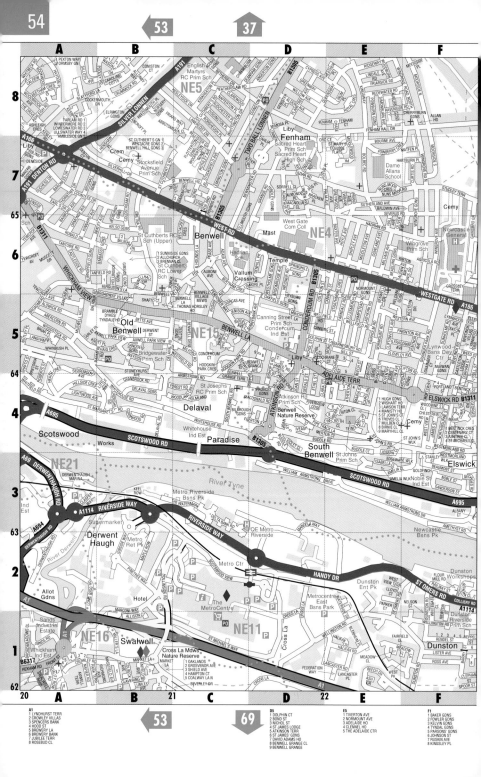

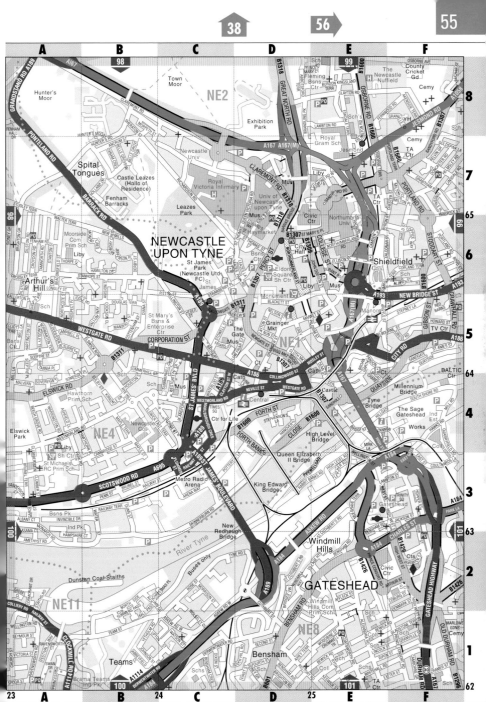

For full street detail of the highlighted area see pages 98, 99, 100 and 101.

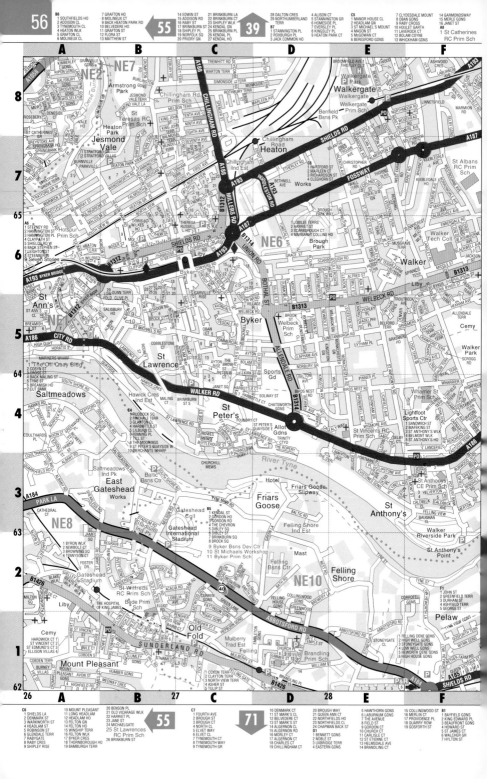

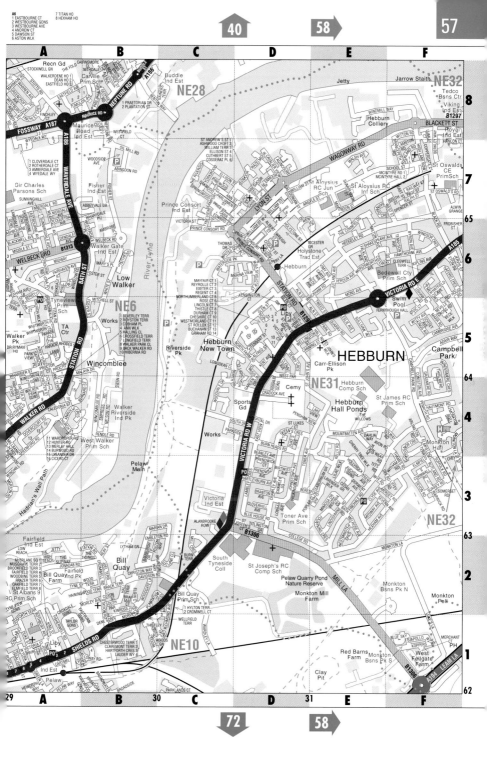

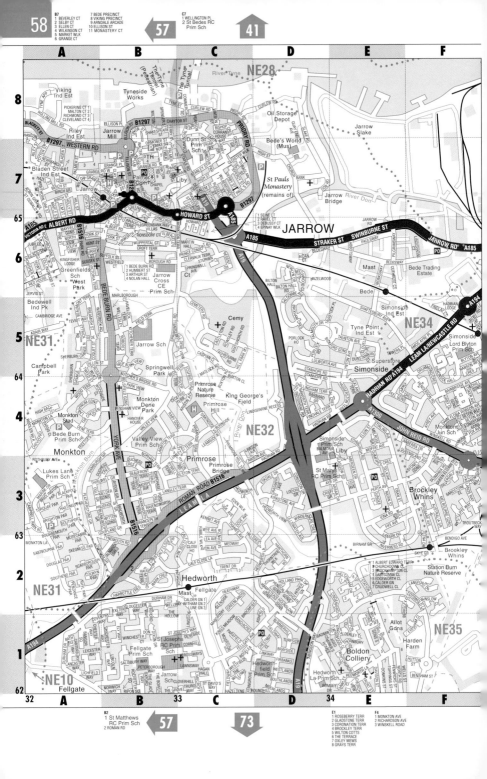

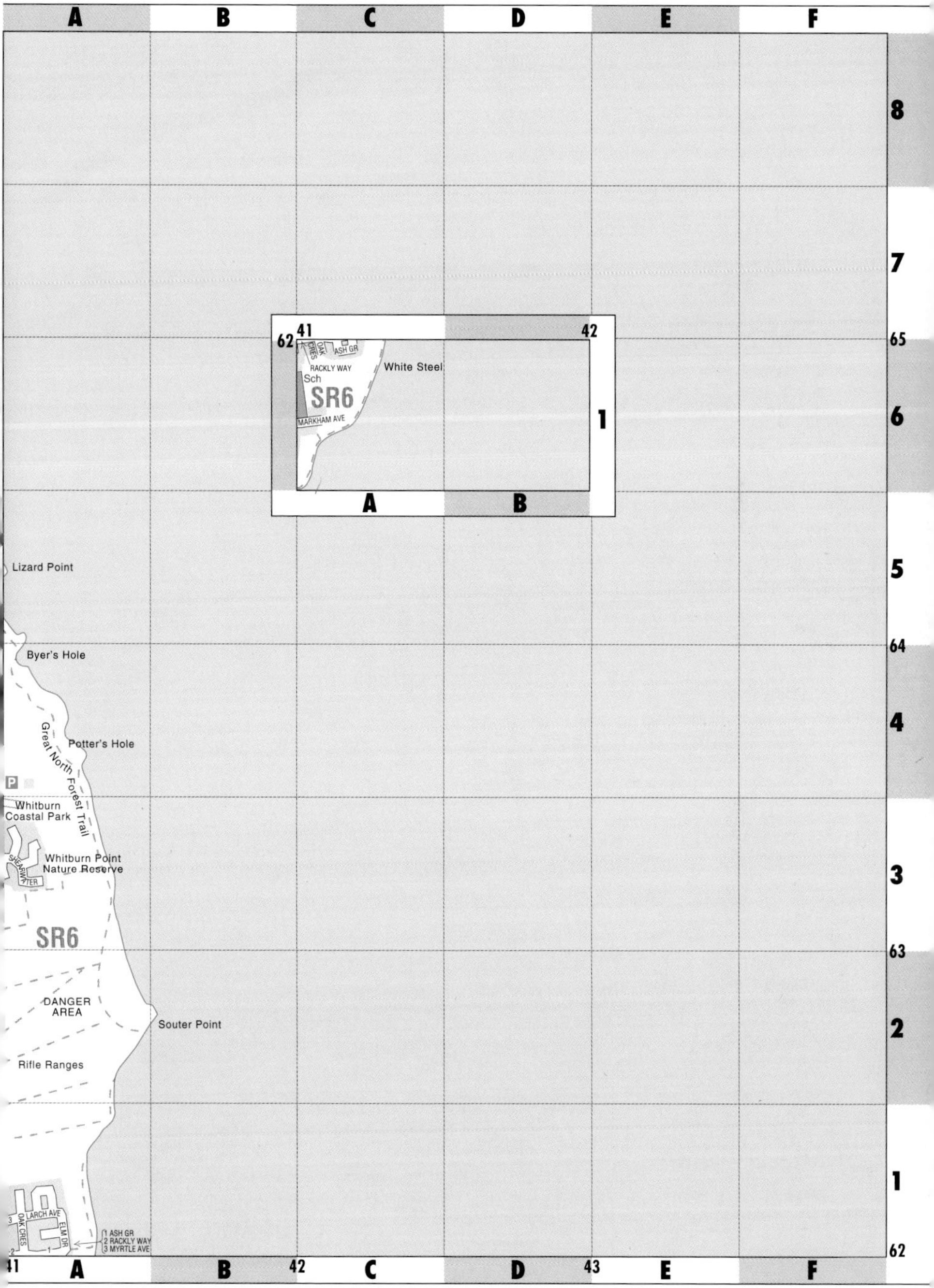

A | B | C | D | E | F

8
7
65
6
5
64
4
3
63
2
1
62

Lizard Point

Byer's Hole

Potter's Hole

Great North Forest Trail

Whitburn
Coastal Park

Whitburn Point
Nature Reserve

SR6

DANGER
AREA

Souter Point

Rifle Ranges

41 A B 42 C D 43 E F 62

White Steel

41
62 41 ASH GR
RACKLY WAY
Sch
SR6
MARKHAM AVE
A B
42

1 ASH GR
2 RACKLY WAY
3 MYRTLE AVE

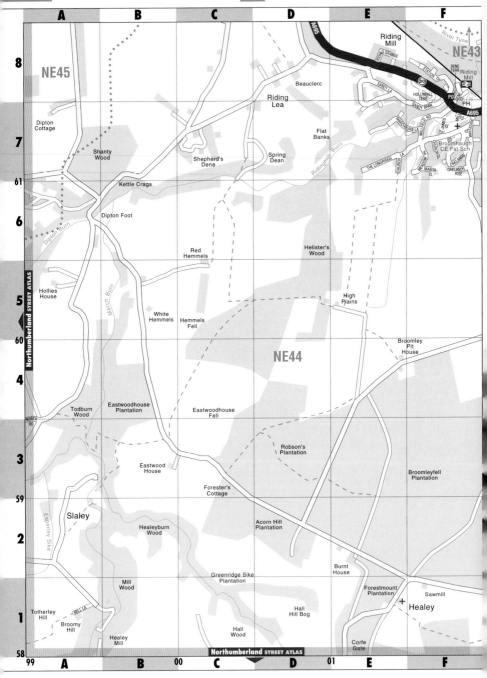

NE45

NE43

Riding
Mill

River Tyne

Dipton
Cottage

Shanty
Wood

Beauclerc

Riding
Lea

Flat
Banks

DENE
TERR

Riding
Mill

HOLLINHILL TERR

SANDY BANK

Broomhaugh
CE Fst Sch

THE LONGRIDGE

Shepherd's
Dene

Spring
Dean

Ridingmill Burn

Kettle Crags

Dipton Foot

OAKLANDS
RISE

Dipton Burn

Red
Hemmels

Helister's
Wood

Hollies
House

High
Plains

Broomley
Pit
House

Match Burn

White
Hemmels

Hemmels
Fell

NE44

Todburn
Wood

Eastwoodhouse
Plantation

Eastwoodhouse
Fell

MORALEE
RD

Robson's
Plantation

Broomleyfell
Plantation

Eastwood
House

Forester's
Cottage

Slaley

Esperley Sike

Healeyburn
Wood

Acorn Hill
Plantation

Burnt
House

Greenridge Sike
Plantation

Forestmount
Plantation

Sawmill

Mill
Wood

Healey

Totherley
Hill

MILL LA

Hall
Hill Bog

Broomy
Hill

Healey
Mill

Hall
Wood

Corfe
Gate

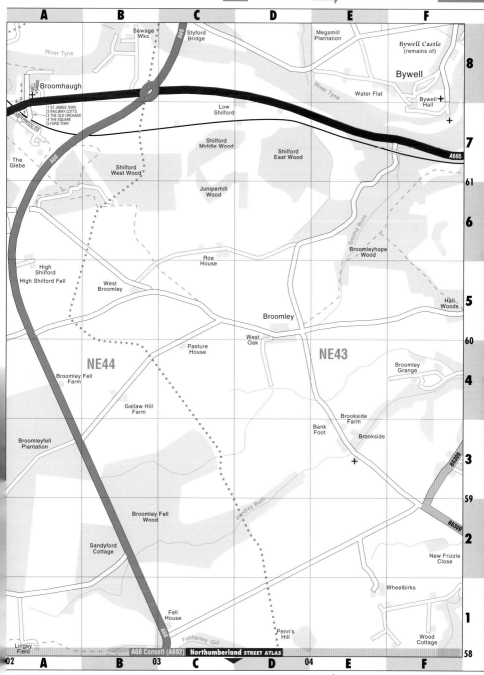

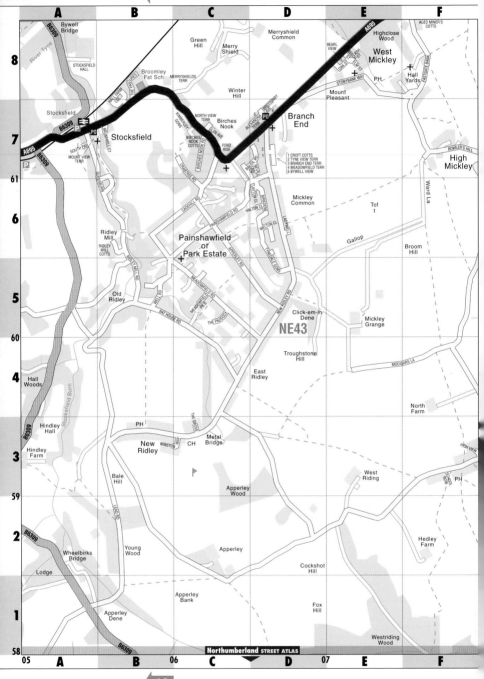

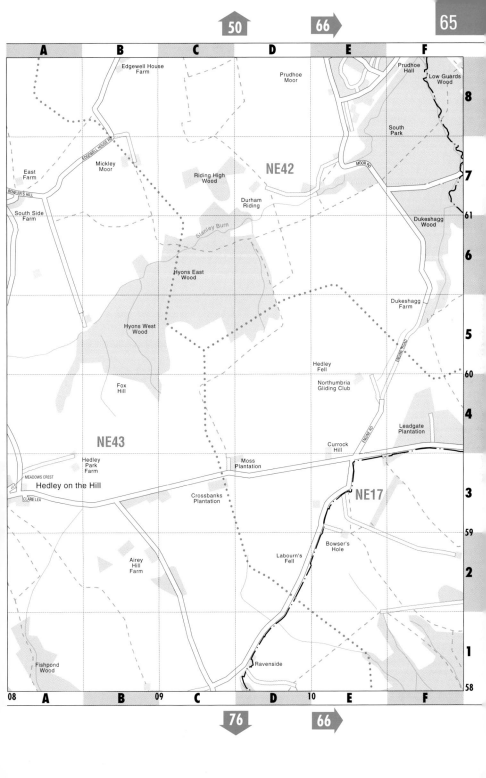

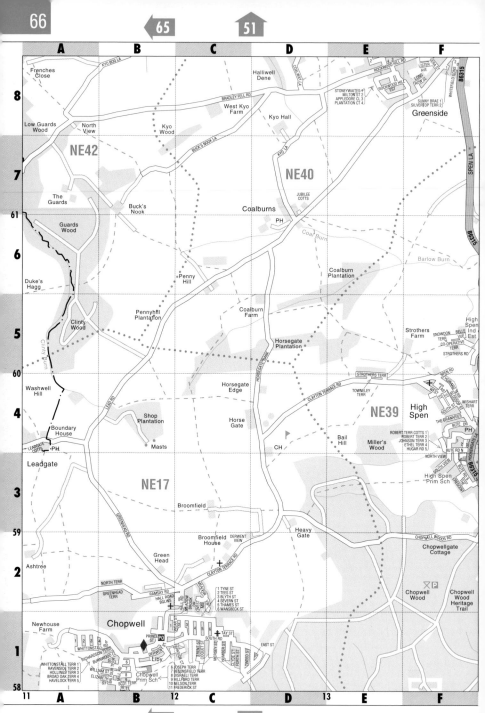

A B C D E F

8

Frenches
Close

KYO BOG LA
Halliwell
Dene

COX WAY LA
ROCKWOOD HILL RD

LISTER TERR
LONG DEAN CL
WHITEFIELD GDNS

B6315

STONEYWAITES 1
MILTON ST 2
APPLEDORE CL 3
PLANTATION CT 4.

ROCKWOOD HILL
EST

SUNNY BRAE 1
SILVERTOP TERR 2

7

Low Guards
Wood

North
View

NE42

BRADLEY FELL RD
West Kyo
Farm

Kyo Hall

Kyo
Wood

Kyo
Wood

BUCK'S NOOK LA

KYO LA

Greenside

NE40

SPEN LA

B6315

61

The
Guards

Buck's
Nook

Coalburns

JUBILEE
COTTS

PH

Coal Burn

Barlow Burn

6

Guards
Wood

Duke's
Hagg

Penny
Hill

Coalburn
Plantation

Clinty Burn

5

Clinty
Wood

Pennyhill
Plantation

Coalburn
Farm

Horsegate
Plantation

Strothers
Farm

High
Spen Ind
Est

SNOWDON
TERR

BELLE
VUE

CO-OPERATIVE
TERR

STROTHERS RD

60

Washwell
Hill

LEAD RD

Horsegate
Edge

HORSEGATE BANK

CLAYTON TERRACE RD

STROTHERS TERR

TOWNELEY
TERR

SPEN RD

WISHART
TERR

4

Boundary
House

LEADGATE
COTTS

PH

Shop
Plantation

Masts

Horse
Gate

CH

Bail
Hill

NE39

Miller's
Wood

ROBERT TERR COTTS 1
ROBERT TERR 2
JOHNSON TERR 3
ETHEL TERR 4
HUGAR RD 5.

High
Spen

THE GRANARIES

BUTE DR

BUTE RD N

NORTH VIEW

PH

B6315

3

Leadgate

NE17

GREENHEAD LA

Broomfield

High Spen
Prim Sch

59

Ashtree

Broomfield
House

DERWENT
VIEW

Heavy
Gate

CHOPWELL WOODS RD

Chopwellgate
Cottage

2

NORTH TERR

GREENHEAD
TERR

RAMSAY RD

Green
Head

CLAYTON TERRACE RD

HALL ROAD
BGLWS

1 TYNE ST
2 TEES ST
3 BLYTH ST
4 SEVERN ST
5 THAMES ST
6 WANSBECK ST

Chopwell
Wood

P

Chopwell
Wood
Heritage
Trail

1

Newhouse
Farm

Chopwell

WHITTONSTALL TERR

RICHARDSON RD

BURNWOOD RD

WILLIAM ST

ELIZABETH ST

SCOTT TERR

Liby

PRINCE RD

PO

DERWENT ST

COLIN ST

SOUTH RD

TAY ST

MERSEY ST

HUMBER RD

EAST ST

TOWER ST

6 JOSEPH TERR
7 BEACONSFIELD TERR
8 DISRAELI TERR
9 HILLFORD TERR
10 NELSON TERR
11 FREDERICK ST

58

WHITTONSTALL TERR 1
RAVENSIDE TERR 2
HOLLINGS TERR 3
BROAD OAK TERR 4
HAVELOCK TERR 5.

Chopwell
Prim Sch

11 A B 12 C 13 E F

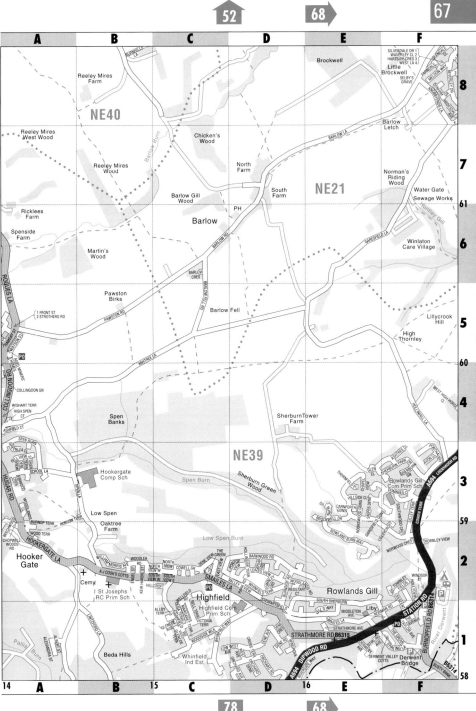

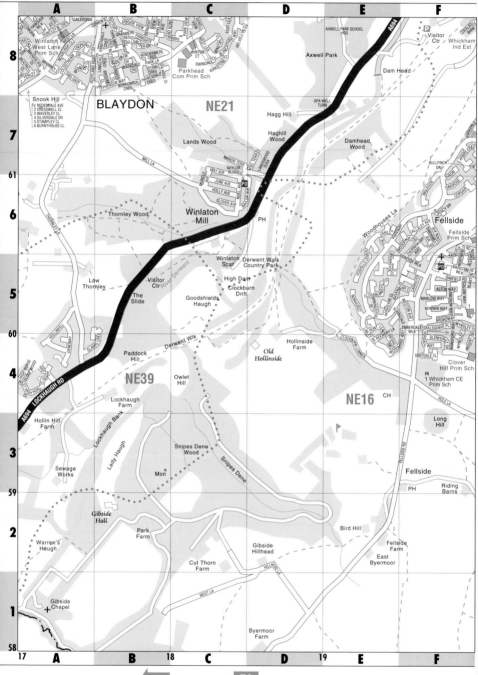

67
53

A   B   C   D   E   F

A694 Visitor Ctr   Whickham Ind Est

AXWELL PARK SCHOOL HSS

8

Winlaton West Lane Prim Sch

Axwell Park

Dam Head

CALEDONIA

Parkhead Com Prim Sch

BLAYDON   **NE21**

Snook Hill
1 REDESDALE AVE
2 CRESSWELL CL
3 WAVERLEY CL
4 SILVERDALE DR
5 STAMPLEY CL
6 BURNTHOUSE CL

SPA WELL TURN

Hagg Hill

7

Lands Wood   Haghill Wood

Damhead Wood

BULLFINCH DRV

MILL LA

61

MANOR TERR   NAYLOR
MAT AVE   BLDGS
JUNE AVE
HOLLY AVE
CLOVER AVE   PO

6

Thornley Wood

Winlaton Mill

PH

Fellside

Woodhouses La

Fellside Prim Sch

PO

Low Thornley

Visitor Ctr

The Slide

Winlaton Scar   Derwent Walk Country Park

High Dam   Clockburn Drift

CLOCKBURN

Goodshields Haugh

River Derwent

OAKFIELD RD

ASTON WAY

MARLOW WAY

NEWMIN WAY

BROADWAY

5

GLENHAUGH WAY

GLAMIS CRES

60

Derwent Wlk

Paddock Hill

Old Hollinside

Hollinside Farm

CLOCKBURN LONNEN

DEEPDALE CL

Clover Hill Prim Sch

4

A694 LOCKHAUGH RD

NE39

Owlet Hill

Whickham CE Prim Sch

NE16   CH

Hollin Hill Farm

Lockhaugh Farm

Long Hill

3

Lockhaugh Bank

Snipes Dene Wood

Snipes Dene

Fellside

PH   Riding Barns

Sewage Works

Lady Haugh

Mon

59

Gibside Hall

Park Farm

Bird Hill

Fellside Farm

East Byermoor

2

Warren's Haugh

Cut Thorn Farm

Gibside Hillhead

HILL LA

WEST LA

1

Gibside Chapel

Byermoor Farm

58

17   A   B   18   C   D   19   E   F

67
79

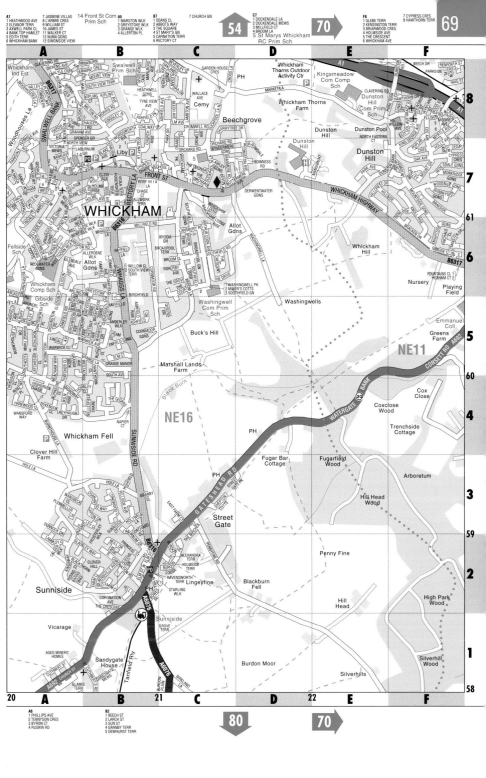

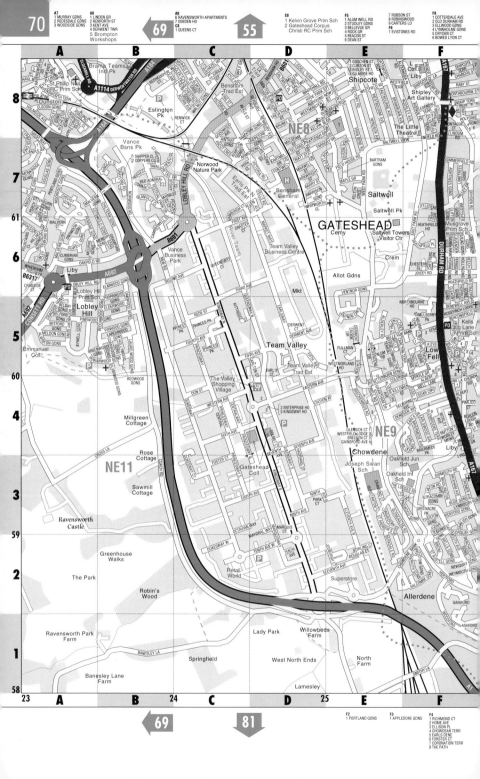

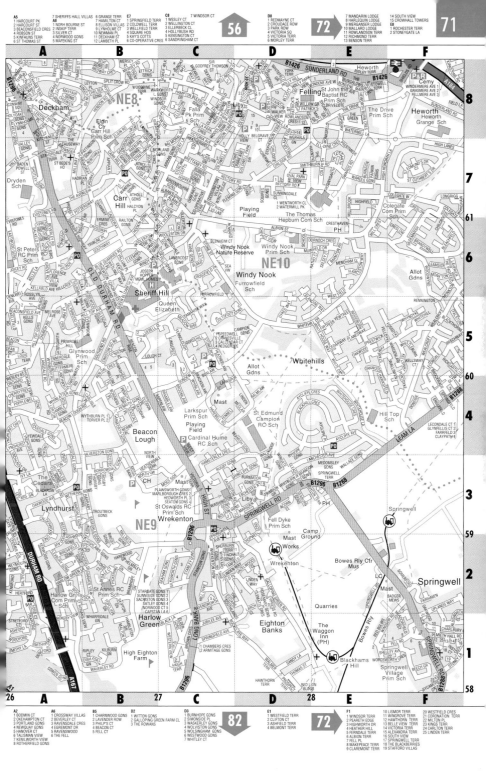

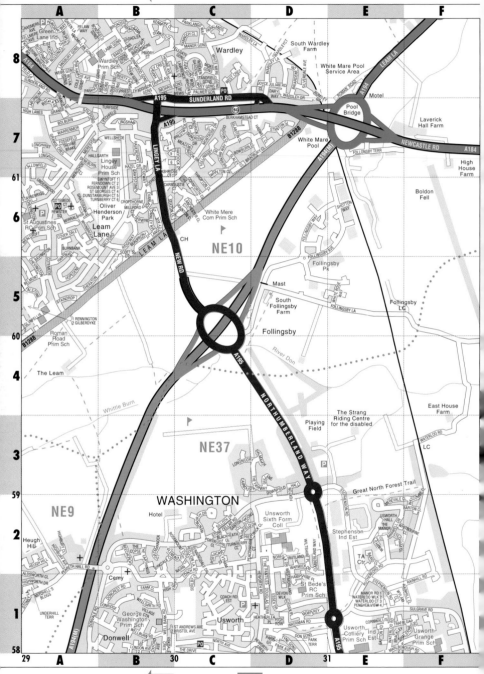

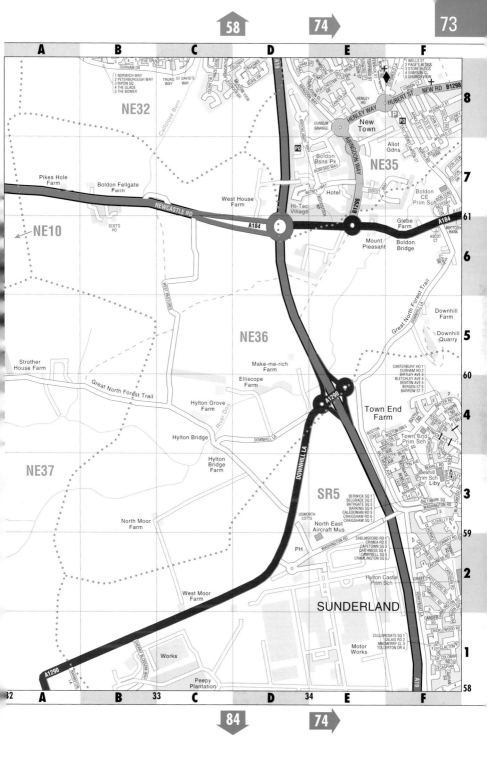

NE35
B1298
NEW RD B1298

Boldon
North Bridge

WHITBURN RD B1299

8

Cleadon Lane
Ind Est

SOUTH END 2
WINDSOR DR 2
GROSVENOR DR 2

Mast

Boldon
Flats
SR6

Boldon Sch

West Boldon Prim Sch

West Boldon

East Boldon
Jun Sch

P&R
LC

East
Boldon

Flats
Bridge

BLUE HOUSE LA

7
WESTERN TERR
FRONT ST

VICTORIA TERR

1 CROSSWAYS
2 STAMON TERR
3 STRUAN TERR
4 BEDE TERR

ADDISON RD
A1184

B1299 STATION RD

East
Boldon

SUNDERLAND RD

61

South
Boldon

Cemy

1 CLAREMOUNT CT
2 EVEREST GR
3 PENNINE GR
4 CHEVIOT HO
5 SHOTLEY GR

East Boldon
Inf Sch

YELLOW LEAS FARM 1
THE ORCHARD 2
PROSPECT TERR 3

D7
1 GRANGE TERR
2 ASHLEIGH VILLAS
3 BIRCHWOOD
4 FERNDALE AVE
5 THE TERRACE
6 ST CHAD'S VILLAS

Low House
Farm

Stadium

A1184

1 ST NICHOLAS RD
2 AVONDALE GDNS
3 WINDERMERE TERR
4 HAMILTON TERR
5 THREE RIVERS CT
6 THE FAIRWAYS
7 MANSION HO

Turner's
Hill

Belle
Vue
Villa

South
Lodge

NE36

Playing
Field

6

Boldon
Hills

Mast

Quarry
Hill

Mundles

Field
House

5

1 BARROW ST
2 BERWICK AVE
3 BRADMAN SQ
4 KING CHARLES CT
5 KING HENRY CT

60

York
Ho

St John Bosco
RC Prim Sch

Downhill

Community
North
Sports Complex

1 KINGSWAY SQ
2 KILLARNEY AVE
3 KESTREL SQ
4 KESTEVEN SQ

Hylton Red
House Sch

Willow Fields
Com Prim Sch

Witherwack

FONTBURN CT 1
ROTHLEY CT 2
WOOLWICH CL 3
WOOLWICH CL 4
WHITCHURCH CL 5
WHITCHURCH RD

4

BLAYDON AVE

1 KENLEY RD
2 KNARESBOROUGH SQ
3 REEDLING CT

Hylton Red
House

Bishop Harland
CE Prim Sch

1 RANGOON SQ
2 RAWMARSH RD
3 RAMILLIES SQ
4 ROCKINGHAM SQ
5 RAEBURN RD
6 REVELSTOKE RD
7 ROCKINGHAM RD

SR5

Cemy

English Martyrs
RC Prim Sch

Allot
Gdns

Playing
Fields

Marley
Pots

WATERBURY RD
OLD
MILL RD

3

1 KIDDERMINSTER SQ
2 KINGSLAND SQ
3 KINGSWOOD SQ
4 BAYSWATER SQ
5 BURKE ST
6 DODDS CT
7 BRENTFORD SQ
8 BALMORAL CT
9 CLOVELLY CT
10 BRENTFORD AVE

Maplewood
Sch

City of Sunderland
College

59

Hylton
Castle

Hylton Red
House
Prim Sch

F2
1 THE POPLARS
2 GROSVENOR ST
3 WALTER THOMAS ST
4 FLORENCE CRES
5 ELMWOOD SQ
6 CARLISLE TERR
7 FITZROY TERR
8 PINEWOOD SQ

Southwick
Ind Est

2

Hylton Dene Nature Reserve
Great North Forest Trail

North
Hylton Road
Ind Est

RIVERBANK RD

WESSINGTON WAY
A1231

Hylton Castle

Castletown

NORTH VIEW

DENE
MEWS

Hylton Retail
Park

HYLTON PARK RD

Business
& Innovation
Ctr

1

Castle View
Acad

1 CROSTHWAITE DR

THE BRIARS

CASTLE VIEW

ST MARGARET'S
CT

KIRKWALL

River Wear

DEAN TERR 1
CLOCKWELL ST 2

SR4

58

A2
1 HEPBURN GR
2 CRAMLINGTON GR
3 Hylton Castle
Prim Sch

B1
1 SHEPPARD TERR
2 STANLEY ST
3 WEST VIEW
4 ASHWOOD GR
5 JOYCE TERR
6 THE GROVE
7 THOMPSON CRES
8 PARKHOUSE AVE
9 JENNIFER AVE

C1
1 WREN GR
2 THRUSH GR
3 EAST VIEW S
4 CASTLE ST S
5 BARRON ST S
6 CHAFFINCH RD
7 THE VILLAS

A1		B1	B2	C1	D1	E1	E2	
1 LORD GORT CL	4 CICERO TERR	1 VEDRA ST	1 CHALFORD RD	1 CHILTON ST	1 DEVONSHIRE TWR	1 CONISCLIFFE PL	1 GLENTHORNE RD	10 ROKER PARK CL
2 MALABURN WAY	5 JULIUS CAESAR ST	2 SUDDICK ST	2 GRANGE TERR	2 FINSBURY ST	2 EGLINTON TWR	2 LENTHORN MEWS	2 DINSDALE RD	11 MIDFIELD DR
3 MOUNT PLEASANT	6 TENNYSON ST	3 USHER ST	3 COLLINGWOOD ST	3 EMPRESS ST	3 HOWARD ST	3 KELPIE GDNS	3 ST ANDREW'S TERR	E4
4 KINGSLEY CL	A3	4 CLOSE ST	4 THE OVAL	4 COLLEGE VIEW	4 ROSEBERY ST	4 LANGEFORD PL	4 ASSOCIATION RD	1 SEABURN CL
5 ALEXANDRA AVE	1 EDMONTON SQ	5 TURNBULL HO	5 BURNBANK	5 NORTH ST	5 DIXON'S SQ	5 DAME DOROTHY CRES	5 COQUETDALE VILLAS	2 CLIFTBOURNE AVE
A2	2 EXMOUTH ST	6 LEE ST	6 CORNHILL RD		6 ALL SAINTS HO	6 VICTOR ST	6 GOALMOUTH CL	3 GARCIA TERR
1 THE POPLARS	3 EDINBURGH SQ	7 PEMBERTON CL	7 NORTH BANK CT		7 SOUTHWICK RD	7 AKELD MEWS	7 TURNSTILE MEWS	4 CAMBOURNE AVE
2 CLARENCE ST	4 EPPING SQ		8 MAYPOLE CL			8 CARLCROFT	8 CLOCKSTAND CL	5 CRESSBOURNE AVE
3 DAVISON TERR	5 EPSOM SQ		9 CHURCH ST			9 ZETLAND SQ	9 PROMOTION CL	6 CALDERBOURNE AVE
	6 MAPLEWOOD AVE					10 HARWOOD CT		7 ASHLEIGH DR

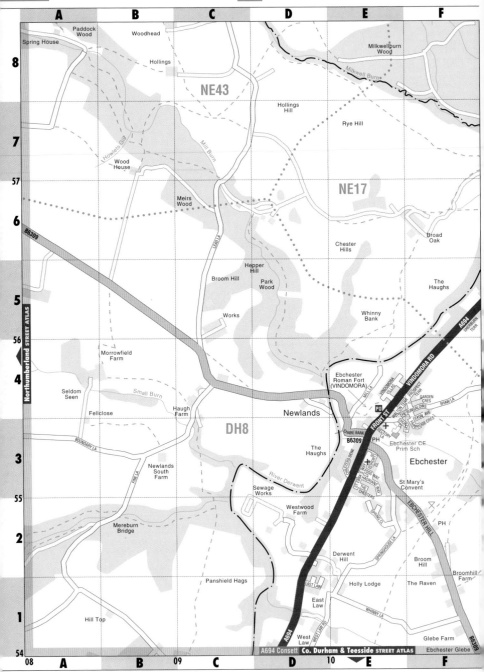

A **B** **C** **D** **E** **F**

Spring House
Paddock Wood
Woodhead
Hollings
Milkwellburn Wood
Milkwell Burn

8

NE43

Hollings Hill
Rye Hill

7

Howlers Gill
Mill Burn
Wood House

57

Meirs Wood

NE17

6

B6309
LEVEL LA
Broad Oak
Chester Hills
Hepper Hill
Broom Hill
Park Wood
The Haughs

5

Works
Whinny Bank

56

Morrowfield Farm
Small Burn

A694
SHOTLEY TERR

4

Seldom Seen
Fellclose
Haugh Farm
BOUNDARY LA
FINE LA

Ebchester Roman Fort (VINDOMORA)
MILL LA
VINDOMORA RD
VINDOMORA VILLAS
WALTON TERR
PROSPECT TERR
THE BUNGALOWS
GARDEN CRES
SHAW LA

DH8
Newlands
PO
FRONT ST
RECTORY
PH
B6309
Ebchester CE Prim Sch
Ebchester
The Haughs
CHARE BANK
CHESTERS DENE
+

3

Newlands South Farm
River Derwent
Sewage Works
+
St Mary's Convent
THE CHESTERS
CROSS WAY
SPRING CL
EBCHESTER HILL

55

Mereburn Bridge
Westwood Farm
SPRINGHOUSE LA
PH

2

Panshield Hags
Derwent Hill
Holly Lodge
Broom Hill
The Raven
Broomhill Farm

EAST LAW
East Law
WHINNY LA

1

Hill Top
A694
West Law
CHESTER LAW RD
Glebe Farm
B6309
Ebchester Glebe

54

08 **A** **B** 09 **C** **D** 10 **E** **F**

A694 Consett **Co. Durham & Teesside** STREET ATLAS

Northumberland STREET ATLAS

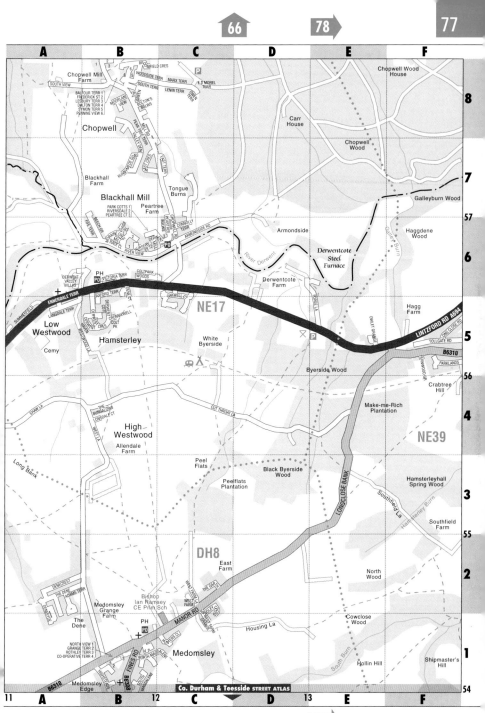

A   B   C   D   E   F

Chopwell Mill Farm

Chopwell Wood House

SOUTH VIEW
BALFOUR TERR 1
FREDERICK ST 2
LESBURY TERR 3
DALTON TERR 4
SYMON TERR 5
PENNINE VIEW 6

MOORLAND VIEW

BR
MFIELD CRES
WOODSIDE TERR
MARX TERR
E D MOREL TERR

Carr House

Chopwell

SOUTH TERR
BOLTON'S BLDGS
LENIN TERR

Chopwell Wood

Blackhall Farm

FIRST TERR
LAST TERR
RUDYARD STREET

Tongue Burns

Galleyburn Wood

Blackhall Mill

PARK COTTS 1
RIVERSDALE 2
PEARTREE CT 3

Peartree Farm

Armondside

Haggdene Wood

ARMONDSIDE RD

River Derwent

Derwentcote Steel Furnace

RIVER VIEW
PO

NE17

Hagg Farm

DERWENT VALLEY VILLAS
PO
VICTORIA TERR
AXFORD TERR

COLTPARK WOODS

OAKWELL CT

Derwentcote Farm

LINTZFORD RD A694

OWLET GRANGE

PINGLE LA

B6310
TOLLGATE RD

Low Westwood

ENNERDALE TERR

LANGDALE TERR

CROMWELL COLT PK

Hamsterley

White Byerside

Byerside Wood

PARKLANDS

Crabtree Hill

NE39

Cemy

SHAW LA

THE BUNGALOWS

CUT THROAT LA

Make-me-Rich Plantation

High Westwood

Allendale Farm

Peel Flats

Black Byerside Wood

Hamsterleyhall Spring Wood

Long Bank

Peelflats Plantation

Southfield Farm

Southfield La

LONGCLOSE BANK

DH8

East Farm

North Wood

Medomsley Grange Farm

DENCREST
THE DENE
ADAMS TERR

Bishop Ian Ramsey CE Prim Sch

WEST FARM

Housing La

Cowclose Wood

The Dene

MANOR RD

PH
PO

Medomsley

Hollin Hill

Shipmaster's Hill

NORTH VIEW 1
GRANGE TERR 2
ROTHLEY TERR 3
CO-OPERATIVE TERR 4

FINES RD

B6310

Medomsley Edge

B6308

11   A   B   12   C   D   13   E   F

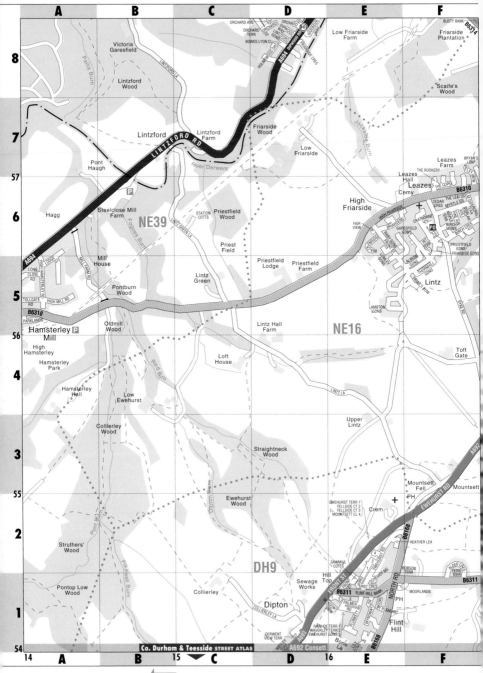

Co. Durham & Teesside STREET ATLAS

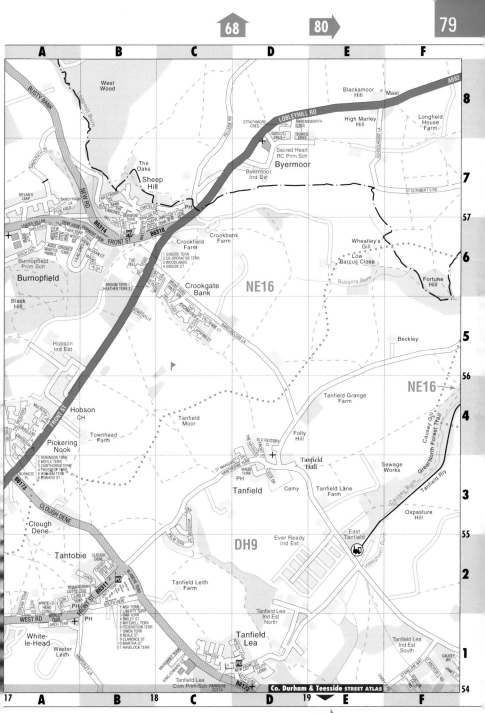

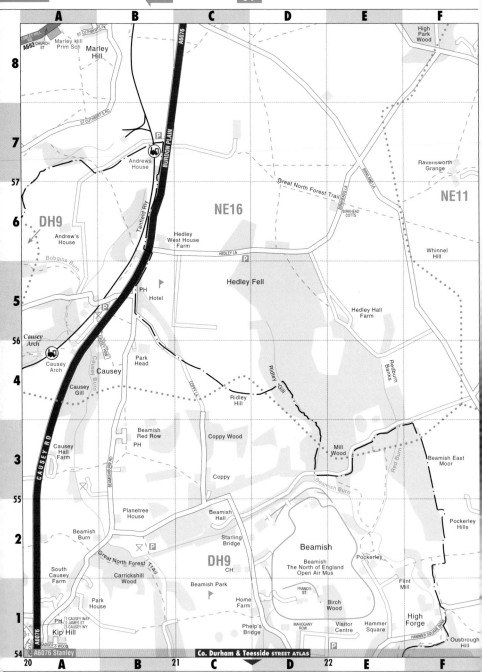

A   B   C   D   E   F

Co. Durham & Teesside STREET ATLAS

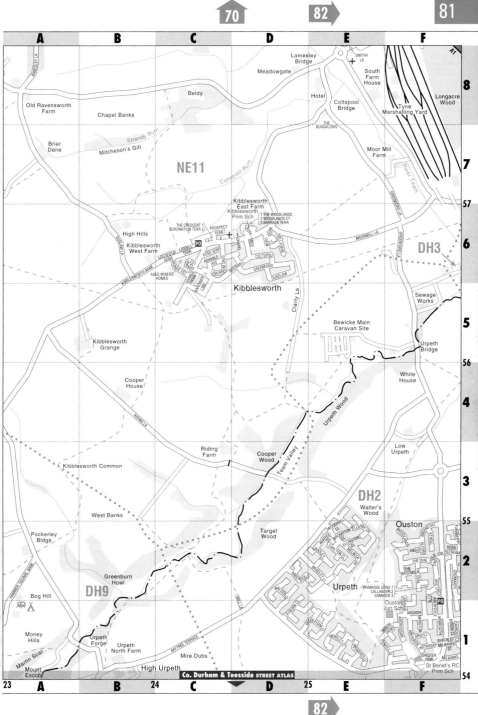

8

Old Ravensworth Farm

Chapel Banks

Beldy

Lamesley Bridge

Meadowgate

SMITHY LA

South Farm House

Hotel

Coltspool Bridge

Tyne Marshalling Yard

Longacre Wood

Briar Dene

Mitcheson's Gill

Strandy Burn

THE BUNGALOWS

Moor Mill Farm

River Team

NE11

Coltspool Burn

7

57

High Hills

Kibblesworth West Farm

OSWALD LA

Kibblesworth East Farm
Kibblesworth Prim Sch

THE CRESCENT 1
CORONATION TERR 2

PROSPECT TERR

1 THE WOODLANDS
2 WOODLANDS CT
3 BARRACK TERR

MOORMILL LA

DH3

6

LOCKEDP CL

LIDDELL TERR

PO

ROSE GDNS

CHAPEL

ARRABALE AVE

MOORMILL

COLTSPOOL

GREENFORD

OUSELAW

KIBBLESWORTH BANK

AGED MINERS HOMES

Kibblesworth

Clarty La

Sewage Works

5

Kibblesworth Grange

Bewicke Main Caravan Site

Urpeth Bridge

56

Cooper House

RIDING LA

White House

Urpeth Wood

4

Kibblesworth Common

Riding Farm

Cooper Wood

Team Valley

Low Urpeth

DH2

Walter's Wood

3

West Banks

Target Wood

Ouston

55

Pockerley Bldgs

ABERNETHY

WOODMAN CL

ELLIASSO DR

KINLOSS

ATHOL

DURHAM ST

ROSS

COLDSTREAM

THE OVAL

2

Bog Hill

Greenburn Howl

DH9

Urpeth

PRIMROSE GDNS 1
CALLANDER 2
CANNOCK 3

Urpeth

THE BROOMS

ARCADIA

ARGYLL

MILBANK ST

Money Hills

Urpeth Forge

Urpeth North Farm

BAYTREE TERRACE

Mire Dubs

Ouston Jun Sch

P PO

1

Martin Scar

Mount Escob

High Urpeth

CHESTER VIEW

St Benet's RC Prim Sch

54

A 23 B 24 C D 25 E F

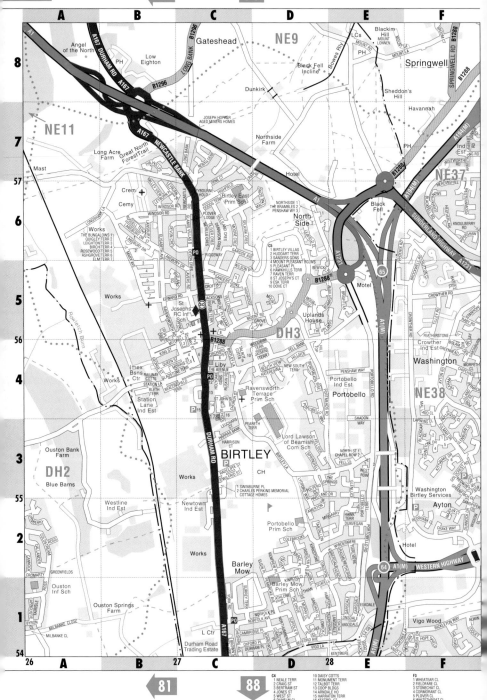

NE9
Gateseshead
Springwell
NE11
NE37
DH3
Washington
NE38
DH2
Blue Barns
BIRTLEY
Portobello
Ayton
Barley
Mow
Vigo Wood

C4
1 NEALE TERR
2 CRAIG ST
3 BERTRAM ST
4 JONES ST
5 WEST ST
6 DUNELM CL
7 CONSTABLES GARTH
8 ORCHARD PK
9 GROVE COTTS
10 DAISY COTTS
11 MONUMENT TERR
12 TALBOT TERR
13 COOP BLDGS
14 ARNDALE HO
15 HARRATON TERR
16 KESTREL CT
17 Birtley St Josephs
RC Junior School

F3
1 WHEATEAR CL
2 FIELDFARE CL
3 STONECHAT CL
4 CORMORANT CL
5 PLOVER CL
6 WHITETHROAT CL
7 GLENHOLME CL
8 TEAL CL
9 WREN CL

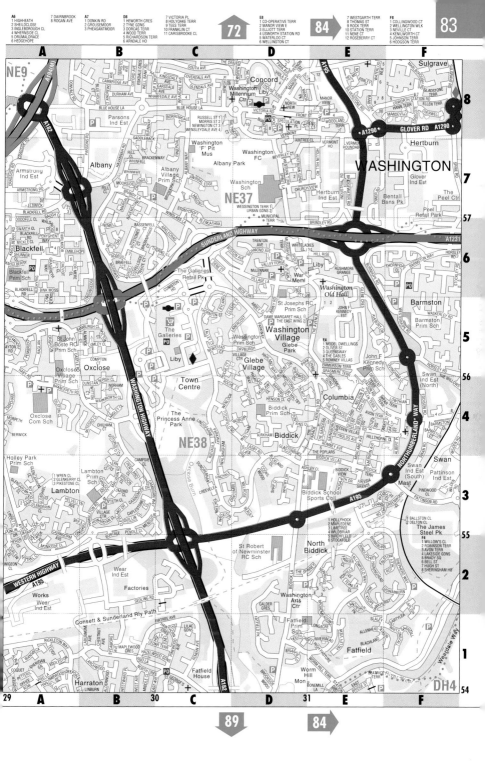

WASHINGTON

NE37

NE38

SR5

SR4

DH4

Peepy Plantation

Works

Hillthorn Farm

Glover Network Ctr

Glover Ind Est

Peel Retail Park

Barmston Water

Hylton Plantation

Test Tracks

Tyne and Wear Fire and Rescue Service HQ

SUNDERLAND HIGHWAY

Pattinson Ind Est

Middle Barmston Farm

Low Barmston Farm

Washington Wetland Ctr

Faraday Cl

Weardale Way

River Wear

Offerton Haugh

High Wood

Manor House Farm

Nab End

White Heugh

Stony Heugh

Sewage Works

Wood House Farm

CH

Ayton's Wood

Offerton Grange Farm

Pennywell Ind Est

THE GRANARIES

Offerton

Offerton Hall Farm

Glebe House Farm

PH

Cox Green

The James Steel Park

Low Lambton

Dawson's Plantation

Penshaw Wood

Penshaw Hill

Flinton Hill Farm

Carr Hill

Great North Forest Trail

The Bottoms

Victoria Viaduct

Low Lambton Farm

Penshaw Monument

CHESTER RD

Wood House

Manor House Farm

Sunrise Ent Pk

Works

Motel

Ferryboat La

WESSINGTON WAY

A19

A1231

A1290

LC

Severn Hos

Horsley Rd

Stockley Rd

Waskerley Rd

Horsley Rd

Wilden Rd

Stanfield Rd

Barmston La

Barmston La

Nissan Way

Cherry Blossom Way

Manderley Way

Monument Park

Pattinson Way

Alston Cl

Lee Dr

Walton Rd

Arncham Gr 1
Kingswood Gr 2
Chalfont Gr 3

Macmerry Cl 1
Tollerton Dr 2
Maydown Cl 3

Offerton Cl 1
Mayfield Rd 2

A183

A19

32

33

34

54

55

56

57

1

2

3

4

5

6

7

8

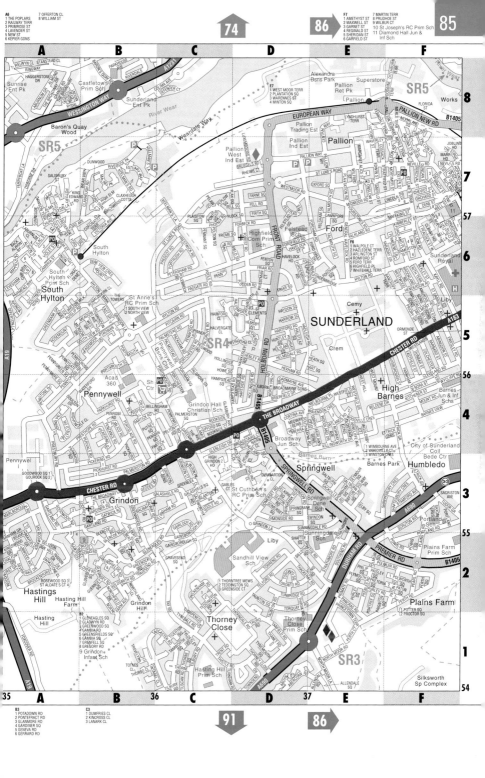

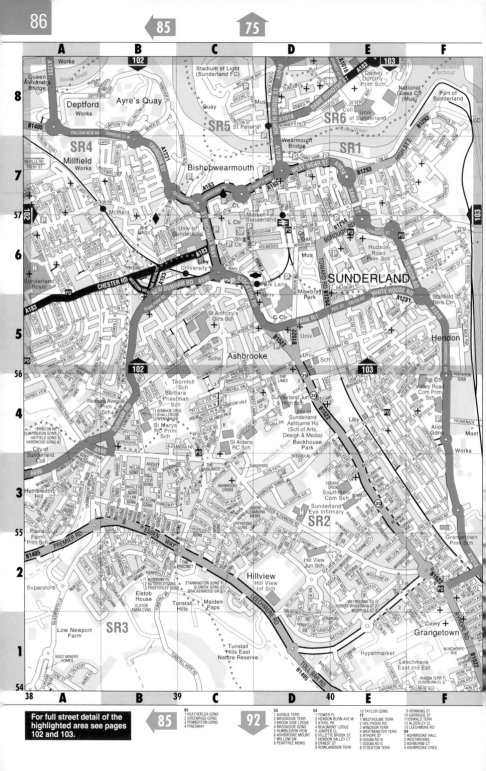

85 75

For full street detail of the highlighted area see pages 102 and 103.

85 92

B3
1 HEATHERLEA GDNS
2 GREENRIGG GDNS
3 PEMBERTON GDNS
4 PINESWAY

C4
1 AVENUE TERR
2 BROOKSIDE TERR
3 BROOK SIDE LODGE
4 BROOKSIDE GDNS
5 HUMBLEDON VIEW
6 ASHBROOKE MOUNT
7 WILLOW GR
8 PEARTREE MEWS

E4
1 TOWER PL
2 HENDON BURN AVE W
3 ATHOL PK
4 BEAUMONT LODGE
5 JUNIPER CL
6 VILLETTE BROOK ST
7 HENDON VALLEY CT
8 ERNEST ST
9 ROWLANDSEN TERR

10 TAYLOR GDNS

F2
1 WESTHOLME TERR
2 HOLYROOD RD
3 WINDSOR TERR
4 WESTMINSTER TERR
5 RYHOPE ST
6 OCEAN RD N
7 OCEAN RD S
8 STOCKTON TERR

9 HEMMING ST
10 GARNEGIE ST
11 OSWALD TERR
12 ALDERLEY CL
13 LEECHMERE RD

D4
1 ASHBROOKE HALL
2 WESTBROOKE
3 ASHBURNE CT
4 ASHBROOKE CRES

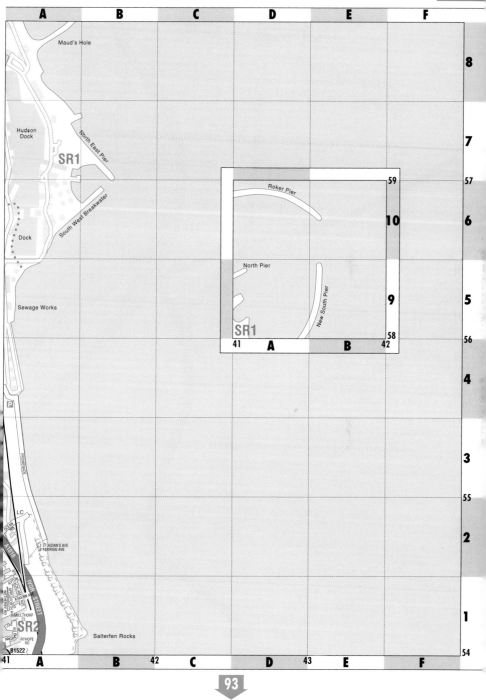

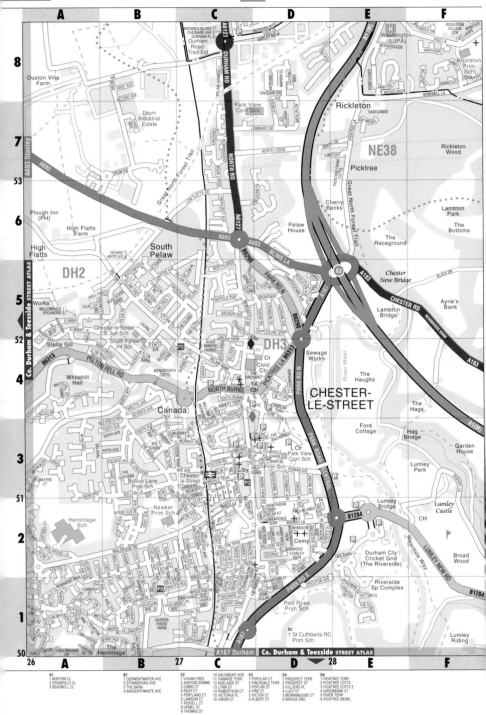

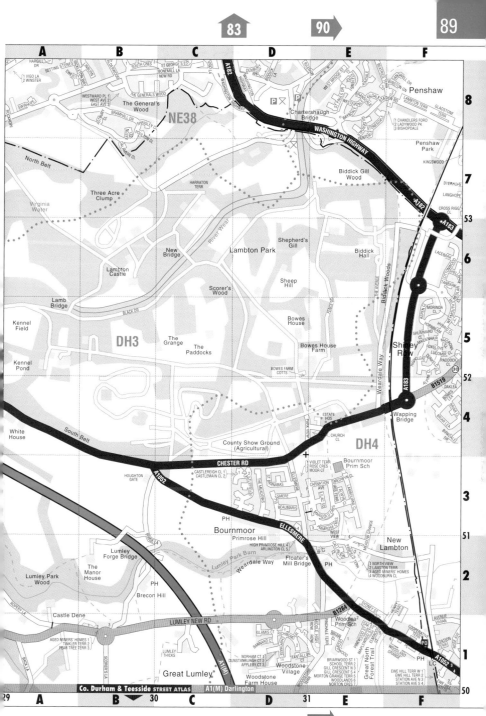

A　B　C　D　E　F

8

7

53

6

5

52

4

3

51

2

1

50

Penshaw
Penshaw Park
Shiney Row
Wapping Bridge
DH4
Bournmoor
Bournmoor Prim Sch
New Lambton
Woodlea Prim Sch
New Lambton
Great North Forest Trail
Great Lumley
Woodstone Village
Woodstone Farm House
Lumley New Rd
Brecon Hill
The Manor House
Lumley Park Wood
Castle Dene
Lumley Forge Bridge
Lumley Thicks
Primrose Hill
Floater's Mill Bridge
Weardale Way
Lumley Park Burn
Bournmoor
Chester Rd
County Show Ground (Agricultural)
Estate Hos
Church Cl
Houghton Gate
White House
South Belt
DH3
Kennel Pond
Kennel Field
Lamb Bridge
The Grange
The Paddocks
Bowes Farm Cotts
Bowes House Farm
Bowes House
Sheep Hill
Scorer's Wood
Lambton Castle
New Bridge
Lambton Park
Shepherd's Gill
Biddick Hall
Biddick Gill Wood
Three Acre Clump
Virginia Water
North Belt
NE38
The General's Wood
Westward Pl
Harraton Terr
Chartershaugh Bridge
Washington Highway
Biddick Woods
Weardale Way
The Avenue

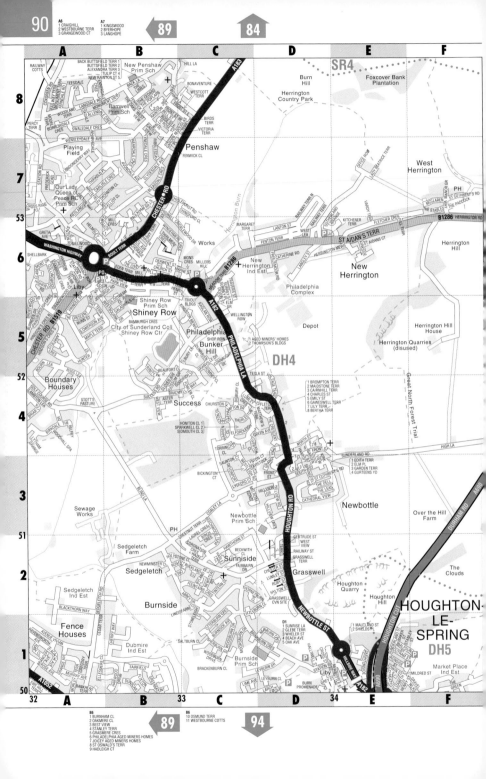

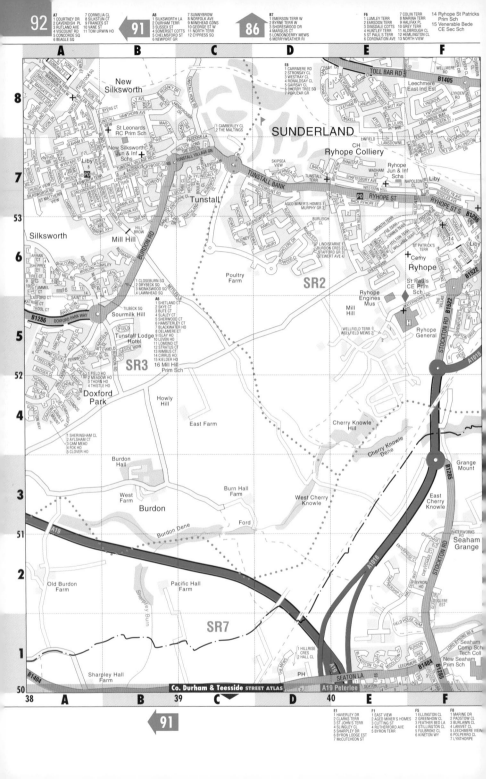

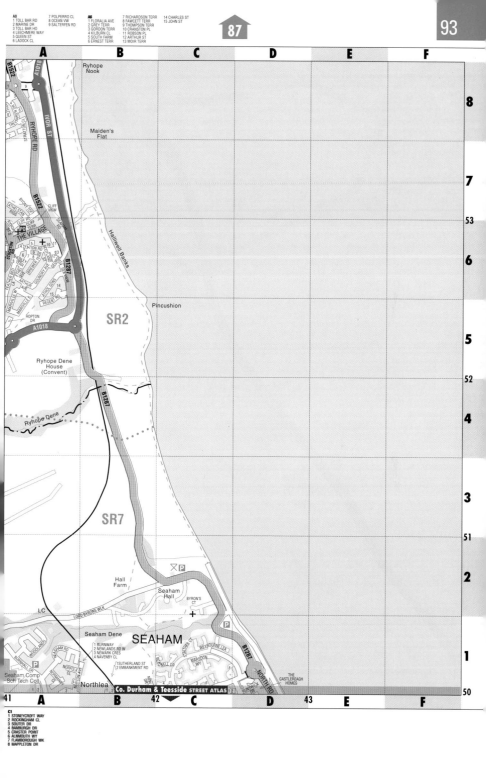

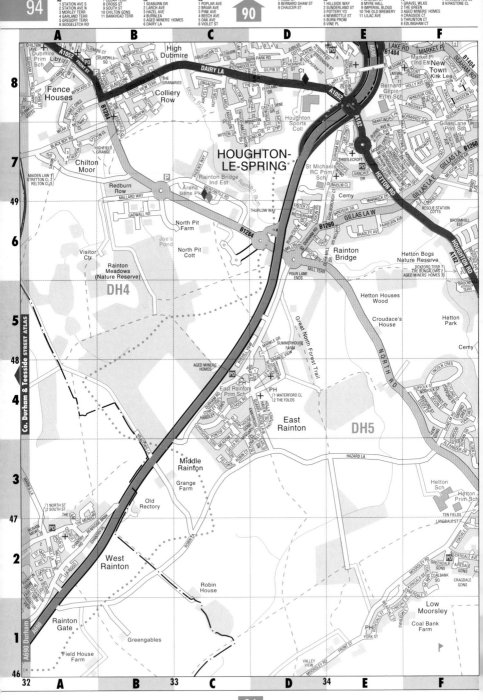

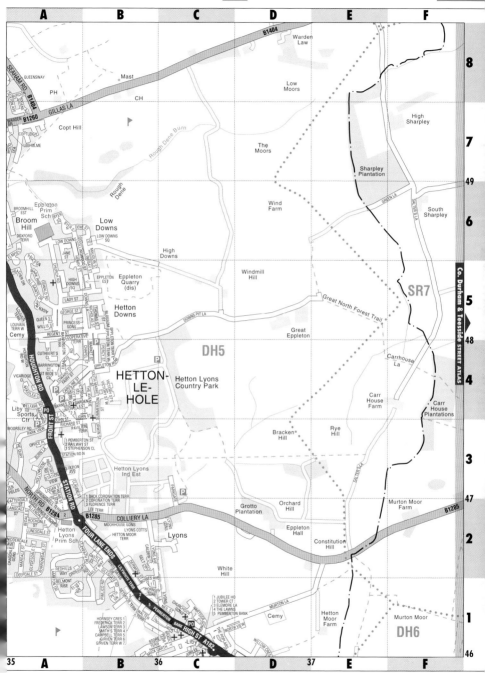

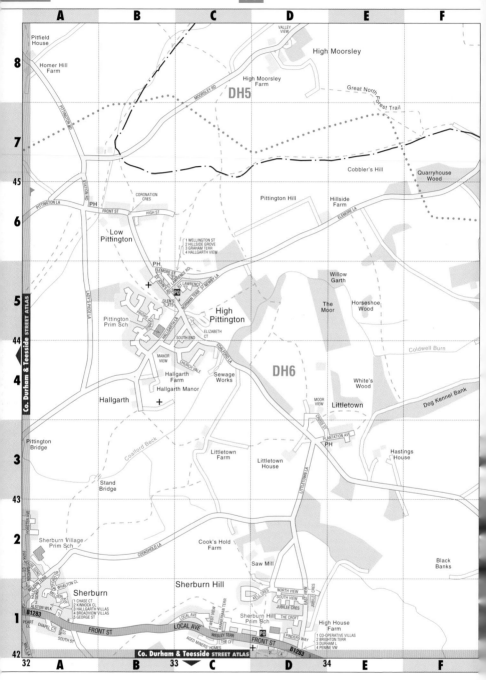

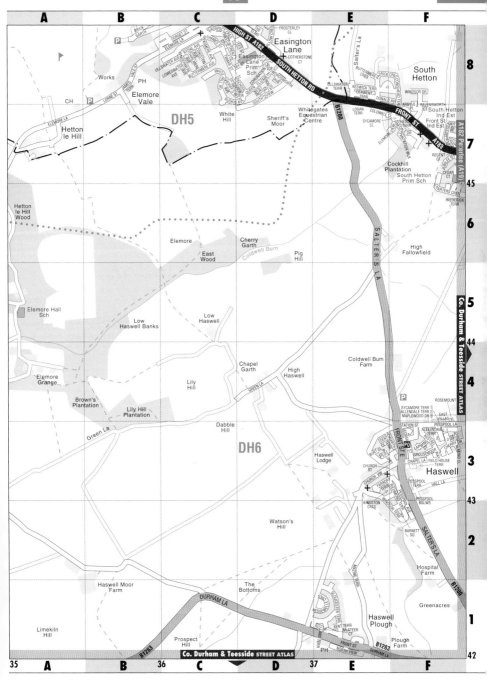

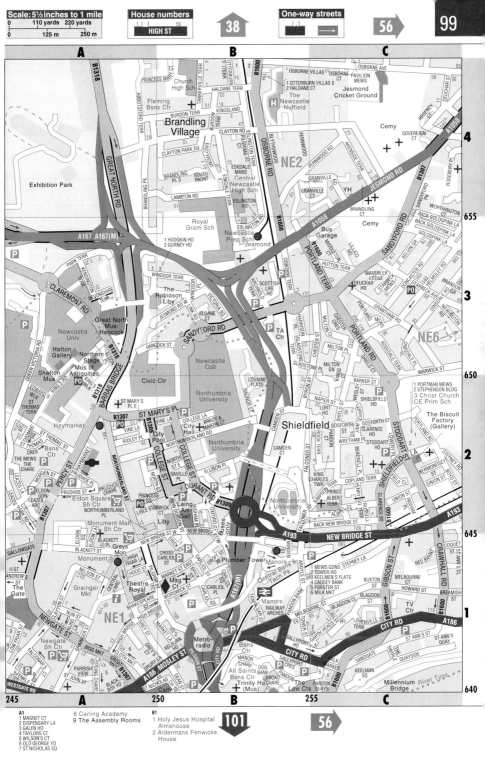

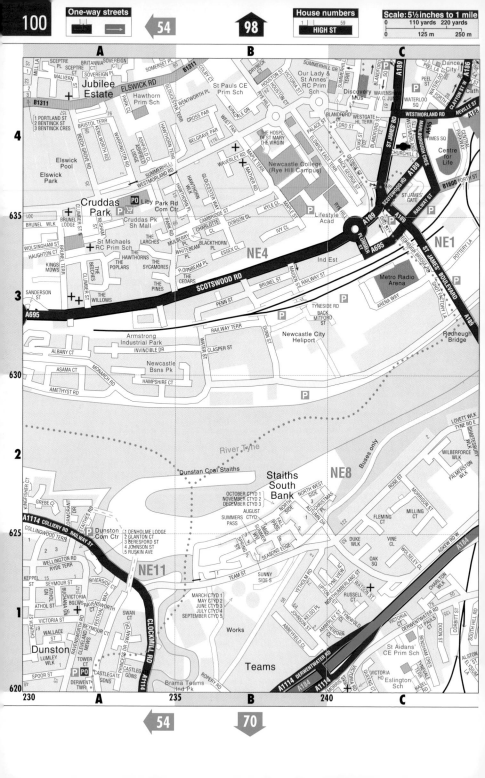

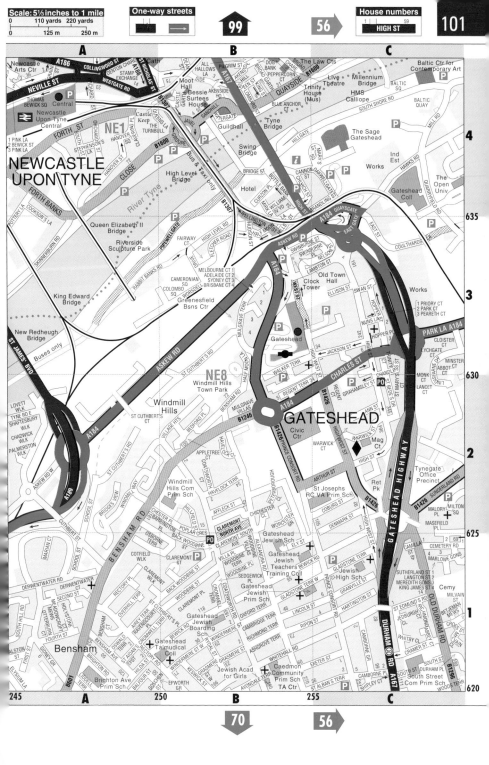

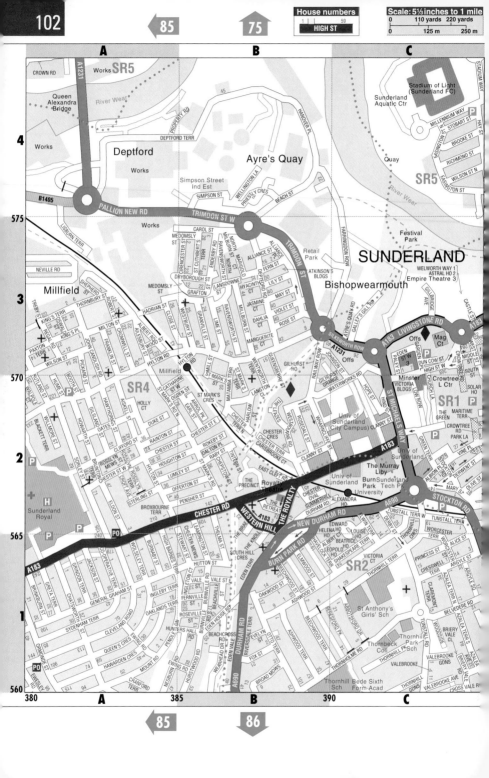

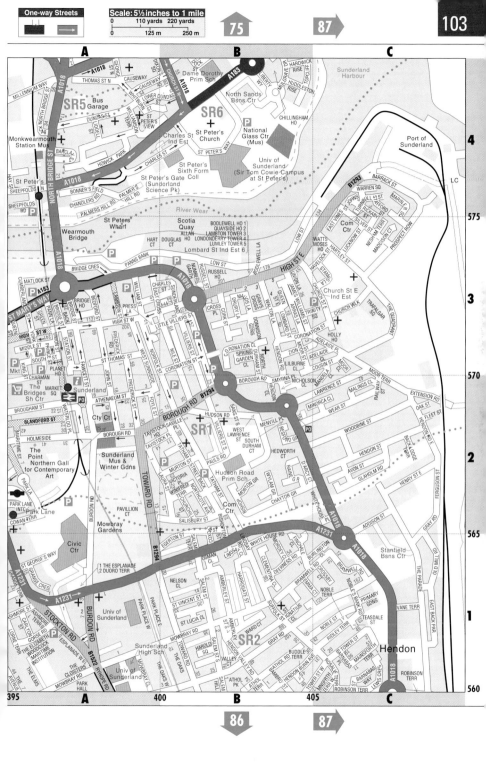

Index

Church Rd 6 Beckenham BR2..........53 C6

Place name May be abbreviated on the map

Location number Present when a number indicates the place's position in a crowded area of mapping

Locality, town or village Shown when more than one place has the same name

Postcode district District for the indexed place

Page and grid square Page number and grid reference for the standard mapping

Cities, towns and villages are listed in CAPITAL LETTERS **Public and commercial buildings** are highlighted in **magenta**
Places of interest are highlighted in blue with a star★

Abbreviations used in the index

Acad	**Academy**	Comm	**Common**	Gd	**Ground**	L	**Leisure**	Prom	**Promenade**
App	**Approach**	Cott	**Cottage**	Gdn	**Garden**	La	**Lane**	Rd	**Road**
Arc	**Arcade**	Cres	**Crescent**	Gn	**Green**	Liby	**Library**	Recn	**Recreation**
Ave	**Avenue**	Cswy	**Causeway**	Gr	**Grove**	Mdw	**Meadow**	Ret	**Retail**
Bglw	**Bungalow**	Ct	**Court**	H	**Hall**	Meml	**Memorial**	Sh	**Shopping**
Bldg	**Building**	Ctr	**Centre**	Ho	**House**	Mkt	**Market**	Sq	**Square**
Bsns, Bus	**Business**	Ctry	**Country**	Hospl	**Hospital**	Mus	**Museum**	St	**Street**
Bvd	**Boulevard**	Cty	**County**	HQ	**Headquarters**	Orch	**Orchard**	Sta	**Station**
Cath	**Cathedral**	Dr	**Drive**	Hts	**Heights**	Pal	**Palace**	Terr	**Terrace**
Cir	**Circus**	Dro	**Drove**	Ind	**Industrial**	Par	**Parade**	TH	**Town Hall**
Cl	**Close**	Ed	**Education**	Inst	**Institute**	Pas	**Passage**	Univ	**University**
Cnr	**Corner**	Emb	**Embankment**	Int	**International**	Pk	**Park**	Wk, Wlk	**Walk**
Coll	**College**	Est	**Estate**	Intc	**Interchange**	Pl	**Place**	Wr	**Water**
Com	**Community**	Ex	**Exhibition**	Junc	**Junction**	Prec	**Precinct**	Yd	**Yard**

Index of towns, villages, streets, hospitals, industrial estates, railway stations, schools, shopping centres, universities and places of interest

Abb–Ala

A

Abbay St SR5 .....75 A1
Abbey Cl
Washington NE38 .....83 D5
Whitley Bay NE25 .....31 D4
Abbey Ct
Gateshead NE8 .....101 C1
5 Hexham NE46 .....45 B5
Shiremoor NE27 .....30 E3
Abbey Dr
Burnside DH4 .....90 C2
Jarrow NE32 .....58 C7
Newcastle upon Tyne NE5 .....36 B4
Tynemouth NE30 .....42 D8
Abbeyfield Cl NE8 .....100 B1
Abbeyfields Fst Sch NE61 .....8 E8
Abbey Gate NE61 .....8 D7
Abbey Mdws NE61 .....8 D7
Abbey Rd NE38 .....83 D5
Abbey Terr
Morpeth NE61 .....3 F1
Shiremoor NE27 .....30 E3
Abbeyvale Dr NE6 .....57 B7
Abbey View
Hexham NE46 .....45 C4
Morpeth NE61 .....3 E1
Abbie Ct NE24 .....17 D7
Abbot Ct NE8 .....101 C3
Abbots Cl NE62 .....11 B8
Abbotsfield Cl SR3 .....91 F5
Abbotsford Gr SR2 .....102 C1
Abbotsford Ho NE24 .....17 C6
Abbotsford Pk NE25 .....31 F4
Abbotsford Rd NE10 .....56 D1
Abbotsford Terr NE2 .....99 A4
Abbotside Cl DH2 .....81 D2
Abbotside Pl NE5 .....36 D2
Abbotsmeade Cl NE5 .....54 C8
Abbotsway NE32 .....58 E6
Abbots Way
Tynemouth NE29 .....41 E8
2 Whickham NE16 .....69 B7
Abbot's Way NE61 .....8 E8
Abbs St SR5 .....75 D1
Abercorn Pl NE28 .....40 E6
Abercorn Rd
Newcastle upon Tyne NE15 .....54 A5
Sunderland SR3 .....91 D8
Abercrombie Pl 2 NE5 .....37 B2
Aberdare Rd SR3 .....91 E7
Aberdeen DH2 .....81 F1
Aberdeen Ct NE3 .....37 D8
Aberdeen Dr NE32 .....58 E3
Aberdeen Tower SR3 .....91 E8
Aberford Cl NE5 .....36 B3
Aberfoyle DH2 .....81 F1
Abernethy DH2 .....81 F2
Abigail Ct NE3 .....38 E5
Abingdon Ct
Blaydon NE21 .....53 C3
Newcastle upon Tyne NE3 .....37 D7
Abingdon Rd NE6 .....57 B7
Abingdon Sq NE23 .....16 C1
Abingdon St SR4 .....85 F5
Abingdon Way NE35 .....73 E7
Abinger St NE4 .....98 B1
Abington DH2 .....81 F1
Aboyne Sq SR3 .....85 D1
Acacia Ave DH4 .....90 A1
Acacia Gr
Hebburn NE31 .....57 E4
South Shields NE34 .....59 F5
Acacia Rd NE10 .....56 B2
Acacia Terr NE63 .....6 D3
Academy 360 SR4 .....85 B4
Acanthus Ave NE4 .....54 D7
Acer Ct SR2 .....86 D4
Acer Dr DH6 .....97 F3
Acklam Ave SR2 .....87 A1
Acomb Ave
Seaton Delaval NE25 .....23 D2
Wallsend NE28 .....40 D7
Acomb Cl NE61 .....9 C5
Acomb Cres NE3 .....38 A8
Acomb Ct
Bedlington NE22 .....11 A1
Gateshead NE9 .....71 B2
Killingworth NE12 .....29 D3
Sunderland SR2 .....86 F1
Acomb Dr NE41 .....51 A7
Acomb Gdns NE5 .....37 C1
Acorn Ave
Bedlington NE22 .....15 F8
Gateshead NE8 .....70 C8
Acorn Cl NE9 .....71 D3
Acorn Rd NE2 .....38 E2
Acorn Sq NE42 .....50 D2
Acreford Ct NE62 .....10 E6
Acton Dr NE29 .....41 D8
Acton Ho 11 NE29 .....42 A4
Acton Pl NE7 .....39 B2
Acton Rd NE5 .....53 F8
Adair Ave NE15 .....54 C6
Adair Way NE31 .....58 A5
Adamsez Ind Est NE15 .....53 F4
Adams Terr DH8 .....77 A2
Ada St
Newcastle upon Tyne NE6 .....56 E6
South Shields NE33 .....42 D1
Adderlane Fst Sch NE42 .....50 E3
Adderlane Rd NE42 .....50 E3
Adderstone Ave NE23 .....22 B5
Adderstone Cres NE2 .....38 F2
Adderstone Ct NE2 .....38 F3
Adderstone Gdns NE29 .....31 B1
Addington Cres NE29 .....41 E6
Addington Dr
Blyth NE24 .....17 E5
Wallsend NE28 .....40 D7
ADDISON 52 F5
Addison Cl 2 NE6 .....56 B6
Addison Ct
Ryton NE40 .....52 B5
7 Wallsend NE28 .....41 A1
Addison Gdns NE10 .....72 B8
Addison Ind Est NE21 .....52 F5
Addison Rd
Newcastle upon Tyne, Lemington NE15 .....53 D7
15 Newcastle upon Tyne NE6 .....56 B6
West Boldon NE36 .....74 A7
Addison St
North Shields NE29 .....42 A4
Sunderland SR2 .....103 C2
Addison Wlk NE34 .....59 A3
Addycombe Terr NE6 .....39 C1
Adelaide Cl SR1 .....103 C3
Adelaide Ct NE8 .....101 B3
Adelaide Ctr The 5 NE4 .....54 E5
Adelaide Ho 3 NE4 .....54 E5
Adelaide Pl SR1 .....103 C3
Adelaide St 12 DH3 .....88 C2
Adelaide Terr NE4 .....54 E4
Adeline Gdns NE3 .....38 A3
Adelphi Cl NE29 .....41 C8
Adelphi Pl NE6 .....56 E5
Aden Tower SR3 .....91 E8
Admington Ct NE62 .....10 F7
Admiral Collingwood Ct 5 NE61 .....9 A8
Admiral Ho 9 NE30 .....42 D7
Admiral Way SR3 .....91 C5
Adolphus St SR6 .....60 F1
Affleck St NE8 .....101 B2
Afton Ct NE34 .....59 C5
Afton Way NE3 .....37 E6
Agar Rd SR3 .....91 D8
Aged Miners' Homes
Annitsford NE23 .....22 B1
Ashington NE63 .....6 A4
2 Ashington, Woodbridge NE63 .....6 F5
Blyth NE24 .....17 B5
Boldon Colliery NE35 .....58 D1
Bournmoor DH4 .....89 E2
Brunswick Village NE13 .....28 A6
Burnopfield NE16 .....79 A6
Cambois NE24 .....12 D4
Chester le Street DH2 .....88 C4
Cramlington NE23 .....21 F7
Dudley NE23 .....29 A6
East Rainton DH5 .....94 C4
Great Lumley DH3 .....89 B1
Hetton-le-Hole DH5 .....94 F6
Hetton-le-Hole DH5 .....95 A2
High Spen NE39 .....67 A4
5 Houghton-le-Spring DH4 .....94 C8
3 Houghton-le-Spring, New Town DH5 .....94 F8
Kibblesworth NE11 .....81 C6
Longhirst NE61 .....5 B7
Mickley Square NE43 .....64 F8
Newbeggin-by-the-Sea NE64 .....7 D3
2 Newcastle upon Tyne NE5 .....36 E3
New Hartley NE25 .....23 E6
New Silksworth SR3 .....86 A1
Prudhoe NE42 .....50 B1
Rowlands Gill NE39 .....67 F1
Ryhope SR2 .....92 E7
Ryton NE40 .....52 E4
2 Seaham SR7 .....92 F1
Sherburn Hill DH6 .....96 C1
Shiney Row DH4 .....90 C5
Shiremoor NE27 .....30 F3
South Shields NE34 .....60 A7
Sunderland SR5 .....74 E2
Sunniside NE16 .....69 A1
Throckley NE15 .....35 B2
Agincourt
Hebburn NE31 .....57 D7
Agincourt *continued*
Killingworth NE12 .....29 D4
Agnes Maria St NE3 .....38 A5
Agricola Ct 1 NE33 .....42 C4
Agricola Gdns NE28 .....40 D7
Agricola Rd NE4 .....54 F6
Aidan Ave NE26 .....24 B6
Aidan Cl
Brunswick Village NE13 .....28 A6
Wallsend NE27 .....30 C1
Aidan Ct
Jarrow NE32 .....58 D6
Longbenton NE7 .....39 C5
Aidan Gr NE61 .....1 E4
Aidan Wlk NE3 .....38 E5
Aiden Way DH5 .....95 A5
Ailesbury St SR4 .....102 A3
Ainderby Rd NE15 .....35 B2
Ainsdale Gdns NE5 .....36 C2
Ainslie Pl NE5 .....37 C2
Ainsworth Ave NE34 .....59 A3
Ainthorpe Cl SR3 .....92 B7
Ainthorpe Gdns NE7 .....39 C4
Aintree Cl
Ashington NE63 .....6 C2
Washington NE37 .....83 D7
Aintree Gdns NE8 .....70 C7
Aintree Rd SR3 .....91 D8
Airedale NE28 .....39 F5
Airedale Gdns DH5 .....94 F2
Aireys Cl DH4 .....94 C8
Airey Terr
Gateshead NE8 .....101 A1
Newcastle upon Tyne NE6 .....57 A5
Airport Freightway NE13 .....26 E2
Airport Ind Est NE3 .....37 D6
Airport Sta NE13 .....26 D3
Airville Mount SR3 .....92 A4
Aisgill Cl NE23 .....22 B6
Aisgill Dr NE5 .....36 C1
Aiskell St SR4 .....102 A2
A J Cook Ct NE63 .....6 C3
A J Cook's Cotts NE39 .....67 B2
Akeld Cl NE23 .....22 B5
Akeld Ct 5 NE3 .....38 E4
Akeld Mews 7 SR6 .....75 E1
Akenside Hill NE1 .....101 B4
Akenside Ho NE1 .....101 B4
Akenside Terr NE2 .....99 C4
Akhurst Sch NE2 .....38 F2
Alamein Ave DH5 .....94 F8
Alanbrooke Row NE31 .....57 C3
Alansway Gdns 8 NE33 .....59 D8

ALBANY 83 B7
Albany Ave NE12........39 D7
Albany Ct NE4...........100 A3
Albany Gdns 2 NE26 ....32 B4
Albany Ho NE5............75 C1
Albany Mews NE3.........38 A2
Albany Rd NE8............56 A3
Albany Street E NE33 ....59 D8
Albany Street W NE33....59 D8
Albany Village Prim Sch
  NE37.....................83 C7
Albany Way NE17.........83 C7
Albatross Way NE24......17 E3
Albemarle Ave NE24......38 D3
Albemarle St 4 NE33.....42 C3
Albert Ave 7 NE28 ......40 B2
Albert Ct SR2...........102 B1
Albert Dr NE9.............70 F4
Albert Edward Terr NE35 ..58 E2
Albert Elliott Prim Sch
  NE34.....................59 C2
Albert Pl
  Gateshead NE9 ....70 F4
  Washington NE38 ....83 F4
Albert Rd
  Bedlington NE22 ....11 E2
  Jarrow NE32............58 A6
  Seaton Sluice NE26.....24 D6
  Sunderland SR4.........102 A3
Albert St
  Blyth NE24...............17 E8
  6 Chester le Street DH3 ..88 C3
  Hebburn NE31...........57 D6
  Newcastle upon Tyne NE2 ..99 C2
  Rowlands Gill NE39.....67 A1
Albert Terr
  5 Longbenton NE12.....29 C1
  7 Whitley Bay NE26.....32 B4
Albion Ct
  Newcastle upon Tyne NE6 ..56 B5
  2 South Shields NE33 ..42 C4
Albion Gdns NE16........78 F5
Albion House 3 NE2 .....42 A5
Albion Pl SR1.............102 C2
Albion Rd NE9, NE30....42 A6
Albion Ret Ctr NE24......17 D8
Albion Road W NE29......42 A5
Albion Row
  Newcastle upon Tyne NE6 ..56 B6
  Newcastle upon Tyne, St
  Lawrence NE6..........56 B5
Albion St
  Gateshead NE10 ....71 D6
  Sunderland SR4.........85 A6
Albion Terr
  6 Gateshead NE9 ....71 F1
  Hexham NE46 ....45 A5
  Lynemouth NE61 ....2 A3
  8 North Shields NE29 ...42 A6
Albion Way
  Blyth NE24...............17 C7
  Cramlington NE23 ....16 D1
Albury Park Rd NE3......42 C7
Albury Pl NE16............69 A5
Albury Rd NE2.............38 E3
Albyn Gdns SR3...........86 A3
Alcester Cl NE62.........10 F7
Alconbury Cl NE24.......17 E5
Alcroft Cl NE5............36 B3
Aldborough St NE24......17 E7
Aldbrough Cl 11 SR2.....92 F6
Aldbrough St NE34.......59 A5
Aldenham Gdns NE30....32 C1
Aldenham Rd SR3........91 E8
Aldenham Tower NE3.....91 E8
Alder Ave NE4............54 D8
Alder Cl
  Hetton-le-Hole DH5......94 F3
  Morpeth NE61............9 A8
Alder Cres DH9...........78 F2
Alder Ct NE25 ....31 E4
Alder Gr NE25.............31 E6
Alderley Cl
  Boldon Colliery NE35....58 E1
  2 Sunderland SR2.......86 F2
Alderley Dr NE12.........29 F4
Alderley Rd NE9..........70 E5
Alderley Way NE21.......16 D1
Aldermans Fenwicks House*
  2 NE1...................99 B1
Alderney Gdns NE5......36 C2
Alder Rd
  Shiremoor NE29.........41 B7
  Wallsend NE28 ....40 E6
Aldershot Rd SR3........91 D7
Aldershot Sq SR3........91 D7
Alder St SR5...............74 B1
Alderton Ct NE62.........10 F7
Alder Walk NE34..........59 F4
Alder Way NE12...........29 C4
Alderwood
  Ashington NE63..........6 C2
  Washington NE38.......89 B8
Alderwood Cres NE6......39 F1
Alderwood Pk NE23.......28 F8
Alderwyk NE10 ....72 B6
Aldsworth Cl NE9.........72 A1
Aldwick Rd NE15.........54 A5
Aldwych Dr NE29.........41 C8
Aldwych Ho NE33.........42 B2
Aldwych Rd SR3..........91 D7
Aldwych Sq SR3..........91 D6
Aldwych St SR3...........91 D7
Alemouth Rd NE46.......45 B5
Alexander Dr DH5.........94 F3
Alexander Pl 12 NE46....45 A5

Alexander Terr
  Hazlerigg NE13..........28 A5
  Sunderland SR6.........75 D3
Alexandra Ave SR5.......74 F1
Alexandra Bus Pk SR4 ..85 E8
Alexandra Cres NE46.....44 F5
Alexandra Dr NE16......69 C8
Alexandra Fst Sch NE63 ..6 F3
Alexandra Gdns
  North Shields NE29 .....41 E6
  Ryton NE40.............52 E4
  Tynemouth NE29 ....41 F6
Alexandra Ho SR2 ......102 C2
Alexandra Pk SR2........86 C4
Alexandra Rd
  Ashington NE63..........6 F3
  Gateshead NE8 ....101 B1
  Morpeth NE61............9 A8
  Newcastle upon Tyne NE6 ..39 B1
Alexandra St
  Rowlands Gill NE39.....67 A1
  Wallsend NE28 ....40 C2
Alexandra Terr
  Bedlington NE22 ....11 B1
  Haswell DH6.............97 F3
  Hexham NE46 ....44 F5
  Penshaw DH4............90 B8
  15 Springwell NE9......71 F1
  Stocksfield NE43........64 D7
  Sunniside NE16.........69 C2
  4 Whitley Bay NE26.....32 B4
Alexandra Way NE23.....22 B5
Alexandrea Way NE28....40 D4
Alford DH2.................81 F2
Alford Ho NE12...........39 C7
Alfred Ave NE22 ....11 B1
Alfred St
  Blyth NE24...............17 E6
  Hebburn NE31...........57 D5
  Whitley Bay NE26.......32 A5
Alnwick Ave
  North Shields NE29 .....41 D4
  Whitley Bay NE26.......32 A5
Alnwick Cl
  Chester le Street DH2 ..88 A1
  Whickham NE16..........69 A7
Alnwick Ct 14 NE6.......56 C7
Alnwick Ct 17 NE6.......56 C7
Alnwick Ind Est NE27....30 F1
Alnwick Pl NE26..........32 B4
Alnwick Rd
  15 Newcastle upon Tyne,
  Heaton NE6..............56 C7
  Newcastle upon Tyne, Lemington
  ....53 C6
Alnwick Sq SR3...........91 E8
Alnwick St
  Newburn NE15...........52 F8
  Wallsend NE28 ....40 C2
Alnwick Terr NE13........28 C7
Aln Wlk NE3...............38 A6
Alpine Ct DH2.............89 F5
Alpine Ct DH2.............88 C3
Alpine Way NE3...........86 A3
Alresford NE12 ....29 C4
Alston Ave
  East Cramlington NE23 ..22 D5
  Newcastle upon Tyne NE6 ..56 C6
Alston Cl
  Tynemouth NE29 ....41 C7
  Wallsend NE28 ....41 A4
Alston Cres SR6..........75 C4
Alstone Ct NE62..........10 F7
Alston Gdns NE15........23 B7
Alston Gr NE26 ....24 B7
Alston Rd
  New Hartley NE25.......23 D6
  Washington NE38.......84 B6
Alston St NE8.............101 A1
Altan Pl NE12.............39 B7
Altree Grange SR5........75 C3
Altrincham Tower SR3 ..91 E8
Alum Well Rd
  11 Gateshead, Low Fell
  NE9......................70 F5
  Gateshead NE9 ....70 F5
Alverston Cl NE15........53 C8
Alverstone Ave NE9......70 E4
Alverstone Rd SR3.......91 D7
Alverthorpe St NE33......59 D8
Alveston Ct NE62.........10 F7
Alwin NE38...............83 A1
Alwin Grange
  Hebburn NE31...........57 D6
  Jarrow NE32............58 A7
Alwinton Ave NE29.......41 D4
Alwinton Cl
  Blyth NE24...............17 C8
  Newcastle upon Tyne NE5 ..37 A4
Alwinton Ct NE24.........17 C8
Alwinton Dr DH2..........88 A1
Alwinton Gdns NE11......70 A5
Alwinton Rd NE27........30 F1
Alwinton Sq 5 NE63......6 F2
Alwinton Terr NE3........38 D5
Alwyn Cl DH4.............89 E3
Amalfi Tower SR3.........91 E8
Amara Sq SR3 ....91 E8
Ambassadors Way NE28 ..41 B8
Amber Ct SR4.............17 C6
Amberdale Ave NE6.......56 A1
Ambergate Cl NE5........37 D3
Ambergate Way NE3.....37 D3
Amberley Chase NE12....29 E4
Amberley Cl NE28........41 A3
Amberley Gdns NE2.......56 C7
Amberley Prim Sch NE12 ..29 E4
Amberley St
  Gateshead NE8 ....100 C1
  Sunderland SR2.........103 B1
Amberley Street S SR2 ..103 B1
Amberley Way NE24......17 E5
Amberley Wlk NE16......69 B5

Amberly Gr NE16 ....69 A5
Amble Ave
  South Shields NE34 .....60 B8
  Whitley Bay NE25 ....32 B4
Amble Cl
  Blyth NE24...............17 C5
  North Shields NE29 .....41 E4
  8 Wide Gr NE2..........56 A7
Amble Pl NE12............29 F1
Ambleside NE15...........35 E3
Ambleside Ave NE9......59 E6
Ambleside Cl NE25.......23 D3
Ambleside Gdns NE9.....71 A4
Ambleside Gn NE5........54 B8
Ambleside Terr SR6......75 C4
Amble Tower SR3.........91 E8
Amble Way NE3...........38 B6
Ambridge Way
  Newcastle upon Tyne NE3 ..37 F5
  Seaton Delaval NE25....23 A4
Ambrose Ct NE21........53 B1
Ambrose Pl NE6..........57 B6
Ambrose Rd SR3..........91 D8
Amec Dr NE28............41 A1
Amec Way NE28 ....40 E1
Amelia Cl NE4.............54 E3
Amelia Gdns SR3.........91 C7
Amelia Wlk NE4..........54 E3
Amen Cnr NE1............101 B4
Amersham Pl 11 NE5....38 A2
Amersham Rd NE24......17 E4
Amesbury Cl NE5.........36 B3
Amethyst Rd NE4 ......100 A2
Amethyst St 51 SR4......85 F7
Amherst Rd NE3..........37 E6
Amos Ayre Pl NE34......58 F5
Amsterdam Rd SR3......91 E8
Amy Cl SR5................75 B2
Ancaster Ave NE12......39 B6
Ancaster Rd NE16.......68 F6
Anchorage The
  Chester le Street DH3 ..88 D1
  Penshaw DH4............90 B6
Ancona St SR4............85 F7
Ancroft Ave NE29........41 F7
Ancroft Pl
  Newcastle upon Tyne NE5 ..54 B8
Ancroft Rd NE25.........23 B3
Ancroft Way NE3.........37 F8
Ancrum St NE2...........98 B3
Anderson Cl NE23........21 E8
Anderson St NE33........59 E8
Andover Pl NE28..........40 E6
Andrew Ct 4 NE6........57 A6
Andrew Rd SR3...........91 D7
Andrews House Sta*
  NE16...................80 B7
Anfield Ct NE3...........37 E5
Anfield Rd NE3............37 E5
Angel of the North* NE9 ..82 A4
Angerton Ave
  Shiremoor NE27.........30 F2
  Tynemouth NE30 ....41 C7
Angerton Gdns 5 NE5 ..54 D8
Angerton Terr NE23 ......28 F8
Anglesey Gdns NE5......36 C2
Anglesey Pl NE4..........98 B1
Anglesey Rd SR3.........91 D7
Anglesey Sq SR3.........91 D7
Angle Terr NE28..........40 F2
Angram Dr SR2...........87 A1
Angram Wlk NE5.........36 C1
Angrove Gdns SR4.......85 F5
Angus DH2.................81 F2
Angus Cl NE12............29 C3
Angus Cres NE23.........41 D3
Angus Rd NE8.............70 C8
Angus Sq SR3.............91 D7
ANICK......................47 F4
Anick Grange Rd NE46 ..45 D6
Anne Dr NE12.............40 A8
Annfield Rd NE23.........16 B2
Annie St SR6..............75 E1
ANNITSFORD..............22 B1
Annitsford Dr NE23 ......22 A1
Ann's Row NE24...........12 E1
Ann St
  Blaydon NE21............53 C3
  Gateshead NE8 ....101 C2
  Hebburn NE31...........57 C7
  Shiremoor NE27.........30 F4
Annville Cres NE6........57 A4
Ann Wlk NE6..............57 A4
Anscomb Gdns NE7......39 A2
Anson Cl NE3..............38 A2
Anson Pl NE5..............36 F3
Anstead Cl NE23.........22 D5
Anthony Rd SR3..........91 D8
Antonine Wlk NE15......54 D8
Antrim Cl NE5............36 A2
Antrim Gdns SR7.........93 E7
Antwerp Rd SR3..........91 C7
Apex Bsns Village NE23 ..22 B7
Apollo Way NE31.........57 F1
Apperley NE5..............37 A4
Apperley Ave NE3........37 C4
Apperley Rd NE43........66 A4
Appian Pl
  Gateshead NE9 ....71 B7
  Throckley NE15.........35 B2
Appleby Ct
  Bournmoor DH4.........89 D1
  Longbenton NE12.......39 B8
  North Shields NE29 .....41 D5

Appleby Gdns
  Gateshead NE9 ....71 A3
  Wallsend NE28 ....41 A4
Appleby Pk NE29.........41 F6
Appleby Rd SR3..........91 D7
Appleby Sq SR3 ....91 D7
Appleby St NE29.........42 A4
Apple Cl NE15............23 C8
Apple Ct NE25............23 D6
Appledore Gdns
  Chester le Street DH3 ..88 D5
  11 Gateshead NE9 .....70 F3
Appledore Rd NE24 .....17 E5
Appleforth Ave SR2......87 A1
Appleton Cl NE11........70 A8
Appletree Ct
  Gateshead NE8 ....101 B2
  Walbottle NE15.........36 A2
Appletree Dr NE42.......50 D3
Appletree Gardens Fst Sch
  NE25....................31 E4
Appletree Gdns
  Newcastle upon Tyne NE6 ..39 F1
  Wallsend NE28 ....40 B3
  Whitley Bay NE25.......31 E3
Appletree La NE45.......47 A5
Appletree Rise NE45.....47 A5
Applewood NE12..........29 F3
Appley Terr SR6..........75 C2
Apsley Cres NE3.........37 E5
Aqua Terr NE64...........4 D4
Aquila Dr NE15...........34 E2
Arbeia Ho NE33...........42 C4
Arbeia Roman Fort & Mus*
  13 NE33................42 C4
Arbroath DH2..............81 F1
Arbroath Rd SR3.........91 D8
Arcade The 2 NE30......42 D7
Arcadia DH2...............81 F1
Arcadia Ave DH4.........88 C5
Arcadia Terr NE24........17 C8
Archbishop Runcie CE Fst
  Sch NE3.................38 D5
Archbold Terr NE2.......99 B3
Archer Rd SR3............91 D8
Archer Sq SR3............91 D8
Archer St NE28............40 D3
Archer Villas NE12........40 D3
Archibald Fst Sch NE3 ..38 C5
Archibald St NE3.........38 C5
Arcot Ave
  Cramlington NE23 ....21 E8
  Whitley Bay NE25.......31 E3
Arcot Dr
  Newcastle upon Tyne NE5 ..53 F8
  Whitley Bay NE25.......31 E3
Arcot Terr 1 NE24.......17 D8
Arden Ave NE3............38 B1
Arden Cl NE28............40 D7
Arden Cres NE23.........37 D1
Ardrossan Rd SR3........91 D7
Arena Bsns Pk DH4......94 C7
Arena Way NE4...........100 C3
Argus Cl NE11............70 B7
Argyle Cl DH9.............80 A1
Argyle Mews NE12.......12 C1
Argyle Pl
  South Hetton DH6.......97 F7
  Tynemouth NE29 ....42 A8
Argyle Sq NE23 ....102 C1
Argyle St
  Blyth NE24...............12 E1
  Hebburn NE31...........57 D7
  Newcastle upon Tyne NE1 ..99 B1
  Sunderland SR2.........102 C1
  Tynemouth NE30 ....42 D8
Argyll DH2.................81 F1
Ariel St NE63..............6 F3
Arisaig DH2................81 F1
Arklecrag NE37...........83 C6
Arkle Rd SR3..............91 D7
Arkleside Pl NE5..........36 D1
Arkle St
  Gateshead NE8 ....70 C8
  Harlerigg NE13 ....28 A4
Arkwright St NE8.........70 C7
Arlbury Ave NE3..........37 F3
Arlington Cl DH4..........89 E3
Arlington Ct NE3..........38 A3
Arlington Gr
  Cramlington NE23 ......16 B2
  Whickham NE16.........69 A6
Arlington Rd NE31........57 F4
Arlington St SR4 51 SR4 ..85 F6
Arlott Ho NE29............41 D3
Armitage Gdns NE9......71 C1
Armondside Rd NE17....77 C6
Armstrong Ave
  Newcastle upon Tyne NE6 ..39 E1
  South Shields NE34 .....59 E6
Armstrong Cl NE63........6 F1
Armstrong Ct NE63.......6 F1
Armstrong Dr NE12......40 A8
Armstrong Ind Est NE37 ..83 A7
Armstrong Ind Pk NE4 ..100 A3
Armstrong Rd
  Newcastle upon Tyne NE15,
  NE4......................54 C4

Armstrong Rd *continued*
Wallsend NE28 . . . . .41 A1
Washington NE37 . . . . .83 A7
Armstrong St
Gateshead NE8 . . . . .70 D7
Woolsington NE5. . . . . .36 B7
Armstrong Terr
Morpeth NE61 . . . . .9 A8
South Shields NE33 . . . . . . .59 C8
Armstrong Way NE63 . . . .11 F8
Arncliffe Ave SR4 . . . . .85 E4
Arncliffe Gdns NE5 . . . . . . .36 C2
Arndale Arc NE32 . . . . .58 B7
Arndale Ho
  1 Birtley DH3. . . . . .82 C4
Newcastle upon Tyne NE3 . .37 E5
  6 Washington NE37. . . . . .83 D8
Arndale Sq NE12. . . . . .39 A6
Arnold Rd SR3. . . . . .91 D8
Arnold St NE35 . . . . .73 F8
Arnside Wlk NE5. . . . . .36 C2
Arran Ct SR3 . . . . .92 A6
Arran Dr NE32 . . . . .58 E3
Arran Gdns NE10 . . . . .71 C7
Arran Pl NE29 . . . . .41 C8
Arras La SR1 . . . . .103 B3
Arrol Pk SR4 . . . . .102 B2
Arrow Cl NE12. . . . . .29 B2
Arthington Way NE34 . . . .59 E5
Arthur Ave SR2 . . . . .93 A6
Arthur Cook Ave NE16 . . .69 C6
ARTHUR'S HILL. 98 A2
Arthur St
  9 Blyth NE24 . . . . .17 E8
Gateshead NE8 . . . . .101 C2
Jarrow NE32 . . . . .58 B6
  12 Ryhope SR2 . . . . .93 A6
Whitburn SR6. . . . . .60 F4
Arthur Terr SR6. . . . . .60 F3
Arundel Cl
Bedlington NE22 . . . . .11 C3
Brunswick Village NE13. . . .28 A5
Arundel Ct
Longbenton NE12. . . . . .39 A6
Newcastle upon Tyne NE3 . .37 C7
Arundel Dr
Newcastle upon Tyne
  NE15. . . . . .53 E7
Whitley Bay NE25 . . . . .31 C4
Arundel Gdns
Gateshead NE9 . . . . .71 A5
Sunderland SR3. . . . . .91 C7
Arundel Rd SR3. . . . . .91 D8
Arundel Sq NE63. . . . . .6 C3
Arundel Wlk NE16 . . . . . . .69 A5
Asama Ct NE4 . . . . .100 A3
Ascot Cl NE28 . . . . .40 D6
Ascot Cres NE38 . . . . .70 C7
Ascot Ct
Newcastle upon Tyne NE3 . .37 C7
Sunderland SR3. . . . . .91 D7
West Boldon NE36. . . . . . . .73 F6
Ascot Gdns NE34 . . . . .59 D7
Ascott Ct NE12 . . . . .39 B6
Ash Ave NE13. . . . . .27 C7
Ash Banks NE61 . . . . .9 A7
Ashberry Gr SR6. . . . . .75 D1
Ashbourne Ave NE6 . . . . . .56 F6
Ashbourne Cl NE27 . . . . . . .30 C5
Ashbourne Cres NE63. . . . . .6 C3
Ashbourne Rd NE31 . . . . . . .72 C2
ASHBROOKE. 86 C5
Ashbrooke NE25 . . . . .31 E5
Ashbrooke Cl NE5 . . . . .36 E5
Ashbrooke Cres **4** SR2 . . .86 D4
Ashbrooke Cross SR2 . . . . .86 C3
Ashbrooke Dr NE20 . . . . . . .25 E7
Ashbrooke Gdns NE28. . . . .40 E3
Ashbrooke Hall **1** SR2 . . .86 D4
Ashbrooke Mount **6** SR2 .86 D4
Ashbrooke Range SR2 . . . . .86 D3
Ashbrooke Rd SR2. . . . . . . .86 C4
Ashbrooke St NE3 . . . . .37 E3
Ashbrooke Terr SR2. . . . . . .86 D4
Ashburne Ct **3** SR2. . . . . .86 D4
Ashburn Rd NE28 . . . . .40 E6
Ashburton Rd NE3 . . . . . . .38 A4
Ashbury NE25 . . . . .31 C6
Ashbury Ho NE30 . . . . .42 C3
Ashby St SR2. . . . . .86 F3
Ash Cl NE46 . . . . .44 E3
Ashcroft Dr NE12 . . . . .39 E7
Ash Ct NE29 . . . . .31 E1
Ashdale
Penshaw DH4 . . . . .89 E8
Ponteland NE20. . . . . .25 E4
Ashdale Cres NE5. . . . . .36 D3
Ashdale Ct SR6. . . . . .75 E2
Ashdown Cl NE12. . . . . .39 B7
Ashdown Rd SR3 . . . . .91 B6
Ashdown Way NE12. . . . . . .39 B7
Asher St NE10 . . . . .71 E5
Ashfield NE32 . . . . .58 D2
Ashfield Ave NE16 . . . . .69 B8
Ashfield Cl NE4. . . . . .100 A4
Ashfield Ct
High Spen NE39. . . . . .67 A4
Killingworth NE12 . . . . .29 E1
Ashfield Gdns NE28 . . . . . . .40 A3
Ashfield Gr
  6 North Shields NE29 . . . .42 A6
Whitley Bay NE26 . . . . .32 A7
Ashfield Lodge NE4 . . . . .100 A4

Ashfield Pk NE16 . . . . .69 B8
Ashfield Rd
Newcastle upon Tyne NE3 . .38 A4
Whickham NE16. . . . . .69 B5
Ashfield Rise NE16. . . . . . . .69 B5
Ashfield Terr
Chester le Street DH3 . . . . .88 D2
  4 Gateshead NE10. . . . . .56 F1
Ryton NE40 . . . . .52 C5
  3 Springwell NE9 . . . . . . .71 E1
Ashford NE9 . . . . .71 A1
Ashford Cl
Blyth NE24. . . . . .17 E5
  4 Tynemouth NE29 . . . . .31 F1
Ashford Gr NE5 . . . . .36 B4
Ashford Rd SR3. . . . . .91 D7
Ashgill NE37. . . . . .83 B6
Ash Gr
Dunston NE11 . . . . .54 E1
Morpeth NE61 . . . . .8 E7
Ryton NE40 . . . . .52 C6
Wallsend NE28 . . . . .40 D1
Whitburn SR6. . . . . .61 A2
Ashgrove Ave NE34 . . . . . . .59 F4
Ashgrove Terr
Birtley DH3 . . . . .82 B5
Gateshead NE8 . . . . .101 B1
Ashill Ct SR2 . . . . .86 D4
ASHINGTON. 6 B3
Ashington Dr NE62. . . . . . . .11 A8
Ashington High Sch Sports
  Coll NE63 . . . . .6 B4
Ashington Hirst Park Mid
  Sch NE63 . . . . .6 A4
Ashington Hospl NE63 . . . . . .6 C3
Ashington L Ctr NE63. . . . . . .6 B4
Ashington Mews NE62 . . . .10 F7
Ashington Rd NE61 . . . . .1 D4
Ashkirk
Dudley NE23 . . . . .29 A8
Sunderland SR3. . . . . .91 E8
Ashkirk Cl DH2 . . . . .88 A1
Ashkirk Way NE25 . . . . .23 D2
Ashleigh DH2. . . . . .88 A5
Ashleigh Cl NE21 . . . . .53 E1
Ashleigh Cres NE5 . . . . .54 A8
Ashleigh Gdns SR6. . . . . . . .60 A2
Ashleigh Gr
Longbenton NE12. . . . . .39 D7
Newcastle upon Tyne NE2 . .38 D2
Sunderland SR6. . . . . .75 C4
Tynemouth NE30 . . . . .42 C8
Ashleigh Rd NE5. . . . . .54 A8
Ashleigh Terr **7** SR6. . . . . .75 E4
Ashleigh Villas **2** NE36. . . .74 A7
Ashley Cl
Killingworth NE12 . . . . .29 F4
Washington NE38 . . . . .83 D3
Ashley Gdns NE62. . . . . .11 A8
Ashley Prim Sch NE34 . . . . .59 C6
Ashley Rd NE34 . . . . .59 C6
Ashley Terr DH3 . . . . .88 C4
Ash Mdws NE38. . . . . .88 E7
Ashmead Cl NE12. . . . . .29 E4
Ashmore St SR2 . . . . .103 A1
Ashmore Terr SR2 . . . . . . .103 A1
Ashover Rd NE3 . . . . .37 D3
Ashridge Cl NE34 . . . . .60 B5
Ashridge Ct NE10 . . . . .72 C7
Ash Sq NE38. . . . . .83 E4
Ash St
Blaydon NE21 . . . . .53 C1
Mickley Square NE43. . . . . .64 E8
Ash Terr DH9 . . . . .78 D1
Ashton Cl NE5. . . . . .36 B4
Ashton Ct NE40 . . . . .52 D4
Ashton Downe **2** DH2. . . . .88 C2
Ashton Rise DH2. . . . . .88 C2
Ashton Way
Sunderland SR3. . . . . .91 C6
Whitley Bay NE26 . . . . .31 E7
Ashtree Cl
Newcastle upon Tyne NE4 . .54 F4
Rowlands Gill NE39 . . . . . . .67 F3
Ash Tree Dr NE22 . . . . .10 F2
Ashtree Gdns NE25 . . . . . . .31 E3
Ashtree Ho NE2 . . . . .98 B4
Ashtree La NE21, NE39. . . . .67 F4
Ashtrees Gdns NE9 . . . . . . .70 F7
Ashvale Ave NE11. . . . . .81 C6
Ashwell Rd SR3. . . . . .91 D7
Ashwood DH3 . . . . .88 D2
Ashwood Ave SR5. . . . . .74 F2
Ashwood Cl
Cramlington NE23 . . . . .16 C2
Longbenton NE12. . . . . .39 E8
Ashwood Cres NE6. . . . . . . .39 F1
Ashwood Croft NE11. . . . . . .81 C7
Ashwood Dr NE63. . . . . .7 B1
Ashwood Gdns NE9. . . . . . . .71 A2
Ashwood Gr
  4 Sunderland SR5 . . . . . .74 B1
Wideopen NE13 . . . . .28 B5
Ashwood Ho NE7 . . . . .39 A4
Ashwood Rd NE46 . . . . .45 C4
Ashwood St SR2 . . . . .102 B1
Ashwood Terr
Greenside NE40. . . . . .51 F1
Sunderland SR2. . . . . .102 B1
Askern Ave SR2. . . . . .87 A1
Askew Rd NE8 . . . . .101 B3
Askew Road W NE8 . . . . . .100 C1
Askrigg Ave
Sunderland SR3. . . . . .86 F1
Wallsend NE28 . . . . .40 D7
Askrigg Cl DH2 . . . . .81 E2

Askrigg Wlk **2** NE5. . . . . . .36 C1
Aspen Cl DH4. . . . . .89 F5
Aspen Ct SR3. . . . . .91 E6
Aspenlaw NE9 . . . . .71 C4
Aspen Terr NE5 . . . . .37 E1
Aspen Way NE24. . . . . .17 D4
Aspley Cl SR3 . . . . .92 A6
Assembly Rooms The **8** **9**
  NE1 . . . . .99 A1
Association Rd **4** SR6. . . . . .75 E2
Astbury Cl NE38 . . . . .89 B8
Aster Pl NE4. . . . . .54 C7
Aster Terr DH4. . . . . .90 B4
Astley Com High Sch
  NE25 . . . . .23 C3
Astley Cl NE32 . . . . .29 D3
Astley Dr NE26. . . . . .31 E8
Astley Gdns
Seaton Delaval NE25 . . . . . .23 C3
Seaton Sluice NE26 . . . . . . .24 B7
Astley Gr NE26 . . . . .24 B7
Astley Rd NE25 . . . . .23 C4
Astley St NE23 . . . . .16 B3
Astley Villas NE26 . . . . .24 B7
Aston Sq SR3. . . . . .91 D7
Aston St NE33 . . . . .59 D7
Aston Way NE16 . . . . .68 F5
Aston Wlk **6** NE6. . . . . .57 A6
Astral Ho SR1 . . . . .102 C3
Athelhampton NE38. . . . . . .84 A5
Athelstan Rigg SR2 . . . . . . .93 A7
Athenaeum St SR1 . . . . . .103 A2
Atherton Dr
Fence Houses DH4 . . . . .94 A7
Newcastle upon Tyne NE4 . .54 E4
Athlone Ct **1** NE24 . . . . . . .17 E8
Athlone Pl DH3 . . . . .82 D1
Athol Gdns
Ryhope SR2 . . . . .93 A6
Whitley Bay NE25 . . . . .31 D3
Athol Gn NE11 . . . . .100 A1
Athol Gr SR3 . . . . .92 A7
Athol Ho NE20. . . . . .25 F6
Atholl DH2 . . . . .81 F2
Athol Pk **3** SR2 . . . . .86 E4
Athol Rd SR2 . . . . .103 B1
Athol St NE11. . . . . .100 A1
Athol Terr SR2. . . . . .103 B1
Atkinson Gdns NE27 . . . . . . .42 A3
Atkinson House Sch NE23 .22 F2
Atkinson Rd
Chester le Street DH3 . . . . .88 D5
Newcastle upon Tyne NE4 . .54 D4
Sunderland SR6 . . . . .75 E4
Atkinson Road Prim Sch
  NE4 . . . . .54 D4
Atkinson's Bldgs SR4 . . . . .102 B3
Atkinson St NE28 . . . . .40 B1
Atkinson Terr
  5 Newcastle upon Tyne
   NE4 . . . . .54 D4
  11 Wallsend NE28 . . . . . . .40 B1
Wallsend NE28 . . . . .40 B1
Atkin St NE12. . . . . .29 B5
Atlantis Rd SR3. . . . . .91 C8
Atley Way NE23 . . . . .15 E2
Atmel Way NE28. . . . . .41 A7
Atmore St NE32 . . . . .29 B5
Attlee Cres NE35. . . . . .97 E1
Attlee Gr SR2. . . . . .92 E8
Attlee Terr NE64 . . . . .7 F5
Attwood Gr SR5 . . . . .75 B2
Aubone Ave NE15. . . . . .54 C6
Auburn Ct NE28. . . . . .41 B2
Auburn Gdns NE4. . . . . .54 E8
Auburn Pl NE61. . . . . .8 E8
Auckland DH2 . . . . .88 A3
Auckland Ave NE34 . . . . . . .60 B6
Auckland Rd NE31 . . . . .57 F7
Auckland Terr NE32 . . . . . . .58 E4
Auden Gr NE4 . . . . .54 E6
Audland Wlk **3** NE5 . . . . . . .36 C1
Audley Ct NE2 . . . . .38 F2
Audley Gdns SR3 . . . . .86 B3
Audley Ho NE3 . . . . .38 A1
Audouins Row NE8 . . . . .70 E8
Augusta Cl NE23 . . . . .28 A6
Augusta Ct NE28. . . . . .40 E6
Augusta Sq SR3 . . . . .91 D7
August Courtyard NE8 . . . .100 B2
August Pl NE33 . . . . .42 D1
Augustus Dr NE22 . . . . .10 E2
Austen Ave NE34 . . . . .59 B4
Austin Sq SR5 . . . . .75 B2
Australia Gr NE34 . . . . .58 F3
Australia Tower SR3 . . . . . .91 B8
Austral Pl NE13 . . . . .28 A5
Austwick Wlk **4** NE5 . . . . . .36 C1
Autumn Cl NE38 . . . . .83 D6
Autumn Dr NE8. . . . . .100 B2
Avalon Dr NE15 . . . . .53 E8
Avalon Rd SR3. . . . . .91 D8
Avebury Ave NE62. . . . . .11 A7
Avebury Dr NE38. . . . . .83 E5
Avebury Pl NE23 . . . . .16 C1
Avenue Cres NE25 . . . . .23 C4
Avenue Rd
Gateshead NE8 . . . . .70 F8
Seaton Delaval NE25 . . . . . .23 C3
Avenue St DH1. . . . . .86 C4
Avenue The
Birtley DH3 . . . . .82 C4
Blaydon NE21 . . . . .53 B2
Bournmoor DH3. . . . . .89 E6
Chester le Street DH2 . . . . .88 B3

Avenue The *continued*
Corbridge NE45. . . . . .46 F6
Gateshead, Carr Hill NE9 . . .71 B7
  7 Gateshead, Felling NE10 .56 D1
Hetton-le-Hole DH5. . . . . . .95 B4
Morpeth NE61. . . . . .8 F6
Rowlands Gill NE39 . . . . . . .67 F1
Seaton Delaval NE25. . . . . .23 E5
Seaton Sluice NE26 . . . . . . .24 A6
Sunderland SR2. . . . . .103 A1
Wallsend NE28 . . . . .40 B1
Washington NE38 . . . . .83 E5
Whitley Bay NE26 . . . . .32 A5
Avenue Vivian
Fence Houses DH4 . . . . .90 A1
Great Lumley DH4 . . . . .89 F1
Aviemore Rd NE36 . . . . .74 B7
Avis Ave NE64 . . . . .7 C3
Avison Ct NE4 . . . . .98 B2
Avison Pl NE4. . . . . .98 B2
Avison St NE4 . . . . .98 B2
Avocet Cl NE24 . . . . .17 E3
Avocet Ho **2** NE29 . . . . .42 A5
Avolon Ct NE4. . . . . .98 B2
Avolon Pl NE4 . . . . .98 B2
Avolon Wlk NE4 . . . . .98 B2
Avon Ave
Hedworth NE32. . . . . .58 C2
North Shields NE29. . . . . . .41 E4
Avon Cl
Rowlands Gill NE39. . . . . . .67 F3
Wallsend NE28 . . . . .40 C4
Avon Cres DH4 . . . . .94 A8
Avon Ct NE25 . . . . .23 D6
Avondale Ave
Blyth NE24. . . . . .17 A5
Longbenton NE12. . . . . .39 D8
Penshaw DH4 . . . . .90 B7
Avondale Cl **1** NE24 . . . . . . .16 F8
Avondale Ct NE3. . . . . .38 D4
Avondale Gdns
Ashington NE63. . . . . .7 A2
West Boldon NE36. . . . . . . .74 A7
Avondale Rd
Newcastle upon Tyne NE6 . .56 C5
Ponteland NE20. . . . . .25 A2
Avondale Terr
Chester le Street DH3 . . . . .88 C2
Gateshead NE8 . . . . .101 B1
West Boldon NE36. . . . . . . .74 A7
Avonlea Way NE5 . . . . .37 C3
Avonmouth Rd SR3 . . . . . . .91 D7
Avonmouth Sq SR3 . . . . . . .91 D7
Avon Rd NE31 . . . . .57 F4
Avon St
Gateshead NE8 . . . . .56 A1
Sunderland SR2. . . . . .103 C2
Avon Terr
Washington NE38 . . . . .83 E4
  3 Washington NE38. . . . .83 F4
Awnless Ct NE34 . . . . .59 C5
Axbridge Cl NE62 . . . . .11 A7
Axbridge Gdns NE4 . . . . . . .54 E5
Axford Terr NE17. . . . . .77 B6
Axminster Ct NE23 . . . . .16 D1
Axwell Dr NE24 . . . . .17 B4
Axwell Ho NE24 . . . . .17 B7
AXWELL PARK 53 E1
Axwell Park Cl **1** NE16 . . . . .69 A7
Axwell Park Rd NE21. . . . . . .53 E1
Axwell Park School Hos
  NE21 . . . . .68 C8
Axwell Park View NE15. . . . .54 B5
Axwell Terr NE16. . . . . .54 A1
Axwell View
Blaydon NE21 . . . . .53 C1
Whickham NE16. . . . . .69 A7
Aycliffe Ave NE9 . . . . .71 E4
Aycliffe Cres NE9 . . . . .71 D4
Aycliffe Pl NE9 . . . . .71 E4
Aydon Ave SR5 . . . . .47 A6
Aydon Cl NE30. . . . . .32 C1
Aydon Cres NE45. . . . . .47 B6
Aydon Dr NE45 . . . . .47 B8
Aydon Gdns
Corbridge NE45. . . . . .47 A6
Longbenton NE12. . . . . .38 F6
Aydon Gr
Corbridge NE45. . . . . .47 A6
Jarrow NE32 . . . . .58 D3
Aydon Ho SR3 . . . . .91 E7
Aydon Pk NE45. . . . . .47 B7
Aydon Road Est NE45 . . . . .47 A6
Aydon Way NE45 . . . . .47 B6
Aydon Wlk NE5 . . . . .36 E1
Aylesbury Dr SR3 . . . . .92 A5
Aylesbury Pl NE12 . . . . .39 B7
Aylesford Mews SR2. . . . . . .86 E2
Aylesford Sq NE24 . . . . .17 E5
Aylsham Cl NE5. . . . . .36 A2
Aylsham Ct SR3. . . . . .92 A4
Aylyth Pl NE3 . . . . .37 F3
Ayr Dr NE32 . . . . .58 E3
AYRE'S QUAY 102 B4
Ayre's Quay Rd SR1 . . . . . .102 C3
Ayre's Terr NE29 . . . . .42 A6
Ayrey Ave NE34 . . . . .58 F4
Aysgarth Ave
Sunderland SR2. . . . . .86 F2
Wallsend NE28 . . . . .40 D7
Aysgarth Gn NE3 . . . . .37 F4
AYTON. 83 B3
Ayton Ave SR2 . . . . .87 A1
Ayton Cl
Newcastle upon Tyne NE5 . .36 E3
Stocksfield NE43 . . . . .64 D6

Ayton Ct NE22 . . . . .10 D2
Ayton Rd NE38. . . . . .82 F4
Ayton Rise NE6 . . . . .56 C5
Ayton St NE6 . . . . .56 D5
Azalea Ave SR2 . . . . .102 C1
Azalea Terrace N SR2 . . . .102 C1
Azalea Terrace S SR2 . . . .102 C1
Azalea Way NE15 . . . . .52 E8
Azure Ct SR3 . . . . .91 D4

B

Back Albion Rd **11** NE30. . . .42 B6
Back Albion St SR4 . . . . .85 D5
Back Beaumont Terr NE3 . . .38 D5
Back Bridge St SR1. . . . . . .103 A3
Back Buttsfield Terr DH4 . . .90 B8
Back Coronation Terr
  DH5. . . . . .95 A2
Back Croft Rd NE24 . . . . . . .17 E8
Back Elmfield Rd **4** NE3 . . .38 C4
Back George St NE4 . . . . . .100 C4
Back Goldspink La NE2 . . . . .99 C3
Back Hawthorn Road W
  NE3 . . . . .38 C4
Back Heaton Park Rd **9**
  NE6 . . . . .56 B6
Back High St NE3 . . . . .38 C4
Back Hylton Rd SR4. . . . . . .102 B3
Back La
Blaydon NE21 . . . . .53 B2
Great Lumley DH3 . . . . .89 A1
Penshaw DH4 . . . . .90 B8
Whitley Bay NE25 . . . . .31 E5
Back Lodge Terr SR1. . . . . .103 C2
Back Maling St NE6. . . . . . . .56 A5
Back Mitford St NE4 . . . . . .100 B3
Back Mowbray Terr SR2 . . . .92 C2
Back New Bridge St NE1,
  NE2 . . . . .99 C2
Back North Bridge St
  SR5. . . . . .103 A4
Back Percy Gdns NE30 . . . . .42 D8
Back Prudhoe Terr **20**
  NE30 . . . . .42 D7
Back Queen Str NE61 . . . . . . .1 F2
Back Riggs **10** NE61 . . . . . . .3 F1
Back Row
Hexham NE46 . . . . .45 B5
Whickham NE16. . . . . .69 B7
Back Ryhope St NE23 . . . . . .92 E7
Back Shipley Rd **11** NE30. . .42 D7
Back St NE21 . . . . .53 B1
Back Stephen St **8** NE6 . . . .56 A4
Back Walker Rd NE6 . . . . . . .57 A4
Back Woodbine St NE8 . . . .101 B1
BACKWORTH. 30 C4
Backworth Bsns Pk NE27. . .30 C4
Backworth La NE23, NE27 . .29 F7
Backworth Park Prim Sch
  NE27 . . . . .30 C5
Backworth Terr NE27. . . . . .30 D1
Baden Cres SR5 . . . . .74 E3
Baden Powell St NE9 . . . . . .71 A7
Baden St DH3 . . . . .88 C2
Bader Ct NE24 . . . . .17 F6
Badger Cl SR3 . . . . .92 A5
Badger Mews NE9 . . . . .71 F2
Badgers Gn NE61 . . . . .3 D2
Badger's Wood DH9. . . . . . . .80 A1
Badminton Ct NE35. . . . . . . .58 E1
Baffin Ct SR3 . . . . .91 F6
Baildon Cl NE28 . . . . .40 C4
Bailey Green Prim Sch
  NE12 . . . . .29 C4
Bailey Sq SR5 . . . . .74 A4
Bailey St DH9 . . . . .79 B2
Bailey Way DH5. . . . . .95 B2
Bainbridge Ave
South Shields NE34 . . . . . . .58 F4
Sunderland SR3. . . . . .86 B3
Bainbridge Holme Cl SR3 . . .86 B3
Bainbridge Holme Rd
  SR3. . . . . .86 B3
Bainford Ave NE15 . . . . .54 A7
Baird Ave NE28 . . . . .41 C2
Baird Cl NE37. . . . . .72 E2
Baird Ct NE38 . . . . .56 B1
Baird St SR5 . . . . .74 A3
Baker Gdns
  1 Dunston NE11 . . . . .54 F1
Gateshead NE10 . . . . .72 B8
Baker Rd NE23 . . . . .15 D1
Baker Sq SR5 . . . . .74 A3
Baker St
Houghton-le-Spring DH5 . . .90 E1
Sunderland SR5 . . . . .74 A3
Bakewell Terr NE6 . . . . .56 D4
Baldersdale Gdns SR3 . . . . .86 B2
Baldwin Ave
Cleadon NE36 . . . . .74 E8
Newcastle upon Tyne NE4 . .54 F2
Balfour Rd NE15 . . . . .54 A6
Balfour St
  2 Blyth NE24. . . . . .17 D8
Gateshead NE8 . . . . .101 A1
Houghton-le-Spring DH5 . . .90 E1
Balfour Terr NE17. . . . . .66 B1
Balgonie Cotts NE40 . . . . . .52 C5
Baliol Rd NE43 . . . . .64 D8
Balkwell Ave NE29. . . . . .41 D5
Balkwell Gn NE29. . . . . .41 E6
Ballast Hill NE24 . . . . .12 A2
Ballast Hill Rd NE29 . . . . . . .42 A3
Balliol Ave NE12. . . . . .39 B7
Balliol Bsns Pk NE12 . . . . . . .39 A8
Balliol Bus Pk E NE12 . . . . . .39 B8

Balliol Gdns NE7 . . . . 39 B5
Balliol Prim Sch NE12 . . . . 39 B6
Ballston Cl NE38 . . . . 83 E3
Balman Rd NE5 . . . . 37 E4
Balmlaw NE9 . . . . 71 D4
Balmoral Ave
  Brockley Whins NE32 . . . . . . 58 E3
  2 Newcastle upon Tyne
  NE3 . . . . 38 E4
Balmoral Cl NE22 . . . . 11 C2
Balmoral Cres NE5 . . . . 94 F7
Balmoral Ct **5** SR5 . . . . 74 A3
Balmoral Dr NE10 . . . . 71 C8
Balmoral Gdns
  Tynemouth NE29 . . . . 41 F7
  Whitley Bay NE26 . . . . 31 F6
Balmoral St NE28 . . . . 40 B2
Balmoral Terr
  Newcastle upon Tyne, Heaton
  NE6 . . . . 56 B8
  Newcastle upon Tyne, South
  Gosforth NE3 . . . . 38 E4
  Sunderland, East Herrington
  SR3 . . . . 91 C7
  Sunderland, Grangetown
  SR2 . . . . 86 F2
Balmoral Way
  Blyth NE24 . . . . 17 C3
  Gateshead NE10 . . . . 71 C8
Balroy Ct NE12 . . . . 39 E7
Baltic Bus Ctr NE8 . . . . 56 B3
Baltic Ct NE33 . . . . 42 E2
Baltic Ctr for Contemporary
  Art* NE8 . . . . 101 C4
Baltic Ind Pk NE28 . . . . 41 E3
Baltic Quay NE8 . . . . 101 C4
Baltic Rd NE10 . . . . 56 D3
Baltic Sq NE8 . . . . 101 C4
Baltimore Ave SR5 . . . . 73 F3
Baltimore Ct NE37 . . . . 83 C8
Baltimore Sq SR5 . . . . 73 F3
Bamborough Ct NE23 . . . . . 29 A8
Bamborough Terr NE30 . . . . 42 A7
Bambro' St SR2 . . . . 103 B1
Bamburgh Cl
  Blyth NE24 . . . . 17 C7
  Washington NE38 . . . . 83 B5
Bamburgh Cres
  Shiney Row DH4 . . . . 90 B5
  Shiremoor NE27 . . . . 30 F3
Bamburgh Ct
  Gateshead NE10 . . . . 70 C7
  Newcastle upon Tyne NE7 . . . 38 F5
Bamburgh Dr
  Gateshead NE10 . . . . 57 B2
  Pegswood NE61 . . . . 4 F3
  4 Seaham NE33 . . . . 93 C1
  Wallsend NE28 . . . . 40 F2
Bamburgh Gdns SR3 . . . . . . 86 B3
Bamburgh Gr
  Jarrow NE32 . . . . 58 A3
  South Shields NE34 . . . . 60 B8
Bamburgh Ho NE5 . . . . 36 E3
Bamburgh Rd
  Longbenton NE12 . . . . 29 F1
  Newcastle upon Tyne NE3 . . . 36 E3
Bamburgh Terr
  19 Newcastle upon Tyne
  NE6 . . . . 56 C6
Bamburgh Wlk NE3 . . . . 38 A6
Bamford Terr NE12 . . . . 29 F1
Bamford Wlk NE34 . . . . 59 D5
Bampton Ave SR6 . . . . 75 C5
Banbury NE37 . . . . 83 E8
Banbury Ave SR5 . . . . 74 A4
Banbury Gdns NE28 . . . . 40 D5
Banbury Rd NE3 . . . . 37 F6
Banbury Terr NE33, NE34 . . 59 D8
Banbury Way
  Blyth NE24 . . . . 17 E5
  North Shields NE29 . . . . 41 D4
Bancroft Terr SR4 . . . . 85 F6
Banesley La NE11 . . . . 70 B1
Banff St SR5 . . . . 74 A4
Bangor Sq NE32 . . . . 58 A1
Bank Ave NE16 . . . . 69 A7
Bank Ct
  Blaydon NE21 . . . . 53 F4
  North Shields NE30 . . . . 42 B6
Bankdale Gdns NE24 . . . . . . 17 A2
Bank Foot Sta NE13 . . . . 37 B6
Bank Head NE46 . . . . 45 B5
Bankhead Rd NE15 . . . . 35 F1
Bankhead Terr **11** DH4 . . 94 A8
Bankside NE61 . . . . 9 A8
Bankside Cl SR2 . . . . 92 E6
Bankside La NE34 . . . . 59 C5
Bankside Rd NE15 . . . . 53 F5
Bankside Wlk NE62 . . . . 11 B8
Bank Top
  Crawcrook NE40 . . . . 51 E3
  Greenside NE40 . . . . 52 B3
  Tynemouth NE30 . . . . 32 C3
Bank Top Hamlet **4** NE4 . 69 A7
Bankwell La NE16 . . . . 101 B4
Bannerman Terr DH6 . . . . . . 96 C1
Bannister Dr NE12 . . . . 40 A8
Bannockburn NE12 . . . . 29 C4
Barbara Priestman Sch
  R2 . . . . 86 B4
Barbara St SR2 . . . . 86 F2
Barbary Dr SR6 . . . . 75 F2
Barbondale Lonnen NE5 . . . 36 C2
Barbour Ave NE34 . . . . 60 A7
Barclay Pl NE5 . . . . 37 B1

Barclay St SR6 . . . . 103 A4
Barcusclose La DH9, NE16 . 79 D5
Bardolph Rd NE29 . . . . 41 D6
Bardon Cl NE5 . . . . 36 F4
Bardon Cres NE25 . . . . 23 F2
Bardon Ct NE34 . . . . 59 E5
Bardsey Pl NE12 . . . . 39 B7
Barehirst St NE33 . . . . 59 B7
Barents Cl **2** NE5 . . . . 36 F2
Baret Rd
  Newcastle upon Tyne,
  Walkergate NE6 . . . . 56 E8
  Newcastle upon Tyne, Walker
  NE6 . . . . 56 E8
Barford Ct NE9 . . . . 71 A2
Barford Dr DH2 . . . . 88 A1
Baring St NE33 . . . . 42 D4
Barker St NE2 . . . . 99 C2
Barking Cres SR5 . . . . 73 F3
Barking Sq SR5 . . . . 73 F3
Barkwood Rd NE39 . . . . 67 D2
BARLEY MOW 82 C2
Barley Mow DH3 . . . . 88 D8
Barley Mow Prim Sch
  DH3 . . . . 82 D1
BARLOW 67 C6
Barlow Cres NE21 . . . . 67 C6
Barlow Fell Rd NE21 . . . . 67 C5
Barlowfield Ct NE21 . . . . 68 A8
Barlow La NE21 . . . . 67 E7
Barlow Rd NE21 . . . . 67 C6
BAR MOOR 51 E4
Barmoor Bank NE61 . . . . 9 C5
Barmoor Dr NE3 . . . . 28 A2
Barmoor La NE40 . . . . 52 B5
Barmoor Pl NE40 . . . . 52 B5
Barmoor Terr NE40 . . . . 52 A5
Barmouth Cl NE28 . . . . 40 D5
Barmouth Rd NE29 . . . . 41 C5
BARMSTON 83 F5
Barmston Cl NE38 . . . . 83 F4
Barmston Ct NE38 . . . . 83 F3
Barmston La NE38 . . . . 84 C6
Barmston Prim Sch NE38 . . 83 F5
Barmston Rd NE38 . . . . 84 A4
Barmston Way NE38 . . . . 83 F6
Barnabas Pl SR2 . . . . 103 C1
Barnard Cl NE22 . . . . 10 E1
Barnard Cres NE31 . . . . 57 F2
Barnard Gn NE3 . . . . 89 D1
Barnard Gn NE3 . . . . 37 E7
Barnard Pk NE32 . . . . 58 D4
Barnard Pk DH5 . . . . 95 A4
Barnes Jun & Inf Schs
  SR4 . . . . 85 F4
Barnes Park Rd NE34 . . . . . . 86 A4
Barnes' Rd NE33 . . . . 59 B8
Barnes St DH5 . . . . 95 A4
Barnes View NE3 . . . . 85 F4
Barnett Cl SR5 . . . . 75 B2
Barnett Sq DH6 . . . . 97 F2
Barningham NE38 . . . . 83 A4
Barningham Cl SR3 . . . . 84 B2
Barns Cl NE32 . . . . 58 A4
Barnstaple Cl NE28 . . . . 40 C5
Barnstaple Rd NE29 . . . . 31 D1
Barnston NE63 . . . . 7 B3
Barn The **3** DH2 . . . . 88 B1
Barnton Rd NE10 . . . . 71 E6
Barnwell Prim Sch DH4 . . . . 90 B8
Barnwood Cl NE28 . . . . 40 D4
Baroness Dr NE15 . . . . 54 A7
Baron's Quay Rd SR5 . . . . . . 85 B8
Baronswood NE3 . . . . 38 B5
Barrack Ct NE4 . . . . 98 C2
Barrack Rd NE2, NE4 . . . . . . 98 B3
Barrack Row DH4 . . . . 90 A6
Barrack St SR1 . . . . 103 C4
Barrack Terr NE11 . . . . 81 D6
Barras Ave
  Annitsford NE23 . . . . 22 B1
  Blyth NE24 . . . . 17 E5
Barras Avenue W NE24 . . . . 17 D5
Barras Bridge NE1 . . . . 99 A2
Barras Dr SR3 . . . . 86 B3
Barrasford Cl
  Ashington NE63 . . . . 6 A2
  Newcastle upon Tyne NE3 . . . 38 A4
Barrasford Dr NE13 . . . . 28 C5
Barrasford Rd NE23 . . . . 22 C6
Barrasford St NE28 . . . . 41 C1
Barras Gdns NE23 . . . . 22 B1
Barras Mews NE23 . . . . 22 F1
Barras Mews NE23 . . . . 22 F1
Barr Cl NE28 . . . . 40 E5
Barrie Sq SR5 . . . . 75 B3
Barrington Ave NE30 . . . . . . 31 F2
Barrington Ct
  Bedlington NE22 . . . . 16 A8
  Hetton-le-Hole DH5 . . . . 95 A4
Barrington Dr NE38 . . . . 83 D4
Barrington Ind Est NE22 . . . 11 F3
Barrington Pl
  Gateshead NE8 . . . . 101 A2
  Newcastle upon Tyne NE4 . . . 98 B2
Barrington Rd
  Bedlington NE22 . . . . 11 B3
  Bedlington NE22 . . . . 11 B3
Barrington St NE33 . . . . 42 C3
Barrington Terr DH5 . . . . 95 A5
Barron Street S **5** SR5 . . 74 C1
Barrowburn Pl NE23 . . . . . . 23 A1
Barrow St SR5 . . . . 73 F4

Barry St
  Dunston NE11 . . . . 54 F1
  Gateshead NE8 . . . . 70 D7
Barton Cl
  Tynemouth NE30 . . . . 32 B1
  Wallsend NE28 . . . . 40 B4
Barton Ct SR6 . . . . 75 C5
Barton Pk SR2 . . . . 92 D7
Bartram Gdns NE8 . . . . 70 E7
Bartram St SR5 . . . . 75 C3
Barwell Cl NE28 . . . . 40 D5
Basil Way NE34 . . . . 59 E3
Basildon Gdns NE28 . . . . 40 C5
Basil Way NE34 . . . . 59 E3
Basingstoke Pl NE12 . . . . . . 39 C7
Baslow Gdns SR3 . . . . 86 B3
Bassenfell Ct NE37 . . . . 83 B6
Bassenthwaite Ave **4**
  DH2 . . . . 88 B1
Bassington Ave NE23 . . . . . . 21 E7
Bassington Cl NE4 . . . . 98 B2
Bassington Dr NE23 . . . . 21 E8
Bassington Ind Est NE23 . . . 21 D8
Bassington La NE23 . . . . 21 D8
Bates La NE21 . . . . 53 F2
Bath Cl NE28 . . . . 40 E5
Bathgate Ave SR5 . . . . 73 F3
Bathgate Cl NE28 . . . . 40 E5
Bathgate Sq SR5 . . . . 73 F3
Bath La
  Blyth NE24 . . . . 17 F7
  Gateshead NE10 . . . . 56 D2
  Hebburn NE31 . . . . 57 E3
Bath Sq NE32 . . . . 58 A1
Bath St NE6 . . . . 57 B6
Bath Terr
  Blyth NE24 . . . . 17 F7
  Newcastle upon Tyne NE3 . . . 38 D5
  Tynemouth NE30 . . . . 42 D7
Batley St NE5 . . . . 73 F3
Battle Hill NE46 . . . . 45 B4
Battle Hill Dr NE28 . . . . 40 D5
Battle Hill Prim Sch NE28 . . 40 D5
Baugh Cl NE37 . . . . 83 A7
Baukham Hills NE46 . . . . 90 B7
Bavington Cl NE10 . . . . 72 A5
Bavington Dr NE5 . . . . 37 D1
Bavington Gdns NE30 . . . . . 32 B1
Bavington Rd NE28 . . . . 40 C5
Bawtry Ct NE28 . . . . 40 C5
Bawtry Gr NE29 . . . . 41 E5
Baxter Ave NE4 . . . . 54 E6
Baxter Ho SR2 . . . . 102 C1
Baxter's Bldgs NE23 . . . . . . 23 D3
Baxter Sq SR5 . . . . 73 F4
Baxterwood Ct NE4 . . . . 98 A2
Baxterwood Gr NE4 . . . . 98 A2
Baybridge Rd NE5 . . . . 36 E3
Bayfield Gdns **1** NE8 . . . . 56 B1
Baysdale DH4 . . . . 89 E8
Bayswater Ave NE34 . . . . . . 74 A3
Bayswater Rd
  Gateshead NE8 . . . . 71 B8
  Newcastle upon Tyne NE2 . . . 38 E2
Bayswater Sq **1** SR5 . . . . 74 A3
Baytree Gdns NE25 . . . . 31 F3
Baytree Terr DH9 . . . . 81 C1
Bay View E NE64 . . . . 7 F5
Bay View W NE64 . . . . 7 E5
Baywood Gr NE28 . . . . 40 C5
Beach Ave
  4 Houghton-le-Spring
  DH4 . . . . 90 D1
  Whitley Bay NE26 . . . . 32 A5
Beachborough Cl **6** NE29 31 F1
Beach Croft Ave NE30 . . . . . 32 B1
Beachcross Rd SR4 . . . . 102 B1
Beaches The NE4 . . . . 100 A3
Beach Rd
  South Shields NE33 . . . . 42 E3
  Tynemouth NE29 . . . . 42 A8
Beach St SR4 . . . . 102 B4
Beach Terr NE64 . . . . 7 F5
Beachville St SR4 . . . . 102 B1
Beachway NE24 . . . . 18 A4
Beach Way NE30 . . . . 32 A1
Beacon Ct
  Brunswick Village NE13 . . . . . 28 A6
  4 Gateshead NE9 . . . . 71 B5
Beacon Ctr NE29 . . . . 42 B5
Beacon Dr
  Brunswick Village NE13 . . . . . 28 A5
  Sunderland SR6 . . . . 75 F1
Beacon Glade NE34 . . . . 60 C6
Beaconhill Fst Sch NE23 . . . 21 E6
BEACONHILL GREEN 21 E6
Beacon Hill Sch NE12 . . . . . 40 B5
Beacon Ho **4** NE8 . . . . 56 B1
Beacon La NE23 . . . . 21 E6
BEACON LOUGH 71 B4
Beacon Lough Rd NE9 . . . . . 71 A4
Beacon Rise NE9 . . . . 71 A4
Beaconsfield Cl NE25 . . . . . . 31 D7
Beaconsfield Cres **3** NE9 . 71 A5
Beaconsfield Rd NE9 . . . . . . 70 F5
Beaconsfield St
  Blyth NE24 . . . . 17 F7
  Newcastle upon Tyne NE4 . . . 98 A2
Beaconside Terr
  Birtley DH3 . . . . 82 B4
  Chopwell NE17 . . . . 66 B1
Beaconside NE34 . . . . 60 C5

Beacon St
  Gateshead NE9 . . . . 71 A5
  North Shields NE30 . . . . 42 C6
  South Shields NE33 . . . . 42 D5
Beadling Gdns NE4 . . . . 54 E6
Beadnell Ave NE29 . . . . 41 D4
Beadnell Cl
  Blaydon NE21 . . . . 68 A8
  3 Chester-le-Street DH2 . 88 A1
Beadnell Ct **1** NE28 . . . . . 40 E5
Beadnell D SR7 . . . . 93 C1
Beadnell Gdns NE27 . . . . . . 30 F3
Beadnell Gr NE25 . . . . 23 F3
Beadnell Pl NE2 . . . . 99 C2
Beadnell Rd NE24 . . . . 17 B5
Beadnell Way NE3 . . . . 38 A6
Beagle Sq **8** SR3 . . . . 92 A7
Beal Cl NE13 . . . . 28 A4
Beal Dr NE12 . . . . 29 F1
Beal Gn NE5 . . . . 37 C4
Beal Gn NE28 . . . . 40 F5
Beal Rd NE27 . . . . 30 D3
Beal Terr NE6 . . . . 56 F4
Beal Way NE3 . . . . 38 B6
Beaminster Way NE3 . . . . . . 37 C5
BEAMISH 80 D2
Beamishburn Rd NE16 . . . . . 80 B3
Beamish Cl NE25 . . . . 40 C5
Beamish Cl NE25 . . . . 31 E3
Beamish Gn NE9 . . . . 71 D4
Beamish The North of
  England Open Air Mus*
  DH9 . . . . 80 C2
Beamish View NE11 . . . . 82 D2
Beamsley Terr NE63 . . . . 6 D3
Beanley Ave
  Hebburn NE31 . . . . 57 D4
  Newcastle upon Tyne NE15 . . 53 C6
Beanley Cres NE30 . . . . 42 D7
Beanley Pl NE7 . . . . 39 A3
Bearl View NE43 . . . . 49 B5
Beatrice Ave NE24 . . . . 17 B4
Beatrice Gdns NE34 . . . . 59 F6
Beatrice Ho SR2 . . . . 102 C1
Beatrice Rd NE6 . . . . 39 B1
Beatrice St
  Ashington NE63 . . . . 6 E4
  Sunderland SR6 . . . . 75 E2
Beatty Ave
  Newcastle upon Tyne NE2 . . . 38 E3
  Sunderland SR5 . . . . 73 F3
Beatty Rd NE22 . . . . 16 B8
Beaufort Cl
  Newcastle upon Tyne NE5 . . . 37 D3
  Shiney Row DH4 . . . . 90 B5
Beaufort Gdns NE28 . . . . . . 40 C5
Beaufort Park Ind Est
  NE46 . . . . 45 D4
Beaufront Ave NE46 . . . . 45 D4
Beaufront Castle Flats
  NE46 . . . . 46 A8
Beaufront Cl NE10 . . . . 72 B6
Beaufront Gdns
  3 Gateshead NE8 . . . . 56 B1
  Newcastle upon Tyne NE5 . . . 37 C1
Beaufront Terr
  Jarrow NE32 . . . . 58 B3
  South Shields NE33 . . . . 59 C8
Beauly NE38 . . . . 83 D3
Beaumaris DH3 . . . . 89 D3
Beaumaris Gdns SR3 . . . . . . 39 A6
Beaumaris Way NE5 . . . . 37 B4
Beaumaris Ct NE25 . . . . 31 D6
Beaumont Dr
  Washington NE38 . . . . 83 D5
  Whitley Bay NE25 . . . . 31 F4
Beaumont Grange NE23 . . . 22 E1
Beaumont Ho NE5 . . . . 37 C2
Beaumont Lodge SR2 . . . . . 86 E4
Beaumont Manor NE24 . . . . 16 F7
Beaumont St
  Blyth NE24 . . . . 17 D8
  Hexham NE46 . . . . 45 B5
  Newcastle upon Tyne NE4 . . . 54 F3
  North Shields NE29 . . . . 42 A5
  Sunderland, Hendon SR2 . . . . 86 E4
  Sunderland, Southwick SR5 . . 75 A2
Beaumont Terr
  Brunswick Village NE13 . . . . . 28 A6
  Jarrow NE32 . . . . 58 A4
  Newcastle upon Tyne, Gosforth
  NE3 . . . . 38 D5
  North Shields NE29 . . . . 42 A4
Beaumont Way NE42 . . . . . . 50 B1
Bebdon Ct NE24 . . . . 17 A8
BEBSIDE 16 C7
Bebside Furnace Rd NE24 . . 16 D8
Bebside Rd NE24 . . . . 16 C7
Beckenham Ave NE36 . . . . . 74 D8
Beckenham Cl NE36 . . . . 74 E8
Beckenham Gdns NE28 . . . . 40 C4
Beckett St NE8 . . . . 56 A4
Beckfoot Cl NE5 . . . . 37 B1
Beckford NE38 . . . . 83 A4
Beckford Cl NE28 . . . . 40 C5
Beckside Gdns NE5 . . . . 36 B1
Beckwith Cl DH4 . . . . 90 C2
Beckwith Rd SR3 . . . . 91 C8
Beda Cotts DH9 . . . . 79 A2
Beda Hill NE21 . . . . 53 C3

Bedale Cl NE28 . . . . 40 C5
Bedale Cres SR5 . . . . 74 A3
Bedale Ct
  Gateshead NE9 . . . . 71 B2
  5 South Shields NE34 . . . . 59 A5
Bedale Dr NE25 . . . . 31 F3
Bedale Gn NE5 . . . . 37 B3
Bedale St DH5 . . . . 95 A2
Bedburn NE38 . . . . 82 F1
Bedburn Ave SR5 . . . . 74 C2
Bede Brook SR3 . . . . 86 A3
Bedeburn Foot NE5 . . . . 36 F5
Bede Ct
  Chester-le-Street DH2 . . . . . . 88 C3
  Gateshead NE8 . . . . 56 A2
  Tynemouth NE30 . . . . 32 C3
Bede Ho **9** SR3 . . . . 91 D7
Bede Ind Est NE32 . . . . 58 E6
Bede Precinct **7** NE32 . . . 58 B7
Bede Prim Sch NE10 . . . . . . 56 B2
Bede Sixth Form Acad
  NE33 . . . . 102 C1
Bede St SR6 . . . . 75 E2
Bede Sq NE32 . . . . 58 E6
Bedesway NE32 . . . . 58 D7
Bede's World (Mus)*
  NE32 . . . . 58 D7
Bede Terr
  Chester-le-Street DH2 . . . . . . 88 B3
  East Boldon NE36 . . . . 74 E7
  Jarrow NE32 . . . . 58 C5
Bedewell Cty Prim Sch
  NE31 . . . . 57 F6
Bedewell Ind Pk NE31 . . . . . 58 A5
Bede Wlk
  Hebburn NE31 . . . . 57 F5
  Newcastle upon Tyne NE3 . . . 38 F5
Bedford Ave
  Birtley DH3 . . . . 82 D1
  Chester-le-Street DH3 . . . . . . 88 D8
  South Shields NE33 . . . . 42 C1
  Wallsend NE28 . . . . 40 A3
Bedford Ct NE30 . . . . 42 B5
Bedford Ho NE30 . . . . 42 B5
Bedford Pl
  Gateshead NE8 . . . . 101 B2
  Newcastle upon Tyne NE5 . . . 36 C1
  New Silksworth SR3 . . . . 92 A8
Bedford St
  Hetton-le-Hole DH5 . . . . 94 F4
  North Shields NE29, NE30 . . . 42 B5
  Sunderland SR1 . . . . 103 A3
Bedford Terr **11** NE29 . . . 42 A6
Bedford Way NE29 . . . . 42 B5
BEDLINGTON 11 A1
Bedlington Bank NE22,
  NE22 . . . . 16 A7
Bedlington Country Pk*
  NE22 . . . . 16 A6
Bedlingtonshire Com High
  Sch NE22 . . . . 11 D2
BEDLINGTON STATION 11 B3
Bedlington Station First Sch
  NE22 . . . . 11 D3
Beech Ave
  Cramlington NE23 . . . . 22 D5
  Dinnington NE13 . . . . 27 B7
  Hexham NE46 . . . . 44 E5
  4 Houghton-le-Spring DH4 94 D8
  Morpeth NE61 . . . . 9 C7
  Newcastle upon Tyne NE3 . . . 37 F6
  Whickham NE16 . . . . 69 C8
  Whitburn SR6 . . . . 60 F1
Beech Cl NE13 . . . . 28 C1
Beechbrooke SR2 . . . . 92 F6
Beech Cl NE13 . . . . 28 C1
Beechcroft
  Newcastle upon Tyne NE3 . . . 38 B2
  Washington NE37 . . . . 72 B2
Beechcroft Ave NE3 . . . . 38 A3
Beech Ct
  Newcastle upon Tyne NE3 . . . 38 A3
  North Shields NE29 . . . . 41 F6
  Ponteland NE20 . . . . 25 A1
  Tynemouth NE29 . . . . 31 E1
Beech Dr
  Corbridge NE45 . . . . 47 B6
  Dunston NE11 . . . . 54 E1
  Ellington NE61 . . . . 1 D5
Beecher St NE24 . . . . 17 B8
Beeches The
  Longbenton NE12 . . . . 39 D6
  Ponteland NE20 . . . . 25 D6
  Stannington NE61 . . . . 14 C4
Beechfield Gdns NE28 . . . . . 40 A3
Beechfield Rd NE3 . . . . 38 B4
Beech Gdns NE9 . . . . 70 F6
Beech Gr
  Bedlington NE22 . . . . 11 A1
  Blackhall Mill NE17 . . . . 77 B8
  Longbenton NE12 . . . . 39 D6
  Prudhoe NE42 . . . . 50 B2
  South Shields NE34 . . . . 59 F4
  Springwell NE9 . . . . 71 F1
  Wallsend NE28 . . . . 40 B2
  Whitley Bay NE26 . . . . 31 F5

BEECHGROVE 69 C8
Beech Grove Ct NE40 . . . .51 F4
Beech Grove Rd NE4 . . . .100 A4
Beech Grove S NE42 . . . . .50 B2
Beech Grove Terr NE4 . . .51 F4
Beech Grove Terrace S
NE40 .51 F4
Beech Hill NE46 . . . . .44 E5
Beech Hill Prim Sch NE5 . .36 F2
Beechlea NE61 . . . . .14 C3
Beecholm Ct SR2 . . . . .86 D3
Beech Sq NE38 . . . . .83 E4
Beech St
Gateshead NE8 . . . . .56 B1
Jarrow NE32 . . . . .58 A7
Mickley Square NE43 . . . . .64 E8
Newcastle upon Tyne NE4 . .54 E5
1 Sunniside NE16 . . . . . . .69 B2
Beech Terr
Ashington NE63 . . . . .6 E2
Burnopfield NE16 . . . . .79 C6
Beechway
Ashington NE63 . . . . .7 A3
Gateshead NE10 . . . . .71 F5
Beech Way NE12 . . . . .29 C4
Beechwood NE39 . . . . .67 A2
Beechwood Ave
Gateshead NE9 . . . . .71 A3
Newcastle upon Tyne NE3 . .38 E6
Ryton NE40 . . . . .52 C5
Stakeford NE62 . . . . .11 A8
Whitley Bay NE25 . . . . .31 D4
Beechwood Cl NE32 . . . . .58 D6
Beechwood Cres NE4 . . . .74 F2
Beechwood Gdns NE11 . . .70 B5
Beechwood Ho NE7 . . . . . .39 A4
Beechwood Pl NE20 . . . . . .25 E7
Beechwoods DH2 . . . . .88 B5
Beechwood St SR2 . . . . .102 B1
Beechwood Terr
Burnside DH4 . . . . .90 C2
Sunderland SR2 . . . . .102 B1
Beeston Ave SR5 . . . . .73 F3
Beetham Cres NE5 . . . . . .54 A8
Beethoven St **10** NE33 . . .42 D2
Begonia Cl NE31 . . . . .57 E3
Beldene Dr SR4 . . . . .85 E4
Belford Ave NE27 . . . . .30 F3
Belford Cl
Gateshead NE8 . . . . .86 D3
Wallsend NE28 . . . . .40 D5
Belford Gdns NE11 . . . . . .70 A5
Belford Rd SR2 . . . . .86 E3
Belford Terr
Newcastle upon Tyne NE6 . .56 E5
Sunderland SR2 . . . . .86 E3
Tynemouth NE30 . . . . .42 A7
Belfry The DH4 . . . . .90 A4
Belgrade Cres SR5 . . . . . .73 F4
Belgrade Sq SR5 . . . . .73 F3
Belgrave Cres NE24 . . . . . .17 F6
Belgrave Ct NE10 . . . . .71 D8
Belgrave Gdns
Ashington NE63 . . . . .7 A2
South Shields NE34 . . . . . .59 F6
Belgrave Par NE4 . . . . . . .100 B4
Belgrave Terr
Gateshead NE10 . . . . .71 D7
South Shields NE33 . . . . . .42 D3
Bellamy Cres NE35 . . . . . .73 F3
Bellburn Ct NE23 . . . . .22 D8
Belle Grove Pl NE2 . . . . . .98 B3
Belle Grove Terr NE2 . . . .98 B3
Belle Grove Villas NE2 . . .98 B3
Belle Grove W NE2 . . . . . . .98 B3
Bellerby Dr DH2 . . . . .81 E2
Belle View Terr **13** NE9 . . .71 F1
Belle Vue NE9 . . . . .66 F5
Belle Vue Ave NE3 . . . . . . .38 D5
Belle Vue Bank NE9 . . . . . .70 E5
Bellevue Cres NE23 . . . . . .16 B2
Belle Vue Cres
South Shields NE33 . . . . . .59 B6
Sunderland SR2 . . . . .86 C4
Belle Vue Dr SR2 . . . . .86 C4
Belle Vue Gr NE9 . . . . .70 F5
Belle Vue Park W SR2 . . . .86 C4
Belle Vue Pk SR2 . . . . .86 C4
Belle Vue Rd SR2 . . . . .86 C4
Belle Vue St NE30 . . . . . . .32 C3
Belle Vue Terr
Crawcrook NE40 . . . . .51 F4
Gateshead NE9 . . . . .70 E5
4 North Shields NE29 . . . .42 A4
Belle Vue Villas NE36 . . . .74 C7
Bellfield Ave NE3 . . . . .37 F6
Bell Gr NE12 . . . . .29 B4
Bellgreen Ave NE3 . . . . . . .28 D1
Bell House Rd SR5 . . . . . . .75 A5
Bellingham Ct NE40 . . . . . .40 D4
Bellingham Ct
Bedlington NE22 . . . . .11 A1
8 Newcastle upon Tyne
NE3 .37 D5
Bellingham Dr NE12 . . . . . .40 A8
Bellingham Ho SR4 . . . . . .85 B4
Bellister Gr NE5 . . . . .54 C7
Bellister Rd NE29 . . . . .41 D6
Belloc Ave NE34 . . . . .59 B3
Bell Rd NE41 . . . . .51 B6
Bellsburn Ct NE63 . . . . .6 E2
Bells Cl
2 Blyth NE24 . . . . .16 F8
Newcastle upon Tyne NE15 . .53 E5
BELL'S CLOSE 53 E6

Bells Close Ind Est NE15 . .53 E5
Bell's Cotts NE40 . . . . .52 A1
Bell's Hill NE61 . . . . .13 D3
Bellshill Cl NE28 . . . . .40 E6
Bells Lonnen NE42 . . . . . . .50 D4
Bell's Pl NE22 . . . . .16 A8
Bell St
Hebburn NE31 . . . . .57 D6
North Shields NE30 . . . . . . .42 B5
Penshaw DH4 . . . . .90 B8
Sunderland SR4 . . . . .85 F6
6 Sunderland NE38 . . . . .83 F4
Bell View NE42 . . . . .50 F3
Bell Villas NE20 . . . . .25 F6
Bellway Ind Est NE12 . . . . .39 F7
Belmont NE10 . . . . .72 A5
Belmont Ave NE25 . . . . . . .31 D4
Belmont Cl NE8 . . . . .56 B3
Belmont Cotts **6** NE5 . . . .36 F3
Belmont Rd SR4 . . . . .85 F5
Belmont Rise DH5 . . . . . . .95 A1
Belmont St NE6 . . . . .56 F3
Belmont Terr **4** NE9 . . . . .71 E1
Belmont Wlk NE6 . . . . .56 F3
Belmount Ave NE3 . . . . . . .28 D1
Belper Cl NE28 . . . . .40 C5
Belsay NE38 . . . . .82 F4
Belsay Ave
Hazlerigg NE13 . . . . .28 A4
South Shields NE34 . . . . . .60 A7
Whitley Bay NE25 . . . . .32 B4
Belsay Cl
Morpeth NE61 . . . . .4 F3
Wallsend NE28 . . . . .40 C5
Belsay Ct NE24 . . . . .17 C7
Belsay Gdns
Dunston NE11 . . . . .70 A5
Newcastle upon Tyne NE3 . .37 F8
Sunderland SR4 . . . . .85 F5
Belsay Gr NE22 . . . . .11 C3
Belsay Ho **7** SR3 . . . . .91 D7
Belsey Pl NE4 . . . . .98 A2
Belsfield Gdns NE32 . . . . . .58 B4
Belsize Pl NE6 . . . . .56 F8
Beltingham NE5 . . . . .36 E1
Belvedere NE29 . . . . .41 F7
Belvedere Ave NE25 . . . . . .31 F4
Belvedere Ct **12** NE6 . . . . .56 C7
Belvedere Gdns NE12 . . . . .39 D6
Belvedere Ho **10** NE6 . . . .56 C7
Belvedere Parkway NE3 . .37 D6
Belvedere Rd SR2 . . . . . .102 C1
Belvedere Ret Pk NE3 . . . .37 C6
Bemersyde Dr NE2 . . . . . . .38 E3
Benbrake Ave NE29 . . . . . .31 E1
Bendigo Ave NE34 . . . . . . .58 F3
Benedict Biscop CE Prim Sch
SR3 .91 D5
Benfield Rd SR6 . . . . .75 F2
Benfield Bsns Pk NE6 . . . .56 E8
Benfield Gr NE26 . . . . .24 B7
Benfield Rd NE6 . . . . .39 E1
Benfield Sch NE6 . . . . .39 E2
Benfleet Ave SR5 . . . . .73 F3
Benjamin Rd NE28 . . . . . . .41 A3
Benjamin St **11** NE40 . . . .51 F1
Bennett Ct
Newcastle upon Tyne
NE15 . . . . .53 C6
Sunderland SR2 . . . . .86 E3
Bennett Gdns **1** NE10 . . .56 D1
Bennett's Wlk NE61 . . . . . . .9 A8
Benridge Bank DH4 . . . . . .94 A2
Benridge Pk NE24 . . . . .17 B3
BENSHAM 101 A1
Bensham Ave NE8 . . . . . .101 A1
Bensham Cres NE8 . . . . .100 C1
Bensham Ct
Gateshead NE8 . . . . .101 A1
South Shields NE34 . . . . . .59 C5
Bensham General Hospl
NE8 .70 D7
Bensham Rd
Gateshead, Bensham
NE8 . . . . .101 A1
Gateshead NE8 . . . . .101 B3
Gateshead, Windmill Hills
NE8 . . . . .101 B2
Bensham St NE35 . . . . .58 F1
Bensham Trad Est NE8 . . .70 D8
Benson Cl NE46 . . . . .44 E4
Benson Pl **20** NE6 . . . . . .56 C6
Benson Rd NE6 . . . . .56 D6
Benson St NE3 . . . . .88 C2
Benson Terr **88** NE10 . . . .71 D8
Bentall Bsns Pk NE37 . . . .83 F7
Bentham Ct SR5 . . . . .74 A4
Bentinck Cres
Newcastle upon Tyne NE4 . .54 F4
Pegswood NE61 . . . . .4 E3
Bentinck Rd NE4 . . . . .54 F5
Bentinck St NE4 . . . . .54 F5
Bentinck Villas NE4 . . . . . .54 F5
Benton Ave SR5 . . . . .73 F4
Benton Bank NE2 . . . . .39 A1
Benton Cl NE7 . . . . .39 B5
Benton Hall Wlk NE7 . . . . .39 D2
Benton La NE12 . . . . .39 B7
Benton Lodge Ave NE7 . . .39 B5
Benton Park Prim Sch
NE7 .39 B4
Benton Park Rd NE7 . . . . . .39 B4
Benton Rd
Biddick Hall NE34 . . . . .59 C2
Newcastle upon Tyne NE7 . .39 B3
Shiremoor NE27 . . . . .30 E1
BENTON SQUARE 30 E1

Benton Square Ind Est
NE12 . . . . .30 B1
Benton Sta NE12 . . . . .39 D6
Benton Way NE28 . . . . .40 B1
Bents Cotts NE33 . . . . .42 E2
Bents Cotts App NE33 . . . .42 E2
Bents Park Rd NE33 . . . . . .42 E3
Bents The SR6 . . . . .75 F7
BENWELL 54 C5
Benwell Dene Terr NE15 . .54 C5
Benwell Gr NE4 . . . . .54 E5
Benwell Grange **9** NE15 . .54 D5
Benwell Grange Ave
NE15 . . . . .54 D5
Benwell Grange Cl **8**
NE15 . . . . .54 D5
Benwell Grange Rd NE15 . .54 C5
Benwell Grange Terr
NE15 . . . . .54 C5
Benwell Hall Dr NE15 . . . . .54 B6
Benwell Hill Gdns NE15 . . .54 C7
Benwell Hill Rd NE5 . . . . . .54 C7
Benwell La NE15 . . . . .54 C5
Benwell Nature Reserve★
NE15 . . . . .54 D4
Benwell Roman Temple★
NE15 . . . . .54 D5
Benwell Vallum Crossing★
NE15 . . . . .54 D6
Benwell Village NE15 . . . . .54 B6
Benwell Village Mews
NE15 . . . . .54 C6
Berberis Way NE15 . . . . . .52 E8
Beresford Ct NE26 . . . . . . .24 D6
Beresford Gdns **6** NE6 . . .56 C5
Beresford Pk SR2 . . . . . . .102 C1
Beresford Rd
Seaton Sluice NE26 . . . . . .24 D5
Tynemouth NE30 . . . . .32 A3
Beresford St NE11 . . . . . .100 A1
Bergen Cl NE29 . . . . .41 B4
Bergen Sq SR5 . . . . .73 F4
Bergen St SR5 . . . . .73 F4
Berkdale Rd NE9 . . . . .70 E2
Berkeley Cl
Boldon Colliery NE35 . . . . . .58 E2
Killingworth NE12 . . . . .29 E4
Sunderland SR3 . . . . .91 C7
Berkeley Sq NE3 . . . . .38 B7
Berkely St NE13 . . . . .42 D2
Berkhamstead Ct NE10 . . .72 C7
Berkley Ave NE21 . . . . .53 E2
Berkley Cl NE28 . . . . .40 C5
Berkley Rd NE29 . . . . .41 D6
Berkley St NE15 . . . . .52 F8
Berkley Terr NE15 . . . . .52 F8
Berkley Way NE31 . . . . .57 E8
Berkshire Cl NE5 . . . . .36 F2
Bermondsey St NE2 . . . . . .99 C2
Bernard Gilpin Prim Sch
DH5 .94 E8
Bernard Shaw St **8** DH4 . .94 D8
Bernard St NE6 . . . . .57 B4
Berrington Dr NE5 . . . . .37 B3
Berrishill Gr NE25 . . . . .31 C6
Berry Cl
Newcastle upon Tyne NE6 . .57 A6
Wallsend NE28 . . . . .40 C5
Berryfield Cl SR3 . . . . .92 A5
Berry Hill NE40 . . . . .52 B1
Berryhill Cl NE21 . . . . .53 D1
Berrymoor NE61 . . . . .6 E4
Bertha Terr DH4 . . . . .90 D4
Bertram Cres NE15 . . . . . . .54 C6
Bertram St
3 Birtley DH3 . . . . .82 C4
South Shields NE33 . . . . . .59 C8
Bertram Terr
Ashington NE63 . . . . .6 D3
Pegswood NE61 . . . . .4 F4
Berwick Ave SR5 . . . . .82 F4
Berwick Ave SR5 . . . . .73 F4
Berwick Cl NE20 . . . . .25 F7
Berwick Ct NE20 . . . . .25 F7
Berwick Dr NE28 . . . . .40 D5
BERWICK HILL 19 A3
Berwick Hill Cotts NE20 . . .19 A4
Berwick Hill Rd
Berwick Hill NE20 . . . . .19 A2
Ponteland NE20 . . . . .25 F8
Berwick Sq SR5 . . . . .73 F3
Berwick Terr NE29 . . . . . . .41 D7
Besford Gr SR1 . . . . .103 B2
Bessemer Rd DH4 . . . . .97 F7
Bessie Surtees House★
NE1 .101 B4
Bessie Terr NE21 . . . . .53 A2
Best View **3** DH4 . . . . .90 B6
Bethnell Ave NE6 . . . . .56 D7
Betjeman Mews NE6 . . . .101 C1
Bet's La NE61 . . . . .54 B5
Bevan Ave SR5 . . . . .92 E6
Bevan Dr NE12 . . . . .38 F6
Bevan Gdns NE10 . . . . .72 A8
Beverley Cres
Gateshead NE9 . . . . .71 A6
Beverley Cres NE9 . . . . . . .71 A6
Beverley Ct
2 Gateshead NE9 . . . . . . .71 A6
1 Jarrow NE32 . . . . .58 B7
Washington NE37 . . . . .83 D7
Beverley Dr
Blaydon NE21 . . . . .67 F3
Stakeford NE62 . . . . .11 A8
Whickham NE16, NE21 . . . .69 C8
Beverley Gdns
Chester le Street DH3 . . . . .88 D2

Beverley Gdns *continued*
Ryton NE40 . . . . .52 A5
Tynemouth NE30 . . . . .32 C2
Beverley Pk NE25 . . . . .31 E4
Beverley Pl NE28 . . . . .40 F3
Beverley Rd
Gateshead NE9 . . . . .71 A6
Sunderland SR2 . . . . .86 E2
Whitley Bay NE25 . . . . .31 F4
Beverley Terr
Newcastle upon Tyne NE6 . .57 A5
Tynemouth NE30 . . . . .32 C3
Walbottle NE15 . . . . .36 A2
Beverley Villas NE30 . . . . .32 C3
Beweshill Cres NE21 . . . . .53 A1
Beweshill La NE21 . . . . . . .53 A3
Bewick Cres NE15 . . . . .53 D7
Bewick Ct NE1 . . . . .99 B2
Bewick Lodge NE28 . . . . . .41 A2
Bewicke Rd NE28 . . . . .41 A2
Bewicke Road Ind Est
NE28 . . . . .41 A1
Bewicke St NE28 . . . . .41 B1
Bewick View DH3 . . . . .82 D5
Bewick Garth NE43 . . . . . . .49 E1
Bewick La NE42 . . . . .50 B4
Bewick Pk NE28 . . . . .40 F5
Bewick St NE8 . . . . .101 B1
Bewick St
Newcastle upon Tyne
NE1 .101 A4
South Shields NE33 . . . . . .59 C8
Bexhill Prim Sch SR5 . . . . .73 F3
Bexhill Rd SR5 . . . . .73 F3
Bexhill Sq
Blyth NE24 . . . . .17 E5
Sunderland SR5 . . . . .73 F3
Bexley Ave NE15 . . . . .54 B6
Bexley Gdns NE28 . . . . .40 D5
Bexley Pl NE16 . . . . .69 A5
Bexley St SR4 . . . . .85 F6
Bickerton Wlk **2** NE5 . . . . .36 E1
Bickington Ct DH4 . . . . .90 C3
Bicknell Ho NE6 . . . . .56 C5
BIDDICK 83 D4
BIDDICK HALL 59 B2
Biddick Hall Dr NE34 . . . . . .59 B4
Biddick Hall Inf Sch NE34 . .59 A3
Biddick Hall Jun Sch
NE34 . . . . .59 B4
Biddick La NE38 . . . . .83 D2
Biddick Prim Sch NE38 . . . .83 D4
Biddick Terr NE38 . . . . .83 E3
Biddick View NE38 . . . . . . .83 E3
Biddick Villas NE38 . . . . . . .83 E3
Biddlestone Cres NE29 . . . .41 D5
Biddlestone Rd NE6 . . . . . .39 C1
Bideford Gdns
Gateshead NE9 . . . . .70 F3
Jarrow NE32 . . . . .58 E5
South Shields NE34 . . . . . .43 A1
Whitley Bay NE26 . . . . .32 A6
Bideford Rd NE16 . . . . .69 A5
Bideford Rd NE1 . . . . .37 E4
Bideford St SR2 . . . . .86 F2
Bigbury Cl DH4 . . . . .90 C4
Bigges Gdns NE28 . . . . .39 F4
Bigg Mkt NE1 . . . . .99 A1
Big Waters Cl NE13 . . . . . . .28 A6
Big Waters Ctry Pk★
NE13 . . . . .28 A7
Bilbrough Gdns NE4 . . . . . .54 D4
BILL QUAY 57 B2
Bill Quay Farm★ NE10 . . .57 A2
Bill Quay Prim Sch NE10 . .57 C2
BILLY MILL 41 D7
Billy Mill Ave NE29 . . . . . . .41 E6
Billy Mill La NE29 . . . . .41 D8
Bilsdale SR6 . . . . .75 F7
Bilsdale Pl NE12 . . . . .38 F6
Bilsmoor Ave NE7 . . . . .39 B2
Bilton Hall Rd NE32 . . . . . . .58 D6
Bilton Hall Rd NE32 . . . . . . .58 C6
Binchester St NE34 . . . . . . .59 A5
Bingfield Gdns NE5 . . . . . . .37 C1
Bingley Cl **8** NE28 . . . . . . .40 E5
Bingley St SR5 . . . . .73 F3
Bink Moss NE37 . . . . .83 A6
Binsby Gdns NE9 . . . . .71 B3
Binswood Ave NE5 . . . . . . .37 C2
Bio Science Ctr NE1 . . . . .100 C4
Bircham Dr NE21 . . . . .53 D1
Birch Ave
Gateshead NE10 . . . . .72 A7
Whitburn SR6 . . . . .60 F1
Birch Cl NE46 . . . . .44 E3
Birch Cres
Burnopfield NE16 . . . . .79 A6
Penshaw DH4 . . . . .90 C2
Birch Ct
Prudhoe NE42 . . . . .50 A2
Silksworth SR3 . . . . .91 E6
Birches Nook Cotts NE43 . .64 C7
Birches Nook Rd NE43 . . . .64 C7
Birches The NE13 . . . . .69 C3
Birchfield NE16 . . . . .69 B5
Birchfield Gdns
Gateshead NE9 . . . . .71 A2
Newcastle upon Tyne NE15 . .53 F7
Birchfield Rd SR2 . . . . .86 B4
Birchgate Cl NE21 . . . . .53 A1
Birch Gr
Jarrow NE32 . . . . .58 A7
Wallsend NE28 . . . . .40 C5
Birchington Ave NE33 . . . . .59 D7

Birch Mews NE16 . . . . .78 F6
Birch Rd NE21 . . . . .53 D3
Birch St NE32 . . . . .58 A7
Birch Terr
Birtley DH3 . . . . .82 B5
Newcastle upon Tyne NE6 . .57 A5
Birchtree Gdns NE25 . . . . . .31 F3
Birchvale Ave **5** NE5 . . . . .37 B2
Birchwood
3 East Boldon NE36 . . . .74 D7
South Hylton SR4 . . . . .85 B7
Birchwood Ave
Newcastle upon Tyne NE7 . .39 C3
Whickham NE16 . . . . .69 A5
Widopen NE13 . . . . .28 C5
Birchwood Cl NE23 . . . . .7 F1
Birchwood Way NE63 . . . . . .7 A1
Birdhill Pl NE34 . . . . .59 C5
Birds Nest Rd NE6 . . . . . . .56 D4
Bird St NE30 . . . . .42 C6
Birds Terr DH4 . . . . .90 D8
Birkdale
South Shields NE33 . . . . . .42 E1
Whitley Bay NE25 . . . . .31 D5
Birkdale Ave SR6 . . . . .75 E7
Birkdale Cl
Newcastle upon Tyne NE7 . .39 C4
Wallsend NE28 . . . . .40 C4
Washington NE37 . . . . .72 B2
Birkdale Dr DH4 . . . . .90 A4
Birkdene NE43 . . . . .64 D6
Birkhead Cotts NE16 . . . . . .80 E6
Birkheads La NE11, NE16 . .80 E6
Birkland La DH9, NE11,
NE16 . . . . .80 E7
Birkshaw Wlk **1** NE5 . . . . .36 E1
Birks Rd NE15 . . . . .35 B6
Birling Pl NE5 . . . . .37 D2
Birnam Gr NE32 . . . . .58 C2
Birney Edge NE20 . . . . .25 C2
Birnham Pl NE3 . . . . .37 F3
Birnie Cl NE4 . . . . .54 E4
Birrell Sq SR5 . . . . .73 F4
Birrell St SR5 . . . . .73 F4
BIRTLEY 82 C3
Birtley Ave
Sunderland SR5 . . . . .73 F4
Tynemouth NE30 . . . . .42 D8
Birtley Cl NE3 . . . . .38 A4
Birtley East Prim Sch
DH3 .82 C4
Birtley Golf Course DH3 . . .82 D3
Birtley La DH3 . . . . .82 D3
Birtley L Ctr DH3 . . . . .82 C4
Birtley St Josephs RC Jun
Sch DH3 . . . . .82 C4
Birtley Villas **1** DH3 . . . . . .82 C4
Birtwistle Ave NE31 . . . . . . .57 D3
Biscop Terr NE32 . . . . .58 C4
Biscuit Factory The★
NE2 .99 C2
Bishopbourne Ct **5** NE29 . .31 F1
Bishop Cres NE32 . . . . .58 C8
Bishopdale
Penshaw DH4 . . . . .89 E8
Wallsend NE28 . . . . .39 F5
Bishopdale Ave NE24 . . . . .17 A8
Bishop Harland CE Prim Sch
SR5 .74 C3
Bishop Ian Ramsey CE Prim
Sch DH8 . . . . .77 C2
Bishop Morton Gr SR1 . . .103 B2
Bishop Ramsay Ct NE34 . .60 A6
Bishop Rock Dr NE12 . . . . .39 A6
Bishop's Ave NE4 . . . . .98 A1
Bishops Cl NE28 . . . . .40 E2
Bishops Ct NE5 . . . . .53 F8
Bishops Dr NE40 . . . . .52 D4
Bishops Mdw NE22 . . . . . . .10 F7
Bishop's Rd NE15 . . . . .54 D5
Bishops Way SR3 . . . . .91 E5
Bishops Wynd DH5 . . . . . . .94 B3
Bishopton St
Blyth NE24 . . . . .17 E6
Sunderland SR2 . . . . .103 B1
Bishopton Way NE46 . . . . . .44 E4
BISHOPWEARMOUTH . . .102 C2
Bisley Ct NE28 . . . . .40 D5
Bisley Dr NE34 . . . . .59 D7
Bittern Cl
Dunston NE11 . . . . .54 F1
Shiremoor NE28 . . . . .41 A1
Biverfield Rd NE42 . . . . .50 E1
Blackberries The **18** NE9 . .71 F1
Black Boy Rd DH4 . . . . .99 A4
Black Boy Yd NE1 . . . . .99 A1
Blackburn Gn NE10 . . . . . . .71 C7
BLACK CALLERTON 36 B8
Blackcap Cl NE38 . . . . .83 D3
Blackclose Bank NE63 . . . . .6 D1
Blackclose Est NE63 . . . . . .6 C2
Blackdene NE63 . . . . .6 D4
Black Dr DH3 . . . . .81 E4
Blackett Cotts NE41 . . . . . . .51 A4
Blackett Ct NE41 . . . . .51 A4
Blackett St
Hebburn NE31, NE32 . . . . .57 F6
Newcastle upon Tyne NE1 . .99 A2
Blackett Terr SR4 . . . . .102 A4
BLACKFELL 83 A4
Blackfell Prim Sch NE37 . . .83 A4
Blackfell Rd NE37 . . . . .82 F5
Blackfriars **8** NE1 . . . . . . .98 C1
Blackfriars★ NE1 . . . . . . .98 C1
Blackfriars Way NE12 . . . . .39 A4
BLACKHALL MILL 77 F2
Blackhams Hill Sta★ NE9 . .71 C1

Blackheath Cl NE37 . . . . .72 C2
Blackheath Ct NE37 . . . . .37 B5
Blackhill Ave NE28 . . . . .40 F6
Blackhill Cres NE9 . . . . .71 D4
Blackhouse La NE40 . . . . .52 B5
Black La
  Blaydon NE21 . . . . .53 A2
  Gateshead NE9 . . . . .71 C1
Blackpool Par NE31 . . . . .58 A3
Black Rd
  Hebburn NE31 . . . . .57 F6
  Sunderland SR2 . . . . .92 F7
Blackrow La
  Gateshead NE9 . . . . .71 A3
  Heddon-on-the-Wall NE15. . .35 A4
Blackstone Ct NE21 . . . . .53 A2
Blackthorn Cl NE16. . . . . .69 A2
Blackthorn Dr
  Blyth NE24 . . . . .17 C4
  Wallsend NE28 . . . . .40 C5
Blackthorne NE10 . . . . .71 F5
Blackthorn Pl NE4 . . . . .100 B3
Blackthorn Way
  Ashington NE63 . . . . .6 B3
  Fence Houses DH4 . . . . .90 A7
Blackwater Ho 7 SR3 . . . .92 A6
Blackwell Ave NE6 . . . . .57 A6
Blackwood Rd SR5 . . . . .74 A3
Bladen St NE32 . . . . .58 A7
Bladen Street Ind Est
  NE32 . . . . .58 A7
Blagdon Ave NE34 . . . . .59 E8
Blagdon Cl
  Morpeth NE61 . . . . .8 E8
  Newcastle upon Tyne NE1. . .99 C1
Blagdon Cres NE23 . . . . .21 E8
Blagdon Ct NE22 . . . . .11 C2
Blagdon Dr NE24 . . . . .17 C3
Blagdon St NE1. . . . . .99 C1
Blagdon Terr
  Cramlington NE23 . . . . .22 B6
  Seaton Burn NE13 . . . . .28 B8
Blake Ave NE16 . . . . .69 B7
BLAKELAW. 37 C2
Blakelaw Rd
  Blakelaw NE5. . . . . .37 C2
  7 Newcastle upon Tyne
  NE5 .37 B2
Blakemoor Pl NE5 . . . . .37 C1
Blaketown NE23 . . . . .23 A1
Blake Wlk NE8. . . . . .56 A2
Blanche Terr DH9 . . . . .79 B2
Blanchland NE38. . . . . .83 E1
Blanchland Ave
  Newcastle upon Tyne
  NE15 . . . . .53 C7
  Wideopen NE13 . . . . .28 B6
Blanchland Dr
  Holywell NE25 . . . . .23 F2
  Sunderland SR5. . . . . .75 C3
Blanchland Terr NE30 . . . . . . .42 B7
Blandford Ct NE4 . . . . .100 C4
Blandford Rd NE29 . . . . .41 D8
Blandford Sq NE1. . . . . .100 C4
Blandford St
  Newcastle upon Tyne
  NE1. . . . . .100 C4
  Sunderland SR1 . . . . .103 A2
Blandford Way NE28 . . . . .40 D5
Blaxton Pl NE16 . . . . .68 F5
BLAYDON. 53 E3
Blaydon Ave SR5. . . . . .74 A4
Blaydon Bank
  Blaydon NE21 . . . . .53 C2
  Blaydon NE21 . . . . .53 C2
Blaydon Bsns Ctr NE21. . . . . .53 E3
Blaydon Bsns Pk NE21. . . . . . .53 E1
BLAYDON BURN. 52 E1
BLAYDON HAUGHS 53 E4
Blaydon Haughs Ind Est
  NE21 . . . . .53 E4
Blaydon Highway NE21. . . . . .53 D3
Blaydon Ind Pk NE21. . . . . . . .53 D3
Blaydon Pool NE21. . . . . .53 D3
Blaydon Trad Pk NE21. . . . . . .53 F3
Blaydon West Prim Sch
  NE21 . . . . .53 C3
Blaykeston Cl SR7 . . . . .92 E1
Blayney Row NE15 . . . . .52 C8
Bleachfield NE10 . . . . .71 F6
BLEACH GREEN 53 C1
Bleasdale Cres DH4. . . . . .90 B7
Blencathra
  4 Tynemouth NE30 . . . . . . .32 A2
  Washington NE37 . . . . .83 C6
Blencathra Way NE21 . . . . . . .68 C8
Blenheim NE12 . . . . .29 D4
Blenheim Ct
  Blyth NE24 . . . . .17 D3
  Gateshead NE10 . . . . .71 C6
Blenheim Dr NE22 . . . . .11 C6
Blenheim Gdns NE61. . . . . . 4 E4
Blenheim Ho 2 NE61. . . . . . . .98 C1
Blenheim Pl NE11. . . . . .54 E1
Blenheim Wlk NE33 . . . . .42 D3
Blenkinsop Ct NE34 . . . . .59 B3
Blenkinsop Gr NE32. . . . . .58 B3
Blenkinsop Mews NE3 . . . . . .28 A1
Blenkinsop St 3 NE28 . . . . . .40 B2
Bletchley Ave NE8 . . . . .73 F4
Blezard Bsns Pk NE13. . . . . . .21 B1
Blezard Ct NE21 . . . . .53 E4
Blind La
  Burnside DH4 . . . . .90 B3
  Chester le Street DH3. . . . . . .88 D6
  New Silksworth SR3 . . . . .92 B7
Blindy La DH5. . . . . .95 C1
Bloomfield Ct SR6 . . . . .75 F2

Bloomfield Dr DH5. . . . . .94 D3
Bloomsbury Ct NE3 . . . . .38 B4
Blossom Gr DH4 . . . . .90 B4
Blossom St DH5 . . . . .95 B5
Blount St NE6 . . . . .56 D6
Blucher Rd
  Killingworth NE12 . . . . .29 C2
  North Shields NE29. . . . . .41 F3
Blucher Terr NE15 . . . . .36 B1
Blue Anchor Ct NE8. . . . . . . .101 B4
Bluebell Cl
  Gateshead NE9 . . . . .71 B5
  Wylam NE41. . . . . .51 B7
Bluebell Dene NE5. . . . . .37 A5
Bluebell Rise NE61. . . . . .8 F7
Bluebell Way NE34 . . . . .59 B5
Blueburn Dr NE12 . . . . .29 F3
Blue House Ct NE37. . . . . .83 B8
Blue House La
  Cleadon SR5, SR6 . . . . .75 A6
  Washington NE37 . . . . .83 C8
Blue House Rd NE31. . . . . .57 D3
Blue Quarries Rd NE16. . . . . . .69 A2
Blue Reef Aquarium*
  NE30. . . . . .32 D1
Blue Row NE15 . . . . .34 F2
Blue Sky Way NE31 . . . . .57 F1
Blue Top Cotts NE23 . . . . .22 D6
Blumer St DH4 . . . . .94 A8
BLYTH 17 E8
Blyth Bebside Cty Mid Sch
  NE24 . . . . .16 F8
Blyth Cl NE23. . . . . .28 F8
Blyth Com Coll NE24 . . . . .16 F7
Blyth Ct
  Newcastle upon Tyne
  NE15. . . . . .53 C7
  South Shields NE34 . . . . .59 C5
Blyth Dr NE61 . . . . .9 E1
Blyth Hospl NE24 . . . . .17 D8
Blyth Rd NE26 . . . . .24 E2
Blyth Sports Ctr NE24 . . . . . . .17 D7
Blyth Sq SR5 . . . . .74 A3
Blyth St
  Chopwell NE17. . . . . .66 C1
  Seaton Delaval NE25 . . . . . . .23 C3
  Sunderland SR5 . . . . .74 A4
Blythswood NE2 . . . . .99 B4
Blyth Terr
  Ashington NE63. . . . . .6 B3
  Birtley DH3 . . . . .82 B4
Blyth to Seaton Sluice Dunes
  Nature Reserve* NE26 . .24 C7
Blyth Tynedale Mid Sch
  NE24 . . . . .17 A7
Blyton Ave
  Ryhope SR2 . . . . .92 E6
  South Shields NE34. . . . . .58 F5
Bob Elliott Ho The 5
  NE24 . . . . .17 E8
Bodlewell Ho SR1 . . . . .103 B3
Bodlewell La SR1 . . . . .103 B3
Bodmin Cl NE3 . . . . .37 F8
Bodmin Ct NE28 . . . . .40 E5
Bodmin Ct 1 NE9 . . . . .71 A2
Bodmin Rd NE28 . . . . .41 C8
Bodmin Sq SR5 . . . . .74 A4
Bodmin Way NE3 . . . . .37 F6
Bog Houses NE23. . . . . .16 C2
Bognor St SR5. . . . . .73 F4
Bohemia Terr NE24 . . . . .17 E6
Boker La NE35. . . . . .74 B8
Bolam Ave
  Blyth NE24 . . . . .17 D7
  Tynemouth NE30 . . . . .32 A1
Bolam Coyne 12 NE6 . . . . . . .56 C5
Bolam Ct NE15 . . . . .35 D1
Bolam Dr NE63 . . . . .6 E2
Bolam Gdns NE28. . . . . .41 B3
Bolam Gr NE30 . . . . .32 A1
Bolam Pl NE22 . . . . .11 C2
Bolam Rd NE12 . . . . .29 C3
Bolam St
  Gateshead NE8 . . . . .70 B8
  Newcastle upon Tyne NE6 . . .56 C5
Bolam Way
  Newcastle upon Tyne NE6 . . .56 C5
  Seaton Delaval NE25 . . . . . . .23 C3
Boland Rd NE61 . . . . .2 A3
Bolbec Rd NE4 . . . . .54 E7
Bolburn NE10. . . . . .72 A7
BOLDON. 74 F6
Boldon Bsns Pk NE35 . . . . . . .73 E7
Boldon CE Prim Sch NE36 .73 F7
Boldon Cl NE28. . . . . .40 E5
BOLDON COLLIERY 58 E1
Boldon Dr NE36. . . . . .74 A7
Boldon Gdns NE9 . . . . .71 C3
Boldon La
  Cleadon SR6 . . . . .59 F1
  East Boldon NE34, NE36. . . . .59 C1
  South Shields NE34 . . . . .59 B5
  Boldon Sch NE35 . . . . .74 A7
Bolingbroke Rd NE29 . . . . . . .41 D6
Bolingbroke St
  Newcastle upon Tyne NE6 . . .56 C5
  4 South Shields NE33 . . . . . .42 D2
Bollihope Dr SR3 . . . . .91 B8
Bolsover Ct NE63 . . . . .6 D3
Bolsover Terr
  Ashington NE63. . . . . .6 D3
  Pegswood NE61. . . . . .9 B8
Bolton's Bghrs NE17 . . . . .77 B8
Bolton CE Prim Sch . . . .
BOMARSUND 11 C6
Bonaventure DH4 . . . . .90 A3
Bonchester Cl NE22. . . . . .10 F2
Bonchester Ct 4 NE28. . . . . .40 E5

Bonchester Pl NE23. . . . . .22 D8
Bond Cl SR5. . . . . .75 C1
Bond Ct NE4 . . . . .54 E5
Bondene Ave NE10. . . . . .71 E8
Bondene Avenue W NE10 .71 E8
Bondene Way NE23 . . . . .16 B2
Bondfield Cl NE28 . . . . .40 F3
Bondfield Gdns NE10 . . . . .72 A8
Bondgate Cl NE46. . . . . .45 B4
Bondgate Ct NE46 . . . . .45 B4
Bondicar Pl 1 NE5 . . . . .37 D1
Bondicar Terr NE24 . . . . .17 E7
Bond St 2 NE4. . . . . .54 D5
Bonemill La
  Chester le Street NE38. . . . . .88 F8
  Washington NE38 . . . . .89 C8
Bonington Way NE5. . . . . .37 B2
Bonner's Field SR6 . . . . .103 A4
Bonnivard Gdns NE23 . . . . . . .23 A1
Bonsall Ct NE34 . . . . .59 D5
Booths Rd NE63 . . . . .6 A4
Booth St
  Gateshead NE10 . . . . .71 D8
  Sunderland SR4. . . . . .102 A2
Bootle St SR5 . . . . .74 A3
Bordeaux Cl SR3 . . . . .91 E6
Bordsley Rd NE29 . . . . .41 C8
Boreham Cl NE28 . . . . .40 D5
Borodin Ave SR5. . . . . .73 F4
Borough Rd
  Jarrow NE32 . . . . .58 B6
  North Shields NE29 . . . . .42 A5
  South Shields NE34 . . . . .60 A5
  Sunderland SR1. . . . . .103 B2
Borrowdale
  Birtley DH3 . . . . .82 D1
  Washington NE37 . . . . .83 C8
  Whickham NE16. . . . . .69 D7
Borrowdale Ave
  Blyth NE24 . . . . .17 A8
  Newcastle upon Tyne NE6. . .56 F7
  Sunderland SR6. . . . . .75 D5
Borrowdale Cl NE36. . . . . .74 C8
Borrowdale Cres
  Blaydon NE21 . . . . .68 B8
  Penshaw DH4 . . . . .90 A8
Borrowdale Gdns NE9. . . . . . . .71 B3
Borrowdale St DH5 . . . . .95 A2
Boscobel Cl NE12. . . . . .38 F6
Boscombe Dr NE28 . . . . .40 C4
Boston Ave
  Newcastle upon Tyne NE7 . . .39 B5
  Washington NE38 . . . . .83 D6
Boston Cl NE28 . . . . .40 D5
Boston Cres SR5. . . . . .73 E4
Boston Ct NE12 . . . . .39 F8
Boston St SR5 . . . . .73 F4
Boswell Ave NE34. . . . . .59 B3
Bosworth Gdns NE6. . . . . .39 D2
Bosworth NE21. . . . . .29 D4
BOTHAL 7 D8
Bothal Ave NE62 . . . . .10 E7
Bothal Bank NE61. . . . . .5 C2
Bothal Cl
  Blyth NE24 . . . . .17 C7
  Pegswood NE61. . . . . .4 E3
Bothal Cotts NE63 . . . . .5 F4
Bothal Mid Sch NE63 . . . . .5 F4
Bothal St NE6 . . . . .56 D6
Bothal Terr NE63 . . . . .5 F4
Botham Ho NE29. . . . . .41 D3
Bottle Bank NE8 . . . . .101 B4
Bottlehouse St NE6 . . . . .56 C4
Boulby Cl SR3 . . . . .92 C7
Boulevard The NE12. . . . . .39 A6
Boulmer Ave NE23 . . . . .16 B2
Boulmer Cl NE3 . . . . .37 F8
Boulmer Ct DH2 . . . . .88 C2
Boulmer Gdns NE13. . . . . .28 B6
Boult Terr DH4. . . . . .90 B6
Boundary Dr NE61 . . . . .9 A7
Boundary Gdns NE7. . . . . .39 A3
BOUNDARY HOUSES 90 A4
Boundary La NE48 . . . . .76 A3
Boundary St SR5 . . . . .75 C2
Boundary Way NE26 . . . . .24 D6
Bourne Ave NE4 . . . . .54 D7
Bournemouth Ct 2 NE28. .40 E5
Bournemouth Gdns
  Newcastle upon Tyne NE5 . . .36 F3
  Whitley Bay NE26 . . . . .32 A6
Bournemouth Par NE31 . . . . . .58 A3
Bournemouth Rd NE29 . . . . . . .41 C5
Bourn Lea DH4. . . . . .90 A5
BOURNMOOR 89 D3
Bournmoor Prim Sch
  DH4 .89 E3
Bourtree Cl NE28 . . . . .40 C4
Bowbank Cl SR3 . . . . .86 B2
Bowburn Ave SR5. . . . . .74 C2
Bowburn Cl NE10 . . . . .72 C7
Bower St SR6 . . . . .75 D4
Bower The NE32 . . . . .73 B8
Bowes Ave DH5. . . . . .95 B1
Bowes Cres NE16 . . . . .79 D8
Bowes Ct
  Blyth NE24 . . . . .17 E7
  Newcastle upon Tyne NE3. . .38 E5
Bowes Farm Cotts DH3 . . . . . .89 D5
Bowes Ho 8 SR3 . . . . .91 D7
Bowes Lea DH4 . . . . .90 A8
Bowes Lyon Ct NE9 . . . . .71 A2
Bowes Lyon Cl 6 NE9 . . . . . .70 F8
Bowes Rly* NE9. . . . . .82 E8
Bowes Rly Ctr Mus* NE9. .71 E2

Bowes St
  Blyth NE24. . . . . .17 E8
  Newcastle upon Tyne NE3. . .38 E5
Bowesville NE16 . . . . .79 B5
Bowes Wlk NE12. . . . . .39 C7
Bowfell Ave NE5 . . . . .37 D3
Bowfell Cl NE5 . . . . .37 D3
Bowfell Gdns NE62. . . . . .11 A8
Bowfield Ave NE3. . . . . .28 C1
Bowler's Hill NE43 . . . . .64 F7
Bowlynn Cl SR3. . . . . .91 E6
Bowman Dr
  Dudley NE23 . . . . .29 B8
  Hexham NE46. . . . . .45 B4
Bowman Pl NE33 . . . . .42 C1
Bowman Sq NE63 . . . . .6 D2
Bowman St SR6 . . . . .90 F1
Bowmont Dr NE23 . . . . .1 E5
Bowmont Dr 2 NE23 . . . . . . .22 D8
Bowmont Wlk DH2. . . . . .88 A1
Bowness Ave NE28. . . . . .40 E6
Bowness Cl NE36 . . . . .74 C7
Bowness Pl NE9. . . . . .71 B4
Bowness Rd
  Newcastle upon Tyne NE5 . . .37 A1
  Whickham NE16. . . . . .69 D7
Bowness St NE5 . . . . .74 A4
Bowness Terr 1 NE28. . . . . . .40 E5
Bowood Cl SR2 . . . . .92 D6
Bowsden Ct NE3. . . . . .38 E5
Bowsden Terr NE3 . . . . .38 E5
Bowtrees SR2 . . . . .86 D3
Boxlaw NE9 . . . . .71 C5
Boyd Cres NE28. . . . . .40 E5
Boyd Rd NE28 . . . . .40 D2
Boyd St
  Newburn NE15. . . . . .52 E8
  Newcastle upon Tyne NE2 . . .99 C2
Boyd Terr
  Newcastle upon Tyne,
  Walbottle NE15. . . . . .36 B1
  5 Newcastle upon Tyne,
  Westerhope NE5. . . . . .36 F3
Boyne Ct 8 NE24 . . . . .17 E8
Boyne Gdns NE27 . . . . .30 E3
Boystones Ct NE37 . . . . .83 B6
Brabourne Gdns 7 NE29 . .31 F1
Brabourne St NE34 . . . . .59 C6
Bracken Ave NE28 . . . . .40 C5
Brackenburn Cl DH4 . . . . .90 C1
Bracken Cl NE13 . . . . .27 B6
Brackendene Dr NE9 . . . . .70 E5
Bracken Dr NE11 . . . . .69 F6
Brackenfield Rd NE3 . . . . .38 B4
Bracken La NE41 . . . . .71 C3
Brackenridge NE16 . . . . .78 E6
Bracken Pl NE4 . . . . .54 D7
Bracken Ridge NE61 . . . . .3 C1
Brackenside NE3 . . . . .28 C1
Brackenway NE37 . . . . .83 B7
Bracken Way NE40 . . . . .52 A2
Brackenwood Gr SR2 . . . . .86 C2
Brackley Gr NE7. . . . . .41 D4
Brackley Gr NE37 . . . . .72 E1
Bracknell Gdns NE5. . . . . .36 C1
Brack Terr NE10 . . . . .57 B2
Bradbury Cl NE10. . . . . .71 B2
Bradbury Ct
  New Hartley NE25 . . . . .23 D6
  Ponteland NE20 . . . . .25 F6
Bradbury Pl NE25 . . . . .23 D6
Bradford Ave
  Sunderland SR5. . . . . .74 A4
  Wallsend NE28 . . . . .40 D5
Bradley Ave
  Houghton-le-Spring DH5 . . . .94 E6
  South Shields NE34 . . . . .60 A6
Bradley Cl DH2 . . . . .88 E2
Bradley Fell La NE41. . . . . .51 C2
Bradley Fell Rd NE40,
  NE42 .66 C8
Bradley Rd NE42. . . . . .50 F3
Bradley Terr DH5. . . . . .95 C1
Bradley View 14 NE40 . . . . . .51 F3
Bradman Dr DH3 . . . . .88 E1
Bradman Sq SR5. . . . . .74 A4
Bradman St SR5 . . . . .74 A4
Bradshaw Sq SR5 . . . . .74 A3
Bradshaw St SR5 . . . . .74 A3
Bradwell Rd NE3. . . . . .37 E5
Bradwell Way DH4. . . . . .90 C4
Brady & Martin Ct NE1. . . . . .99 B2
Brady Sq 5 NE38. . . . . .83 F4
Brady St SR4 . . . . .85 F7
Braebridge Pl NE3 . . . . .38 A1
Braefell Ct NE37 . . . . .83 B6
Braemar Ct NE10 . . . . .57 B2
Braemar Dr NE34 . . . . .60 A8
Braemar Gdns
  Sunderland, East Herrington
  SR3 . . . . .91 C6
  Sunderland, Hillview SR3 . . . .86 B3
  Whitley Bay NE25. . . . . .31 C4
Braeside
  Dunston NE11 . . . . .69 F7
  Sunderland SR2. . . . . .86 B2
Braeside Cl NE30 . . . . .32 A3
Brae The SR2. . . . . .102 B2
Brahman Ave NE34 . . . . .59 B4
Braintree Gdns NE3. . . . . .37 F4
Braithwaite Rd NE3. . . . . .28 A3
Brama Teams Ind Pk NE8. .70 B8
Bramble Ct NE24 . . . . .17 C8
Bramble Dykes NE15 . . . . .54 B6
Bramblelaw NE9 . . . . .71 C4
Brambles The DH3 . . . . .88 D6
Brambling Lea NE22 . . . . .11 C2
Bramhall Dr NE38. . . . . .89 B8

Bramham Ct NE34 . . . . .59 E5
Bramhope Gn NE9 . . . . .71 B2
Bramley Cl SR4 . . . . .85 A3
Bramley Ct
  8 Hexham NE46. . . . . .45 B4
  Newcastle upon Tyne NE7 . . .39 E3
Brampton Ave NE6 . . . . .56 F4
Brampton Ct NE23 . . . . .22 C8
Brampton Gdns
  Gateshead NE9 . . . . .71 A3
  Throckley NE15 . . . . .35 E2
  Wallsend NE28 . . . . .41 A4
Brampton Pl NE22 . . . . .41 E5
Brampton Rd NE34. . . . . .59 A5
Bramwell Cl NE17 . . . . .38 E5
Bramwell Rd SR2 . . . . .103 B1
Brancepeth Ave
  Fence Houses DH4 . . . . .90 A1
  Newcastle upon Tyne NE4 . . .54 E5
Brancepeth Cl NE15. . . . . .53 C7
Brancepeth Rd
  Hebburn NE31. . . . . .57 F7
  Washington NE38 . . . . .83 A4
Brancepeth Terr NE32. . . . . . .58 B3
BRANCH END 64 D7
Branch St NE21. . . . . .53 B1
Branckenpeth Mews NE3. . . . .28 B1
Brand Ave NE4 . . . . .54 E7
Brandling Ct
  14 Gateshead NE10 . . . . .56 D1
  Newcastle upon Tyne NE2 . . .99 C4
  South Shields NE34. . . . . .60 A4
Brandling Dr NE3. . . . . .28 C1
Brandling Mews NE3 . . . . .28 C1
Brandling Pk NE2. . . . . .99 A4
Brandling Place S NE2 . . . . . . .99 C4
Brandling Prim Sch NE10 .56 D1
Brandling St
  Gateshead NE8 . . . . .101 C4
  Sunderland SR6. . . . . .75 E2
Brandling Street S SR6 . . . . . .75 E2
Brandling Terr 3 NE30. . . . . .42 B6
BRANDLING VILLAGE 99 B4
Brandon Ave NE27 . . . . .30 E3
Brandon Cl
  Blaydon NE21 . . . . .68 A8
  Blyth NE24 . . . . .17 B8
  Houghton-le-Spring DH4. . . . .94 D3
Brandon Gdns NE9. . . . . .71 D3
Brandon Gr NE2 . . . . .99 C3
Brandon Rd
  Newcastle upon Tyne NE3. . .37 F6
  North Shields NE29. . . . . .41 D6
Brandy La NE37. . . . . .83 B7
Brandywell NE10. . . . . .71 F6
Branken St NE29 . . . . .42 A5
Bransdale DH4 . . . . .89 E8
Bransdale Ave SR6. . . . . .75 F7
Branston St SR5 . . . . .75 B2
Branton Ave NE31. . . . . .57 D3
Brantwood Ave NE25. . . . . . . .31 D4
Brantwood Ct NE21 . . . . .53 D2
Branxton Cres NE6. . . . . .56 F5
Brass Thill Way NE13 . . . . .42 E2
Bray Cl NE28 . . . . .40 D5
Braydon Dr NE29 . . . . .41 E3
Brayside NE32 . . . . .58 D1
Breamish Dr NE38 . . . . .88 F8
Breamish Ho NE1. . . . . .56 A5
Breamish St
  Jarrow NE32 . . . . .58 A5
  Newcastle upon Tyne NE1. . .56 A5
Brearley Way NE10. . . . . .71 C8
Breckenbeds Rd NE9 . . . . .70 E4
Brecken Ct NE9 . . . . .70 E4
Breckon Cl NE63. . . . . .6 A4
Brecon Cl NE5 . . . . .37 B4
Bredon Cl NE38. . . . . .83 B3
Brendale Ave NE5. . . . . .36 E3
BRENKLEY 20 D3
Brenkley Ave NE27 . . . . .30 F2
Brenkley Cl NE13 . . . . .27 B5
Brenkley Ct NE13 . . . . .28 B8
Brenkley Way NE13 . . . . .21 B1
Brenlynn Cl SR3 . . . . .91 E6
Brennan Cl
  Ashington NE63. . . . . .7 A3
  Newcastle upon Tyne NE15. . .54 B6
Brentford Ave
  7 Hylton Castle SR5. . . . . . .74 A3
  Sunderland SR5. . . . . .74 A3
Brentford Sq 4 SR5. . . . . .74 A3
Brentwood Ave
  Newbiggin-by-the-Sea
  NE64 . . . . .7 D5
  Newcastle upon Tyne NE2 . . .38 D2
Brentwood Cl NE25 . . . . .23 C2
Brentwood Gdns
  Gateshead NE9. . . . . .71 A3
  Newcastle upon Tyne NE2 . . .38 D2
  Sunderland SR3. . . . . .86 B3
  Whickham NE16. . . . . .69 B8
Brentwood Gr NE28. . . . . .40 D1
Brentwood Ho 7 NE33 . . . . . .42 D2
Brentwood Rd DH4 . . . . .90 A5
Brettanby Gdns NE40 . . . . . . .52 C6
Brettanby Rd NE10. . . . . .71 E7
Brett Cl NE7 . . . . .39 D3
Bretton Gdns NE7. . . . . .39 C2
Brewer's La NE28, NE29. . . . . .41 C3
Brewer Terr SR2 . . . . .93 A6
Brewery Bank 6 NE16 . . . . . .54 A1

Brewery Bond NE29........42 B4
Brewery La
 Gateshead NE10.........56 D2
 Ponteland NE20..........25 E6
 South Shields NE33......42 B2
 5 Whickham NE16........54 A1
Brewery St **3** NE24......17 F8
Brewery Stables **1** NE1..98 C1
Brewhouse Bank NE30....42 C6
Briar Ave
 2 Houghton-le-Spring
 DH4......................94 D8
 Whitley Bay NE26........32 A6
Briar Cl
 Blaydon NE21............53 A2
 Great Lumley DH4........89 E1
 Shiney Row DH4..........89 F4
 Wallsend NE28...........40 C5
Briar Ct NE26............32 A5
Briardale
 Bedlington NE22.........10 E1
 Dinnington NE13.........27 B7
Briardale Rd NE14........17 A8
Briardene
 Ashington NE63..........6 B2
 Burnopfield NE16........78 E6
Briardene Cl NE13........91 C6
Briardene Cres NE3......38 A3
Briardene Dr NE10.......72 D8
Briar Edge NE12.........39 D8
Briarfield NE38..........83 D1
Briarfield Rd NE13.......38 B4
Briarhill DH2............88 A5
Briar La NE15............35 E1
Briarlea NE61...........9 E4
Briar Lea DH4............89 F4
Briar Pl NE15............54 A5
Briar Rd NE39............67 D2
Briarside NE37...........37 A3
Briars The SR5...........74 B1
Briarsyde NE12...........39 E6
Briarsyde Cl NE16........68 E5
Briar Terr NE16..........79 C6
Briar Vale NE25..........31 D3
Briarwood NE23..........29 B8
Briarwood Ave NE3.......38 E6
Briarwood Cres
 3 Dunston NE11.......69 F8
 Newcastle upon Tyne NE6..79 C3
Briarwood Rd NE24.......17 F6
Briarwood St DH4........89 E1
Briary The NE15.........35 C2
Brick Garth DH5.........95 C1
Brick Row SR2...........92 E7
Bridekirk NE37...........83 C7
Bridge Cotts NE23.......29 B8
Bridge Cres SR1.........103 A1
BRIDGE END..............45 C6
Bridge End
 6 Chester le Street DH3..88 C4
 Hexham NE46............45 C6
Bridge End Ind Est NE46..45 C6
Bridge House SR1........103 A3
Bridge Pk NE3...........38 C8
Bridge Rd NE61..........2 A2
Bridge Road S NE29......41 E3
Bridges St Ctr The SR1..103 A2
Bridge St
 Blaydon NE21...........53 C4
 Blyth NE24..............17 F7
 Gateshead NE8..........101 B4
 Morpeth NE61...........8 F8
 Newbiggin-by-the-Sea NE64..7 E4
 Seaton Burn NE13.......28 B8
 Sunderland SR1.........103 A2
Bridges The **10** NE33....42 D1
Bridges View NE8........101 A2
Bridge Terr
 Bedlington NE22.........11 C3
 Shiremoor NE27.........30 F4
Bridgewater Ct
 Newcastle upon Tyne
 NE15....................53 C7
 Wallsend NE28...........40 C4
Bridgewater Prim Sch
 NE15....................54 B5
Bridgewater Rd NE37....43 B7
Bridle Path
 East Boldon NE36.......74 C7
 Sunderland SR3.........91 C8
Bridle The NE27.........31 B2
Bridlington Ave NE9......70 F3
Bridlington Cl NE28......40 D5
Bridlington Pl NE31......58 A3
Bridport Rd DH1.........31 D1
Brierdene Cl NE26.......31 F8
Brier Dene Cres NE26....31 F8
Brierdene Ct NE26.......31 E8
Brierdene Rd NE26.......24 F1
Brierdene View NE26.....31 E8
Brierfield Gr SR4........86 B8
Brierley Cl NE24.........17 B7
Brierley Rd NE24........17 B7
Briermede Ave NE9......70 F4
Briermede Pk NE9.......70 F4
Briery Hill La NE61.......14 C3
Brieryside NE5..........37 D2
Briery Vale Cl SR2.......102 C1
Briery Vale Rd SR2.......86 C4
Brigham Ave NE3........38 E3
Brigham Pl NE33.........42 C3
Brightlea DH3...........82 E5
Brightman Rd NE29......42 A6
Brighton Avenue Prim Sch
 NE8....................101 A1

Brighton Cl NE28.........40 E5
Brighton Gdns NE8.......70 E7
Brighton Gr
 Newcastle upon Tyne NE4..98 A1
 North Shields NE29......41 F6
 Whitley Bay NE26.......31 F6
Brighton Par NE31.......58 A3
Brighton Rd NE8.........70 E8
Brighton Terr DH4........96 D1
Bright St
 South Shields NE33......42 E2
 Sunderland SR5.........75 E1
Brignall Gdns NE15......54 A7
Brignall Rise SR3........86 B2
Brigside Cotts NE13......28 C8
Brindley Rd NE37........83 E6
Brinkburn
 Blaydon NE21............68 A8
 Washington NE38........83 E2
Brinkburn Ave
 Blyth NE24..............17 F6
 Cramlington NE23........22 C6
 Gateshead NE8..........70 E8
 Whickham NE16.........69 B8
Brinkburn Cl
 Blaydon NE21...........68 A8
 Newcastle upon Tyne NE6..56 B6
Brinkburn Cres
 Ashington NE63..........6 E4
 Burnside DH4............90 C1
Brinkburn Ct
 3 Newcastle upon Tyne
 NE6....................56 B6
 3 North Shields NE30....41 C1
Brinkburn Gdns NE11....86 A8
Brinkburn La **21** NE6....56 B6
Brinkburn Pl **25** NE6....56 B6
Brinkburn Sq **7** NE6....56 B5
Brinkburn St
 25 Heaton NE6........56 B6
 7 Newcastle upon Tyne
 NE6....................56 B6
 Newcastle upon Tyne, St
 Lawrence NE6...........56 B5
 North Shields NE30......41 C1
 South Shields NE34......59 B6
 Sunderland SR4.........102 A1
Brinkburn Street S NE6..56 C4
Brisbane Ave NE34.......58 F3
Brisbane Ct NE8.........101 B3
Brisbane St SR5.........74 A3
Brislee Ave NE30........42 C7
Brislee Gdns NE3........37 E4
Bristlecone SR3.........91 E5
Bristol Ave
 Sunderland SR5.........73 F4
 Washington NE37........83 B8
Bristol Dr NE28..........40 D5
Bristol St NE25..........23 D6
Bristol Terr NE4.........100 A4
Bristol Wlk NE25........23 D6
Britannia Ct NE4........100 A4
Britannia Pl NE4........98 A1
Britannia Rd SR3........92 A7
Britannia Terr NE4.......94 A8
Brittania Ho NE28.......40 F1
Brittania Pl NE4.........98 A1
Brixham Ave NE9.........70 F3
Brixham Cres NE32......58 D5
Brixham Gdns SR3.......86 B3
Broadacre NE10.........72 B8
Broadbank NE10.........72 B8
Broad Chare NE1........101 B4
Broadfield Pl NE34.......59 D5
Broad Garth NE1.........101 B4
Broadgates NE46.........45 B4
Broad Landing NE33......42 B3
Broadlands SR6..........75 A7
Broadlea NE10...........72 B8
Broadmayne Ave SR4....85 D4
Broadmayne Gdns SR4...85 D4
Broad Mdws
 Newcastle upon Tyne NE3..37 F3
 Sunderland SR2.........102 B1
Broadmeadows
 Sunderland SR3.........91 B6
 Washington NE38........83 E2
Broadmeadows Cl NE16..68 E4
Broadmead Way NE15...54 A5
Broadoak NE10..........72 B8
Broad Oak Terr NE17....66 B1
Broadpark NE10.........72 B8
Broadpool Gn NE16......69 C6
Broadpool Terr NE16.....69 C6
Broadsheath Terr SR5...74 F2
Broadside NE10..........72 B8
Broadstairs Ct SR4.......85 D4
Broadstone Gr NE5......36 C1
Broadstone Way NE28...40 C4
Broadview Villas DH6....96 A1
Broadwater NE10........72 B8
Broadway
 Blyth NE24..............17 E6
 Chester le Street DH3....88 D5
 Gateshead NE9..........71 B7
 Guide Post NE62.........10 F7
 Newcastle upon Tyne NE15..53 D7
 Ponteland NE20.........25 D4
 Whickham NE16.........69 A4
Broadway Circ NE24......17 E7
Broadway Cl NE30........32 B3
Broadway Cres NE24.....17 E6
Broadway Ct
 Newcastle upon Tyne NE3..38 C7
 Wallsend NE28...........38 C7
Broadway E NE3.........38 C7

Broadway East Fst Sch
 NE3....................38 D7
Broadway Gdns NE3......38 D7
Broadway Jun Sch SR4..85 D4
Broadway The
 Houghton-le-Spring DH4..94 E8
 Sunderland, Castletown SR5..85 A8
 Sunderland, Grindon SR4..85 B3
 Sunderland, Springwell SR4..85 D4
 Tynemouth NE30.........32 B2
Broadway Villas NE15....54 B6
Broadway W NE3.........38 B7
Broadwell Ct NE3........38 F4
Broadwood Prim Sch
 NE15....................53 F7
Broadwood Rd NE15.....53 F7
Broadwood View DH3....88 D2
Brockenhurst Dr SR4....85 A2
Brock Farm Ct NE30.....42 B6
Brockhampton Ct NE35..58 E2
Brock La NE62.........11 F5
Brockley Ave NE34.......59 B4
Brockley St SR5.........74 A3
Brockley Terr **4** NE33..58 E1
BROCKLEY WHINS.......58 E2
Brockley Whins Sta NE32..58 F2
Brockley Whins Sta NE32..58 F2
Brock St NE6............56 B5
Brockwade NE10........71 F4
Brockwell Cl NE21.......53 A1
Brockwell Ct NE24.......17 C5
Brockwell Dr NE39......67 E3
Brockwell Ho NE5........37 C2
Brockwell Mid Sch NE23..22 B8
Brockwell Rd NE38......22 B8
Brockwell St **1** NE4....17 C4
Brockwood Cl NE63......6 B1
Brodie Cl NE34..........59 C4
Brodrick Cl NE3.........37 D5
Brodrick St **13** NE33....42 D3
Brokenheugh NE5........36 F1
Bromarsh Ct SR6.........75 F1
Bromford Rd NE3........37 D5
Bromley Ave NE25.......31 E4
Bromley Ct NE3..........37 D7
Brompton Cl DH2........81 E2
Brompton Terr DH4......90 D4
Bromsgrove Cl **6** NE28..40 E5
Bronte St NE8...........56 B1
Brookbank Cl SR3........91 F5
Brook Ct NE22...........11 A1
Brooke Ave
 West Boldon NE35.......74 B8
 Whickham NE16.........69 A8
Brooke St SR5...........102 C4
Brooke's Wlk NE34.......59 A2
Brookfield
 Newcastle upon Tyne NE3..38 B2
 Shiremoor NE27.........30 E2
Brookfield Cres NE5......36 C1
Brookfield Terr NE6......57 A1
Brookland Dr NE12......29 E3
Brookland Rd SR4........85 F6
Brooklands NE20........25 A3
Brooklands Way NE35...73 D8
Brookland Terr NE29....31 B1
Brookside
 Dudley NE23............29 A7
 Houghton-le-Spring DH4..94 D6
Brookside Ave
 Blyth NE24..............17 B7
 Brunswick Village NE13..28 A6
Brookside Cres NE5......37 D1
Brookside Gdns **3** SR2..86 C4
Brook Side Lodge **3** SR2..86 C4
Brookside Terr **2** SR2..86 C4
Brookside Wood NE38...83 D1
Brooksmead NE38.......40 A4
Brook St
 Newcastle upon Tyne NE6..56 D5
 Whitley Bay NE26.......32 B6
Brookvale Ave NE3......38 A4
Broom Cl
 Blaydon NE21...........68 B8
 Morpeth NE61...........9 A7
 Whickham NE16.........69 C6
Broom Ct NE9...........82 F8
Broome Cl NE3...........37 E5
Broomfield NE32.........58 C2
Broomfield Ave
 Newcastle upon Tyne NE6..39 E1
 Wallsend NE28...........40 C5
Broomfield Cres NE17....37 B8
Broomfield Rd NE3.......38 B4
Broom Gn NE16.........69 C6
BROOMHAUGH..........63 A8
Broomhaugh CE Fst Sch
 NE44....................62 F7
Broomhaugh Ct NE46....45 C4
BROOM HILL............95 A6
Broomhill Est DH5.......94 F6
Broomhill Gdns NE5......37 C3
Broomhill Rd NE42.......50 E3
Broomhill Terr DH5......94 F5
Broomhouse Farm Ct **6**
 NE42....................50 D3
Broomhouse La NE42....50 D3
Broomhouse Rd NE42...50 F3
Broom La NE16..........69 C6
Broomlaw NE9...........71 C4
Broomlea NE29..........31 B1
Broomlea Cl NE62.......11 B8
Broomlee **6**...........6 E2
Broomlee Cl NE7........39 D3
Broomlee Rd NE12......29 D3

BROOMLEY..............63 D5
Broomley Ct NE3........37 F7
Broomley Fst Sch NE43..64 B8
Broomley Wlk NE3.......37 F7
Broomridge Ave NE15...54 D6
Broomshields Ave SR5...75 B3
Broomshields Cl SR5....75 B3
Brooms The DH2.........81 F2
Broom Terr
 Burnopfield NE16.......79 C6
 Whickham NE16.........69 C6
Broom Wood Ct NE42...50 B1
Broomy Hill Rd NE15....35 D2
Broomylinn Pl NE23......22 C8
Brotherlea Rd NE37......37 F7
Brougham St SR1........103 A2
Brough Ct **3** NE6........56 C7
Brough Gdns NE28......41 A4
Brough Park Way NE6...56 D7
Brough St **3** NE6.......56 C7
Broughton Cl NE5.......37 A4
Broughton Rd NE33......42 D2
Brough Way **20** NE6....56 C7
Brown Cres NE9.........71 C1
Browne Rd SR6..........75 E3
Browning Cl NE34.......59 B3
Browning Sq NE8.........56 A2
Brownlow Cl NE7........39 E3
Brownlow Rd NE34......59 C6
Browning Dr NE23.......22 C5
Brownriggs Ct NE37.....83 B6
Brown's Bldgs DH2.......81 C1
Brownsea Pl NE9........71 A7
Browntop Pl NE34.......59 C5
Brow The **7**............56 C5
Broxbourne Terr SR4....102 A2
Broxburn Cl NE28.......40 E5
Broxburn Cl NE5........37 C3
Broxholm Rd NE6........39 B1
Bruce Cl
 Newcastle upon Tyne NE5..36 F2
 Whiteleas NE34.........59 C4
Bruce Gdns NE5.........54 C7
Brumell Dr NE61.........1 A6
Brummell Ct NE43.......64 B7
Brundon Ave NE5........31 F7
Brunel Dr SR6...........75 F2
Brunel Lodge NE4.......100 A3
Brunel St
 Gateshead NE8.........70 D8
 Newcastle upon Tyne NE4..100 A3
Brunel Terr NE4.........100 A3
Brunel Wlk NE4.........100 A3
Brunswick Gr NE13......28 A6
BRUNSWICK IND EST...27 F6
Brunswick Ind Est NE13..27 F6
Brunswick Park Ind Est
 NE13....................28 A6
Brunswick Rd
 Shiremoor NE27.........30 F2
 Sunderland SR5.........74 A4
Brunswick Sq NE27......30 F2
Brunswick St NE33.......42 C1
BRUNSWICK VILLAGE...28 A6
Brunton Ave
 Newcastle upon Tyne NE3..37 F6
 Wallsend NE28...........41 B3
Brunton Cl NE27.........30 F2
Brunton Gr NE37........37 F6
Brunton La
 Hazlerigg NE13.........27 E2
 Newcastle upon Tyne, Brunton
 Park NE3, NE13.........28 B2
 Newcastle upon Tyne, Kingston
 Park NE3................37 C7
Brunton Mews NE13.....27 F2
Brunton Rd NE13........28 B1
Brunton Rd NE3.........37 F6
Brunton Sq NE29.........41 D3
Brunton Terr SR4........102 A2
Brunton Way
 Cramlington NE23.......16 B2
 Gateshead NE10........57 B2
Brussels Rd
 Sunderland SR4.........85 D7
 Wallsend NE28...........40 B1
Bryan's Leap NE16......79 A7
Bryden Ct NE34.........59 D5
Bryers St SR6...........60 F1
Buchanan Gn NE11.....100 A1
Buchanan St NE31.......57 D5
Buckingham SR3........91 E8
Buckingham Cl **1** NE6..75 F8
Buckingham St NE4......98 B1
Buckland Cl
 Burnside DH4...........90 C2
 Washington NE38........83 D3
Buck's Nook La NE40....66 C7
Buckthorne Gr NE7.......39 C3
Buddle Arts Ctr* NE28...40 B2
Buddle Ct NE4..........54 E4
Buddle Ind Est NE28.....54 D4
Buddle Rd NE4..........54 D4
Buddle St NE28..........40 A4
Buddle Terr
 8 Shiremoor NE27....30 E1
 Sunderland SR2.........103 B1
Bude Ct NE28...........40 C4
Bude Gdns NE9.........70 F3
Bude Gr NE29...........31 D1
Budle Cl
 Blyth NE24..............17 C7
 Newcastle upon Tyne NE3..38 A4
Budleigh Rd NE3........38 A4
Budworth Ave NE26.....24 D5
Bugatti Ind Est NE29.....41 C5
Buller's Gn NE61........3 E1
Bullfinch Dr NE16.......69 A7

Bullion La DH2..........88 B3
Bullion Lane Prim Sch
 DH2....................88 B3
Bulman's La NE29.......42 A8
Bulmer Ho NE34.........60 A7
Bulmer Rd NE34.........60 A7
Bungalows The
 Birtley DH3.............82 B6
 Elchester DH8..........76 F4
 Gateshead NE10........71 E8
 Hetton-le-Hole DH5......94 F6
 Kibblesworth NE11......81 E8
 Medomsley NE17.........77 B4
 Wallsend NE28...........40 F3
BUNKER HILL...........90 C5
Bunyan Ave NE34.......59 A3
Burdale Ave NE5........37 A1
BURDON................92 B3
Burdon Ave
 Cramlington NE23.......21 F7
 Houghton-le-Spring DH5...95 A8
Burdon Cl SR6..........59 E1
Burdon Cres
 Cleadon SR6............59 E1
 Ryhope SR2.............92 E6
 Seaham SR7............92 F1
Burdon La
 Ryhope SR2, SR3.......92 C5
 Silksworth SR3..........91 F3
Burdon Lodge NE16......59 E1
Burdon Main Row NE29..42 A4
Burdon Pk NE16.........59 C2
Burdon Plain NE16.......80 B7
Burdon Rd
 Cleadon SR6............59 E1
 Silksworth, Doxford Park
 SR3....................91 E2
 Silksworth, Mill Hill SR3..92 B6
 Sunderland SR1, SR2....103 A1
Burdon St NE29..........41 D3
Burdon Terr
 Bedlington NE22.........10 E1
 Newcastle upon Tyne NE2..99 B4
Burford Ct NE7..........39 A4
Burford Gdns SR3........86 B3
Burford La NE46.........45 C4
Burford St NE6..........56 B5
Burghley Gdns NE61.....4 F4
Burghley Rd NE10.......71 C6
Burgoyne Ct NE37.......83 D8
Burgoyne Terr NE61.....51 A6
Burke St **3** SR5........74 A3
Burlawn Cl **3** SR2.......92 F8
Burleigh Cl SR2.........92 F8
Burleigh St **1** NE33....42 D2
Burlington Ct
 Newcastle upon Tyne NE2..99 B4
 Wallsend NE28...........40 E7
Burlington Gdns NE6....56 B8
Burlison Gdns NE10.....56 C2
Burnaby Dr NE40........52 B4
Burnaby St SR4.........102 A1
Burn Ave
 2 Longbenton NE12...39 D8
 1 Wallsend NE28......40 B2
Burnbank
 Gateshead NE10........72 A6
 Seaton Burn NE13.......28 B8
 5 Sunderland SR5....75 B2
Burnbridge NE13........28 A8
Burnbridge NE13........28 A8
Burncroft **10** NE46....45 A4
Burn Crook DH5.........94 D6
Burnden Gr DH4.........90 A5
Burnet Cl NE28..........40 C5
Burnet Ct NE63.........6 B1
Burney Villas NE8.......56 A1
Burnfoot NE42..........79 A4
Burnfoot Terr NE26......32 A2
Burnfoot Way NE3.......37 E3
Burnhall Dr SR7.........93 A1
Burnham Ave NE15......53 B7
Burnham Cl
 Blyth NE24..............17 E5
 1 Newcastle upon Tyne NE4..90 B6
Burnham Gr
 East Boldon NE36.......74 D7
 Newcastle upon Tyne NE6..56 E4
Burnham St NE34........59 C6
Burn Heads Rd NE31....57 D4
Burnhills Gdns NE40.....52 A1
Burnhills La NE40........52 A1
Burnhope Dr SR5........75 B3
Burnhope Gdns **1** NE9..71 E3
Burnhope Rd NE38......83 E6
Burn La
 Hetton-le-Hole DH5......95 A3
 Hexham NE46...........45 A6
Burnland Terr NE44.....44 F5
Burnlea **4** DH4.........94 C8
Burnlea Gdns NE23......23 B2
Burnley St NE21.........53 C2
Burnmoor Gn NE9.......71 D3
BURNOPFIELD...........79 A6
Burnopfield Gdns NE15..54 A1
Burnopfield Prim Sch
 NE16....................79 A6
Burnopfield Rd NE39....67 F1
Burnop Terr NE39.......67 A2
Burn Park Rd
 Houghton-le-Spring DH4..94 D8
 Sunderland SR2.........102 B1
Burn Prom **5** DH4......94 E8
Burn Rd NE21...........53 A1
Burns Ave
 Blyth NE24..............17 C5
 West Boldon NE35.......74 B8

Burns Avenue N DH5......94 E7
Burns Avenue S DH5......94 E7
Burns Cl
　Biddick Hall NE34..........59 B3
　West Rainton DH4...........94 A2
　Whickham NE16.............69 B5
Burns Cres NE16...........98 E8
BURNSIDE.................90 B2
Burnside
　Ashington NE63.............7 A3
　Bedlington NE22...........11 D3
　East Boldon NE36..........74 E7
　Gateshead NE10...........71 E7
　Holywell NE25.............23 F1
　Jarrow NE32...............58 C4
　Morpeth NE61..............4 A1
　Newcastle upon Tyne NE2..98 B3
　Ovington NE42.............49 D4
　Ponteland NE20............25 B3
Burnside Ave
　Burnside DH4..............90 C1
　Dudley NE23...............29 B8
Burnside Bsns & Fnt Coll
　NE28....................40 D2
Burnside Cl
　Blyth NE24................17 B8
　Ovingham NE42............50 A4
　Seghill NE23..............22 E1
　Whickham NE16............69 A4
Burnside Cotts
　Annitsford NE23...........29 C8
　Mickley Square NE43......49 E1
Burnside Fst Sch NE23....16 C1
Burnside Prim Sch DH4....90 D1
Burnside Rd
　Newcastle upon Tyne NE3..38 C7
　Rowlands Gill NE39........67 D2
　Tynemouth NE30...........32 B3
Burnside The NE5...........36 E1
Burnside View NE23........22 E1
Burns St NE32..............58 B7
Burnstones NE5.............36 E1
Burn Terr
　Hebburn NE31..............57 C2
　Shiney Row DH4............90 B6
　Wallsend NE28.............40 F2
Burnthouse Cl NE21.......68 A8
Burnthouse La
　Whickham NE16............69 A5
　Whickham NE16............69 A6
　Whickham, Whickham Fell
　NE16....................69 A5
Burnt House Rd NE25......31 E3
Burnt Houses NE40.........52 B1
Burntland Ave SR5..........74 F2
Burn View
　Dudley NE23...............29 B8
　Hedworth NE32............73 D8
Burnville Rd SR4..........102 B1
Burnville Rd SR4..........102 B1
Burnway
　Seaham SR7...............93 A1
　Washington NE37..........83 B8
Burnwood Cl NE17..........66 B1
BURRADON..................29 C6
Burradon Farm Cotts
　NE23....................29 C5
Burradon Prim Sch NE23...29 C5
Burradon Rd NE23..........29 C7
Burrow St ⑤ NE33..........42 C3
Burscough Cres NE5........75 D2
Burstow Ave NE6............56 E3
Burswell Ave NE6..........44 F5
Burswell Villas NE46......44 F5
Burt Ave NE6...............41 E5
Burt Cl DH6................97 E3
Burt Cres NE23.............29 B8
Burt Memorial Homes
　NE62....................10 E5
Burt Rd NE22...............11 E3
Burtree NE38...............83 B3
Burt St NE24...............17 E8
Burt Terr
　Morpeth NE61..............9 A8
　Walbottle NE15...........36 A2
Burwell Ave NE5...........53 F8
Burwood Cl NE6.............57 A4
Burwood Rd
　Newcastle upon Tyne NE6..56 F3
　Tynemouth NE29...........41 C8
Business & Innovation Ctr
　SR5.....................74 F1
Buston Terr NE2............38 F1
Busty Bank
　Burnopfield NE16..........79 B7
　Burnopfield NE16, NE39...79 A8
Butcher's Bridge Rd NE32 58 B4
Butcher's La NE61..........4 F5
Bute Ct ⑤ SR3.............42 A6
Bute Dr NE11...............64 F4
Buteland Rd NE15..........53 F7
Buteland Terr NE64.........7 D4
Bute Road N NE39..........66 F4
Bute Road S NE39..........66 F3
Bute St DH9................79 A2
Butsfield Gdns SR3........86 B2
Butterburn Cl NE17........39 E4
Butterfield Cl NE40........51 F4
Buttermere
　Cleadon SR6...............60 A1
　Gateshead NE10...........72 A8
Buttermere Cl
　Chester le Street DH2.....88 C2
　Killingworth NE12.........29 C3

Buttermere Cl continued
⑧ Newcastle upon Tyne
　NE5.....................37 B1
Buttermere Cres
　Blaydon NE21.............68 B8
　South Hetton DH6.........97 E8
Buttermere Gdns
　Gateshead NE9............71 A5
　South Shields NE34........59 E6
Buttermere Rd NE30........32 A2
Buttermere St SR2.........86 E2
Buttermere Way NE24......12 B1
Butterwell Dr NE61.........4 E3
Buttsfield Terr NE34.......90 B8
Buxton Cl
　Jarrow NE32...............58 C5
　Wallsend NE28............40 D5
Buxton Gdns
　Blakelaw NE5.............37 A3
　Newcastle upon Tyne NE5..36 F3
　Sunderland SR3...........86 B3
Buxton Gn ② NE5..........36 F3
Buxton Rd NE32............58 C5
Buxton St NE1.............99 C1
Byemoor Sacred Heart RC
　Prim Sch NE16............79 D7
Byerhope ② DH4............90 A7
BYERMOOR.................79 D7
Byermoor Ind Est NE16....79 D7
Byers Ct SR3...............92 B8
Byer Sq DH5................95 A6
Byer St DH5................95 A6
Byeways The NE12..........39 B6
Byewell Terr NE26.........24 D6
Bygate Cl NE3.............37 E3
Bygate Rd NE25............31 E4
BYKER.....................56 C5
Byker Bank NE6............56 A5
Byker Bridge NE1, NE6....56 A4
Byker Bsns Development Ctr
　NE6.....................56 B5
Byker Cres 17 NE6..........56 C5
Byker Sta NE6..............56 C6
Byker St NE6..............56 F6
Byker Terr NE6.............56 F6
Byland Cl NE4.............90 C2
Byland St NE38............83 C5
Byland St NE6.............56 F6
Bylands Gdns SR3..........86 B3
Byony Toft SR2............93 A7
Byrness NE5...............36 E1
Byrness Cl NE3.............37 C4
Byrness St ⑤ NE28........40 E5
Byrness Row NE23..........22 C8
Byrne Terrace W ② SR3...92 B7
Byron Ave
　Blyth NE24................17 C6
　Hebburn NE31.............57 F6
　⑭ Wallsend NE28..........41 A1
　West Boldon NE35.........74 A8
Byron Cl
　Guide Post NE62...........10 E7
　Ouston DH2...............82 A1
Byron Ct
　Newcastle upon Tyne NE5..36 C2
　④ Whickham NE16.........69 A8
Byron Rd NE37.............92 F2
Byron Lodge Est ⑥ SR7....92 E1
Byron Pl NE63..............6 F2
Byron Rd SR5..............75 A2
Byron's Ct SR7.............93 C2
Byron St
　Newcastle upon Tyne NE2..99 B2
　Ouston DH2...............81 F1
　⑭ South Shields NE33.....59 D8
　Sunderland SR5...........75 C1
Byron Terr
　Houghton-le-Spring DH5...94 E7
　⑤ Seaham SR7............92 F1
Byron Wlk NE8.............56 A2
By-Way The NE15...........35 D1
BYWELL....................63 F8
Bywell Ave
　Hexham NE46..............45 D4
　Newcastle upon Tyne, Denton
　Burn NE15...............53 E7
　Newcastle upon Tyne, Fawdon
　NE3.....................37 F8
　South Shields NE34........60 A7
　Sunderland SR5...........75 C3
Bywell Cl NE40............51 E3
Bywell Gdns
　Dunston NE11.............70 A5
　Gateshead NE9............71 B6
Bywell Gr NE27.............31 A3
Bywell Home Farm NE43..48 F3
Bywell Rd
　Ashington NE63............6 D2
　Cleadon SR6..............74 F8
Bywell St NE6..............56 F6
Bywell Terr NE32...........58 B3
Bywell View NE43..........64 D7

C

Cadehill Rd NE43..........64 C6
Cadlestone Ct NE23........22 D8
Caedmon Com Prim Sch
　NE8....................101 B1
Caedmon Hall* NE8........70 F8
Caernarvon Cl NE5.........37 B4
Caernarvon Dr SR3.........91 C6
Caer Urfa Cl NE33.........42 C4
Caesar's Wlk ⑧ NE33......42 C4
Caesar Way NE28...........40 E4
Cairncross SR5.............74 A1

Cairnglass Gn NE23.........22 D8
Cairngorm Ave NE38.......83 A2
Cairnhill Terr DH4.........90 D4
Cairnside SR3..............91 C7
Cairnside S SR3............91 B7
Cairnsmore Cl
　Cramlington NE23.........22 B4
　Newcastle upon Tyne NE28..57 B8
Cairnsmore Dr NE38........83 B3
Cairns Rd SR5.............75 C4
Cairns Sq SR5.............75 C4
Cairns Way NE3............37 F7
Cairo St SR2...............86 F3
Caithness Rd SR5..........73 F2
Caithness Sq SR5..........73 F2
Calais Rd SR5..............73 F1
Calandra Chase NE2........98 B4
Caldbeck Ave NE6..........56 F3
Caldbeck Cl NE6...........56 F3
Calderbourne Ave ⑥ SR6..75 E4
Calder Cres NE38..........83 D1
Calder Ct 18 SR3...........91 F6
Calderdale NE28...........39 F5
Calderdale Ave NE6.......56 F7
Calder Gn NE32............58 C2
Calder Green
　Bolden Colliery NE35......58 E2
　Hedworth NE32............58 C2
Calder Wlk NE16...........69 A2
Calderwood Cres NE9......71 A3
Caldew Cres NE5...........54 A8
Caldew Ct DH5.............95 B2
Caldwell Rd NE3...........37 F8
Caledonia NE21............68 A8
Caledonian Rd SR5.........73 F3
Caledonian St NE31........57 D7
Caledonia St NE6..........57 A4
Calf Close Dr NE32........58 B2
Calf Close NE32...........58 C2
Calf Close NE32...........58 C2
Calf Close Wlk NE32.......58 C2
California NE21............53 B1
California Gdns 18 NE61...9 A8
Callaley Ave NE16.........68 F6
Callaly Ave SR5............22 C6
Callaly Cl NE61............4 F3
Callaly Way NE6...........56 D4
Callander DH2.............82 A2
Callendar Ct NE9..........71 C5
Callerdale Rd NE24........17 A7
CALLERTON................36 B6
Callerton NE12............29 D5
Callerton Ave NE29........41 C6
Callerton Cl
⑧ Ashington NE63..........6 F2
　Cramlington NE23.........22 C6
Callerton Ct NE20..........25 E4
Callerton La NE5, NE15,
　NE20...................25 E4
CALLERTON LANE END....35 E7
Callerton Lane End Cotts
　NE5....................35 E7
Callerton Parkway Sta
　NE13...................26 E1
Callerton Pl NE4...........98 A1
Callerton View NE5........36 A8
Callington Cl DH4.........89 E2
Callington Dr SR2.........92 F7
Callum Dr NE3.............60 A8
Calow Way NE16...........68 F5
Calthwaite Cl SR5.........74 B2
Calver St NE34.............59 E5
Calvus Dr NE15............34 F2
Camberley Cl SR3..........92 C8
Camberley Rd NE28........41 A4
Camberwell Cl NE11.......70 B6
Camberwell Way NE11.....91 D5
Cambo Ave
　Bedlington NE22..........11 C1
　Whitley Bay NE25.........31 D3
Cambo Cl
　Blyth NE24................17 C7
　Newcastle upon Tyne NE3..38 D5
　Wallsend NE28............40 D6
Cambo Dr NE23.............22 C6
Cambo Gn NE5.............37 C2
CAMBOIS..................12 C5
Cambois Fst Sch NE24....12 C4
Cambo Pl NE30.............32 A1
Camborne Gr NE8..........101 C1
Camborne Pl NE8..........101 C1
Cambourne Ave ⑥ SR6....75 E4
Cambria Gn SR4............85 A6
Cambrian St NE32..........58 C7
Cambrian Way NE38.......83 B3
Cambria St SR4............85 A6
Cambridge Ave
　Hebburn NE31.............57 F5
　Longbenton NE12..........39 D8
　Wallsend NE28............40 A1
　Washington NE37..........83 B8
　Whitley Bay NE26.........32 A5
Cambridge Cres DH4.......90 A6
Cambridge Pl DH3..........82 C1
Cambridge Rd
　New Silksworth SR3.......92 A7
　Stakeford NE62...........11 A7
Cambridge St NE4.........100 B4
Cambridge St NE10.........101 B1
Camden St NE1.............99 B2
Camden Sq NE30............42 C6
Camden St
　Newcastle upon Tyne NE1,
　NE2.....................99 B2
　North Shields NE30.......42 B5
　Sunderland SR5...........75 A1
Camelford Ct NE15.........53 C8

Cameron Cl NE34...........59 C3
Cameronian Sq NE8........101 B3
Cameron Rd NE42..........50 D2
Camerton Pl NE28..........40 E7
Camilla Rd NE15...........34 F2
Camilla St NE8............101 C1
Cam Mead SR3.............92 A4
CAMPBELL PARK...........57 F5
Campbell Park Rd NE31...57 F5
Campbell Pl NE4...........98 A1
Campbell St SR5...........73 F2
Campbell Sq SR5...........73 F2
Campbell Terr DH5.........95 B1
CAMPERDOWN.............29 C5
Camperdown NE5..........36 F1
Camperdown Ave
　Chester le Street DH3.....88 D5
　Killingworth NE12.........29 B4
Camperdown Ind Est
　NE12...................29 B5
Campion Gdns NE10........71 D5
Campion Way NE63.........6 C2
Campsie Cl NE38...........83 B3
Campsie Ct NE32...........32 A1
Camp Terr NF79...........42 A6
Campus Martius NE15......34 E2
Campville NE29.............31 D3
Camperra Dr NE34.........58 F4
Camperra Rd SR4..........85 D4
Candelford Cl NE7.........39 D3
Candlish St NE33..........42 D2
Canning St
　Hebburn NE31.............57 E5
　Newcastle upon Tyne NE4..54 E5
Canning Street Prim Sch
　NE4....................54 D5
Cannock
　Killingworth NE12.........29 D4
　Ouston DH2...............82 A2
Cannock Dr NE7...........39 A4
Cannon St NE18............101 B4
Canonbie Sq NE23.........22 D8
Canon Cockin St SR2......86 F4
Canon Gr NE32.............58 C7
Canon Savage Dr NE46....44 E4
CANTERBURY..............83 D3
Canterbury Cl
　Newcastle upon Tyne
　NE15...................36 B3
　Silksworth SR3...........91 F5
Canterbury Ave NE28.....40 D6
Canterbury Cl
　Ashington NE63............6 F2
　Longbenton NE12.........39 A7
Canterbury Ho SR5........73 F4
Canterbury Rd NE23........74 A3
Canterbury St
　Newcastle upon Tyne NE6..56 B6
　South Shields NE33.......59 D8
Canterbury Way
　Hedworth NE32............58 A1
　Widopen NE13.............26 B6
Capercaillie Lodge NE23...2 B2
Capetown Rd SR5..........73 F2
Capetown Sq SR5...........73 F2
Caplestone Cl NE38........83 B3
Capstan La NE37...........92 F2
Captains Row The NE33....59 B8
Captains Wharf NE33.......42 C3
Capulet Gr NE34...........59 A5
Capulet Terr SR2..........86 E4
Caradoc Cl NE38...........83 B3
Caraway Wlk NE34.........59 E2
Carden Ave NE34..........60 B5
Caragh Rd DH7............88 C1
Cardiff Sq SR5.............73 F1
Cardigan Gr NE30..........32 A3
Cardigan Rd SR5...........31 D3
Cardigan Terr NE6.........56 B7
Cardinal Cl
　Longbenton NE12.........39 A6
　Newcastle upon Tyne NE15..36 B3
Cardinal Hume RC Sch
　NE9....................71 C4
Cardinals Ct ⑤ SR3........91 F5
Cardonnel St NE29.........42 A4
Cardwell St SR6............75 E1
Careen Cres SR3............91 B7
Carew Ct NE23..............22 B5
Carew Cres NE23...........22 C6
Carham Cl
　Corbridge NE45............47 B5
　Newcastle upon Tyne NE3..38 D6
Carisbrooke NE42..........50 A1
Carisbrooke Cl NE37.......83 D8
Carisbrooke Ct 11 NE37...83 D8
Carisbrooke Ct SR1.......102 B2
Carisbrooke Rd NE23......74 A3
Caris St NE8, NE9.........71 A8
Carlcroft Pl NE23..........22 C5
Carley Hill NE4...........98 A1
CARLEY HILL..............75 A4
Carley Lodge SR5..........75 B3
Carley Rd SR5.............75 B3
Carley Ho NE4.............98 A1
Carling Acad* ⑧ NE1......99 A1
Carlingford Rd DH4........89 B1
Carliol Pl NE1.............99 B1
Carliol Sq NE1.............99 B1
Carliol St NE1.............99 B1
Carlisle Cl NE27...........30 C1
Carlisle Cres DH4..........90 B7
Carlisle Ct ⑪ NE10........71 C8
Carlisle Ho SR3............91 D7
Carlisle Pl NE10...........71 C8
Carlisle Pl NE10...........56 D1

Carlisle Terr
⑧ Shiremoor NE27.........30 E1
⑥ Sunderland SR5.........74 F2
Carlisle View ⑧ NE61......8 F8
Carlisle Way NE27.........30 C1
Carlow Dr NE62............11 D8
Carlton Ave NE24...........17 C3
Carlton Cl DH2.............81 E2
Carlton Cres SR3...........91 C7
Carlton Ct
　Gateshead NE11...........70 C5
　North Shields NE29.......41 F5
Carlton Gdns NE15.........53 E7
Carlton Gr NE63.............6 F1
Carlton Grange NE3........38 A3
Carlton Ho NE64.............7 E5
Carlton Rd NE12............39 D6
Carlton St NE24.............17 F7
Carlton Terr
　Blyth NE24................17 D8
　Newcastle upon Tyne NE3..70 F5
⑭ Springwell NC7..........71 F1
Carlyle Cres NE9...........69 A8
Carlyle Ct ④ NE28.........41 A1
Carlyle St ⑪ NE28.........41 A1
Carlyon St SR2............103 A1
Carmel Gr NE23.............16 A1
Carnaby Cl NE42...........50 D3
Carnaby Rd NE6............55 D4
Carnation Ave NE6.........56 B4
Carnation Terr ⑤ NE16...69 B7
Carnegie Cl NE34..........59 C4
Carnegie St ⑩ SR2........86 F2
Carnforth Cl NE28.........40 E7
Carnforth Gdns
　Gateshead NE9............71 B4
　Rowlands Gill NE39.......67 E3
Carnoustie
　Ouston DH2...............82 A1
　Washington NE37..........72 C3
Carnoustie Cl
　Newcastle upon Tyne NE7..39 C4
　North Seaton NE63........7 A3
Carnoustie Ct
　Gateshead NE10...........72 B6
　Whitley Bay NE25.........31 C5
Carnoustie Dr NE34........59 F3
Carol Gdns NE7............39 B3
Caroline Cotts NE5.........54 B8
Caroline Gdns NE28........41 A3
Caroline St
　Hetton-le-Hole DH5........95 A4
　Jarrow NE32..............58 A7
　Newcastle upon Tyne NE4..53 B4
Carol St NE4..............102 B3
Carolyn Cl NE12............39 C6
Carolyn Cres NE26.........31 E7
Carolyn Way NE26.........31 F7
Carpenter St NE33.........42 B2
Carr Field NE20.............25 F7
Carr Hill Prim Sch NE9....71 B7
Carr Hill Rd N10, NE9.....71 B7
Carrick Dr NE24............17 D4
Carrigill Dr NE12..........39 A6
Carrington Cl NE23.........22 F1
Carrmere Rd SR2...........86 E1
Carrock Ct SR3.............91 F6
Carroll Wlk NE34...........59 A5
Carrowmore Rd DH2........88 C1
Carrs Cl NE42..............50 F3
Carrsfield NE45.............47 A5
Carrside Mews ④ NE24...17 C4
Carr St
　Blyth NE24................17 C4
　Hebburn NE31.............57 D7
Carrsyde Cl NE16..........68 F5
Carsdale Rd NE3...........38 A5
Carter Ave NE31...........57 E6
Carters Lo ⑨ NE9.........70 F5
Cartington Ave NE27......30 F2
Cartington Ct NE3..........37 E7
Cartington Rd NE29.......41 E5
Cartington Terr NE6........39 C1
Cartmel Ct DH2............88 A2
Cartmel Gn NE5............70 D7
Cartmel Gr NE8............70 D7
Cartmel Pk NE10...........57 A1
Cartwright Rd SR5.........74 B1
Carville Gdns NE28.........57 B8
Carville Prim Sch NE28....57 B8
Carville Rd NE28...........40 B1
Carville Rise NE6..........56 C6
Carville Station Cotts
　NE28...................40 C1
Carvoran ④ NE34..........40 F4
Carwarding Pl NE5.........37 C2
Caseton Cl NE25............31 C6
Caspian Cl NE32...........58 C5
Caspian Rd SR5............73 F1
Caspian Sq SR5............73 F1
Castellan Rd NE6..........36 B3
Castle Bank NE61...........9 A8
Castle Cl
　Chester le Street DH3.....88 D2
　Hetton-le-Hole DH5........95 B2
　Morpeth NE61..............8 F8
⑦ Newcastle upon Tyne
　NE3....................37 D5
　Prudhoe NE42.............50 C3

Castle Cl continued
Wickham NE16...........69 A7
Castle Ct NE20............25 E6
Castledale Ave NE24.....17 A6
Castledene Ct
  Newcastle upon Tyne NE3...38 F4
  Sunderland SR5.............74 A2
Castle Dene Gr DH4.......94 D8
Castle Farm Mews NE2....38 F3
Castlefields DH4............89 D3
Castlefields Dr NE42......50 E3
Castlefields Wood Nature
  Reserve* NE42.............50 D4
Castleford Rd SR5..........73 F2
Castle Fst Sch NE42........50 B2
Castle Garth NE1..........101 B4
Castlegate Gdns NE8.....100 A1
Castle Gn 10 SR3...........91 D7
Castle Hill Ho NE41........51 C5
Castle Island Way NE63..11 F8
Castle Keep* NE1..........101 A4
Castle Lea NE42............50 B3
Castle Leazes (Halls of
  Residence) NE2............98 B3
Castlemain Cl DH4........89 D3
Castle Mdws NE61..........8 F2
Castle Mews SR3..........91 D7
Castlenook Pl NE15......53 F7
Castle Rd
  Prudhoe NE42..............50 B3
  Washington NE38..........83 A5
Castlereagh Homes The
  SR7......................93 D1
Castlereagh St SR3........92 A7
Castlereigh Cl DH4........89 D3
Castle Riggs DH2..........88 B3
Castles Farm Rd NE2, NE7.38 F4
Castles Gn NE12............29 E3
Castleside Rd NE15.......54 A6
Castle Sq
  Backworth NE27...........30 B5
  19 Morpeth NE61...........9 A8
Castle St
  Hazlerigg NE13............28 A4
  Morpeth NE61..............9 A8
  Newcastle upon Tyne NE3...102 C3
Castle Street S 4 SR5....74 C1
Castle Terr NE63............6 A6
Castleton Cl
  Cramlington NE23.........16 A1
  Newcastle upon Tyne NE2...38 F2
Castleton Gr NE2...........38 F2
Castleton Lodge NE4.....54 F5
Castletown Rd SR5........74 C2
Castletown Way SR5......74 D2
Castle View
  Chester le Street DH3....88 C5
  Horsley NE15..............50 C8
  Ovingham NE42.............50 B4
  Penshaw DH4...............90 B8
  Prudhoe NE42..............50 B4
  Sunderland SR5............74 B1
Castle View Acad SR5....74 A1
Castleway NE61.............4 F3
Castle Way NE13...........27 B7
Castle Wlk NE61.............9 A7
Castlewood Cl NE5.........36 D2
Catcheside Cl NE16.......69 A5
Cateran Way NE23.........22 C4
Catharine Street W SR4..102 A2
Cathedral Ct NE8...........56 A3
Cathedral View DH4......90 D3
Catherine Cookson Ct
  NE33......................42 E1
Catherine Rd DH4..........90 D6
Catherine St 3 NE33.....42 D3
Catherine View 9 NE40..51 F3
Catholic Row NE22........15 E8
Catkin Wlk NE40...........52 A3
Cato Sq SR5................75 A2
Cato St SR5................75 A2
Catrail Pl NE23.............22 C8
Cattle Market NE46........45 B4
Catton Gr NE16............69 B3
Catton Pl NE28.............40 E6
CAULDWELL..................59 E7
Cauldwell Ave
  South Shields NE34........59 E7
  Whitley Bay NE25..........31 D3
Cauldwell Cl NE34.........31 E4
Cauldwell La NE25.........31 E4
Cauldwell Pl NE34.........59 E7
Cauldwell Villas NE34....59 E7
Causeway
  Gateshead NE9............71 B6
  Sunderland SR6..........103 A4
Causeway The
  Gateshead NE9............71 A8
  Throckley NE15...........35 D1
CAUSEY.....................80 B4
Causey Arch* NE16.......80 A4
Causey Arch Sta* NE16...80 A4
Causey Bank NE1..........99 B1
Causey Bldgs 8 NE16.....80 B4
Causey Brae NE46.........44 F3
Causey Hill Rd NE46......44 F3
Causey Hill Way NE46....44 E3
Causey Ho NE46...........38 C3
Causey Pk NE46...........44 F4
Causey Rd DH9, NE16....80 A3
Causey Row NE16..........80 B4
Causey St NE3.............38 C4

Causey Way
  Hexham NE46..............44 F3
  Kip Hill DH9..............80 A1
Cavalier View NE31........57 D7
Cavalier Way SR3...........91 F7
Cavell Rd SR5...............74 A2
Cavendish Gdns NE63......6 D3
Cavendish Pl
  Burnopfield NE16.........79 A4
  Newcastle upon Tyne NE2...38 F1
  New Silksworth SR3.......91 F7
Cavendish Rd NE2..........38 F1
Cavendish Sq NE61..........4 E3
Cavendish Terr NE63........6 D3
Caversham Rd NE5.........36 B3
Cawburn Cl NE7...........39 E3
Cawdell Ct NE30...........42 B5
Cawfields Ct NE12.........38 F6
Cawnpore Sq SR4..........85 E7
Cawthorne Terr NE16......79 A4
Caxton Way DH3............88 D8
Caxton Wlk NE34...........59 A2
Caynham Cl NE29..........41 E8
Cayton Gr NE5.............36 B2
Cecil Ct
  Ponteland NE20............25 F6
  Wallsend NE28.............57 B8
Cecil St NE29..............42 A5
Cecil Terr NE46.............45 B5
Cedar Cl
  Bedlington NE22...........10 F2
  Whitley Bay NE25.........31 F3
Cedar Cres
  Burnopfield NE16..........78 F6
  Dunston NE11.............69 F7
  Gateshead NE9............70 F4
Cedar Ct
  South Hetton DH6.........97 F7
  Sunderland SR2............86 D4
  Tynemouth NE29...........31 E1
Cedar Dr NE32..............73 C8
Cedar Gr
  Blyth NE24................17 C4
  Hebburn NE31..............57 E3
  Ryton NE40................52 C6
  South Shields NE34........59 F5
  Wallsend NE28.............40 D2
  Whitburn SR6..............60 F7
Cedar Rd NE4..............54 D7
Cedars DH2................88 B5
Cedars Cres SR2...........86 E3
Cedars Gn NE9.............71 A3
Cedars Pk SR2.............86 E3
Cedars Sch The NE9.......71 A3
Cedars The
  Gateshead NE9............71 C2
  Newcastle upon Tyne NE4..100 B3
  Penshaw DH4...............90 B8
  Sunderland SR2............86 D4
  Whickham NE16............69 B4
Cedar Terr
  Ashington NE63.............6 E2
  Fence Houses DH4.........90 A1
  Washington NE38..........83 C1
Cedartree Gdns NE25.....31 E3
Cedarway NE10............71 E5
Cedar Way NE12............29 C3
Cedarwood DH4............89 C1
Cedarwood Ave 3 NE6....40 A1
Cedarwood Gr SR2........86 B2
Cedric Cres SR2............86 B4
Celadon Cl NE15...........53 C8
Celandine Cl NE3...........38 D7
Celandine Ct NE63..........6 B1
Celandine Way NE10......71 E5
Cellar Hill Terr DH4........90 D2
Celtic Cl SR6...............59 E1
Celtic Cres SR6............59 E1
Cemetery App NE34.......59 E8
Cemetery Rd
  Gateshead NE8...........101 C1
  Jarrow NE32...............58 C5
Centenary Ave NE34......60 A6
Centenary Cotts NE22....15 F8
Centenary Ct NE11........99 A1
Central Arc NE1...........99 A1
Central Ave
  Guide Post NE62..........10 E2
  North Shields NE29........41 E5
  South Shields NE34........59 F6
  Whitburn SR6..............60 F1
Central County Fst Sch
  NE63......................6 D3
Central Gdns NE34.........59 F6
Central Newcastle High Sch
  NE2......................99 B4
Central Newcastle High Sch
  (Jun Dept) 6 NE3.........38 C4
Central Parkway
  Newbiggin-by-the-Sea
  NE11.......................7 D4
  Newcastle upon Tyne NE1..100 C4
Central Sta (Metro) NE1..101 A4
Centralway NE11...........70 C4
Central Way SR4...........85 E8
Centre for Life* NE1......100 C4
Centurion Way NE22......10 E2
Centurion Rd NE15.........53 E5
Centurion Way
  Gateshead NE9............71 B6
  Heddon-on-the-Wall NE15..34 D2
Ceolfrid Terr NE32.........58 C4
Cestria Prim Sch DH3.....88 C3
Cestrium Ct NE28..........40 E4
Chacombe NE38............83 D3
Chadderton Dr NE5........36 B3

Chadwick St NE28..........40 B1
Chadwick Wlk NE8.......101 A2
Chaffinch Ct NE63..........6 B2
Chaffinch Rd 6 SR5.......54 C1
Chaffinch Way NE12.......29 C4
Chainbridge Ind Est NE21.53 F4
Chainbridge Rd
  Blaydon, Derwenthaugh
  NE21......................53 F4
  Blaydon NE21..............53 D3
Chains Dr NE45............46 F6
Chalfont Gr SR4...........85 A2
Chalfont Rd NE6...........56 F4
Chalford Rd 1 SR5........75 B2
Challoner's Gdns NE16....3 E1
Chaloner Pl 2 NE4.........6 F8
Chamberlain St
  Blyth NE24................17 C6
  Crawcrook NE40...........51 F4
Chambers Cres NE9.......71 C1
Chancery La NE4 CT......54 A1
Chandler Ct NE2...........38 F2
Chandlers Ford NE29......41 F6
Chandlers Quay NE6.......56 C4
Chandless St NE8.........101 C3
Chandos SR3...............92 A4
Chandos St NE8............70 F8
Chandra Pl 3 NE5.........37 B2
Chantry Cl SR3.............91 E5
Chantry Dr NE13...........28 B6
Chantry Est NE45..........46 F6
Chantry Ho NE4............94 A2
Chantry Mews 2 NE61.....9 A8
Chantry Mid Sch NE61....3 E1
Chantry Pl
  9 Morpeth NE61............9 A8
  West Rainton DH4.........94 A2
Chapel Ave NE16...........79 B6
Chapel Cl
  Kibblesworth NE11........81 D6
  Newcastle upon Tyne NE3..28 D1
Chapel Ct
  Newburn NE15.............52 E8
  Seaton Burn NE13.........28 B8
  Sherburn DH6..............96 A1
Chapel Grange NE5........36 A3
Chapel Ho NE13.............42 E1
Chapel House Dr NE5......36 C1
Chapel House Gr NE5......36 C1
Chapel House Rd NE5......36 C1
Chapel La
  Haswell DH6...............97 F3
  Whitley Bay NE25..........31 E4
  Wylam NE41................51 A6
Chapel Park Sh Ctr NE5..36 D4
Chapel Pl NE13.............28 D6
Chapel Rd NE32............58 B7
Chapel Row
  Birtley DH3................82 E3
  Mickley Square NE43......49 E1
Chapel St
  Hetton-le-Hole DH5........95 B4
  North Shields NE29........41 E5
  Thornley DH6..............79 B2
Chapel View
  Brunswick Village NE13...28 A6
  Rowlands Gill NE39........67 E3
Chapelville NE13...........28 B8
Chapman Back St 24 NE6.56 C7
Chapman St SR4............75 E4
Chapter Row NE33.........42 C3
Chare Bank DH8............76 F3
Chare The NE1..............99 A2
Chareway NE46.............45 A6
Chareway La NE46.........45 A6
Charlbury Cl NE9...........71 F1
Charlcote Cres NE36......74 D7
Charles Ave
  Longbenton NE12..........39 D8
  Newcastle upon Tyne NE3..37 E6
  Shiremoor NE27...........30 F4
  Whitley Bay NE25..........31 F5
Charles Baker Wlk NE34..60 B7
Charles Ct 18 NE6..........56 C7
Charles Dr NE23............29 B8
Charles Perkins Memorial
  Cottage Homes DH3......82 C3
Charles St
  Boldon Colliery NE35......73 F8
  Gateshead NE8...........101 C2
  Hazlerigg NE13............28 A5
  Newbottle DH4............90 D4
  Pegswood NE61.............4 F3
  14 Ryhope SR2.............93 A6
  Sunderland, Monkwearmouth
  SR6......................103 A4
  Sunderland SR1..........103 B3
Charles Street Ind Est
  SR6.......................103 A4
Charleswood NE3..........38 D8
Charlie St NE40............51 F1
Charlotte Mews 7 NE1....98 C1
Charlotte Sq NE1..........98 C1
Charlotte St
  Crawcrook NE40...........51 E3
  South Shields NE33........42 B6
  South Shields NE33........42 C2
  Wallsend NE28............40 C2
Charlotte Terr 12 NE33...42 D2
Charlton Cl NE61...........44 F2
Charlton Ct NE25...........31 D3
Charlton Gdns NE61........9 B7
Charlton Gr SR6............75 A8
Charlton Mews NE15......53 D6

Charlton Rd SR5............75 C3
Charlton St
  Ashington NE63.............6 C4
  Blyth NE24................17 D7
  Newcastle upon Tyne NE15.53 D6
Charlton Villas NE40.......52 B1
Charlton Wlk NE8..........100 C1
Charman St SR1............103 A3
Charminster Gdns NE6....39 C1
Charnwood Ave NE12.....39 A6
Charnwood Ct NE33........42 E2
Charnwood Gdns 1 NE9.71 B5
Charter Dr SR3.............91 C7
Charters Cres DH6.........97 F6
Chase Ct
  Sherburn DH6..............96 A1
  Whickham NE16............69 B7
Chasedale Cres NE24.....17 A7
Chase Farm Dr NE24......16 F7
Chase Mdws NE24.........16 F6
Chase Mews NE24.........16 F7
Chase The
  Hexham NE46..............44 F3
  Longbenton NE12..........29 A2
  North Shields NE29........41 F6
  Washington NE38.........82 F1
Chatham Cl NE25...........23 D1
Chatham Rd SR5...........74 A2
Chathill Cl
  Morpeth NE61..............9 B6
  Newcastle upon Tyne NE3..31 D5
Chathill Terr NE6...........56 F5
Chatsworth Cres SR4.....86 A4
Chatsworth Ct 8 NE3.....31 D5
Chatsworth Dr NE22......11 C3
Chatsworth Gdns
  3 Newcastle upon Tyne
  NE5......................36 F3
  Newcastle upon Tyne, Walker
  NE6......................56 D4
  Whitley Bay NE25..........31 E3
Chatsworth Pl NE16.......69 A5
Chatsworth Rd NE32......58 C5
Chatsworth St SR4........102 A1
Chatsworth Street S SR4.86 A4
Chatterton St SR5..........75 A2
Chatton Ave
  Cramlington NE23.........22 C6
  South Shields NE34........60 B8
Chatton Cl
  Chester le Street DH2.....88 A1
  Morpeth NE61..............9 C5
Chatton St NE28............41 C1
Chatton Wynd NE3.........38 A7
Chaucer Ave NE34.........59 A3
Chaucer Cl 8 NE8..........56 A2
Chaucer St NE8.............56 A2
Chaytor Gr SR1............103 B2
Chaytor St NE32............58 B8
Cheadle Ave
  Cramlington NE23.........16 A1
  Wallsend NE28.............40 E6
Cheadle Rd SR5............74 A2
Cheam Cl NE16............69 B5
Cheam Rd SR5..............74 A2
Cheddar Gdns NE9........70 F3
Cheeseburn Gdns 8 NE5.54 D8
Cheldon Cl NE25...........31 C6
Chelford Cl NE28...........40 E7
Chelmsford Gr NE2........56 A7
Chelmsford Rd SR5........74 A2
Chelmsford Sq SR5........74 A3
Chelmsford St 5 SR3......92 A8
Chelsea Gdns NE8.........54 D6
Chelsea Gr NE4............98 A1
Cheltenham Rd SR5.......74 A2
Cheltenham Dr NE35......58 E2
Cheltenham Rd SR5.......74 A2
Cheltenham Sq SR5.......74 A2
Cheltenham Terr NE6.....56 B7
Chelton Cl NE13............28 B4
Chepstow Gdns NE8......70 D7
Chepstow St SR4..........102 B2
Cherribank SR2.............92 E6
Cherry Banks DH3.........88 D5
Cherry Blossom Way
  NE37......................73 B1
Cherryburn Cotts NE43..49 E2
Cherryburn (Mus)* NE43.49 F2
Cherry Cotts DH9..........79 B2
Cherry Dr NE9.............97 F3
Cherry Gr
  Killingworth NE12.........29 C4
  Prudhoe NE42..............50 B3
Cherrytree Cl NE12........29 F2
Cherrytree Ct NE22........11 D2
Cherrytree Dr NE16........69 C8
Cherry Tree Dr NE22......10 F1
Cherrytree Gdns
  Gateshead NE9............71 A4
  Whitley Bay NE25..........31 F3
Cherry Tree La NE15......50 C8
Cherry Tree Gdns NE41..51 A6
Cherry Trees NE24.........17 D6
Cherry Tree Sq 6 SR2....92 E8
Cherry Tree Wlk NE31....57 E4
Cherry Way
  Fence Houses DH4.........90 B1
  Killingworth NE12.........29 C4
Cherrywood NE6...........39 E1
Cherrywood Gdns SR3....92 B7
Cherwell NE37..............83 F8
Cherwell Rd SR8...........29 C1
Cherwell Sq NE12..........29 C1
Chesham Gdns NE5.......36 B2

Cheshire Ave DH3...........82 C1
Cheshire Cl NE63............6 A4
Cheshire Ct NE31...........57 D5
Cheshire Gdns NE28......40 A3
Cheshire Gr NE34..........60 B7
Chesils The NE12...........39 A5
Chesmond Dr NE21........53 C3
Chessar Ave NE5...........37 B2
Chester Ave NE28..........40 F3
Chester Cl NE20............25 B4
Chester Cres
  Newcastle upon Tyne NE2..99 C3
  Sunderland SR1...........102 B2
Chesterfield Rd NE4.......54 F4
Chester Gdns NE34........59 E7
Chester Gr
  Blyth NE24................17 C6
  Seghill NE23................22 E1
Chesterhill NE23............22 B5
CHESTER-LE-STREET......88 E4
Chester-le-Street CE Jun
  Sch DH2..................88 B5
Chester-le-Street Com Hospl
  DH3......................88 C3
Chester-le-Street Sta
  DH3......................88 C3
Chester Mews SR4........102 B2
Chester Oval SR2.........102 B2
Chester Pl NE8............101 B2
Chester Rd
  Bournmoor DH3, DH4......89 D3
  Chester le Street DH3.....88 B1
  Penshaw DH4...............90 B7
  Shiney Row DH4, DH4......89 A3
  Sunderland, Grindon SR4..85 B3
  Sunderland, High Barnes SR1,
  SR2, SR4..................85 C5
  Sunderland SR1, SR4.....102 B2
Chesters 5 NE28..........40 F4
Chesters Ave NE12........39 A5
Chesters Cl NE9...........70 F6
Chesters Ct NE12..........39 A6
Chesters Dene NE40......76 E3
Chesters Gdns NE40......51 E4
Chesters Pk NE9...........70 F6
Chester Sq NE61.............2 A3
Chester St
  Newbottle DH4............90 D2
  Newcastle upon Tyne NE2..99 C3
  Sunderland SR4...........102 A2
Chesters The
  Ebchester DH8.............76 E3
  Newcastle upon Tyne NE5..36 C1
  Whitley Bay NE25..........31 E6
Chester Street E SR4.....102 A2
Chester Street W SR4....102 A2
Chester Terr SR1..........102 B2
Chester Terrace N SR4...102 A2
Chesterton Rd NE34......59 B3
Chester View DH2...........9 F1
Chester Way NE32.........58 B4
Chesterwood Dr NE28....40 A2
Chesterwood Terr NE10..57 F2
Chestnut Ave
  Blyth NE24................12 C1
  Newcastle upon Tyne NE5..37 E2
  Washington NE38..........83 B1
  Whickham NE16............69 B5
  Whitley Bay NE25..........31 F4
Chestnut Cl
  Hedworth NE32.............58 D1
  Killingworth NE12..........29 B4
Chestnut Cres SR5.........74 F3
Chestnut Gdns NE8........58 D1
Chestnut Gr NE34..........59 F4
Chestnut St
  Ashington NE63.............9 D1
  Wallsend NE28.............40 C1
Chestnut Terr DH4.........90 C3
Cheswick Dr NE3...........38 D6
Cheswick Rd NE25.........23 E2
Chevin Cl NE6..............40 B1
Chevington
  Gateshead NE10...........72 A5
  Leam Lane NE10..........72 A6
Chevington Cl NE61.........4 B8
Chevington Gdns 6 NE5..37 D1
Chevington Gr NE25.......31 D7
Cheviot Cl
  Blaydon NE21..............53 C3
  Ellington NE61.............1 D4
  Tynemouth NE29...........31 F2
  Washington NE37..........83 A6
Cheviot Ct
  Blaydon NE21..............53 C3
  Morpeth NE61..............9 C6
  Newcastle upon Tyne NE7..39 A4
  1 Stobhillgate NE61.......9 A8
  Whitley Bay NE26..........32 C4
Cheviot Gdns NE11.........70 A3
Cheviot La 2 SR2..........92 E8
Cheviot Gr NE61.............4 E3
Cheviot Grange NE23......29 B8
Cheviot Ho NE36...........74 E7
Cheviot Mews DH9.........78 E3
Cheviot Mount NE6.........56 F6
Cheviot Prim Sch NE5....37 C4
Cheviot Rd
  Blaydon NE21..............53 C3
  Chester le Street DH2.....88 B3
  Hebburn NE32..............58 A2
  South Shields NE34........60 A2
Cheviot St SR4.............85 F7
Cheviot View
  Ashington NE63.............6 E5
  Brunswick Village NE13...28 A6
  Gateshead NE10...........71 D6

Cheviot View *continued*
Longbenton NE12 39 C6
Ponteland NE20 26 A5
Prudhoe NE42 50 E2
Seghill NE23 22 F1
Whitley Bay NE26 32 B5
Cheviot Way
Hexham NE46 45 A4
Stakeford NE62 11 B8
Chevron The 4 NE6 56 B5
Chevychase Ct SR7 92 F2
Cheyne Rd NE42 50 C2
Cheyne The SR3 92 A5
Chichester Ave NE23 21 F8
Chichester Cl
Ashington NE63 7 A2
Gateshead NE8 101 B2
Newcastle upon Tyne NE3 37 D8
Chichester Gr NE22 10 F2
Chichester Pl NE33 59 C8
Chichester Rd
South Shields NE33 42 D1
Sunderland SR6 75 E4
Chichester Road E NE33 42 D1
Chichester Sta NE33 59 C8
Chichester Way NE32 58 B1
Chicken Rd NE28 40 A4
Chick's La 4 SR6 75 F8
Chigwell Cl DH4 90 B7
Chilcote NE10 71 D7
Chilcrosse NE10 71 F6
Chilham Ct
Tynemouth NE29 41 B8
Washington NE38 83 B4
Chillingham Cl NE24 17 B5
Chillingham Cres NE63 6 C3
Chillingham Ct 19 NE6 56 C7
Chillingham Dr
Chester le Street DH2 88 A1
North Shields NE29 41 D4
Chillingham Ho SR6 103 B4
Chillingham Ind Est NE6 56 C7
Chillingham Rd NE6 56 C8
Chillingham Road Prim Sch
NE6 56 C8
Chillingham Road Sta
NE6 56 D7
Chillingham Terr NE32 58 D4
Chilside Rd NE10 71 D7
Chiltern Ave DH2 88 B2
Chiltern Cl
Ashington NE63 6 F1
Washington NE38 83 B3
Chiltern Dr NE12 29 B1
Chiltern Gdns NE11 70 B7
Chiltern Rd NE29 31 F2
Chilton Ave DH4 94 A8
Chilton Gdns 10 DH4 94 A8
CHILTON MOOR 94 A7
Chilton St 1 SR5 75 C1
Chimney Mills NE2 98 C4
China St SR2 86 E4
Chingford Cl DH4 90 C7
Chipchase NE38 82 F4
Chipchase Ave NE23 22 B6
Chipchase Cl
Bedlington NE22 10 D1
Pegswood NE61 4 F3
Chipchase Cres NE5 36 E3
Chipchase Ct
Bournmoor DH4 89 D1
New Hartley NE25 23 D6
Seaham SR7 92 F2
Chipchase Mews NE3 28 A1
Chipchase Terr NE32 58 B3
Chippendale Pl NE2 98 B4
Chip The NE61 8 F5
Chirdon Cres NE46 45 C4
Chirnside NE23 22 B4
CHIRTON 41 F5
Chirton Ave
North Shields NE29 41 F5
South Shields NE34 60 C6
Chirton Dene Quays NE28 41 F2
Chirton Dene Way NE29 42 A3
Chirton Gn
Blyth NE24 17 B5
North Shields NE29 41 F5
Chirton Gr NE34 60 C6
Chirton Hill Dr NE29 41 C7
Chirton La NE29 41 E5
Chirton Lodge NE28 41 E5
Chirton West View NE29 41 F5
Chirton Wynd NE6 56 C5
Chisholm Pl 6 NE46 45 B5
Chislehurst Rd DH4 90 B7
Chiswick Gdns NE8 71 A8
Chiswick Rd SR5 74 A2
Chiswick Sq SR5 74 A2
Chollerford Ave
North Shields NE29 41 D6
Whitley Bay NE25 32 B4
Chollerford Cl NE3 38 A4
Chollerford Mews NE25 23 F2
Chollerton Dr
Bedlington NE22 11 A1
Longbenton NE12 40 A8
CHOPPINGTON 10 E5
Choppington Fst Sch
NE62 10 E5
Choppington Rd
Bedlington NE22, NE62 10 F2
Morpeth NE61 9 B6
CHOPWELL 66 B1
Chopwell Gdns NE9 71 D2
Chopwell Prim Sch NE17 66 B1
Chopwell Rd NE17 77 C6
Chopwell Wood Heritage
Trail* NE39 66 F2
Chopwell Woods Rd NE39 67 A3
Chorley Pl NE6 56 E5
Chowdean Terr 4 NE9 70 F4
CHOWDENE 70 E4
Chowdene Bank NE11,
NE9 70 F2
Christal Terr SR6 75 D3
Christ Church CE Prim Sch
Newcastle upon Tyne NE2 99 C2
14 North Shields NE30 42 A6
Christie Terr NE6 56 F5
Christmas Pl NE8 100 B2
Christon Cl NE3 38 E5
Christon Rd NE3 38 D5
Christon Way NE10 57 B2
Christopher Rd NE6 56 E7
Chudleigh Gdns NE5 36 B2
Church Ave
Choppington NE62 10 E5
Newcastle upon Tyne NE3 38 D5
West Sleekburn NE62 11 D7
Church Bank
Jarrow NE32 58 D7
Newburn NE15 52 F7
Sunderland SR5 75 A1
Wallsend NE28 40 D2
Churchburn Dr NE61 8 F6
Church Chare
Chester le Street DH3 88 D3
Ponteland NE20 25 F7
Whickham NE16 69 B7
Church Cl
Bedlington NE22 15 F8
Bournmoor DH4 89 E4
Dinnington NE13 27 B7
Ebchester DH8 76 E3
Riding Mill NE44 62 F7
Whitley Bay NE25 31 C4
Church Ct
Bedlington NE22 15 F8
10 Gateshead NE10 56 D1
Churchdown Cl NE35 58 E2
Churcher Gdns NE28 40 A4
Church Flatt NE20 25 F7
Church Gn 7 NE16 69 B7
Church High Sch NE2 99 B4
Churchill Ave
Sunderland SR5 75 A2
Whitley Bay NE25 31 F3
Churchill Com Coll NE28 40 F4
Churchill Ct NE25 31 E4
Churchill Gdns NE2 39 A1
Churchill Mews NE6 56 C4
Churchill Sq DH4 94 B8
Churchill St
Newcastle upon Tyne
NE1 100 C4
Sunderland SR1 103 B2
Wallsend NE28 40 F4
Church La
Bedlington NE22 16 A7
Gateshead NE9 71 B6
Newcastle upon Tyne NE3 38 D5
Riding Mill NE44 62 E7
Sunderland SR1 102 C2
Whitburn SR6 75 F8
Churchlands NE46 45 D4
Church Mews
Ashington NE63 6 B4
Backworth NE27 30 C5
Church Pl NE10 56 D1
Church Rd
Backworth NE27 30 C5
Gateshead NE9 71 A5
Hetton-le-Hole DH5 95 A5
Newburn NE15 52 F7
Newcastle upon Tyne NE3 38 D5
Stannington NE61 14 C3
Wylam NE41 51 A6
Church Rise
Ryton NE40 52 E5
Whickham NE16 69 B7
Church Row 1 NE46 45 B5
Churchside Gdns DH5 95 C1
Church Sq NE61 2 B3
Church St
Birtley DH3 82 C4
Blaydon NE21 53 B1
Blyth NE24 17 E8
Cramlington NE23 22 B6
Dunston NE11 100 A1
Gateshead, Felling NE10 71 D8
Gateshead NE8 101 B4
Haswell DH6 97 E3
Hebburn NE31 57 D7
7 Houghton-le-Spring DH4,
DH5 94 E8
Newcastle upon Tyne NE6 57 A4
North Shields NE30 42 B6
Penshaw DH4 90 B6
Sunderland, South Hylton
SR4 85 A6
9 Sunderland SR5 75 B2
Sunniside NE16 69 A1
West Rainton DH4 94 A2
Church Street E SR1 103 C3
Church Street East Ind Est
SR1 102 B3
Church Street N SR6 103 B4
Church Terr NE21 53 C3
Church Vale DH6 96 C4
Church View
Boldon Colliery NE35 58 E1
Earsdon NE25 31 A5
Haswell DH6 97 F3
New Silksworth SR3 92 A7
Church View *continued*
Wallsend NE28 40 D2
Washington NE37 83 D7
Churchwalk Ho NE6 57 A5
Church Way
Earsdon NE25 31 A6
North Shields NE29, NE30 42 A6
South Shields NE33 42 C3
Church Wlk
Morpeth NE61 8 E8
Newcastle upon Tyne NE6 57 A5
Sunderland SR1 103 C3
Churston Cl DH4 90 C4
Cicero Ct NE6 57 A4
Cicero Terr 4 SR5 75 A2
Cinderford Cl NE35 58 E2
Circle Pl NE46 45 A5
Circle The NE32 58 C4
Cirencester St SR4 102 B3
Cirrus Ho 14 SR3 92 A6
Citadel E NE12 29 D3
Citadel W NE12 29 D3
Citygate NE4 98 C1
City Hall NE1 99 B2
City of Sunderland Coll
(Bede Ctr) SR3 85 F3
City of Sunderland Coll
(Hylton Ctr) SR5 74 E2
City of Sunderland Coll
(Shiney Row Ctr) DH4 90 B5
City of Sunderland Coll
(Usworth Sixth Form Coll)
NE37 83 D7
City Pool NE1 99 B2
City Rd NE1 99 C1
City Way SR3 91 C6
Civic Ct NE31 57 F5
Clacton Rd SR5 73 F1
Clanfield Ct NE3 38 F4
Clanny Ho SR4 85 F6
Clanny St SR1 102 B2
Clapham Ave NE6 56 D5
Clara Ave NE27 30 F4
Clarabad Terr NE12 30 A1
Clarance Pl NE3 38 E5
Clara St
Blaydon NE21 53 B1
Newcastle upon Tyne NE4 54 D4
CLARA VALE 51 E6
Clara Vale Nature Reserve*
NE40 51 E6
Clare Lea NE43 65 A3
Claremont Ave
Newcastle upon Tyne
NE15 53 D7
Sunderland SR6 75 E3
Claremont Cres NE26 31 E7
Claremont Ct NE26 31 E8
Claremont Dr DH4 90 A6
Claremont Gdns
East Boldon NE36 74 D7
Whitley Bay NE26 31 F6
Claremont North Ave
NE8 101 B2
Claremont Pl
Gateshead NE8 101 B1
Newcastle upon Tyne NE2 98 C3
Claremont Rd
Newcastle upon Tyne NE2 98 B4
Sunderland SR6 75 E3
Whitley Bay NE26 31 F7
Claremont South Ave
NE8 101 B1
Claremont St
Gateshead NE8 101 B1
Newcastle upon Tyne NE2 98 C3
Claremont Terr
Blyth NE24 17 D7
Gateshead NE10 57 B1
Newcastle upon Tyne NE2 98 C3
9 Springwell NE9 71 F1
Sunderland SR2 102 C1
Claremont Wlk NE8 101 A1
Claremount Ct NE36 74 B7
Clarence Cres 3 NE26 32 B4
Clarence Ho NE2 99 C2
Clarence St
Newcastle upon Tyne NE1,
NE2 99 C2
Seaton Sluice NE26 24 D5
2 Sunderland SR5 75 A2
Tantobie DH9 79 B2
Clarence Terr DH3 88 C3
Clarendon Mews NE3 28 C2
Clarendon Rd NE6 39 C1
Clarendon Sq SR5 75 B3
Clarewood Ave NE34 60 A8
Clarewood Ct NE4 98 B2
Clarewood Gn NE4 98 A2
Clarewood Pl NE5 54 C8
Clarke's Terr NE23 29 A6
Clarke Terr NE10 71 C8
Clarks Field NE61 8 E8
Clarks Hill Wlk NE15 52 F7
Clarks Terr 2 SR7 92 E1
Clasper Ct 11 NE33 42 C4
Clasper St NE4 100 B3
Clasper Way NE16 54 A3
Claude St
10 Crawcrook NE40 51 F3
Hetton-le-Hole DH5 95 A3
Claudius Ct 4 NE33 42 C4
Claverdon St NE5 36 B4
Clavering Pl NE1 101 A4
Clavering Rd
Blaydon NE21 53 C1
Whickham NE16 54 B1
Clavering Sq NE11 69 F8
Clavering St NE28 41 B1
Clavering Way NE21 53 E2
Claverley Dr NE27 30 C5
Claxheugh Cotts SR4 85 B7
Claxheugh Rd SR4 85 B7
Claymere Rd SR2 86 E1
Claypath NE10 71 F4
Claypath La NE33 42 D2
Claypath Rd DH5 95 B2
Claypath St 4 NE6 56 A6
Claypit Cl NE33 42 C4
Claypool Ct NE34 59 C5
Clayside House 4 NE33 42 D1
Clayton Park Sq NE2 99 B4
Clayton Rd NE2 99 B4
Clayton St
Bedlington NE22 11 D3
Dudley NE23 28 F8
Jarrow NE32 58 B7
Newcastle upon Tyne NE1 99 A1
Clayton Street W
12 Newcastle upon Tyne
NE1 98 C1
Newcastle upon Tyne NE1 100 C4
Clayton Terr
Gateshead NE8 56 C1
Heddon-on-the-Wall NE15 34 F2
Clayton Terrace Rd
Chopwell NE17 66 C2
High Spen NE13, NE39 66 D4
Clayworth Rd NE3 28 B1
CLEADON 60 B1
Cleadon Gdns
Gateshead NE9 71 D3
Wallsend NE28 41 A5
Cleadon Hill Dr NE34 60 A4
Cleadon Hill Rd NE34 60 B4
Cleadon Hills Nature
Reserve* SR6 60 B3
Cleadon La
Cleadon SR6 60 C1
East Boldon NE36, SR6 74 E8
Cleadon Lane Ind Est
NE36 74 E8
CLEADON LEA 59 E1
Cleadon Lea SR6 59 F1
Cleadon Mdws SR6 60 A2
Cleadon Old Hall SR6 60 A1
CLEADON PARK 60 A4
Cleadon St NE6 56 E6
Cleadon Twrs NE34 60 B4
Cleadon Village CE Prim Sch
SR6 59 F1
Cleasby Gdns NE9 70 F6
Cleasewell Terr NE62 11 A7
Cleaside Ave NE34 60 A4
Cleaswell Hill NE62 10 F7
Cleaswell Hill Special Sch
NE62 10 F7
Cleehill Dr NE29 31 F1
Cleeve Ct NE38 83 C5
Cleghorn St 4 NE6 56 C8
Clegwell Terr NE31 57 F6
Clematis Cres NE9 71 D2
Clement Ave NE22 11 C1
Clementina Cl SR2 103 B1
Clement St NE9 70 F5
Clennel Ave NE31 57 D5
Clennel Ho 4 NE4 54 E5
Clent Way NE12 39 A6
Clephan St NE11 54 F1
Clervaux Terr NE32 58 C6
Cleveland Ave
Chester le Street DH2 88 B2
Newbeggin-by-the-Sea NE64 7 D4
North Shields NE29 41 F6
Cleveland Cres NE29 42 A6
Cleveland Ct
Jarrow NE32 58 A7
9 South Shields NE33 42 C4
Cleveland Dr NE38 83 B3
Cleveland Gdns
Newcastle upon Tyne NE7 39 A3
Wallsend NE28 41 B3
Cleveland Mews NE11 100 A1
Cleveland Rd
North Shields NE29 42 A6
Sunderland SR4 85 F5
Sunderland SR4 102 A1
Cleveland St 3 NE33 42 D4
Cleveland Terr
Newbeggin-by-the-Sea
NE64 7 D4
North Shields NE29 42 A6
Cleveland View SR6 75 E6
Clickemin NE20 26 A6
Cliffe Ct SR6 75 F4
Cliffe Pk SR6 75 F4
Clifford Gdns 4 NE40 51 F3
Clifford Rd NE6 56 D5
Clifford's Fort NE30 42 C6
Clifford St
Blaydon NE21 53 C3
Chester le Street DH3 88 C1
Newcastle upon Tyne NE6 56 B6
North Shields NE30 42 C6
Sunderland SR4 102 A2
Clifford Terr
Chester le Street DH3 88 C2
Crawcrook NE40 51 F3
Cliff Rd SR2 93 A6
Cliff Row NE26 32 C4
Cliffside NE34 60 C6
Cliff Terr SR2 93 A6
Cliff View SR2 93 A6
CLIFTON 9 A2
Clifton Ave
South Shields NE34 59 E7
Clifton Ave *continued*
8 Wallsend NE28 40 B2
Cliftonbourne Ave 2 SR6 75 E4
Clifton Cl
Ryton NE40 52 E4
Stakeford NE62 11 A8
Clifton Ct
2 Gateshead NE9 71 E1
Newcastle upon Tyne NE3 37 D7
Whitley Bay NE26 31 E7
Clifton Gdns
Blyth NE24 17 D4
Gateshead NE9 70 F7
North Shields NE29 41 E3
Clifton Gr NE25 31 E6
Clifton La NE61 9 B2
Clifton Rd
Cramlington NE23 22 C5
Newcastle upon Tyne NE4 54 F5
Sunderland SR6 75 E4
Clifton Terr
Longbenton NE12 39 D7
South Shields NE33 59 C8
Whitley Bay NE26 32 B5
Cliftonville Ave NE4 54 E5
Cliftonville Gdns NE26 32 A6
Clifton Wlk NE5 36 B2
Climbing Tree Wlk NE61 4 E3
Clintburn Ct NE23 22 C8
Clinton Pl
Newcastle upon Tyne NE3 28 B2
Sunderland SR3 91 C6
Clipsham Cl 1 NE12 39 B6
Clipstone Ave NE6 56 E3
Clipstone Cl NE15 35 C2
Clitheroe Gdns NE22 10 D2
Clive Pl NE6 56 B5
Clive St
North Shields NE29 42 B5
9 South Shields NE34 59 A4
Clockburn Lonnen NE16 68 E4
Clockburnsyde Cl NE16 68 E5
Clockmill Rd NE11, NE8 100 A1
Clockstand Cl 8 SR6 75 E2
Clockwell St SR5 74 F1
Cloggs The NE20 25 F7
Cloister Ave NE34 59 A5
Cloister Ct NE8 101 C3
Cloister Garth NE7 38 F5
Cloisters The
Newcastle upon Tyne NE7 38 F5
South Shields NE34 59 F7
Sunderland SR2 103 A1
Cloister Wlk NE32 58 C7
Close NE1 101 A4
Closeburn Sq SR3 92 B6
Close E The DH2 88 C5
Closefield Gr NE25 31 E4
Close St
Sunderland, Millfield
SR4 102 A3
4 Sunderland SR5 75 B1
Close The
Blaydon NE21 53 A1
Blyth NE24 12 E1
Burnopfield NE16 79 C7
Chester le Street DH2 88 C5
Cleadon SR6 59 F1
Houghton-le-Spring DH5 94 F8
Newcastle upon Tyne NE5 53 E8
Ponteland NE20 25 E5
Prudhoe NE42 50 E3
Seghill NE23 22 F1
Stannington NE61 14 C3
Cloth Mkt NE1 99 A1
CLOUGH DENE 79 A3
Clough Dene
Tantobie DH9 79 B2
Tantobie, Pickering Nook
NE16 79 A3
Clough La NE1 99 A1
Clousden Dr NE12 29 E1
Clousden Grange NE12 29 E1
Clovelly Ave NE4 54 E5
Clovelly Gdns
Bedlington NE22 15 F8
Whitley Bay NE26 32 A6
Clovelly Pl
Jarrow NE32 58 E5
Ponteland NE20 25 C2
Clovelly Sq 6 SR5 74 A3
Clover Ave
Shiney Row DH4 90 B4
Winlaton Mill NE21 68 C6
Cloverdale NE22 10 E1
Cloverdale Ct NE6 57 A7
Cloverdale Gdns
Newcastle upon Tyne NE7 39 B3
Whickham NE16 69 B5
Cloverfield NE27 30 D2
Cloverfield Ave NE3 37 F6
Cloverhill NE32 58 C1
Clover Hill NE16 69 B2
Cloverhill Ave NE31 57 D3
Cloverhill Cl NE23 22 A1
Cloverhill Dr NE40 52 A4
Clover Hill Prim Sch NE16 68 F4
Clover Ho SR3 92 A4
Clumber St NE4 100 A3
Clumber Street N NE4 100 A3
Clyde Ave NE31 57 E3
Clyde Ct 10 SR3 91 F6
Clydedale Ave NE12 39 D8
Clydesdale Ave DH4 90 B7
Clydesdale Mount 7 NE6 56 C5

Clydesdale Rd NE6............56 C5
Clydesdale St DH5.............95 A2
Clyde St
  Chopwell NE17................66 C1
  Gateshead NE8...............71 A8
Clyvedon Rise NE34............60 A3
Coach House Ct NE9.........71 B6
Coach La
  Brunswick Village NE13........27 E4
  Hazlerigg NE13...............28 B4
  Newcastle upon Tyne NE7.....39 C4
  North Shields NE29...........42 A5
Coach Open NE28...............41 B1
Coach Rd
  Kibblesworth NE11............70 B3
  Throckley NE15..............35 C1
  Washington NE37.............72 C2
Coach Road Est NE37.........72 C1
Coach Road Gn NE10.........56 C2
Coalbank Rd DH5..............94 F2
Coalbank Sq DH5..............94 F2
COALBURNS...................66 D7
Coalburn Terr NE61.............9 D4
Coaley La DH4................90 C3
Coalford La DH6..............96 C4
Coal La NE42.................49 D4
Coalway Dr NE16.............69 B8
Coalway La
  Greenside NE40, NE41........51 D1
  Whickham NE16..............69 B7
Coalway Lane N NE16.........54 B1
Coanwood Dr NE23............22 C5
Coanwood Gdns NE11........70 B5
Coanwood Rd NE15...........54 B4
Coanwood Way NE16.........69 B3
Coast Rd
  Newcastle upon Tyne NE6, NE7,
  NE28.......................39 E2
  North Shields NE28, NE29....41 C6
  South Shields NE34, SR6.....60 D6
  Wallsend NE28...............40 C4
Coatsworth Ct NE8..........101 B2
Coatsworth Rd NE8..........101 B1
Cobalt Bus Pk NE27...........40 E8
Cobalt Ct NE15...............53 C8
Cobalt Park Way NE27........40 F8
Cobbett Cres NE34............59 B3
Cobbler's La NE43............49 B8
Cobblestone NE26.............56 B5
Cobden Rd NE23..............22 C4
Cobden St
  2 Gateshead NE8............56 A1
  2 Wallsend NE28..........40 B2
Cobden Terr NE8..............56 A1
Cobham Pl NE6................57 A4
Cobham Sq SR5...............75 B2
Coble Dene NE29.............41 E2
Coble Landing NE33...........42 B3
Coburg St
  Blyth NE24...................17 F7
  Gateshead NE8.............101 C2
  North Shields NE30...........42 B6
Coburn Ct NE23...............29 C5
Cochrane Ct NE4..............54 A4
Cochrane Park Ave NE7......39 C2
Cochrane St NE4..............54 E5
Cochrane Terr NE13...........27 B7
Cochran St NE21..............53 C4
Cockburn Terr NE29...........41 D3
Cockermouth Gn NE5.........54 A8
Cockermouth Rd SR5.........73 F2
Cockshaw NE46...............45 A5
Cockshaw Ct **7** NE46......45 A5
Cockshaw Terr **9** NE46....45 A5
Cockshott Dean NE42.........50 C3
Cohen Ct NE8.................70 E8
Cohort Cl DH8................76 E3
Coity La NE46................45 A5
Colbeck Terr **3** NE30.....42 D7
Colbourne Ave NE23..........15 E1
Colbourne Cres NE23.........15 E1
Colbury Ct NE23..............16 A2
Colby Ct NE4................100 B4
Colchester St NE34...........59 A5
Colchester Terr SR4..........85 F5
Coldbeck Ct NE23.............15 F2
Coldingham Gdns NE5........37 D2
Coldside Gdns NE5............36 B3
Coldstream DH3..............82 A2
Coldstream Ave SR5..........75 B2
Coldstream Cl DH4...........90 B5
Coldstream Dr NE21..........68 A8
Coldstream Gdns NE15.......54 B7
Coldstream Way NE29........41 C8
Coldwell Cl DH6..............97 F7
Coldwell La NE10..............71 C7
Coldwell Park Ave NE10......71 D7
Coldwell Park Dr NE10........71 D7
Coldwell Rd NE42.............50 F3
Coldwell St NE10..............71 D7
Coldwell Terr **2** NE10....71 C7
Colebridge Cl NE5............37 C3
Colebrooke DH3..............82 B2
Colegate NE10................71 F7
Colegate Com Prim Sch
  NE10.......................71 F7
Colegate W NE10.............71 F7
Cole Gdns NE10..............72 A8
Colepeth NE10................71 E7
Coleridge Ave
  Gateshead NE9...............70 E4
  South Shields NE33...........42 E1
Coleridge Rd SR5.............74 B2

Coleridge Sq NE31............57 E6
Coley Gn NE5................36 B4
Coley Hill Cl NE5.............36 C4
Coley Terr SR6...............75 E3
Colgrove Pl NE3..............37 E5
Colgrove Way NE3............37 F5
Colima Ave SR5..............85 C8
Colin Terr **7** SR2..........92 F6
College Burn Rd SR3.........91 E5
College Dr NE33..............59 E8
College La
  Longbenton NE12.............39 C6
  Newcastle upon Tyne NE1....99 B2
College Pl NE63................6 E2
College Rd
  Ashington NE63...............6 E2
  Hebburn NE31................57 D2
College St NE1...............99 B2
College View **4** SR5.......75 C1
Collier Cl NE15...............35 D1
Colliery La DH4...............78 D1
Colliery La
  Hetton-le-Hole DH5...........95 B2
  Newcastle upon Tyne NE4....98 B1
Colliery Rd NE11.............56 C2
COLLIERY ROW................94 B8
Collin Ave NE34..............60 B5
Collingdon Gn NE39..........67 A4
Collingdon Rd NE39..........67 A4
COLLINGWOOD................22 B4
Collingwood Ave NE28.......40 B4
Collingwood Cl NE23.........21 F8
Collingwood Cotts NE20.....25 B7
Collingwood Cres NE20......25 D4
Collingwood Ct **1** NE37...83 F8
Collingwood Dr
  Hexham NE46................44 F2
  Shiney Row DH4..............90 A6
Collingwood Gdns NE10.....56 D2
Collingwood Ho
  North Shields NE29...........41 F5
  South Shields NE33...........42 F5
Collingwood Mansions
  NE29.......................42 B4
Collingwood Mews NE3......38 C5
Collingwood Pl NE62.........11 A7
Collingwood Prim Sch
  NE29.......................41 D5
Collingwood Rd
  Earsdon NE25................31 A3
  Newbiggin-by-the-Sea NE64...7 D5
Collingwood Sch & Media
  Arts Coll NE61................9 B7
Collingwood Sh Ctr NE29...31 F1
Collingwood St
  3 Gateshead NE10.........56 D1
  Hebburn NE31................58 A6
  Hetton-le-Hole DH5..........95 A6
  Newcastle upon Tyne NE1...101 A4
  South Shields NE33...........59 C8
  3 Sunderland SR5.........75 B2
Collingwood Terr
  Blyth NE24...................17 E7
  Dunston NE11...............100 A1
  4 Newcastle upon Tyne
  NE2.........................38 F1
  Tynemouth NE30.............42 D7
  Whitley Bay NE26............32 C4
Collingwood View NE29......41 F5
Collywell Bay Rd NE26.......24 D5
Collywell Ct NE26............24 D6
Colman Ave NE34.............59 B3
Colman Ct NE11...............70 D4
Colnbrook Cl NE3.............37 D7
Colombo Rd SR5..............73 F1
Colombo Sq NE8.............101 B3
Colston St NE4...............54 D6
Colston Way NE25............31 D7
Coltere Ave NE36.............74 E7
Colton Gdns NE9.............71 A3
Coltpark NE5.................36 B4
Coltpark Pl NE23.............22 B5
Coltpark Woods NE17.........77 B6
Colt Pk NE17.................77 B5
Coltsfoot Gdns NE10.........71 C5
Coltspool NE10...............81 D6
Columba St SR5...............75 B2
Columba Wlk NE3.............38 E5
COLUMBIA....................83 E4
Columbia Grange NE3........37 E5
Columbia Terr NE24..........17 E6
Colwell Pl NE5................36 F2
Colwell Rd
  Ashington NE63...............6 F1
  Shiremoor NE27..............30 F2
  3 Tynemouth NE29.........31 F1
Colwyne Pl NE5...............37 B2
Colwyn Par NE31..............58 A2
Colwyn Rd DH1...............53 B7
Comet Row NE12..............29 C2
Comet Sq **3** NE37..........92 A7
Comical Cnr NE33.............42 B4
Comma Ct NE11...............70 B7
Commercial Pl **4** NE46....45 B4
Commercial Rd
  8 Blyth NE24.............17 E8
  Jarrow NE32.................58 C8
  Newcastle upon Tyne, Byker
  NE6........................56 C5
  Newcastle upon Tyne, South
  Gosforth NE3................38 C5
  South Shields NE33...........42 B1
  Sunderland SR2..............86 F4
Commercial St **9** NE21....53 B1
Commissioners' Wharf
  NE29.......................42 A2
Community North Sports
  Complex SR5................74 C4

Compton Ave NE34............59 D7
Compton Ct NE38.............83 B5
Compton Rd NE29.............41 F5
CONCORD....................83 D8
Concorde Ho NE25............23 E1
Concorde Sq **5** SR3.......92 A7
Concorde Way NE32...........58 B6
Concordia L Ctr NE23.........22 A6
Condercum Ct NE15...........54 C5
Condercum Ind Est NE4......54 D5
Condercum Rd NE4...........54 D5
Cone Terr DH3................88 D4
Conewood Ho NE3.............37 F6
Coneygarth Pl **7** NE63.....6 F5
Conhope La NE15, NE4.......54 D5
Conifer Cl NE21...............68 B8
Conifer Ct NE12...............39 F8
Coniscliffe Ave NE3..........37 F4
Coniscliffe Pl **3** NE8......75 E1
Coniscliffe Terr DH6..........97 F8
Coniston
  Birtley DH3..................82 D2
  Gateshead NE10..............72 A8
Coniston Ave
  Easington Lane DH5..........97 C8
  Hebburn NE31................57 F6
  Newbiggin-by-the-Sea NE64...7 C3
  Newcastle upon Tyne NE2....38 D8
  South Shields NE34..........60 B8
  Whitley Bay NE26............32 A5
Coniston Cl
  Chester le Street DH2........88 C2
  Killingworth NE12............29 C3
  Newburn NE15...............52 E7
Coniston Cres NE21..........53 C1
Coniston Ct
  Ashington NE63...............6 E4
  Chopwell NE17...............66 C1
  Hebburn NE31................57 D6
  Jarrow NE32.................58 A5
  Newcastle upon Tyne NE5....54 A8
Coniston Dr NE32.............58 D3
Coniston Gdns NE9...........71 B5
Coniston Grange NE36.......74 B7
Coniston Ho NE38.............83 C6
Coniston Pl NE9...............71 B5
Coniston Rd
  Blyth NE24...................12 A1
  Newcastle upon Tyne NE2....32 A2
  Wallsend NE28................41 A4
Connaught Cl NE12...........39 D7
Connaught Gdns NE12.......39 D7
Connaught Terr NE32.........58 B6
Conningsby Cl NE3............38 D8
Conniscliffe Ct NE46.........44 F3
Conniscliffe Rd NE46........44 F3
Connolly Terr NE17...........77 C6
Conqueror Ct NE11...........70 A5
Consort Pl **8** NE12.........39 A6
Constable Cl NE40............52 C4
Constable Gdns NE34........60 A8
Constables Garth **7** DH3...82 C4
Content St NE21...............53 C1
Convent Rd NE4..............54 D7
Conway Cl
  Bedlington NE22.............10 D1
  Newburn NE15...............52 D4
Conway Dr NE7...............39 A4
Conway Gdns
  Sunderland SR3..............91 C7
  Wallsend NE28...............40 A4
Conway Gr NE26...............24 B7
Conway Rd SR5...............73 F2
Conway Sq
  Gateshead NE9...............71 A8
  Sunderland SR5..............73 F2
Conyers Ave DH2.............88 B5
Conyers Gdns DH2............88 B5
Conyers Pl DH2...............88 B5
Conyers Rd
  Chester le Street DH2........88 C5
  Newcastle upon Tyne NE6....56 C6
Cook Cl NE33.................59 B8
Cook Gdns NE10..............72 B8
Cookshold La DH6............96 B2
Cookson Cl
  Corbridge NE45..............46 F6
  Newcastle upon Tyne NE4....54 A4
Cookson House NE33.........42 C3
Cookson's La NE1............101 A4
Cookson St NE4...............98 A1
Cook Sq SR5.................74 A2
Cooks Wood NE38............83 D3
Coomassie Rd NE24..........17 E7
Coomside NE23...............22 C4
Coop Bldgs **13** DH3.........82 A4
Co-operative Cres **6**
  NE10.......................71 C7
Co-operative St DH3..........88 C4
Cooperative Terr
  Great Lumley DH4............89 F1
  Hetton-le-Hole DH5..........95 A5
Co-Operative Terr
  Backworth NE27.............30 F4
  Brunswick Village NE13.......28 A6
  Burnopfield NE16............79 B6
  Gateshead NE16.............71 C7
  High Spen NE39..............66 F5
  Longbenton NE12............39 A8
  Medomsley DH8..............77 B1
  1 Shiremoor NE27.........30 E1
  Sunderland SR4.............102 A1
  1 Washington NE37.......83 E8
Co-operative Villas DH6....96 D1
Coopers Ct NE45.............46 F6
Cooper St SR6...............75 E1
Coopers Field NE61...........9 B8

Coopies Haugh NE61..........9 C7
Coopies La NE61..............9 C7
Coopies Lane Ind Est NE61...9 C7
Coopies Way NE61.............9 C7
Copeland Terr NE2............99 C2
Copley Ave SR5...............59 C2
Copley Dr SR3................86 B2
Copperas La NE15.............53 F7
Copper Chare NE1..............3 F1
Coppergate Ct NE31...........57 F7
Coppers Cl NE11..............70 B7
Coppice The NE26.............24 C6
Coppice Way NE2.............99 C2
Coppy La DH9, NE16..........80 C4
Copse The
  Blaydon NE21.................53 F2
  Burnopfield NE16.............78 F6
  Longbenton NE12............29 E1
  Newcastle upon Tyne NE3....38 D8
  Prudhoe NE42................50 E2
  Washington NE37.............72 B2
Copthleigh DH5...............95 A7
Coquet NE38.................82 F1
Coquet Ave
  Blyth NE24...................17 E5
  Newcastle upon Tyne NE3....38 B6
  South Shields NE34...........60 B8
  Whitley Bay NE26............32 A5
Coquet Bldgs NE15............36 B1
Coquetdale Ave NE6..........57 A6
Coquetdale Cl NE61...........63 A1
Coquetdale Villas **5** SR6...75 E2
Coquet Dr NE61................1 E5
Coquet Gr NE15...............35 C2
Coquet Ho **16** SR3.........91 F6
Coquet Park Fst Sch NE26..31 F7
Coquet Terr
  Dudley NE23.................28 F8
  Newcastle upon Tyne NE6....56 B8
Corbridge Ave NE3............38 B6
Corbridge CE Fst Sch
  NE45.......................47 A6
Corbridge Cl NE28............40 E6
Corbridge Mid Sch NE45....46 F7
Corbridge Rd
  Hexham NE46................45 D4
  Newcastle upon Tyne NE6....56 C6
Corbridge Roman Site*
  ....46 E6
Corbridge St NE6.............56 B6
Corbridge Sta NE45..........46 F4
Corby Gate SR2...............86 D4
Corby Gdns NE6..............56 F6
Corby Hall Dr SR2............86 D4
Corbiere Cl SR3...............91 E6
Corbitt St NE8...............100 C1
CORBRIDGE...................47 B5
Corbridge Ave NE3............38 B6
Corchester La NE46, NE45...46 C7
Corchester Rd NE22..........10 F2
Corchester Terr NE45.........46 F6
Corchester Twrs NE45........46 E7
Corchester Wlk NE7...........39 C4
Corfu Rd SR5.................74 A2
Corinthian Sq SR5............74 A2
Cork St SR1..................103 B3
Cormorant Cl
  Ashington NE63...............6 E1
  Blyth NE24...................17 F4
  4 Washington NE38.......82 F3
Cormorant Dr NE11..........100 A2
Cornbank Cl SR3..............92 A5
Cornbank Cl SR3..............84 A4
Cornelia Cl **7** SR3.........92 A7
Cornel Mews NE7.............39 C3
Cornel Rd NE7................39 C3
Corney St NE33...............59 B7
Cornfields The NE31..........57 E6
Cornforth Cl
  Ashington NE63...............6 B2
  Gateshead NE10..............72 C6
Cornhill
  Hedworth NE32..............58 C1
  Newcastle upon Tyne NE5....36 F1
Cornhill Ave NE3.............37 F7
Cornhill Cres NE29...........41 D7
Cornhill Rd
  Cramlington NE23............22 C6
  6 Sunderland SR5.........75 B2
Corn Mill Dr DH6.............94 D6
Cornmoor Gdns NE16........69 B5
Cornmoor Rd NE16...........69 B5
Cornthwaite Dr SR6..........75 E8
Cornwall Ct NE12.............72 E1
Cornwallis Sq NE33..........42 B1
Cornwallis St **13** NE33....42 C3
Cornwall Rd NE31............57 F3
Cornwell Cres NE22..........16 B8
Cornwell Ct NE3..............38 F4
Coronation Ave
  8 Ryhope SR2............92 F6
  Sunniside NE16..............69 B2
Coronation Bglws NE12......38 D5
Coronation Cl SR1...........103 B3
Coronation Cotts NE61........2 A3
Coronation Cres
  Burnside DH4................90 C2
  High Pittington DH6..........96 B6
  Whitley Bay NE25............31 F4
Coronation Gn DH5...........97 D8

Coronation Rd
  Newcastle upon Tyne NE25...36 B3
  Seaton Delaval NE25.........23 C3
  Sunniside NE16..............69 B2
Coronation St
  Annitsford NE23..............22 B1
  Blyth NE24...................17 E6
  Chester le Street DH3........88 D1
  Newbiggin-by-the-Sea NE64...7 E5
  North Shields NE29...........42 A4
  Ryton NE40..................52 E4
  South Shields NE33...........42 C2
  Sunderland SR1.............103 B3
  Wallsend NE28...............40 C2
Coronation Terr
  3 Boldon Colliery NE35...58 E1
  Chester le Street DH3........88 D1
  7 Gateshead NE9.........70 F4
  Hetton-le-Hole DH5...........95 A2
  Kibblesworth NE11...........81 C6
  21 Springwell NE9........71 F1
  Sunderland SR4..............85 B6
  Tynemouth NE29.............31 B1
Corporation Rd SR2..........86 F4
Corporation St NE4...........98 C1
Corporation Yd **9** NE61....3 F3
Correction House Bank
  NE30.......................42 C6
Corrighan Terr DH5...........94 C4
Corrofell Gdns NE10..........56 F4
Cory Ct SR4..................85 B6
Corsair NE16.................68 F6
Corsenside NE5...............36 F1
Corstopitum **3** NE28.......40 F4
Corstorphine Town NE33....42 B3
Cortina Ave SR4..............85 D4
Corvan Terr DH9..............79 A2
Cosford Ct NE3...............37 C7
Cosgrove Ct NE7.............39 A5
Cossack Terr SR4............85 F7
Cosserat Pl NE31.............57 D7
Cosser St NE24...............17 B4
Coston Dr NE33...............42 C3
Cosyn St NE6.................56 A5
Cotehill Dr NE20.............25 B4
Cotehill Rd **2** NE5.........37 B1
Cotemede NE10...............72 A6
Cotemede Ct NE10............72 A6
Cotfield Wlk NE8............101 A1
Cotgarth The NE10............71 E7
Cotherstone Ct
  Easington Lane DH5..........97 D8
  Sunderland SR3..............91 E6
Cotman Gdns NE34...........59 D2
Cotswold Ave
  Chester le Street DH2........88 B1
  Longbenton NE12............29 B1
Cotswold Cl NE38.............83 B4
Cotswold Dr
  Ashington NE63...............6 E1
  Whitley Bay NE25............31 F3
Cotswold Gdns
  Dunston NE11...............100 A7
  Newcastle upon Tyne NE7....39 A3
  Wallsend NE35...............58 F2
Cotswold Rd
  Sunderland SR5..............74 A2
  Tynemouth NE29.............31 E2
Cotswold Sq SR5..............74 A2
Cottage Farm NE7............39 D3
Cottage La NE5...............37 A1
Cottenham Chare NE4........98 B1
Cottenham St NE4............98 B1
Cotterdale NE28..............39 F5
Cotterdale Ave **2** NE8.....70 F8
Cotter Riggs Pl NE5..........36 B2
Cotter Riggs Wlk NE5.........36 B2
Cottersloe Gdns NE5.........36 B3
Cottingvale NE61..............3 F2
Cottingwood Ct NE4..........98 B2
Cottingwood Gdns
  Morpeth NE61................3 F2
  Newcastle upon Tyne NE4....98 B2
Cottingwood Gn NE24.......17 C3
Cottingwood La NE61.........3 F2
Cottonwood
  Shiney Row DH4.............89 F6
  Silksworth SR3..............91 E5
Coulson Cl NE46..............44 F2
Coulson Park Fst Sch NE63..6 F2
Coulthards La NE8..........101 C3
Coulthards Pl NE8............56 A4
Coulton Dr NE36..............74 D7
Council Ave DH4..............90 B6
Council Rd NE63...............6 C4
Counden Rd **4** NE5........36 E3
Countess Ave NE26...........32 A5
Countess Dr NE26............32 A5
County Mews NE33............42 D1
Coupland Gr NE32...........58 B3
Coupland Rd NE63.............6 C3
Courtfield Rd NE6............56 F6
Courtney Ct NE3..............37 C7
Courtney Dr SR3..............91 F5
Court Rd NE22................16 B8
Court The NE16...............69 C6
Cousin St SR1...............103 B2
Coutts Rd NE6................56 E8
Coventry Gdns
  Newcastle upon Tyne NE4....54 E4
  North Shields NE29...........41 E4
Coventry Way NE32...........58 B3
Coverdale
  Gateshead NE10..............72 A6
  Wallsend NE28...............39 F5
Coverdale Ave
  Blyth NE24...................17 A7

Coverdale Ave continued
Washington NE37 . . . . .83 C8
Coverdale Wlk NE33 . . . . . .59 C7
Coverley Rd NE5 . . . . .74 B2
Covers The
Longbenton NE12 . . . . .39 E6
Morpeth NE61 . . . . .9 A7
Wallsend NE28 . . . . .40 B3
Whickham NE16 . . . . .53 F1
Cove The DH4 . . . . .90 B6
Cowan Cl NE21 . . . . .53 A4
Cowans Ave NE21 . . . . .29 C4
Cowans Ho NE15 . . . . .53 C6
Cowan Terr SR2 . . . . .103 A2
Cowdray Ct NE3 . . . . .37 C7
Cowdray Rd SR5 . . . . .74 B2
Cowdrey Ho NE29 . . . . .41 D3
Cowell Gr NE3 . . . . .67 C2
Cowen Gdns NE9 . . . . .71 A1
Cowen Rd NE21 . . . . .53 D3
Cowen St
Blaydon NE21 . . . . .68 B8
Newcastle upon Tyne NE6 . . .56 F6
Cowen Terr NE39 . . . . .67 F3
Cowgarth NE46 . . . . .45 A5
COWGATE 37 D1
Cow La NE45 . . . . .46 F7
Cowie Cres DH5 . . . . .94 C4
Cowley Pl NE24 . . . . .17 B8
Cowley Rd NE24 . . . . .12 B1
Cowpath Gdns NE10 . . . . . .57 A1
COWPEN 17 A8
Cowpen Hall Rd NE24 . . . . .17 A8
COWPEN NEW TOWN 17 B8
Cowpen Rd
Blyth, Cowpen NE24 . . . . . . .17 A8
Blyth NE24 . . . . .17 C8
Coxfoot Cl NE34 . . . . .59 C5
COX GREEN 84 B3
Coxgreen Rd DH4, SR4 . . . .84 B2
COXLODGE 38 A5
Coxlodge Rd NE3 . . . . .38 A5
Coxlodge Terr NE3 . . . . .38 A5
Coxon St
Gateshead NE10 . . . . .57 B2
Sunderland SR2 . . . . .103 B1
Coxon Terr NE6 . . . . .56 C1
Crabtree Rd NE43 . . . . .64 C7
Cradock Ave NE31 . . . . .57 D4
Craggyknowe NE37 . . . . .82 F6
Craghall Dene NE2 . . . . .38 E4
Craghall Dene Ave NE2 . . . .38 E4
Cragleas NE16 . . . . .79 A4
Cragside
Brunswick Village NE13 . . . .28 B6
Chester le Street DH2 . . . . . .88 A4
Corbridge NE45 . . . . .47 B7
Cramlington NE23 . . . . .22 B5
Newcastle upon Tyne NE7 . . .39 B3
South Shields NE34 . . . . .60 B5
Whitley Bay NE26 . . . . .31 E7
Cragside Ave NE29 . . . . .41 D8
Cragside CE Fst Sch NE23 .22 B4
Cragside Ct
Dunston NE11 . . . . .70 A6
Houghton-le-Spring DH5 . . .94 F8
Cragside Gdns
Bedlington NE22 . . . . .11 C3
Dunston NE11 . . . . .70 A5
Killingworth NE12 . . . . .29 F4
Wallsend NE28 . . . . .40 F3
Cragside Ho SR3 . . . . .10 D7
Cragside Prim Sch NE7 . . . .39 A3
Cragside Rd NE37 . . . . .83 A7
Cragston Ave NE5 . . . . .37 C3
Cragston Cl NE5 . . . . .37 C2
Cragston Gdns NE24 . . . . . .17 B7
Cragaivon Rd SR5 . . . . .74 B2
Craig Cres NE23 . . . . .29 A8
Craigend NE23 . . . . .22 B5
Craiglands The DH4 . . . . . . .90 D5
Craigmillar Ave NE5 . . . . . . .36 F3
Craigmillar Cl NE5 . . . . .36 F3
Craigmill Pk NE24 . . . . .17 A8
Craigmont Ct NE12 . . . . . . .39 D6
Craigshaw Rd SR5 . . . . .73 F3
Craigshaw Sq SR5 . . . . .73 F3
Craig St DH3 . . . . .82 C4
Craigwell Ct NE61 . . . . .1 E6
Craigwell Dr SR3 . . . . .92 A4
Craik Park (Morpeth Town
AFC) NE61 . . . . .8 D6
Crake Way NE38 . . . . .82 F2
Cramer St NE8 . . . . .101 C1
CRAMLINGTON 21 F5
Cramlington Eastlea Fst Sch
NE23 . . . . .22 C8
Cramlington Hillcrest Sch
NE23 . . . . .22 B6
Cramlington Learning Village
NE23 . . . . .22 A4
Cramlington Northburn Fst
Sch NE23 . . . . .16 A1
Cramlington Parkside Mid
Sch NE23 . . . . .22 B7
Cramlington Rd SR5 . . . . . . .73 F2
Cramlington Sq SR5 . . . . . . .73 F2
Cramlington Sta NE23 . . . . .21 F7
Cramlington Terr
 Blyth NE24 . . . . .17 C4
 Shiremoor NE27 . . . . .30 E1
CRAMLINGTON VILLAGE . .22 B7
Cramond Ct NE9 . . . . .70 E3
Cramond Way NE23 . . . . . . .22 B4
Cranberry Dr NE38 . . . . .83 E3
Cranberry Rd SR5 . . . . .74 B2
Cranberry Sq SR5 . . . . .74 A2

Cranborne SR3 . . . . .91 C6
Cranbourne St NE30 . . . . . .32 B3
Cranbrook SR3 . . . . .86 A3
Cranbrook Ave NE3 . . . . . . .37 E7
Cranbrook Ct NE3 . . . . .37 E7
Cranbrook Dr NE42 . . . . .50 B2
Cranbrook Rd NE15 . . . . . . .54 B4
Cranemarsh Cl NE63 . . . . . . .6 C1
Craneshaugh Cl NE46 . . . . .45 E4
Cranesville NE9 . . . . .71 C5
Craneswater Ave NE26 . . . .24 F1
Cranfield Pl NE15 . . . . .53 C7
Cranford Gdns NE15 . . . . . . .53 E7
Cranford St NE34 . . . . .59 C6
Cranford Terr SR4 . . . . .102 A1
Cranham Cl NE12 . . . . .29 F4
Cranlea NE3 . . . . .37 C6
Cranleigh Ave NE3 . . . . .37 C7
Cranleigh Gr NE42 . . . . .50 D3
Cranleigh Pl NE25 . . . . .31 D6
Cranleigh Rd SR5 . . . . .74 B2
Cranshaw Pl NE23 . . . . .22 C5
Cranston Pl SR2 . . . . .93 A6
Crantock Rd NE3 . . . . .37 F5
Cranwell Ct NE3 . . . . .37 C7
Cranwell Dr NE13 . . . . .28 B6
Craster Ave
Longbenton NE12 . . . . .29 F1
Shiremoor NE27 . . . . .30 F3
South Shields NE34 . . . . .60 B8
Craster Cl
Blyth NE24 . . . . .17 C7
Whitley Bay NE25 . . . . .31 D7
Craster Ct NE11 . . . . .70 C6
Craster Gdns NE28 . . . . .40 F3
Craster Point SR7 . . . . . . .93 C1
Craster Rd NE29 . . . . .41 D5
Craster Sq NE3 . . . . .38 A6
Craster Terr NE7 . . . . .39 B2
Craster Walk NE63 . . . . .5 F4
Crathie DH3 . . . . .82 C7
Crathorne Ct NE16 . . . . .78 F6
Craven Ct SR6 . . . . .75 F1
CRAWCROOK 51 E4
Crawcrook La NE40, NE41 . .51 D5
Crawcrook St Agnes RC Prim
Sch NE40 . . . . .51 E4
Crawcrook Terr NE40 . . . . . .51 E3
Crawford Cotts NE61 . . . . . . .4 A1
Crawford St SR3 . . . . .91 F6
Crawford Pl NE25 . . . . .31 E4
Crawford St NE24 . . . . .12 D1
Crawford Terr
Morpeth NE61 . . . . .4 A1
Newcastle upon Tyne NE6 . . .56 F5
Crawhall Cres NE61 . . . . .8 E7
Crawhall Rd NE1 . . . . .99 C1
Crawley Ave NE31 . . . . .57 D3
Crawley Gdns NE16 . . . . . . .69 C7
Crawley Rd NE28 . . . . .40 B1
Crawley Sq NE31 . . . . .57 D3
Craythorne Gdns NE24 . . . .39 D2
Creevelea NE38 . . . . .83 C3
Creighton Ave NE3 . . . . .37 E4
Creland Way NE5 . . . . .37 C3
Crescent Ave NE46 . . . . .44 F5
Crescent The
Chester le Street DH2 . . . . . .88 B3
Cleadon SR6 . . . . .74 F8
 Dunston NE11 . . . . .69 B8
Hetton-le-Hole DH5 . . . . .95 A3
High Spen NE39 . . . . .66 F3
Jarrow NE32 . . . . .58 A4
Kibblesworth NE11 . . . . .81 C6
Morpeth NE61 . . . . .8 F6
Newbottle DH4 . . . . .90 B4
Newcastle upon Tyne, Kenton
Bankfoot NE13 . . . . .37 B6
Newcastle upon Tyne NE7 . . .39 B5
New Silksworth SR3 . . . . . . .86 A1
Pontland NE20 . . . . .26 A1
Rowlands Gill NE39 . . . . .67 F2
Ryton NE40 . . . . .52 D5
Seghill NE23 . . . . .22 F1
Shiney Row DH4 . . . . .90 A5
South Shields NE34 . . . . .59 F5
Sunniside NE16 . . . . .69 B2
 Throckley NE15 . . . . .35 D2
Tynemouth NE30 . . . . .40 D8
Wallsend NE28 . . . . .40 B3
Whickham NE16 . . . . .69 C6
Whitley Bay NE26 . . . . .32 B4
Wylam NE41 . . . . .51 B5
Crescent Vale NE26 . . . . . . .32 A4
Crescent Way NE12 . . . . . . .39 E8
Crescent Way N NE12 . . . . .39 E8
Crescent Way S NE12 . . . . . .39 E8
Creslow NE10 . . . . .71 F6
Cressbourne Ave SR6 . . .75 E4
CRESSWELL 2 A7
Cresswell Ave
Longbenton NE12 . . . . .29 F1
Seaton Sluice NE26 . . . . .24 C6
Tynemouth NE29 . . . . .41 E8
Cresswell Cl
Blaydon NE21 . . . . .68 A8
Whitley Bay NE25 . . . . .31 E3
Cresswell Dr
Blyth NE24 . . . . .17 C5
Newcastle upon Tyne NE3 . . .37 E7
Cresswell Home Farm Cotts
NE61 . . . . .2 A7
Cresswell Rd
Ellington NE61 . . . . .1 E6
Wallsend NE28 . . . . .40 A1
Cresswell St NE6 . . . . .56 D6
Cresswell Terr
Ashington NE63 . . . . .6 C4

Cresswell Terr continued
Sunderland SR2 . . . . .102 C1
Cresthaven NE10 . . . . .71 E6
Crest The
Bedlington NE22 . . . . .10 E1
Dinnington NE13 . . . . .27 B7
Seaton Sluice NE26 . . . . .24 E4
Crichton Ave DH3 . . . . .88 D1
Cricket Terr NE16 . . . . .79 A6
Cricklewood Dr DH4 . . . . . . .90 B6
Cricklewood Rd SR5 . . . . . . .74 A1
Criddle St NE8 . . . . .56 A4
Crieff Gr NE32 . . . . .58 D3
Crieff Sq SR5 . . . . .73 F2
Crigdon Hill NE5 . . . . .36 F1
Crighton NE38 . . . . .83 A5
Crimdon Gr DH4 . . . . .94 C7
Crimea Rd SR5 . . . . .73 F2
Crindledykes NE38 . . . . .83 E2
Cripps Ave NE10 . . . . .72 B8
Crocus Cl NE21 . . . . .53 A2
Croft Ave
Longbenton NE12 . . . . .39 E7
Sunderland SR4 . . . . .102 A2
Wallsend NE28 . . . . .40 C2
Croft Cl NE40 . . . . .52 C4
Croft Cotts NE43 . . . . .64 D7
Croftdale Rd NE21 . . . . .53 B2
Crofter Cl NE23 . . . . .22 A1
Crofthead Dr NE23 . . . . .22 A4
Croft Ho NE42 . . . . .50 A4
Crofton Mill Ho NE24 . . . .17 F7
Crofton Mill Ind Est NE24 . .17 F7
Crofton St
Blyth NE24 . . . . .17 E7
South Shields NE34 . . . . .59 C6
Croft Rd NE24 . . . . .17 E7
Crofts NE46 . . . . .45 B8
Crofts Cl NE45 . . . . .47 B5
Croftside DH3 . . . . .82 C5
Croftside Ave SR6 . . . . . . .75 F8
Croftside Ho
 Silksworth SR3 . . . . .91 F5
 Whitburn SR6 . . . . .60 F1
Croft's La NE15 . . . . .50 C8
Crofts Pk NE61 . . . . .9 E5
Croft St NE1 . . . . .99 B2
Crofts The NE20 . . . . .25 F6
Croftsway NE4 . . . . .54 A4
Crofts Way NE45 . . . . .47 A6
Croft Terr
 Hexham NE46 . . . . .45 A4
Horsley NE15 . . . . .50 C8
Jarrow NE32 . . . . .58 B6
Croft The
Hexham NE46 . . . . .44 F5
Killingworth NE12 . . . . .29 E4
Nedderton NE22 . . . . .15 A8
Ryton NE40 . . . . .52 D4
Sherburn Hill DH6 . . . . .96 C1
Croft View
Crawcrook NE40 . . . . .51 E3
Ovingham NE42 . . . . .50 A3
Croft Villas NE40 . . . . .51 E3
Croftway Fst Sch NE24 . . . . .17 E6
Croftwell Cl NE21 . . . . .53 D1
Cromarty DH2 . . . . .81 F2
Cromarty St SR6 . . . . .75 D2
Cromdale Pl NE5 . . . . .37 B1
Cromer Ave NE9 . . . . .70 F3
Cromer Ct NE9 . . . . .71 A3
Cromer Gdns
Newcastle upon Tyne NE2 . . .38 E3
Whitley Bay NE26 . . . . .32 A6
Crompton Rd NE6 . . . . .56 B8
Cromwell Ave NE21 . . . . . . .53 B2
Cromwell Ct
Newcastle upon Tyne
NE10 . . . . .57 C2
Ryton NE21 . . . . .53 A4
Cromwell Pl NE21 . . . . .53 A1
Cromwell Rd
Gateshead NE10 . . . . .57 B4
Whickham NE16 . . . . .69 C8
Cromwell St
Gateshead NE8 . . . . .56 A1
 Newcastle upon Tyne NE6 .56 A4
Sunderland SR4 . . . . .102 A3
Cromwell Terr
Gateshead NE8 . . . . .101 A1
North Shields NE29 . . . . .41 F6
Crondall St NE33 . . . . .59 D7
Cronin Ave NE34 . . . . .59 B4
Cronniewell NE17 . . . . .77 B5
CROOKGATE BANK 79 C6
Crookham Gr NE61 . . . . .9 B5
Crookham Way NE23 . . . . . .22 C4
CROOKHILL 52 D5
Crookhill Prim Sch NE40 . . .52 E5
Crookhill Terr NE40 . . . . .52 E5
Croome Gdns NE61 . . . . .9 C5
Cropthorne NE10 . . . . .72 B6
Crosby Gdns NE9 . . . . .71 B3
Crosland Pk NE23 . . . . .21 F6
Cross Ave NE28 . . . . .39 F4
Crossbank Rd NE5 . . . . .37 B3
Crossbrook Rd NE5 . . . . . .37 D2
Crosby Ct SR2 . . . . .103 C1
Cross Carliol St NE1 . . . . . . .99 B1
Cross Dr NE40 . . . . .52 C4
Crossfell NE20 . . . . .25 C4
Crossfield Pk NE10 . . . . .71 C7
Crossfield Terr NE6 . . . . .57 A4
Crossgate NE33 . . . . .42 C2

Crossgate Rd DH5 . . . . .95 A2
Crossgill NE37 . . . . .83 B7
Crossgreen Rd NE15 . . . . . . .54 B4
Cross Keys La NE9 . . . . .70 F5
Cross La
Dunston NE11 . . . . .54 D2
Kibblesworth NE11 . . . . .70 B4
Cross Lane Meadows Nature
Reserve* NE16 . . . . .54 C1
Crosslaw NE5 . . . . .36 F1
Crosslea Ave SR3 . . . . .86 B3
Crossley Terr
Longbenton NE12 . . . . .29 F1
Newcastle upon Tyne NE4 . . .98 A2
Cross Morpeth St NE2 . . . . .98 B4
Cross Par NE4 . . . . .100 B4
Cross Pl SR1 . . . . .103 B3
Cross Rigg Cl
Penshaw DH4 . . . . .90 A7
Shiney Row DH4 . . . . .89 F7
Cross Row
Gateshead NE8 . . . . .56 B1
Ryton NE40 . . . . .52 E4
Cross Sheraton St NE2 . . . .98 B4
Cross St
 Fence Houses DH4 . . . . . .94 A8
Gateshead NE8 . . . . .101 C1
High Pittington DH6 . . . . .96 D3
Houghton-le-Spring DH4 . . . .90 D1
Newcastle upon Tyne NE1 . . .98 C1
Newcastle upon Tyne, St Ann's
NE6 . . . . .56 A5
Prudhoe NE42 . . . . .50 D3
Cross Terr NE39 . . . . .67 D1
Cross Vale Rd SR2 . . . . .86 C4
Cross Villa Place No 1
NE4 .98 C1
Cross Villa Place No 2
NE4 .98 C1
Cross Villa Place No 3
NE4 .98 C1
Cross Villa Place No 4
NE4 .98 B1
Cross Villa Place No 5
NE4 .98 B1
Crossway
Gateshead NE9 . . . . .71 B6
Guide Post NE62 . . . . .10 F7
Newcastle upon Tyne NE2 . . .38 E3
South Shields NE34 . . . . .60 A5
Tynemouth NE30 . . . . .42 C8
Crossway Ct NE5 . . . . .37 F3
Crossways
East Boldon NE36 . . . . .74 E2
Hedworth NE32 . . . . .58 E2
Jarrow NE32 . . . . .58 B6
Crossways The NE13 . . . . . .28 A4
Crossway The
Newcastle upon Tyne, Kenton
NE3 .37 F4
Newcastle upon Tyne, Lemington
NE15 . . . . .53 D2
Cross Way The NE10 . . . . . . .71 A6
Crossway Villas NE9 . . . . .71 A6
Crostbuate Gr SR5 . . . . . . .74 A1
Croudace Row NE10 . . . . . .71 D8
Crow Bank NE28 . . . . .40 C2
Crowhall La NE10 . . . . .71 D8
Crow Hall La NE23 . . . . .21 F7
Crow Hall Rd NE23 . . . . .15 F1
Crowhall Towers NE10 . . .71 D8
Crowley Ave NE16 . . . . .69 C8
Crowley Gdns NE21 . . . . . . .53 C2
Crowley Rd NE15 . . . . .51 D7
Crowley Villas NE16 . . . . .54 A1
Crown & Anchor Cotts
NE15 . . . . .50 C8
Crown Rd SR5 . . . . .75 A1
Crown St
Blyth NE24 . . . . .17 F7
 Morpeth NE61 . . . . .9 A8
Crown Terr NE40 . . . . .52 B1
Crowther Ind Est
Birtley NE38 . . . . .82 F4
Washington NE38 . . . . .82 F5
Crowther Rd NE38 . . . . .82 F5
Crowtree L Ctr SR1 . . . . . . .102 C2
Crowtree Rd SR1 . . . . .102 C3
Croxdale Ct NE34 . . . . .59 A5
Croxdale Gdns NE10 . . . . . . .57 A2
Croxdale Terr
Gateshead NE10 . . . . .57 A1
Greenside NE40 . . . . .52 C1
Croydon Rd NE4 . . . . .98 A2
Crozier St SR5 . . . . .75 C1
CRUDDAS PARK 100 A4
Cruddas Park Sh Mall
NE4 . . . . .100 A4
Crudwell Cl NE35 . . . . .58 E2
Crummock Ave SR6 . . . . .75 C4
Crummock Ct NE28 . . . . .41 A4
Crummock Rd NE5 . . . . .54 B8
Crumstone Ct NE12 . . . . .29 E4
Crusade Wlk NE32 . . . . .58 A5
Cty Cricket Gd NE2 . . . . .99 C4
Cuillin Cl NE38 . . . . .83 B3
Culford Pl NE28 . . . . .40 E6
CULLERCOATS 32 D3
Cullercoats Prim Sch
NE30 . . . . .32 C3
Cullercoats Rd SR5 . . . . .73 F1
Cullercoats Sq SR5 . . . . .73 F1
Cullercoats St NE6 . . . . .56 E6
Cullercoats Sta NE30 . . . . . .32 C3
Culloden Wlk NE12 . . . . .29 D4
Culzean Ho SR3 . . . . .91 D7

Cumberland Ave
Bedlington NE22 . . . . .10 E1
Newbeggin-by-the-Sea NE64 . .7 D4
Cumberland Pl
Birtley DH3 . . . . .82 D1
South Shields NE34 . . . . .60 B7
Cumberland Rd
New Silksworth SR3 . . . . .92 A8
Shiremoor NE27 . . . . .41 B7
Cumberland St
Sunderland SR1 . . . . .103 A3
Wallsend NE28 . . . . .40 C2
Wallsend, Willington Quay
NE28 . . . . .41 B1
Cumberland Way NE37 . . . . .72 C2
Cumberland Wlk NE7 . . . . . .39 B4
Cumbrian Ave
Chester le Street DH2 . . . . . .88 C2
Sunderland SR5 . . . . .75 C5
Cumbrian Gdns NE11 . . . . . .70 A6
Cumbria Wlk NE4 . . . . .98 A1
Cummings St NE24 . . . . .17 E8
Curlew Cl
Ashington NE63 . . . . .11 E8
Longbenton NE12 . . . . .39 A7
Ryton NE40 . . . . .52 C4
Washington NE38 . . . . .83 A2
Curlew Hill NE61 . . . . .8 E8
Curlew Ho NE33 . . . . .42 D3
Curlew Rd NE32 . . . . .58 C8
Curlew Way NE24 . . . . .17 E4
Curly Kews NE61 . . . . .8 E8
Curran House NE32 . . . . .58 C8
Curren Gdns NE10 . . . . .56 C2
Curtis Rd NE4 . . . . .54 C4
Curzon Pl
Gateshead NE8 . . . . .101 B4
 Newcastle upon Tyne
NE5 .37 B2
Curzon Road W NE28 . . . . . .40 B1
Curzon St NE8 . . . . .70 E8
Cushat Cl NE6 . . . . .56 C5
Cushy Cow La NE40 . . . . .52 C4
Customs House The*
NE33 . . . . .42 B2
Cut Bank NE1 . . . . .56 A5
Cuthbert Ct NE32 . . . . .58 E6
Cuthbertson Ct SR6 . . . . . . .75 E5
Cuthbert St
Gateshead NE8 . . . . .101 A2
Hebburn NE31 . . . . .57 F6
Sunniside NE16 . . . . .69 A1
Cuthbert Wlk NE3 . . . . .38 E5
Cut Throat La NE17, NE39 . . .77 C4
Cutting St SR7 . . . . .92 F1
Cygnet Cl
Ashington NE63 . . . . .11 D8
Newcastle upon Tyne NE5 . . .36 D4
Cyncopa Way NE5 . . . . .37 D2
Cypress Ave NE4 . . . . .54 D8
Cypress Cres
Blyth NE24 . . . . .17 E7
Dunston NE11 . . . . .70 A7
Cypress Dr NE24 . . . . .17 E7
Cypress Gdns
Blyth NE24 . . . . .17 E7
Killingworth NE12 . . . . .29 C4
Cypress Gr NE40 . . . . .52 C6
Cypress Rd NE6 . . . . .71 D2
Cypress Sq SR3 . . . . .92 A8
Cyprus Gdns NE9 . . . . .71 A6

D

Dachet Rd NE25 . . . . .31 D7
Dacre Ct NE61 . . . . .4 A1
Dacre Rd SR6 . . . . .75 D4
Dacre St
Morpeth NE61 . . . . .3 F1
South Shields NE33 . . . . .59 C8
Daffodil Cl NE21 . . . . .53 B2
Dahlia Cl SR4 . . . . .102 B3
Dahlia Pl NE4 . . . . .54 D7
Dahlia Way NE31 . . . . .57 E4
Dainton Cl DH4 . . . . .90 C4
Dairnbrook NE37 . . . . .83 A6
Dairy La DH4 . . . . .94 C8
Daisy Cotts DH4 . . . . .82 C4
Dalamere Cl NE38 . . . . .89 B7
Dalegarth Gr SR6 . . . . .75 C5
Dale Rd NE25 . . . . .31 D4
Dale St
Cambois NE24 . . . . .12 E1
Crawcrook NE40 . . . . .51 F4
South Shields NE33 . . . . .42 D3
Dales The NE5 . . . . .37 E2
Dale Terr SR6 . . . . .75 E3
Dale Top NE25 . . . . .23 F1
Dale View Gdns NE40 . . . . . .51 F3
Dalla St SR4 . . . . .85 A7
Dally Mews NE3 . . . . .28 B1
Dalmahoy NE37 . . . . .72 D3
Dalmatia Terr NE24 . . . . .17 E6
Dalston Pl NE24 . . . . .17 E4
Dalton Ave NE24 . . . . .2 A3
Dalton Cl NE23 . . . . .22 B6
Dalton Cres NE6 . . . . .56 B6
Dalton Ct NE28 . . . . .39 F5
Dalton Pl
Newcastle upon Tyne NE5 . . .36 C3
Sunderland SR4 . . . . .102 B2
Daltons La NE33 . . . . .42 B2
Dalton St
Newcastle upon Tyne NE6 . . .56 B5

Dalton St *continued*
Newcastle upon Tyne NE6 . . . 56 B6
Dalton Terr NE17 . . . 77 B8
Dalton Way DH4 . . . 90 A7
Dame Allans Junior Sch NE12 . . . 39 D8
Dame Allans Sch NE4 . . . 54 E7
Dame Dorothy Cres 5 SR6 . . . 75 E1
Dame Dorothy Prim Sch SR6 . . . 103 B4
Dame Dorothy St SR6 . . . 103 A4
Dame Flora Robson Ave NE34 . . . 58 F4
Dame Margaret Hall NE38 . . . 83 E5
Damside 6 NE61 . . . 9 A8
Danby Cl
Silksworth SR3 . . . 92 B6
Washington NE38 . . . 88 F8
Danby Gdns NE6 . . . 39 D1
Dance City* NE1 . . . 100 C4
Danville Rd SR6 . . . 75 E4
D'arcy Ct SR1 . . . 103 B2
Darden Cl NE12 . . . 29 F4
Darden Lough NE5 . . . 36 F1
Darenth St NE34 . . . 59 C6
Darien Ave SR6 . . . 75 D4
Dark La
Morpeth NE61 . . . 4 A1
Pegswood NE61 . . . 4 E3
Darley Ct 15 SR3 . . . 91 F6
Darley Pl NE15 . . . 54 A5
Darnell Pl NE4 . . . 98 B2
Darnley Rd NE63 . . . 6 C3
Darras Ct NE33 . . . 42 D1
Darras Dr NE29 . . . 41 C7
DARRAS HALL . . . 25 D3
Darras Hall Fst Sch NE20 . . . 25 C3
Darras Mews NE20 . . . 25 C4
Darras Rd NE20 . . . 25 D4
Darrell St NE13 . . . 28 A6
Dartford Cl NE25 . . . 23 E3
Dartford Rd
South Shields NE33 . . . 42 F2
Sunderland SR6 . . . 75 D4
Dartmouth Ave NE9 . . . 70 F2
Darvall Cl NE25 . . . 31 D7
Darwin Cres NE3 . . . 37 F3
Darwin St SR5 . . . 74 F2
Daryl Cl NE21 . . . 53 A1
Daryl Way NE10 . . . 72 D8
Davenport Dr NE3 . . . 28 B1
David Adams Ho 7 NE15 . . . 54 D5
David Gdns SR6 . . . 75 F3
Davidson Cotts NE2 . . . 38 E3
Davidson Rd NE10 . . . 57 B2
Davidson St NE10 . . . 71 D8
David St NE28 . . . 40 B2
David Terr 8 NE40 . . . 51 F3
Davison Ave
New Silksworth SR3 . . . 92 B7
Whitley Bay NE26 . . . 31 F6
Davison St
Blyth NE24 . . . 17 E8
Boldon Colliery NE35 . . . 58 E1
Newburn NE15 . . . 52 E8
Davison Terr 3 SR5 . . . 75 A2
Davy Bank NE28 . . . 40 D1
Dawlish Cl NE29 . . . 41 D8
Dawlish Gdns NE9 . . . 70 F3
Dawlish Pl NE5 . . . 36 C3
Dawson Pl NE61 . . . 3 F1
Dawson Sq 4 NE30 . . . 42 D7
Dawson St 5 NE6 . . . 57 A6
Dawson Terr SR4 . . . 85 A7
Daylesford Dr NE3 . . . 38 F4
Daylesford Rd NE23 . . . 16 A2
Dayshield NE5 . . . 36 F1
Deacon Cl NE15 . . . 36 B2
Deacon Ct NE12 . . . 39 A7
Deaconsfield Cl SR3 . . . 91 F5
Deadridge La NE45 . . . 47 B7
Deal Cl NE24 . . . 17 E4
Dean Ct 6 NE24 . . . 17 D8
Deanery St NE22 . . . 10 F1
Deanham Gdns
12 Cowgate NE5 . . . 37 D1
Newcastle upon Tyne NE5 . . . 54 D8
Dean Ho NE6 . . . 57 A8
Dean Rd
South Shields, Dean NE33 . . . 59 C8
South Shields NE33 . . . 59 B7
DEANS . . . 59 C7
Deans Ave NE64 . . . 7 C5
Deans Cl 1 NE16 . . . 69 B7
Deansfield Cl SR3 . . . 91 F5
Deansfield Gr NE15 . . . 36 B3
Dean St
Gateshead NE9 . . . 71 A5
Hexham NE46 . . . 45 C5
Newcastle upon Tyne NE1 . . . 99 B1
Dean Terr
Ryton NE40 . . . 52 C5
South Shields NE33 . . . 59 B7
Sunderland SR5 . . . 75 A1
Dean View Dr NE24 . . . 17 B8
Dearham Gr NE23 . . . 16 A2
Debden Ho 7 NE11 . . . 70 A8
Debdon Gdns NE6 . . . 39 D1
Debdon Pl NE23 . . . 22 B6
Debdon Rd NE63 . . . 6 F2
Debussy Ct NE32 . . . 58 C6
December Ctyd NE8 . . . 100 B2
DECKHAM . . . 71 A8
Deckham St 11 NE8 . . . 71 A8
Deckham Terr NE8, NE9 . . . 71 A8
Deel Ho 2 SR3 . . . 91 D7
Deepbrook Rd 5 NE5 . . . 37 C1
Deepdale
Wallsend NE28 . . . 39 F5
Washington NE38 . . . 83 A1
Deepdale Cl NE16 . . . 68 F4
Deepdale Cres NE5 . . . 37 E2
Deepdale Gdns NE12 . . . 29 C3
Deepdale Gn NE5 . . . 37 E2
Deepdale Rd NE30 . . . 32 B2
Deepdale St DH5 . . . 95 A2
Deepdene Gr SR6 . . . 75 E5
Deepdene Rd SR6 . . . 75 D5
Deerbolt Pl NE12 . . . 39 C7
Deer Bush NE5 . . . 36 F1
Dee Rd NE31 . . . 57 F3
Deerfell Cl NE63 . . . 6 B2
Deerness Rd SR2 . . . 103 B1
Deer Park Way NE21 . . . 53 E1
Dees Ave NE28 . . . 40 B3
Dee St NE32 . . . 58 C7
Defender Ct SR5 . . . 85 C8
Defoe Ave NE34 . . . 59 C3
Deighton Wlk NE5 . . . 36 F1
Delacour Rd NE21 . . . 53 C3
Delamere Cres NE23 . . . 16 A2
Delamere Ct 8 SR3 . . . 92 A6
Delamere Rd NE3 . . . 37 F5
DELAVAL . . . 54 C4
Delaval DH2 . . . 88 A3
Delaval Ave
North Shields NE29 . . . 41 E6
Seaton Delaval NE25 . . . 23 C3
Delaval Cres NE24 . . . 17 B4
Delaval Ct
Bedlington NE22 . . . 11 C2
Longbenton NE12 . . . 29 E1
15 South Shields NE33 . . . 42 D1
Delaval Gdns
Blyth NE24 . . . 17 B4
Newcastle upon Tyne NE15 . . . 54 B4
Delaval Mid Sch NE24 . . . 17 D5
Delaval Rd
Longbenton NE12 . . . 29 D1
Newcastle upon Tyne, Delaval NE15 . . . 54 B4
Newcastle upon Tyne, Old Benwell NE15 . . . 54 B5
Whitley Bay NE26 . . . 32 C4
Delaval St NE24 . . . 17 B4
Delaval Terr
Blyth NE24 . . . 17 E8
Newcastle upon Tyne NE3 . . . 38 A4
Delaval Trad Est NE25 . . . 23 C5
Delhi Cres NE40 . . . 52 A3
Delhi Gdns NE40 . . . 52 A3
Delhi View NE40 . . . 52 A3
Dellfield Dr SR4 . . . 85 A4
Dell The
Morpeth NE61 . . . 3 E3
Newbottle DH4 . . . 90 D3
Delta Bank Rd NE11 . . . 54 C3
Delton Cl NE38 . . . 83 E3
De Merley Rd NE61 . . . 3 F1
Demesne Dr NE22 . . . 15 F8
Demesne The NE63 . . . 7 B2
De Mowbray Way NE61 . . . 3 D2
Dempsey Rd NE13 . . . 28 B4
Denbeigh Pl NE12 . . . 39 C7
Denbigh Ave
Sunderland SR6 . . . 75 D4
Wallsend NE28 . . . 41 A3
Denbigh Com Prim Sch NE28 . . . 41 A3
Denby Cl NE23 . . . 16 A2
Dene Ave
Brunswick Village NE13 . . . 28 A6
Hexham NE46 . . . 45 C4
Houghton-le-Spring DH5 . . . 95 A7
Killingworth NE12 . . . 29 A2
Newcastle upon Tyne, Denton Burn NE15 . . . 53 D7
Newcastle upon Tyne, South Gosforth NE3 . . . 38 E4
Rowlands Gill NE39 . . . 67 D1
Ryton NE40 . . . 52 D5
Denebank NE25 . . . 31 E5
Dene Bank View NE3 . . . 37 E3
Deneburn NE10 . . . 72 A7
Dene Cl
Newcastle upon Tyne NE7 . . . 39 A1
Ovingham NE42 . . . 50 B5
Riding Mill NE44 . . . 62 F8
Ryton NE40 . . . 52 D5
Dene Cres
Newcastle upon Tyne NE3 . . . 38 E4
Rowlands Gill NE39 . . . 67 D1
Ryton NE40 . . . 52 D5
Wallsend NE28 . . . 40 D2
Whitley Bay NE26 . . . 31 F6
Denecrest DH8 . . . 77 A2
Denecroft NE41 . . . 51 A6
Dene Ct
Birtley DH3 . . . 82 C7
Hamsterley NE17 . . . 77 B6
Newcastle upon Tyne NE7 . . . 39 B1
Washington NE38 . . . 83 C6
Dene Farm Cotts NE15 . . . 35 E2
Deneford NE9 . . . 71 A1
Dene Garth NE42 . . . 50 A5
Dene Gdns
Gateshead NE10 . . . 57 B1
Houghton-le-Spring DH5 . . . 94 F7
Newcastle upon Tyne NE15 . . . 53 D6
Whitley Bay NE25 . . . 31 E5
Dene Gr
Newcastle upon Tyne NE3 . . . 38 E4
Prudhoe NE42 . . . 50 B3
Dene Gr *continued*
Seghill NE23 . . . 23 B2
Deneholm
Wallsend NE28 . . . 40 D3
Whitley Bay NE25 . . . 31 E5
Dene La SR6 . . . 75 D4
Denelands NE46 . . . 45 C5
Dene Mews SR5 . . . 74 C1
Dene Pk
Hexham NE46 . . . 45 C4
Ponteland NE20 . . . 25 B3
Sunderland SR5 . . . 74 C1
Dene Rd
Blaydon NE21 . . . 53 D3
Guide Post NE62 . . . 10 E7
Rowlands Gill NE39 . . . 67 D1
Sunderland SR5 . . . 74 C1
Tynemouth NE30 . . . 42 C8
Wylam NE41 . . . 51 B7
Deneside
Dunston NE11 . . . 69 F7
Hedworth NE32 . . . 58 C1
Newcastle upon Tyne, Denton Burn NE15 . . . 54 A7
Newcastle upon Tyne NE5 . . . 36 F4
Seghill NE23 . . . 23 A2
South Shields NE34 . . . 60 C6
Dene Side NE21 . . . 53 D2
Deneside Ave NE9 . . . 70 F4
Deneside Cl NE15 . . . 35 D2
Deneside Ct
Newcastle upon Tyne NE2 . . . 56 A8
Whitley Bay NE26 . . . 31 E8
Dene St
Hetton-le-Hole DH5 . . . 95 B6
Holywell NE25 . . . 23 F2
New Silksworth SR3 . . . 86 A1
Prudhoe NE42 . . . 50 E3
Sunderland SR4 . . . 85 F7
Denesyde DH8 . . . 77 A2
Dene Terr
Blaydon NE21 . . . 53 B2
Jarrow NE32 . . . 58 A4
Newburn NE15 . . . 52 F8
Newcastle upon Tyne NE3 . . . 38 E4
Ovington NE42 . . . 49 D4
Riding Mill NE44 . . . 62 F8
Dene Terrace E NE41 . . . 51 A7
Dene Terrace W NE41 . . . 51 A7
Dene The
Medomsley DH8 . . . 77 A2
West Rainton DH4 . . . 94 A2
Whitley Bay NE25 . . . 31 E5
Wylam NE41 . . . 51 B6
Dene View
Ashington NE63 . . . 6 B3
Bedlington NE22 . . . 11 C1
Burnopfield NE16 . . . 79 A6
Ellington NE61 . . . 1 E4
High Spen NE39 . . . 67 A3
Newcastle upon Tyne NE3 . . . 38 E4
Rowlands Gill NE39 . . . 67 C2
Dene View Cres SR4 . . . 85 B6
Dene View Ct NE24 . . . 17 B7
Dene View Dr NE24 . . . 17 B8
Dene View E NE22 . . . 11 C1
Dene View W NE22 . . . 16 B8
Dene Villas DH3 . . . 88 D1
Deneway NE39 . . . 68 A4
Denewell Ave
Gateshead NE9 . . . 70 F5
Newcastle upon Tyne NE7 . . . 39 A3
Denewood NE12 . . . 29 E2
Denewood Ct 3 NE28 . . . 41 A2
Denham Ave SR6 . . . 75 D4
Denham Dr NE25 . . . 23 D2
Denham Gr NE21 . . . 67 F8
Denham Wlk NE5 . . . 36 C3
Denhill Pk NE15 . . . 54 D6
Denholm Ave NE23 . . . 16 A2
Denholme Lodge NE11 . . . 100 A1
Denmark Ct 10 NE6 . . . 56 C7
Denmark Ctr 14 NE33 . . . 42 C3
Denmark St
Gateshead NE8 . . . 101 C2
2 Newcastle upon Tyne NE6 . . . 56 C6
Dennison Cres DH3 . . . 82 C6
Denshaw Cl NE23 . . . 16 B2
Dent Cl DH6 . . . 97 E3
Dentdale DH4 . . . 89 E8
Denton Ave
Newcastle upon Tyne NE15 . . . 53 D6
North Shields NE29 . . . 41 C6
DENTON BURN . . . 53 E7
Denton Chare NE1 . . . 101 A4
Denton Ct NE5 . . . 54 A7
Denton Dene Nature Reserve* NE15 . . . 53 F6
Denton Gate NE5 . . . 37 A3
Denton Gdns NE15 . . . 54 C5
Denton Gr NE5 . . . 37 A3
Denton Park Ho NE5 . . . 36 E2
Denton Park Sh Ctr NE5 . . . 36 E2
Denton Rd NE15 . . . 53 F6
Denton View NE21 . . . 53 B2
Dent St
Blyth NE24 . . . 17 F6
Sunderland SR6 . . . 75 D4
Denver Gdns NE6 . . . 56 E5
Denway Gr NE26 . . . 24 B7
Denwick Ave NE15 . . . 53 C6
Denwick Terr NE30 . . . 42 C7
Depot Rd NE6 . . . 56 D7
DEPTFORD . . . 102 A4
Deptford Rd
Gateshead NE8 . . . 56 A4
Deptford Rd *continued*
Sunderland SR4 . . . 102 B3
Deptford Terr SR4 . . . 102 A4
Derby Cres NE31 . . . 57 D5
Derby Ct NE4 . . . 98 B2
Derby Gdns NE28 . . . 40 A3
Derby St
Jarrow NE32 . . . 58 C7
Newcastle upon Tyne NE4 . . . 98 B2
South Shields NE33 . . . 42 C2
Sunderland SR2 . . . 102 C2
Derby Terr NE33 . . . 42 D2
Dereham Cl NE26 . . . 24 D5
Dereham Ct NE5 . . . 37 B4
Dereham Rd NE26 . . . 24 D5
Dereham Terr NE62 . . . 11 C8
Dereham Way NE29 . . . 41 B8
Derry Ave SR6 . . . 75 E4
Derwent Ave
Gateshead NE11 . . . 70 D5
Hebburn NE31 . . . 57 E3
Newburn NE15 . . . 52 E7
Rowlands Gill NE39 . . . 67 E1
Derwent Cote NE17 . . . 77 B5
Derwentcote Steel Furnace* NE17 . . . 77 E6
Derwent Cres
Hamsterley NE17 . . . 77 B5
Whickham NE16 . . . 69 B8
Derwent Crook Dr NE9 . . . 70 E5
Derwent Ct
Gateshead NE11 . . . 70 D5
Newcastle upon Tyne NE7 . . . 39 A4
Derwentdale Gdns NE7 . . . 39 B3
Derwent Gdns
Gateshead NE9 . . . 71 A5
Wallsend NE28 . . . 41 A4
DERWENT HAUGH . . . 54 B2
Derwenthaugh Ind Est NE16 . . . 53 F3
Derwenthaugh Marina NE21 . . . 54 A3
Derwenthaugh Rd NE21 . . . 54 A3
Derwent Haven NE17 . . . 77 B5
Derwent Rd
Hexham NE46 . . . 45 C4
Seaton Sluice NE26 . . . 24 C6
Tynemouth NE30 . . . 32 B2
Derwent St
Blackhall Mill NE17 . . . 77 C6
Chopwell NE17 . . . 66 B1
Hetton-le-Hole DH5 . . . 95 B2
Newcastle upon Tyne NE15 . . . 54 B5
Penshaw DH4 . . . 90 B6
Sunderland SR1 . . . 102 C2
Derwent Terr
Burnopfield NE16 . . . 79 B7
South Hetton DH6 . . . 97 E8
Washington NE38 . . . 83 E4
Derwent Tower 4 NE11 . . . 100 A1
Derwent Valley Cotts NE39 . . . 67 F1
Derwent Valley Villas NE17 . . . 77 A6
Derwent View
Blaydon NE21 . . . 53 B1
Burnopfield NE16 . . . 79 B6
Chopwell NE17 . . . 66 C2
Derwent View Terr DH9 . . . 78 D1
Derwent Walk Ctry Pk* NE16, NE21, NE39 . . . 68 C5
Derwentwater Ave 1 DH2 . . . 88 B1
Derwentwater Ct NE8 . . . 101 A1
Derwentwater Gdns NE16 . . . 69 D7
Derwentwater Rd
Gateshead NE8 . . . 100 C1
Gateshead NE9 . . . 70 B8
Newbeggin-by-the-Sea NE64 . . . 7 C3
Derwentwater Terr NE33 . . . 59 C8
Derwent Way
Blaydon NE21 . . . 53 E1
Killingworth NE12 . . . 29 C3
Deuchar Ho NE2 . . . 99 C3
Deuchar St NE2 . . . 99 C4
Devon Ave NE16 . . . 69 C7
Devon Cl NE63 . . . 5 F4
Devon Cres DH3 . . . 82 B6
Devon Dr SR3 . . . 92 A8
Devon Gdns
Gateshead NE9 . . . 70 F7
South Shields NE34 . . . 60 B7
Devonport DH4 . . . 90 C3
Devon Rd
Hebburn NE31 . . . 57 F3
Tynemouth NE29 . . . 31 D1
Devonshire Dr NE27 . . . 30 C1
Devonshire Gdns NE28 . . . 40 A3
Devonshire Pl NE2 . . . 38 F1
Devonshire St
South Shields NE33 . . . 59 B7
Sunderland SR5 . . . 75 C1
Devonshire Terr
Newcastle upon Tyne NE2 . . . 99 A3
7 Whitley Bay NE26 . . . 32 B4
Devonshire Twr 1 SR5 . . . 75 D1
Devon St
Hetton-le-Hole DH5 . . . 94 F4
Penshaw DH4 . . . 90 C6
Devon Wlk NE37 . . . 72 D1
Devonworth Pl NE24 . . . 17 A7
De Walden Sq NE61 . . . 4 E3
De Walden Terr NE61 . . . 4 F3
Dewberry Cl NE24 . . . 17 C4
Dewhurst Terr 5 NE16 . . . 69 B2
Dewley NE23 . . . 22 B5
Dewley Ct NE23 . . . 22 B5
Dewley Pl NE5 . . . 36 E4
Dewley Rd NE5 . . . 37 B1
Dewsgreen NE23 . . . 22 B6
Dexter Ho NE29 . . . 41 D3
Dexter Way NE10 . . . 71 C8
Deyncourt NE20 . . . 25 D2
Deyncourt Cl NE20 . . . 25 D1
Diamond Ct NE3 . . . 37 D5
Diamond Hall Jun & Inf Sch 11 SR4 . . . 85 F7
Diamond Sq 5 NE46 . . . 45 B4
Diana St NE4 . . . 98 B1
Dibley Sq 5 NE6 . . . 56 B5
Dibley St 6 NE6 . . . 56 B5
Dickens Ave
Biddick Hall NE34 . . . 59 B3
Whickham NE16 . . . 69 A8
Dickens St
Houghton-le-Spring DH4 . . . 94 D8
Sunderland SR5 . . . 75 A1
Dickens Wlk NE5 . . . 36 C3
Dickson Dr NE46 . . . 44 E3
Dick St 12 NE40 . . . 51 F3
Didcot Ave NE29 . . . 41 E4
Didcot Way NE36 . . . 73 E7
Dillon St NE32 . . . 58 A5
DILSTON . . . 46 D3
Dilston Ave
Hexham NE46 . . . 45 D
Whitley Bay NE25 . . . 32 B
Dilston Cl
Pegswood NE61 . . . 5 A
Shiremoor NE27 . . . 30 F
Washington NE38 . . . 83 A
Dilston Dr
Ashington NE63 . . . 6 D
Newcastle upon Tyne NE5 . . . 36 E
Dilston Gdns SR4 . . . 85 F
Dilston Grange NE28 . . . 41 A
Dilston Haugh Cotts NE45 . . . 46 D
Dilston Rd NE4 . . . 98 A
Dilston Terr
Jarrow NE32 . . . 58 C
Newcastle upon Tyne NE3 . . . 38 E
Dilston West Cotts NE45 . . . 46 C
Dimbula Gdns NE7 . . . 39 D
Dinmont Pl NE23 . . . 22 B
DINNINGTON . . . 27 A
Dinnington Fst Sch NE13 . . . 27 C
Dinsdale Ave NE28 . . . 40 C
Dinsdale Cotts 3 SR2 . . . 92 F
Dinsdale Pl NE2 . . . 99 C
Dinsdale Rd
Newcastle upon Tyne NE2 . . . 99 C
2 Sunderland SR6 . . . 75 E
Dinsdale St SR2 . . . 92 F
Dinsdale Street S SR2 . . . 92 F
Dipe La NE36 . . . 74 B
DIPTON . . . 78 D
Dipton Ave NE4 . . . 54 E
Dipton Cl NE46 . . . 45 E
Dipton Gdns SR3 . . . 86 B
Dipton Gr NE23 . . . 22 B
Dipton Mill Rd NE46 . . . 45 B
Dipton Rd NE25 . . . 31 D
Dipwood Rd NE39 . . . 67 E
Dipwood Way NE39 . . . 78 D
Discovery Ct SR3 . . . 91 F
Discovery Mus* NE1 . . . 100 C
Dishforth Gn NE9 . . . 71 E
Dispensary La 2 NE1 . . . 99 A
Disraeli St
Blyth NE24 . . . 17 D
Blyth NE24 . . . 17 E
Fence Houses DH4 . . . 94 E
Disraeli Terr NE17 . . . 66 E
Dissington Pl
Newcastle upon Tyne NE5 . . . 54 C
Whickham NE16 . . . 69 A
Ditchburn Terr SR4 . . . 85
Dixon Ave DH8 . . . 76
Dixon Pl NE11 . . . 69
Dixon Rd DH5 . . . 94
Dixon's Sq SR6 . . . 103
Dixon St
Gateshead NE8 . . . 100 C
South Shields NE33 . . . 42 C
Dobson Cl NE4 . . . 100
Dobson Cres NE6 . . . 56
Dockendale La 1 NE16 . . . 69
Dockendale Mews 2 NE16 . . . 69
Dock Rd NE29 . . . 42
Dock Road S NE29 . . . 42
Dock St
South Shields NE33 . . . 59
Sunderland SR6 . . . 75
Dockwray Cl NE30 . . . 42
Dockwray Sq NE30 . . . 42
Doddfell Cl NE37 . . . 83
Doddington Cl NE15 . . . 53
Doddington Dr NE23 . . . 22
Doddington Villas NE10 . . . 71
Dodds Ct 3 SR5 . . . 74
Dodds Farm NE3 . . . 38
Dodds Terr DH3 . . . 82
Dodsworth N NE40 . . . 52
Dodsworth Terr NE40 . . . 52
Dodsworth Villas NE40 . . . 52
Dog Bank NE1 . . . 101
Dogger Bank NE61 . . . 3
Dolphin Ct 1 NE4 . . . 54
Dolphin Quay NE29 . . . 42
Dolphin St NE4 . . . 54
Dolphin Villas NE13 . . . 28
Dominies Cl NE39 . . . 67
Donald Ave DH6 . . . 97
Donald St NE3 . . . 38
Doncaster Rd NE2 . . . 99

Doncrest Rd NE37 . . . . .72 B1
Don Dixon Dr NE32 . . . . . . .58 B1
Don Gdns
  Washington NE37 . . . . .72 D1
  West Boldon NE36 . . . . . . .73 F7
Donkin Rd ■ NE37 . . . . .82 F7
Donkins St NE35 . . . . .58 E1
Donkin Terr
  Crawcrook NE40 . . . . .51 E3
  North Shields NE30 . . . . . . .42 C7
Donnington Ho ■ SR3 . . . . . .91 D7
Donnington Ct SR5 . . . . .74 A1
Donnington Ct NE3 . . . . .38 F4
Donnison Gdns SR1 . . . . . . .103 B3
Don Rd NE32 . . . . .58 D7
Donridge NE37 . . . . .72 B1
Donside NE10 . . . . .71 F4
Don St NE11 . . . . .70 C4
Donvale Rd NE37 . . . . .72 A1
Don View NE36 . . . . .74 A7
DONWELL 72 B1
Dorcas Ave NE15 . . . . .54 C5
Dorcas Terr ■ NE37 . . . . . . .83 D8
Dorchester Cl NE5 . . . . .36 B3
Dorchester Ct NE25 . . . . . . .23 C6
Dorchester Gdns NE9 . . . . . .70 F2
Doris Wilkes Ho NE6 . . . . . . .56 B6
Dorking Ave NE29 . . . . .41 C4
Dorking Ct NE24 . . . . .17 E4
Dorking Rd NE5 . . . . .75 E4
Dornoch Cres NE10 . . . . .71 E6
Dorrington Rd NE3 . . . . .37 E7
Dorset Ave
  Birtley DH3 . . . . .82 D1
  Hebburn NE31 . . . . .57 F5
  South Shields NE34 . . . . . . .60 B7
  Sunderland SR6 . . . . .75 E4
  Wallsend NE28 . . . . .40 A3
Dorset Cl NE23 . . . . .5 F4
Dorset Gr NE29 . . . . .31 D1
Dorset Rd
  Gateshead NE8 . . . . .56 A4
  Newcastle upon Tyne NE15 . .53 F6
Dorset St DH5 . . . . .97 C8
Dotland Cl NE46 . . . . .45 E4
Double Row NE25 . . . . .23 B5
Douglas Ave NE3 . . . . .38 A4
Douglas Bader Ho ■
  NE24 . . . . .17 F6
Douglas Cl NE34 . . . . .59 C4
Douglas Ct
  Gateshead NE11 . . . . .70 E2
  Sunderland SR1 . . . . .103 B3
Douglas Gdns NE11 . . . . .70 A7
Douglas Par NE31 . . . . .58 D2
Douglas Rd SR6 . . . . .75 E4
Douglas St ■ NE28 . . . . .40 B2
Douglas St NE28 . . . . .41 A1
Douglas Terr
  Newcastle upon Tyne NE4 . . .98 B1
  Penshaw DH4 . . . . .90 C8
  Washington NE37 . . . . .72 D1
Doulting Cl NE12 . . . . .39 B6
Doulton Dr SR4 . . . . .85 A4
Dove Ave NE32 . . . . .58 C3
Dove Cl NE12 . . . . .29 C4
Dovecote Cl NE25 . . . . .31 C6
Dovecote Rd NE12 . . . . .39 E7
Dovecrest Ct ■ NE28 . . . . . . .40 F4
Dove Ct
  ■ Birtley DH3 . . . . .82 C5
  Tynemouth NE30 . . . . .32 C3
Dovedale Ave NE24 . . . . .17 A8
Dovedale Ct ■ NE34 . . . . . . .59 A5
Dovedale Gdns
  Gateshead NE9 . . . . .71 A4
  Newcastle upon Tyne NE7 . . .39 B3
Dovedale Rd SR6 . . . . .75 C5
Dove Ho NE30 . . . . .32 C3
Dover Cl
  Bedlington NE22 . . . . .10 D1
  Newcastle upon Tyne NE5 . . .36 C3
Dovercourt Rd NE6 . . . . .57 A4
Dove Row NE30 . . . . .32 C2
Dowding La NE3 . . . . .37 D3
Dowling Ave NE25 . . . . .31 F4
Down at the Farm* DH5 . .91 B2
Downend Rd NE5 . . . . .36 E3
Downfield NE37 . . . . .72 D3
Downham NE5 . . . . .36 F1
Downham Ct NE33 . . . . .42 C1
DOWNHILL 74 B4
Downhill La
  Sunderland SR5, NE36 . . . . .73 F3
  Town End Farm SR5 . . . . . . .73 D3
  West Boldon NE36 . . . . .73 D4
Downing Dr NE61 . . . . .8 E7
Downs La DH5 . . . . .95 B5
Downs Pit La DH5 . . . . .95 C5
Downswood NE12 . . . . .29 F3
Doxford Ave NE6 . . . . .56 C7
Doxford Gdns ■ NE5 . . . . . . .37 D1
Doxford International Bus Pk
  SR3 .91 C5
Doxford Park Ho NE61 . . . . . .91 E6
Doxford Park Way SR3 . . . . .91 E6
Doxford Pl NE23 . . . . .22 B5
Doxford Terr NE5 . . . . .94 F6
Drake Cl NE33 . . . . .59 B8
Drawback NE42 . . . . .50 D1
Drawback Cl NE42 . . . . .50 D2
Drayton Rd
  Newcastle upon Tyne NE3 . . .37 E4
  Sunderland SR6 . . . . .75 D4
Drey The NE20 . . . . .25 B3
Drivecote NE10 . . . . .71 E8
Drive Prim Sch The NE10 . . .71 E8

Drive The
  Birtley DH3 . . . . .82 D1
  Gateshead, Felling NE10 . . . .71 E8
  Gateshead, Saltwell NE9 . . . .70 F6
  Newcastle upon Tyne, East
    Denton NE5 . . . . .54 A8
  Newcastle upon Tyne, Gosforth
    NE3 . . . . .38 C3
  Newcastle upon Tyne NE7 . . .39 B4
  Stannington NE61 . . . . .14 D6
  Tranwell NE61 . . . . .8 C3
  Tynemouth NE30 . . . . .42 D8
  Wallsend NE28 . . . . .40 B2
  Washington NE37 . . . . .72 C1
  Whickham NE16 . . . . .69 C6
Dronfield Cl ■ DH2 . . . . .88 A1
Drove Rd NE15 . . . . .35 B3
Dr Pit Cotts NE22 . . . . .10 F1
Dr Ryman Ho NE6 . . . . .57 A5
Drumaldrace ■ NE37 . . . . . . .83 A6
Drum Ind Est DH2 . . . . .88 B7
Drummond Cres NE34 . . . . . .58 F5
Drummond Rd NE3 . . . . .37 F4
Drummond Terr NE30 . . . . . .42 B6
Drumoyne Cl SR3 . . . . .91 B6
Drumoyne Gdns NE26 . . . . . .31 D3
Drum Rd DH2, DH3 . . . . .88 B8
Drumsheugh Pl NE5 . . . . .91 B2
Druridge Ave SR6 . . . . .75 E5
Druridge Cres
  Blyth NE24 . . . . .17 B5
  South Shields NE34 . . . . .60 B8
Druridge Dr
  Blyth NE24 . . . . .17 B5
  Newcastle upon Tyne NE5 . . .37 D1
Drury La
  Newcastle upon Tyne NE1 . . .99 A1
  Sunderland SR1 . . . . .103 B3
  Tynemouth NE29 . . . . .41 C7
Drybeck Ct
  Cramlington NE23 . . . . .22 D8
  Newcastle upon Tyne NE4 . . .98 B1
Drybeck Sq SR3 . . . . .92 B6
Drybeck Wlk NE27 . . . . .30 C1
Dryborough St SR4 . . . . .102 B3
Dryburgh NE38 . . . . .83 D5
Dryburgh Cl NE29 . . . . .41 E8
Dryden Cl NE34 . . . . .59 B2
Dryden Ct ■ NE9 . . . . .70 F8
Dryden Rd NE9 . . . . .70 F7
Dryden Sch NE9 . . . . .71 A7
Dryden St SR5 . . . . .75 A2
Drysdale Cres NE13 . . . . .28 B6
Drysdale Ct NE13 . . . . .28 B6
Dubmire Cotts DH4 . . . . .94 A8
Dubmire Ct DH4 . . . . .94 A8
Dubmire Ind Est DH4 . . . . . . .94 A8
Dubmire Prim Sch DH4 . . . . .94 A8
Duchess Cres NE32 . . . . .58 C7
Duchess Crescent E NE32 .58 B3
Duchess Dr NE15 . . . . .54 A7
Duchess St NE26 . . . . .32 A5
Duckets Dean NE42 . . . . .50 D3
Duckpool La NE16 . . . . .69 C8
Duckpool Lane N NE16 . . . . .69 C8
Duddon Pl NE9 . . . . .71 B4
DUDLEY 29 A7
Dudley Ave SR6 . . . . .75 D4
Dudley Bsns Ctr NE23 . . . . . .22 A2
Dudley Ct NE23 . . . . .29 B8
Dudley Gdns SR3 . . . . .91 C7
Dudley Ho NE4 . . . . .98 B2
Dudley La
  Annitsford NE23 . . . . .22 A2
  Cramlington, Collingwood
    NE23 . . . . .22 A4
  Cramlington, Hall Close
    NE23 . . . . .22 A4
  Seaton Burn NE13, NE23 . . . .28 D8
Dudley Lane Cotts NE13 . . . .28 C8
Dugdale Ct ■ NE6 . . . . .37 D5
Duke of Northumberland Ct
  NE28 . . . . .40 E5
Duke's Ave NE31 . . . . .57 D4
Dukes Cott NE15 . . . . .52 F7
Duke's Ct NE6 . . . . .58 D4
Dukesfield NE23 . . . . .22 B6
Duke's Gdns NE24 . . . . .17 C8
Dukes Mdw NE13 . . . . .36 E8
Dukes Meadow NE27 . . . . . .30 B5
Duke St
  Ashington NE63 . . . . .6 C4
  Gateshead NE10 . . . . .57 A1
  Newcastle upon Tyne NE1 .100 C4
  North Shields NE29 . . . . .42 B4
  Sunderland SR4 . . . . .102 A2
  Whitley Bay NE26 . . . . .32 A5
Duke Street N SR6 . . . . .75 D2
Dukeshay NE11 . . . . .70 C4
Dukes Way NE42 . . . . .50 E4
Dukesway C NE11 . . . . .70 C2
Dukesway NE11 . . . . .70 C2
Duke Wlk NE8 . . . . .100 C1
Dulverton Cl NE5 . . . . .36 C3
Dulverton Ave NE33 . . . . . . .59 D7
Dulverton Ct NE12 . . . . .38 F2
Dumas Wlk NE5 . . . . .36 C3
Dumbarton Cl SR4 . . . . .85 D3
Dumfries Cl ■ SR4 . . . . .85 D3
Dumfries Cres NE32 . . . . .58 E3
Dunbar Cl NE5 . . . . .36 C3
Dunbar St SR4 . . . . .85 F5
Dunblane Cres NE5 . . . . .36 C3
Dunblane Dr NE24 . . . . .17 E4
Dunblane Rd SR6 . . . . .75 E4

Dunbreck Gr SR4 . . . . .86 A4
Duncan Gdns NE61 . . . . .8 F7
Duncan St
  Gateshead NE8 . . . . .56 B1
  Newcastle upon Tyne NE6 . . .57 A5
  Sunderland SR4 . . . . .85 F7
Dunces Hos NE61 . . . . .9 D7
Dun Cow St SR1 . . . . .102 C3
Dundas St SR6 . . . . .103 A4
Dundas Way NE10 . . . . .71 C8
Dundee Cl NE5 . . . . .36 C3
Dundee Ct NE32 . . . . .58 E3
Dundrennan NE38 . . . . .83 C3
Dunelm SR2 . . . . .86 B4
Dunelm Cl ■ DH3 . . . . .82 C4
Dunelm Dr
  Houghton-le-Spring DH4 . . . .94 D7
  West Boldon NE36 . . . . .74 B8
Dunelm Grange NE35 . . . . . .73 E8
Dunelm Rd DH5 . . . . .94 F4
Dunelm S NE34 . . . . .86 B4
Dunelm St NE33 . . . . .42 D2
Dunford Gdns NE5 . . . . .36 D4
Dunholm Cl DH5 . . . . .94 E7
Dunholme Rd NE4 . . . . .54 F5
Dunira Cl NE2 . . . . .38 F2
Dunira Ho NE2 . . . . .38 F2
Dunkeld Cl
  Blyth NE24 . . . . .17 E4
  Gateshead NE10 . . . . .72 C8
  Shiney Row DH4 . . . . .89 F5
Dunkirk Ave DH5 . . . . .94 F7
Dunlin Cl NE40 . . . . .52 E4
Dunlin Ct NE61 . . . . .2 A3
Dunlin Dr
  Blyth NE24 . . . . .17 E4
  Washington NE38 . . . . .82 F3
Dunlop Cl NE7 . . . . .39 C4
Dunlop Cres NE34 . . . . .60 A6
Dunmoor Cl NE3 . . . . .38 A4
Dunmoor Ct DH2 . . . . .88 A1
Dunmore Ave NE34 . . . . .75 E4
Dunmorlie St NE6 . . . . .56 D6
Dunn Ave SR3 . . . . .86 A1
Dunn Rd NE21 . . . . .53 E4
Dunning St SR1 . . . . .102 C3
Dunnlynn Cl SR3 . . . . .91 E6
Dunnock Ct NE15 . . . . .53 D6
Dunnock Dr
  Sunnside NE16 . . . . .69 A3
  Washington NE38 . . . . .82 F3
Dunnock Lodge NE15 . . . . . .53 D6
Dunns Terr NE2 . . . . .38 A4
Dunn's Terr NE2 . . . . .98 B4
Dunn Street Prim Sch
  NE32 . . . . .58 C7
Dunns Way NE21 . . . . .53 C2
Dunn Terr NE6 . . . . .56 B6
Dunnykirk Ave ■ NE3 . . . . . .37 D5
Dunraven Cl NE3 . . . . .28 A1
Dunrobin Pl NE5 . . . . .36 C3
Dunsany Terr DH4 . . . . .90 B1
Dunsdale Dr NE23 . . . . .22 D8
Dunsdale Rd NE25 . . . . .23 E2
Dunsgreen NE20 . . . . .25 E5
Dunsgreen Ct NE20 . . . . .25 E5
Dunsley Gdns NE13 . . . . .27 B7
Dunslow Croft NE15 . . . . .33 C1
Dunsmuir Gr NE8 . . . . .70 D8
Dunstable Pl NE5 . . . . .36 B3
Dunstanburgh Cl NE22 . . . . .10 D1
Dunstanburgh Ct
  Bedlington NE22 . . . . .10 D1
  Newcastle upon Tyne NE6 . . .56 D5
  Washington NE38 . . . . .83 B4
Dunstanburgh Rd NE6 . . . . . .56 D5
Dunstan Cl DH2 . . . . .88 A1
Dunstan Wlk NE5 . . . . .36 F1
Dunster Ho ■ SR3 . . . . .91 D7
DUNSTON 100 A1
Dunston Bank NE11 . . . . .69 F7
Dunston Ent Pk NE11 . . . . . .54 E2
DUNSTON HILL 69 E7
Dunston Hill Com Prim Sch
  NE11 . . . . .69 E8
Dunston Hill Hospl NE11 . . . .69 D7
Dunston Pl NE11 . . . . .17 B8
Dunston Pool NE11 . . . . .69 E8
Dunston Rd NE11 . . . . .54 F1
Dunston Riverside Prim Sch
  NE11 . . . . .70 A8
Dunston Sta NE11 . . . . .70 A8
Dunston Workshops NE11 .54 F2
Dunvegan DH3 . . . . .82 E2
Dunvegan Ave DH2 . . . . .88 B1
Dunwood NE4 . . . . .85 B7
Dunwoodie Terr ■ NE46 . . . .45 A5
Du004 Terr SR2 . . . . .103 A1
Durant Rd NE1 . . . . .99 B2
Durban St NE24 . . . . .17 D8
Durham Ave NE37 . . . . .72 D2
Durham Cl NE22 . . . . .10 D2
Durham Ct NE31 . . . . .57 D5
Durham Gr NE32 . . . . .58 B2
Durham Ho NE5 . . . . .73 F4
Durham La
  Haswell DH6 . . . . .97 C1
  Sherburn Hill DH6 . . . . .96 D1
Durham Pl
  Birtley DH3 . . . . .82 D1
  Gateshead NE8 . . . . .101 C4
Durham Rd
  Birtley DH3 . . . . .82 C3

Durham Rd continued
  Chester le Street, Barley Mow
    DH3 . . . . .88 C8
  Chester le Street DH3 . . . . . .88 C1
  Cramlington NE23 . . . . .16 C1
  East Rainton DH5 . . . . .94 C4
  Gateshead NE8, NE9 . . . . . . .70 F6
  Houghton-le-Spring DH5 . . . .90 F3
  Houghton-le-Spring DH5 . . . .94 E7
  Sunderland SR3 . . . . .85 E2
Durham Road Trad Est
  Barley Mow DH3 . . . . .82 C1
  Chester le Street DH3 . . . . . .88 C8
Durham St
  Fence Houses DH4 . . . . .94 A8
  ■ Gateshead NE10 . . . . .71 D8
  Newcastle upon Tyne NE4 . . .54 F5
  Wallsend NE28 . . . . .40 C2
Durham Street W NE28 . . . . .40 C2
Durham Terr SR3 . . . . .86 A1
Durken Bsns Pk NE23 . . . . . .22 F7
Dutton Cl NE21 . . . . .53 E4
Duxbury Pk NE38 . . . . .89 D8
Duxfield Rd NE7 . . . . .39 B3
Dwyer Cres SR2 . . . . .92 F6
Dyer Sq SR5 . . . . .75 B2
Dykefield Ave NE3 . . . . .37 E7
Dyke Heads La NE40 . . . . . . .52 B1
Dykelands Rd SR6 . . . . .75 E5
Dykelands Way NE34 . . . . . . .58 F3
Dykenook Cl NE16 . . . . .69 A4
Dykes Way NE10 . . . . .71 D5
Dymock Ct NE3 . . . . .37 B5

E

Eaglescliffe Dr NE7 . . . . .39 D2
Ealing Cl NE3 . . . . .37 B6
Ealing Dr NE30 . . . . .32 C1
Ealing Sq NE23 . . . . .21 D6
Eardulph Ave DH3 . . . . .88 D3
Earl Grey Way NE29 . . . . .41 F3
Earlington Ct NE12 . . . . .29 E1
Earls Ct
  Gateshead DH98 . . . . .70 D5
  Prudhoe NE42 . . . . .50 E4
  Sunderland SR5 . . . . .75 A4
Earls Dene ■ NE9 . . . . .70 F4
Earls Dr NE9 . . . . .70 F4
Earl's Dr NE15 . . . . .54 A7
Earls Gn DH5 . . . . .17 C8
Earlsmeadow NE27 . . . . .30 F4
Earls Park North Trad Est
  NE11 . . . . .70 C7
Earl St SR4 . . . . .102 B2
Earlston St SR5 . . . . .75 A4
Earlston Way NE23 . . . . .16 B4
Earsway DH98, NE11, NE82 .70 D5
Earsdon Cl ■ NE5 . . . . .70 F4
Earsdon Gr NE24 . . . . .17 D3
Earlswood Pk NE9 . . . . .70 F4
Earnshaw Way NE25 . . . . . . .31 D7
EARSDON 31 A5
Earsdon Cl NE25 . . . . .37 A1
Earsdon Ct NE25 . . . . .31 D4
Earsdon Rd
  Houghton-le-Spring NE3 . . . .94 F8
  Newcastle upon Tyne NE3 . . .37 E3
  Shiremoor NE27 . . . . .30 E4
  Whitley Bay NE25 . . . . .31 C4
Earsdon Terr
  ■ Ryhope SR2 . . . . .92 F6
  ■ Shiremoor NE27 . . . . .30 F1
Earsdon View NE27 . . . . .30 F4
Earth Balance* NE22 . . . . . .11 C5
Easby Cl NE3 . . . . .38 D8
Easby Rd NE38 . . . . .83 D4
Easdale Ave NE3 . . . . .28 C1
Easedale NE26 . . . . .24 C6
Easedale Gdns NE9 . . . . .71 B3
Easington Ave
  Cramlington NE23 . . . . .16 B3
  Gateshead NE9 . . . . .71 C3
Easington Lane Prim Sch
  DH5 .97 D8
Easington St SR5 . . . . .102 C4
Easington Street N SR5 . .102 C4
East Acres
  Blaydon NE21 . . . . .53 D1
  Dinnington NE13 . . . . .27 C8
East Ave
  Longbenton NE12 . . . . .39 D6
  South Shields NE34 . . . . .60 A6
  Washington NE38 . . . . .83 B1
  Whitley Bay NE25 . . . . .31 E5
East Back Par SR2 . . . . .103 C3
East Bailey NE12 . . . . .29 F3
East Benton Cotts NE12 . . . .39 E5
EAST BOLDON 74 D7
East Boldon Inf Sch NE34 .74 D7
East Boldon Jun Sch
  NE36 . . . . .74 D7
East Boldon Rd SR6 . . . . .59 F1
East Boldon Sta NE36 . . . . . .74 E8
Eastbourne Ave
  Gateshead NE8 . . . . .70 E8
  Newcastle upon Tyne NE6 . . .57 A6
Eastbourne Ct ■ NE6 . . . . . .57 A6
Eastbourne Gdns
  Cramlington NE23 . . . . .21 D6
  Newcastle upon Tyne NE6 . . .57 A6
  Whitley Bay NE26 . . . . .32 A6
Eastbourne Gr ■ SR2 . . . . . .92 F6
Eastbourne Par NE31 . . . . . . .58 A2
Eastbourne Sq SR5 . . . . .75 A4

East Bridge St DH4 . . . . .83 E1
Eastburn Gdns NE10 . . . . . . .57 B2
Eastbury Ave ■ NE15 . . . . . .53 F8
Eastcheap NE6 . . . . .39 C1
East Cl NE34 . . . . .60 A6
East Cleft Rd SR2 . . . . .102 B2
Eastcliffe Ave NE3 . . . . .38 A3
Eastcombe Cl NE35 . . . . .58 E2
Eastcote Terr NE6 . . . . .56 F4
EAST CRAMLINGTON 22 E5
East Cramlington Ind Est
  NE23 . . . . .22 E5
East Cres NE22 . . . . .11 D2
East Cross St SR1 . . . . .103 A3
EAST DENTON 37 A1
East Dr
  Blyth NE24 . . . . .17 C4
  Cleadon NE36 . . . . .74 F8
East End NE26 . . . . .24 E4
Easten Terr NE28 . . . . .41 C1
Easterfield Ct NE61 . . . . .4 A1
Easter Gdns ■ NE9 . . . . .70 D4
Eastern Gdns ■ NE10 . . . . . .56 D1
Eastern Way
  Newcastle upon Tyne NE5 . . .37 D2
  Ponteland NE20 . . . . .25 D3
East Farm Ct NE16 . . . . .69 C3
East Farm Terr NE23 . . . . . . .22 B6
EASTFIELD 22 D8
Eastfield Ave
  Newcastle upon Tyne NE28,
    NE6 . . . . .57 A8
  Whitley Bay NE25 . . . . .31 D4
Eastfield Ho NE6 . . . . .57 A8
Eastfield Rd
  Longbenton NE12 . . . . .39 D6
  South Shields NE34 . . . . .59 F8
Eastfields NE46 . . . . .45 D4
East Fields SR6 . . . . .75 F8
Eastfield St SR4 . . . . .85 F5
Eastfield Terr NE12 . . . . .39 D6
East Ford Rd NE62 . . . . .11 C8
East Forest Hall Rd NE12 . .39 E8
East Front ■ NE2 . . . . .99 B4
Eastgarth
  Kenton Bankfoot NE5 . . . . . .37 A5
  Newcastle upon Tyne NE5 . . .37 A5
Eastgate
  Choppington NE62 . . . . .10 F5
  Hexham NE46 . . . . .45 B4
East Gate
  Gateshead NE8 . . . . .101 C3
  Morpeth NE61 . . . . .9 A6
Eastgate Bank NE43 . . . . . . .64 F8
Eastgate Gdns NE4 . . . . .54 E4
EAST GATESHEAD 56 B3
East George Potts St ■
  NE33 . . . . .42 D1
East George St NE30 . . . . . . .42 C6
East Gr SR4 . . . . .85 B5
East Grange
  Holywell NE25 . . . . .23 F2
  Sunderland SR5 . . . . .75 C3
Eastgreen NE62 . . . . .10 F5
EAST HARTFORD 16 B3
East Hartford Sch NE23 . . . .16 B3
EAST HERRINGTON 91 C6
East Herrington Prim Sch
  SR3 .91 C7
East Hill Rd NE8 . . . . .56 B1
East Holborn NE33 . . . . .42 B2
EAST HOLYWELL 30 E7
EAST HOWDON 41 C2
Eastlands
  Blaydon NE21 . . . . .53 B1
  Chester le Street NE38 . . . . .88 E7
  Newcastle upon Tyne NE7 . . .39 A3
East Law DH8 . . . . .76 D1
East Lea
  Blaydon NE21 . . . . .68 C8
  Newbiggin-by-the-Sea NE64 . .7 F1
Eastleigh Cl NE35 . . . . .73 E8
East Loan NE61 . . . . .4 A2
East Moffet St ■ NE33 . . . . .42 D1
East Moor Rd SR4 . . . . .85 F7
East Oakwood NE46 . . . . . . .45 E8
East Parade
  Newcastle upon Tyne NE26 . .32 B6
  Whitley Bay NE26 . . . . .32 B6
East Par NE26 . . . . .32 B5
East Park Gdns NE21 . . . . . . .53 C1
East Park Rd NE9 . . . . .70 F6
East Park View NE24 . . . . . . .18 A2
East Pastures NE63 . . . . .6 B2
East Percy St NE30 . . . . .42 C6
EAST RAINTON 94 D4
East Rainton Prim Sch
  DH5 .94 C4
East Riggs NE22 . . . . .15 F8
East Sea View NE64 . . . . .7 F5
East SLEEKBURN 11 A3
East St
  Chopwell NE17 . . . . .66 D1
  Gateshead NE8 . . . . .101 C3
  Hebburn NE31 . . . . .57 F7
  High Spen NE39 . . . . .66 F4
  Mickley Square NE43 . . . . . .49 F1
  ■ South Shields NE33 . . . . . .42 D1
  Tynemouth NE30 . . . . .42 D7
East Stainton St ■ NE33 . .42 D1
East Stevenson St ■
  NE33 . . . . .42 D1
East Tanfield Sta* DH9 . .79 D2
East Terr
  Chopwell NE17 . . . . .77 C7
  Stakeford NE62 . . . . .11 C7

East Thorp NE5 . . . . .36 F5
East View
🖪 Bedlington NE22. . . . . .11 D3
Blaydon NE21 . . . . .53 D3
Boldon Colliery NE35. . . . . .73 F8
Burnopfield NE16. . . . . .79 A6
Crawcrook NE40 . . . . .51 E6
Hebburn NE31. . . . . .57 D4
Morpeth NE61 . . . . .9 A8
New Hartley NE25 . . . . .23 C5
Rowlands Gill NE39 . . . . . . .67 C2
Ryhope SR2. . . . . .92 E6
🗖 Seaham SR7. . . . . .92 F1
Seghill NE23 . . . . .22 F2
Sherburn Hill DH6 . . . . .96 D1
Stakeford NE62 . . . . .11 C7
Sunderland, Castletown SR5 74 C1
Sunderland, Monkwearmouth
SR6. . . . . .75 E3
Wideopen NE13. . . . . .28 B7
East View Ave NE23 . . . . . . .22 B6
East View S 🖪 SR5. . . . . . .74 C1
East View Terr
Dudley NE23 . . . . .29 A8
Fordley NE23 . . . . .29 A8
Gateshead NE10 . . . . .71 F6
Whickham NE16. . . . . .69 B8
East Villas DH6 . . . . .97 F4
East Vines SR1. . . . . .103 C3
Eastward Gn NE25. . . . . . . .31 D4
Eastward Ct NE34. . . . . .60 B5
East Wing The NE38. . . . . . .83 E5
Eastwood Ave NE24. . . . . . .17 D3
Eastwood Cl NE23 . . . . .29 C5
Eastwood Ct NE12 . . . . .39 D7
Eastwood Gdns
Gateshead, Low Fell NE9. . . .71 A6
Gateshead, Old Fold NE10. . .56 C2
Newcastle upon Tyne NE3 . . .37 F4
Eastwood Grange Ct
NE46 . . . . .45 E4
Eastwood Grange Rd
NE46 . . . . .45 D4
Eastwood Pl NE23 . . . . .16 C2
Eastwoods Rd NE42. . . . . . .50 F3
Eastwood Villas NE42 . . . . .50 F4
Eaton Cl NE38 . . . . .89 B8
Eaton Pl NE4 . . . . .54 F5
Eavers Ct NE34 . . . . .59 C5
Ebba Wlk NE3 . . . . .38 D5
EBCHESTER 76 F3
Ebchester Ave NE9. . . . . . . .71 D3
Ebchester CE Prim Sch
DH8 .76 E3
Ebchester Cl NE3 . . . . .37 C5
Ebchester Hill DH8 . . . . . . .76 F2
Ebchester Roman Fort
(Vindomora)* DH8 . . . . . . .76 E4
Ebchester St NE34 . . . . .59 A5
Ebdon La SR6 . . . . .75 D4
Ebor St
Newcastle upon Tyne NE6 . . .56 C8
South Shields NE34. . . . . . . .59 A4
Eccles Ct NE27 . . . . .30 C5
Eccles Ind Est NE27 . . . . . . .30 C4
Eccles Terr 🗖 NE27 . . . . . . .30 C1
Eccleston Cl NE27 . . . . .30 C4
Eccleston Rd NE33 . . . . .42 E2
Ecgfrid Terr NE32 . . . . .58 C4
Eddison Rd NE38 . . . . .83 F4
Eddleston NE38. . . . . .83 A1
Eddleston Ave NE3. . . . . . . .38 A3
Eddrington Gr NE5. . . . . . . .36 C2
Ede Ave
Dunston NE11 . . . . .69 F8
South Shields NE34. . . . . . . .60 A8
Eden Ave
Bedlington NE22 . . . . .16 A8
🖪 Wallsend NE28 . . . . .40 B1
Eden Dale NE40 . . . . .51 F4
Edendale Ave
Blyth NE24. . . . . .17 B8
Newcastle upon Tyne NE6 . . .56 C6
Edendale Ct
Blyth NE24. . . . . .17 B8
🗖 South Shields NE34 . . . . .59 A4
Edendale Ho NE24 . . . . .17 B8
Edendale Terr NE8 . . . . .70 F8
Edengarth 🗖 NE30 . . . . . . .32 A2
Eden Gr NE61. . . . . .9 A6
Eden House Rd SR2, SR4. .102 B1
Eden Pl NE30. . . . . .32 A1
Eden St NE28 . . . . .40 B1
Eden Street W SR1 . . . . . . .102 C3
Eden Terr
Lynemouth NE61 . . . . .2 A3
Penshaw DH4 . . . . .90 B6
Sunderland SR2 . . . . .102 B1
Eden Vale SR2 . . . . .102 B1
Eden Villas NE38 . . . . .83 E4
Eden Wlk NE32 . . . . .58 C3
Edgar St NE13 . . . . .38 F5
Edgecote NE37 . . . . .83 F8
Edgefield Ave NE3 . . . . .37 F5
Edgefield Dr NE23 . . . . .16 C2
Edgehill NE61 . . . . .9 B8
Edge Hill NE20. . . . . .25 C1
Edgehill Cl NE20 . . . . .25 C1
Edge Mount NE12. . . . . .29 E4
Edgeware Ct SR5 . . . . .75 A3

Edgeware Wlk NE4 . . . . .54 E3
Edgewell Ave NE42 . . . . . . .50 B1
Edgewell Grange NE42 . . . .50 C2
Edgewell House Rd NE42,
NE43 . . . . .65 B8
Edgewell Rd NE42 . . . . .50 B1
Edgewood
Hexham NE46 . . . . .45 D4
Ponteland NE20. . . . . .25 D2
Edgewood Ave NE22 . . . . . . .11 C1
Edgeworth Cl NE35. . . . . . . .58 E2
Edgeworth Cres SR6. . . . . . .75 D2
Edgmond Ct SR2. . . . . .92 E8
Edgware Rd NE8. . . . . .71 A8
Edhill Ave NE34. . . . . .59 A4
Edhill Gdns NE34 . . . . .58 F4
Edinburgh Ct NE3 . . . . .37 D8
Edinburgh Dr NE22 . . . . . . .10 E2
Edinburgh Rd NE32. . . . . . . .58 E4
Edinburgh Sq 🖪 SR5 . . . . . .75 A3
Edington Gdns NE40 . . . . . .51 E6
Edington Gr NE30. . . . . .32 A1
Edington Rd NE30 . . . . .32 A1
Edison Ct SR5 . . . . .75 A3
Edison Gdns NE10 . . . . .70 E7
Edith Ave NE21 . . . . .53 C2
Edith Moffat Ho 🖪 NE29 . .42 A6
Edith St
Jarrow NE32 . . . . .58 A7
Sunderland, Hendon SR2. . . .86 E4
Sunderland, Monkwearmouth
SR5. . . . . .75 C2
Tynemouth NE30 . . . . .42 C8
Edith Terr
Newbottle DH4 . . . . .90 D3
🖪 Whickham NE16. . . . . . . .69 A7
Edlingham Cl NE3 . . . . .38 A1
Edlingham Ct 🗖 DH5 . . . . . .94 F8
Edmonton Sq 🖪 SR5. . . . . .75 A3
E D Morel Terr NE17 . . . . . . .77 C8
Edmund Pl NE9. . . . . .70 F5
Edmund Rd NE27 . . . . .30 D1
Edna Terr NE5 . . . . .37 A3
Edrich Ho NE29 . . . . .41 D3
Edward Burdis St SR5. . . . . .75 B7
Edward Graveling Ho
NE30 . . . . .42 C6
Edward Ho SR2. . . . . .102 C2
Edward Pl NE4 . . . . .98 B1
Edward Rd
Bedlington NE22 . . . . .11 D3
🖪 Cramlington NE23 . . . . . .21 D6
Wallsend NE28 . . . . .40 F3
Edwards Rd NE26. . . . . .32 C4
Edward St
Blyth NE24. . . . . .17 D7
Burnopfield NE16. . . . . .79 A4
Chester le Street DH3. . . . . . .88 C3
Crawcrook NE40 . . . . .51 E3
Hebburn NE31. . . . . .57 C6
Newcastle upon Tyne NE3 . . .38 C5
New Silksworth SR3 . . . . . . .92 A7
Pegswood NE61. . . . . .4 F3
Edward's Wlk NE11 . . . . .99 A2
Edwina Gdns NE29 . . . . .41 F7
Edwin Gr NE28 . . . . .41 A3
Edwin Ave NE12 . . . . .39 E8
Edwin's Avenue S NE12 . . .39 E8
Edwin St
Brunswick Village NE13. . . . .28 A6
Houghton-le-Spring DH5 . . . .90 E1
🖾 Newcastle upon Tyne
NE6. . . . . .56 B6
Sunderland SR4 . . . . .85 E7
Edwin Terr NE40 . . . . .52 C2
Egerton Rd NE34 . . . . .59 C6
Egerton St
Newcastle upon Tyne NE4 . . .54 D4
Sunderland SR2 . . . . .103 B1
Eggleston Dr SR3. . . . . .86 A2
Egham Rd NE5 . . . . .36 C2
Eglesfield Rd NE33. . . . . . . .59 C8
Eglingham Ave NE30 . . . . . .32 C1
Eglingham Cl NE61 . . . . .9 B6
Eglinton St N SR5. . . . . .75 C1
Eglinton St SR5. . . . . .75 C1
Eglinton Twr 🖪 SR5. . . . . . .75 D1
Egremont Dr 🖪 NE9 . . . . . .71 A6
Egremont Pl NE26 . . . . .32 B4
Egremont Way NE23 . . . . . .16 C2
Egton Terr DH3 . . . . .82 C5
Eider Cl NE24. . . . . .17 E3
Eider Wlk NE12 . . . . .29 C4
Eighteenth Ave NE24 . . . . . .17 D5
Eighth Ave
Ashington NE63 . . . . .6 E2
Blyth NE24. . . . . .17 D6
Chester le Street DH2. . . . . . .88 B3
Gateshead NE11 . . . . .70 D3
Morpeth NE61. . . . . .9 B7
Newcastle upon Tyne NE6 . . .56 C8
Eighth Row NE63 . . . . .6 D1
EIGHTON BANKS 71 D1
Eighton Terr NE9. . . . . .71 E3
Eilansgate NE46 . . . . .45 A5
Eilansgate Terr NE46. . . . . .45 A5
Eilanville NE46. . . . . .45 A5
Eishort Way NE12. . . . . .39 B6
Eland Cl NE3 . . . . .37 D5
Eland Edge NE20 . . . . .25 F6
ELAND GREEN 25 E8
Eland La NE20 . . . . .25 F7
Eland View NE20. . . . . .25 F6
Elberfeld Ct NE32 . . . . .58 B6

Elder Gdns NE9. . . . . .71 C1
Elder Gr
🖪 Gateshead NE9 . . . . .70 F5
South Shields NE34. . . . . . . .59 F3
Elder Sq NE63 . . . . .6 B2
Elderwood Gdns NE11 . . . . .70 B5
Eldon Cl 🖪 NE28 . . . . .41 B1
Eldon Gdn NE1 . . . . .99 A2
Eldon La NE1 . . . . .99 A1
Eldon Pl
Newcastle upon Tyne,
Lemington NE15 . . . . .53 D7
Newcastle upon Tyne NE1 . . .99 A3
Eldon Rd
Hexham NE46 . . . . .45 D4
Newcastle upon Tyne NE15 . .53 D7
Eldon Sq NE1. . . . . .99 A2
Eldon Square Sh Ctr NE1. .99 A2
Eldon St
Gateshead NE8 . . . . .56 A2
South Shields NE33. . . . . . . .42 B1
Sunderland SR4 . . . . .102 A2
Wallsend NE28 . . . . .41 B2
Eleanor St
South Shields NE33. . . . . . . .42 D3
Tynemouth NE30 . . . . .32 C3
Eleanor Terr
Crawcrook NE40 . . . . .52 A4
🖪 Whickham NE16 . . . . .69 A7
Elemore Hall Sch DH6 . . . . .97 A5
Elemore La
Easington Lane DH5. . . . . . . .97 A7
High Pittington DH6. . . . . . . .96 E6
Hetton-le-Hole DH5. . . . . . . .96 B5
ELEMORE VALE. 97 B8
Elemore View DH6 . . . . .97 F7
Elenbel Ave NE22 . . . . .11 C1
Eleventh Ave
Blyth NE24. . . . . .17 E6
Chester le Street DH2 . . . . . .88 B3
Gateshead NE11 . . . . .70 E2
Morpeth NE61. . . . . .9 B7
Eleventh Avenue N NE11 . .70 E3
Eleventh Row NE63 . . . . .4 B3
Elfin Way NE24 . . . . .17 F4
Elford Cl NE25 . . . . .31 D5
Elfordleigh DH4. . . . . .90 C4
Elgar Ave 🖪 NE5 . . . . .36 C2
Elgin Ave NE28 . . . . .40 F4
Elgin Cl
Bedlington NE22 . . . . .11 D2
Cramlington NE23 . . . . .21 D6
Tynemouth NE29 . . . . .41 C6
Elgin Ct NE10. . . . . .57 B2
Elgin Gdns NE6 . . . . .56 F6
Elgin Pl DH3 . . . . .82 D2
Elgin Rd NE9 . . . . .71 B8
Elgin St NE32 . . . . .58 E4
Elgy Rd NE3 . . . . .38 B3
Elisabeth Ave DH3 . . . . .82 B6
Elizabeth Cres NE23 . . . . . . .29 A8
Elizabeth Ct
High Pittington NE12. . . . . . .96 C5
Longbenton NE12. . . . . .30 A1
Elizabeth Diamond Gdns
NE33 . . . . .59 B8
Elizabeth Dr NE12 . . . . .40 A8
Elizabeth Rd NE28 . . . . .41 A2
Elizabeth St
Chopwell NE17. . . . . .66 B1
East Cramlington NE23 . . . . .22 F5
Houghton-le-Spring DH5 . . . .90 E1
Newcastle upon Tyne NE6 . . .56 A6
🗖 South Shields SR2 . . . . . .42 D2
Sunderland, Castletown SR5 74 B1
Sunderland, Monkwearmouth
SR5. . . . . .75 C3
Elizabeth Woodcock
Maritime Inst The SR2. .103 A1
Ell-Dene Cres NE10. . . . . . . .71 E7
Ellen Ct 🖪 NE32. . . . . .58 B7
Ellen Terr NE37 . . . . .83 F8
Ellerbeck Cl 🖪 NE10 . . . . . .71 C8
Ellersmere Gdns NE30 . . . . .32 B2
Ellerton Way
Cramlington NE23 . . . . .16 C2
🖪 Longbenton NE12 . . . . . .71 C8
Ellesmere DH4 . . . . .89 D3
Ellesmere Ave
🗣 Newcastle upon Tyne, South
Gosforth NE3 . . . . .38 C4
Newcastle upon Tyne,
Walkergate NE5. . . . . .56 E8
Newcastle upon Tyne,
Westerhope NE5. . . . . .37 A2
Ellesmere Cl NE34. . . . . .90 A1
Ellesmere Ct
Grangetown SR2 . . . . .86 E1
Sunderland SR2 . . . . .86 E1
Ellesmere Gdns NE62 . . . . .11 C8
Ellesmere Rd NE4 . . . . .54 E5
Ellesmere Terr SR6. . . . . . . .75 E3
ELLINGTON 1 D4
Ellington Cl
Newcastle upon Tyne
NE15 . . . . .53 B7
🖪 Ryhope SR2 . . . . .92 F5
Urpeth DH2 . . . . .81 E2
Ellington Fst Sch NE61 . . . . .1 E5
Ellington Terr NE63. . . . . .5 F4
Ellington Way NE61 . . . . .1 C4
Elliot Dr NE10 . . . . .71 D8
Elliot Cl NE61 . . . . .9 B7
Elliot Rd NE10 . . . . .56 B1
Elliot Gdns NE34. . . . . .59 D2
Elliot Dr NE10 . . . . .71 D8
Elliott Gdns NE28 . . . . .40 A4

Elliott St NE24 . . . . .17 C4
Elliott Terr
Newcastle upon Tyne NE4 . . .98 A1
🖪 Washington NE37 . . . . . . .83 E8
Elliott Terrace Ind Est
NE4 .98 A1
Ellison Pl
🖪 Gateshead NE9 . . . . .70 F4
Jarrow NE32 . . . . .58 B8
Newcastle upon Tyne NE1 . . .99 B2
Ellison Rd NE11, NE8 . . . . . . .69 F8
Ellison St
Gateshead NE8 . . . . .101 C3
Hebburn NE31. . . . . .57 C7
Hebburn NE31. . . . . .57 D6
🖪 Jarrow NE32 . . . . .58 B7
Ellison Terr NE40 . . . . .51 F1
Ellison Villas
🖪 Gateshead NE8 . . . . .71 A8
Mount Pleasant. 56 A1
Ellis Rd SR5 . . . . .75 A3
Ellis Sq
Pegswood NE61. . . . . .4 F3
Sunderland SR5 . . . . .75 B3
Ellwood Gdns 🖪 NE9 . . . . .70 F8
Elm Ave
Dinnington NE13 . . . . .27 B7
Dunston NE11 . . . . .69 F7
South Shields NE34. . . . . . . .59 F4
Whickham NE16. . . . . .69 C8
Elm Bank Rd NE41 . . . . .51 B5
Elm Cl
Cramlington NE23 . . . . .16 C2
Hexham NE46 . . . . .44 E3
Elmcroft Rd NE12 . . . . .39 E7
Elm Ct NE16. . . . . .69 B5
Elm Dr
Bedlington NE22 . . . . .15 F8
Whitburn SR6. . . . . .61 A2
Elmfield DH5 . . . . .95 A6
Elmfield Cl SR3 . . . . .91 C6
Elmfield Gdns
Newcastle upon Tyne NE3 . . .38 B4
Wallsend NE28 . . . . .39 F4
Whitley Bay NE25 . . . . .31 D3
Elmfield Gr NE3 . . . . .38 B4
Elmfield Pk NE3 . . . . .38 B3
Elmfield Rd
Hebburn NE31. . . . . .57 F3
Newcastle upon Tyne NE3 . . .38 C3
Throckley NE15 . . . . .35 E2
Elmfield Sq NE3 . . . . .38 B4
Elmfield Terr
Gateshead NE10 . . . . .57 A1
Hebburn NE31. . . . . .57 F4
Elm Gr
Burnopfield NE16. . . . . .78 F6
Killingworth NE12 . . . . .29 D1
Newcastle upon Tyne NE3 . . .37 F7
Shiney Row DH4 . . . . .90 C5
South Shields NE34. . . . . . . .59 F4
Elm Pl DH4 . . . . .90 D3
Elm Rd
Blaydon NE21 . . . . .53 D2
Ponteland NE20. . . . . .26 A5
Tynemouth NE29 . . . . .41 A7
Elmsford Gr NE12 . . . . .39 B6
Elmsleigh Gdns SR6 . . . . . . .60 A2
Elm St
Chester le Street DH3. . . . . . .88 C3
Jarrow NE32 . . . . .58 A7
Mickley Square NE43. . . . . . .64 E8
Seaton Burn NE13. . . . . .28 C8
Sunniside NE16 . . . . .69 B2
Elms The
Easington Lane DH5 . . . . . . .97 D8
Ellington NE61 . . . . .1 B4
Newcastle upon Tyne NE3 . . .38 B3
Sunderland SR2 . . . . .103 A1
Elm Street W NE16. . . . . . . .69 B2
Elm Terr
Birtley DH3 . . . . .82 B5
Tantobie DH9 . . . . .79 B2
Elmtree Dr NE40 . . . . .52 B2
Elmtree Gdns NE25 . . . . .31 E3
Elmtree Gr NE3 . . . . .38 B3
Elm Trees NE24 . . . . .17 D6
Elmway DH2. . . . . .88 A5
Elmwood NE15 . . . . .53 C8
Elmwood Ave
Sunderland SR5 . . . . .74 F3
Wallsend NE28 . . . . .40 F2
Wideopen NE13. . . . . .28 A6
Elmwood Cres NE6 . . . . .39 F1
Elmwood Dr NE20 . . . . .25 E7
Elmwood Gdns NE11 . . . . . . .70 B6
Elmwood Gr NE26 . . . . .32 A6
Elmwood Ho NE7 . . . . .39 A4
Elmwood Mews NE13 . . . . . .28 B4
Elmwood Rd NE25 . . . . .31 E4
Elmwood Sq 🖪 SR5. . . . . . .74 F2
Elmwood St
Great Lumley DH4 . . . . .89 E1
Sunderland SR2. . . . . .102 B1
Elrick Cl NE5 . . . . .36 C2
Elrington Gdns NE5 . . . . . . .54 B8
Elsdon Ave
New Hartley NE25. . . . . .23 D7
Seaton Delaval NE25 . . . . . . .23 D7
Elsdonburn Rd SR3 . . . . .91 E5
Elsdon Cl NE24 . . . . .17 A8
Elsdon Ct NE16 . . . . .69 A5
Elsdon Dr
Ashington NE63 . . . . .6 F3
Longbenton NE12. . . . . .39 F8
Elsdon Gdns NE11 . . . . .70 A8
Elsdon Pl 🖪 NE29 . . . . .42 A4

Elsdon Rd
Newcastle upon Tyne NE3 . . .38 C5
Whickham NE16. . . . . .69 A6
Elsdon St NE29 . . . . .42 A4
Elsdon Terr
North Shields NE29 . . . . .41 D4
🗖 Wallsend NE28 . . . . .40 B1
Elsham Gn NE3 . . . . .37 E6
Elsing Cl NE5 . . . . .37 B4
Elstob Farm Cvns SR3. . . . . .86 B2
Elstob Pl
Newcastle upon Tyne NE6 . . .56 E4
Sunderland SR3 . . . . .86 B3
Elston Cl NE5. . . . . .36 C2
Elstree Ct NE3 . . . . .37 B7
Elstree Gdns NE24 . . . . .17 D3
Elstree Sq SR5. . . . . .75 A3
ELSWICK 54 F3
Elswick East Terr NE4 . . . .100 B4
Elswick Pool NE4 . . . . .100 A4
Elswick Rd
Newcastle upon Tyne
NE4. . . . . .100 A4
Washington NE37 . . . . .83 A7
Elswick Row NE4 . . . . .98 B1
Elswick St NE4. . . . . .98 B1
Elswick Way Ind Est NE34. .59 A6
Elsworth Gn NE5. . . . . .36 C3
Elterwater Rd DH2 . . . . .88 B1
Elton St E NE28 . . . . .40 A1
Elton Street W NE28 . . . . . . .40 A1
ELTRINGHAM 50 A3
Eltringham Cl NE28. . . . . . . .40 A2
Eltringham Cotts NE43 . . . . .49 F1
Eltringham Rd NE42 . . . . . . .50 A2
Elvaston Cres NE3 . . . . .37 D3
Elvaston Dr NE46 . . . . .45 B3
Elvaston Gr NE46 . . . . .45 A3
Elvaston Park Rd NE46. . . . .45 A3
Elvaston Rd
Hexham NE46 . . . . .45 B4
Ryton NE40 . . . . .52 C6
Elvet Cl
Brunswick Village NE13. . . . .28 B6
🖪 Newcastle upon Tyne
NE6. . . . . .56 C7
Elvet Ct NE6. . . . . .56 C7
Elvet Gn
Chester le Street DH2. . . . . . .88 C2
Hetton-le-Hole DH5. . . . . . . .95 A1
Elvet Way 🖪 NE6 . . . . .56 C7
Elvington St SR6 . . . . .75 E3
Elwin Cl NE26 . . . . .24 D5
Elwin Pl NE26 . . . . .24 D5
Elwin Terr SR2 . . . . .102 C2
Ely Cl NE12 . . . . .39 D4
Elysium La NE8 . . . . .101 A1
Ely St NE8 . . . . .101 B1
Ely Way NE32 . . . . .58 B1
Embankment Rd SR7. . . . . . .93 B1
Embassy Gdns NE15 . . . . . . .54 B8
Embleton NE37 . . . . .83 A6
Emblehope Dr NE3 . . . . .38 A4
Emblehope Ho SR3 . . . . .91 E8
Embleton Ave
Newcastle upon Tyne NE3 . . .38 A6
South Shields NE34. . . . . . . .60 B8
Wallsend NE28 . . . . .40 E5
Embleton Cres NE29 . . . . . . .41 C8
Embleton Dr
Blyth NE24. . . . . .17 C5
Chester le Street DH2. . . . . . .88 A1
Embleton Gdns
Gateshead NE10 . . . . .56 D1
🖪 Newcastle upon Tyne
NE5. . . . . .37 D1
Embleton Rd
Gateshead NE10 . . . . .57 B2
Tynemouth NE29 . . . . .41 C8
Emden Rd NE3 . . . . .37 F6
Emily Davison Ave NE61. . . .8 E3
Emily St
Gateshead NE8 . . . . .56 B1
Newbottle DH4 . . . . .90 D4
Newcastle upon Tyne NE6 . . .56 C6
Emlyn Rd NE34 . . . . .59 C6
Emma Ct SR2 . . . . .103 B1
Emmanuel Coll NE11 . . . . . .70 A5
Emma View 🖾 NE40 . . . . . . .51 F3
Emmaville NE40 . . . . .52 A4
Emmaville Prim Sch NE40 . .52 A4
Embrook Cl DH5. . . . . .94 D4
Emmerson Cl NE27. . . . . . . .30 C5
Emmerson Pl NE27 . . . . .30 E3
Emmerson Rd NE64. . . . . .7 D5
Emmerson Terr NE38 . . . . . .83 B5
Emmerson Terrace W 🖬
SR3 .92 B7
Emperor Way SR3 . . . . .91 C5
Empire Theatre* NE1 . . . . .102 C3
Empress Rd NE6 . . . . .57 B4
Empress St 🖪 SR5. . . . . . . .75 C1
Emsworth Rd SR5. . . . . .75 A3
Enderby Dr NE46 . . . . .44 E3
Enderby Rd SR4 . . . . .102 B3
Enfield Ave NE16 . . . . .69 B6
Enfield Gdns NE16. . . . . .69 B5
Enfield Rd NE9 . . . . .70 F8
Enfield St SR4 . . . . .85 F7
Engel St NE39 . . . . .67 B2
Engine Inn Rd NE28 . . . . . . .40 F4
Engine La NE9 . . . . .70 F5
Engine Rd
Bardon Mill NE17. . . . . .65 E4
Prudhoe NE42 . . . . .65 F5
Englefield NE10 . . . . .71 F4
Englefield Cl NE3 . . . . .37 D7

Englemann Way SR3 . . . . . .91 E5
English Martyrs RC Prim Sch
  Newcastle upon Tyne NE5 . . .54 C8
  Sunderland SR2 . . . . .74 F2
Enid Ave SR6 . . . . .75 D3
Enid St NE13 . . . . .28 A4
Ennerdale
  Birtley DH3 . . . . .82 D2
  Gateshead NE10 . . . . .72 A8
  Sunderland SR2 . . . . .86 C4
  Washington NE37 . . . . .83 C7
Ennerdale Cres
  Blaydon NE21 . . . . .68 B8
  Penshaw DH4 . . . . .90 A8
Ennerdale Gdns
  Gateshead NE9 . . . . .71 A5
  Wallsend NE28 . . . . .41 A4
Ennerdale Pl DH2 . . . . .88 C1
Ennerdale Rd
  Blyth NE24 . . . . .16 F8
  Newcastle upon Tyne NE6 . . .56 F6
  Tynemouth NE30 . . . . .32 A2
Ennerdale St DH5 . . . . .94 F2
Ennerdale Terr NE17 . . . . . .77 A5
Ennerdale Wlk NE16 . . . . . .68 F5
Ennis Cl NE62 . . . . .11 D8
Ennismore Ct NE12 . . . . . . .39 D6
Ensign Ho NE30 . . . . .42 D7
Enslin St NC6 . . . . .56 F3
Enterprise Ct
  Cramlington NE23 . . . . .15 F1
  Seaham SR7 . . . . .92 F2
Enterprise Ho NE11 . . . . . . .70 D4
Epinay Bsns & Ent Sch
  NE32 . . . . .58 C6
Epinay Wlk NE32 . . . . .58 C6
Epping Cl NE23 . . . . .21 D6
Epping Sq **4** SR5 . . . . .75 A3
Eppleton Est DH5 . . . . .95 B4
Eppleton Prim Sch DH5 . . . .95 A3
Eppleton Row DH5 . . . . .95 B4
Eppleton Terrace E DH5 . . . .95 B4
Eppleton Terrace W DH5 . . . .95 B4
Epsom Cl NE29 . . . . .41 F4
Epsom Ct NE3 . . . . .37 C7
Epsom Dr DH3 . . . . 6 C2
Epsom Sq **5** SR5 . . . . .75 A3
Epsom Way NE24 . . . . .17 D3
Epwell Gr NE23 . . . . .16 C2
Epworth Gr NE8 . . . . .101 B1
Equitable St NE28. . . . . .40 B1
Erick St NE1 . . . . .99 B1
Eric Tolhurst Ctr **12** NE24 . .17 F8
Erin Sq SR5 . . . . .75 A3
Erith Terr SR4 . . . . .85 F6
Ermine Cres NE9 . . . . .71 B6
Ernest Mackley Ho NE34 . . .59 A5
Ernest St
  5 Sunderland SR2 . . . . . . .86 E4
  West Boldon NE35. . . . . . . .74 A8
Ernwill Ave SR5. . . . . .74 B1

Essen Way SR3 . . . . .86 B3
Essex Cl
  Ashington NE63. . . . . .6 A4
  Newcastle upon Tyne NE4 . . .100 B3
Essex Ct NE7 . . . . .72 D1
Essex Gdns
  Gateshead NE9 . . . . .70 F7
  South Shields NE34 . . . . . . .60 C7
  Wallsend NE28 . . . . .40 E3
Essex Gr SR3 . . . . .92 A8
Essex St DH5 . . . . .94 F4
Estate Houses DH4 . . . . .89 E4
Esther Campbell Ct
  NE2 . . . . .98 C3
Esther Sq NE38 . . . . .83 E4
Estherlaw NE37 . . . . .83 B6
Esthwaite Ave DH2. . . . . . . .88 B1
Eston Ct
  Blyth NE24 . . . . .17 B8
  Wallsend NE28 . . . . .39 F5
Eston Gr SR5 . . . . .75 C3
Estuary Way SR5 . . . . .85 B7
Etal Ave
  North Shields NE29. . . . . . . .41 D4
  Whitley Bay NE25 . . . . .32 B4
Etal Cl NE27 . . . . .30 F3
Etal Cres
  Jarrow NE32. . . . . .58 E4
  Shiremoor NE27 . . . . .30 F3
Etal Ct **1** NE29 . . . . .42 A6
Etal House NE63 . . . . .6 F4
Etal La NE5 . . . . .37 B3
Etal Pl NE3 . . . . .38 A7
Etal Rd NE24 . . . . .17 B3
Etal Way NE5 . . . . .37 B4
Ethel Ave
  Blaydon NE21 . . . . .53 C2
  Ryhope SR2 . . . . .93 A6
Ethel St
  Dudley NE23 . . . . .29 A6
  Newcastle upon Tyne NE4 . . .54 D4
Ethel Terr
  7 Hexham NE46. . . . . .45 A4
  High Spen NE39. . . . . .66 F3
  South Shields NE34 . . . . . . .59 B5
  Sunderland SR5 . . . . .74 B1
Etherley Rd NE6 . . . . .56 D7
Etherstone Ave NE7. . . . . . . .39 C3
Eton Cl NE23 . . . . .16 C2
Eton Sq NE31. . . . . .57 F6
Ettrick Cl NE12 . . . . .29 C4
Ettrick Gdns
  Gateshead NE8 . . . . .71 B8
  Sunderland SR4 . . . . .85 F4
Ettrick Gr SR4 . . . . .85 F4
Ettrick Lodge NE3 . . . . .38 D4
Ettrick Rd NE32. . . . . .58 A5
European Way SR4. . . . . . . .85 E8
Euryalus Ct NE33 . . . . .42 E1
Eustace Ave NE29. . . . . .41 E5
Euston Ct SR5 . . . . .75 A4
Evanlade NE10. . . . . .72 B6
Eva St NE15 . . . . .53 C6
Evelyn St SR2. . . . . .102 B1
Evelyn Terr NE11 . . . . .53 C3
Evenwood Gdns NE9 . . . . . . .71 B5
Everard St NE23 . . . . .16 B3
Everest Gr NE36 . . . . .74 A7
Everest Sq SR5 . . . . .75 A4
Ever Ready Ind Est DH9 . . . .12 D2
Eversleigh Pl NE15. . . . . . . .35 E2
Eversley Cres SR5 . . . . .75 B3
Eversley Pl
  7 Newcastle upon Tyne
    NE6. . . . . .56 B7
  Wallsend NE28 . . . . .40 F3
Everton La SR5 . . . . .85 A6
Evesham SR4. . . . . .85 A6
Evesham Ave NE26. . . . . . . .31 F6
Evesham Cl NE35 . . . . .58 F1
Evesham Garth NE3 . . . . . . .37 E3
Evesham Pl NE23 . . . . .21 D7
Evistones Gdns NE9 . . . . . . .56 E3
Evistones Rd NE9 . . . . .71 A7
Ewart Cres NE34. . . . . .58 D4
Ewart Ct NE3 . . . . .38 A7
Ewbank Ave NE4 . . . . .54 E7
Ewe Hill Cotts DH4 . . . . . . .89 F1
Ewe Hill Terr DH4 . . . . .89 F1
Ewe Hill Terrace W DH4. . . .89 F1
Ewehurst Cres DH9 . . . . . . .78 E1
Ewehurst Gdns DH9. . . . . . .78 E1
Ewehurst Pk DH9 . . . . .78 E2
Ewehurst Rd DH9. . . . . .78 E2
Ewen Ct NE23 . . . . .41 B8
Ewesley NE38. . . . . .89 A8
Ewesley Cl NE5 . . . . .37 A1
Ewesley Gdns NE13 . . . . . . .28 B6
Ewesley Rd SR4 . . . . .85 F5
Ewing Rd SR4 . . . . .102 A1
Excelsior Academy NE15 . . .53 F6
Exchange Bldgs NE26. . . . . .32 B5
Exelby **1** DH3 . . . . .38 D8
Exeter Cl
  Ashington NE63. . . . . .7 A2
  Cramlington NE23 . . . . .21 E6
Exeter Ct NE31. . . . . .57 D5
Exeter Rd
  Tynemouth NE29 . . . . .31 C1
  Wallsend NE28 . . . . .40 A5
Exeter St
  Gateshead NE8 . . . . .101 C1
  Newcastle upon Tyne NE6 . . .57 A4
  Sunderland SR4. . . . . .85 F7
Exmouth Rd NE29 . . . . .41 C5
Exmouth Sq SR5. . . . . .75 A3
Exmouth St **2** SR5 . . . . . . .75 A3
Extension Rd SR1. . . . . .103 C2

Eyemouth Ct **2** NE34 . . . . .59 A5
Eyemouth La SR5 . . . . .75 A4
Eyemouth Rd NE29. . . . . . . .41 C5

F

Faber Rd SR5. . . . . .75 A3
Factory Rd NE21. . . . . .53 D4
Fairbairn Dr DH4 . . . . .90 C2
Fairburn Ave
  Houghton-le-Spring DH5 . . . .94 E6
  Newcastle upon Tyne NE7 . . .39 C4
Fairdale Ave NE7 . . . . .39 C4
Fairfield
  Fence Houses DH4 . . . . .90 B1
  Hexham NE46 . . . . .44 F4
  Longbenton NE12. . . . . .38 F6
Fairfield Ave
  Blyth NE24 . . . . .17 D4
  3 Longbenton NE12. . . . . .39 D4
  Whickham NE16. . . . . .69 A5
Fairfield Cl NE11. . . . . .54 E1
Fairfield Cres NE46 . . . . .45 E8
Fairfield Dr
  Ashington NE63. . . . . .7 A2
  Tynemouth NE30 . . . . .32 B2
  Whitburn SR6. . . . . .60 F2
  Whitley Bay NE25 . . . . .31 D4
Fairfield Gn NE25 . . . . .31 C4
Fairfield Ind Est NE10. . . . . .57 A2
Fairfield Ind Pk NE10 . . . . . .57 A2
Fairfield Rd NE2 . . . . .38 D1
Fairfields NE40 . . . . .52 B5
Fairfield Terr NE10 . . . . .57 A2
Fair Gn NE25 . . . . .31 C4
Fairgreen Cl SR3 . . . . .91 F5
Fairhaven NE9. . . . . .71 F2
Fairhaven Ave NE6. . . . . . . .56 C5
Fairhill Cl NE7. . . . . .39 C4
Fairholme Ave NE34 . . . . . . .59 F6
Fairholme Rd SR3 . . . . .86 C2
Fairholm Rd NE4 . . . . .54 E5
Fairisle DH2. . . . . .82 A1
Fairlands E SR6. . . . . .75 D2
Fairlands W SR6. . . . . .75 D2
Fairlawn Gdns SR4. . . . . . . .85 E4
Fairles St NE33 . . . . .42 D4
Fairmead Way SR4. . . . . . . .85 A6
Fairmile Dr SR3 . . . . .92 A4
Fairmont Way NE7 . . . . .39 C4
FAIR MOOR 3 C4
Fairney Cl NE20. . . . . .25 F6
Fairney Edge NE20. . . . . . . .25 F6
Fairnley Wlk NE5 . . . . .37 A2
Fairspring **3** NE5. . . . . .37 A2
Fairview NE62 . . . . .11 A8
Fair View
  Burnopfield NE16. . . . . .78 E6
  Prudhoe NE42. . . . . .50 C2
  West Rainton DH4. . . . . . . .94 A2
Fairview Ave NE34 . . . . .59 F7
Fairview Gn NE7. . . . . .39 C4
Fairville Cl NE23 . . . . .16 B2
Fairville Cres NE7. . . . . .39 C4
Fairway
  Morpeth NE61 . . . . .9 B6
  Stakeford NE62 . . . . .11 A8
Fairway Cl NE3 . . . . .38 A3
Fairway Ct NE8 . . . . .101 B3
Fairways
  New Silksworth SR3 . . . . . . .92 B7
  Whitley Bay NE25 . . . . .31 D5
Fairways Ave NE7. . . . . .39 C4
Fairways The NE36. . . . . . . .74 A7
Fairway The
  Newcastle upon Tyne NE3 . . .38 B8
  Ryton NE21 . . . . .53 A4
  Washington NE37 . . . . .72 D3
Fairwood Rd NE46 . . . . .45 D8
Fairy St DH5. . . . . .95 A4
Falconar's Ct NE1 . . . . .99 A1
Falconar St NE2 . . . . .99 B2
Falconer St NE6 . . . . .99 B2
Falcon Cl NE63 . . . . .6 A4
Falcon Hill NE61. . . . . .8 D7
Falcon Pl NE12 . . . . .39 A7
Falcon Terr NE41. . . . . .51 B6
Falcon Way NE34 . . . . .59 B4
Faldo Dr NE63 . . . . .6 F4
Faldonside NE6. . . . . .39 D2
Falkirk NE12. . . . . .29 D4
Falkland Ave
  Hebburn NE31. . . . . .57 E6
  Newcastle upon Tyne NE3 . . .37 F3
Falkland Rd SR4 . . . . .85 E6
Falla Park Cres NE10 . . . . . .71 C8
Falla Park Prim Sch NE10 . . .71 C8
Falla Park Rd NE10 . . . . .71 C8
Falloden Ave NE3. . . . . .37 F8
Falloden Gdns NE5 . . . . .37 D2
Falloden Rd NE21 . . . . .01 D5
Fallowfeld NE10 . . . . .72 A7
Fallowfield Ave NE3. . . . . . . .37 F6
Fallowfield Way
  Ashington NE63. . . . . .6 B2
  Washington NE38 . . . . .83 E2
Fallow Park Ave NE24. . . . . .17 C6
Fallow Rd NE34. . . . . .60 D6
Fal Pass NE15 . . . . .100 B3
Falmouth Dr DH4. . . . . .90 C2
Falmouth Rd
  Newcastle upon Tyne NE6 . . .56 B7
  North Shields NE29 . . . . . . .41 C5
  Sunderland SR4. . . . . .85 E7
  Tynemouth NE29 . . . . .41 C5
Falmouth Sq SR4 . . . . .85 E6
Falmouth Wlk NE23 . . . . . . .22 A8

Falsgrave Pl NE16. . . . . .68 F5
Falstaff Rd NE29. . . . . .41 D6
Falstone
  Gateshead NE10 . . . . .72 A5
  Washington NE38 . . . . .83 F2
Falstone Ave
  Newcastle upon Tyne
    NE15. . . . . .53 E8
  South Shields NE34 . . . . . . .60 A6
Falstone Cl NE12 . . . . .40 A8
Falstone Cres NE63 . . . . .6 E1
Falstone Sq NE3. . . . . .38 A6
Falstone Way NE46 . . . . .44 F3
Falston Rd NE24 . . . . .17 C5
Faraday Cl NE38. . . . . .84 B5
Faraday Gr
  Gateshead NE8 . . . . .70 E7
  Sunderland SR4. . . . . .85 F6
Faraday Terr DH6. . . . . .97 E3
Farbridge Cres DH8. . . . . . . .76 F3
Farding Lake Ct NE34 . . . . . .60 C6
Farding Sq NE34. . . . . .60 C6
Fareham Gr NE35. . . . . .73 D8
Fareham Way NE23 . . . . .22 B7
Farleigh Ct NE3. . . . . .37 A1
Farm Cl
  Sunnisde NE16 . . . . .69 B2
  Washington NE37 . . . . .72 B1
Farm Cotts NE25. . . . . .23 F2
Farm Hill Rd SR6 . . . . .60 A2
Farm St NE6 . . . . .56 C5
Farmstead Ct NE22 . . . . .15 D5
Farm View NE10 . . . . .72 A7
Farm Well Pl **5** NE42. . . . . .50 D3
Farnborough Cl SR3 . . . . . . .91 F5
Farnborough Dr SR3 . . . . . . .92 B8
Farn Ct NE3 . . . . .37 D8
Farndale Ave
  Stakeford NE62 . . . . .11 A8
  Sunderland SR6. . . . . .75 F6
Farndale Cl
  Blaydon NE21 . . . . .67 B8
  Dinnington NE13 . . . . .27 B7
Farndale Ct NE24 . . . . .17 D4
Farndale Rd NE4. . . . . .54 E5
Farne Ave
  Ashington NE63. . . . . .6 C2
  Newcastle upon Tyne NE3 . . .38 A7
  South Shields NE34 . . . . . . .60 B8
Farne Prim Sch NE3 . . . . . . .37 A3
Farne Rd NE27. . . . . .30 F3
Farne Sq SR4. . . . . .85 D7
Farne Terr NE6 . . . . .56 E6
Farnham Cl NE15 . . . . .53 D6
Farnham Gr NE24 . . . . .17 D4
Farnham Rd NE34. . . . . .59 C6
Farnham St NE15. . . . . .53 C6
Farnham Terr SR4 . . . . .85 F4
Farnley Rd NE6 . . . . .39 C1
Farnon Rd NE3 . . . . .38 A5
Farnsworth Ct NE2 . . . . .38 F1
Farquhar St **5** NE2 . . . . . . .38 F1
Farrfield NE10 . . . . .71 F4
Farrier Cl NE38 . . . . .83 E2
Farriers Ct NE12. . . . . .40 C5
FARRINGDON 91 D8
Farringdon Prim Sch SR3 . . .91 D8
Farringdon Rd NE30 . . . . . . .32 A2
Farringdon Row SR4 . . . . . . .102 C3
Farrow Dr SR6. . . . . .60 E1
Farthings The NE37 . . . . . . .72 B2
FATFIELD 83 E1
Fatfield Pk NE38. . . . . .83 D1
Fatfield Prim Sch NE38 . . . . .83 D1
Fatfield Rd NE38. . . . . .83 E4
Fatherly Terr DH4. . . . . .94 B8
Faversham Ct NE3 . . . . .37 D7
Faversham Pl NE23 . . . . .22 B8
Fawcett St SR1 . . . . .103 A2
Fawcett Terr **8** SR2. . . . . . .93 A6
Fawcett Way NE33 . . . . .42 C3
FAWDON 37 E7
Fawdon Cl NE3 . . . . .37 F8
Fawdon Gr NE61. . . . . .4 D3
Fawdon House Farm NE61 . .4 D5
Fawdon La NE3 . . . . .37 F7
Fawdon Park Ct NE3 . . . . . . .37 F6
Fawdon Park Rd
  Fawdon NE3. . . . . .37 F6
  Newcastle upon Tyne NE3 . . .37 F6
Fawdon Pl NE29 . . . . .41 C7
Fawdon Sta NE3. . . . . .37 F6
Fawdon Wlk NE3 . . . . .37 D7
Fawlee Gn NE5 . . . . .37 C4
Fawley Cl NE35. . . . . .58 E1
Fawn Rd SR4. . . . . .85 C6
Feather Bed La SR2. . . . . . . .93 A6
Featherstone NE38. . . . . . . .82 F5
Featherstone Gr
  Bedlington NE22 . . . . .10 E2
  Brunton Park NE3 . . . . .28 A1
  Jarrow NE32. . . . . .58 A3
  Newcastle upon Tyne SR6 . . .75 F2
Federation Terr DH9 . . . . . . .79 B2
Federation Way NE11 . . . . . .54 E1
Fee Terr SR2 . . . . .93 A6
Feetham Ave NE12. . . . . . . .40 A8
Feetham Ct NE12 . . . . .30 A1
Felixstowe Dr NE7 . . . . .39 D3
Fell Bank DH3 . . . . .82 D4

Fell Cl
  Birtley DH3 . . . . .82 E3
  Sunniside NE16 . . . . .69 B2
  Washington NE37 . . . . .83 B7
Fell Dene NE16 . . . . .82 C5
Fell Ct **8** NE9 . . . . .71 F1
Felldyke NE10 . . . . .72 C6
Fell Dyke Prim Sch NE9 . . . .71 D3
FELLGATE 58 A1
Fellgate Ave NE32 . . . . .58 C1
Fellgate Gdns NE10 . . . . . . .72 C8
Fellgate Prim Sch NE32 . . . .58 B1
Fellgate Sta NE32. . . . . .58 C2
FELLING 71 D8
Felling Bsns Ctr NE10. . . . . .56 D2
Felling Dene Gdns NE10 . . . .56 E1
Felling Gate NE10. . . . . .56 C1
Felling House Gdns NE10 . . .56 E2
FELLING SHORE. 56 E2
Felling Shore Ind Est
  NE10 . . . . .56 D3
Felling Sta NE10. . . . . .56 D1
Felling View NE16 . . . . .56 D1
Fellmere Ave NE10. . . . . . . .72 A8
Fell Pl **7** NE9 . . . . .71 F1
Fell Rd
  Springwell NE9 . . . . .71 F1
  Sunderland SR4 . . . . .85 D7
Fellsdyke Ct NE9. . . . . .71 C6
Fellside
  Birtley DH3 . . . . .82 D3
  Ponteland NE20. . . . . .25 B1
  South Shields NE34 . . . . . . .60 B5
FELLSIDE
  Sunniside. 68 F3
  Whickham 68 F6
Fellside Ave NE16. . . . . .69 B3
Fellside Cl NE20 . . . . .25 B1
Fellside Ct
  Dipton DH9 . . . . .78 E2
  Washington NE37 . . . . .83 B6
  Whickham NE16. . . . . .69 A7
Fellside Prim Sch NE16 . . . . .68 F6
Fellside Rd
  Byermoor NE16 . . . . .79 C8
  Sunniside NE16 . . . . .68 F3
Fellside The NE15 . . . . .37 F4
Fells Rd NE11. . . . . .70 D7
Fells The **9** NE9 . . . . .71 A6
Fells Way The NE16 . . . . .79 B6
Fell The NE16 . . . . .79 B6
Fell View
  16 Crawcrook NE40 . . . . . .51 F3
  High Spen NE39. . . . . .67 A3
Fell View W **1** NE40 . . . . . .51 F3
Fell Way The NE5 . . . . .36 D1
Felsham Sq SR4. . . . . .85 E7
Felstead Cres SR4 . . . . .85 D7
Felstead Pl NE24 . . . . .17 D4
Felstead Sch SR4 . . . . .85 D6
Felstead Sq SR4. . . . . .85 D6
Felthorpe Ct NE5 . . . . .37 B4
Felton Ave
  Newcastle upon Tyne NE3 . . .38 A6
  South Shields NE34 . . . . . . .60 A7
  Whitley Bay NE25 . . . . .32 B4
Felton Cl
  Morpeth NE61 . . . . .9 B6
  Shiremoor NE27 . . . . .30 F3
Felton Cres NE8 . . . . .70 E7
Felton Dr NE12 . . . . .29 F1
Felton Gn NE6 . . . . .56 C6
Felton Ho **10** NE6. . . . . . . .56 C6
Felton Terr NE63 . . . . .6 D2
Felton Wlk **18** NE6. . . . . . .56 C6
FENCE HOUSES 94 A8
Fencer Ct NE3 . . . . .38 C8
Fence Rd DH3 . . . . .89 E5
Fencer Hill Pk NE3 . . . . .38 C8
FENHAM 54 D7
Fenham Chase NE4. . . . . . . .54 C8
Fenham Hall Dr NE4 . . . . . . .54 E8
Fenham Rd
  Lynemouth NE61 . . . . .1 F3
  Newcastle upon Tyne NE4 . . .98 A3
Fenkle St NE1 . . . . .99 A1
Fennel NE9 . . . . .71 C4
Fennel Gr NE34 . . . . .59 E3
Fenning Pl **3** NE6. . . . . . . .56 C6
Fenside Rd SR2 . . . . .92 F8
Fenton Cl DH2. . . . . .88 A2
Fenton Sq SR4 . . . . .85 D6
Fenton Terr DH4 . . . . .90 D6
Fenton Wlk NE5 . . . . .37 A2
Fenwick Ave
  Blyth NE24 . . . . .17 D5
  South Shields NE34 . . . . . . .59 A5
Fenwick Cl
  4 Newcastle upon Tyne
    NE2 . . . . .38 F1
  Penshaw DH4 . . . . .90 B8
  Shiremoor NE27 . . . . .30 D3
Fenwick Gr
  4 Hexham NE46. . . . . .45 A4
  Morpeth NE61 . . . . .4 A1
Fenwick St NE35 . . . . .58 E1
Fenwick Terr
  3 Newcastle upon Tyne
    NE2. . . . . .38 F1
  North Shields NE29 . . . . . . .42 A6

Ferguson Cres NE13 28 A4
Ferguson's La NE15 54 B6
Ferguson St SR2 103 C2
Fern Ave
Cramlington NE23 16 B2
Newcastle upon Tyne, Fawdon NE3 38 A7
Newcastle upon Tyne, Jesmond NE2 38 F1
North Shields NE29 41 F6
Sunderland SR5 75 A2
Whitburn SR6 60 F2
Fernbank NE26 24 C6
Fernclough NE9 71 C5
Fern Ct NE62 10 E7
Ferndale Ave
4 East Boldon NE36 74 D7
Newcastle upon Tyne NE3 28 D1
Wallsend NE28 40 C2
Ferndale Cl NE24 17 A8
Ferndale Gr NE36 74 D7
Ferndale Rd DH4 90 A8
Ferndale Terr
5 Springwell NE9 71 F1
Sunderland SR4 85 E8
Ferndene
Longbenton NE12 39 D7
Wallsend NE28 40 E4
Ferndene Cres SR4 85 F6
Ferndene Ct NE3 38 D4
Ferndene Gr
Newcastle upon Tyne NE7 39 C3
Ryton NE40 52 D6
Fern Dene Rd NE8 70 E8
Ferndown Ct
Gateshead NE10 72 B7
Ryton NE40 52 D4
Fern Dr
Cleadon SR6 59 F1
Dudley NE23 29 B8
Fordley NE23 29 B8
Fern Gdns NE9 70 F6
Ferngrove NE32 73 C8
Fernhill Ave NE16 69 A7
Fernlea NE23 29 B8
Fernlea Cl NE38 83 E2
Fernlea Gdns NE40 52 A4
Fernlea Gn NE3 37 F5
Fernley Villas NE23 22 D6
Fern St SR4 102 B3
Fernsway SR3 86 B3
Fern Terr DH9 78 F1
Fernville Ave NE16 69 B2
Fernville Rd NE3 38 B3
Fernville St SR4 102 B1
Fernway NE61 9 B8
Fernwood NE2 99 B4
Fernwood Ave NE3 38 D6
Fernwood Cl SR3 92 A5
Fernwood Gr NE39 77 F5
Fernwood Rd
Newcastle upon Tyne, Jesmond NE2 99 B4
Newcastle upon Tyne, Lemington NE15 53 D6
Fernyhough Hall NE31 57 F5
Ferrand Dr DH4 94 D8
Ferriby Cl NE3 38 D8
Ferrisdale Way NE3 37 F7
Ferry App NE33 42 C3
Ferryboat La
Sunderland, Castletown SR5 85 A7
Sunderland, Hylton Castle SR5 73 F2
Ferrydene Ave NE3 37 F4
Ferry Landing NE42 49 F3
Ferry Mews
North Shields NE29 42 B4
South Shields NE33 42 B3
Ferry Rd NE46 45 C6
Ferry St
Jarrow NE32 58 B8
South Shields NE33 42 B3
Festival Cotts NE12 29 B5
Festival Park Dr NE11 70 B7
Festival Way NE11, NE8 100 A1
Fetcham Ct NE3 37 C7
Fewster Sq NE10 72 A6
Field Cl NE2 99 C2
Fieldfare Cl 2 NE38 82 F3
Fieldfare Ct NE16 79 C5
Fieldfare Ho 9 NE24 17 F8
Field Ho
9 North Shields NE30 42 B6
Silksworth SR3 92 A5
Fieldhouse Cl NE61 9 F5
Field House Farm SR7 92 F1
Fieldhouse La NE61 9 E5
Field House Rd NE8 70 E7
Field House Terr DH6 97 F3
Fielding Ct NE34 59 A3
Fielding Pl NE9 71 B8
Field La NE10 72 A8
Fieldside
East Rainton DH5 94 C3
Whitburn SR6 60 E1
Field Sq SR4 85 D6
Field St
8 Gateshead NE10 56 D1
Newcastle upon Tyne NE3 38 E5
Field Terr
Jarrow NE32 58 B5
4 Throckley NE15 35 D2
Fieldway NE32 73 D8
Fife Ave
Brockley Whins NE32 58 E3
Chester le Street DH2 88 C3
Fife St NE8 56 A1
Fife Terr NE17 77 B6
Fifteenth Ave NE24 17 D6
Fifth Ave
Ashington NE63 6 E3
Blyth NE24 17 D6
Chester le Street DH2 88 B3
Gateshead DH98, NE11 70 D5
Morpeth NE61 9 B7
Newcastle upon Tyne NE6 56 C7
Fifth Row NE61 1 A3
Filey Cl NE23 22 B8
Filton Cl NE23 22 B8
Finchale NE38 83 C3
Finchale Cl
Dunston NE11 69 F6
Houghton-le-Spring DH4 94 D8
Sunderland SR2 103 B1
Finchale Gdns
Gateshead NE9 71 C2
Throckley NE15 35 D3
Finchale Rd NE31 57 E3
Finchale Terr
Great Lumley DH4 89 E1
Jarrow NE32 58 D4
2 Newcastle upon Tyne NE6 56 C4
Finchdale Cl NE29 41 F4
Finchdale Terr 2 DH3 88 C3
Finchley Cres NE6 57 A8
Finchley Ct NE6 57 A8
Findlay Ct NE34 58 F5
Findon Gr NE29 41 E4
Fine La DH8 76 B3
Fines Rd DH8 77 B1
Finsbury Ave NE6 56 E6
Finsbury St 2 SR5 75 C1
Finsmere Pl 1 NE5 37 B1
Finstock Ct NE3 38 F4
Firbank Ave NE30 32 B2
Firbanks NE32 58 D1
Fire Station Cotts SR6 75 D4
Firfield Rd NE5 37 D2
Fir Gr
Ellington NE61 1 D4
South Shields NE34 59 F5
Fir St NE32 58 A7
First Ave
Ashington NE63 6 E4
Blyth NE24 17 D6
Chester le Street DH2 88 B8
Gateshead NE11 70 C6
Morpeth NE61 9 B7
Newcastle upon Tyne NE6 56 C7
North Shields NE29 41 C4
Firs The NE3 38 B4
First Row
Ashington NE63 6 A4
Ellington NE61 1 E4
Linton NE61 1 A3
First St NE8 101 A1
Fir Terr NE16 79 B6
Firth Sq SR4 85 D7
Firtree Ave
Longbenton NE12 29 D1
Wallsend NE6 40 A1
Washington NE38 83 C1
Firtree Cres NE12 29 C1
Firtree Gdns NE25 31 F3
Firtree Rd NE16 69 A6
Firtrees
Chester le Street DH2 88 B5
Gateshead NE10 71 E5
Firtrees Ave NE28 41 B3
Firwood Cres NE39 67 A3
Firwood Gdns NE11 70 B5
Fisher Ind Est NE6 57 B7
Fisher La NE13, NE23 21 B5
Fisher St NE6 57 B7
Fisherwell Rd NE10 57 A1
Fish Quay NE30 42 C6
Fitzpatrick Pl NE33 42 E2
Fitzroy Terr 7 SR5 74 F2
Fitzsimmons Ave NE28 40 B3
Flagg Ct NE33 42 D3
Flag Ho NE33 42 E1
Flag Lo NE33 42 E1
Flamborough Walk 7 SR7 93 C1
Flaunden Cl NE34 60 B5
Flaxby Cl NE3 38 D8
Flax Sq SR4 85 C7
Fleet St SR1 103 C2
Fleming Bsns Ctr NE2 99 B4
Fleming Ct NE8 100 C2
Fleming Gdns NE10 71 D7
Fletcher Cres DH4 90 E6
Fletcher Ho NE29 41 E3
Fletcher Rd NE8 101 B3
Fletcher Terr DH4 90 D4
Flexbury Gdns
Gateshead, Lyndhurst NE9 71 A2
Gateshead, Mount Pleasant NE10 71 C8
Newcastle upon Tyne NE15 53 E7
FLINT HILL 78 E1
Flint Hill Bank DH9 78 E1
Flixton DH4 90 B1
Flock Sq SR4 85 D7
Flodden NE12 29 D4
Flodden Rd SR4 85 D6
Flodden St NE6 56 D5
Floral Dene SR4 85 A6
Floralia Ave 1 SR2 93 A6
Flora St 12 NE6 56 B6
Florence Ave NE9 71 A6
Florence Cres 4 SR5 74 F2
Florence St NE21 53 B1
Florence Terr DH5 95 A2
Florida St SR4 85 F8
Florin Ct NE22 15 D5
Flotterton Gdns NE5 54 C7
Flour Mill Rd NE11 54 F2
Folds The
East Rainton DH5 94 D4
Fence Houses DH4 94 B8
Fold The
Burnopfield NE16 79 A7
Newcastle upon Tyne NE6 57 A8
Silksworth SR3 92 B5
Whitley Bay NE25 31 E5
Folldon Ave SR6 75 D3
FOLLINGSBY 72 D5
Follingsby Ave NE10 72 D6
Follingsby Dr NE10 72 C7
Follingsby La NE10 72 E5
Follingsby Pk NE10 72 D5
Follingsby Way NE10 72 D6
Follonsby Terr NE10 72 E7
Folly La NE40 52 B2
Folly The NE36 74 A7
Folly Yd NE40 52 C2
Fontburn NE61 1 E6
Fontburn Cres 2 NE63 6 F3
Fontburn Ct
North Shields NE29 41 D4
Sunderland SR5 74 F4
Fontburn Gdns NE61 8 E7
Fontburn Pl NE7 39 A5
Fontburn Rd
Bedlington NE22 11 C1
Seaton Delaval NE25 23 D3
Fontburn Terr NE30 42 B6
Fonteyn Pl NE23 16 B2
Font Side NE61 3 A1
Fontwell Dr NE8 70 D7
Forbeck Rd SR4 85 D6
Forber Ave NE34 60 B6
Forbes Terr SR2 92 E6
FORD 85 E6
Ford Ave
Ashington NE63 6 D2
North Shields NE29 41 D4
Sunderland SR4 85 A6
Ford Cres
Jarrow NE32 58 B3
Shiremoor NE27 30 E3
Sunderland SR4 85 A6
Ford Dr NE24 17 C7
Fordenbridge Cres SR4 85 E6
Fordenbridge Rd SR4 85 D6
Fordenbridge Sq SR4 85 E6
Fordfield Rd SR4 85 D6
Ford Gr NE3 38 B7
Ford Hall Dr SR4 85 E6
Fordham Rd SR4 85 E6
Fordham Sq SR4 85 E6
Fordland Pl SR4 85 F6
FORDLEY 29 B8
Fordley Com Prim Sch NE23 29 B8
Fordmoss Wlk 7 NE5 37 A2
Ford Oval SR4 85 B7
Ford Pk NE62 11 C8
Ford Rise NE43 64 C7
Ford St NE6 56 A5
Ford Terr
Guide Post NE62 10 F7
Riding Mill NE44 63 A8
5 Sunderland SR4 85 F6
Wallsend NE28 40 F2
Ford The NE42 50 C3
Ford View NE23 22 A1
Fore St NE2 56 A8
Forest Ave NE12 39 E8
Forestborn Ct 5 NE5 36 F2
Forest Dr NE38 88 F8
Forest Gate NE12 30 A1
FOREST HALL 39 E8
Forest Hall Prim Sch 2 NE12 29 D1
Forest Hall Rd NE12 29 E1
Forest Rd
Newcastle upon Tyne NE15 54 C4
South Shields NE33 42 C2
Sunderland SR4 85 D6
Forest Road Ind Est 5 NE33 42 C2
Forest Villa NE12 39 E8
Forest Way NE23 22 F1
Forfar St SR6 75 D2
Forge Cl NE17 77 B6
Forge La
Bournmoor DH3 89 B2
Hamsterley Mill NE17 77 E5
Forge Rd NE11, NE8 70 A8
Forge The SR4 85 F7
Forge Wlk NE15 35 F1
Forres Pl NE23 22 B8
Forrest Rd 5 NE28 40 A1
Forster Ave
Bedlington NE22 10 E1
Sherburn DH6 96 A2
South Shields NE34 59 E6
Forster Ct 6 NE9 70 F4
Forster St
Blyth NE24 17 F7
Newcastle upon Tyne NE1 99 C1
Sunderland SR6 75 E1
Forsyth Rd NE2 38 E1
Forsyth St NE29 31 B1
Forth Banks NE1 101 A4
Forth Ct
7 Silksworth SR3 91 F6
South Shields NE34 59 C5
Forth La NE1 101 A4
Forth Pl NE1 100 C4
Forth St
Chopwell NE17 66 C1
Newcastle upon Tyne NE1 101 A4
Fortrose Ave SR3 86 A3
Fort Sq 2 NE33 42 C4
Fort St NE33 42 D4
Forum Ct NE22 10 F1
Forum Sh Ctr The 2 NE28 40 B1
Forum The NE15 53 F7
Forum Way NE23 22 A6
Fossdyke NE10 71 F5
Fossefeld NE10 72 A7
Fosse Law NE15 35 E1
Fosse Terr NE9 71 B6
Fossway NE6 56 E7
Foss Way
Ebchester DH8 76 E3
South Shields NE34 59 B5
Foster Ct NE11 70 C3
Foster Dr NE8 56 B2
Foster St
Newcastle upon Tyne, Low Walker NE6 57 B6
Newcastle upon Tyne, Wincomblee NE6 57 B5
Foundary Ct NE6 56 C4
Foundry Ct NE6 56 C4
Foundry Ind Est NE46 45 C6
Foundry La NE6 56 A6
Fountain Cl NE22 10 F1
Fountain Gr NE34 59 F8
Fountain Head Bank NE26 24 C6
Fountain La NE21 53 C3
Fountain Row NE2 98 B3
Fountains Cl
Dunston NE11 69 F6
Washington NE38 83 D4
Fountains Cres
Burnside DH4 90 C2
Hebburn NE31 57 E3
Fouracres Rd NE5 37 E2
Four Lane Ends
Hetton-le-Hole DH5 95 B2
Houghton-le-Spring DH5 94 D6
Four Lane Ends Sta NE7 39 C5
Fourstones 6 NE5 37 A2
Fourstones Cl NE3 37 D5
Fourstones Rd SR4 85 E6
Fourteenth Ave NE24 17 D6
Fourth Ave
Ashington NE63 6 D3
Blyth NE24 17 D6
Chester le Street DH2 88 B3
Gateshead NE11 70 C5
Morpeth NE61 9 B7
1 Newcastle upon Tyne NE6 56 C7
Fourth Row NE61 1 A3
Fourth St NE8 101 A1
Fowberry Cres NE4 54 E7
Fowberry Rd NE15 53 F4
Fowler Cl DH4 90 C4
Fowler Gdns 2 NE11 54 F1
Fowler St NE33 42 C3
Fox and Hounds La NE15 54 C6
Fox and Hounds Rd NE5 54 C7
Fox Ave NE34 59 A4
Foxcover NE63 6 F1
Foxcover La SR3 91 B7
Foxcover Rd
Sunderland, Middle Herrington SR3 91 A8
Sunderland, Offerton SR4 84 F2
Fox Covert La NE20 25 D6
Foxglove DH4 89 F5
Foxglove Cl NE24 17 C4
Foxglove Ct NE34 59 B4
Foxhill Cl NE63 6 B1
Foxhills Cl NE38 83 E2
Foxhills Covert NE16 68 E5
Foxhills The NE16 68 E6
Fox Ho SR3 92 A4
Foxhomes NE32 73 D8
Foxhunters Light Ind Site NE25 31 F3
Foxhunters Rd NE25 31 F3
Foxlair Cl SR3 92 A4
Fox Lea Wlk NE23 22 E1
Foxley NE37 83 E8
Foxley Cl NE12 29 F4
Fox St
Gateshead NE10 56 C1
Sunderland SR2 102 B1
Foxton Ave
Newcastle upon Tyne NE3 37 F7
Tynemouth NE30 32 B3
Foxton Cl NE29 41 E3
Foxton Ct SR6 60 A1
Foxton Gn NE3 37 E5
Foxton Hall NE37 72 D3
Foxton Way NE10 57 B2
Foyle St SR1 103 A2
Framlington Ho NE2 98 C3
Framlington Pl NE2 98 C3
Frances St
Blaydon NE21 53 A2
9 New Silksworth SR3 92 A7
Frances Ville NE62 10 E4
Francis Rd DH5 95 A4
Francis St
Beamish DH9 80 D1
Sunderland SR6 75 D2
Francis Way NE27 30 D1
Frank Bushell Ho NE34 59 C5
Frankham St 1 NE5 36 F2
Frankland Dr NE25 31 E3
Franklin Ct 10 NE37 83 D8
Franklin Pk NE21 53 E4
Franklin St
South Shields NE33 42 C2
Sunderland SR4 102 A3
Franklyn Ave NE26 24 B7
Frank Pl NE29 42 A6
Frank St
Greenside NE40 51 F1
Sunderland SR5 75 B2
Wallsend NE28 40 B1
Fraser Cl NE33 59 B8
Frater Terr NE28 41 C2
Frazer Terr NE10 57 A1
Freda St SR5 74 F1
Frederick Gdns DH4 90 A7
Frederick Rd SR1 103 A3
Frederick St
Chopwell NE17 77 B8
South Shields NE33 42 C1
Sunderland, South Hylton SR4 85 A6
Sunderland SR1 103 A2
Frederick Terr
Hetton-le-Hole DH5 95 B1
South Hetton DH6 97 F6
3 Whitburn SR6 60 F1
Freehold Ave NE62 10 F7
Freehold St 5 NE24 17 F8
Freeman Hospl NE7 39 A4
Freeman Rd NE3, NE7 38 F4
Freeman Way
Ashington NE63 6 F1
Whitley Bay NE26 31 E7
Freesia Grange NE38 83 E3
Freezemoor Rd DH4 90 D6
Fremantle Rd NE34 60 B5
Frenchman's Row NE15 35 B2
Frenchman's Way NE34 60 B8
French St NE24 17 E8
Frensham NE38 84 A4
Frenton Cl NE5 36 C2
Friarage Ave SR6 75 D3
Friar Rd SR4 85 D6
Friars NE1 98 C1
Friars Dene Rd NE10 56 C2
Friarsfield Cl SR3 91 E5
Friars Gate NE61 8 D7
FRIARS GOOSE 56 D3
Friarside Cres NE39 78 D8
Friarside Gdns
Burnopfield NE16 78 F6
Whickham NE16 69 A6
Friarside Rd NE4 54 E8
Friar Sq SR4 85 D6
Friar's Row NE16 78 F5
Friars St NE1 98 C1
Friars Way NE5 54 C8
Friar Way NE32 58 C7
Friary Gdns NE10 56 C1
Frinton Pk SR3 86 A3
Frobisher Ct SR3 91 F6
Frobisher St NE31 58 A6
Frome Gdns NE9 70 F2
Frome Pl NE23 22 B8
Frome Sq SR4 85 C6
Front Rd SR4 85 D6
Front St
Annitsford NE23 22 B1
Blaydon NE21 53 B1
Blyth NE24 16 E7
Boldon Colliery NE35 58 E1
Burnopfield, Hobson NE16 79 A4
Burnopfield, Lintz NE16 78 E6
Burnopfield NE16 79 B6
Chester le Street DH3 88 C3
Cleadon SR6 60 A1
Corbridge NE45 46 F5
Cramlington NE23 22 B6
Dinnington NE13 27 B7
Dipton DH9 78 E
Earsdon NE25 31 A5
East Boldon NE36 74 C
Ebchester DH8 76 E
Ellington NE61 1 C
Fence Houses DH4 94 A8
Guide Post NE62 10 E7
Haswell DH6 97 E1
Hetton-le-Hole DH5 95 A
Hetton-le-Hole, Low Moorsley DH5 94 E
High Pittington DH6 96 B6
High Spen NE39 67 A
Killingworth NE12, NE23 29 B
Longbenton NE7, NE12 39 C
Newbeggin-by-the-Sea NE64 7 E
Newbottle DH4 90 D
Newbottle DH4 90 D
North Shields NE29 41 E
Prudhoe, Hagg Bank NE41 50 F
Prudhoe NE42 50 D
Seghill NE23 22 F
Sherburn DH6 96 A
Sherburn Hill DH6 96 D
South Hetton DH6 97 F
Tanfield DH9 79 D
Tantobie DH9 79 B
Tynemouth, Cullercoats NE30 32 C
Tynemouth NE30 42 D
Tynemouth, Preston NE29 42 A

Front St continued
Washington NE37 . . . . .83 D8
Whickham NE16. . . . . .69 B7
Whickham, Swalwell NE16 . . .54 A1
Whitburn SR6. . . . . .75 F8
Whitley Bay NE25 . . . . .31 E4
Front Street Com Prim Sch
14 NE16. . . . . .69 A7
Front Street E
Bedlington NE22 . . . . .16 A8
Haswell DH6 . . . . .97 F3
Penshaw DH4 . . . . .90 B8
Front Street Ind Est DH6 . .97 F7
Front Street W
Bedlington NE22 . . . . .15 F8
Penshaw DH4 . . . . .90 B8
Frosterley Cl DH5. . . . . .97 D8
Frosterley Gdns SR3 . . . . . .86 B2
Frosterley Pl NE4. . . . . .98 A2
Frosterley Wlk NE16 . . . . . .69 B3
Frost Mews NE33 . . . . .42 C1
Froude Ave NE34 . . . . .59 C3
Fuchsia Gdns NE31 . . . . . . .57 E3
Fuchsia Pl NE5 . . . . .37 D2
Fulbrook Cl **5** SR2 . . . . . . .92 F5
Fulbrook Cl NE23 . . . . .16 B2
Fulbrook Rd NE3 . . . . .37 F5
Fuller Rd SR2. . . . . .86 C4
Fullerton Pl NE9 . . . . .71 A8
Fulmar Dr
Blyth NE24. . . . . .17 E3
Washington NE38 . . . . .82 F3
Fulmar Lodge NE3 . . . . .42 F2
Fulmar Wlk SR6 . . . . .60 F2
FULWELL 75 C4
Fulwell Ave NE34 . . . . .60 B7
Fulwell Grn NE5. . . . . .37 B1
Fulwell Inf Sch SR6. . . . . . .75 D4
Fulwell Jun Sch SR6. . . . . . .75 C4
Fulwell Quarry Nature
Reserve★ SR5. . . . . .75 A5
Fulwell Rd SR6. . . . . .75 C2
Fulwell Windmill★ SR5. . . . .75 C2
Furnace Bank NE22 . . . . . . .11 D1
Furness Ct **1** SR3. . . . . . . .91 F6
Furrowfield NE10 . . . . .71 C6
Furrowfield Sch NE10. . . . . .71 C6
Furzefield Rd NE3 . . . . .38 B4
Fylingdale Dr SR3 . . . . .92 C2
Fylingdale Dr **3** SR3 . . . . . .91 F5

G

Gables Ct SR4 . . . . .85 C3
Gables The
3 Blyth NE24. . . . . .17 D8
Newcastle upon Tyne NE13 . .37 B8
4 Washington NE38. . . . . . .83 E4
Gadwall Rd NE24 . . . . .94 B6
Gainers Terr NE28. . . . . . .57 C8
Gainford
Chester le Street DH2. . . . . .88 A3
Gateshead NE9 . . . . .70 F2
Gainsborough Ave
Washington NE38 . . . . .83 C4
Whiteleas NE34. . . . . .59 D2
Gainsborough Cl NE25 . . . .31 C1
Gainsborough Cres
Gateshead NE9 . . . . .71 B7
Shiney Row DH4 . . . . .90 A5
Gainsborough Pl NE23 . . . .22 B3
Gainsborough Sq SR4. . . . .85 C2
Gainsbro Gr NE4 . . . . .54 F6
Gainsford Ave NE9 . . . . . . .70 E4
Gairloch Cl NE23. . . . . .16 B1
Gairloch Dr NE38 . . . . .83 A3
Gairloch Rd SR4 . . . . .85 C3
Gairsay Cl **2** SR2 . . . . . . .92 E8
Galashiels Gr DH4 . . . . . . .90 B5
Galashiels Rd SR4 . . . . . . .85 C3
Galashiels Sq SR4 . . . . . . .85 C3
Gale Ho **8** NE1. . . . . .99 A1
Gallalaw Terr NE3. . . . . . . .38 F5
Gallant Terr NE28 . . . . .41 C1
Galleries Sh Ctr The NE38 .83 D5
Galley's Gill Rd SR1. . . . . .102 C3
Galloping Green Farm Cl **2**
NE9. . . . . .71 D2
Galloping Green Rd NE9 . . .71 D2
Galloway Rd NE6 . . . . .57 B8
Gallowgate NE1 . . . . .98 C1
Gallowhill La NE15, NE42. . .50 B7
Gallows Bank NE46 . . . . . . .45 B3
Galsworthy Rd
Biddick Hall NE34 . . . . .59 B3
Sunderland SR4. . . . . .85 C3
Whiteleas NE34. . . . . .59 C3
Galway Rd SR4 . . . . .85 C3
Galway Sq SR4 . . . . .85 B3
Gambia Rd **4** SR4 . . . . . . .85 B2
Gambia Sq SR4 . . . . .85 B2
Ganton Ave NE23 . . . . .22 B4
Ganton Cl NE37 . . . . .72 C2
Ganton Ct NE34 . . . . .59 F3
Gaprigg Ct NE46 . . . . .45 B4
Gaprigg La NE46. . . . . .45 A4
Garasdale Cl NE24 . . . . . . .17 D4
Garcia Dr NE63. . . . . .6 F3
Garcia Terr **3** SR6 . . . . . . .75 E4
Garden City Villas NE63 . . .6 D3
Garden Cl NE13. . . . . .28 B8
Garden Cres DH8 . . . . .76 F4
Garden Croft NE12 . . . . . . .39 E8
Garden Ct DH6 . . . . .96 A2
Garden Dr NE31 . . . . .57 D4
Garden Est DH5. . . . . .95 B4

Front St continued
Washington NE37 . . . . .83 D8
Garden House Cres NE16. . .69 C8
Garden House Est NE40 . . .51 E4
Garden House Farm DH2. . .88 B1
Garden La
Cleadon SR6 . . . . .74 F8
South Shields NE33 . . . . .42 C2
Garden Pk **9** NE28 . . . . . . .40 F4
Garden Pl
Penshaw DH4 . . . . .90 B7
Sunderland SR1. . . . . 102 C3
Garden St
Blaydon NE21. . . . . .53 C3
Newbottle DH4 . . . . .90 D3
Newcastle upon Tyne NE4. . . .38 C4
Gardens The
Chester le Street DH2. . . . . . .88 B3
Washington NE38 . . . . .83 E4
Whitley Bay NE25 . . . . .31 F4
Garden Terr
10 Blaydon NE21 . . . . .53 B1
Crawcrook NE40. . . . . .51 F4
Crawcrook, Ryton Woodside
NE40 . . . . .52 A3
Earsdon NE25 . . . . .31 A5
Hexham NE46 . . . . .45 A5
Newbottle DH4 . . . . .90 D3
Gardiner Rd SR4 . . . . .85 B3
Gardiner Sq
Kibblesworth NE11. . . . . .81 C6
4 Sunderland SR4 . . . . .85 B3
Gardner Pk NE29 . . . . .41 F5
Gardner Pl NE29. . . . . .42 B5
Garesfield Gdns
Burnopfield NE16. . . . . .78 F6
Rowlands Gill NE39 . . . . .67 E6
Garesfield La NE21, NE39 . .67 E6
Gareston Cl NE24 . . . . .17 B7
Garfield St **6** SR4 . . . . . . .85 F7
Garforth Cl NE23. . . . . .22 A4
Garland Terr **4** DH4 . . . . . .94 A8
Garleigh Cl NE12 . . . . .29 F3
Garmondsway **14** NE6 . . . . .56 C5
Garner Cl NE5 . . . . .36 D3
Garnet St **3** SR4 . . . . .85 F7
Garrett Cl NE28 . . . . .40 F3
Garrick Cl NE29 . . . . .41 C2
Garrick St NE33 . . . . .59 C8
Garrigill NE38 . . . . .83 F1
Garsdale DH3. . . . . .82 B5
Garsdale Ave NE37. . . . . . . .83 C8
Garsdale Rd NE26. . . . . .24 E1
Garside Ave DH3. . . . . .82 C6
Garstin Cl NE7 . . . . .39 E3
Garth Cotts NE46 . . . . .45 A4
Garth Cres
Blaydon NE21. . . . . .53 B1
South Shields NE34 . . . . .43 A1
Garth Farm Rd NE21 . . . . . .53 B1
Garthfield Cl NE5 . . . . .37 A3
Garthfield Cnr NE5 . . . . . . .37 A3
Garthfield Cres NE5 . . . . . .37 A3
Garth Heads NE1 . . . . .99 C1
Garth Sixteen NE12 . . . . . .29 D4
Garth The
7 Blaydon NE21 . . . . .53 B1
Medomsley DH8. . . . . .77 C2
Newcastle upon Tyne, Kenton
NE3. . . . . .37 F4
Newcastle upon Tyne NE5. . . .36 E1
Garth Thirty Three NE12 . . .29 E3
Garth Thirty Two NE12 . . . .29 E3
Garth Twenty NE12. . . . . . . .29 E3
Garth Twenty Five NE12 . . .29 F3
Garth Twenty Four NE12. . .29 E3
Garth Twenty One NE12 . . .29 E3
Garth Twenty Seven NE12 . .29 F3
Garth Twenty Two NE12 . . .29 E3
Gartland Rd SR4 . . . . .85 B3
Garvey Villas N10, NE9. . . . .71 C6
Garwood St NE33 . . . . .59 B8
Gas House La NE61. . . . . . . .4 A1
Gaskell Ave NE34 . . . . .59 B3
Gas La NE21. . . . . .53 C4
Gatacre St NE24 . . . . .17 E8
Gateley Ave NE24 . . . . .17 D4
Gatesgarth NE9. . . . . .71 A5
Gatesgarth Gr SR6 . . . . . . .75 D5
GATESHEAD
. . . . .55 E2
. . . . 101 C2
Gateshead Coll (Academy for
Sport) NE8 . . . . .56 B3
Gateshead Coll (Baltic Ctr)
NE8 . . . . 101 C4
Gateshead Coll (Skills Acad)
NE11 . . . . 101 A4
Gateshead Corpus Christi RC
Prim Sch **2** NE8 . . . . . . .70 D8
Gateshead Highway NE8 101 C2
Gateshead International Stad
(Athletics Gd) NE10 . . . . .56 C3
Gateshead Jewis Academy
Girls NE8 . . . . 101 B1
Gateshead Jewish Boarding
Sch NE8 . . . . 101 B1
Gateshead Jewish Prim Sch
NE8 . . . . 101 B1
Gateshead Jewish Sch
NE8 . . . . 101 B1
Gateshead Jewish Teachers
Training Coll NE8. . . . . . 101 B1
Gateshead Millenium
Bridge★ NE8 . . . . 101 C4
Gateshead Rd NE16. . . . . . .69 C3
Gateshead Rd NE16. . . . . . 101 B3
Gateshead Stadium Sta
NE8 .56 A2

Gateshead Talmudical Coll
NE8 . . . . 101 B1
Gate The NE11 . . . . .98 C1
Gatwick Ct NE3 . . . . .37 C7
Gatwick Rd SR4 . . . . .85 B3
Gaughan Ct NE6 . . . . .56 F3
Gawsevell Terr DH4 . . . . . . .90 D4
Gayhurst Cres SR3 . . . . . . .92 B6
Gayton Rd NE37 . . . . .72 E1
Geddes Rd SR4 . . . . .85 C3
Gellesfield Chare NE16. . . .69 B3
Gelt Cres DH1 . . . . .78 A4
General Graham St SR4 . . 102 A1
General Havelock Rd SR4 . .85 E6
General's Wood The NE38 . .89 B8
Geneva Rd SR4 . . . . .85 B3
Genister Pl NE4. . . . . .54 D8
Geoffrey St
Whitburn SR6. . . . . .60 F1
Whiteleas NE34 . . . . .59 C3
George Rd
Bedlington NE22 . . . . .11 D2
Washington NE38 . . . . .87 B8
George Scott St NE33 . . . . .42 D4
George Smith Gdns NE10. . .56 C2
George Sq **6** NE30 . . . . . . .42 B6
Georges Rd
Newcastle upon Tyne, Elswick
NE4. . . . . .54 F3
Newcastle upon Tyne NE4. . . .54 F3
George St
Ashington NE63. . . . . .6 E4
Birtley DH3 . . . . .82 B4
Blaydon NE21. . . . . .53 D3
Blyth NE24. . . . . .17 E6
Brunswick Village NE13 . . . . .28 A6
Chester le Street DH3. . . . . . .88 D2
5 Crawcrook NE40. . . . . . . .51 F3
5 Gateshead NE10 . . . . . . .56 F1
Haswell DH6 . . . . .97 F3
Hetton-le-Hole DH5. . . . . . . .95 A5
Newcastle upon Tyne, Coxlodge
NE3. . . . . .38 A5
Newcastle upon Tyne NE1,
NE4. . . . . 100 C4
North Shields NE30 . . . . .42 B6
Ryhope SR2 . . . . .93 A6
Sherburn DH6 . . . . .96 A1
Walbottle NE15 . . . . .35 F2
Wallsend NE28 . . . . .41 B1
Whickham NE16. . . . . .69 A7
George Stephenson High Sch
NE12 . . . . .29 D3
George Stephenson's
Cottage★ NE41. . . . . .51 D7
George Stephenson Way
NE29 . . . . .42 A3
George Street N SR6. . . . . .92 A8
George Street N SR6. . . . . 103 A4
George Street W **10** SR3 . . .92 A8
George's View NE29 . . . . . . .29 A7
George Washington Prim
Sch NE37 . . . . .72 C1
Georgian Ct
Longbenton NE12. . . . . .29 B1
Sunderland SR4. . . . . .86 A4
Gerald St
Newcastle upon Tyne NE4. . . .54 D4
Whiteleas NE34. . . . . .59 C3
Gerrard Cl
Cramlington NE23. . . . . .22 B4
Whitley Bay NE26 . . . . .24 E1
Gerrard Rd
6 Sunderland SR4 . . . . .85 B3
Whitley Bay NE26 . . . . .24 F1
Gertrude St DH4 . . . . .90 D2
Ghyll Edge NE61. . . . . .3 C1
Gibbon's Wlk NE34 . . . . . . .59 A2
Gibbs St **3** DH2 . . . . .88 C2
Gibside DH2. . . . . .88 A1
Gibside Chapel★ NE16 . . . .68 A1
Gibside Cres NE16 . . . . . . .79 D8
Gibside Ct
Burnopfield NE16. . . . . .79 B6
Dunston NE11 . . . . .69 F6
Gibside Gdns NE15. . . . . . .54 B6
Gibside Hall★ NE16. . . . . . .68 A1
Gibside Rd NE16 . . . . .69 A5
Gibside Terr NE16. . . . . . . .79 B6
Gibside View NE21. . . . . . . .68 B8
Gibside Way NE11 . . . . .54 B2
Gibson Ct NE35 . . . . .73 F8
Gibson Fields NE46. . . . . . .45 B4
Gibson Ho **8** NE46. . . . . . . .45 A4
Gibson Pl **8** NE46. . . . . . . .45 A5
Gibsons Ct NE21 . . . . .53 C2
Gibson St
Newbeggin-by-the-Sea
NE64. . . . . .7 D4
Newcastle upon Tyne NE1. . . .99 C1
Wallsend NE28 . . . . .40 F5
Gibson Terr NE40 . . . . .52 A4
Gifford Sq SR4. . . . . .85 C4
Gilberdyke NE10 . . . . .72 A6
Gilbert Rd SR4 . . . . .85 B2
Gilbert Sq SR4 . . . . .85 B2
Gilbert St NE33 . . . . .59 C8
Gilderdale DH4 . . . . .89 E8
Gilderdale Way NE23 . . . . . .22 A3
Gilesgate NE46 . . . . .45 A5
Gilesgate Ct **10** NE46. . . . . .45 A5
Giles Pl **13** NE46 . . . . .45 A5
Gilhespy Green Cvn Pk
NE24 . . . . .17 F4
Gilhurst Grange SR1. . . . . 102 B2
Gillas La DH5. . . . . .95 A7
Gillas Lane E DH5. . . . . . . .94 F7

Gillas Lane Prim Sch DH5 .94 F7
Gillas Lane W DH5. . . . . . . .94 E6
Gillbridge Ave SR2. . . . . . .102 C3
Gill Burn NE39. . . . . .67 E3
Gill Crescent N DH4 . . . . . .89 E1
Gill Crescent S DH4 . . . . . .89 E1
Gill Ct NE13 . . . . .28 A6
Gillhurst Ho SR1. . . . . .102 B3
Gillies St NE6. . . . . .56 D6
Gilliland Cres DH3 . . . . . . .82 C6
Gillingham Rd SR4. . . . . . . .85 C3
Gillside Ct **4** NE34 . . . . . . .59 A5
Gill Side Gr SR6 . . . . .75 E2
Gill St NE4 . . . . .54 E5
Gillwood Ct DH4. . . . . .89 E1
Gilmore Cl NE5 . . . . .36 D3
Gilmore Ho NE8 . . . . .70 E8
Gilpin St SR4. . . . . .94 D8
Gilsland Ave NE28 . . . . .40 F3
Gilsland Gr NE23. . . . . .16 B1
Gilsland St SR4 . . . . .102 A2
Gilwell Way NE3. . . . . .28 B1
Gingler La NE40 . . . . .52 A2
Girven Terr DH5 . . . . .95 B1
Girven Terrace W DH5 . . . . .95 B1
Gisburn Ct NF73 . . . . .16 B1
Gishford Way NE5 . . . . .37 B2
Givens St SR6 . . . . .75 E2
Gladeley Way NE16 . . . . . . .69 B2
Glade The
Newcastle upon Tyne NE3 . . .73 B8
Walbottle NE15 . . . . .36 A2
Gladewell Ct NE62 . . . . . . .10 E7
Gladstonbury Pl NE12. . . . .39 C7
Gladstone Ave NE26. . . . . . .31 F6
Gladstone Pl NE2 . . . . .99 B3
Gladstone St
Blyth NE24. . . . . .17 D8
Blyth NE24. . . . . .17 E8
Fence Houses DH4 . . . . .94 B8
Hebburn NE31, NE32 . . . . . . .58 A6
Morpeth NE61. . . . . .9 A8
Newcastle upon Tyne NE15 . .53 C6
Sunderland SR6. . . . . .75 D1
3 Wallsend NE28 . . . . .41 B1
Gladstone Terr
Bedlington NE22 . . . . .11 A1
Birtley DH3 . . . . .82 B4
2 Boldon Colliery NE35 . . . .58 E1
Gateshead NE8 . . . . 101 C1
Newcastle upon Tyne NE2. . . .99 B3
Penshaw DH4 . . . . .90 A8
Washington NE37 . . . . .83 F8
8 Whitley Bay NE26. . . . . . .32 B4
Gladstone Terrace W
NE8 . . . . 101 B1
Gladwyn Rd **2** SR4 . . . . . . .85 B2
Gladwyn Sq SR4 . . . . .85 B2
Glaholm Rd SR2 . . . . .103 C2
Glaisdale Ct NE34. . . . . . . .59 A4
Glaisdale Dr SR6. . . . . .75 E6
Glaisdale Rd NE7 . . . . .39 A5
Glamis Ave
Newcastle upon Tyne NE3 . . .28 C1
Sunderland SR4. . . . . .85 C4
Glamis Cres NE39. . . . . . . .68 B4
Glamis Ct
Bournmoor DH4. . . . . .89 D1
South Shields NE34 . . . . .59 F3
Glamis Terr NE16 . . . . .69 A1
Glamis Villas DH3 . . . . .82 C6
Glanmore Rd **8** SR4 . . . . . .85 B3
Glantlees NE5 . . . . .37 A2
Glanton Cl NE28 . . . . .40 C4
Glanton Ct NE11 . . . . 100 A1
Glanton Ho NE24 . . . . .17 B8
Glanton Rd
Hexham NE46 . . . . .45 D4
Tynemouth NE29 . . . . .41 D5
Glanton Sq SR4. . . . . .85 C3
Glanton Wynd NE3 . . . . .38 B7
Glanville Cl NE11 . . . . .70 B7
Glanville Rd SR3. . . . . .91 D5
Glasbury Ave SR4 . . . . .85 C4
Glasgow Rd NE32 . . . . .58 C3
Glassey Terr NE22 . . . . .11 D1
Glasshouse St NE6. . . . . . .56 C4
Glastonbury NE38. . . . . . . .83 D4
Glastonbury Gr NE2. . . . . . .38 F2
Glazebury Way NE23 . . . . . .16 A3
Glebe Ave
Longbenton NE12. . . . . .39 D7
Whickham NE16. . . . . .69 B7
Glebe Cl
Newcastle upon Tyne NE5. . . .36 D2
Ponteland NE20 . . . . .25 E7
Glebe Cres
Longbenton NE12. . . . . .29 D1
Washington NE38 . . . . .83 E6
Glebe Ct NE22 . . . . .10 F1
Glebe Dr SR7 . . . . .92 F2
Glebe Farm NE62 . . . . .10 F8
Glebelands NE45. . . . . .47 A6
Glebe Mews NE22 . . . . .10 F1
Glebe Rd
Bedlington NE22 . . . . .10 F1
Longbenton NE12. . . . . .29 D1
Glebe Rise NE16. . . . . .69 B7
Glebe St NE4 . . . . .54 E6

Glebe Terr
Choppington NE62. . . . . .10 E4
1 Dunston NE11 . . . . .69 F8
2 Houghton-le-Spring DH4 .90 D1
Longbenton NE12. . . . . .29 D1
Glebe The
21 South Shields NE33 . . . . .42 D1
Stannington NE61. . . . . .14 C4
GLEBE VILLAGE 83 D5
Glebe Villas NE12 . . . . .29 C1
Glebe Wlk NE16 . . . . .69 B7
Glenallen Gdns NE30. . . . . .32 C1
Glen Ave NE41 . . . . .64 C7
Glenavon Ave DH2 . . . . .88 B4
Glen Barr NE33 . . . . .88 B4
Glenbrooke Terr NE9 . . . . . .70 F4
Glenburn Cl NE38. . . . . .82 F3
Glencarron Cl NE38 . . . . . . .83 A3
Glen Cl NE39 . . . . .67 E3
Glencoe NE12 . . . . .29 D4
Glencoe Ave
Chester le Street DH2. . . . . . .88 B4
Cramlington NE23 . . . . .22 B3
Glencoe Rd SR4 . . . . .85 B2
Glencoe Rise NE39. . . . . . . .67 C1
Glencoe Sq SR4 . . . . .85 B3
Glencoe Terr NE39 . . . . . . .67 C1
Glencourse NE36 . . . . .74 E7
Glen Ct NE31. . . . . .57 D5
Glendale Ave
Blyth NE24. . . . . .16 E8
Newcastle upon Tyne NE5. . . .38 A4
North Shields NE29 . . . . .41 F6
Stakeford NE62 . . . . .11 A8
Wallsend NE28 . . . . .40 B4
Washington NE37 . . . . .83 C8
Whickham NE16. . . . . .69 A6
Whitley Bay NE26 . . . . .32 A7
Glendale Cl
Blaydon NE21. . . . . .67 F8
Newcastle upon Tyne NE5. . . .36 D3
Sunderland SR3. . . . . .91 C6
Glendale Gdns
Gateshead NE9 . . . . .71 B5
Stakeford NE62 . . . . .11 A8
Glendale Gr NE29 . . . . .41 F6
Glendale Rd
Ashington NE63. . . . . .7 A2
Shiremoor NE27 . . . . .31 A3
Glendale Terr **6** NE6 . . . . . .56 C6
Glendford Pl NE24 . . . . .17 D4
Glendower Ave NE29 . . . . . .41 D6
Glendyn Cl NE7. . . . . .39 A1
Gleneagle Cl NE5. . . . . .36 D3
Gleneagles
South Shields NE33 . . . . .42 F1
Whitley Bay NE25 . . . . .31 D6
Gleneagles Cl NE7 . . . . . . .39 C5
Gleneagles Ct NE25 . . . . . .31 D6
Gleneagles Dr NE37. . . . . . .72 C2
Gleneagles Rd
Gateshead NE9 . . . . .70 E3
Sunderland SR4. . . . . .85 B2
Gleneagles Sq **1** SR4. . . . .85 B2
Glenesk Gdns SR2 . . . . . . .86 C2
Glenesk Rd SR2 . . . . .86 C3
Glenfield Ave NE23. . . . . . . .16 B1
Glenfield Rd
Longbenton NE12. . . . . .39 B7
Longbenton NE12. . . . . .39 C7
Glengarvan Cl NE38. . . . . . .83 A3
Glenholme Cl **7** NE38 . . . . .82 F3
Glenhurst Dr
Newcastle upon Tyne NE5. . . .36 D3
Whickham NE16. . . . . .68 F4
Glenhurst Gr NE34 . . . . . . .59 F6
Glenkerry Cl NE38 . . . . .83 A3
Glenleigh Dr SR4 . . . . .85 C4
Glenluce Cl NE23 . . . . .22 B4
Glenluce Dr NE23 . . . . .22 B3
Glen Luce Dr SR2. . . . . .86 F2
Glenmeads NE31 . . . . .72 E7
Glenmore Ave DH2. . . . . . . .58 C4
Glenmuir Ave NE73 . . . . . . .22 A3
Glenorrin Cl NE38 . . . . .83 A3
Glen Path SR2 . . . . .86 D3
Glenridge Ave **2** NE6. . . . . .39 B1
Glenroy Gdns DH2. . . . . . . .88 B4
Glen's Flats DH6. . . . . .96 B5
Glenshiel Cl NE38 . . . . .83 A3
Glenside
Ellington NE61. . . . . .1 E5
Hedworth NE32 . . . . .58 C2
Glenside Ct NE9. . . . . .70 E4
Glen St NE31. . . . . .57 D5
Glen Terr
Chester le Street DH2. . . . . . .88 A4
Hexham NE46 . . . . .44 F5
Washington NE38 . . . . .83 E6
Glen Tho SR2 . . . . .86 D3
Glenthorne Rd **1** SR6 . . . . .75 E2
Glenthorn Rd NE2 . . . . .38 E2
Glenthorpe Ave SR6. . . . . . .75 E2
Glenthorpe Ho NE33 . . . . . .42 D1
Glenuce NE23 . . . . .82 E3
Glenwood NE63. . . . . .6 C2
Glenwood Wlk NE5 . . . . . . .36 D3
Gloria Ave NE25 . . . . .31 D5
Glossop St NE39 . . . . .66 F4
Gloucester Ave SR6 . . . . . . .75 E4
Gloucester St NE3 . . . . .37 C8
Gloucester Pl NE34 . . . . . . .60 A5
Gloucester Rd
Newcastle upon Tyne NE4. . . .98 A1
Shiremoor NE29 . . . . .41 B7

Gloucester St NE25 . . . . .23 D6
Gloucester Terr
  Haswell DH6 . . . . .97 E1
  Newcastle upon Tyne NE4 .100 A4
Gloucester Way
  Hedworth NE32 . . . . .58 B2
  Newcastle upon Tyne NE4 .100 B4
Glover Ind Est NE37 . . . . .83 F7
Glover Network Ctr NE37 . .83 F7
Glover Rd
  Sunderland SR4 . . . . .85 B2
  Washington NE37 . . . . .83 F8
Glovers Pl **6** NE46 . . . . .45 A5
Glover Sq SR4 . . . . .85 B2
Glynfellis NE10 . . . . .71 F4
Glynfellis Ct NE10 . . . . .71 F5
Glynwood Cl NE23 . . . . .16 B1
Glynwood Gdns NE9 . . . . . . .71 A5
Glynwood Prim Sch NE12 . .71 A5
Goalmouth Cl **6** SR6 . . . . . .75 C2
Goathland Ave NE12 . . . . . . .39 C6
Goathland Cl SR3 . . . . .92 C7
Goathland Dr SR3 . . . . .92 B6
Goathland Prim Sch NE12 .39 C6
Godfrey Rd SR4 . . . . .85 B3
Gofton Wlk NE5 . . . . .37 A2
Goldcrest Rd NE38 . . . . .82 F3
Goldfinch Cl NE4 . . . . .54 F4
Goldlynn Dr SR3 . . . . .91 E6
Goldsbrough Ct NE2 . . . . . . .98 C3
Goldsmith Rd SR4 . . . . .85 B2
Goldspink La NE2 . . . . .56 A7
Goldstone Ct NE12 . . . . .29 E4
Goldthorpe Cl NE23 . . . . .16 B1
Golf Course Rd DH4 . . . . .90 A4
Gompertz Gdns NE33 . . . . . . .59 B8
Gooch Ave NE22 . . . . .11 A4
Goodrich Cl DH4 . . . . .90 C5
Goodwood NE12 . . . . .29 E3
Goodwood Ave NE8 . . . . .70 C8
Goodwood Cl NE5 . . . . .36 D3
Goodwood Ct NE63 . . . . .6 D2
Goodwood Rd SR4 . . . . .85 A3
Goodwood Sq SR4 . . . . .85 A3
Goole Rd SR4 . . . . .85 C3
Goose Hill NE61 . . . . .9 A8
Gordon Ave
  1 Newcastle upon Tyne
    NE3 . . . . .38 C4
  Sunderland SR5 . . . . .85 A8
Gordon Ct **9** NE10 . . . . .56 D1
Gordon Dr NE36 . . . . .74 D7
Gordon Ho
  2 Newcastle upon Tyne
    NE6 . . . . .56 B5
Gordon Rd
  Blyth NE24 . . . . .17 F6
  3 Newcastle upon Tyne
    NE6 . . . . .56 B5
  South Shields NE34 . . . . .59 C6
  Sunderland SR4 . . . . .85 B2
Gordon Sq
  Newcastle upon Tyne NE6 . .56 B5
  Whitley Bay NE26 . . . . .32 C4
Gordon St NE33 . . . . .59 D8
Gordon Terr
  Bedlington NE22 . . . . .16 A8
  Prudhoe NE42 . . . . .50 D2
  3 Ryhope SR2 . . . . .93 A6
  Sunderland SR5 . . . . .75 A2
  Whitley Bay NE26 . . . . .32 C5
Gorleston Way SR3 . . . . .92 A4
Gorse Ave NE34 . . . . .60 A5
Gorsedene Ave NE26 . . . . . . .24 F1
Gorsedene Rd NE26 . . . . .24 F1
Gorsehill NE9 . . . . .71 C5
Gorse Hill Way NE5 . . . . .37 C3
Gorse Rd SR2 . . . . .103 A1
Gorseway NE61 . . . . .8 D7
Goschen St
  Blyth NE24 . . . . .17 D8
  Gateshead NE8 . . . . .70 D8
  Sunderland SR5 . . . . .75 A2
GOSFORTH 38 C6
Gosforth Ave NE34 . . . . .59 C3
Gosforth Bsns Pk NE12 . . . .38 F7
Gosforth Central Mid Sch
    NE3 . . . . .38 D6
Gosforth East Mid Sch
    NE3 . . . . .38 D7
Gosforth High Sch NE3 . . . .38 C6
Gosforth Jun High Sch
    NE3 . . . . .38 B5
Gosforth Park Ave NE12 . .39 A7
Gosforth Park Fst Sch
    NE3 . . . . .38 B8
Gosforth Park Villas NE13 .28 C4
Gosforth Park Way NE13 . .39 A8
Gosforth Sh Ctr NE3 . . . . . .38 C4
Gosforth St
  10 Gateshead NE10 . . . . . . .56 D1
  Newcastle upon Tyne NE2 . .99 C2
Gosforth Terr
  Gateshead NE10 . . . . .56 F1
  Newcastle upon Tyne NE3 . .38 E5
Gosport Way NE24 . . . . .17 E5
Gossington NE38 . . . . .84 A5
Goswick Ave NE7 . . . . .39 B3
Goswick Dr NE3 . . . . .37 F8
Goundry Ave SR2 . . . . .93 A6
Gourock Sq SR4 . . . . .85 A3
Gowanburn
  Cramlington NE23 . . . . .22 A3
  Washington NE38 . . . . .83 F2

Gowan Terr NE2 . . . . .38 F1
Gower Rd SR5 . . . . .75 A2
Gower St NE6 . . . . .57 A4
Gower Wlk NE10 . . . . .71 C8
Gowland Ave NE4 . . . . .54 E6
Grace Ct NE33 . . . . .59 C8
Gracefield Cl NE5 . . . . .36 D3
Grace Gdns NE28 . . . . .40 A4
Grace Ho NE29 . . . . .41 E3
Grace St
  Dunston NE11 . . . . .69 F8
  Newcastle upon Tyne, Byker
    NE6 . . . . .56 C6
  Newcastle upon Tyne, Walker
    NE6 . . . . .56 D6
Gradys Yd NE15 . . . . .35 D3
Grafton Cl **5** NE6 . . . . .56 B6
Grafton Ho **1** NE6 . . . . .56 B6
Grafton Rd NE26 . . . . .32 C4
Grafton St
  11 Newcastle upon Tyne
    NE6 . . . . .56 B6
  Sunderland SR4 . . . . .85 B3
Gragareth Way NE37 . . . . . . .83 A6
Graham Ave NE16 . . . . .69 B8
Graham Park Rd NE3 . . . . . . .38 C3
Graham Rd NE31 . . . . .57 D5
Grahamsley St NE8 . . . . . . .101 C2
Graham St NE33 . . . . .42 D2
Graham Terr DH4 . . . . .96 B5
Grainger Ct NE4 . . . . .54 F5
Grainger Mkt NE1 . . . . .99 A1
Grainger Park Rd NE4 . . . . . .54 F5
Grainger St NE1 . . . . .99 A1
Graingerville N NE4 . . . . .98 A1
Graingerville S NE4 . . . . .98 A1
Grampian Ave DH2 . . . . .88 B2
Grampian Cl **2** NE29 . . . . . . .31 F1
Grampian Gdns NE11 . . . . . . .70 B6
Grampian Gr NE36 . . . . .74 B7
Grampian Pl NE12 . . . . .29 B1
Granaries The
  Fence Houses DH4 . . . . .94 B8
  High Spen NE39 . . . . .66 F4
  Sunderland SR4 . . . . .84 F3
Granby Cl
  Sunderland SR3 . . . . .86 B3
  Sunniside NE16 . . . . .69 B3
Granby Terr **4** NE6 . . . . .56 E5
Grand Par NE30 . . . . .32 D1
Grandstand Rd NE2 . . . . .38 B2
Grandstand The NE61 . . . . . . .8 D6
Grange Ave
  Bedlington NE22 . . . . .11 E3
  Fence Houses DH4 . . . . .90 A1
  Longbenton NE12 . . . . .39 E6
  Shiremoor NE27 . . . . .30 F4
Grange Cl
  Blyth NE24 . . . . .17 D4
  Tynemouth NE30 . . . . .32 B2
  Wallsend NE28 . . . . .40 C2
  Whitley Bay NE25 . . . . .31 D4
Grange Cres
  Gateshead NE10 . . . . .72 A7
  Ryton NE40 . . . . .52 C4
  Sunderland SR3 . . . . .103 A1
Grange Ct
  Gateshead NE10 . . . . .72 A7
  6 Gateshead NE9 . . . . .58 B7
  Morpeth NE61 . . . . .9 A7
  Prudhoe NE42 . . . . .50 D2
  Ryton NE40 . . . . .52 C4
Grange Dr NE40 . . . . .52 C4
Grange Farm Dr NE16 . . . . . .69 A5
Grange Fst Sch NE3 . . . . .38 B6
Grange La NE16 . . . . .69 B5
Grange Lonnen NE40 . . . . . . .52 B5
Grange Manor NE16 . . . . .69 B5
Grangemere Cl SR2 . . . . .86 F1
Grange Nook NE16 . . . . .69 A5
Grange Park Ave
  Bedlington NE22 . . . . .11 E3
  Sunderland SR5 . . . . .75 C2
Grange Park Prim Sch
    SR5 . . . . .75 C2
Grange Pk NE25 . . . . .31 D4
Grange Pl NE32 . . . . .58 B7
Grange Rd
  Gateshead NE10 . . . . .72 A7
  Jarrow NE32 . . . . .58 B7
  Morpeth NE61 . . . . .9 A6
  Newburn NE15 . . . . .52 E8
  Newcastle upon Tyne, Fenham
    NE4 . . . . .54 D7
  Newcastle upon Tyne, Gosforth
    NE3 . . . . .38 C7
  Ponteland NE20 . . . . .25 F7
  Ryton NE40 . . . . .52 C5
  Sunderland SR5 . . . . .85 A8
Grange Road W NE32 . . . . . .58 A7
Grangeside Ct **8** NE29 . . . .31 F1
Grange Street S SR2 . . . . . . .86 F2
Grange Terr
  1 East Boldon NE36 . . . . . .74 D7
  6 Gateshead NE9 . . . . .71 A8
  Kibblesworth NE11 . . . . .81 C6
  Medomsley DH8 . . . . .77 B1
  Prudhoe NE42 . . . . .50 D2
  3 Sunderland, High Southwick
    SR5 . . . . .75 B2
  Sunderland SR2 . . . . .103 A1
Grange The
  Bedlington NE22 . . . . .10 A1
  East Boldon NE36 . . . . .74 D7

Grange View
  East Rainton DH5 . . . . .94 D5
  Newbottle DH4 . . . . .90 D3
  Ryton NE40 . . . . .52 C4
  Sunderland SR5 . . . . .75 C3
Grange Villas NE28 . . . . .40 C2
Grange Wlk **8** NE16 . . . . . . .69 A5
Grangewood Cl DH4 . . . . . . .90 A5
Grangewood Ct **3** DH4 . . .90 A6
Grantham Dr NE9 . . . . .70 E4
Grantham Pl NE23 . . . . .22 A4
Grantham Rd
  Newcastle upon Tyne NE2 . .99 C3
  Sunderland SR6 . . . . .75 E2
Grantham St NE24 . . . . .17 F6
Grant St NE32 . . . . .58 A7
Granville Ave
  Longbenton NE12 . . . . .29 E1
  Seaton Sluice NE26 . . . . .24 D5
Granville Cres NE12 . . . . .39 E7
Granville Ct NE12 . . . . .99 C4
Granville Dr
  Longbenton NE12 . . . . .39 E7
  Newcastle upon Tyne NE5 . .36 D3
  Shiney Row DH4 . . . . .90 A4
Granville Gdns
  Newcastle upon Tyne NE2 . .56 A8
  Stakeford NE62 . . . . .11 A8
Granville Lodge NE12 . . . . . .39 E8
Granville Rd
  Newcastle upon Tyne, Gosforth
    NE3 . . . . .38 D7
  Newcastle upon Tyne, Jesmond
    NE2 . . . . .99 C4
Granville St
  Gateshead NE8 . . . . .101 C1
  Sunderland SR4 . . . . .102 B3
Grasmere
  Birtley DH3 . . . . .82 E2
  Cleadon SR6 . . . . .60 A1
Grasmere Ave
  Easington Lane DH5 . . . . . . .97 C8
  Gateshead NE10 . . . . .71 F8
  Hedworth NE32 . . . . .58 D3
  Newburn NE15 . . . . .52 E7
  Newcastle upon Tyne NE6 . .56 F5
Grasmere Cres
  Blaydon NE21 . . . . .68 B8
  5 Penshaw DH4 . . . . .90 B6
  Sunderland SR5 . . . . .75 C3
  Whitley Bay NE26 . . . . .31 F7
Grasmere Ct
  Killingworth NE12 . . . . .29 C3
  Newburn NE15 . . . . .52 E7
Grasmere Gdns
  South Shields NE34 . . . . .59 E4
  Washington NE38 . . . . .83 E4
Grasmere Ho NE6 . . . . .56 E5
Grasmere Pl **2** NE3 . . . . . . .38 C7
Grasmere Rd
  Chester le Street DH2 . . . . . .88 B1
  Hebburn NE31 . . . . .57 F4
  Wallsend NE28 . . . . .40 A1
  Whickham NE16 . . . . .69 C7
Grasmere St NE8 . . . . .101 B1
Grasmere Street W NE8 . .101 B1
Grasmere Terr
  Newbiggin-by-the-Sea
    NE64 . . . . .7 D4
  Washington NE38 . . . . .83 E5
Grasmoor Pl NE15 . . . . .53 B7
Grassbanks NE10 . . . . .72 A6
Grassholme Mdws SR3 . . . .86 B2
Grassholm Pl NE12 . . . . .39 A7
Grassington Dr NE23 . . . . . . .22 A4
Grasslees NE38 . . . . .88 F8
Grassmere Cl NE10 . . . . .72 A6
GRASSWELL 90 D2
Grasswell Cvn Site DH4 . .90 D2
Grasswell Dr NE5 . . . . .37 D3
Grasswell Terr DH4 . . . . .90 D2
Gravel Wlks DH5 . . . . .90 F1
Gravesend Rd SR4 . . . . .85 B2
Gravesend Sq SR4 . . . . .85 C2
Gray Ave
  Chester le Street DH2 . . . . . .88 B2
  Wideopen NE13 . . . . .28 C7
Gray Ct SR2 . . . . .86 D4
Graylands NE38 . . . . .88 E8
Grayling Ct SR3 . . . . .91 C5
Grayling Rd NE11 . . . . .70 B7
Gray Rd
  Sunderland SR2 . . . . .103 B1
  Sunderland SR2 . . . . .103 C2
Grays Cross SR1 . . . . .103 B3
Gray St NE12 . . . . .12 E1
Grays Terr **8** NE35 . . . . .58 E1
Graystones NE10 . . . . .72 B6
Gray's Wlk NE34 . . . . .59 A2
Greathead St NE33 . . . . .59 C4
Great Lime Rd
  Dudley NE12, NE13, NE23 . .29 A5
  Longbenton NE12 . . . . .29 D1
GREAT LUMLEY 89 C1
Great North Mus, Hancock*
    NE2 . . . . .99 B3
Great North Rd
  Newcastle upon Tyne, Gosforth
    NE3 . . . . .38 C7
  Newcastle upon Tyne, West
    Jesmond NE2 . . . . .38 D2
  Stannington NE61 . . . . .9 A4
Great Parkway NE13 . . . . . . .27 F2
Great Park Way NE13 . . . . . .28 A3
Grebe Cl
  Ashington NE63 . . . . .11 C6
  Blyth NE24 . . . . .17 E5
  Dunston NE11 . . . . .100 A2

Grebe Ct **6** NE2 . . . . .38 F1
Greely Rd NE5 . . . . .36 F2
Grecnacre Pk NE9 . . . . .70 E3
Green Acres
  Morpeth NE61 . . . . .8 E7
  Ponteland NE20 . . . . .25 C1
Greenacres Cl NE40 . . . . .52 A3
Green Ave DH4 . . . . .90 D4
Greenbank
  Blaydon NE21 . . . . .53 C2
  Jarrow NE32 . . . . .58 B7
Green Bank NE46 . . . . .45 C4
Greenbank Dr SR4 . . . . .85 A5
Greenbank St **4** DH3 . . . . .88 D4
Greenbank Villas NE32 . . . . .58 B7
Greenbourne Gdns NE10 . .71 C7
Green Cl
  Stannington NE61 . . . . .14 C4
  Tynemouth NE30 . . . . .32 B1
  Whitley Bay NE25 . . . . .31 D4
Green Cres NE23 . . . . .28 F8
Greencroft NE63 . . . . .6 C2
Greencroft Ave
  Corbridge NE45 . . . . .47 A6
  Newcastle upon Tyne NE6 . .57 A8
Greendale Cl NE24 . . . . .17 A8
Greendale Gdns DH5 . . . . . . .94 F2
Greendyke NE15 . . . . .37 A5
Greener Ct NE42 . . . . .50 B1
Greenesfield Bsns Ctr
    NE8 . . . . .101 B3
Greenfield Ave NE6 . . . . .37 A2
Greenfield Dr NE62 . . . . .10 E6
Greenfield Pl
  Newcastle upon Tyne NE4 . .98 C1
  Ryton NE40 . . . . .52 D5
Greenfield Rd NE3 . . . . .28 B1
Greenfields DH2 . . . . .82 A2
Greenfield Terr **2** NE10 . . .56 F1
Greenfields Com Prim Sch
    NE13 . . . . .28 C6
Greenfields Sch NE31 . . . . . .58 A6
Greenfinch Cl NE38 . . . . .82 F3
Greenford NE11 . . . . .81 D6
Greenford La DH2, NE11 . . .81 F6
Greenford Rd NE6 . . . . .57 A4
Green Gr NE40 . . . . .52 B3
Greenhaugh NE12 . . . . .29 B1
Greenhaugh Rd NE25 . . . . . .31 B5
Greenhead NE38 . . . . .82 F4
Greenhead Rd NE17 . . . . .66 B3
Greenhead Terr NE17 . . . . . .66 B2
Greenhills NE12 . . . . .29 D5
Greenhill View **5** NE4 . . . . .37 E2
Greenholme Cl NE23 . . . . . . .16 B1
Greenhow Cl **2** SR2 . . . . . . .92 F5
Green La
  Ashington NE63 . . . . .6 C3
  Dudley NE23 . . . . .28 F8
  East Boldon NE36 . . . . .74 E6
  Gateshead, Felling NE10 . . .56 D2
  Gateshead, Pelaw NE10 . . . .57 A1
  Haswell DH6 . . . . .97 B3
  Killingworth NE12 . . . . .29 C2
  Morpeth NE61 . . . . .8 A5
Green Lane Gdns NE10 . . . . .56 C2
Green Lane Ind Est
  Bill Quay NE10 . . . . .57 A1
  Wardley NE10 . . . . .72 A8
Greenlaw NE5 . . . . .53 E8
Greenlaw Rd NE23 . . . . .22 A3
Greenlea NE29 . . . . .31 B1
Greenlea Cl
  High Spen NE39 . . . . .67 A3
  Sunderland SR4 . . . . .85 C3
Greenlee Dr NE7 . . . . .39 D3
Greenmount DH4 . . . . .90 B1
Greenock Rd SR4 . . . . .85 B2
Green Pk NE28 . . . . .39 E3
Greenrigg
  Blaydon NE21 . . . . .53 D1
  Seaton Sluice NE26 . . . . .24 C5
Greenrigg Gdns **2** SR3 . . .86 B3
Greenrigg Pl NE27 . . . . .30 F4
Greenriggs Ave NE3 . . . . . . .28 D1
Greenrising **2** NE42 . . . . . .49 D4
Greenshields Rd SR4 . . . . . .85 B2
Greenside **5** SR4 . . . . .85 B2
GREENSIDE 52 A1
Greenside
  Ashington NE63 . . . . .6 C4
  South Shields NE34 . . . . .60 B6
Greenside Ave
  Brunswick Village NE13 . . . .28 A6
  Wallsend NE28 . . . . .40 F3
Greenside Cres NE15 . . . . . . .54 A7
Greenside Ct SR3 . . . . .85 C2
Greenside Dr **3** NE32 . . . . .58 C3
Greenside Prim Sch NE40 .51 F1
Greenside Rd
  Crawcrook NE40 . . . . .51 F3
  Greenside NE40 . . . . .51 F2

Green Terr SR1 . . . . .102 C2
Green The
  Chester le Street DH2 . . . . . .88 B3
  Chopwell NE17 . . . . .77 B8
  Gateshead NE10 . . . . .71 E8
  Houghton-le-Spring DH5 . . .90 F1
  Newcastle upon Tyne NE3 . .37 F3
  New Silksworth SR3 . . . . . . .92 C7
  Ovington NE42 . . . . .49 C4
  Ponteland NE20 . . . . .25 F7
  Rowlands Gill NE39 . . . . .67 C2
  Sunderland, Bishopwearmouth
    SR1 . . . . .102 C2
  Sunderland, Southwick SR5 .75 A1
  Walbottle NE15 . . . . .35 F1
  Whitley Bay NE25 . . . . .31 E6
Greentree Sq NE5 . . . . .37 B2
Greenway
  Newcastle upon Tyne, Fenham
    NE4 . . . . .54 D8
  Newcastle upon Tyne NE5 . .36 B3
  Whitley Bay NE25 . . . . .31 D4
Greenway The SR4 . . . . .85 C4
Greenwell Cl NE21 . . . . .53 A1
Greenwell Dr NE42 . . . . .50 B3
Greenwell Terr NE40 . . . . . . .51 E4
Greenwich Pl NE8 . . . . .54 A4
Greenwood NE12 . . . . .29 F3
Greenwood Ave
  Bedlington NE22 . . . . .11 D3
  Houghton-le-Spring DH4 . . .94 C8
  2 Wallsend NE28 . . . . .40 A1
Greenwood Cl NE38 . . . . .83 F3
Greenwood Gdns
  Dunston NE11 . . . . .70 B5
  Gateshead NE10 . . . . .56 D2
Greenwood Rd SR4 . . . . .85 B3
Greenwood Sq **3** SR4 . . . .85 B3
Greetlands Rd SR2 . . . . .92 E6
Gregory Rd **1** SR4 . . . . .85 B2
Gregory Terr DH4 . . . . .90 A1
Gregson Terr SR7 . . . . .92 F1
Grenada Cl NE26 . . . . .31 F8
Grenada Dr NE26 . . . . .31 F8
Grenada Pl NE26 . . . . .31 F8
Grenfell Sq **7** SR4 . . . . .85 B2
Grenville Ct
  Cramlington NE23 . . . . .22 A1
  Ponteland NE20 . . . . .25 A4
Grenville Dr NE3 . . . . .28 B1
Grenville Terr NE1 . . . . .99 C1
Grenville Way NE20 . . . . .25 A4
Gresford St NE33 . . . . .59 C6
Gresham Cl NE23 . . . . .22 B4
Greta Ave DH4 . . . . .90 A6
Greta Gdns NE33 . . . . .59 D8
Greta St NE3 . . . . .102 A1
Gretna Dr NE32 . . . . .58 F2
Gretna Rd NE15 . . . . .54 B6
Gretton Pl NE7 . . . . .39 A3
Grey Ave NE23 . . . . .22 A3
Greybourne Gdns SR2 . . . . .86 C2
Greyfriars La NE12 . . . . .39 A6
Grey Lady Wlk NE42 . . . . . . .50 D3
Grey Pl **15** NE42 . . . . .9 A8
Grey's Ct NE1 . . . . .99 A1
Grey St
  Brunswick Village NE13 . . . .28 A6
  Houghton-le-Spring DH4 . . .90 D3
  Newcastle upon Tyne NE1 . .99 A1
  North Shields NE30 . . . . .42 B6
  Wallsend NE28 . . . . .40 C2
Greystead Cl NE5 . . . . .36 D3
Greystead Rd NE25 . . . . .31 B5
Greystoke Ave
  Newcastle upon Tyne NE2 . .56 A7
  Sunderland SR2 . . . . .86 C2
  Whickham NE16 . . . . .69 B7
Greystoke Pk NE3 . . . . .38 C6
Greystoke Pl NE23 . . . . .22 B3
Greystoke Wlk **2** NE16 . . . .69 A5
Greystone Pl SR5 . . . . .75 C2
Grey Terr **10** SR2 . . . . .92 F6
Greywood Ave NE4 . . . . .54 E7
Grieves' Row NE23 . . . . .29 A6
Grieve St NE12 . . . . .12 D1
Griffith Terr **84** NE27 . . . . . .30 E2
Grimsby St NE24 . . . . .17 E4
Grindleford Ct NE34 . . . . .59 E3
GRINDON 85 B3
Grindon Ave SR4 . . . . .85 B4
Grindon Cl
  Cramlington NE23 . . . . .22 A4
  Whickham NE16 . . . . .69 B8
Grindon Ct SR4 . . . . .85 C4
Grindon Gdns SR4 . . . . .85 C3
Grindon Hall Christian Sch
    SR4 . . . . .85 C3
Grindon La NE9 SR4 . . . . .85 B3
Grindon La
  Sunderland, South Hylton
    SR4 . . . . .85 B3
  Sunderland, Springwell SR3,
    SR4 . . . . .85 D2
Grindon Pk SR4 . . . . .85 C4
Grindon Terr SR4 . . . . .102 A4
Grinstead Cl NE34 . . . . .59 F7
Grisdale Gdns NE9 . . . . .71 A4
Grisdale St SR6 . . . . .75 C
Groat Mkt NE1 . . . . .99 A1

Grosvenor Ave
Newcastle upon Tyne NE2 . . . 38 F1
Whickham NE16 . . . 69 B8
Grosvenor Cl NE23 . . . 22 A3
Grosvenor Cres NE31 . . . 57 F4
Grosvenor Ct NE5 . . . 36 D3
Grosvenor Dr
Cleadon SR6 . . . 74 E8
South Shields NE34 . . . 59 F8
Whitley Bay NE26 . . . 32 A4
Grosvenor Gdns
Newcastle upon Tyne NE2 . . . 56 A8
South Shields NE34 . . . 59 F6
Wallsend NE28 . . . 41 A3
Grosvenor Mews
1 North Shields NE29 . . . 42 A6
4 South Shields NE33 . . . 59 E8
Grosvenor Pl
Blyth NE24 . . . 16 F6
Newcastle upon Tyne NE2 . . . 38 F1
North Shields NE29 . . . 42 A6
Grosvenor Rd
Newcastle upon Tyne NE2 . . . 38 F1
South Shields NE33 . . . 59 E8
Grosvenor St SR5 . . . 75 A2
Grosvenor Villas 1 NE2 . . . 38 F1
Grosvenor Way NE5 . . . 36 D3
Grotto Gdns NE34 . . . 60 D6
Grotto Rd NE34 . . . 60 D6
Grousemoor
Haswell DH6 . . . 97 F3
2 Washington NE37 . . . 83 A7
Grousemoor Dr NE63 . . . 6 C1
Grove Ave NE3 . . . 38 D4
Grove Cotts 9 DH3 . . . 82 C4
Grove Ho NE3 . . . 38 D4
Grove Park Ave NE3 . . . 38 D4
Grove Park Cres NE3 . . . 38 D4
Grove Park Sq NE3 . . . 38 D4
Grove Rd
Gateshead NE9 . . . 71 A6
Walbottle NE15 . . . 35 F2
Grove Terr
Burnopfield NE16 . . . 79 B6
Sunniside NE16 . . . 69 B1
Grove The
Hedworth NE32 . . . 73 B8
Houghton-le-Spring DH5 . . . 94 D6
Longbenton NE12 . . . 39 D6
Newcastle upon Tyne, Gosforth NE3 . . . 38 D4
Newcastle upon Tyne, Jesmond NE2 . . . 38 F2
Newcastle upon Tyne NE5 . . . 36 D1
Ponteland NE20 . . . 25 D5
Rowlands Gill NE39 . . . 67 F1
Ryhope SR2 . . . 92 F6
Stocksfield NE43 . . . 64 C3
Sunderland, Ashbrooke SR2 . 86 D4
6 Sunderland SR5 . . . 74 B1
Whickham NE16 . . . 69 C6
Whitley Bay NE25 . . . 31 F4
Grove View DH3 . . . 82 D5
Guardian Ct NE26 . . . 32 C4
Guardians Ct NE20 . . . 25 F7
Gubeon Wood NE61 . . . 8 C2
Guelder Rd NE7 . . . 39 C3
Guernsey Rd SR4 . . . 85 B2
Guernsey Sq SR4 . . . 85 B2
Guessburn NE43 . . . 64 B6
GUIDE POST . . . 10 F6
Guide Post Mid Sch NE62 . 10 F7
Guildford Pl NE6 . . . 56 B7
Guildford Sq NE61 . . . 2 A3
Guildford St SR2 . . . 86 E4
Guillemot Cl NE24 . . . 17 E5
Guillemot Row NE12 . . . 29 C4
Guillimot Ho NE33 . . . 42 D5
Guisborough Dr NE29 . . . 41 B8
Guisborough St SR4 . . . 85 F5
Gullane NE37 . . . 72 D3
Gullane Cl NE10 . . . 57 C2
Gunnerston Gr 1 NE3 . . . 37 D5
Gunnerton Cl NE23 . . . 22 B4
Gunnerton Pl NE29 . . . 41 D6
Gunn St NE11 . . . 69 F8
Gurney Ho NE2 . . . 99 B3
Gurteen Yd DH4 . . . 90 D3
Gut Rd NE28 . . . 40 F1
Guyzance Ave NE3 . . . 38 B6

H

Hackwood Pk NE46 . . . 45 B3
Hackworth Gdns NE41 . . . 51 B6
Hackworth Way NE29 . . . 41 F3
Haddington Rd NE25 . . . 31 D7
Haddon Cl NE25 . . . 31 B5
Haddon Gn NE25 . . . 31 B5
Haddon Rd SR2 . . . 86 F2
Haddricks Mill Ct 1 NE3 . . 38 E4
Haddricks Mill Rd NE3 . . . 38 E4
Hadleigh Ct 9 DH4 . . . 90 B6
Hadleigh Rd SR4 . . . 85 D5
Hadrian Ave DH3 . . . 88 D5
Hadrian Ct
Killingworth NE12 . . . 29 E3
Ponteland NE20 . . . 25 B1
Hadrian Gdns NE21 . . . 53 D1
Hadrian Ho 2 NE15 . . . 35 D2
Hadrian Lodge NE34 . . . 58 F5
Hadrian Park Prim Sch NE28 . . . 40 E7
Hadrian Pl
Gateshead NE9 . . . 71 B7
Throckley NE15 . . . 35 E2
Hadrian Prim Sch NE33 . . . 42 C4
Hadrian Rd
Blyth NE24 . . . 17 C3
Jarrow NE32 . . . 58 D4
Newcastle upon Tyne NE4 . . . 54 E6
Simonside NE32, NE34 . . . 58 E4
Wallsend NE28 . . . 40 D1
Hadrian Road Sta NE28 . . . 40 E2
Hadrian Sch NE15 . . . 54 C6
Hadrians Ct NE11 . . . 70 D3
Hadrian St SR4 . . . 102 A3
Hadrian's Wall* NE15 . . . 34 D3
Hadrians Way DH8 . . . 76 E3
Hadstone Pl 3 NE5 . . . 37 C1
Hagan Hall NE32 . . . 58 C1
Hagg Bank Cotts NE41 . . . 50 F5
Haggerston Cl NE5 . . . 37 B4
Haggerston Cres NE5 . . . 37 B4
Haggerston Ct NE5 . . . 37 B4
Haggerstone Dr SR5 . . . 85 A8
Haggerstone Mews NE21 . . 53 C1
Haggerston Terr NE32 . . . 58 E4
Haggie Ave NE28 . . . 40 D3
Hahnemann Ct SR5 . . . 75 B2
Haig Ave NE25 . . . 31 F3
Haig Cres NE15 . . . 54 B5
Haigh Terr NE9 . . . 71 C1
Haig Rd NE22 . . . 16 B8
Haig St NE11 . . . 69 F8
Hailsham Ave NE12 . . . 39 C7
Hainford Cl SR4 . . . 85 C5
Haininghead NE38 . . . 83 E2
Hainingwood Terr NE10 . . . 57 B2
Halcyon Pl NE9 . . . 71 B7
Haldane Ct NE2 . . . 99 B4
Haldane St NE63 . . . 6 C4
Haldane Terr NE2 . . . 99 B4
Halesworth Dr SR4 . . . 85 D5
Halewood Ave NE3 . . . 37 E4
Half Fields Rd NE21 . . . 53 B1
Half Moon La
Gateshead NE8 . . . 101 B2
Tynemouth NE30 . . . 42 D7
Half Moon St NE62 . . . 11 B8
Halidon Rd SR2 . . . 86 D1
Halidon Sq SR2 . . . 86 D1
Halifax Pl
Dunston NE11 . . . 54 E1
9 Ryhope SR2 . . . 92 F6
Halifax Rd NE11 . . . 54 E1
Halkirk Way NE23 . . . 16 A1
Hall Ave NE4 . . . 54 E6
Hall Cl
Seaham SR7 . . . 92 D1
West Rainton DH4 . . . 94 A2
HALL CLOSE . . . 22 B6
Hall Dene Way SR7 . . . 92 F2
Hall Dr NE12 . . . 29 C5
Halleypike Cl NE7 . . . 39 D3
Hall Farm Cl NE43 . . . 64 B8
Hall Farm Rd SR3 . . . 92 A5
Hallfield Cl SR3 . . . 92 A5
HALLGARTH . . . 96 B4
Hallgarth NE10 . . . 72 A7
Hall Garth NE3 . . . 38 C8
Hallgarth Ct SR6 . . . 75 F1
Hallgarth Ho NE33 . . . 59 C8
Hallgarth La DH6 . . . 96 B5
Hallgarth Rd NE21 . . . 53 B2
Hallgarth View DH6 . . . 96 C5
Hallgarth Villas DH6 . . . 96 A1
Hallgate NE46 . . . 45 B5
Hall Gdns
Gateshead NE10 . . . 71 D7
Seaton Sluice NE26 . . . 24 A6
Sherburn DH6 . . . 96 A1
West Boldon NE36 . . . 74 A7
Hall Gn NE24 . . . 17 B7
Halling Cl NE6 . . . 57 A4
Hallington Dr NE25 . . . 23 D3
Hallington Mews NE12 . . . 29 C3
Halliwell St DH4 . . . 90 D1
Hall La
Haswell DH6 . . . 97 F3
Houghton-le-Spring DH5 . . . 94 F7
West Rainton DH4 . . . 94 A2
Hallow Dr NE15 . . . 35 D1
Hall Pk NE21 . . . 53 A4
Hall Rd
Chopwell NE17 . . . 66 C2
Hebburn NE31 . . . 57 E5
Washington NE37 . . . 83 E8
Hall Road Bglws NE17 . . . 66 B2
Hallside Rd NE24 . . . 17 B6
Hallstile Bank NE46 . . . 45 B5
Hall Terr
Blyth NE24 . . . 17 E8
Gateshead NE10 . . . 57 B2
Hall View SR6 . . . 75 F8
Hallwood Cl NE22 . . . 15 A8
Halstead Pl 2 NE33 . . . 42 D1
Halstead Sq SR4 . . . 85 D5
Halterburn Cl NE3 . . . 38 A4
Halton Cl NE43 . . . 64 D6
Halton Dr
Backworth NE27 . . . 30 D3
Wideopen NE13 . . . 28 B6
Halton Way NE3 . . . 28 A1
Halvergate Cl SR4 . . . 85 C5
Hamar Cl NE29 . . . 41 C4
Hambard Way NE38 . . . 83 D4
Hambledon Ave
Chester le Street DH2 . . . 88 B2
Tynemouth NE30 . . . 32 A3
Hambledon Cl NE35 . . . 73 E8
Hambledon Gdns NE7 . . . 39 A3
Hambledon St NE24 . . . 17 D8
Hambleton Ct NE63 . . . 6 F1
Hambleton Gn NE9 . . . 71 B1
Hambleton Rd NE38 . . . 83 B3
Hamilton Cres
Newcastle upon Tyne NE4 . . . 98 B2
Tynemouth NE29 . . . 41 C8
Hamilton Ct
7 Gateshead NE8 . . . 71 A8
Sunderland SR6 . . . 75 F2
Hamilton Dr NE26 . . . 31 F8
Hamilton Pl NE4 . . . 98 B2
Hamilton Terr
14 Morpeth NE61 . . . 9 A8
West Boldon NE36 . . . 74 A7
Hamilton Way 2 NE26 . . . 31 F8
Hammer Square Bank DH9 . . . 80 F1
Hammerton Ct 6 NE28 . . . 40 A1
Hampden Rd SR6 . . . 75 E2
Hampden St NE33 . . . 59 C8
Hampshire Ct NE4 . . . 100 A2
Hampshire Gdns NE28 . . . 40 E4
Hampshire Pl NE37 . . . 72 D1
Hampshire Way NE34 . . . 60 C7
Hampstead Cl NE24 . . . 17 C3
Hampstead Gdns NE32 . . . 58 D2
Hampstead Rd
Newcastle upon Tyne NE4 . . . 54 E5
Sunderland SR4 . . . 85 D4
Hampstead Sq SR4 . . . 85 C4
Hampton Cl NE23 . . . 22 D7
Hampton Ct
Chester le Street DH3 . . . 88 D7
Whickham NE16 . . . 54 B1
Hampton Dr
Gateshead NE10 . . . 71 C8
Whitley Bay NE25 . . . 31 C4
Hampton Rd NE30 . . . 32 A2
HAMSTERLEY . . . 77 B5
Hamsterley Cres
Gateshead NE9 . . . 71 C3
Newcastle upon Tyne NE15 . . . 53 B7
Hamsterley Ct 6 SR3 . . . 92 A6
Hamsterley Dr NE12 . . . 29 C4
HAMSTERLEY MILL . . . 78 A5
Hanby Gdns SR3 . . . 86 A3
Hancock St NE1, NE2 . . . 99 A3
Handel St NE33 . . . 42 D2
Handley Cres DH5 . . . 94 C4
Handley Cross DH8 . . . 77 C2
Handy Dr NE11 . . . 54 E2
Hangmans La SR3, SR7 . . . 91 E3
Hanlon Ct
Hebburn NE32 . . . 57 F7
Jarrow NE32 . . . 58 A8
Hannington Pl 3 NE6 . . . 56 A6
Hannington St 2 NE6 . . . 56 A6
Hann Terr NE37 . . . 83 F8
Hanover Cl 2 NE5 . . . 36 C2
Hanover Ct
Annitsford NE23 . . . 22 B1
5 Gateshead NE9 . . . 71 A2
Hanover Dr NE21 . . . 53 A1
Hanover Gdns 3 NE28 . . . 41 A1
Hanover House NE32 . . . 58 B4
Hanover Pl
Cramlington NE23 . . . 16 A2
Sunderland SR4 . . . 102 B4
Hanover Sq NE1 . . . 101 A4
Hanover St NE1 . . . 101 A4
Hanover Wlk
Blaydon NE21 . . . 68 A8
1 Newcastle upon Tyne NE5 . . . 36 C2
Harbord Terr NE26 . . . 23 F5
Harbottle Ave
Newcastle upon Tyne NE3 . . . 38 A6
Shiremoor NE27 . . . 31 A2
Harbottle Cres NE32 . . . 58 B2
Harbottle Ct NE6 . . . 56 C4
Harbottle St 4 NE6 . . . 56 C4
Harbour View
Cambois NE22 . . . 12 B3
South Shields NE33 . . . 42 D5
Sunderland SR6 . . . 75 F2
Harcourt Pk 1 NE9 . . . 71 A5
Harcourt Rd SR2 . . . 86 D1
Harcourt St 2 NE9 . . . 71 A5
Hardgate Rd SR2 . . . 86 D1
Hardie Ave NE16 . . . 69 A8
Hardie Dr NE36 . . . 74 B7
Hardman Gdns NE40 . . . 52 D5
Hardwick Ct NE8 . . . 56 A1
Hardwick Pl NE3 . . . 38 A3
Hardwick Rise SR6 . . . 103 B4
Hardyards Ct NE34 . . . 59 C5
Hardy Ave NE34 . . . 59 B3
Hardy Ct 5 NE30 . . . 42 B6
Hardy Gr NE28 . . . 40 A5
Hardy Sq SR5 . . . 75 A2
Harebell Rd NE9 . . . 71 C4
Harehills Ave NE5 . . . 37 D3
Harehills Tower NE3 . . . 37 E3
Harelaw Dr
Ashington NE63 . . . 6 B1
Sunderland SR6 . . . 75 E1
Harelaw Gr NE5 . . . 36 D1
Hareshaw Rd NE25 . . . 31 B5
Hareside NE23 . . . 22 A5
Hareside Cl NE15 . . . 52 F8
Hareside Ct NE15 . . . 52 F8
Hareside Fst Sch NE23 . . . 22 A5
Hareside Wlk NE15 . . . 52 F8
Harewood Cl
Whickham NE16 . . . 69 A4
Whitley Bay NE25 . . . 31 B4
Harewood Cres NE25 . . . 31 B4
Harewood Ct NE25 . . . 31 B4
Harewood Dr NE22 . . . 11 C2
Harewood Gdns
Pegswood NE61 . . . 4 E4
Sunderland SR3 . . . 86 A3
Harewood Gn NE9 . . . 71 B2
Harewood Rd NE3 . . . 38 C6
Hareydene NE5 . . . 36 F5
Hargill Dr NE38 . . . 83 A1
Hargrave Ct NE24 . . . 17 C6
Harland Way NE38 . . . 83 D5
Harlebury NE27 . . . 30 C1
Harle Cl
Newcastle upon Tyne NE5 . . . 36 E1
Sunniside DH4 . . . 90 C2
Harlequin Lodge 8 NE10 . 71 D8
Harle Rd NE27 . . . 30 D3
Harle St NE28 . . . 40 B2
Harleston Way NE10 . . . 71 E6
Harley Terr NE3 . . . 38 D5
Harlow Ave
Backworth NE27 . . . 30 D3
Newcastle upon Tyne NE3 . . . 37 F7
Harlow Cl NE23 . . . 16 A1
HARLOW GREEN . . . 71 B1
Harlow Green Com Prim Sch NE9 . . . 71 A2
Harlow Green La NE9 . . . 71 A2
HARLOW HILL . . . 33 A5
Harlow Pl NE7 . . . 39 B3
Harlow St SR4 . . . 102 B2
Harnham Ave NE29 . . . 41 D5
Harnham Gdns NE5 . . . 37 C1
Harnham Gr NE23 . . . 22 A5
Harold Sq SR2 . . . 103 B1
Harold St NE32 . . . 58 C7
Harperley Dr SR3 . . . 86 B2
Harperley La DH9 . . . 79 B1
Harper St NE24 . . . 17 D7
Harraby Gdns NE9 . . . 71 B3
Harras Bank DH3 . . . 82 C3
HARRATON . . . 83 B1
Harraton Terr
15 Birtley DH3 . . . 82 C4
Bournmoor DH3 . . . 89 C7
Harriet Pl 22 NE6 . . . 56 C6
Harriet St
Blaydon NE21 . . . 53 C2
Newcastle upon Tyne NE6 . . . 56 D6
Harrington Gdns NE62 . . . 11 C8
Harrington St 4 NE28 . . . 40 B2
Harrington Way NE63 . . . 6 F4
Harriot Dr NE12 . . . 29 B2
Harrison Ct
Annitsford NE23 . . . 29 B8
Birtley DH3 . . . 82 C3
Harrison Gdns NE8 . . . 70 D7
Harrison Pl NE2 . . . 99 B3
Harrison Rd NE28 . . . 41 A3
Harrogate Ct 4 NE63 . . . 6 F5
Harrogate St SR2 . . . 103 B1
Harrow Cres DH4 . . . 90 A6
Harrow Gdns NE13 . . . 28 C5
Harrow Sq SR4 . . . 85 D5
Harrow St NE27 . . . 30 E4
Hartburn NE10 . . . 72 A6
Hartburn Dr NE5 . . . 36 D3
Hartburn Pl NE4 . . . 54 F7
Hartburn Rd NE30 . . . 32 A1
Hartburn Terr NE25 . . . 23 D3
Hartburn Wlk NE3 . . . 37 D5
Hart Ct SR1 . . . 103 A3
Hartford NE12 . . . 29 D5
Hartford Bank NE23 . . . 15 C4
Hartford Bridge Farm NE22 . . . 15 C5
Hartford Cres
Ashington NE63 . . . 6 D2
Bedlington NE22 . . . 15 E8
Hartford Ct NE22 . . . 15 E8
Hartford Cvn Pk NE22 . . . 15 B5
Hartford Dr NE22 . . . 15 C5
Hartford Ho NE4 . . . 98 B2
Hartford Rd
Bedlington NE22 . . . 15 D6
Newcastle upon Tyne NE3 . . . 38 D7
South Shields NE34 . . . 59 A5
Sunderland SR4 . . . 85 D5
Hartford Road E NE22 . . . 15 F8
Hartford Road W NE22 . . . 15 F8
Hartford St 1 NE6 . . . 56 C8
Harthope NE61 . . . 1 E5
Harthope Ave SR5 . . . 74 C3
Harthope Cl NE38 . . . 88 F8
Harthope Dr NE29 . . . 41 E3
Hartington Rd NE30 . . . 32 B2
Hartington St
Gateshead NE8 . . . 101 C1
Newcastle upon Tyne NE4 . . . 98 A1
Sunderland SR6 . . . 75 E1
Hartington Terr NE33 . . . 59 D8
Hartland Dr DH3 . . . 82 D3
Hartlands NE22 . . . 15 E8
Hartleigh Pl NE24 . . . 17 B7
HARTLEY . . . 24 E4
Hartley Ave NE26 . . . 31 E5
Hartleyburn Ave NE31 . . . 57 D3
Hartley Ct
Brunswick Village NE13 . . . 27 F5
New Hartley NE25 . . . 23 D6
Hartley Gdns NE25 . . . 23 C3
Hartley Ho NE26 . . . 31 F5
Hartley La
Holywell NE25 . . . 31 B7
Whitley Bay NE25, NE26 . . . 24 C2
Hartley Sq NE26 . . . 24 D4
Hartley St
Seaton Delaval NE25 . . . 23 C3
Sunderland SR1 . . . 103 C3
Hartley Street N NE25 . . . 23 C3
Hartley Terr NE24 . . . 17 C4
Hartoft Cl DH4 . . . 90 D3
HARTON . . . 59 F6
Harton Down Hill Nature Reserve* NE34 . . . 60 C8
Harton Gr NE34 . . . 59 E7
Harton House Rd NE34 . . . 59 F7
Harton House Road E NE34 . . . 60 A7
Harton Inf Sch NE34 . . . 60 B6
Harton Jun Sch NE34 . . . 60 A6
Harton La NE34 . . . 59 D6
Harton Lea NE34 . . . 59 F6
HARTON NOOK . . . 59 F5
Harton Quay NE33 . . . 42 B2
Harton Rise NE34 . . . 60 A7
Harton Tech Coll NE34 . . . 60 A6
Harton View NE36 . . . 74 A7
Hartside
Birtley DH3 . . . 82 D1
Newcastle upon Tyne NE15 . . 53 C7
Hartside Cres
Backworth NE27 . . . 30 D4
Blaydon NE21 . . . 68 A8
Cramlington NE23 . . . 16 A2
Hartside Gdns
Easington Lane DH5 . . . 95 C1
Newcastle upon Tyne NE2 . . . 38 F1
Hartside Pl NE3 . . . 28 C1
Hartside Rd SR4 . . . 85 D4
Hartside Sq SR4 . . . 85 D4
Hart Sq SR4 . . . 85 E5
Hart Terr SR6 . . . 75 F6
Harvard Rd NE3 . . . 37 E6
Harvest Cl SR3 . . . 91 F5
Harvey Cl
Ashington NE63 . . . 7 A3
Washington NE38 . . . 82 F5
Harvey Combe NE12 . . . 29 B3
Harvey Cres NE10 . . . 72 B8
Harwood Cl
Cramlington NE23 . . . 22 A5
Washington NE38 . . . 83 A1
Harwood Ct 10 SR6 . . . 75 E1
Harwood Dr
Fence Houses DH4 . . . 90 B1
Killingworth NE12 . . . 30 A3
Hascombe Cl NE25 . . . 31 D6
Haslemere Dr SR3 . . . 86 A3
Hassop Way NE22 . . . 10 F2
Hasting Hill Prim Sch SR3 . . . 85 C1
Hastings Ave
Longbenton NE12 . . . 39 D7
Newcastle upon Tyne NE3 . . . 37 D7
Seaton Sluice NE26 . . . 24 B7
Whitley Bay NE26 . . . 24 F1
Hastings Ct
Bedlington NE22 . . . 11 C2
New Hartley NE25 . . . 23 D6
Hastings Dr NE30 . . . 42 C8
Hastings Gdns NE25 . . . 23 D6
HASTINGS HILL . . . 85 A2
Hastings Par NE31 . . . 58 A3
Hastings St
Cramlington NE23 . . . 22 C5
Sunderland SR2 . . . 86 E3
Hastings Terr
Cramlington NE23 . . . 16 D1
New Hartley NE25 . . . 23 D7
Sunderland SR2 . . . 86 F3
HASWELL . . . 97 F3
Haswell Cl NE10 . . . 72 D7
Haswell Gdns NE30 . . . 42 A6
HASWELL PLOUGH . . . 97 E1
Hatfield Ave NE31 . . . 57 F6
Hatfield Dr NE23 . . . 23 A2
Hatfield Gdns
Sunderland SR3 . . . 86 A3
Whitley Bay NE25 . . . 31 B5
Hatfield Ho 10 NE29 . . . 42 A4
Hatfield Sq 11 NE33 . . . 42 D3
Hathaway Gdns SR3 . . . 86 A3
Hathersage Gdns NE34 . . . 59 D5
Hatherton Ave NE30 . . . 32 B3
Hathery La NE24 . . . 16 D5
Hatton Gallery* NE1 . . . 99 A3
Haugh La
Hexham NE46 . . . 45 B5
Ryton NE15, NE40 . . . 52 E6
Ryton, Ryton Haugh NE21 . . 53 A5
Haugh Lane Ind Est NE46 . 45 A6
Haughs The 2 NE42 . . . 50 D3
Haughton Cres
Hedworth NE32 . . . 58 B2
Newcastle upon Tyne NE5 . . . 36 E1
Haughton Ct NE4 . . . 100 A3
Haughton Terr NE24 . . . 17 E7
Hautmont Rd NE31 . . . 57 F4
Hauxley NE12 . . . 29 D5
Hauxley Dr
Cramlington NE23 . . . 16 A1
Newcastle upon Tyne NE3 . . . 37 F7
Hauxley Gdns NE5 . . . 37 D2
Havanna NE12 . . . 29 D5
Havannah Cres NE13 . . . 27 B6
Havannah Nature Reserve* NE13 . . . 27 E4
Havannah Rd NE37 . . . 83 B7
Havant Gdns NE13 . . . 28 B7
Havelock Cl NE8 . . . 101 B2
Havelock Cres NE22 . . . 11 F3
Havelock Ct SR4 . . . 85 D6
Havelock Ho SR4 . . . 85 D6
Havelock Mews NE22 . . . 11 F3

Havelock PI NE4 . . . . .98 B1
Havelock Rd NE27 . . . . .30 D3
Havelock St
  Blyth NE24 . . . . .17 E8
  South Shields NE33 . . . . .42 B1
  South Shields NE33 . . . . .42 C1
  Sunderland SR1 . . . . .103 C3
Havelock Terr
  Chopwell NE17 . . . . .66 B1
  Gateshead NE8 . . . . .101 B2
  Jarrow NE32 . . . . .58 B5
  Sunderland SR2 . . . . .102 B1
  Tantobie DH9 . . . . .79 B2
Havelock Villas NE22 . . . . . .11 F3
Haven Ct
  Blyth NE24 . . . . .17 C6
  Sunderland SR6 . . . . .75 F1
Haven The
  North Shields NE29 . . . . .42 A3
  Penshaw DH4 . . . . .90 B6
  Prudhoe NE42 . . . . .50 D2
Haven View NE62 . . . . .7 E4
Havercroft NE10 . . . . .72 B7
Haverley Dr 🔢 SR7 . . . . .92 E1
Haversham CI NE7 . . . . .39 A5
Haversham Pk SR5 . . . . .75 C5
Hawarden Cres SR4 . . . . . .102 A1
Hawes Ave DH2 . . . . .88 C1
Hawes Ct SR6 . . . . .75 C5
Haweswater Cres NE21 . . . .68 B8
Haweswater Ct NE34 . . . . . . .59 D6
Haweswater Cres NE64 . . . . . .7 C4
Hawick Cres NE6 . . . . .56 B4
Hawick Crescent Ind Est
  NE6 . . . . .56 B4
Hawkesley Rd SR4 . . . . .85 D5
Hawkey's La NE29 . . . . .41 F6
Hawkhills Terr 🔢 DH3 . . . . . .82 C5
Hawkhurst NE38 . . . . .83 E2
Hawkins Ct SR3 . . . . .91 F6
Hawkmoor CI NE63 . . . . .6 C1
Hawksbury NE16 . . . . .69 A7
Hawks Edge NE12 . . . . .29 A1
Hawksfeld NE10 . . . . .71 E4
Hawkshead St NE33 . . . . . . .37 D7
Hawkshead PI NE9 . . . . .71 B4
Hawksley NE5 . . . . .36 F2
Hawk's Nest NE38 . . . . .56 A4
Hawk Terr DH3 . . . . .82 E2
Hawkwell CI NE15 . . . . .35 D1
Hawkwell Rise NE15 . . . . . . .35 D1
Hawsker CI SR3 . . . . .92 C7
Hawthorn Ave
  Brunswick Village NE13 . . . . .28 A6
  New Silksworth SR3 . . . . .92 B8
Hawthorn CI NE16 . . . . .69 B5
Hawthorn Cres NE38 . . . . . .83 C1
Hawthorn Ct
  Morpeth NE61 . . . . .9 B6
  Newcastle upon Tyne NE3 . . . .38 C4
Hawthorn Dr
  Dunston NE11 . . . . .69 F8
  Hedworth NE32 . . . . .58 D2
Hawthorne Ave
  North Shields NE31 . . . . .57 F6
  South Shields NE34 . . . . .59 F4
Hawthorne Gdns NE9 . . . . . .70 F6
Hawthorne Rd 🔢 NE24 . . . . .17 F7
Hawthorne Terr DH9 . . . . . .79 D3
Hawthorn Fst Sch NE63 . . . . .6 D1
Hawthorn Gdns
  🔢 Gateshead NE10 . . . . .56 D1
  Newcastle upon Tyne NE3 . . . .37 F4
  Ryton NE40 . . . . .52 E4
  Tynemouth NE29 . . . . .41 F7
  Whitley Bay NE26 . . . . .31 F5
Hawthorn Gr NE28 . . . . .40 B2
Hawthorn Mews 🔢 NE3 . . . .38 C4
Hawthorn PI
  Killingworth NE12 . . . . .29 C4
  Newcastle upon Tyne NE4 . . .100 A4
Hawthorn Prim Sch NE4 . .100 A4
Hawthorn Rd
  Ashington NE63 . . . . .6 E3
  Blaydon NE21 . . . . .53 C1
  Newcastle upon Tyne NE3 . . . .38 C4
Hawthorn Road W NE3 . . . .38 C4
Hawthorn St
  Burnside DH4 . . . . .90 C2
  Jarrow NE32 . . . . .58 C2
  Sunderland SR4 . . . . .102 A2
  Walbottle NE15 . . . . .35 F2
Hawthorns The
  East Boldon NE36 . . . . .74 D7
  Gateshead NE9 . . . . .71 D1
  Newcastle upon Tyne NE4 . . .100 A3
Hawthorn Terr
  Chester le Street DH3 . . . . . .88 D2
  Crawcrook NE40 . . . . .51 E3
  Dunston NE11 . . . . .69 F8
  Gateshead NE9 . . . . .71 D1
  Newcastle upon Tyne NE4 . . .100 A4
  🔢 Springwell NE9 . . . . .71 F1
  Sunderland SR5 . . . . .75 E6
Hawthorn Villas NE23 . . . . .22 C6
Hawthorn Way NE20 . . . . . . .25 D3
Hawthorn Wlk NE4 . . . . . . .100 B4
Haydock Dr NE10 . . . . .72 C7
Haydon CI NE38 . . . . .83 E1
Haydon CI NE3 . . . . .37 F8
Haydon Dr
  Howdon NE28 . . . . .41 A2
  Whitley Bay NE25 . . . . .31 F3
Haydon Gdns NE27 . . . . .30 D4
Haydon Rd NE63 . . . . .6 D2

Haydon Sq SR4 . . . . .85 D5
Hayes Wlk NE13 . . . . .28 B6
Hayfield La NE16 . . . . .69 B6
Hayhole Rd NE29 . . . . .41 E2
Haylands Sq NE34 . . . . .59 D5
Hayleazes Rd NE15 . . . . .53 F7
Haymarket NE1 . . . . .99 A2
Haymarket Sta NE1 . . . . .99 A2
Haynyng The NE10 . . . . .71 E7
Hayricks The DH9 . . . . .79 D4
Hay St SR5 . . . . .102 C4
Hayton Ave NE34 . . . . .60 A5
Hayton CI NE23 . . . . .22 C7
Hayton Rd NE30 . . . . .32 A2
Hayward Ave NE25 . . . . .23 D3
Hazard La DH5 . . . . .94 E3
Hazel Ave
  🔢 Houghton-le-Spring
  DH4 . . . . .94 D2
  New Silksworth SR3 . . . . .92 B8
  Tynemouth NE30 . . . . .41 F7
Hazel Ct NE12 . . . . .39 D7
Hazeldene
  Hedworth NE32 . . . . .73 C8
  Whitley Bay NE25 . . . . .31 E5
Hazeldene Ave NE3 . . . . .37 C5
Hazeldene Ct NE30 . . . . .42 C7
Hazeley Gr 🔢 NE3 . . . . .37 B5
Hazeley Way NE3 . . . . .37 B5
Hazel Gr
  Burnopfield NE16 . . . . .79 C6
  Chester le Street DH2 . . . . . . .88 A5
  Ellington NE61 . . . . .1 E5
  Gateshead NE10 . . . . .72 B7
  Killingworth NE12 . . . . .29 B2
  South Shields NE34 . . . . .59 F4
Hazel Rd
  Blaydon NE21 . . . . .53 D2
  Gateshead NE8 . . . . .70 C8
Hazel St NE32 . . . . .58 A7
Hazel Terr DH4 . . . . .90 C2
Hazelwood
  Jarrow NE32 . . . . .58 D6
  Killingworth NE12 . . . . .29 F3
Hazelwood Ave
  Newbiggin-by-the-Sea
  NE64 . . . . .7 D5
  Newcastle upon Tyne NE2 . . . .38 E2
  Sunderland SR5 . . . . .74 F2
Hazelwood CI NE9 . . . . .71 D2
Hazelwood Com Prim Sch 🔢
  NE13 . . . . .28 A6
Hazelwood Gdns NE38 . . . . .83 C1
Hazelwood Terr 🔢 NE4 . . . .41 A3
Hazledene Terr 🔢 SR4 . . . .85 F6
Hazlerigg 28 A4
Hazlitt Ave NE34 . . . . .59 B3
Hazlitt PI NE23 . . . . .23 A1
Headlam Gn 🔢 NE6 . . . . . . .56 C5
Headlam Ho 🔢 NE6 . . . . . . .56 C6
Headlam St 🔢 NE6 . . . . .56 C6
Headlam View 🔢 NE28 . . . . .41 A2
HEALEY 62 F1
Healey Dr NE38 . . . . .86 B2
Heartsbourne Dr NE34 . . . . .59 F3
Heath CI NE11 . . . . .70 B7
Heathcote Gdns NE7 . . . . . . .37 B3
Heath Cres NE15 . . . . .54 A4
Heathdale Gdns NE7 . . . . . . .39 B3
Heather CI SR6 . . . . .60 A2
Heatherdale Terr NE9 . . . . . .71 B3
Heather Dr DH5 . . . . .95 A5
Heather Hill NE9 . . . . .71 F1
Heatherlaw
  Gateshead NE9 . . . . .71 C5
  Washington NE37 . . . . .82 F6
Heather Lea
  Bebside NE24 . . . . .16 E7
  Dipton DH9 . . . . .78 E2
Heatherlea Gdns 🔢 SR3 . . .86 B3
Heather Lea La 🔢 NE42 . . . .50 D3
Heatherlea PI NE37 . . . . .72 D1
Heatherlee Gdns NE62 . . . . .11 A8
Heather PI
  Crawcrook NE40 . . . . .52 A4
  Newcastle upon Tyne NE4 . . . .54 E8
Heatherslaw Rd NE5 . . . . . . .54 C8
Heather Terr NE16 . . . . .79 B6
Heatherwell Gn NE10 . . . . . .71 C7
Heatheryhill NE46 . . . . .44 A4
Heathery La NE3 . . . . .38 E7
Heathfield
  Morpeth NE61 . . . . .9 B6
  Shiremoor NE27 . . . . .30 D2
  Sunderland SR2 . . . . .86 C2
Heathfield Cres NE5 . . . . . . .37 D3
Heathfield Farm NE40 . . . . .52 A1
Heathfield Gdns NE40 . . . . .52 A1
Heathfield Ho NE10 . . . . .70 F6
Heathfield PI
  Gateshead NE10 . . . . .56 C1
  Newcastle upon Tyne NE3 . . . .28 D1
Heathfield Rd NE42 . . . . .70 F6
Heath Grange DH5 . . . . .90 E1
Heath Hill NE15 . . . . .34 F2
Heath Sq SR4 . . . . .85 D5
Heathway NE32 . . . . .58 C2
Heathwell Gdns NE16 . . . . . .54 A8
Heathwell Rd NE15 . . . . .53 F7
Heathwood Ave 🔢 NE16 . . .69 A7
HEATON 56 D7
Heaton CI NE6 . . . . .56 B7

Heaton Gdns NE34 . . . . .59 C2
Heaton Gr NE6 . . . . .56 B7
Heaton Hall Rd NE6 . . . . .56 B7
Heaton Manor Sch NE7 . . . . .39 A2
Heaton Park Ct 🔢 NE6 . . . . .56 B7
Heaton Park Rd NE6 . . . . . . .56 B7
Heaton Park View NE6 . . . . .56 B7
Heaton Rd NE6 . . . . .56 B6
Heaton Rd NE6 . . . . .56 B7
Heaton Terr
  Newcastle upon Tyne NE6 . . . .56 A6
  North Shields NE29 . . . . .41 E6
Heaton Wlk 🔢 NE6 . . . . .56 B6
HEBBURN. 57 E5
Hebburn Comp Sch NE31 . .57 E4
HEBBURN HALL PONDS . .57 C4
HEBBURN NEW TOWN 57 C7
Hebburn Sta NE31 . . . . .57 D6
Hebburn Swimming Pool
  NE31 . . . . .57 F5
Heber St NE1 . . . . .98 C1
HEBRON 3 F8
Hebron Way NE11 . . . . .4 E4
Hebron PI 🔢 NE63 . . . . .6 F3
Hebron Way NE23 . . . . .22 A5
Hector St NE27 . . . . .30 F4
Heddon Ave NE13 . . . . .28 A4
Heddon Banks NE15 . . . . . . .34 E1
Heddon CI
  Newcastle upon Tyne NE3 . . . .38 A6
  Ryton NE40 . . . . .52 D5
HEDDON-ON-THE-WALL . .34 F2
Heddon St Andrew's CE Fst
  Sch NE15 . . . . .34 E2
Heddon View
  Blaydon NE21 . . . . .53 B2
  Ryton NE40 . . . . .52 D5
Heddon Way NE34 . . . . .59 B6
Hedge CI NE11 . . . . .70 B7
HEDGEFIELD 52 E5
Hedgefield Ave NE21 . . . . . . .52 F5
Hedgefield Cotts NE21 . . . . .52 F5
Hedgefield Ct NE21 . . . . .52 F5
Hedgefield Gr NE24 . . . . .17 C3
Hedgefield View NE23 . . . . . .22 A1
Hedgehope
  Sheriff Hill NE9 . . . . .71 C5
  🔢 Washington NE37 . . . . . . .83 A6
Hedgehope Rd NE5 . . . . .37 A4
Hedgelea NE40 . . . . .52 B5
Hedgelea Rd DH5 . . . . .94 C3
Hedgeley Rd
  Hebburn NE31 . . . . .57 E6
  North Shields NE29 . . . . .41 D7
  Tynemouth NE30 . . . . .41 D7
Hedgeley Terr NE6 . . . . .56 F6
Hedgerow Mews NE63 . . . . . .6 B2
Hedley Ave NE24 . . . . .17 F6
Hedley CI 🔢 NE33 . . . . .42 C4
Hedley Ct NE6 . . . . .17 F6
Hedley PI NE33 . . . . .40 B1
Hedley Rd
  North Shields NE29 . . . . .41 F3
  Seaton Delaval NE25 . . . . . . .23 E2
  Wallsend NE28 . . . . .41 B6
Hedley St
  Gateshead NE8 . . . . .70 D8
  Newcastle upon Tyne NE3 . . . .38 C5
  🔢 South Shields NE33 . . . . . .42 C4
Hedley Terr
  Newcastle upon Tyne NE3 . . . .38 C5
  Ryhope SR2 . . . . .93 A6
  South Hetton DH6 . . . . .97 F7
Hedworth 58 D1
Hedworth Ave NE34 . . . . .59 A4
Hedworth Ct SR1 . . . . .103 B2
Hedworthfield Prim Sch
  NE32 . . . . .58 D1
Hedworth La
  Boldon Colliery NE35 . . . . .58 E1
  Hedworth NE32 . . . . .58 D2
Hedworth Lane Prim Sch
  NE35 . . . . .58 D1
Hedworth PI NE9 . . . . .71 C3
Hedworth St DH3 . . . . .88 C3
Hedworth Terr DH4 . . . . .90 B6
Hedworth View NE32 . . . . . . .58 D3
Heighley St NE15 . . . . .53 F5
Heightley Ct NE4 . . . . .12 C7
Helena Ave NE26 . . . . .32 B5
Helena Ho SR2 . . . . .102 B1
Helen St
  Blaydon NE21 . . . . .53 A2
  East Cramlington NE23 . . . . . .22 F5
  Sunderland SR6 . . . . .75 E4
Hellpool La NE46 . . . . .44 F5
Helmdon NE37 . . . . .83 E8
Helmsdale Ave 🔢 NE10 . . . .56 D1
Helmsdale Rd SR4 . . . . .85 D5
Helmsley CI NE24 . . . . .17 C3
Helmsley Ct SR5 . . . . .74 E3
Helmsley Dr NE28 . . . . .40 F2
Helmsley Rd NE2 . . . . .99 C3
Helston Ct NE15 . . . . .34 E5
Helvellyn Ave NE38 . . . . .83 A3
Helvellyn CI NE21 . . . . .68 A8
Helvellyn Rd SR2 . . . . .86 F4
Hemel St DH3 . . . . .88 C2
Hemlington CI 🔢 SR2 . . . . . .92 F6
Hemming St 🔢 SR2 . . . . . . .86 F2
Hemsley CI SR4 . . . . .85 D5
Hemsley Rd NE33 . . . . .42 A1
Hencotes NE46 . . . . .45 A4
Hencotes Ct 🔢 NE46 . . . . . .45 A4
Hencotes Mews 🔢 NE46 . . .45 A4

Henderson Ave NE16 . . . . . . .69 A8
Henderson CI NE46 . . . . .44 F3
Henderson Ct NE29 . . . . .41 F3
Henderson Gdns NE10 . . . . .72 B8
Henderson Rd
  South Shields NE34 . . . . .58 F4
  Sunderland SR4 . . . . .85 F6
  Wallsend NE28 . . . . .40 B3
  Wallsend NE28 . . . . .40 B4
Henderson's Bldgs NE64 . . .7 F5
Hendersyde CI NE5 . . . . .37 B3
HENDON. 103 C1
Hendon Burn Ave SR2 . . . .103 B1
Hendon Burn Avenue W 🔢
  SR2. . . . . .86 E4
Hendon CI
  North Shields NE29 . . . . .42 A3
  Sunderland SR1 . . . . .103 B2
Hendon Gdns NE32 . . . . .58 D2
Hendon Ho NE63 . . . . .6 A4
Hendon Rd
  Gateshead NE8, NE9 . . . . . . .71 B8
  Sunderland, Hendon SR1,
  SR2 .103 C3
  Sunderland SR1 . . . . .103 B3
Hendon Road E SR1 . . . . . .103 C2
Hendon St SR1 . . . . .103 C2
Hendon Valley Ct 🔢 SR2 . .86 E4
Hendon Valley Rd 🔢 SR2 . .86 E4
Henley CI NE23 . . . . .22 D7
Henley Gdns NE28 . . . . .41 B4
Henley Ho NE15 . . . . .73 E8
Henley Rd
  Sunderland SR4 . . . . .85 D5
  Tynemouth NE30 . . . . .32 C1
Henley Sq NE61 . . . . .2 A3
Henley Way NE35 . . . . .73 E8
Henlow Rd NE15 . . . . .53 C7
Henry Nelson St NE33 . . . . .42 C2
Henry Robson Way NE33 . .42 C2
Henry Sq 🔢 NE2 . . . . .99 C2
Henry St
  Hetton-le-Hole DH5 . . . . .95 A5
  Houghton-le-Spring DH5 . . . .90 E1
  Newcastle upon Tyne NE3 . . . .38 C5
  North Shields NE29 . . . . .42 A4
  Shiney Row DH4 . . . . .90 B6
  South Shields NE33 . . . . .42 A4
Henry Street E SR2 . . . . . .103 C2
Henry Terr DH4 . . . . .89 F2
Hensby Ct NE5 . . . . .37 B4
Henshaw Ct NE63 . . . . .6 B2
Henshaw Gr NE25 . . . . .23 F2
Henshaw PI NE5 . . . . .54 B7
Henshelwood Terr 🔢 NE2 . .38 E1
Henson CI NE38 . . . . .83 D4
Hepburn Ave NE3 . . . . .37 D8
Hepburn Gdns NE10 . . . . . . .56 C1
Hepburn Gr SR5 . . . . .73 F1
Hepple Ct NE24 . . . . .17 C6
Hepple Rd NE64 . . . . .7 C3
Hepple Way NE3 . . . . .38 A6
HEPSCOTT 9 F5
Hepscott Dr NE25 . . . . .31 D6
Hepscott Manor Cotts
  NE61 . . . . .9 D3
Hepscott Terr NE33 . . . . .59 D8
Hepscott Wlk NE61 . . . . .4 E3
Herbert St NE6 . . . . .56 A1
Herbert Terr SR5 . . . . .75 B5
Herd CI NE21 . . . . .53 A1
Herd House La NE21 . . . . . . .52 F2
Herdinghill NE37 . . . . .82 F6
Herdlaw NE23 . . . . .22 A6
Hereford Ct
  Newcastle upon Tyne NE3 . . . .37 D8
  Sunderland SR2 . . . . .86 D1
Hereford Rd SR2 . . . . .86 D1
Hereford Sq SR2 . . . . .86 D1
Hereford Way NE32 . . . . .58 B2
Heritage CI NE8 . . . . .100 C1
Hermiston NE25 . . . . .31 E5
Hermitage Gdns DH2 . . . . . .88 B1
Hermitage Pk DH3 . . . . .88 C1
Hermitage Sta DH2 . . . . .88 A2
Heron CI
  Ashington NE63 . . . . .6 E1
  Blyth NE24 . . . . .17 E4
  Washington NE38 . . . . .83 A2
Heron Dr NE33 . . . . .42 C4
Heron PI NE12 . . . . .39 A7
Heron Villas NE34 . . . . .59 B4
Heron Way 🔢 NE5 . . . . .37 A3
Herring Gull CI NE24 . . . . . .17 E3
Herrington Country Park*
  DH4 . . . . .90 D8
Herrington Mews DH4 . . . . .90 E6
Herrington Rd SR3, DH4 . . .91 B6
Hersham CI NE23 . . . . .22 D7
Hester Ave NE25 . . . . .23 E3
Hester Bglws NE25 . . . . .23 E3
Hester Gdns NE25 . . . . .23 E3
Heswall Rd NE23 . . . . .16 A2
Hetherset CI SR4 . . . . .85 D5
Hetton Bogs Nature
  Reserve* DH4 . . . . .94 F6

HETTON DOWNS 95 B5
HETTON LE HILL 97 A7
HETTON LE HOLE. 95 A5
Hetton Lyons Ctry Pk*
  DH5 . . . . .95 C4
Hetton Lyons Ind Est NE35 .95 B3
Hetton Lyons Prim Sch
  DH5 . . . . .95 B5
Hetton Moor Terr DH5 . . . . .95 B2
Hetton Prim Sch DH5 . . . . . .94 F3
Hetton Rd DH5 . . . . .94 E7
Hetton Sch DH5 . . . . .94 F2
Heugh Hill NE9 . . . . .72 A3
Heughan CI SR4 . . . . .85 D5
Hewitson Terr NE10 . . . . .71 C8
Hewitt Ave SR2 . . . . .92 E8
Hewley Cres NE37 . . . . .71 F8
HEWORTH 71 F8
Heworth Burn Cres NE10 . .56 F1
Heworth Cres 🔢 NE37 . . . . .83 D8
Heworth Ct 🔢 NE34 . . . . . . .59 C5
Heworth Dene Gdns NE10 .56 E1
Heworth Grange Sch
  NE10 .71 F8
Heworth Rd NE37 . . . . .72 D1
Heworth Sta (BR & Metro)
  NE10 .71 F8
Heworth Way NE10 . . . . .72 A8
Hewson PI NE9 . . . . .71 B6
HEXHAM. 45 A5
Hexham NE38. . . . . .82 F4
Hexham Abbey* NE46 . . . . .45 B5
Hexham Ave
  Cramlington NE23 . . . . .22 D7
  Hebburn NE31 . . . . .57 E3
Hexham Bsns Pk NE46 . . . . .45 A6
Hexham Ct NE23 . . . . .41 C7
Hexham Ct NE11 . . . . .69 F6
Hexham East Fst Sch
  NE46 .45 C4
Hexham General Hospl
  NE46 .45 A4
Hexham Ho 🔢 NE6 . . . . .57 A6
Hexham Mid Sch NE46 . . . . .45 A4
Hexham Old Rd NE21,
  NE40 .52 E5
Hexham Priory Sch NE46 . .45 C4
Hexham Race Course
  NE46 .44 D1
Hexham Rd
  Heddon-on-the-Wall NE15 . . .34 E2
  Sunderland SR4 . . . . .85 D5
  Throckley NE15 . . . . .35 C2
  Whickham NE16 . . . . .54 A1
Hexham Sta NE46 . . . . .45 C5
Hextol Cres NE46 . . . . .45 A4
Hextol Ct NE46 . . . . .44 F4
Hextol Gdns NE15 . . . . .53 F7
Hextol Terr NE46 . . . . .44 F4
Heybrook Ave NE29 . . . . .41 F8
Heyburn Gdns NE15 . . . . . . .54 D5
Hibernian Rd NE32 . . . . .58 B7
Hibernia Rd NE15 . . . . .37 C4
Hickling Ct NE5 . . . . .37 C4
Hickstead CI NE28 . . . . .40 E7
Hickstead Gr NE23 . . . . .22 D7
Hiddleston Ave NE7 . . . . .39 B5
Higham PI NE1 . . . . .99 B3
High Axwell NE21 . . . . .53 D2
High Back CI NE32 . . . . .58 A4
HIGH BARNES. 85 B5
High Barnes Terr SR4 . . . . .102 A1
Highbridge NE3 . . . . .38 C7
High Bridge NE1, NE99 . . . . .99 A1
Highburn NE23 . . . . .22 A5
Highbury
  Gateshead NE10 . . . . .71 E8
  Newcastle upon Tyne NE2 . . . .38 D2
  Whitley Bay NE25 . . . . .31 E5
Highbury Ave NE9 . . . . .72 A2
Highbury CI NE9 . . . . .72 A2
Highbury PI NE29 . . . . .41 F6
HIGH CALLERTON 25 E2
High Chare DH3 . . . . .88 C3
HIGH CHURCH 8 F7
High CI NE21 . . . . .50 F1
Highclere Ho NE3 . . . . .89 F5
Highclere Dr SR2 . . . . .92 D6
Highcliffe Gdns NE8 . . . . . . .71 A8
High Croft NE37 . . . . .72 C8
High Croft CI NE31 . . . . .57 F5
Highcroft Dr NE64 . . . . .60 E1
Highcroft PI SR2 . . . . .92 F8
Highcross Rd NE30 . . . . .32 A3
Highcrofts NE15 . . . . .50 C6
High Dene NE7 . . . . .39 B3
High Dewley Burn NE15 . . . .35 D2
High Downs Sq DH5 . . . . . . .95 A4
HIGH DUBMIRE 90 B4
High Elm Sr4 . . . . .85 B2
HIGHFIELD 67 C7
Highfield
  Birtley DH3 . . . . .82 C4
  Blyth NE24 . . . . .17 F6
  Prudhoe NE42 . . . . .50 D7
  Sunniside NE16 . . . . .69 B3
Highfield Ave NE12 . . . . .39 D7
Highfield CI NE5 . . . . .36 F2
Highfield Comm Prim Sch
  Rowlands Gill NE39 . . . . .78 A8
  Sunderland SR4 . . . . .85 C6
Highfield Cres DH3 . . . . .88 C1
Highfield Ct NE10 . . . . .71 E8
Highfield Dr
  Ashington NE63 . . . . .7 A1

Highfield Dr continued
Fence Houses DH4 . . . . 94 B7
South Shields NE34 . . . . . . 59 F8
Highfield Gdns DH3 . . . . 88 C5
Highfield Grange DH4 . . 94 B7
Highfield La NE42 . . . . 50 C1
Highfield Pl
 Brunswick Village NE13 . . . 28 A1
 6 Sunderland SR4 . . . . 85 F6
Highfield Rd
 Gateshead NE8 . . . . 56 A1
 Newcastle upon Tyne NE5 . . 36 F3
 Rowlands Gill NE39 . . . . . 67 C1
 Shiney Row DH4 . . . . 90 A6
 South Shields NE33, NE34 . . 59 F8
Highfield Rise DH3 . . . . 88 C5
Highfields Mid Sch NE42 . . 50 C2
Highfield Terr
 Newcastle upon Tyne NE4 . . 57 A4
 Prudhoe NE42 . . . . 50 B2
HIGH FLATTS 88 A6
High Flatworth NE29 . . . . 41 B4
Highford Gdns NE61 . . . . . 8 E7
Highford La NE46 . . . . 44 E4
HIGH FORGE 00 F1
High Friar La NE1 . . . . . . 99 A1
HIGH FRIARSIDE 78 E6
High Friarside NE16 . . . . 78 E6
High Gables **9** NE46 . . . 45 B4
Highgate NE32 . . . . 58 D2
Highgate Rd NE4 . . . . 85 D5
High Gate The NE3 . . . . 37 E4
High Gosforth Park
(Newcastle Race Course)
 NE3 . . . . 28 D2
High Gr NE40 . . . . 72 D4
Highgreen Chase NE16 . . 69 A4
High Grindon Ho SR4 . . . 85 C3
Highgrove NE5 . . . . 36 D2
High Hamsterley Rd NE39 78 A5
Highheath **1** NE37 . . . . . 83 A6
HIGH HEATON 39 A3
High Hedgefield Terr
 NE21 . . . . 52 E5
High Heworth La NE10 . . 71 E7
High Horse Cl NE39 . . . . 68 A4
High Horse Close Wood
 NE39 . . . . 68 A4
High House Cl NE61 . . . . 8 D8
High House Rd NE10 . . . 56 E1
High La DH4 . . . . 90 F4
Highland Rd NE5 . . . . 37 D3
High Lane Row NE8 . . . . 57 F7
High Lanes NE10 . . . . 71 F7
High Laws NE3 . . . . 38 F4
Highlaws Gdns NE9 . . . . 71 B2
High Level Rd NE8 . . . . 101 B3
High Market NE63 . . . . 6 A4
High Mdw NE32 . . . . 37 C3
High Mdws NE3 . . . . 37 E3
High Meadow NE34 . . . . 59 F8
HIGH MICKLEY 64 F7
High Mill Rd NE39 . . . . . . 78 A5
Highmoor NE61 . . . . 8 D7
High Moor Ct NE5 . . . . . . 37 E2
High Moor Pl NE34 . . . . 59 C5
HIGH MOORSIDE 96 D8
HIGH MOORSLEY 96 D8
High Pasture NE38 . . . . . 83 E1
HIGH PIT 22 D6
High PITTINGTON 96 C5
High Pk NE61 . . . . 9 A7
High Primrose Hill DH4 . . 89 D3
High Quay
 Blyth NE24 . . . . 17 F8
 Newcastle upon Tyne NE1 . . 56 A5
High Rd The NE34 . . . . . . 40 A6
High Reach NE10 . . . . 57 A2
High Reins NE46 . . . . 44 E5
Highridge DH3 . . . . 82 C5
High Ridge
 Bedlington NE22 . . . . 10 E1
 Hazlerigg NE13 . . . . 28 B4
High Row
 Great Lumley DH4 . . . . . . 89 E1
 Newcastle upon Tyne NE15 . . 53 C6
 Ryton NE40 . . . . 52 E4
 Washington NE37 . . . . 72 D1
High Sandgrove SR6 . . . . 60 A1
High Shaw NE42 . . . . 50 B1
HIGH SHIELDS 42 B1
Highside Dr SR3 . . . . 86 A3
HIGH SOUTHWICK 75 B3
HIGH SPEN 66 F4
High Spen Cty Jun Sch NE39 . . 67 A4
High Spen Ind Est NE39 . . 66 F5
High Spen Prim Sch NE39 66 F3
High St
 Blyth NE24 . . . . 17 D7
 Blyth NE24 . . . . 17 E7
 Choppington NE62 . . . . . . 10 E6
 Easington Lane DH5 . . . . . 95 C1
 Gateshead, Felling NE10 . . 71 C3
 Gateshead NE8 . . . . 101 C3
 Gateshead, Wrekenton NE9 71 C1
 Guide Post NE62 . . . . 10 E7
 High Pittington DH6 . . . . 96 B6
 Jarrow NE32 . . . . 58 C7
 Jarrow NE32 . . . . 58 D7
 Newbiggin-by-the-Sea NE64 . . 7 F5
 Newburn NE15 . . . . 52 F7
 Newcastle upon Tyne NE3 . . 38 C4
 Sunderland SR4 . . . . 85 A6
Highstead Ave NE23 . . . . 16 A1
Highsteads DH4 . . . . 77 B1
High Stobhill NE61 . . . . . . 9 A4
High Street Bk NE3 . . . . 38 C5

High Street E
 Sunderland SR1 . . . . 103 B3
 Wallsend NE28 . . . . 40 C1
High Street W
 Sunderland SR1 . . . . 103 A3
 Wallsend NE28, NE6 . . . . 40 A1
High Swinburne Pl NE4 . . 98 B1
Hightree Cl SR3 . . . . 91 F5
HIGH URPETH 81 B1
High View
 Hedley on the Hill NE43 . . 64 F3
 Ponteland NE20 . . . . 25 D2
 Wallsend NE28 . . . . 40 B3
High View N NE28 . . . . . . 40 B4
High Well Gdns NE16 . . 53 F6
Highwell La **4** NE61 . . . 36 E1
High West St NE8 . . . . . 101 C2
HIGH WESTWOOD 77 B4
Highwood Rd NE15 . . . . 53 F7
Highworth Dr
 Newcastle upon Tyne NE7 . . 39 D3
 3 Springwell NE9 . . . . . 71 F1
Hilda Pk DH2 . . . . 88 B5
Hilda St
 Gateshead NE8 . . . . 101 A1
 Sunderland SR6 . . . . 75 D3
Hilda Terr **7** NE15 . . . . 35 D2
Hilden Bldgs NE7 . . . . . . 39 C2
Hilden Gdns NE7 . . . . . . 39 C2
Hillary Ave NE12 . . . . 39 E8
Hill Ave NE23 . . . . 23 A2
Hill Brow SR3 . . . . 92 B6
Hillcrest
 Ashington NE63 . . . . 7 A2
 Hedworth NE32 . . . . 58 D2
 Prudhoe NE42 . . . . 50 D2
 South Shields NE34 . . . . . 60 B5
 Sunderland SR3 . . . . 91 B8
 Whitley Bay NE25 . . . . . . 31 E5
Hill Crest
 Burnopfield NE16 . . . . 79 B6
 Gateshead NE10 . . . . 71 E6
Hillcrest Ave NE62 . . . . . 10 F8
Hillcrest Ct NE42 . . . . . . 50 D2
Hillcrest Dr
 Dunston NE11 . . . . 69 E7
 Hexham NE46 . . . . 45 C4
Hill Crest Gdns NE2 . . . . 38 E4
Hillcroft
 Gateshead 71 A6
 Rowlands Gill NE39 . . . . . 67 C2
Hill Croft NE15 . . . . 33 C1
Hill Dyke NE9 . . . . 71 C2
Hillfield NE25 . . . . 31 D5
Hillfield Gdns SR3 . . . . . 86 B3
Hillfield St NE8 . . . . 101 B2
Hillgate NE8 . . . . 101 B4
Hill Gate NE61 . . . . 9 A8
Hill Head Dr NE5 . . . . . . 36 D1
Hillhead La NE11 . . . . 70 A6
Hillhead La NE16 . . . . 68 D2
Hillhead Parkway NE5 . . 36 C2
Hillhead Rd NE34 . . . . . . 36 D2
Hillheads Ct NE25 . . . . . 32 A4
Hillheads Rd NE25, NE26 . . 32 A4
Hillhead Way NE5 . . . . . 36 C2
Hill House Rd NE15 . . . . 35 C2
Hillingdon Gr SR3 . . . . . 85 A2
Hill La DH4 . . . . 84 C1
Hill Park Rd NE32 . . . . . 58 C5
Hill Pk NE20 . . . . 25 D2
Hill Rise
 Crawcrook NE40 . . . . 51 F3
 Washington NE38 . . . . 83 E6
Hillrise Cres SR7 . . . . . . 92 D1
Hills Ct NE21 . . . . 53 E4
Hillsden Rd NE5 . . . . 31 D7
Hillside
 Ashington NE63 . . . . 6 C4
 Birtley DH3 . . . . 82 D4
 Blaydon NE21 . . . . 53 B2
 Chester le Street DH3 . . . 88 C4
 Dunston NE11 . . . . 69 F7
 Killingworth NE12 . . . . . . 29 E2
 Morpeth NE61 . . . . 8 F7
 Ponteland NE20 . . . . 25 C1
 South Shields NE34 . . . . . 60 B4
 Sunderland SR3 . . . . 86 C3
 West Boldon NE36 . . . . . . 74 A7
Hillside Ave NE15 . . . . . 53 F8
Hillside Cres NE15 . . . . . 54 A4
Hillside Dr SR6 . . . . 75 E4
Hillside Gdns SR3 . . . . . 86 C3
Hillside Grove DH6 . . . . . 96 B5
Hillside Pl NE9 . . . . 71 A6
Hillside Rd NE46 . . . . 45 D4
Hillside Way DH4 . . . . . . 90 E1
Hillsleigh Rd NE5 . . . . . . 37 D2
Hills St NE8 . . . . 101 B3
Hill St
 Corbridge NE45 . . . . 46 F5
 Jarrow NE32 . . . . 58 A7
 New Silksworth SR3 . . . . . 92 A7
 South Shields NE33 . . . . . 42 B1
Hillsview Ave NE3 . . . . . 37 E5
Hill Terr DH4 . . . . 90 E6
Hill The NE42 . . . . 50 B4
Hillthorne Cl NE38 . . . . . 83 E4
HILL TOP 41 A8
Hill Top
 Birtley DH3 . . . . 82 D4
 Blaydon NE21 . . . . 53 B1
Hill Top Ave NE9 . . . . . . 71 B5
Hill Top Cl NE62 . . . . 10 F8

Hilltop Gdns SR3 . . . . . . 92 C7
Hill Top Gdns NE9 . . . . . 71 A5
Hilltop Ho NE5 . . . . 37 A2
Hill Top Sch NE10 . . . . . 71 E4
Hilltop View SR6 . . . . . . 60 E2
HILLVIEW 86 C2
Hillview SR3 . . . . 91 B7
Hillview Cres DH4 . . . . . 90 D3
Hill View Gdns SR3 . . . . 86 B3
Hillview Gr DH4 . . . . 90 D3
Hill View Inf Sch SR2 . . 86 D2
Hill View Jun Sch SR2 . . 86 D2
Hill View Rd DH4 . . . . . . 90 D3
Hill View Rd SR2 . . . . . . 86 D2
Hilton Ave NE5 . . . . 37 B2
Hilton Cl NE23 . . . . 16 A2
Hilton Prim Sch NE5 . . . 37 B2
Hindley Cl NE40 . . . . 51 E3
Hindley Gdns NE4 . . . . . 54 D7
Hindmarch Dr NE35, NE36 . . 74 B7
Hindmarsh Dr **6** NE63 . . 6 F5
Hindson's Crescent N
 DH4 . . . . 90 A5
Hindson's Crescent S
 DH4 . . . . 90 A5
Hind St SR1 . . . . 102 C2
Hinkley Cl SR3 . . . . 92 B6
Hippingstones La NE45 . . 46 F6
Hipsburn Dr SR3 . . . . 86 A3
Hiram Dr NE36 . . . . 74 D7
HIRST 6 E3
Hirst Head NE22 . . . . 11 A1
Hirst High Tech Coll NE63 . . 7 A2
Hirst Terrace N NE22 . . 11 A1
Hirst Villas NE22 . . . . . . 11 A1
Histon Ct NE5 . . . . 37 B3
Histon Way NE5 . . . . 37 B3
Hi-Tec Village NE35 . . . . 73 D7
Hither Gn NE32 . . . . 58 D2
Hobart NE26 . . . . 31 F7
Hobart Ave NE34 . . . . . . 59 C5
Hobart Gdns NE7 . . . . . . 39 A5
HOBSON 79 A4
Hobson Ind Est NE16 . . . 79 A5
Hodgkin Ho NE2 . . . . 99 A3
Hodgkin Park Cres NE15 . . 54 C5
Hodgkin Park Rd NE15 . . 54 C5
Hodgson's Rd NE24 . . . . 12 D1
Hodgson Terr **6** NE37 . . 83 F8
Hodkin Gdns NE9 . . . . . . 71 B6
Hogarth Cotts NE22 . . . . 16 A4
Hogarth Dr NE38 . . . . . . 83 E3
Hogarth Rd NE34 . . . . . . 59 C3
Holbein Rd NE34 . . . . . . 59 C3
Holborn Ho NE33 . . . . . . 42 E1
Holborn Pl NE5 . . . . 36 E1
Holborn Sq SR4 . . . . 85 D5
Holburn Cl NE40 . . . . 52 E5
Holburn Gdns NE40 . . . 52 E5
Holburn La NE40 . . . . 52 D6
Holburn Lane Ct NE40 . . 52 D6
Holburn Way NE40 . . . . 52 D5
Holburn Wlk NE40 . . . . 52 D5
Holden Pl NE5 . . . . 37 D2
Holder House La NE34 . . 59 E2
Holder House Way NE34 . . 59 E2
Holderness Rd
 Newcastle upon Tyne NE6 . . 39 B1
 Wallsend NE28 . . . . 41 B3
Hole La
 Sunniside NE16 . . . . 69 B3
 Whickham NE16 . . . . 68 F4
Holeyn Hall Rd NE41 . . . 51 A7
Holeyn Rd NE15 . . . . 35 C1
Holland Dr NE2 . . . . 98 B3
Holland Park Dr NE32 . . 58 D2
Holland Pk NE28 . . . . . . 39 E3
Holley Park Prim Sch
 NE38 . . . . 83 A3
Hollinghill Rd NE25 . . . . 23 E2
Hollings Cres NE28 . . . . 40 B4
Hollingside Way NE34 . . 59 D5
Hollings Terr NE17 . . . . 66 A1
Hollington Ave NE12 . . . . 39 B6
Hollington Cl NE12 . . . . 39 B6
Hollinhill NE39 . . . . 68 A5
Hollinhill La NE39 . . . . . . 67 F4
Hollin Hill Rd NE37 . . . . 83 E2
Hollinhill Terr NE44 . . . . 63 A2
Hollinside Cl NE16 . . . . . 69 A5
Hollinside Gdns NE15 . . 54 B6
Hollinside Rd
 Sunderland SR4 . . . . 85 D4
 Whickham NE11 . . . . 54 C5
Hollinside Sq SR4 . . . . . 85 C5
Hollinside Terr NE9 . . . . 67 D2
Hollon St NE61 . . . . 3 E1
Hollowdene DH5 . . . . 95 A3
Hollow The
 Ashington NE63 . . . . 7 B2
 Hedworth NE32 . . . . 58 B2
Holly Ave
 Dunston NE11 . . . . 69 F7
 Earsdon NE25 . . . . 31 B5
 Houghton-le-Spring DH5 . . 94 F8
 Longbenton NE12 . . . . . . 29 D1
 Morpeth NE61 . . . . 8 E7
 Newcastle upon Tyne, Fawdon NE3 . . 37 F6
 Newcastle upon Tyne, Jesmond NE2 . . 38 F1
 New Silksworth SR3 . . . . . 92 B8
 Ryton NE40 . . . . 52 C6

Holly Ave continued
 South Shields NE34 . . . . . 60 A5
 Wallsend NE28 . . . . 40 C1
 Whitburn SR6 . . . . 75 F8
 Whitley Bay NE26 . . . . . . 32 A5
 Winlaton Mill NE21 . . . . . 68 C6
Holly Avenue W NE2 . . . 38 E1
Holly Bush Gdns NE40 . . 52 E4
Hollybush Rd **4** NE10 . . 71 C8
Hollycarrside Rd SR2 . . 92 E8
Holly Cl
 Hexham NE46 . . . . 44 E3
 Killingworth NE12 . . . . . . 29 C4
Holly Cres NE38 . . . . 83 C1
Hollycrest DH2 . . . . 88 B5
Holly Ct
 Newcastle upon Tyne NE5 . . 37 B2
 Sunderland SR4 . . . . 102 A2
 Whitley Bay NE26 . . . . . . 31 F5
Hollydene
 Kibblesworth NE11 . . . . . 81 D6
 Rowlands Gill NE39 . . . . . 67 F2
Holly Gdns NE9 . . . . 70 F6
Holly Gr NE42 . . . . 50 E2
Holly Haven DH5 . . . . 94 D4
Holly Hill NE10 . . . . 71 D8
Holly Ho NE5 . . . . 103 C3
Hollyhock
 Ashington NE63 . . . . 6 D3
 Jarrow NE32 . . . . 58 A7
Hollys The DH3 . . . . 82 B7
Holly Terr NE16 . . . . 79 C5
Holly View NE10 . . . . 71 C8
Holly Rd NE29 . . . . 41 D6
Holly St
 Ashington NE63 . . . . 6 D3
 Jarrow NE32 . . . . 58 A7
Hollywell Ave
 Newcastle upon Tyne, Gosforth
 NE3 . . . . 38 D6
 Sunderland SR5 . . . . 74 F2
 Wallsend NE6 . . . . 40 A1
Hollywood Cres NE3 . . . 38 D6
Hollywood Gdns NE11 . . 70 B5
Holman Cl NE33 . . . . 42 C2
Holmcroft NE34 . . . . 7 E5
Holmdale
 Ashington NE63 . . . . 6 C2
 Hexham NE46 . . . . 45 C4
Holme Ave
 Newcastle upon Tyne NE6 . . 39 F1
 Whickham NE16 . . . . 69 B7
Holme Gdns
 Sunderland SR3 . . . . 86 B3
 Wallsend NE28 . . . . 41 A2
Holme Rise NE16 . . . . . . 69 B7
Holmesdale Rd NE5 . . . . 37 D1
Holmeside NE1 . . . . 103 A2
Holmewood Dr NE39 . . 78 D8
Holmfield Ave NE34 . . . 59 E7
Holm Gdns NE25 . . . . . . 31 D4
Holmland NE15 . . . . 31 E5
Holmlands NE25 . . . . 31 E5
Holmlands Cl NE25 . . . . 31 E5
Holmlands Park N SR2 . . 86 C4
Holmlands Park S SR3 . . 86 C4
Holmside Ave NE11 . . . . 70 A8
Holmside Terr NE16 . . . 69 C2
Holmwood Ave
 Newbiggin-by-the-Sea
 NE64 . . . . 7 D5
 Whitley Bay NE25 . . . . . . 31 D4
Holmwood Gr NE2 . . . . . 38 D2
Holwick Cl NE38 . . . . 83 A2
HOLY CROSS 40 D3
Holy Cross RC Prim Sch
 NE28 . . . . 40 C4
Hoylfields NE27 . . . . 30 E2
Holy Island **11** NE46 . . . 45 B5
Holy Jesus Bglws NE2 . . 98 B4
Holy Jesus Hospital
 Almshouse* **1** NE1 . . 99 B1
Holylake Sq SR4 . . . . 85 D5
Holyoake Gdns
 Birtley DH3 . . . . 82 D4
 Gateshead NE9 . . . . 70 F8
Holyoake St NE42 . . . . . 50 D3
Holyoake Terr
 8 Newcastle upon Tyne NE3 . . 83 D8
Holyrood Rd **2** SR2 . . . 86 F2
Holystone Ave
 Blyth NE24 . . . . 17 C5
 Newcastle upon Tyne NE25 . . 38 B6
 Whitley Bay NE25 . . . . . . 32 A4
Holystone Cl
 Blyth NE24 . . . . 17 B5
 Burnside DH4 . . . . 90 B2
Holystone Cres NE7 . . . . 39 B3
Holystone Dr NE27 . . . . 30 C2
Holystone Gdns NE29 . . 41 D8
Holystone Prim Sch NE27 . . 30 C2
Holystone St **11** NE31 . . 57 D6
Holystone Trad Est NE12 . . 29 B8
Holystone Way NE12, NE27 40 C8
Holy Trinity CE VA Sch
 NE34 . . . . 59 B4

HOLYWELL 23 F2
Holywell Ave
 Holywell NE25 . . . . 23 F2
 Newcastle upon Tyne NE6 . . 56 E3
 Whitley Bay NE26 . . . . . . 31 F6
Holywell Cl
 Blaydon NE21 . . . . 53 D1
 Holywell NE25 . . . . 23 F2
 Newcastle upon Tyne NE6 . . 98 B2
Holywell Dene Nature
 Reserve* NE26 . . . . 24 B2
Holywell Dene Rd NE25 . . 23 F2
Holywell Est Sch NE25 . . 23 F2
Holywell La NE16 . . . . . . 69 B3
Holywell Mews NE16 . . . 31 F6
Holywell Terr NE27 . . . . 30 D1
Home Ave **2** NE9 . . . . . 70 F4
Homedale NE42 . . . . 50 E2
Homedale Pl NE42 . . . . . 50 E1
Homedale Terr NE42 . . . 50 D2
Homedowne Ho NE3 . . . 38 C5
Home Farm Cl NE63 . . . . 5 F4
Homeforth Ho NE3 . . . . . 38 C5
Home Pk NE28 . . . . 39 E3
Homeprior Ho NE25 . . . . 31 E4
Homeside Pl **6** NE6 . . . . 56 B7
Homestall Cl NE34 . . . . . 59 D5
Honeycomb Cl **7** SR3 . . 91 F5
Honeycrook Dr NE7 . . . . 39 E3
Honeysuckle Ave NE34 . . 59 B5
Honeysuckle Cl SR3 . . . . 92 A5
Honister Ave NE2 . . . . . . 38 C3
Honister Cl NE15 . . . . . . 53 D7
Honister Dr SR5 . . . . 75 C3
Honister Pl NE15 . . . . . . 53 D7
Honister Rd NE30 . . . . . . 32 B2
Honister Way NE24 . . . . 17 C3
Honiton Cl DH4 . . . . 90 C4
Honiton Ct NE3 . . . . 37 B6
Honiton Way NE28 . . . . 41 B8
Hood Cl SR5 . . . . 75 C1
Hood St NE21 . . . . 53 A1
Hood St
 Morpeth NE61 . . . . 3 F1
 Newcastle upon Tyne NE1 . . 99 A1
 4 Whickham NE16 . . . . 54 A1
HOOKER GATE 67 A2
Hookergate Comp Sch
 NE39 . . . . 67 B3
Hookergate La NE39 . . . 67 A2
Hopedene NE10 . . . . 72 A5
Hope Shield NE38 . . . . . . 82 F1
Hope St
 Jarrow NE32 . . . . 58 C7
 Sunderland SR1 . . . . 102 C2
Hope View SR2 . . . . 92 F7
Hopgarth Ct DH3 . . . . . . 88 D4
Hopgarth Gdns DH3 . . . 88 E7
Hopkins Ct SR4 . . . . 85 F7
Hopkins Wlk NE34 . . . . . 59 A2
Hopper Pl NE8 . . . . 101 C3
Hopper Rd NE10 . . . . 71 C7
Hopper St
 5 North Shields NE29 . . 41 F5
 6 Wallsend NE28 . . . . . 40 B2
Horatio St
 Newcastle upon Tyne NE1 . . 56 A5
 Sunderland SR6 . . . . 75 E1
Hornbeam DH4 . . . . 89 F5
Hornbeam Pl NE4 . . . . . 100 B3
Horncliffe Gdns NE16 . . 69 C8
Horncliffe Pl NE15 . . . . . 35 B2
Horncliffe Wlk NE15 . . . 53 A7
Horning Ct NE13 . . . . . . 28 B5
Hornsea Cl NE13 . . . . 28 B5
Hornsey Cres DH5 . . . . . 95 B1
Hornsey Terr DH5 . . . . . 95 B1
Horse Crofts NE21 . . . . . 53 C3
Horsegate Bank NE17,
 NE40 . . . . 66 D3
Horsham Gdns SR3 . . . . 86 A3
Horsley Ave NE39 . . . . . 41 E4
HORSLEY 50 D8
Horsley Ave
 Crawcrook NE40 . . . . 51 E3
 Shiremoor NE27 . . . . 30 F2
Horsley Bus Ctr NE15 . . 33 C1
Horsley Cl NE62 . . . . 10 F8
Horsley Ct NE3 . . . . 37 E6
Horsley Gdns
 Dunston NE11 . . . . 70 A8
 Holywell NE25 . . . . 23 F2
Horsley Gr SR3 . . . . 86 A3
HORSLEY HILL 60 B8
Horsley Hill Rd NE33 . . . 42 E1
Horsley Hill Sq NE34 . . . 60 B7
Horsley Rd
 Newcastle upon Tyne NE7 . . 39 A2
 Ovingham NE42 . . . . 50 A5
 Shiremoor NE27 . . . . 30 A8
Horsley Terr
 Newcastle upon Tyne NE6 . . 56 F5
 12 Tynemouth NE30 . . . 42 D7
Horsley Vale NE34 . . . . . 60 A8
Horsley View
 Howdon NE28 . . . . 41 A2
 Prudhoe NE42 . . . . 50 B2
Horsley Wood Cotts NE15 50 D7
Horton Ave
 Bedlington NE22 . . . . 15 F8
 Shiremoor NE27 . . . . 30 F2
 Whiteleas NE34 . . . . 59 D3

Horton Cres NE13 . . . . .27 B7
Hortondale Gr NE24 . . . . .17 B7
Horton Dr NE23 . . . . .16 B2
Horton Grange Fst Sch
NE24 .16 F8
Horton Manor NE24 . . . . .16 D7
Horton Pl NE27 . . . . .17 B4
Horton Rd NE22, NE24 . . . . . .16 C5
Horton St **3** NE24 . . . . .17 F7
Horwood Ave NE5 . . . . .36 E2
Hospital Dr NE31 . . . . .57 D4
Hospital La NE15 . . . . .53 B8
Hospital of King James The
. . . . .56 B1
Hospl of St Mary the Virgin
The NE4 . . . . .100 B4
Hotch Pudding Pl NE5 . . . . . .36 F1
Hotspur Ave
Bedlington NE22 . . . . .15 F8
South Shields NE34 . . . . . . .59 F7
Whitley Bay NE25 . . . . .32 A4
Hotspur Prim Sch NE22 . . . . .56 A6
Hotspur St NE28 . . . . .40 A5
Hotspur St
Newcastle upon Tyne NE6 . . .56 A7
Tynemouth NE30 . . . . .42 D8
HOUGHTON 34 D2
Houghton Ave
Newcastle upon Tyne NE5 . . .37 E3
Tynemouth NE30 . . . . .32 B3
Houghton Cut DH5 . . . . .90 E1
Houghton Gate DH3 . . . . .89 B3
HOUGHTON-LE-SPRING 94 D7
Houghton Rd
Hetton-le-Hole DH5 . . . . . . .95 A4
Newbottle DH4 . . . . .90 D3
Houghton Road W DH5 . . . . .95 A4
Houghtonside 90 E1
Houghton Sports Coll
DH4 .94 D8
Houghton St **3** SR4 . . . . . .102 A2
Houlet Garth **10** NE6 . . . . . .56 C5
Houlsyke Cl SR3 . . . . .92 C7
Houndelee Pl NE5 . . . . .37 C1
Houndslow Dr NE63 . . . . .6 B2
Hounslow Gdns NE28 . . . . . . .58 D2
Housesteads NE28 . . . . .41 A2
Housesteads Gdns NE12 . . . .36 A6
House Terr NE37 . . . . .83 D8
Housing La DH8 . . . . .77 D1
Housteads **6** NE28 . . . . .40 F4
Houston Ct NE4 . . . . .100 B4
Houston St NE4 . . . . .100 B4
Houxty Rd NE25 . . . . .31 B5
Hovingham Gdns SR3 . . . . . . .86 A3
Howard Cl NE27 . . . . .30 C1
Howard Gr NE61 . . . . .4 E2
Howard Ho NE3 . . . . .38 C4
Howardian Cl NE38 . . . . .83 B3
Howard Pl NE3 . . . . .38 C5
Howard Rd NE61 . . . . .4 A1
Howard St
4 Gateshead, Mount Pleasant
NE8 .56 B1
Gateshead, Windy Nook
NE10 . . . . .71 C6
Jarrow NE32 . . . . .58 C6
Newcastle upon Tyne NE1 . . .99 C1
North Shields NE30 . . . . . . .42 B5
3 Sunderland SR5 . . . . . . .75 D1
Howard Terr
High Spen NE39 . . . . .66 F4
6 Morpeth NE61 . . . . .3 A6
Howard Walk NE63 . . . . .6 F5
Howarth St SR4 . . . . .102 A2
Howarth Terr DH6 . . . . .97 F3
Howat Ave NE5 . . . . .37 E1
Howburn Cres NE61 . . . . .4 E3
Howburn Ct NE61 . . . . .4 A3
Howdene Rd NE15 . . . . .53 F6
HOWDON 41 B2
Howdon Green Ind Est
NE28 . . . . .41 B2
Howdon La NE28 . . . . .41 A2
HOWDON PANS 41 C1
Howdon Rd
North Shields, Howdon Pans
NE28 . . . . .41 C2
North Shields, Redburn Dene
NE28, NE29 . . . . .41 A3
Howdon Sta NE28 . . . . .41 A2
Howe Sq SR4 . . . . .85 C5
Howe St
Gateshead NE8 . . . . .56 A1
Hebburn NE31 . . . . .58 A6
Howick Ave NE3 . . . . .38 A7
Howick Pk NE6 . . . . .103 A4
Howlett Hall Rd NE15 . . . . . . .53 F6
Howley Ave NE5 . . . . .74 D2
Hownam Cl NE3 . . . . .38 A4
Hoy Cres SR7 . . . . .92 F1
Hoylake Ave NE7 . . . . .39 C5
Hoyle Ave NE4 . . . . .54 E6
Hoyle Fold SR3 . . . . .92 A4
Hubert St NE35 . . . . .73 F8
Hucklow Gdns NE34 . . . . .59 D5
Huddart Terr **2** DH3 . . . . . . .82 C5
Huddleston Rd NE6 . . . . .56 C5
Huddleston Rise SR6 . . . . . . .103 B4
Hudshaw NE26 . . . . .32 C4
Hudshaw Gdns NE46 . . . . . . .45 D4
Hudson Ave
Bedlington NE22 . . . . .11 B1
Dudley NE23 . . . . .29 B8

Hudson Rd SR1 . . . . .103 B2
Hudson Road Prim Sch
SR1 . . . . .103 B2
Hudson St
Gateshead NE8 . . . . .101 B4
North Shields NE30 . . . . . . .42 C6
South Shields NE33 . . . . . . .59 B6
Hugar Rd NE39 . . . . .67 A3
Hugh Ave NE27 . . . . .30 F4
Hugh Gdns NE4 . . . . .54 E4
Hugh St
Sunderland SR6 . . . . .75 E4
Wallsend NE28 . . . . .40 B1
7 Washington NE38 . . . . . .83 F4
Hull St NE4 . . . . .54 F5
Hulne Ave NE30 . . . . .32 A1
Hulne Terr NE15 . . . . .53 C6
Humber St **1** SR3 . . . . .91 F6
Humber Gdns NE8 . . . . .56 B1
Humbert St NE61 . . . . .66 C1
Humbert St NE32 . . . . .58 B6
HUMBLEDON 85 F3
Humbledon Pk SR3 . . . . .86 A3
Humbledon View **5** SR4 . . . .85 F3
Humford Gn NE24 . . . . .16 F7
Humford Ho NE24 . . . . .17 B6
Humford Way NE22 . . . . .16 F7
Humsford Gr NE23 . . . . .22 C8
Humshaugh Cl NE12 . . . . .40 A8
Humshaugh Rd NE29 . . . . . . .41 C6
Hunn's Buildings NE26 . . . . . .10 E5
Hunstanton Ct NE9 . . . . .70 E3
Huntcliffe Ave NE6 . . . . .57 A5
Huntcliffe Gdns NE6 . . . . .39 D1
Huntcliffe Ho NE34 . . . . .59 C3
Hunter Ave NE24 . . . . .17 F6
Hunter Cl NE36 . . . . .74 D6
Hunter Ho NE1 . . . . .99 B1
Hunters Cl DH8 . . . . .77 C1
Hunters Ct NE28 . . . . .40 C2
Hunters Hall Rd SR4 . . . . . . .102 B1
Hunters Lodge NE28 . . . . .40 C2
Hunter's Moor Cl NE2 . . . . . . .98 B4
Hunter's Pl NE2 . . . . .98 B4
Hunter's Rd
Newcastle upon Tyne, South
Gosforth NE3 . . . . .38 F5
Newcastle upon Tyne, Spital
Tongues NE2 . . . . .98 B3
Hunter St
Shiney Row DH4 . . . . .90 A5
South Shields NE33 . . . . . . .42 D1
Hunter Terr SR2 . . . . .86 E3
Huntingdon Pl NE30 . . . . .37 D8
Huntingdon Gdns SR3 . . . . . .86 A3
Huntingdon Pl NE30 . . . . .32 D7
Huntington Av NE23 . . . . .22 D7
Hunt Lea NE16 . . . . .68 C5
Huntley Cres NE21 . . . . .68 A8
Huntley Sq SR4 . . . . .85 A8
Huntley Terr **4** SR2 . . . . . . .92 F6
Huntly Rd NE25 . . . . .31 D7
Huntsmoor Ho NE2 . . . . .98 B3
Hunworth Cl SR4 . . . . .85 D5
Hurst Terr NE6 . . . . .56 E6
Hurstwood Rd NE4 . . . . .64 A4
Hurworth Ave NE34 . . . . .60 B7
Hurworth Pl NE32 . . . . .58 B6
Hutton Cl
Chester le Street DH3 . . . . . .88 E1
Houghton-le-Spring DH4 . . . .94 C8
Washington NE37 . . . . .83 B6
Hutton Ho NE29 . . . . .41 E3
Hutton Row NE33 . . . . .42 E2
Hutton St
Boldon Colliery NE35 . . . . . .58 F1
Newcastle upon Tyne NE3 . . .38 A5
Sunderland SR4 . . . . .102 A3
Hutton Terr
Gateshead NE9 . . . . .70 F4
Newcastle upon Tyne NE2 . . .99 C3
Huxley Cl NE34 . . . . .59 B2
Huxley Cres NE8 . . . . .70 D3
Hyacinth Ct SR4 . . . . .102 B3
Hybrid Cl DH4 . . . . .89 F5
Hyde Park St NE8 . . . . .70 D8
Hyde Pk NE28 . . . . .39 F3
Hyde St
South Shields NE33 . . . . . . .42 D5
Sunderland SR2 . . . . .86 F4
Hyde Terr NE3 . . . . .38 D5
Hylton Ave NE34 . . . . .60 B7
Hylton Bank SR4 . . . . .85 B6
HYLTON CASTLE 74 A2
Hylton Castle* SR5 . . . . .74 B2
Hylton Castle Prim Sch **3**
SR5 .74 A2
Hylton Castle Rd SR5 . . . . . . .74 A1
Hylton Cl NE22 . . . . .10 D1
Hylton Ct SR3 . . . . .85 E1
Isabella St NE4 . . . . .54 E3
Hylton Dene Nature
Reserve* SR5 . . . . .74 B2
Hylton Grange SR5 . . . . .84 F8
Hylton La NE36, SR5 . . . . . . .74 A5
Hylton Park Rd SR5 . . . . .74 F1
Hylton Rd
Jarrow NE32 . . . . .58 C3
Sunderland SR4 . . . . .85 D5
Sunderland SR4 . . . . .85 D5
HYLTON RED HOUSE 74 D4
Hylton Red House Prim Sch
SR5 .74 E4
Hylton Red House Sch
SR5 .74 E4
Hylton Retail Park SR5 . . . . . .74 D1

Hylton St
Gateshead NE8 . . . . .56 B1
Newbottle DH4 . . . . .90 D2
17 North Shields NE29 . . . .42 A5
7 Old Fold NE8, NE10 . . . .56 B1
Sunderland SR4 . . . . .102 A2
Hylton Terr
Newcastle upon Tyne
NE6 .57 C2
6 North Shields NE29 . . . .42 A5
Ryhope SR2 . . . . .92 E6
Hylton Wlk SR4 . . . . .85 A5
Hymers Ave NE34 . . . . .58 F4
Hyperion Ave NE34 . . . . .59 A5

I

Ilderton Pl NE5 . . . . .53 E8
Ilford Ave NE23 . . . . .16 A1
Ilford Pl NE8, NE9 . . . . .71 A8
Ilford Rd
Newcastle upon Tyne NE2 . . .38 D3
Wallsend NE28 . . . . .40 F3
Ilford Road Sta NE2 . . . . .38 D3
Ilfracombe Ave NE4 . . . . .54 E5
Ilfracombe Gdns
Gateshead NE9 . . . . .70 F3
Whitley Bay NE26 . . . . .31 F6
Illingworth Ho NE29 . . . . .41 E3
Ilminster Ct NE3 . . . . .37 C6
Imeary Gr **9** NE33 . . . . .42 D1
Imeary St NE33 . . . . .42 D1
Imperial Bldgs **1** DH4 . . . . .94 E8
Inchberry Cl NE4 . . . . .54 D4
Inchcliffe Cres NE5 . . . . .37 C2
Industrial Rd NE37 . . . . .83 E7
Industry Rd NE6 . . . . .39 D2
Ingham Gr NE23 . . . . .16 A1
Ingham Grange NE33 . . . . . . .42 E1
Ingham Pl NE2 . . . . .99 C2
Ingham Terr NE24 . . . . .17 D7
Ingleborough Cl **3** NE37 . .83 A6
Ingleby Terr
Lynemouth NE61 . . . . .2 A3
Sunderland SR4 . . . . .102 A1
Ingleby Way NE24 . . . . .17 D3
Ingleside
South Shields NE34 . . . . . . .60 B6
Whickham NE16 . . . . .69 B6
Ingleton Ct SR4 . . . . .102 B1
Ingleton Rd SR4 . . . . .85 A5
Ingleton Gdns NE24 . . . . .17 C3
Inglewood Cl NE24 . . . . .16 F7
Inglewood Pl NE3 . . . . .28 C1
Ingoe Ave NE25 . . . . .37 F7
Ingoe St NE24 . . . . .17 C7
Ingoe St NE28 . . . . .41 C2
Ingoldsby Ct SR4 . . . . .85 E4
Ingram Ave NE3 . . . . .37 F8
Ingram Cl
Chester le Street DH2 . . . . . .88 A1
Wallsend NE28 . . . . .40 F5
Ingram Dr
Blyth NE24 . . . . .17 B7
Newcastle upon Tyne NE5 . . .36 D4
Ingram Terr NE6 . . . . .57 A6
Ingram Rd NE37 . . . . .72 D1
Inkerman St SR5 . . . . .75 A1
Inkerman Rd NE37 . . . . .72 D1
Inleborough Dr NE40 . . . . .52 D4
Innesmoor NE31 . . . . .57 D7
Inskip Ho NE34 . . . . .59 C5
Inskip Terr NE8 . . . . .70 F8
Inst for Higher Rabbinical
Studies 101 B1
Institute Rd NE63 . . . . .6 B4
Intake Way NE40 . . . . .44 F2
Inverness Rd NE32 . . . . .58 E2
Inverness St 75 D2
Invertay St 38 E5
Invincible Dr NE4 . . . . .100 A3
Iolanthe Cres NE6 . . . . .56 E7
Iolanthe Terr NE33 . . . . .42 E1
Iona Cl **10** NE26 . . . . .40 F4
Iona Rd
Brockley Whins NE32 . . . . . .58 E3
Sunderland SR4 . . . . .85 A5
Iona St NE10 . . . . .71 B7
Ipswich Cl NE24 . . . . .54 D4
Ireland Ho NE4 . . . . .98 A2
Irene Ave SR2 . . . . .86 F1
Iris Cl NE21 . . . . .53 A2
Iris Cres DH2 . . . . .81 F2
Iris Pl NE4 . . . . .54 B4
Iris Steedman Ho NE4 . . . . . . .98 A2
Iris Terr
Bournmoor DH4 . . . . .89 E3
Crawcrook NE40 . . . . .51 F3
Ironside St NE10 . . . . .90 L1
Irthing Ave NE6 . . . . .56 F6
Irthing Ho NE6 . . . . .56 F6
Irton St NE3 . . . . .38 C5
Irvine Ho **7** NE12 . . . . .39 D8
Irwin Ave NE28 . . . . .40 D3
Isabella Cl NE4 . . . . .54 E3
Isabella Rd NE4 . . . . .54 E3
Isabella Wlk NE15 . . . . .35 D1
Islay Ho **9** SR3 . . . . .92 A6
Ivanhoe NE25 . . . . .31 E5
Ivanhoe Cres SR2 . . . . .86 E4
Ivanhoe Terr
11 Chester le Street DH3 . .88 C2
Dipton DH9 . . . . .78 E1
Ivanhoe View NE61 . . . . .71 B2
Iveagh Cl NE4 . . . . .54 D4
Iveson Rd NE46 . . . . .44 E3
Ivor St SR2 . . . . .87 A1
Ivy Ave
Newbiggin-by-the-Sea
NE64 .7 C5

Ivy Ave continued
Ryton NE40 . . . . .52 C6
Ivy Cl
Newcastle upon Tyne
NE4 . . . . .100 B3
Ryton NE40 . . . . .52 C6
Ivy La NE9 . . . . .71 A3
Ivymount Rd NE6 . . . . .39 B1
Ivy Pl DH9 . . . . .79 C3
Ivy Rd
Longbenton NE12 . . . . .39 E8
Newcastle upon Tyne, Gosforth
NE3 .38 C4
Newcastle upon Tyne,
Walkergate NE6 . . . . .56 F8
Ivy Road Prim Sch NE12 . . . .39 E8
Ivy St NE13 . . . . .28 C8
Ivy Terr
Crawcrook NE40 . . . . .51 E3
Penshaw DH4 . . . . .90 B6

J

Jack Common Ho **3** NE6 . . .56 B7
Jackson Ave NE20 . . . . .25 F7
Jackson Rd NE41 . . . . .51 B6
Jacksons Pl DH3 . . . . .82 C5
Jackson St
Gateshead NE8 . . . . .101 C3
Newcastle upon Tyne NE6 . . .56 F6
North Shields NE30 . . . . . . .42 B6
Sunderland SR4 . . . . .102 A1
Jackson Street W NE30 . . . . .42 B6
Jackson Terr **18** NE61 . . . . . .9 A8
Jack's Terr NE34 . . . . .59 C5
Jacobins Chare **9** NE1 . . . .98 C1
Jacques St SR4 . . . . .85 F8
Jacques Terr DH2 . . . . .88 B4
Jade Cl NE15 . . . . .53 C8
James Armitage St SR5 . . . . .75 B2
James Ave NE27 . . . . .30 F4
James Mather St NE33 . . . . . .42 D3
Jameson Dr NE45 . . . . .47 B7
James Pl St NE6 . . . . .56 A6
James St
Kip Hill DH9 . . . . .79 F1
Newcastle upon Tyne, Elswick
NE4 .54 F4
Newcastle upon Tyne NE5 . . .36 F2
Sunderland SR5 . . . . .75 A2
Newcastle upon Tyne NE6 . . .69 A7
James Steel Pk The*
NE38 . . . . .84 A2
James Terr
Easington Lane DH5 . . . . . . .97 B8
Fence Houses DH4 . . . . . . .94 A8
Wallsend NE28 . . . . .40 B1
10 Wallsend NE28 . . . . . . .40 B1
Jane Williams St SR1 . . . . . .103 B3
Jane Eyre Terr NE8 . . . . .56 B1
Jane St
Hetton-le-Hole DH5 . . . . . . .95 A6
23 Newcastle upon Tyne
NE6 .56 C6
Jane Terr NE6 . . . . .56 C6
Janet Sq NE6 . . . . .56 C5
Janet St
18 Newcastle upon Tyne, St
Lawrence NE6 . . . . .56 C5
Newcastle upon Tyne, St Peters
NE6 .56 C4
Janus Cl NE5 . . . . .36 C4
JARROW 58 D6
Jarrow Cross CE Prim Sch
NE32 . . . . .58 B6
Jarrow Rd NE32, NE34 . . . . . .58 F6
Jarrow Sch (Cornhill)
NE32 . . . . .58 B1
Jarrow Sch (Field Terrace)
NE32 . . . . .58 B6
Jarrow Sta NE32 . . . . .58 B7
Jasmin Ave NE34 . . . . .36 C4
Jasmine Cl NE6 . . . . .39 E1
Jasmine Ct
Ashington NE63 . . . . .6 C1
Sunderland SR4 . . . . .102 B3
Jasmine Terr DH3 . . . . .82 D4
Jasmine Villas **7** NE16 . . . . .69 A7
Jasper Ave NE40 . . . . .52 B1
Javel Groupe NE1 . . . . .101 B4
Jaycroft Ct NE30 . . . . .42 B5
Jedburgh Cl
Gateshead NE8 . . . . .101 C1
Newcastle upon Tyne NE5 . . .36 C4
Tynemouth NE29 . . . . .41 E8
Jedburgh St NE11 . . . . .70 E2
Jedburgh Rd DH4 . . . . .90 B6
Jedmoor NE31 . . . . .57 D7
Jefferson Cl SR5 . . . . .75 C4
Jefferson Pl NE4 . . . . .98 B2
Jellicoe Rd NE6 . . . . .56 E3
Jenifer Gr NE7 . . . . .39 A4
Jenison Ave NE15 . . . . .54 C5
Jennifer Ave **9** SR5 . . . . . . .74 B1
Jersey Sq NE61 . . . . .2 A3
Jervis St NE31 . . . . .57 F6
JESMOND 38 E1
Jesmond Dene* NE2 . . . . .39 A2
Jesmond Dene Rd
Newcastle upon Tyne, Jesmond
NE2 .38 F2
Newcastle upon Tyne, West
Jesmond NE2 . . . . .38 D3
Jesmond Gdns
Newcastle upon Tyne NE2 . . .39 D1
Whitelaws NE34 . . . . .59 C3

Jesmond Park Ct **1** NE7 . . .39 B1
Jesmond Park E NE7 . . . . .39 B1
Jesmond Park W NE7 . . . . . . .39 A2
Jesmond Pl **1** NE2 . . . . .38 E1
Jesmond Rd NE2 . . . . .99 C4
Jesmond Road W NE2 . . . . . .98 B3
Jesmond Sta NE2 . . . . .99 B3
Jesmond Terr NE26 . . . . .32 B4
JESMOND VALE 56 A7
Jesmond Vale NE2 . . . . .56 A7
Jesmond Vale La NE6 . . . . . . .56 B8
Jesmond Vale Terr NE6 . . . . . .56 B8
Jessel St NE9 . . . . .70 F4
Jetty The NE10 . . . . .57 A2
Jewish High Sch NE8 . . . . . .101 C1
Joan Ave SR2 . . . . .86 F1
Joannah St SR5 . . . . .75 C3
Joan St NE4 . . . . .54 D4
Jobling Ave NE21 . . . . .53 B2
Jobling Cres NE61 . . . . .9 B6
Jobling Rd SR4 . . . . .85 F7
Joel Terr NE10 . . . . .57 B2
John Ave NE40 . . . . .52 B1
John Brown Ct NE27 . . . . .17 A4
John Candlish Rd SR4 . . . . . .102 A1
John Clay St
3 South Shields, Dean
NE33 . . . . .59 B8
3 South Shields NE33 . . . .42 D1
John Dobson St NE1, NE99 . .99 B2
John F Kennedy Est NE38 . . .83 E5
John F Kennedy Prim Sch
NE38 . . . . .83 E5
John & Margaret Common
Homes for Aged Miners **5**
NE24 . . . . .16 F8
John Reid Rd NE34 . . . . .59 C4
Johnson St
6 Dunston NE11 . . . . .54 F1
Gateshead NE8 . . . . .100 B1
Newcastle upon Tyne NE15 . .53 C6
South Shields NE33 . . . . . . .59 C7
Sunderland SR1 . . . . .102 C3
Johnson's Villas NE62 . . . . . .10 B7
Johnson Terr
High Spen NE39 . . . . .66 F4
5 Washington NE37 . . . . . .83 F8
John Spence Community
High Sch NE29 . . . . .42 A8
John St
Ashington NE63 . . . . .6 C4
Blyth NE24 . . . . .17 B8
Boldon Colliery NE35 . . . . . .73 F8
Earsdon NE25 . . . . .31 A5
Fence Houses DH4 . . . . . . .94 A8
Gateshead, Old Fold NE8 . . .56 B1
Hetton-le-Hole DH5 . . . . . . .95 A3
Houghton-le-Spring DH5 . . . .94 F8
Newcastle upon Tyne NE3 . . .38 A5
Pegswood NE61 . . . . .4 E3
Prudhoe NE42 . . . . .50 E3
15 Ryhope SR2 . . . . .93 A6
Sunderland, South Hylton
SR4 . . . . .85 A3
Sunderland SR1 . . . . .103 A3
Tynemouth NE30 . . . . .32 C3
Washington NE38 . . . . .40 B2
Johnston Ave NE31 . . . . .57 D3
Johnston Cl SR5 . . . . .75 A3
John Taylor Ct SR5 . . . . .75 A3
John Wesley Ct NE42 . . . . . . .50 D2
John Williamson St NE33 . . . .59 D6
Joicey Aged Miners Homes
7 DH4 . . . . .90 B6
Joicey Rd NE9 . . . . .70 F6
Joicey Sq NE10 . . . . .57 A1
Jolliffe St DH3 . . . . .88 D3
Jonadab Rd NE10 . . . . .57 A2
Jonadab St NE10 . . . . .57 A2
Jones St **4** DH3 . . . . .82 C4
Jonquil Cl NE5 . . . . .54 E4
Joseph Cl NE4 . . . . .54 E4
Joseph Hopper Aged Miners'
Homes DH3 . . . . .82 C3
Joseph Hopper Meml Homes
NE9 .71 C6
Joseph Swan Sch NE9 . . . . . .71 C3
Joseph Terr NE17 . . . . .66 B7
Journal Tyne Theatre*
NE1 .98 C1
Jowett Sq SR5 . . . . .75 A3
Joyce Cl NE10 . . . . .72 D8
Joyce Terr **6** SR5 . . . . .74 B1
Jubilee Bldgs **8** NE46 . . . . .45 B6
Jubilee Cotts
Greenside NE40 . . . . .66 D2
Houghton-le-Spring DH4 . . . .94 D8
Lynemouth NE61 . . . . .2 A1
Jubilee Cres
Newcastle upon Tyne NE13 . .38 A8
Sherburn Hill DH6 . . . . .96 D3
Jubilee Ct
Annitsford NE23 . . . . .22 B3
Blyth NE24 . . . . .17 D8
Gateshead NE9 . . . . .71 C3
Hebburn NE31 . . . . .58 Ae
Jubilee Est NE63 . . . . .6 D3
Jubilee Ho NE65 . . . . .95 C
Jubilee Ind Est NE63 . . . . . . .6 D
Jubilee Lodge NE23 . . . . .22 B
Jubilee Mews
Bedlington NE22 . . . . .11 D
Newcastle upon Tyne NE3 . . .38 B2
Jubilee Rd
Blyth NE24 . . . . .17 D

Jubilee Rd continued
Newcastle upon Tyne, Coxlodge
NE3 . . . . .38 B5
Newcastle upon Tyne NE1 . . .99 C1
Ovington NE42 . . . . .49 C4
Jubilee Sq
Easington Lane DH5 . . . . .95 C1
South Hetton DH6 . . . . .97 F7
Jubilee Terr
Bedlington NE22 . . . . .11 B2
Crawcrook NE40 . . . . .51 E3
Newbeggin-by-the-Sea NE64 . . .7 E4
Seaton Burn NE13 . . . . .28 B8
Tantobie DH9 . . . . .79 A2
Washington NE38 . . . . .84 A2
☑ Whickham NE16 . . . . .54 A1
Jubilee Terrs NE11 . . . . .56 D6
Julian Ave
Newcastle upon Tyne NE6 . . . .56 E7
South Shields NE33 . . . . .42 C4
Julian Rd NE10 . . . . .72 D8
Julian St NE33 . . . . .42 C4
Juliet Ave NE29 . . . . .41 D6
Juliet St NE63 . . . . .6 C4
Julius Caesar St ☑ SR5 . . . . . .75 A2
Julius Ct NE33 . . . . .42 C4
July Courtyard NE8 . . . . .100 B1
June Ave NE21 . . . . .68 C6
June Courtyard NE8 . . . . .100 B1
Juniper Cl
Blyth NE24 . . . . .17 C4
Newcastle upon Tyne NE3 . . .28 D1
☑ Sunderland SR2 . . . . .86 E4
Juniper Ct NE21 . . . . .53 C3
Juniper Wlk NE5 . . . . .36 D4
Jutland Ave NE31 . . . . .57 E6

K

Kane Gdns NE10 . . . . .71 C6
Kateregina DH3 . . . . .82 D4
Katherine St NE63 . . . . .6 E4
Katrine Cl DH2 . . . . .88 B1
Katrine Ct SR3 . . . . .92 A5
Kayll Rd SR4 . . . . .85 F6
Kay's Cotts ☑ NE12 . . . . .71 C7
Kearsley Cl NE25 . . . . .23 D3
Kearton Ave NE5 . . . . .36 C3
Keats Ave
Blyth NE24 . . . . .17 C5
Sunderland SR5 . . . . .75 A2
West Boldon NE35 . . . . .74 B8
Keats Rd NE15 . . . . .53 A6
Keats Wlk
Biddick Hall NE34 . . . . .59 A3
Gateshead NE8 . . . . .56 A2
Keeble Ct NE63 . . . . .7 A2
Keebledale Ave NE56 . . . . .56 F7
Keebledale Ho NE6 . . . . .56 F7
Keele Dr NE23 . . . . .21 D6
Keelmans Ho ☑ NE24 . . . . . . .17 E8
Keelman's La SR4 . . . . .85 C7
Keelman's Rd SR4 . . . . .85 B7
Keelmans Terr NE24 . . . . .17 E8
Keelmen's Flats NE11 . . . . .99 C1
Keel Row NE11 . . . . .54 B3
Keel Row Sh Ctr ☑ NE24 . .17 E8
Keighley Ave NE10 . . . . .71 C7
Keighley Sq SR5 . . . . .74 A4
Keir Hardie Ave NE10 . . . . .72 A8
Keir Hardie Ct NE64 . . . . .7 E5
Keir Hardie St
Fence Houses DH4 . . . . .94 B8
Rowlands Gill NE39 . . . . .67 B2
Keir Hardie Way SR5 . . . . .75 C1
Keith Cl NE4 . . . . .54 E4
Keith Sq SR5 . . . . .74 B4
Kelburn Ho NE1 . . . . .99 B1
Keldane Gdns NE4 . . . . .54 E6
Kelfield Gr NE23 . . . . .16 B2
Kelham Sq SR5 . . . . .74 A4
Kell Cres DH6 . . . . .96 D1
Kellfield Ave NE9 . . . . .71 A6
Kellfield Rd NE9 . . . . .71 A6
Kells Gdns NE15 . . . . .71 A5
Kells La NE9 . . . . .70 F5
Kells Lane Prim Sch NE9 . . . . .70 F5
Kellsway NE10 . . . . .71 F5
Kell's Way NE39 . . . . .67 C1
Kellsway Ct NE10 . . . . .71 F5
Kelly Rd NE31 . . . . .57 E3
Kelman Sq NE1 . . . . .99 C1
Kelpie Gdns ☑ SR6 . . . . .75 E1
Kelsey Way NE23 . . . . .16 B2
Kelso Cl NE5 . . . . .36 C4
Kelso Dr NE29 . . . . .41 E8
Kelso Gdns
Bedlington NE22 . . . . .11 C1
Newcastle upon Tyne NE15 . . .54 B6
Wallsend NE28 . . . . .41 A4
Kelso Gr DH4 . . . . .90 A6
Kelson Way NE5 . . . . .36 C4
Kelso Pl NE8 . . . . .100 B1
Kelston Way NE5 . . . . .37 C2
Kelvin Gdns ☑ NE11 . . . . .54 F1
Kelvin Gr
Cleadon SR6 . . . . .59 E1
Gateshead NE8 . . . . .70 D8
Newcastle upon Tyne NE2 . . . .99 C3
South Shields NE33 . . . . .42 A1
Tynemouth NE29 . . . . .42 A8
Kelvin Grove Prim Sch ☑
NE8 . . . . .70 E8
Kelvin Pl NE12 . . . . .30 A1
Kemble Cl NE23 . . . . .16 B2

Kemble Sq SR5 . . . . .74 B4
Kempton Gdns NE8 . . . . .70 C7
Kendal DH3 . . . . .82 E2
Kendal Ave
Blyth NE24 . . . . .17 D6
Tynemouth NE30 . . . . .32 B2
Kendal Cres NE9 . . . . .71 B5
Kendal Dr
Cramlington NE23 . . . . .22 C8
East Boldon NE36 . . . . .74 C8
Kendal Wlk NE5 . . . . .36 E3
Kendal Gdns NE28 . . . . .41 A4
Kendal Ho ☑ NE6 . . . . .56 B6
Kendal Ho ☑ NE6 . . . . .56 B6
Kendal Pl ☑ NE6 . . . . .56 B6
Kendal Rise NE22 . . . . .10 D2
Kendal St ☑ NE6 . . . . .56 B5
Kendor Gr NE61 . . . . .8 F6
Kenilworth NE12 . . . . .29 D4
Kenilworth Ct
Newcastle upon Tyne
NE4 . . . . .100 A4
☑ Washington NE37 . . . . .83 F8
Kenilworth Rd
Ashington NE63 . . . . .6 C3
Killingworth NE12 . . . . .29 C4
Newcastle upon Tyne NE4 . .100 A4
Whitley Bay NE25 . . . . .31 F4
Kenilworth Sq SR5 . . . . .74 C4
Kenilworth View ☑ NE9 . . . . .71 A2
Kenley Rd
Newcastle upon Tyne NE5 . . . .54 A8
Sunderland SR5 . . . . .74 C4
Kenmoor Way NE5 . . . . .36 C3
Kenmore Cl NE10 . . . . .72 B8
Kenmore Cres NE40 . . . . .52 B2
Kennersdene NE30 . . . . .42 C8
Kennet Ave NE32 . . . . .58 C3
Kennet Sq SR5 . . . . .74 B4
Kennford NE9 . . . . .71 A2
Kennington Gr NE6 . . . . .56 E5
Kensington Ave NE3 . . . . .38 C7
Kensington Cl NE25 . . . . .31 F5
Kensington Ct
☑ Gateshead NE10 . . . . .71 C8
Hebburn NE31 . . . . .57 D5
South Shields NE33 . . . . .59 E8
Kensington Gdns
☑ North Shields NE30 . . . . . . .42 B6
Wallsend NE28 . . . . .39 E3
Whitley Bay NE25 . . . . .31 F5
Kensington Gr ☑ NE30 . . . . . .42 B7
Kensington Terr
☑ Newcastle upon Tyne NE2 . .99 A3
Kensington Villas ☑ NE5 . . .36 E3
Kent Ave
☑ Dunston NE11 . . . . .70 A8
Hebburn NE31 . . . . .57 D5
Wallsend NE28 . . . . .40 F2
Kentchester Rd SR5 . . . . .74 C4
Kent Cl NE63 . . . . .6 A4
Kent Ct NE3 . . . . .37 D8
Kent Gdns DH5 . . . . .94 F4
Kentmere NE3 . . . . .82 E1
Kentmere Ave
Newcastle upon Tyne NE6 . . . .56 F7
Sunderland SR5 . . . . .75 C5
Kentmere Cl NE23 . . . . .23 A2
Kentmere Gn NE6 . . . . .56 F6
KENTON 37 E4
Kenton Ave NE3 . . . . .38 A3
Kenton Bank NE5 . . . . .37 C5
Kenton Rd
Newcastle upon Tyne NE3 . . . .38 A3
Tynemouth NE29 . . . . .41 C7
Kenton St NE6 . . . . .37 E4
Kent Pl NE34 . . . . .60 A6
Kent Terr DH6 . . . . .97 E1
Kentucky Rd SR5 . . . . .74 A4
Kenwood Gdns NE9 . . . . .71 A2
Kenya Rd SR5 . . . . .74 C4
Kepier Gdns ☑ SR4 . . . . .85 A6
Keppel St
Dunston NE11 . . . . .54 F1
☑ South Shields NE33 . . . . . . .42 C3
Kepwell Bank Top NE42 . . . . . .50 D3
Kepwell Ct NE42 . . . . .50 D3
Kepwell Rd NE42 . . . . .50 C2
Kerry Cl NE24 . . . . .17 E8
Kerry Sq SR5 . . . . .74 B4
Kestesven Sq SR5 . . . . .74 B4
Keston Dr NE23 . . . . .16 B2
Kestrel Cl NE38 . . . . .83 A2
Kestrel Ct ☑ DH3 . . . . .82 C4
Kestrel Dr NE63 . . . . .6 A2
Kestrel Lodge Flats ☑
NE33 . . . . .42 D3
Kestrel Mews ☑ NE16 . . . . . . .69 A7
Kestrel Pl NE12 . . . . .39 A7
Kestrel Sq SR5 . . . . .74 B4
Kestrel Way
North Shields NE29 . . . . .42 A3
South Shields NE34 . . . . .59 B4
Keswick Ave SR6 . . . . .75 D4
Keswick Dr NE30 . . . . .32 B2
Keswick Gdns NE28 . . . . .41 A3
Keswick Gr NE5 . . . . .54 A8

Keswick St NE8 . . . . .101 B1
Keswick St DH6 . . . . .97 E8
Kettering Pl NE23 . . . . .22 C8
Kettering Sq SR5 . . . . .74 B4
Kettlewell Terr ☑ NE30 . . . . . .42 B6
Kew Gdns NE40 . . . . .39 B6
Kew Gdns NE16 . . . . .31 F6
Keyes Gdns NE2 . . . . .38 E3
KIBBLESWORTH 81 D5
Kibblesworth Bank NE11 . . . . .81 B6
Kibblesworth Prim Sch
NE11 . . . . .81 D6
Kidderminster Dr NE5 . . . . .36 C3
Kidderminster Sq SR5 . . . . .74 B3
Kidderminster Sq SR5 . . . . .74 B3
Kidd Sq SR5 . . . . .74 B4
Kidland Cl NE63 . . . . .6 F4
Kidlandlee Gn NE5 . . . . .37 A4
Kidlandlee Pl NE5 . . . . .37 A4
Kidsgrove Sq SR5 . . . . .74 B3
Kielder NE38 . . . . .82 F4
Kielder Ave NE23 . . . . .21 D6
Kielder Cl
Blyth NE24 . . . . .17 B5
Killingworth NE12 . . . . .29 C4
Newcastle upon Iyne NE5 . . . .37 A4
Kielder Dr NE63 . . . . .6 C3
Kielder Gdns
Jarrow NE32 . . . . .58 B3
Stakeford NE62 . . . . .6 A1
Kielder Ho ☑ SR3 . . . . .92 A6
Kielder Pl NE5 . . . . .31 B5
Kielder Rd
Earsdon NE25 . . . . .31 B5
Newcastle upon Tyne NE15 . . .53 C7
Kielder Terr NE30 . . . . .42 B6
Kielder Way NE3 . . . . .38 B7
Kilburn Cl ☑ SR2 . . . . .93 A6
Kilburne Cl NE7 . . . . .39 E3
Kilburn Gdns NE29 . . . . .41 D2
Kilburn Gn NE9 . . . . .71 B1
Kildale DH4 . . . . .89 E8
Kildare Sq SR5 . . . . .74 B4
Kilkenny Ave SR5 . . . . .74 B4
Killarney Ave SR5 . . . . .74 B4
Killarney Sq SR5 . . . . .74 B4
Killiebrigs NE15 . . . . .34 E2
Killin Cl NE23 . . . . .16 C3
KILLINGWORTH 29 D3
Killingworth Ave NE27 . . . . .30 C3
Killingworth Ctr The
NE12 . . . . .29 D3
Killingworth Dr
Killingworth NE12 . . . . .29 B2
Newcastle upon Tyne SR3,
SR4 . . . . .85 E4
Killingworth Hall NE12 . . . . . . .29 E2
Killingworth La NE27 . . . . .30 A5
Killingworth Rd
Killingworth NE12 . . . . .29 B2
Newcastle upon Tyne NE3 . . . .38 F5
Killingworth Way NE12,
NE27 . . . . .29 D4
Killowen St NE9 . . . . .71 A4
Kiln Rise NE16 . . . . .69 A4
Kilnshaw Pl NE3 . . . . .28 D1
Kilsyth Ave NE29 . . . . .31 E2
Kilsyth Sq SR5 . . . . .74 B4
Kimberley NE38 . . . . .84 A5
Kimberley Ave NE29 . . . . .41 E6
Kimberley Gdns
Newcastle upon Tyne NE2 . . . .56 A8
Stocksfield NE43 . . . . .64 C7
Kimberley St
Blyth NE24 . . . . .17 D8
Newcastle upon Tyne NE6 . . . .56 C5
Kimberley Terr ☑ NE24 . . . . . .17 E8
Kincross Cl ☑ SR4 . . . . .85 C3
Kineton Way ☑ SR2 . . . . .92 F5
Kinfauns Terr ☑ NE9 . . . . .71 A5
Kingarth Ave SR6 . . . . .75 E5
King Charles Ct SR5 . . . . .74 A4
King Charles Twr NE2 . . . . .99 C2
Kingdom Pl NE62 . . . . .22 A3
King Edward Pl ☑ NE8 . . . . . . .56 B1
King Edward Prim Sch
NE30 . . . . .42 B7
King Edward Rd
Newcastle upon Tyne NE6 . . . .39 B1
Ryton NE40 . . . . .52 E4
Sunderland SR4 . . . . .85 D4
Tynemouth NE30 . . . . .42 B7
King Edward St
Gateshead NE8 . . . . .56 B1
Tanfield Lea DH9 . . . . .79 C1
King Edward VI Sch NE1 . . . .3 F2
Kingfisher Bvd NE15 . . . . .53 D5
Kingfisher Cl NE63 . . . . .6 F6
Kingfisher Ct NE11 . . . . .100 A2
Kingfisher Lodge NE32 . . . . . . .58 A6
Kingfisher Rd NE12 . . . . .39 A7
Kingfisher Way
Blyth NE24 . . . . .17 F4
Shiremoor NE28 . . . . .41 A6
King George Ave NE11 . . . . .69 F8
King George Rd
Newcastle upon Tyne NE3 . . . .37 E6
South Shields NE34 . . . . .59 E5
King George's Rd NE64 . . . . . . .7 D5
Kingham Ct NE3 . . . . .37 E4
King Henry Ct SR5 . . . . .74 A4
Kinghorn Sq SR5 . . . . .74 B4
King James St SR5 . . . . .74 A4
King James St NE8 . . . . .101 C1
King John's Ct NE20 . . . . .25 A4
King John St NE6 . . . . .56 B8
King John Terr NE6 . . . . .56 B8
Kings Ave
Hebburn NE31 . . . . .57 F5
Sunderland SR6 . . . . .75 C5

King's Ave NE61 . . . . .3 F1
Kingsbridge NE12 . . . . .38 F7
Kingsbridge Cl NE29 . . . . .41 E4
Kingsbury Ct NE12 . . . . .39 A6
Kings Cl NE8 . . . . .56 B1
Kingsclere Ave NE29 . . . . .39 B6
Kingsclere Sq SR5 . . . . .74 B4
Kings Ct NE2 . . . . .99 C2
Kingsdale Ave
Blyth NE24 . . . . .17 A7
Washington NE37 . . . . .83 C8
Kingsdale Rd NE12 . . . . .38 F7
King's Dr
Greenside NE40 . . . . .52 B1
Whitley Bay NE26 . . . . .32 A4
Kingsgate ☑ NE46 . . . . .45 A5
Kingsgate Terr NE46 . . . . .45 A5
King's Gdns NE24 . . . . .17 C8
Kingsland NE2 . . . . .99 B4
Kingsland Sq SR5 . . . . .74 B3
Kingsley Ave
Biddick Hall NE34 . . . . .59 A3
Newcastle upon Tyne NE3 . . . .28 D1
Kingsley Cl SR5 . . . . .74 A4
Kingsley Pl ☑ SR4 . . . . .75 A1
Kingsley Pl
☑ Dunston NE11 . . . . .54 F1
☑ Newcastle upon Tyne
NE6 . . . . .56 B7
Wallsend NE28 . . . . .40 F3
Whitley Bay NE26 . . . . .31 F6
Kingsley Rd NE61 . . . . .2 A2
Kingsley Terr
Crawcrook NE40 . . . . .51 E3
Newcastle upon Tyne NE4 . . . .98 A1
Kings Lodge NE30 . . . . .42 B6
Kings Meadow NE32 . . . . .58 C5
Kingsmeadow Com Comp
Sch NE11 . . . . .69 E8
Kings Meadows NE4 . . . . .100 A3
Kingsmere DH3 . . . . .82 D1
Kingsmere Gdns NE6 . . . . .57 A4
King's Pk NE62 . . . . .10 F5
King's Pl SR4 . . . . .102 A3
King's Rd
Bedlington NE22 . . . . .11 D2
Newcastle upon Tyne NE1,
NE2 . . . . .99 A2
Whitley Bay NE26 . . . . .32 A6
King's Rd The SR5 . . . . .75 A2
Kings Road N NE28 . . . . .40 B8
Kings Road S NE28 . . . . .40 B3
Kings School NE30 . . . . .42 B6
King St
Birtley DH3 . . . . .82 B4
Blyth NE24 . . . . .17 E8
Gateshead, Bensham NE8 . . . .70 C8
Gateshead, Pelaw NE10 . . . . . .57 A1
Newbeggin-by-the-Sea NE64 . . .7 E5
Newcastle upon Tyne NE1 . .101 B4
North Shields NE30 . . . . .42 B6
South Shields NE33 . . . . .42 C4
Sunderland, Fulwell SR6 . . . . .75 D4
Sunderland SR1 . . . . .103 A3
Kings Terr SR6 . . . . .75 F1
Kings Terr ☑ SR4 . . . . .102 A3
Kingston Ave NE6 . . . . .56 D4
Kingston Cl NE26 . . . . .31 F8
Kingston Cres DH6 . . . . .97 E2
Kingston Ct ☑ NE26 . . . . .31 F8
Kingston Dr NE26 . . . . .31 F8
Kingston Gn NE6 . . . . .56 D5
Kingston Mews DH4 . . . . .90 C5
KINGSTON PARK 37 C6
Kingston Park Ave NE3 . . . . .37 C6
Kingston Park Ctr NE3 . . . . .37 C6
Kingston Park Prim Sch
NE3 . . . . .37 C5
Kingston Park Rd NE3 . . . . .37 F7
Kingston Rd NE8 . . . . .70 C8
Kingston St ☑ NE6 . . . . .56 D5
Kingston Terr NE6 . . . . .56 D5
Kingston Way NE3 . . . . .37 D2
Kingston Way ☑ NE26 . . . . . . .31 F8
Kings Vale NE28 . . . . .40 C4
Kingsway
Blyth NE24 . . . . .17 B6
Houghton-le-Spring DH5 . . . . .94 F8
Newcastle upon Tyne NE4 . . . .54 B8
Ponteland NE20 . . . . .25 E6
South Shields NE33 . . . . .59 B8
Sunmside NE16 . . . . .69 A2
Tynemouth NE30 . . . . .42 C8
Kingsway Ave NE3 . . . . .38 C7
Kingsway Ho NE11 . . . . .70 A4
Kingsway N NE11 . . . . .70 A7
Kingsway Rd SR5 . . . . .74 B4
Kingsway S NE11 . . . . .70 D3
Kingsway Sq SR5 . . . . .74 B4
Kingswell NE61 . . . . .9 B7
Kings Wlk NE5 . . . . .36 C4
King's Wlk NE1 . . . . .99 A2
Kingswood ☑ DH4 . . . . .90 A7
Kingswood Ave NE2 . . . . .38 D3
Kingswood Cl NE35 . . . . .58 E3
Kingswood Cl ☑ NE30 . . . . . . .42 D7
Kingswood Gr NE20 . . . . .25 C4
Kingswood Rd NE23 . . . . .85 A2
Kingswood Sq SR5 . . . . .74 B4
Kinlett NE38 . . . . .84 A5
Kinloch Ct NE23 . . . . .16 B4
Kinloss Sq NE23 . . . . .22 C8
Kinnaird Ave NE15 . . . . .54 B6
Kinnock Cl DH6 . . . . .96 A1
Kinross Ct DH3 . . . . .82 D2
Kinross Dr NE10 . . . . .57 B2

Kinross Dr NE3 . . . . .37 F5
Kinsale Sq SR5 . . . . .74 B4
Kinver Dr NE5 . . . . .36 C3
KIP HILL 80 A1
Kipling Ave
Hebburn NE31 . . . . .57 F6
West Boldon NE35 . . . . .74 B8
Whickham NE16 . . . . .69 B8
Kipling St SR5 . . . . .75 A1
Kipling Wlk NE8 . . . . .56 A2
Kirby Cl NE34 . . . . .59 A4
Kirkbride Pl NE23 . . . . .22 C8
Kirkdale Ct ☑ NE34 . . . . .59 A4
Kirkdale Gn NE4 . . . . .100 B4
Kirkdale Sq SR5 . . . . .74 B3
Kirkdale St DH5 . . . . .94 F2
Kirkham NE38 . . . . .83 D4
Kirkham Ave NE3 . . . . .37 C7
Kirkharle Dr NE61 . . . . .9 C8
Kirklands NE23 . . . . .29 C5
Kirkleatham Gdns NE6 . . . . .39 D2
Kirkley Ave NE34 . . . . .60 A6
Kirkley Cl NE3 . . . . .38 B6
Kirkley Dr
Ashington NE63 . . . . .6 E2
Ponteland NE20 . . . . .25 E7
Kirkley Lodge NE3 . . . . .38 B6
Kirkley Rd NE27 . . . . .30 F2
Kirklinton Rd NE30 . . . . .32 A2
Kirknewton Cl ☑ NE5 . . . . .54 F8
Kirk St NE6 . . . . .56 C5
Kirkstone Ave NE15 . . . . .53 D7
Kirkstone Cl DH3 . . . . .82 D2
Kirkstone Dr
Hedworth NE32 . . . . .58 D3
Sunderland SR5 . . . . .75 C3
Tynemouth NE30 . . . . .32 A2
Kirkstone Cl
Blaydon NE21 . . . . .68 C8
☑ Houghton-le-Spring DH5 . .94 F8
Kirkstone Gdns NE7 . . . . .39 C2
Kirkstone Rd NE10 . . . . .71 F8
Kirk View DH4 . . . . .90 D3
Kirkwall Cl SR5 . . . . .74 A1
Kirkwood NE23 . . . . .29 C5
Kirkwood Dr NE3 . . . . .37 F5
Kirkwood Gdns NE10 . . . . .72 B8
Kirkwood Pl NE3 . . . . .28 B1
Kirton Ave NE4 . . . . .54 E6
Kirton Park Terr NE29,
NE30 . . . . .42 A7
Kirton Way NE23 . . . . .22 C8
Kismet St SR5 . . . . .75 A2
Kitchener Rd SR6 . . . . .60 F4
Kitchener St
Gateshead NE9 . . . . .71 A8
Sunderland SR4 . . . . .85 F4
Kitchener Terr
Jarrow NE32 . . . . .58 B5
New Herrington DH4 . . . . .90 D6
North Shields NE30 . . . . .42 C7
Sunderland SR2 . . . . .86 F2
Kittiwake Cl
Blyth NE24 . . . . .17 E3
Shiremoor NE28 . . . . .41 A7
Kittiwake Dr NE38 . . . . .82 F3
Kittiwake Ho NE26 . . . . .32 B5
Kittiwake St NE11 . . . . .70 C5
Kitty Brewster Ind Est
NE24 . . . . .12 B1
Kitty Brewster Rd 16 F8
KLONDYKE 17 F1
Knaresborough Cl NE22 . . . . . .10 D2
Knaresborough Sq SR5 . . . . . . .74 C4
Knaresdale DH3 . . . . .82 D2
Knarsdale Ave NE29 . . . . .41 D6
Knarsdale Pl ☑ NE5 . . . . .36 E1
Knightsbridge
Newcastle upon Tyne NE3 . . . .38 C6
Sunderland SR3 . . . . .91 B8
Knightsbridge Ct NE13 . . . . . . .38 C6
Knightside Gdns NE11 . . . . .70 A7
Knightside Pl NE5 . . . . .36 F8
Knivestone Ct NE12 . . . . .29 E4
Knobbyends La NE21 . . . . .67 F8
Knoll Rise NE11 . . . . .69 F7
Knollside Cl SR3 . . . . .91 F5
Knoll The
Ellington NE61 . . . . .1 C5
Sunderland SR2 . . . . .102 B1
Knoplaw Prim Sch NE5 . . . . . . .36 C3
Knott Memorial Flats ☑
NE30 . . . . .42 D7
Knott Pl NE15 . . . . .54 B5
Knoulberry NE37 . . . . .83 A6
Knoulberry Rd NE37 . . . . .83 A6
Knowledge Hill NE21 . . . . .53 B1
Knowle Pl NE12 . . . . .39 B5
Knowsley Ct NE3 . . . . .37 B5
Knox Cl NE22 . . . . .10 F2
Knox Rd NE22 . . . . .16 B8
Knox Sq SR5 . . . . .75 A2
Knutsford Wlk NE23 . . . . .22 C8
Koppers Way NE31 . . . . .57 F1
Kristin Ave NE32 . . . . .58 C4
Kyffin View NE34 . . . . .60 B5
Kyle Cl NE4 . . . . .100 B4
Kyle Rd NE8 . . . . .70 C8
Kylins The NE61 . . . . .9 A6

Kyloe Ave NE25 . . . . .23 D2
Kyloe Cl NE3 . . . . .37 E7
Kyloe Pl
  Bedlington NE22 . . . . .10 F1
  Newcastle upon Tyne NE5 . .37 A3
Kyloe Villas NE5 . . . . .37 A3
Kyo Bog La NE41, NE42 . .51 B1
Kyo La NE40 . . . . .66 D7

L

Laburnum Ave
  Blyth NE24 . . . . .17 D8
  Gateshead NE10 . . . . .72 A7
  Newcastle upon Tyne NE6 . .56 F8
  Wallsend NE28 . . . . .40 B2
  Washington NE38 . . . . .83 B1
  Whitley Bay NE26 . . . . .32 A5
Laburnum Cl SR4 . . . . .85 A6
Laburnum Cres NE11 . . . . . . .81 C6
Laburnum Ct NE12 . . . . .29 C4
Laburnum Gdns
  6 Gateshead, Felling
    NE10 . . . . .56 D1
  Gateshead, Low Fell NE9 . . . .70 F6
  Jarrow NE32 . . . . .58 A4
Laburnum Gr
  Cleadon SR6 . . . . .60 A1
  Hebburn NE31 . . . . .57 E3
  South Shields NE34 . . . . .59 F5
  Sunderland SR5 . . . . .85 A8
  Sunniside NE16 . . . . .69 A7
  Whickham NE16 . . . . .69 A7
Laburnum Ho NE28 . . . . . . .40 C1
Laburnum Rd SR6 . . . . .75 D3
Laburnum Terr
  Ashington NE63 . . . . .6 D3
  Wylam NE41 . . . . .51 A6
Laburnum Ct NE62 . . . . .10 E7
Lacebark
  Shiney Row DH4 . . . . .89 F6
  Silksworth SR3 . . . . .91 E4
Ladock Cl 6 SR2 . . . . .93 A8
Ladybank NE5 . . . . .36 B4
Lady Beatrice Terr DH4 . . .90 E7
Lacarter's La NE45 . . . . . . .46 F3
Ladyhaugh Dr NE16 . . . . . . .69 A4
Ladykirk Rd NE4 . . . . .54 E5
Ladykirk Way NE23 . . . . . . .21 E6
Ladyrigg NE20 . . . . .25 D4
Ladysmith St NE33 . . . . . . .42 D2
Lady's Piece La DH6 . . . . . .96 A5
Lady St DH5 . . . . .95 A5
Lady's Wlk
  Morpeth NE61 . . . . .3 E1
  South Shields NE33 . . . . .42 C4
Ladywell NE43 . . . . .64 D6
Ladywell Rd NE21 . . . . .53 C2
Ladywell Way NE20 . . . . . . .25 D7
Ladywood Pk DH4 . . . . .89 F8
Laet St NE29 . . . . .42 B5
Laindon Ave SR6 . . . . .75 D4
Laing Art Gall★ NE1 . . . . .99 B2
Laing Gr NE28 . . . . .41 B3
Laith Rd NE3 . . . . .37 E5
Lake App NE21 . . . . .53 F1
Lake Ave NE34 . . . . .60 C6
Lake Ct SR3 . . . . .92 A6
Lake Rd DH5 . . . . .94 E8
Lakeside
  Blaydon NE21 . . . . .53 F1
  South Shields NE34 . . . . .60 D6
Lakeside Centre The
  NE12 . . . . .29 D3
Lakeside Gdns 4 NE38 . .83 F4
Lake View NE31 . . . . .57 E4
Laleham Ct NE3 . . . . .37 D7
Lamara Dr SR5 . . . . .73 C3
Lambden Cl NE29 . . . . .41 E3
Lambert Rd NE12 . . . . .29 B4
Lambert Sq NE3 . . . . .38 A5
Lambeth Pl NE8 . . . . .71 A8
Lambley Ave NE30 . . . . .32 B2
Lambley Cl NE16 . . . . .69 A2
Lambley Cres NE31 . . . . . . .57 D3
Lambourn Ave
  Longbenton NE12 . . . . .39 C7
  North Shields NE29 . . . . .41 E4
Lambourne Cl DH4 . . . . .89 E3
Lambourne Rd SR2 . . . . . . .86 C3
Lambrook Ho NE24 . . . . . . .17 A7
Lamb St
  East Cramlington NE23 . . . . .22 F5
  Newcastle upon Tyne NE6 . . .57 A5
Lamb Terr 6 NE27 . . . . . . .30 E1
LAMBTON 83 A3
Lambton Ave NE16 . . . . . . .69 C8
Lambton Cl NE40 . . . . .51 F4
Lambton Ct
  Sunderland SR3 . . . . .91 C7
  Washington NE38 . . . . .88 E8
Lambton Dr DH5 . . . . .95 A1
Lambton Gdns NE16 . . . . . .78 E5
Lambton Lea DH4 . . . . .90 A4
Lambton Prim Sch NE38 . .83 B3
Lambton Rd
  Hebburn NE31 . . . . .57 F7
  Newcastle upon Tyne NE2 . . .99 B4
Lambton St
  Chester le Street DH3 . . . . . . .88 D2
  Gateshead NE8 . . . . .101 B3
  Sunderland SR1 . . . . .103 A3
Lambton Terr
  Jarrow NE32 . . . . .58 B4

Lambton Terr continued
  Penshaw DH4 . . . . .89 F8
Lambton Tower SR1 . . . . . .103 B3
Lamonby Way NE23 . . . . . . .22 A4
Lampeter Cl NE5 . . . . .37 B4
Lampton St NE31 . . . . .57 C7
Lampton Ct NE22 . . . . .11 C2
Lanark Cl
  8 Springwell SR4 . . . . . . .85 C3
  Tynemouth NE29 . . . . .41 C8
Lanark Dr NE32 . . . . .58 E2
Lancaster Ct NE3 . . . . .37 D7
Lancaster Dr NE28 . . . . .40 D7
Lancaster Ho NE23 . . . . .22 D5
Lancaster Rd NE11 . . . . .54 E1
Lancaster St NE4 . . . . .98 B1
Lancaster Terr
  Chester le Street DH3 . . . . . . .88 D2
  Morpeth NE61 . . . . .4 A1
Lancaster Way NE32 . . . . . .58 A1
Lancastrian Rd NE23 . . . . . .22 A5
Lancefield Ave NE6 . . . . . . .56 F4
Lancet Ct NE8 . . . . .101 C2
Lanchester Ave NE9 . . . . . . .71 E3
Lanchester Cl NE10 . . . . . . .72 C6
Lanchester Gn NE22 . . . . . .10 F2
Lanchester Pk NE38 . . . . . .83 E2
Lancing Ct NE3 . . . . .37 C7
Landscape Terr NE40 . . . . . .52 B1
Landsdowne Gdns NE62 . .11 A8
Landseer Gdns
  Gateshead NE9 . . . . .71 B7
  Whiteleas NE34 . . . . .59 D2
Landswood Terr NE21 . . . . .68 A7
Lane Cnr NE34 . . . . .59 C5
Lane Head NE40 . . . . .52 C5
Lanercost NE38 . . . . .83 D5
Lanercost Ave NE21 . . . . . . .53 B2
Lanercost Dr NE5 . . . . .54 C8
Lanercost Gdns
  Gateshead NE10 . . . . .71 C6
  Throckley NE15 . . . . .35 D2
Lanercost Pk NE23 . . . . .22 D5
Lanercost Rd NE29 . . . . .41 E5
Lanesborough Ct NE3 . . . . .38 A3
Langdale
  Birtley DH3 . . . . .82 E1
  Washington NE37 . . . . .83 C7
  Whitley Bay NE25 . . . . .31 E5
Langdale Cl NE12 . . . . .39 A6
Langdale Cres NE21 . . . . . . .68 B8
Langdale Dr NE23 . . . . .21 E6
Langdale Gdns
  Newcastle upon Tyne NE6 . . .57 A6
  Wallsend NE28 . . . . .41 A5
Langdale Rd
  Gateshead NE9 . . . . .71 A5
  Sunderland SR5 . . . . .90 A8
Langdale St DH5 . . . . .95 A2
Langdale Terr NE17 . . . . . . .77 A5
Langdale Way NE36 . . . . . . .74 C7
Langdon Cl NE29 . . . . .31 F1
Langdon Rd NE5 . . . . .36 F2
Langeeford Pl 4 SR6 . . . . .75 E1
Langford Dr NE35 . . . . .58 F2
Langham Rd NE15 . . . . .54 A5
Langholm Rd NE29 . . . . .41 C8
Langholm Rd
  East Boldon NE36 . . . . .74 D8
  Newcastle upon Tyne NE3 . . .38 C7
Langhope 3 DH4 . . . . .90 A7
Langhorn Cl NE6 . . . . .56 B7
Langhurst SR2 . . . . .92 E8
Langleeford Rd NE5 . . . . . . .37 A4
Langley Ave
  Blyth NE24 . . . . .17 B8
  Gateshead NE10 . . . . .72 B6
  Shiremoor NE27 . . . . .31 A3
  Whitley Bay NE25 . . . . .31 D3
Langley Cl NE38 . . . . .83 A1
Langley Fst Sch NE25 . . . . .31 D3
Langley Mere 8 NE12 . . . .39 B8
Langley Rd
  Ashington NE63 . . . . .6 C3
  Newcastle upon Tyne, Walker
    NE6 . . . . .56 F6
  Newcastle upon Tyne, West
    Denton NE5 . . . . .53 F8
  North Shields NE29 . . . . .41 D6
  Sunderland SR3 . . . . .86 B2
Langley St DH4 . . . . .90 B2
Langley Tarn 1 NE29 . . . . .42 A4
Langley Terr NE32 . . . . .58 B3
Langport Rd SR2 . . . . .86 D3
Langton Cl SR4 . . . . .102 B2
Langton Ct NE20 . . . . .26 A6
Langton Dr NE23 . . . . .16 C2
Langton St NE8 . . . . .101 C1
Langton Terr
  Bournmoor DH4 . . . . .89 E2
  Newcastle upon Tyne NE7 . . .39 B2
Langwell Cres NE63 . . . . . . .6 C4
Langwell Terr NE61 . . . . .4 F4
Lanivet Cl 4 SR2 . . . . .92 F8
Lannerwood 5 NE29 . . . . .42 A4
Lansbury Cl DH3 . . . . .82 B6
Lansbury Ct NE11 . . . . .88 A5
Lansbury Dr DH3 . . . . .82 B5
Lansbury Gdns NE10 . . . . . .72 A8
Lansbury Rd NE16 . . . . .69 C6
Lansbury Way SR5 . . . . .74 B1
Lansdowne SR2 . . . . .92 E7
Lansdowne Cres NE3 . . . . . .38 C5
Lansdowne Ct NE46 . . . . . . .44 F3
Lansdowne Gdns NE2 . . . . .56 A8
Lansdowne Pl NE3 . . . . .38 C5
Lansdowne Rd NE12 . . . . . .39 D8

Lansdowne St SR4 . . . . . . .102 B3
Lansdowne Terr
  Newcastle upon Tyne NE3 . . .38 C5
  North Shields NE30 . . . . .41 F6
Lansdowne Terrace E
  NE3 . . . . .38 C5
Lansdowne Terrace W
  NE29 . . . . .41 F6
Lanthwaite Rd NE9 . . . . .71 A4
Lanton St DH4 . . . . .90 D6
Lapford Dr NE23 . . . . .16 C1
Lapwing Cl
  Burnopfield NE16 . . . . .79 C5
  Washington NE38 . . . . .82 F3
Lapwing Ct
  Burnopfield NE16 . . . . .79 C5
  Haswell DH6 . . . . .97 F3
  South Shields NE34 . . . . .59 E5
L'Arbre Cres NE16 . . . . .68 F7
Larch Ave
  Houghton-le-Spring DH4 . . . .90 D1
  South Shields NE34 . . . . .60 A5
  Whitburn SR6 . . . . .61 A2
Larch Cl NE9 . . . . .71 D2
Larches The
  Burnopfield NE16 . . . . .79 B7
  Newcastle upon Tyne NE4 . .100 A3
Larch Gr NE24 . . . . .17 C4
Larchlea NE20 . . . . .25 C2
Larchlea S NE20 . . . . .25 C2
Larch Rd NE21 . . . . .53 D3
Larch St 6 NE16 . . . . .69 B7
Larch Terr DH9 . . . . .79 A1
Larchwood NE38 . . . . .83 B1
Larchwood Ave
  Newcastle upon Tyne, Fawdon
    NE3 . . . . .37 F7
  Newcastle upon Tyne,
    Walkergate NE6 . . . . .56 E8
  Wideopen NE13 . . . . .28 C5
Larchwood Dr NE61 . . . . .8 D2
Larchwood Gdns NE11 . . . .70 B5
Larchwood Gr SR2 . . . . .86 C2
Lea Ave NE32 . . . . .58 C2
Leabank NE15 . . . . .53 D8
Leaburn Terr NE42 . . . . .50 B2
LEADGATE 66 A3
Leadgate Cotts NE17 . . . . . .66 A4
Lead La
  Greenside NE40 . . . . .52 B1
  High Spen NE17, NE40 . . . . .66 D6
  Stocksfield NE43 . . . . .64 B2
Leafield NE63 . . . . .6 F4
Leafield Cl DH3 . . . . .82 D6
Leafield Cres NE34 . . . . .60 A8
Lea Gn DH3 . . . . .82 C6
Leagreen Ct NE3 . . . . .38 A5
Leaholme Cres NE24 . . . . . .17 C6
Lealholm Rd NE7 . . . . .39 A5
Leam Gdns NE10 . . . . .72 C8
Leamington St SR4 . . . . . . .102 B1
Leam La
  Gateshead NE10 . . . . .72 B6
  Jarrow NE32 . . . . .58 C3
LEAM LANE 72 A6
Leam La/Newcastle Rd NE32,
  NE34 . . . . .58 F5
Leamside
  Gateshead NE10 . . . . .71 F6
  Jarrow NE32 . . . . .58 C4
Leander Ave
  Chester le Street DH3 . . . . . . .88 D7
  Stakeford NE62 . . . . .11 B8
Leander Ct NE10 . . . . .72 C8
Leander Dr NE35 . . . . .73 E8
Leaplish NE38 . . . . .83 F2
Lea Rigg DH4 . . . . .94 A2
Leas The
  Newbottle DH4 . . . . .90 D3
  Whitley Bay NE25 . . . . .31 D4
Leaside NE34 . . . . .59 C5
Leatham SR2 . . . . .92 E8
Leaway NE42 . . . . .50 B2
LEAZES 78 F6
Leazes Arc NE1 . . . . .99 A2
Leazes Cres
  Hexham NE46 . . . . .44 F5
  Newcastle upon Tyne NE1 . . .98 C2
Leazes Ct NE4 . . . . .98 B2
Leazes La
  Corbridge NE45 . . . . .47 A8
  Hexham NE46 . . . . .44 E5
  Newcastle upon Tyne NE1 . . .99 A2
Leazes Par NE2 . . . . .98 B3
Leazes Park Rd NE1 . . . . . . .99 A2
Leazes Parkway NE15 . . . . .35 D1
Leazes Pk NE46 . . . . .44 E5
Leazes Terr
  Corbridge NE45 . . . . .46 F6
  Hexham NE46 . . . . .44 F5
  Newcastle upon Tyne NE1 . . .98 C2
Leazes The
  Burnopfield NE16 . . . . .78 F6
  South Shields NE34 . . . . .59 D6
  Sunderland SR1 . . . . .102 B2
  Throckley NE15 . . . . .35 C1
Leazes View
  Ovingham NE42 . . . . .49 D4
  Rowlands Gill NE39 . . . . .67 D2
LEAZES VILLAGE 98 C2
Leazes Villas NE16 . . . . .79 A6
Lecondale NE10 . . . . .71 F5
Lecondale Ct NE10 . . . . .71 F5
Ledbury Rd SR2 . . . . .86 D3
Leechmere Cres SR7 . . . . . .92 F1
Leechmere Ind Est SR2 . . .86 E1

Leechmere Rd
  18 Grangetown SR2 . . . . . . .86 F2
  Sunderland SR2 . . . . .86 D1
Leechmere View 5 SR2 . .92 F8
Leechmere Way SR2 . . . . . . .92 F8
Lee Cl NE38 . . . . .84 B6
Leeds St SR6 . . . . .75 E2
Leeholme DH5 . . . . .94 F7
Leeming Gdns NE9 . . . . .71 B6
Lee St
  Annitsford NE23 . . . . .22 B1
  Fordley NE23 . . . . .29 B8
  6 Sunderland, Fulwell SR5 . .75 D4
  Sunderland, Southwick
    SR5 . . . . .75 B1
Lee Terr DH5 . . . . .95 B2
Legg Ave NE22 . . . . .11 E3
Legges Dr NE13 . . . . .20 D6
Legion Gr NE15 . . . . .53 F7
Legion Rd NE15 . . . . .53 F7
Leicester Cl NE28 . . . . .40 A5
Leicester St NE6 . . . . .56 E5
Leicester Way NE32 . . . . . . .58 A1
Leighton Rd SR2 . . . . .86 D2
Leighton St
  7 Newcastle upon Tyne
    NE6 . . . . .56 A6
  South Shields NE33 . . . . .42 E2
Leighton Terr DH3 . . . . .82 B5
Leith Ct NE34 . . . . .59 C5
Leith Gdns DH9 . . . . .79 D1
Leland Pl NE61 . . . . .4 A1
LEMINGTON 53 C7
Lemington Gdns NE5 . . . . . .54 C7
Lemington Rd NE15 . . . . . . .53 B6
Lemington Riverside Prim
  Sch NE15 . . . . .53 B6
Lemon St NE33 . . . . .59 B6
Lena Ave NE25 . . . . .31 E4
Lenin Terr NE17 . . . . .77 B6
Lenore Terr NE40 . . . . .52 B2
Lenthorn Mews 2 SR6 . . . .75 E1
Leominster Rd SR2 . . . . .86 D2
Leopold Ho SR2 . . . . .102 C1
Leopold St NE32 . . . . .58 B6
Lesbury Ave
  Ashington NE63 . . . . .6 F2
  Shiremoor NE27 . . . . .30 E3
  Stakeford NE62 . . . . .6 A1
  Wallsend NE28 . . . . .40 F3
Lesbury Chase NE3 . . . . .38 B7
Lesbury Gdns NE13 . . . . . . .28 C6
Lesbury Rd NE6 . . . . .56 B8
Lesbury St NE28 . . . . .41 C1
Lesbury Terr NE17 . . . . .77 B8
Lesley Ct NE3 . . . . .38 C5
Leslie Ave NE31 . . . . .57 E4
Leslie Cl NE40 . . . . .52 E4
Leslie Cres NE3 . . . . .38 C3
Leslies View NE61 . . . . .1 B2
Letch Way NE15 . . . . .53 F7
Letchwell Villas NE12 . . . . .29 E1
Leuchars Ct DH3 . . . . .82 C3
Leven Ave DH2 . . . . .88 B1
Leven Ho 10 SR3 . . . . .92 A6
Levens Wlk NE23 . . . . .21 E7
Levisham Cl SR3 . . . . .92 C7
Lewis Cres SR2 . . . . .103 C1
Lewis Dr NE4 . . . . .54 F6
Lewis Gdns NE34 . . . . .59 C3
Leybourne Ave NE12 . . . . . .29 D1
Leybourne Dene NE12 . . . . .29 D1
Leybourne Hold DH3 . . . . . .82 C5
Leyburn Cl
  Houghton-le-Spring DH4 . . . .90 D1
  Urpeth DH2 . . . . .81 D1
Leyburn Ct NE23 . . . . .22 A4
Leyburn Dr NE7 . . . . .39 A3
Leyburn Gr DH4 . . . . .90 D1
Leyburn Pl DH3 . . . . .82 B6
Leyfield Cl SR3 . . . . .92 B5
Leyton Pl NE8 . . . . .71 B8
Liberty Ho NE2 . . . . .38 E1
Liberty Terr DH9 . . . . .79 B2
Liberty Way SR6 . . . . .103 B4
Liburn Cl NE36 . . . . .74 C8
Lichfield Ave NE6 . . . . .56 E4
Lichfield Cl
  Ashington NE63 . . . . .6 F2
  Newcastle upon Tyne NE3 . . .37 E7
Lichfield Rd SR5 . . . . .75 A3
Lichfield Way NE32 . . . . . . .58 A1
Lidcombe Ct SR3 . . . . .92 C7
Liddell Ct SR6 . . . . .75 E1
Liddell St
  North Shields NE29, NE30 . . .42 B5
  Sunderland SR6 . . . . .103 A4
Liddell Terr
  Gateshead NE8 . . . . .70 D8
  Kibblesworth NE11 . . . . .81 C6
Liddle Ave NE16 . . . . .98 A1
Liddle Rd NE4 . . . . .98 A1
Liddles St 11 NE22 . . . . . . .11 D3
Lieven St NE13 . . . . .20 B3
Lifestyle Acad The NE4 . .100 C4
Liffey Rd NE31 . . . . .57 A6
Lightbourne Rd NE6 . . . . . . .57 A6
Lightfoot Sports Ctr NE6 . .56 F4
Lightwood Ave NE15 . . . . . .54 A7
Lilac Ave
  Blyth NE24 . . . . .17 D8
  6 Houghton-le-Spring DH5 .94 E8
  Longbenton NE12 . . . . .29 C4
  New Silksworth SR3 . . . . .92 B8
  South Shields NE34 . . . . .60 A5
  Whitburn SR6 . . . . .60 F7
Lilac Cl NE5 . . . . .36 B4
Lilac Cres NE16 . . . . .79 A6

Lilac Ct
Ashington NE63 . . . . 6 C1
Ellington NE61 . . . . 1 E6
Lilac Gdns
Cleadon SR6 . . . . 60 A2
Washington NE38 . . . . 70 F6
Whickham NE16 . . . . 69 A6
Lilac Rd NE6 . . . . 40 A1
Lilac Sq DH4 . . . . 89 E3
Lilac St SR4 . . . . 85 A6
Lilac Wlk NE31 . . . . 57 E3
Lilburn Cl 6 NE6 . . . . 56 C4
Lilburne Cl SR1 . . . . 103 B3
Lilburn Gdns NE3 . . . . 38 F4
Lilburn Pl SR5 . . . . 75 A1
Lilburn Rd NE27 . . . . 30 E2
Lilburn St NE29 . . . . 41 F5
Lilian Ave
Sunderland SR2 . . . . 92 E8
Wallsend NE28 . . . . 40 A1
Lilleycroft NE39 . . . . 67 F2
Lilley Gr SR5 . . . . 74 B1
Lilley Terr NE39 . . . . 67 F3
Lillico Ho NE2 . . . . 99 C3
Lily Ave
Bedlington NE22 . . . . 16 B8
Newcastle upon Tyne NE2 . . 38 F1
Lily Bank NE28 . . . . 40 C2
Lily Cl NE21 . . . . 53 A2
Lily Cres
Newcastle upon Tyne NE2 . . 38 E1
Whitburn SR6 . . . . 60 F3
Lily Est NE15 . . . . 35 D3
Lily Gdns DH9 . . . . 78 E1
Lily St SR4 . . . . 102 B3
Lily Terr
Newbottle DH4 . . . . 90 D4
Newcastle upon Tyne NE5 . . 37 A3
Lilywhite Terr DH5 . . . . . . 95 B1
Lime Ave DH4 . . . . 90 C1
Limecroft NE32 . . . . 58 C1
Lime Gr
Prudhoe NE42 . . . . 50 B3
Ryton NE40 . . . . 52 C5
Limekiln Ct NE28 . . . . 40 D2
Limekiln Rd NE28 . . . . 40 D2
Limes Ave NE24 . . . . 12 D1
Lime St
Blaydon NE21 . . . . 53 D1
Newcastle upon Tyne NE1,
NE6 . . . . 56 A3
Sunderland SR4 . . . . 102 B3
Throckley NE15 . . . . 35 D3
Limes The
Penshaw DH4 . . . . 90 B8
Stannington NE61 . . . . 14 C3
Sunderland SR2 . . . . 86 D4
Limestone La NE20 . . . . . . 25 B7
Limetree NE38 . . . . 83 E2
Limetrees Gdns NE9 . . . . . 70 F7
Limewood Ct NE2 . . . . 98 B4
Limewood Gr NE13 . . . . . . 28 B3
Linacre Cl NE3 . . . . 37 B6
Linbridge Dr NE5 . . . . 36 E1
Linburn NE38 . . . . 89 B8
Lincoln Ave
New Silksworth SR3 . . . . . . 92 A8
Wallsend NE28 . . . . 40 A3
Lincoln Cres DH5 . . . . 94 F4
Lincoln Ct NE31 . . . . 57 D5
Lincoln Gn NE3 . . . . 28 C1
Lincoln Rd
Cramlington NE23 . . . . 16 C1
South Shields NE34 . . . . . . 60 B7
Lincoln St
Gateshead NE8 . . . . 101 B1
Sunderland SR4 . . . . 85 F7
Lincoln Way NE32 . . . . 58 B1
Lincrest Ct NE5 . . . . 36 F2
Lindale Ave NE16 . . . . 69 A5
Lindale Rd NE4 . . . . 54 E8
Lindean Pl NE23 . . . . 21 F6
Linden NE9 . . . . 71 D4
Linden Ave
Newcastle upon Tyne, Fenham
NE4 . . . . 54 D7
Newcastle upon Tyne, Gosforth
NE3 . . . . 38 C4
Linden Cl NE62 . . . . 11 A8
Linden Gdns SR2 . . . . 86 C3
Linden Gr
1 Dunston NE11 . . . . 70 A8
Houghton-le-Spring DH4 . . 94 D8
Linden Rd
Blaydon NE21 . . . . 53 D2
Longbenton NE12 . . . . 39 D6
Newcastle upon Tyne NE3 . . 38 C4
Seaton Delaval NE25 . . . . . 23 B3
Sunderland SR2 . . . . 86 C3
Linden Terr
Longbenton NE12 . . . . 39 D6
25 Springwell NE9 . . . . 71 F1
Whitley Bay NE26 . . . . 32 B5
Linden Way
Ellington NE61 . . . . 1 D5
Gateshead NE9 . . . . 71 D2
Ponteland NE20 . . . . 25 C3
Lindfield Ave NE5 . . . . 37 C1
Lindisfarne
Ryhope SR2 . . . . 92 E4
Washington NE38 . . . . 83 C4
Lindisfarne Ave DH3 . . . . . 88 D3
Lindisfarne Cl
Burnside DH4 . . . . 90 C2

Lindisfarne Cl continued
Chester le Street DH2 . . . . . 88 A1
2 Morpeth NE61 . . . . 9 A6
Newcastle upon Tyne, Jesmond
NE2 . . . . 38 F2
Newcastle upon Tyne NE5 . . 36 F1
Pegswood NE61 . . . . 5 A4
Lindisfarne Ct NE32 . . . . . . 58 F6
Lindisfarne Dr NE8 . . . . . . 101 C2
Lindisfarne La NE61 . . . . 9 A6
Lindisfarne Pl NE28 . . . . . . 40 D3
Lindisfarne Rd
Hebburn NE31 . . . . 57 E3
Jarrow NE32 . . . . 58 D4
Newcastle upon Tyne NE2 . . 38 F2
Lindisfarne Recess NE32 . . 58 D4
Lindisfarne Terr NE30 . . . . 42 A7
Lindisfarne Wlk NE62 . . . . 10 E7
Lindom Ave DH3 . . . . 88 D3
Lindon Rd NE23 . . . . 99 B3
Lindrick Ct NE10 . . . . 72 C7
Lindsay Ave NE24 . . . . 17 C8
Lindsay Cl SR2 . . . . 103 B1
Lindsay Ct SR6 . . . . 60 F2
Lindsay Rd SR5 . . . . 103 B1
Lindsay St DH5 . . . . 95 B5
Lindsey Cl NE23 . . . . 21 E6
Lindum Rd NE9 . . . . 70 F8
Linefield Ct 92 E7
Lingcroft NE9 . . . . 71 C5
Lingdale Ave NE6 . . . . 75 E6
Lingey Gdns NE10 . . . . 72 C8
Lingey House Prim Sch
NE10 . . . . 72 B7
Lingey La NE10 . . . . 72 B7
Lingfield DH5 . . . . 94 F7
Lingholme DH2 . . . . 88 A4
Lingmell NE37 . . . . 83 B6
Lingshaw NE10 . . . . 72 B7
Lingside NE32 . . . . 58 C1
Linhope Ave NE3 . . . . 37 F7
Linhope Rd NE5 . . . . 36 F2
Link Ave NE22 . . . . 10 D1
Link Rd
Hazlerigg NE13 . . . . 28 A4
Newcastle upon Tyne NE5 . . 37 C2
Links Ave
Tynemouth NE30 . . . . 32 C2
Byermoor NE16 . . . . 31 F7
Links Ct NE26 . . . . 32 A7
Links Gn NE3 . . . . 38 D6
Links Green Wlk NE3 . . . . . 38 D6
Links Rd
Blyth NE24 . . . . 17 F4
Seaton Sluice NE24 . . . . . . 18 A2
Tynemouth NE30 . . . . 32 C2
Links The NE26 . . . . 32 A7
Links View
Ashington NE63 . . . . 12 A8
Blyth NE24 . . . . 17 C4
Links Wlk NE5 . . . . 36 F2
Linkway NE32 . . . . 58 D1
Linley Hill NE16 . . . . 68 E4
Linnel Dr NE15 . . . . 53 E7
Linnet Cl NE38 . . . . 83 A3
Linnet Ct NE63 . . . . 6 A1
Linnet Gr SR5 . . . . 74 C1
Linnetsfield NE6 . . . . 56 F8
Linney Gdns NE34 . . . . 59 A4
Linnheads NE42 . . . . 50 B1
Linshiels Gdns 1 NE63 . . . 6 F2
Linskell SR2 . . . . 92 E8
Linskill Pl
Newcastle upon Tyne NE3 . . 37 F3
North Shields NE30 . . . . . . 42 B7
Linskill St NE30 . . . . 42 B5
Linskill Terr
North Shields NE30 . . . . . . 42 B7
Tynemouth NE30 . . . . 42 B7
Linslade Wlk NE23 . . . . 21 F6
Lintfort NE38 . . . . 88 E7
Linthorpe Ct 1 NE34 . . . . . 59 A5
Linthorpe Rd
Newcastle upon Tyne NE3 . . 38 C2
Tynemouth NE30 . . . . 32 B1
LINTON 1 B3
Linton NE12 . . . . 29 D5
Linton Fst Sch NE61 . . . . . . 1 A3
Linton Rd
Gateshead NE9 . . . . 70 F3
Newbiggin NE24 . . . . 24 E1
Lintonville Ent Pk NE61 . . . 6 D5
Lintonville Parkway NE63 . . 6 C5
Lintonville Rd NE63 . . . . . . 6 C5
Lintonville Terr NE63 . . . . . 6 C5
LINTZ 78 F5
LINTZFORD 78 B7
Lintzford Gdns
Newcastle upon Tyne
NE15 . . . . 54 E4
Rowlands Gill NE39 . . . . . . 78 D8
Lintzford La NE39 . . . . 67 B1
Lintzford Rd NE39 . . . . 78 C7
Lintz Green La NE16, NE39 . 78 C6
Lintz La NE16 . . . . 78 E4
Lintz Terr NE16 . . . . 78 F6
Linum Pl NE4 . . . . 54 E8
Linwood Pl NE3 . . . . 28 C1
Lion Wlk NE29 . . . . 42 A5
Lisa Ave SR4 . . . . 85 A5
Lisburn Terr SR4 . . . . 102 A3
Lish Ave NE26 . . . . 32 C4
Lishman Terr NE40 . . . . 52 A4
Lisle Gr NE28 . . . . 40 B2
Lisle Pl DH3 . . . . 88 C3
Lisle Rd NE34 . . . . 60 A6

Lisle St
Newcastle upon Tyne NE1 . . 99 A2
Wallsend NE28 . . . . 40 B2
Lismore Ave NE33 . . . . 59 D7
Lismore Pl NE15 . . . . 54 D6
Lismor Terr 10 NE9 . . . . . . 71 F1
Lister Ave
Dunston NE11 . . . . 54 F1
Greenside NE40 . . . . 66 F8
Lister Cl DH5 . . . . 94 D6
Listers La NE1 . . . . 71 A8
Lister St NE15 . . . . 53 F5
Litchfield Cres 2 NE21 . . . 53 B1
Litchfield La NE21 . . . . 53 B1
Litchfield St 1 NE21 . . . . . 53 B1
Litchfield Terr 3 NE21 . . . 53 B1
Little Bedford St NE29,
NE30 . . . . 42 B5
Little Bldgs NE42 . . . . 49 D4
Littleburn Cl DH4 . . . . 90 C2
Littledene NE9 . . . . 70 F7
Little Dene NE2 . . . . 38 D3
Little Theatre The NE8 . . . . 70 F8
LITTLETOWN 96 E4
Littletown La HH6 . . . . 96 D3
Little Villiers St SR1 . . . . . 103 B3
Little Way NE15 . . . . 54 B4
Litton Cl 14 SR3 . . . . 91 F6
Littondale NE28 . . . . 39 F4
Live Theatre★ NE1 . . . . . . 101 B4
Livingstone Pl 8 NE33 . . . 42 C4
Livingstone Sq SR2 . . . . . . 86 F1
Livingstone St NE33 . . . . . . 42 D4
Livingstone View NE30 . . . 42 C7
Lizard La NE34, SR6 . . . . . . 60 E4
Lizard View SR6 . . . . 60 E2
Lloyd Ave DH5 . . . . 94 C4
Lloyd Ct NE11 . . . . 54 B4
Lloyd St 6 NE40 . . . . 51 F3
LOANSDEAN 8 F5
Lobban Ave NE31 . . . . 57 D4
Lobelia Ave NE10 . . . . 56 B2
Lobelia Cl NE5 . . . . 36 B3
Lobley Gdns NE11 . . . . 70 A6
LOBLEY HILL 70 A5
Lobley Hill Prim Sch
NE11 . . . . 70 A6
Lobleyhill Rd
Byermoor NE16 . . . . 79 D8
Sunniside NE16 . . . . 79 D8
Lobley Hill Rd NE11, NE8 . . 70 C7
Local Ave NE6 . . . . 96 C1
Locarno Pl NE64 . . . . 7 E4
Lochcraig Pl NE23 . . . . 21 F6
Lochfield Gdns NE11 . . . . . 81 C6
Lochmaben Terr SR5 . . . . . 75 D2
Lockerbie Gdns NE15 . . . . . 53 E7
Lockerbie Rd NE23 . . . . 21 F6
Lockhaugh Rd NE39 . . . . . . 68 A4
Locksley Cl NE29 . . . . 31 B1
Locomotion Way
Killingworth NE12 . . . . 29 B5
North Shields NE29 . . . . . . 42 A4
Locomotive Ct NE42 . . . . . . 50 C2
Lodge St NE39 . . . . 78 A5
Lodgeside Mdw SR3 . . . . . . 92 B5
Lodges Rd The NE9 . . . . . . 70 F3
Lodore Ct 8 SR3 . . . . 91 F6
Lodore Gr NE32 . . . . 58 D3
Lodore Rd NE2 . . . . 38 D3
Lodsworth Dr NE23 . . . . . . 22 A4
Lofthill 6 SR3 . . . . 91 E5
Logan Rd NE6 . . . . 39 F1
Logan St DH5 . . . . 95 A3
Logan Terr DH6 . . . . 97 E8
Lola St NE13 . . . . 27 F5
Lombard Dr DH3 . . . . 88 D7
Lombard St
Newcastle upon Tyne
NE1 . . . . 101 B4
Sunderland SR1 . . . . 103 B3
Lombard Street Ind Est
SR1 . . . . 102 B3
Lomond Cl NE38 . . . . 83 B3
Lomond Ct 11 SR3 . . . . 92 A6
Lomond Pl DH2 . . . . 88 B1
London Ave NE37 . . . . 72 B1
Londonderry Mews 5
SR3 . . . . 92 B7
Londonderry St SR3 . . . . . . 92 A7
Londonderry Terr SR3 . . . . 92 A7
Londonderry Tower SR1 . 103 B3
Londonbrough Ct NE37 . . . . 39 A4
Longacre
Houghton-le-Spring DH4 . . 94 C8
Washington NE38 . . . . 83 E1
Long Bank
Birtley DH3 . . . . 82 C7
Gateshead NE9 . . . . 71 C7
LONGBENTON 39 C8
Longbenton Com Coll
NE12 . . . . 39 C7
Longbenton Sta NE12 . . . . 39 A5
Longborough Ct NE7 . . . . . 39 A4
Longclose Bank DH8,
NE39 . . . . 77 E3
Long Close Rd NE39 . . . . . . 77 F5
Long Crag NE37 . . . . 83 A5
Longdean Cl NE31 . . . . 57 C5
Longdean Pk DH3 . . . . 88 D2
Long Dr NE61 . . . . 8 F5
Longfellow St DH5 . . . . 94 E7
Longfield Cl NE34 . . . . 59 D4
Longfield Rd SR6 . . . . 75 D3
Long Gair NE21 . . . . 68 A8
Long Headlam 11 NE6 . . . . 56 C6
LONGHIRST 4 F7

Longhirst
Gateshead NE10 . . . . 72 A7
Killingworth NE12 . . . . 29 D5
Newcastle upon Tyne NE5 . . 36 F2
Longhirst Ct NE61 . . . . 4 F4
Longhirst Dr
Cramlington NE23 . . . . 22 A4
Widdopen NE13 . . . . 28 B5
Longhirst Rd NE61 . . . . 4 F4
Longhirst Village NE61 . . . . 4 F4
Longlands 11 NE6 . . . . 45 A4
Longlands Dr DH5 . . . . 94 E7
Longleat Gdns
Pegswood NE61 . . . . 4 E4
10 South Shields NE33 . . . 42 D3
Longley St NE4 . . . . 98 A2
Long Meadow Ct NE40 . . . 52 A4
Longmeadows
Ponteland NE20 . . . . 25 B3
Sunderland SR3 . . . . 91 C6
Longniddry NE37 . . . . 72 C3
Longniddry Ct NE9 . . . . 70 E3
Long Pk NE64 . . . . 7 D4
Longridge Ave
Newcastle upon Tyne NE7 . . 39 D2
Washington NE38 . . . . 83 B3
Longridge Ct NE22 . . . . 11 A4
Longridge Dr NE26 . . . . 31 E7
Long Ridge Rd NE21, NE40 . 52 D2
Longridge Sq SR2 . . . . 86 D2
Longridge Way
Bedlington NE22 . . . . 11 A4
Cramlington NE23 . . . . 21 F6
Longrigg NE10 . . . . 72 A7
Long Rigg NE16 . . . . 54 A8
Longriggs The NE44 . . . . . . 62 E7
Long Row NE33 . . . . 42 B4
Long Row Cl NE40 . . . . 66 F8
Longshank La DH3 . . . . 82 A6
Longstaff Gdns NE34 . . . . . 58 F4
Longston Ave NE30 . . . . . . 32 B2
Longstone Ct NE12 . . . . 29 E4
Longstone Sq NE5 . . . . 36 D1
Longwood Cl NE16 . . . . 69 B3
Lonnen Ave NE4 . . . . 54 D7
Lonnen Dr NE16 . . . . 69 A8
Lonnen The
Ryton NE40 . . . . 52 E5
South Shields NE34 . . . . . . 60 B4
Lonsdale DH3 . . . . 82 D1
Lonsdale Ave
Blyth NE24 . . . . 16 E8
Sunderland SR6 . . . . 75 E7
Lonsdale Ct
Medomsley NE17 . . . . 77 B8
South Shields NE34 . . . . . . 59 A4
Lonsdale Gdns NE28 . . . . . 41 A4
Lonsdale Rd SR6 . . . . 75 E7
Lonsdale Terr NE2 . . . . 38 E2
Loraine Terr NE15 . . . . 53 C6
Lord Blyton Prim Sch
NE34 . . . . 59 E4
Lord Byrons Wlk SR7 . . . . . 93 B1
Lordenshaw NE5 . . . . 36 F2
Lord Gort Cl 1 SR5 . . . . . . 75 A1
Lord Lawson of Beamish
Com Sch DH3 . . . . 82 D3
Lord Nelson St NE33 . . . . . 59 B6
Lord St
Newcastle upon Tyne
NE1 . . . . 100 C4
New Silksworth SR3 . . . . . . 92 B7
South Shields NE33 . . . . . . 42 E1
Lorne St DH5 . . . . 94 F8
Lorne Terr SR2 . . . . 103 A1
Lorrain Rd NE34 . . . . 59 D2
Lort Ho NE2 . . . . 99 C2
Lorton Ave NE30 . . . . 32 A2
Lorton Rd NE9 . . . . 71 A4
Losh Terr NE6 . . . . 56 F6
Lossiemouth Rd NE29 . . . . 41 C5
Lothian Cl
Birtley DH3 . . . . 82 D1
Sunderland SR4 . . . . 85 D3
Lothian Ct NE5 . . . . 37 C3
Lotus Cl NE5 . . . . 36 B3
Lotus Pl NE4 . . . . 54 D7
Loudon St NE34 . . . . 59 C5
Loughborough Ave
Sunderland SR2 . . . . 86 C3
Tynemouth NE30 . . . . 32 C1
Loughrow Pk NE46 . . . . 45 B2
Lough Ct NE9 . . . . 71 B5
Loughrigg Ave NE23 . . . . . . 21 F5
Louie Terr NE9 . . . . 71 A5
Louis Ave SR6 . . . . 75 D3
Louise Ho SR2 . . . . 102 C1
Louise Terr DH3 . . . . 88 C3
Louisville NE20 . . . . 25 F7
Loup St SR2 . . . . 53 C3
Louvain Terr
Guide Post NE62 . . . . 10 F7
Hetton-le-Hole DH5 . . . . . . 94 F3
Louvain Terrace W DH5 . . . 95 A5
Lovaine Ave
8 North Shields NE29 . . . . 42 A5
Whitley Bay NE25 . . . . 32 A4
Lovaine Flats NE1 . . . . 99 B2
Lovaine Pl NE29 . . . . 42 A5
Lovaine Place W 6 NE29 . . 42 A5
Lovaine Row NE30 . . . . 42 E8
Lovaine Terr NE29 . . . . 42 A6
Love Ave NE23 . . . . 29 B8
Love Avenue Cotts NE23 . . 29 B8
Love La NE1 . . . . 99 C1
Loveless Gdns NE10 . . . . . . 72 B8

Lovett Wlk NE8 . . . . 100 C3
Lowbiggin NE5 . . . . 36 E5
Low Burswell NE46 . . . . 44 F5
Low Chare DH3 . . . . 88 D3
Low Cl NE42 . . . . 50 E3
Lowdham Ave NE29 . . . . . . 41 E4
Lowdon Ct NE2 . . . . 98 C3
LOW DOWNS 95 B6
Low Downs Rd DH5 . . . . . . 95 A6
Low Downs Sq DH5 . . . . . . 95 B6
Lower Crone St NE27 . . . . . 30 F4
Lower Dundas St SR6 . . . . 103 A4
Lower Rudyerd St NE29 . . . 42 B5
Lowerson Ave DH4 . . . . 90 A5
Lowery Pl NE23 . . . . 99 C2
Loweswater Ave
Chester le Street DH2 . . . . . 88 B1
Easington Lane DH5 . . . . . . 97 C8
Loweswater Cl NE24 . . . . . 11 F1
Loweswater Rd
Gateshead NE9 . . . . 71 A4
Newcastle upon Tyne NE5 . . 54 B8
Loweswood Cl NE7 . . . . 39 A1
Low Farm NE61 . . . . 1 D4
LOW FELL 70 F5
Lowfield Terr NE6 . . . . 56 F4
Lowfield Wlk NE16 . . . . 69 A4
Low Flatts Rd DH3 . . . . 88 C6
Low Fold NE6 . . . . 56 B5
Low Friar St NE1 . . . . 99 A1
LOW GATE 44 A4
Low Gosforth Ct NE3 . . . . . 28 D1
LOW GREENSIDE 52 A2
Low Haugh NE20 . . . . 25 F7
Low Heworth La NE10 . . . . 56 F1
Lowick Cl DH3 . . . . 82 D1
Lowick Ct 6 NE3 . . . . 38 E4
Low Lane NE3 . . . . 28 C3
Lowland Cl SR3 . . . . 92 A5
Lowlands Ct NE5 . . . . 36 F1
LOW LIGHTS 42 C6
Low Main Pl NE23 . . . . 22 B6
Low Mdw SR6 . . . . 60 A1
Low Mill Villas NE21 . . . . . 53 C2
LOW MOORSLEY 94 F1
Lownds Terr NE6 . . . . 56 E6
LOW PITTINGTON 96 B6
LOW PRUDHOE 50 D4
Low Prudhoe Ind Est
NE42 . . . . 50 D4
Low Quay NE24 . . . . 17 F8
Low Reach NE10 . . . . 57 A2
Lowrey's La NE9 . . . . 70 F5
Low Row
Ryton NE40 . . . . 52 E3
Sunderland SR1 . . . . 102 C2
Lowry Gdns NE34 . . . . 59 D2
Lowry Rd SR6 . . . . 75 E5
LOW SOUTHWICK 75 A1
Low St SR1 . . . . 103 B3
Low Stobhill NE61 . . . . 9 A4
Lowther Ave DH2 . . . . 88 B2
Lowther Cl NE63 . . . . 6 F1
Lowther Ct NE63 . . . . 21 E6
Lowthian Cres NE6 . . . . 56 E5
Lowthian Terr NE38 . . . . . . 83 F4
LOW WALKER 57 B6
Low Well Gdns NE10 . . . . . 56 E1
Low West Ave NE39 . . . . . . 67 D1
LOW WESTWOOD 77 A5
Loxton Sq NE23 . . . . 22 A3
Lucknow St SR1 . . . . 103 C3
Lucock St NE14 . . . . 59 B5
Lucombe Cl NE34 . . . . 89 F5
Lucy St
Blaydon NE21 . . . . 53 D3
4 Chester le Street DH3 . . 88 C4
Ludlow Ave NE29 . . . . 41 E8
Ludlow Ct NE3 . . . . 37 E7
Ludlow Dr NE25 . . . . 31 B5
Ludlow Rd SR2 . . . . 86 D3
Luffness Dr NE34 . . . . 59 F3
Luke's La NE10, NE31 . . . . . 57 F1
Lukes Lane Prim Sch
NE31 . . . . 58 A3
Lulsgate SR5 . . . . 74 A1
Lulworth Ave NE32 . . . . 58 D5
Lulworth Ct SR3 . . . . 91 C7
Lulworth Gdns SR2 . . . . . . 86 C3
Lumley Ave
South Shields NE34 . . . . . . 60 B6
Whickham NE16 . . . . 54 B1
Lumley Cl
Chester le Street DH2 . . . . . 88 B3
Washington NE38 . . . . 83 B5
Lumley Cres DH4 . . . . 90 C4
Lumley Ct
Bedlington NE22 . . . . 11 C2
Hebburn NE31 . . . . 57 F8
Sunderland SR3 . . . . 91 C7
Lumley Gdns
Burnopfield NE16 . . . . 78 E5
Gateshead NE8 . . . . 56 B1
Lumley New Rd DH3, DH4 . . 89 C1
Lumley St
Houghton-le-Spring DH4 . . 90 D2
Sunderland SR4 . . . . 102 B2
Lumley Terr
Chester le Street DH3 . . . . . 88 D2
Jarrow NE32 . . . . 58 C4
1 Ryhope SR2 . . . . 92 F6
Lumley Thicks DH3 . . . . 89 C1
Lumley Tower SR1 . . . . 103 B3
Lumley Way NE23 . . . . 28 A1

Lumley Wlk NE11 . . . . 100 A1
Lumsden's La NE61 . . . . 3 F1
Lunedale Ave SR6 . . . . 75 C5
Lune Gn NE32 . . . . 58 C2
Lune Green NE32 . . . . 58 C2
Lunedale St DH5 . . . . 95 A2
Lupin Cl NE6 . . . . 36 C4
Luss Ave NE32 . . . . 58 E3
Lutterworth Cl NE12 . . . . 39 B6
Lutterworth Pl NE12 . . . . 39 B6
Lutterworth Rd
  Longbenton NE12 . . . . 39 B5
  Sunderland SR2 . . . . 86 C3
Luxembourg Rd SR4 . . . . 85 D7
Lychgate Ct NE8 . . . . 101 C3
Lydbury Cl NE23 . . . . 16 C1
Lydcott NE38 . . . . 84 B5
Lyden Gate NE9 . . . . 71 A3
Lydford Ct
  Newbottle DH4 . . . . 90 C3
  Newcastle upon Tyne NE3 . . 37 C6
Lydford Way DH3 . . . . 82 D3
Lydney Cl NE15 . . . . 35 C1
Lyncroft NE63 . . . . 6 C2
Lyncroft Rd NE29 . . . . 41 E6
Lyndale NE23 . . . . 16 C1
Lynden Gdns NE5 . . . . 37 A3
Lynden Rd SR2 . . . . 92 B8
LYNDHURST 71 A3
Lyndhurst Ave
  Chester le Street DH3 . . . . 88 C6
  Gateshead NE9 . . . . 71 A4
  Newcastle upon Tyne NE2 . . 38 C2
Lyndhurst Cl NE21 . . . . 68 A8
Lyndhurst Cres NE9 . . . . 71 A4
Lyndhurst Dr NE9 . . . . 71 A3
Lyndhurst Gdns NE2 . . . . 38 D2
Lyndhurst Gn NE9 . . . . 70 F4
Lyndhurst Gr NE9 . . . . 71 A4
Lyndhurst Lodge NE25 . . . . 31 E5
Lyndhurst Rd
  Ashington NE63 . . . . 6 F1
  Longbenton NE12 . . . . 39 D7
  Whitley Bay NE25 . . . . 31 E5
Lyndhurst St NE33 . . . . 42 D2
Lyndhurst Terr
  Sunderland SR4 . . . . 85 E8
  1 Whickham NE16 . . . . 54 A1
Lyndon Cl NE36 . . . . 74 B7
Lyndon Dr NE36 . . . . 74 B7
Lyndon Gr NE36 . . . . 74 B7
Lyndon Wlk NE24 . . . . 16 F8
Lyneburn Grange NE61 . . . . 1 D5
LYNEMOUTH 2 D2
Lynemouth Fst Sch NE61 . . 2 B3
Lynemouth Rd NE61 . . . . 1 D4
Lyne Terr NE61 . . . . 1 F3
Lynfield NE26 . . . . 31 E7
Lynfield Ct NE5 . . . . 37 B3
Lynfield Pl NE5 . . . . 37 B3
Lynford Gdns SR2 . . . . 86 C3
Lyngrove SR2 . . . . 92 F8
Lynholme Ct 8 NE8 . . . . 71 A8
Lynholm Gr NE12 . . . . 39 D8
Lynmouth Pl NE7 . . . . 39 B3
Lynmouth Rd
  Gateshead NE9 . . . . 70 F3
  North Shields NE29 . . . . 41 C5
Lynndale Ave NE24 . . . . 17 A7
Lynnholm Cl NE7 . . . . 39 B2
Lynnholme Gdns
  Gateshead, Deckham NE9 . . 71 A8
  4 Gateshead NE9 . . . . 70 F8
Lynn Rd
  Tynemouth NE29 . . . . 41 D7
  Wallsend NE28 . . . . 40 A1
Lynn St
  Blyth NE24 . . . . 17 D7
  15 Chester le Street DH3 . . 88 C2
Lynnwood Ave NE4 . . . . 54 F5
Lynnwood Ct NE3 . . . . 37 C3
Lynthorpe 7 SR2 . . . . 92 F8
Lynthorpe Gr SR6 . . . . 75 E3
Lynton Ave NE32 . . . . 58 E5
Lynton Ct
  Newbottle DH4 . . . . 90 C3
  Newcastle upon Tyne NE5 . . 37 B3
Lynton Pl NE5 . . . . 37 B3
Lynton Way NE5 . . . . 37 B3
Lynwood Ave
  Blaydon NE21 . . . . 53 C3
  Newbeggin-by-the-Sea NE64 . 7 D5
  Sunderland SR4 . . . . 85 A2
Lynwood Bsns Dev Ctr
  NE4 . . . . 54 F5
Lynwood Cl NE20 . . . . 25 C2
Lynwood Way NE34 . . . . 59 F5
Lyon St
  Tynemouth NE29 . . . . 41 D7
LYONS 95 C2
Lyons Ave DH5 . . . . 95 B2
Lyons Cotts DH5 . . . . 95 B2
Lyons Ct NE6 . . . . 57 A1
Lyons Gdns NE6 . . . . 95 C2
Lyons La DH5 . . . . 95 C1
Lyon St NE31 . . . . 57 D7
Lyric Ct NE29 . . . . 41 C8
Lysander Dr NE6 . . . . 57 A4
Lysdon Ave NE25 . . . . 23 D6
Lyster Cl SR7 . . . . 92 E1
Lytchfeld NE10 . . . . 72 B7
Lytham Cl
  Cramlington NE23 . . . . 21 E6
  Wallsend NE28 . . . . 40 E7
  Washington NE37 . . . . 72 C2
Lytham Dr NE25 . . . . 31 D5
Lytham Gn NE10 . . . . 57 B2

Lytham Grange DH4 . . . . 90 A4
Lytham Pl NE6 . . . . 56 E5
Lythe Way NE12 . . . . 39 C6

M

Mabel St NE21 . . . . 53 C3
MacAdam St NE8 . . . . 70 D7
McAnany Ave NE34 . . . . 59 D5
McAteer Ct DH6 . . . . 97 E1
McClaren Way DH4 . . . . 90 F7
McCracken Cl NE3 . . . . 38 C8
McCracken Dr NE12 . . . . 28 C7
McCutcheon St 7 SR7 . . . . 92 E1
MacDonald Rd NE4 . . . . 54 D4
McErlane Sq NE10 . . . . 57 A1
McEwan Gdns NE4 . . . . 54 F5
McGowen Ct 5 NE6 . . . . 56 C5
McIlvenna Gdns NE28 . . . . 40 B4
McIntyre Hall NE31 . . . . 57 F7
McIntyre Rd NE31 . . . . 57 F7
McKendrick Villas NE5 . . . . 37 D1
McLennan Ct NE38 . . . . 83 D6
Maclynn Cl SR3 . . . . 91 E6
Macmerry Cl SR5 . . . . 84 F8
Macmillan Gdns NE10 . . . . 72 A8
McNamara Rd NE28 . . . . 40 F3
Mcnulty Ct NE23 . . . . 28 F8
Maddison Ct SR1 . . . . 103 C3
Maddison Gdns NE23 . . . . 22 E1
Maddison St NE24 . . . . 17 E8
Maddox Rd NE12 . . . . 39 D6
Madeira Ave NE26 . . . . 31 F7
Madeira Cl NE5 . . . . 36 C4
Madeira Terr 8 NE33 . . . . 42 D1
Madras St NE34 . . . . 59 A4
Madrona Cl DH4 . . . . 89 F5
Mafeking Pl NE29 . . . . 31 B1
Mafeking St
  5 Gateshead NE9 . . . . 71 A8
  Newcastle upon Tyne NE6 . . 56 F3
  Sunderland SR4 . . . . 85 F7
Magdalene Ct NE2 . . . . 98 B4
Magdalene Pl SR4 . . . . 85 F7
Magenta Cres NE5 . . . . 36 C4
Magnet Ct 1 NE1 . . . . 99 A1
Magnolia Ave NE4 . . . . 54 D7
Magnolia Ct NE63 . . . . 6 C1
Magnolia Dr NE63 . . . . 6 C1
Magnolia Gr NE61 . . . . 79 B6
Magpie Ct NE63 . . . . 6 B2
Mahogany Row DH9 . . . . 80 F1
Maidenhair NE31 . . . . 89 F5
Maiden La NE40 . . . . 52 A2
Maiden Law NE34 . . . . 94 A7
Maidens Croft NE46 . . . . 44 F4
Maiden St NE4 . . . . 100 B3
Maiden's Wlk NE46 . . . . 45 C4
Maidstone Cl SR3 . . . . 91 D6
Maidstone Terr DH4 . . . . 90 D4
Main Cres NE28 . . . . 39 F4
Main Rd
  Dinnington NE13 . . . . 27 C6
  Newcastle upon Tyne NE3 . . 37 B6
  Ryton NE40 . . . . 52 B5
  Wylam NE41 . . . . 51 B6
Mainsforth Terr SR7 . . . . 103 C1
Mainsforth Terrace W
  SR2 . . . . 86 E4
Mains Park Rd DH3 . . . . 88 D3
Mains Pl NE61 . . . . 3 F1
Main St
  Corbridge NE45 . . . . 47 A5
  Crawcrook NE40 . . . . 51 E6
Mainstone Cl NE23 . . . . 22 A6
Main Street N NE23 . . . . 22 F1
Main Street S NE23 . . . . 22 F1
Maitland Terr NE64 . . . . 7 D4
Makendon St NE31 . . . . 57 E7
Makepeace Terr 8 NE9 . . . . 71 F1
Malaburn Way 5 SR5 . . . . 75 A1
Malaga Cl NE5 . . . . 36 B4
Malaya Dr NE6 . . . . 57 B5
Malcolm Ct NE25 . . . . 31 D4
Malcolm St NE6 . . . . 56 F5
Malden Cl NE23 . . . . 21 F6
Maling Ct NE6 . . . . 56 B4
Maling Pk SR4 . . . . 85 B7
Malings Cl SR1 . . . . 103 C2
Maling Rd NE6 . . . . 56 A5
Mallard Cl
  Ashington NE63 . . . . 11 D8
  Washington NE38 . . . . 82 F4
Mallard Ct NE12 . . . . 29 C4
Mallard Lodge 10 NE10 . . . . 71 D8
Mallard Way
  Blyth NE24 . . . . 17 F3
  Fence Houses DH4 . . . . 94 B7
  Shiremoor NE28 . . . . 41 A6
Mallowburn Cres NE3 . . . . 37 C4
Malmo Cl NE29 . . . . 41 B5
Malone Gdns DH3 . . . . 82 D6
Malory Pl NE8 . . . . 101 C2
Maltby Cl
  2 Silksworth SR3 . . . . 91 E5
  Washington NE38 . . . . 83 D4
Maltings The SR3 . . . . 92 C7
Maltkiln NE6 . . . . 45 A4
Malton Cl
  Blyth NE24 . . . . 17 B7
  Newcastle upon Tyne NE15 . 53 E6
Malton Cres NE29 . . . . 41 F4
Malton Ct NE32 . . . . 58 A7
Malton Gdns NE28 . . . . 40 B4
Malton Gn NE9 . . . . 71 B1
Malvern Ave DH2 . . . . 88 B2
Malvern Cl NE63 . . . . 6 F1

Malvern Ct
  Cleadon SR6 . . . . 59 F1
  Dunston NE11 . . . . 70 A6
  Newcastle upon Tyne NE15 . 53 B7
Malvern Gdns
  Dunston NE11 . . . . 70 A7
  Sunderland SR6 . . . . 75 E3
Malvern Rd
  Seaton Sluice NE26 . . . . 24 D5
  Tynemouth NE29 . . . . 41 E8
  Wallsend NE28 . . . . 41 A3
  Washington NE38 . . . . 83 B3
Malvern St
  Newcastle upon Tyne
    NE4 . . . . 100 A4
  South Shields NE33 . . . . 59 C7
Malvins Close Fst Sch
  NE24 . . . . 17 C7
Malvins Close Rd NE24 . . . . 17 C7
Malvins Rd NE24 . . . . 17 B8
Manchester St NE61 . . . . 3 F1
Mandale Cres NE30 . . . . 32 A3
Mandarin Ct NE5 . . . . 36 C3
Mandarin Lodge 7 NE10 . . . . 71 D8
Mandarin Way NE10 . . . . 54 D3
Mandela Cl SR1 . . . . 103 C3
Mandela Way NE11 . . . . 54 D3
Mandeville NE37 . . . . 83 F8
Mandleston Cl SR2 . . . . 92 D6
Manet Gdns NE34 . . . . 59 D4
Mangrove Cl NE5 . . . . 36 C4
Manila St SR2 . . . . 86 E4
Manisty Ho NE4 . . . . 54 E4
Manley View NE61 . . . . 7 A3
Manningford Cl NE23 . . . . 22 A5
Manningford Dr SR3 . . . . 91 E5
Manor Ave
  Longbenton NE7 . . . . 39 C5
  Newburn NE15 . . . . 52 F8
Manor Chare NE1 . . . . 99 B1
Manor Cl
  Newcastle upon Tyne NE3 . . 38 C5
  Riding Mill NE44 . . . . 62 F7
Manor Cotts NE45 . . . . 46 F6
Manor Ct
  Newbiggin-by-the-Sea
    NE64 . . . . 7 E5
  South Shields NE33 . . . . 42 E1
Manor Dr
  Longbenton NE7 . . . . 39 C5
  Newbiggin-by-the-Sea NE64 . 7 E5
Manorfields NE12 . . . . 39 D6
Manor Gdns
  Gateshead NE10 . . . . 72 C8
  Longbenton NE7 . . . . 39 C5
Manor Gr
  Longbenton NE7 . . . . 39 C5
  Newburn NE15 . . . . 52 F7
  New Herrington DH4 . . . . 90 E2
Manor House Cl 1 NE6 . . . . 56 C5
Manor House Farm Cotts
  NE5 . . . . 37 D4
Manor House Rd NE2 . . . . 38 F1
Manor Pk
  Corbridge NE45 . . . . 46 F6
  High Heaton NE7 . . . . 39 C4
  Washington NE37 . . . . 83 D8
Manor Pl NE7 . . . . 39 C5
Manor Rd
  Longbenton NE7 . . . . 39 C5
  Medomsley DH8 . . . . 77 C1
  Tynemouth NE30 . . . . 42 D7
  Washington NE37 . . . . 83 D8
Manors Sta NE1 . . . . 99 B1
Manors Sta (Metro) NE1 . . . . 99 B1
Manors The NE42 . . . . 50 E3
Manor Terr
  Blaydon NE21 . . . . 53 A1
  Winlaton Mill NE21 . . . . 68 C7
Manor The NE37 . . . . 72 E2
Manor View
  High Pittington DH6 . . . . 96 B4
  Newbiggin-by-the-Sea NE64 . 7 E5
  Washington NE37 . . . . 83 D8
Manor View E 2 NE37 . . . . 83 E8
Manor Walks Sh Ctr NE23 22 A6
Manorway
  Hedworth NE32 . . . . 58 C1
  Tynemouth NE30 . . . . 42 D8
Manor Wlk NE7 . . . . 39 C5
Mansell Pl NE3 . . . . 37 F3
Manse Terr NE24 . . . . 16 E7
Mansfield Cres SR6 . . . . 75 E2
Mansfield Ct NE36 . . . . 74 A7
Mansfield Pl NE4 . . . . 98 B1
Mansfield St NE4 . . . . 98 B1
Mansion Ho NE16 . . . . 74 A7
Mansion Hts NE11 . . . . 69 E7
Manston Cl SR3 . . . . 91 D6
Manx Sq SR5 . . . . 75 B3
Maple Ave
  Dunston NE11 . . . . 70 A7
  New Silksworth SR3 . . . . 92 B8
  Whitley Bay NE25 . . . . 31 F4
Maplebeck Cl SR3 . . . . 91 D5
Maple Cl
  Killingworth NE12 . . . . 29 C4
  New Hartley NE25 . . . . 23 D6
Mapledene NE38 . . . . 83 E2
Mapledene Rd NE3 . . . . 37 F6
Maple Gr
  Gateshead, Felling NE10 . . 71 D8
  Gateshead, Saltwell NE8 . . 71 A7
  Prudhoe NE42 . . . . 50 B2

Maple Gr continued
  South Shields NE34 . . . . 59 F5
  Whitburn SR6 . . . . 60 F1
Maple Rd NE21 . . . . 53 C2
Maple Row NE11 . . . . 54 B2
Maple St
  Ashington NE63 . . . . 6 D3
  Jarrow NE32 . . . . 58 A7
  Newcastle upon Tyne NE4 . . 100 B4
Maple Terr
  Burnopfield NE16 . . . . 78 F6
  Newcastle upon Tyne NE4 . . 100 B4
  Shiney Row DH4 . . . . 90 A5
Maplewood
  Chester le Street DH2 . . . . 88 B4
  Newcastle upon Tyne NE6 . . 56 E8
Maplewood Ave SR5 . . . . 74 F3
Maplewood Cres NE38 . . . . 83 B1
Maplewood Dr DH6 . . . . 97 F3
Maplewood Sch SR5 . . . . 74 E3
Maplewood St DH4 . . . . 89 E1
Mapperley Dr NE15 . . . . 53 C7
Mappleton Dr 8 SR7 . . . . 93 C1
Marblet Ct NE11 . . . . 70 B7
Marbury Cl SR3 . . . . 91 D6
Marchburn La NE44 . . . . 62 E7
March Courtyard NE8 . . . . 100 B1
March Rd NE23 . . . . 29 B7
March Terr NE13 . . . . 27 A7
Marcia Ave SR6 . . . . 75 D3
Marconi Way NE11 . . . . 54 A4
Marcross Cl NE15 . . . . 36 B2
Marcross Dr SR3 . . . . 91 E5
Mardale NE37 . . . . 83 B7
Mardale Gdns NE9 . . . . 71 A3
Mardale Rd NE5 . . . . 37 B1
Mardale St DH5 . . . . 95 A2
MARDEN 32 B2
Marden Ave NE30 . . . . 32 C3
Marden Bridge Mid Sch
  NE25 . . . . 32 A4
Marden Cl NE8 . . . . 70 D7
Marden Cres NE26 . . . . 32 C4
Marden Ct NE26 . . . . 24 B7
Marden Farm Dr NE30 . . . . 32 B3
Marden Quarry 8 NE25 . . . . 32 A3
Marden Rd NE26 . . . . 32 B3
Marden Road S NE25 . . . . 32 B4
Marden Terr NE30 . . . . 32 C3
Mareburn Cres NE10 . . . . 71 E8
Maree Cl SR3 . . . . 91 E5
Margaret Alice St SR4 . . . . 85 E7
Margaret Collins Ho NE6 . . 56 D6
Margaret Cotts NE26 . . . . 31 F2
Margaret Dr NE12 . . . . 40 A8
Margaret Gr NE34 . . . . 59 A5
Margaret Rd NE26 . . . . 32 C4
Margaret St SR2 . . . . 87 A2
Margaret Sutton Sch
  NE34 . . . . 59 D6
Margaret Terr
  Penshaw DH4 . . . . 90 C6
  Rowlands Gill NE39 . . . . 67 C1
  Tanfield Lea DH9 . . . . 79 C1
Margate St SR3 . . . . 92 A8
Marguerite Ct SR4 . . . . 102 B3
Maria Cl NE15 . . . . 35 D1
Marian Ct NE34 . . . . 101 A1
Marian Dr NE10 . . . . 57 C3
Marian Way
  Ponteland NE20 . . . . 25 B2
  South Shields NE34 . . . . 59 F3
Marie Curie Dr NE4 . . . . 54 F4
Marigold Ave NE10 . . . . 56 B2
Marigold Cres DH4 . . . . 89 E3
Marigold Ct SR4 . . . . 102 B3
Marigold Wlk NE34 . . . . 59 B5
Marina App NE33 . . . . 42 E2
Marina Ave SR6 . . . . 75 D3
Marina Ct SR6 . . . . 75 D3
Marina Dr
  South Shields NE33 . . . . 42 E3
  Whitley Bay NE25 . . . . 31 C4
Marina Gr SR6 . . . . 75 D3
Marina Terr
  8 Ryhope SR2 . . . . 92 F6
  Whitburn SR6 . . . . 60 F1
Marina View
  Hebburn NE31 . . . . 57 D6
  Wallsend NE28 . . . . 40 F2
Marine App NE33 . . . . 42 E2
Marine Ave 2 NE26 . . . . 31 F5
Marine Court E NE26 . . . . 32 A6
Marine Court W NE26 . . . . 32 A6
Marine Dr
  Jarrow NE31 . . . . 58 A3
  2 Ryhope SR2 . . . . 93 A8
Marine Gdns NE26 . . . . 32 A6
Marine Park Fst Sch
  NE26 . . . . 32 A6
Marine Park Prim Sch
  NE33 . . . . 42 D3
Mariners' Cotts NE33 . . . . 42 E3
Mariners' La NE30 . . . . 42 C7
Mariners Point 8 NE30 . . . . 42 D7
Mariner Sq NE1 . . . . 103 C4
Mariners Wharf NE1 . . . . 45 A5
Marine Terr NE24 . . . . 17 E7
Marine View NE26 . . . . 24 C7
Marine Wlk SR6 . . . . 75 F2
Marion St SR2 . . . . 86 E4
Maritime Pl 4 NE61 . . . . 3 F1
Maritime St SR1 . . . . 103 A2
Maritime Terr SR1 . . . . 102 C2

Marius Ave NE15 . . . . 34 F2
Mariville E SR2 . . . . 93 A5
Mariville W SR2 . . . . 93 A5
Marjorie St NE23 . . . . 22 F5
Markby Cl 8 SR3 . . . . 91 E5
Market Cres DH4 . . . . 90 C6
Market La
  Dunston NE11, NE16 . . . . 69 D8
  Newcastle upon Tyne NE1 . . 99 B1
Market Pl
  Bedlington NE22 . . . . 15 F8
  Blyth NE24 . . . . 17 E8
  Corbridge NE45 . . . . 46 F5
  2 Hexham NE46 . . . . 45 B5
  Houghton-le-Spring DH5 . . 94 F8
  4 Morpeth NE61 . . . . 8 F8
  South Shields NE33 . . . . 42 C3
Market Place Ind Est DH5 90 F1
Market Sq
  Jarrow NE32 . . . . 58 B7
  Lynemouth NE61 . . . . 2 B2
  Sunderland SR1 . . . . 103 A2
Market St
  Blyth NE24 . . . . 17 E8
  Dudley NE23 . . . . 29 A8
  Hetton-le-Hole DH5 . . . . 95 B4
  Hexham NE46 . . . . 45 B5
  Newcastle upon Tyne NE1 . . 99 B1
Market Street E NE1 . . . . 99 B1
Market Walk 5 NE32 . . . . 58 B7
Market Way NE11 . . . . 70 D6
Markham Ave SR6 . . . . 61 A1
Markham St SR2 . . . . 87 A2
Markington Dr SR2 . . . . 92 F5
Markle Gr DH5 . . . . 94 D5
Mark Rise DH5 . . . . 95 A5
Mark's La DH4 . . . . 94 A3
Marlboro Ave NE15 . . . . 34 F5
Marlborough App NE3 . . . . 38 C7
Marlborough Ave NE3 . . . . 38 C7
Marlborough Cres
  Gateshead NE11 . . . . 71 C3
  Newcastle upon Tyne NE1 . . 100 C4
Marlborough Ct
  Houghton-le-Spring DH5 . . 94 E6
  Jarrow NE32 . . . . 58 B5
  Newcastle upon Tyne NE3 . . 38 A3
Marlborough House NE26 . 31 F6
Marlborough Rd
  Sunderland SR4 . . . . 85 A3
  Washington NE37 . . . . 83 F8
Marlborough Street N
  NE33 . . . . 59 D8
Marlborough Street S
  NE33 . . . . 59 D8
Marlborough Terr NE62 . . 10 F4
Marleen Ave NE6 . . . . 56 C8
Marleen Ct 2 NE6 . . . . 56 C8
Marlesford Cl SR3 . . . . 91 D6
Marley Cres SR5 . . . . 74 F3
MARLEY HILL 80 A8
Marley Hill Prim Sch
  NE16 . . . . 80 A8
MARLEY POTS 74 F3
Marlfield Ct NE5 . . . . 37 B3
Marlow Dr SR3 . . . . 91 D5
Marlowe Gdns NE8 . . . . 101 C1
Marlowe Pl DH5 . . . . 94 F7
Marlow Pl NE12 . . . . 39 C6
Marlow St NE24 . . . . 17 D7
Marlow Way NE16 . . . . 68 F5
Marmion Rd NE6 . . . . 57 A4
Marmion Terr NE25 . . . . 31 E4
Marne St DH4 . . . . 90 C6
Marondale Ave NE6 . . . . 56 F7
Marquis Ave NE5 . . . . 36 C5
Marquis Cl NE12 . . . . 39 C5
Marquis Ct
  Gateshead NE11 . . . . 70 C3
  4 New Silksworth SR3 . . 92 B7
  Prudhoe NE42 . . . . 50 E3
Marquisway NE11 . . . . 70 D2
Marr Ho SR4 . . . . 85 F7
Marris Ho NE2 . . . . 98 C3
Marr Rd NE31 . . . . 57 F5
MARSDEN 60 C5
Marsden Ave SR6 . . . . 60 F1
Marsden Cl DH4 . . . . 94 C8
Marsden Gr
  Gateshead NE9 . . . . 71 D3
  Whitburn SR6 . . . . 60 C6
Marsden La
  Newcastle upon Tyne NE5 . . 37 A3
  South Shields NE34 . . . . 60 C5
Marsden Old Quarry Nature
  Reserve* NE34 . . . . 60 C5
Marsden Prim Sch SR6 . . 60 F3
Marsden Rd
  Cleadon SR6 . . . . 74 F8
  South Shields NE34 . . . . 60 A7
Marsden View SR6 . . . . 60 A7
Marsden Way SR7 . . . . 93 C1
Marshall Cl NE63 . . . . 5 D7
Marshall St SR6 . . . . 75 D4
Marshall Wallis Rd NE33 . 59 C8
Marsham Cl
  Gateshead SR6 . . . . 60 A2
  Newcastle upon Tyne NE15 . 53 E2
Marsham Rd 8 NE5 . . . . 36 E3
Marsh Ct NE11 . . . . 70 B3
Marshes' Houses NE62 . . 11 D7
Marshmont Ave NE30 . . . . 32 C1
Marske Terr NE6 . . . . 56 F5
Marston NE12 . . . . 28 A1
Marston Wlk 1 NE16 . . . . 68 F5
Martello Gdns NE9 . . . . 79 B2
Martha St DH9 . . . . 79 D2

Martin Ct NE38 . . . . .82 F2
Martindale Ave SR6 . . . . . .75 C5
Martindale Pk DH5 . . . . . . .94 E8
Martindale Pl NE25 . . . . . .23 E3
Martindale Wlk NE12 . . . . .29 C3
Martin Hall NE32 . . . . .58 C6
Martin Rd NE28. . . . . .41 A2
Martin Terr **7** SR4 . . . . . . .85 F7
Martin Way NE13 . . . . .28 A6
Marwell Dr NE37. . . . . .72 E2
Marwood Ct NE25. . . . . . . .31 D6
Marx Terr NE17 . . . . .77 C8
Mary Agnes St NE3 . . . . . .38 A5
Mary Ave DH3 . . . . .82 B6
Maryhill Cl NE4 . . . . .54 E4
Mary Magdalene Bglws
  NE2 . . . . .98 A4
Maryside Pl NE40 . . . . .51 F7
Mary's Pl NE6. . . . . .57 B6
Mary St
  Blaydon NE21 . . . . .53 C3
  Blaydon, Winlaton NE21 . .53 A2
  New Silksworth SR3 . . . . .92 A8
  Sunderland SR1 . . . . .102 C2
Mary Terr NE5 . . . . .37 A3
Mascot Ho **3** NE1 . . . . . . .98 C1
Masefield Ave NE16. . . . . .54 B1
Masefield Dr NE34 . . . . . . .59 A2
Masefield Pl NE8 . . . . .101 C2
Mason Ave NE26. . . . . .32 B5
Mason Rd NE28. . . . . .40 A4
Mason St
  Brunswick Village NE13. . .28 A6
  4 Newcastle upon Tyne
    NE6. . . . . .56 C5
Mason View NE13 . . . . .28 B8
Massingham Way NE34. . .59 B5
Master Mariners' Homes
  NE30 . . . . .42 C7
Master's Cres NF47 . . . . . .59 B2
Mast La NE30. . . . . .32 B3
Matamba Terr NE4 . . . . . .102 B2
Matanzas St SR2. . . . . .86 E3
Matfen Ave
  Hazlerigg NE13 . . . . .28 A4
  Shiremoor NE27 . . . . .31 A2
Matfen Cl
  Blyth NE24. . . . . .17 C2
Matfen Ct DH2. . . . . .88 A3
Matfen Dr SR3 . . . . .91 D6
Matfen Gdns NE28 . . . . . . .40 F5
Matfen Pl
  Newcastle upon Tyne, Fawdon
    NE3 . . . . .38 A6
  Newcastle upon Tyne, Fenham
    NE4. . . . . .54 F7
Matfen Terr NE6 . . . . .7 D3
Mather Rd NE4 . . . . .100 B4
Mathesons Gdns NE61 . . . . .8 F8
Matlock Ave NE3 . . . . .37 D3
Matlock Gdns NE5 . . . . . . .36 F3
Matlock Rd NE32 . . . . .58 C6
Matlock Sq NE61 . . . . .2 A2
Matlock St SR1 . . . . .103 A3
Matthew Bank NE2 . . . . . .38 E3
Matthew Cl NE6 . . . . .56 B6
Matthew Rd NE24. . . . . . . .17 F5
Matthew St **15** NE6 . . . . .56 B6
Maude Gdns **7** NE28 . . . .40 B1
Maudlin Pl **2** NE5. . . . . . .37 D1
Maudlin St DH5. . . . . .95 B6
Mauds La SR1 . . . . .103 B3
Maud St
  Newcastle upon Tyne
    NE15. . . . . .53 C6
  Sunderland SR6. . . . . .75 E4
Maud Terr NE64. . . . . .7 E5
Maud Terr
  5 Shiremoor NE27. . . . . .30 E1
  Tanfield DH9 . . . . .79 D3
Maughan St NE24. . . . . . . .17 F7
Maurice Rd NE3 . . . . .58 B8
Maurice Road Ind Est
  NE28 . . . . .57 B8
Mautland St DH4 . . . . .90 E1
Maxton Cl SR3. . . . . .91 D5
Maxwell NE33 . . . . .42 C2
Maxwell St Ind Est **6**
  NE33 . . . . .42 C2
Maxwell St
  Gateshead NE8 . . . . .70 D7
  South Shields NE33 . . . . . .42 C2
  2 Sunderland SR4 . . . . .85 F7
May Ave
  Ryton NE40 . . . . .52 C6
  Winlaton NE40 . . . . .68 C7
Maybury Villas NE12 . . . . .39 A5
May Courtyard NE8 . . . . .100 B1
Maydown Cl SR5. . . . . .84 F8
Mayfair Ct NE31 . . . . .57 D5
Mayfair Gdns
  Gateshead NE8 . . . . .71 A8
  Ponteland NE20 . . . . .25 F6
  South Shields NE34 . . . . . .59 E7
Mayfair Rd NE2. . . . . .38 D2
MAYFIELD 22 C6
Mayfield
  Morpeth NE61 . . . . .8 E7
  Whickham NE16. . . . . .69 A5
Mayfield Ave
  Cramlington NE23 . . . . . . .22 C6
  Throckley NE15 . . . . .35 E1
Mayfield Ct SR6 . . . . .75 C3
Mayfield Dr SR6 . . . . .75 B8
Mayfield Gdns
  Jarrow NE32 . . . . .58 A6
  Throckley NE15 . . . . .35 E1

Mayfield Gdns continued
  Wallsend NE28 . . . . .40 A3
Mayfield Gr SR4 . . . . .85 A2
Mayfield Pl NE13 . . . . .28 A5
Mayfield Rd
  Newcastle upon Tyne NE3 . .38 C4
  Sunderland SR4 . . . . .85 A6
Mayfield Terr NE5. . . . . . . .37 E1
May Gr SR6 . . . . .60 F3
Mayo Dr **1** SR3 . . . . .91 E5
Mayoral Way NE11 . . . . . . .70 D3
Maypole Cl **8** SR5. . . . . . .75 B2
May St
  Birtley NE21 . . . . .82 C4
  Blaydon NE21 . . . . .53 B1
  South Shields NE33 . . . . . .42 D1
  Sunderland SR4 . . . . .102 B3
Mayswood Rd SR6 . . . . . . .75 D3
Maytree House NE4. . . . . .100 A4
Maywood Cl NE3 . . . . .37 E4
Mazine Terr DH6. . . . . .97 E2
Meacham Way NE16 . . . . .69 A5
Mead Ave NE12 . . . . .39 E8
Mead Cres NE12 . . . . .39 F8
Meadowbank NE23. . . . . . .99 A4
Meadow Bank Dr NE62. . .10 E6
Meadowbrook Dr NE10. . .72 C7
Meadow Brook Dr NE17. .66 C2
Meadow Cl
  Blaydon NE21 . . . . .52 F1
  Dunston NE11. . . . . .54 E1
  Houghton-le-Spring DH5 . .94 F7
  Longbenton NE12. . . . . . . .39 F7
  Ryton NE40 . . . . .52 D5
  Seghill NE23 . . . . .22 F2
Meadowcroft Mews NE8 101 A1
Meadow Ct
  Bedlington NE22 . . . . .10 E1
  Ponteland NE20 . . . . .25 E5
Meadowdale Cres
  Bedlington NE22 . . . . .10 D1
  Newcastle upon Tyne NE5 .37 D3
Meadowdale Mid Sch
  NE22 . . . . .10 E1
Meadow Dr
  Seaton Burn NE13. . . . . . .28 C8
  Sunderland, East Herrington
    SR3. . . . . .91 B6
  Sunderland, South Hylton
    SR4. . . . . .85 A5
Meadowfield
  Ashington NE63. . . . . .7 A2
  Ponteland NE20 . . . . .25 E7
  Whitley Bay NE25 . . . . . . .31 D5
Meadowfield Ave NE3 . . . .38 A6
Meadowfield Cres NE40 . .52 A2
Meadowfield Ct NE20 . . . .25 E7
Meadowfield Dr SR6. . . . . .60 B1
Meadowfield Est NE9 . . . .71 F1
Meadowfield Gdns NE10 . .72 A6
Meadowfield Ind Est
  NE20 . . . . .25 E6
Meadowfield Park S NE43 64 C5
Meadowfield Pk NE20 . . . .25 E7
Meadowfield Rd
  Newcastle upon Tyne NE3 . .38 B4
  Stocksfield NE43 . . . . .64 C5
Meadowfield Terr
  Longbenton NE12. . . . . . . .29 F1
  Stocksfield NE43 . . . . .64 D7
Meadow Gdns SR3 . . . . . . .86 B3
Meadow Gr SR4 . . . . .85 B5
Meadow Grange DH4 . . . . .89 E2
Meadow Ho SR3 . . . . .92 A5
Meadow La
  Cravcrook NE40 . . . . .52 A4
  Dunston NE11 . . . . .54 F1
  Sunderland SR3 . . . . .91 B6
Meadow Laws NE34. . . . . .60 A4
Meadow Pk NE44 . . . . .62 F7
Meadow Rd
  Newcastle upon Tyne
    NE15. . . . . .53 D8
  Seaton Sluice NE26 . . . . . .24 B6
  Wallsend NE28 . . . . .40 F1
  Whitley Bay NE25 . . . . . . .31 D4
Meadow Rise
  Gateshead NE9 . . . . .71 C1
  Newcastle upon Tyne NE5 . .37 B4
Meadows Crest NE43. . . . .65 A3
Meadowside SR2 . . . . .86 B4
Meadows La DH4, DH5. . . .94 B3
Meadow St DH5 . . . . .94 C3
Meadows The
  Bournmoor DH4. . . . . .89 D3
  Burnopfield NE16. . . . . . . .79 A4
  New Hartley NE25 . . . . . . .23 D6
  Ryton NE40 . . . . .52 D5
  Seaham Grange SR7 . . . . .92 D1
  West Rainton NE9 . . . . . . .94 A3
Meadowsweet Cl **3** NE24.17 C4
Meadow Terr DH4 . . . . .90 C6
Meadowvale
  Backworth NE27 . . . . .30 D3
  Ponteland NE20 . . . . .25 A2
  Shiremoor NE27 . . . . .30 D3
Meadow Vale SR2. . . . . . . .86 C4
Meadow View
  Chopwell NE17 . . . . .66 C2
  Dipton DH9 . . . . .78 E1
  Hedworth NE32 . . . . .73 D8
  New Hartley NE25 . . . . . . .23 D6
  North Shields NE29 . . . . . .41 E4
  Sunderland SR3 . . . . .91 B5
Meadow Well Ind NE11 . . .41 E4
Meadow Well Way **2**
  NE29 . . . . .41 E4
Meadow Wlk NE40 . . . . . . .52 D5

Mead Way NE12 . . . . .39 F8
Meadway Dr NE12 . . . . . . .39 F8
Mead Wlk NE6. . . . . .56 F6
Means Ct NE23 . . . . .29 B5
Means St NE23 . . . . .29 B5
Medburn Ave NE30. . . . . . .32 C2
Medburn Rd
  Newcastle upon Tyne
    NE15. . . . . .53 C7
  Seaton Delaval NE25 . . . . .23 E2
Medina Cl SR3. . . . . .91 D6
Medlar NE9. . . . . .71 D4
Medlar Cl DH4. . . . . .89 F6
MEDOMSLEY 77 C1
Medomsley Gdns NE9 . . . .71 E4
Medomsley St
  Sunderland SR4 . . . . .102 A3
  Sunderland SR4 . . . . .102 A3
Medway NE32 . . . . .58 C2
Medway Ave NE31 . . . . . . .57 E3
Medway Cl DH4 . . . . .94 A7
Medway Cres NE8 . . . . . . .71 B8
Medway Gdns
  Sunderland SR4. . . . . .85 D4
  Tynemouth NE30. . . . . . . .42 A7
Medway Pl NE23 . . . . .16 D1
Medwood Ct NE3 . . . . .37 E5
Medwyn Cl
  Blyth NE24. . . . . .17 D5
  Bournmoor DH4. . . . . .89 E3
Megstone Ave SR3 . . . . . . .22 A5
Megstone Ct NE12 . . . . . . .29 E4
Melbeck Dr DH2. . . . . .82 E1
Melbourne Cres NE25 . . . .31 E3
Melbourne Ct
  Gateshead NE8 . . . . .101 B3
  Newcastle upon Tyne NE1. .99 C1
Melbourne Gdns NE34 . . .58 F3
Melbourne Pl SR4 . . . . . . .85 E4
Melbourne St
  Melbury NE25. . . . . .71 D6
Melbury Cl SR6. . . . . .75 D3
Melbury Rd NE7 . . . . .39 A1
Meldon Ave
  Newcastle upon Tyne NE3 . .37 F7
  Sherburn DH6 . . . . .96 A1
  South Shields NE34 . . . . . .59 E6
Meldon Cl NE28 . . . . .40 E3
Meldon Ct NE40 . . . . .51 E3
Meldon Gdns
  Dunston NE11 . . . . .70 A5
  Stakeford NE62 . . . . .10 F8
Meldon Ho NE7 . . . . .17 B8
Meldon Rd SR4 . . . . .85 A3
Meldon St NE28 . . . . .41 C1
Meldon Terr
  Greenside NE40. . . . . .51 F1
  Newcastle-by-the-Sea NE64.7 D3
  Newcastle upon Tyne NE6 . .56 B8
Meldon Way NE21 . . . . . . .67 F8
Melford Pl NE20 . . . . .31 D1
Melgarve Dr SR3 . . . . .91 E5
Melkington Ct NE5 . . . . . . .37 B3
Melkridge Gdns NE7 . . . . .39 D3
Melkridge Pl NE23 . . . . . . .22 A5
Mellendean Ct NE5 . . . . . .37 A3
Melling Rd NE23 . . . . .22 A6
Melmerby Cl NE3 . . . . .38 D7
Melness Rd NE13 . . . . .28 A5
Melock Ct NE13 . . . . .28 A5
Melrose NE38. . . . . .83 D3
Melrose Ave
  Backworth NE27 . . . . .30 C5
  Bebside NE22 . . . . .11 D1
  Gateshead NE9 . . . . .71 A1
  Hebburn NE31 . . . . .57 E3
  Seaton Delaval NE25. . . . .23 D2
  Tynemouth NE30 . . . . .32 A2
  Whitley Bay NE25 . . . . . . .31 F4
Melrose Cl
  Newcastle upon Tyne, Bell's
    Close NE15. . . . . .53 E6
  Newcastle upon Tyne NE3 . .28 D2
Melrose Ct NE22. . . . . .11 D2
Melrose Gdns
  Newbottle DH4 . . . . .90 C3
  Sunderland SR6 . . . . .75 E3
  Wallsend NE28 . . . . .40 A4
Melrose Gr NE32. . . . . .58 C4
Melrose Terr
  Bedlington NE22 . . . . .11 D2
  Newcastle-by-the-Sea NE64.7 D3
Melrose Villas NE22 . . . . . .11 D2
Melsonby Cl SR3. . . . . .91 D6
Meltham Ct NE15 . . . . .36 B2
Meltham Dr SR3 . . . . .91 E5
Melton Ave NE6 . . . . .56 F5
Melton Cres NE26. . . . . . . .24 D5
Melton Dr NE25 . . . . .23 D6
MELTON PARK 28 C1
Melvaig Cl SR3 . . . . .91 E5
Melville Ave NE24 . . . . . . .17 D5
Melville Gdns NE25 . . . . . .31 C4
Melville Gr NE7. . . . . .39 A4
Melville St DH3 . . . . .88 C3
Melvin Pl **5** NE5 . . . . . . .37 B2
Melvyn Gdns SR6 . . . . .75 E3
Membury Cl **4** SR3 . . . . .91 E5
Memorial Sq NE64 . . . . .7 D5
Menai Ct **3** SR3 . . . . .91 D6
Menceforth Cotts DH2 . . . .88 B4
Mendham Cl NE10 . . . . . . .71 E6
Mendip Ave DH2. . . . . .88 C2
Mendip Cl
  Ashington NE63. . . . . .6 E1
  Tynemouth NE29 . . . . .31 F1
Mendip Dr NE38 . . . . .83 B3
Mendip Gdns NE11. . . . . . .70 B6

Mendip Way NE12 . . . . . . .38 F6
Mentieth Ct NE38 . . . . .83 B3
Menvill Pl SR1. . . . . .103 B2
Mercantile Rd DH4 . . . . . . .94 C7
Merchant Ct NE31 . . . . . . .57 F1
Merchants Wharf NE6 . . . .56 C4
Mercia Way NE15 . . . . .53 E5
Meredith Gdns NE8 . . . . . .101 C1
Mere Knolls Rd SR6. . . . . .75 E4
Meresyde NE10 . . . . .72 A7
Meresyde Ct NE10 . . . . . . .72 A7
Merevale Cl NE37 . . . . .72 E2
Merganser Lodge **9**
  NE10 . . . . .71 D8
Meridian Way NE7. . . . . . . .39 D3
Meridian Ho **3** NE33. . . .59 E8
Merlay Dr NE13 . . . . .27 B6
Merlay Hall NE6 . . . . .57 A4
Merle Gdns
  15 Newcastle upon Tyne
    NE6. . . . . .56 C5
Merle Terr SR4 . . . . .85 F7
Merley Gate NE61. . . . . .9 A6
Merlin Cres NE28 . . . . .40 F3
Merlin Ct NE10 . . . . .56 D1
Merlin Dr DH3. . . . . .88 D7
Merlin Pl NE12 . . . . .39 A7
Merlin Way
  Earsdon NE27 . . . . .31 A1
  Shiremoor NE27 . . . . .41 A8
Merrick Ho **3** SR3. . . . . . .91 F6
Merrington Cl
  New Hartley NE25 . . . . . . .23 D7
  Silksworth SR3 . . . . .91 D6
Merrion Cl SR3 . . . . .91 D6
Merryfield Gdns SR6 . . . . .75 E3
Merryshields Terr NE43 . .64 C8
Merryweather Rise **6**
  SR3. . . . . .92 B7
Mersey Ct **1** SR3 . . . . . . .91 F6
Mersey Pl NE8 . . . . .71 B8
Mersey Rd
  Gateshead NE8 . . . . .71 B8
  Hebburn NE31 . . . . .57 F3
Mersey St NE17. . . . . .66 C1
Merton Ct NE4. . . . . .54 D4
Merton Rd NE20 . . . . .25 E6
Merton Sq NE64 . . . . .7 E8
Merton Way NE20 . . . . . . .25 E6
Methuen St NE9 . . . . .71 A8
Methven Way NE23 . . . . . .16 C2
Metrocentre East Bus Pk
  NE11 . . . . .54 D2
MetroCentre The NE11 . . .54 D2
Metro Ctr Sta NE11 . . . . . .54 D2
Metroradio NE1. . . . . .99 B1
Metro Radio Arena*
  NE4 . . . . .100 C3
Metro Ret Pk NE11. . . . . . .54 C3
Metro Riverside Bus Pk
  NE11 . . . . .54 C3
Mews Ct DH5. . . . . .94 E8
Mews Gdns NE1 . . . . .99 B1
Mews The
  Blaydon NE21 . . . . .53 E2
  Fence Houses DH4 . . . . . . .94 A7
  Gateshead NE12 . . . . .58 D7
  Newcastle upon Tyne NE1. .99 A1
  North Shields NE30 . . . . . .42 A6
  Sunderland SR3 . . . . .91 B7
  Tynemouth NE30 . . . . .42 C8
Michaelgate **24** NE6 . . .56 C6
Mickle Cl NE37 . . . . .83 A6
Mickleton Gdns SR3 . . . . .86 B2
Micklewood Cl NE61. . . . . .4 E6
Mickley Fst Sch NE43 . . . .49 E1
MICKLEY SQUARE 49 E1
Middlebrook NE20 . . . . . . .25 D4
Middle Chare DH3 . . . . . . .88 D3
Middle Cl NE38 . . . . .83 B1
Middle Dr
  Ponteland NE20. . . . . .25 C3
  Woolsington NE13. . . . . . .26 F1
Middle Engine La
  Shiremoor NE27, NE28,
    NE29. . . . . .41 A7
  Wallsend NE27, NE28, NE29 .40 F5
Middle Farm Ct NE23 . . . .22 B7
Middlefields Ind Est NE33 59 B8
Middle Garth **1** NE5 . . . .37 D2
Middle Gate
  Morpeth NE61 . . . . .8 F6
  Newcastle upon Tyne NE5. .36 F1
Middle Gn NE25 . . . . .31 C4
Middleham Cl DH2. . . . . . .81 E1
Middleham Ct SR5. . . . . . . .74 A3
MIDDLE HERRINGTON. . .91 B8
MIDDLE RAINTON 94 F7
Middle Row
  Gateshead NE10 . . . . .89 E1
  Ryton NE40 . . . . .52 E3
Middle St
  Blyth NE24. . . . . .17 B4
  Corbridge NE45 . . . . .46 F5
  Newcastle upon Tyne NE6. .56 F6
  Sunderland SR1. . . . . .102 C3
  Sunderland SR3 . . . . .103 A3
  Tynemouth NE30 . . . . .42 C7
Middle Street E NE6 . . . . . .56 F5
Middleton Ave
  Newcastle upon Tyne NE4 . .54 E6
  Rowlands Gill NE39 . . . . . .78 A4
Middleton Cl SR7 . . . . .92 E1
Middleton Ct NE1 . . . . .99 C1
Middleton St NE24. . . . . . .17 F7
Middlewood Pk NE4 . . . . . .54 E7
Midfield Dr **11** SR6. . . . . .75 E2

Midgley Dr SR3. . . . . .91 E5
Midhurst Ave NE34. . . . . . .60 A8
Midhurst Cl SR3 . . . . .91 D6
Midhurst Rd NE12 . . . . . . .39 D7
Midlothian Cl SR4 . . . . . . .85 D3
Midmoor Rd SR4 . . . . .85 E7
Midsomer Cl SR3 . . . . .91 D5
Mid Summer Way NE8 . . .100 B2
Midway NE6 . . . . .57 A6
Milbanke Cl DH2. . . . . .81 F1
Milbanke St DH2. . . . . .81 F1
Milburn Cl
  Chester le Street DH3 . . . .88 C2
  Hexham NE46 . . . . .44 F2
Milburn Dr NE15. . . . . .54 B6
Milburn Rd NE63. . . . . .6 D2
Milburn Terr
  Shiney Row DH4 . . . . .90 B6
  Stakeford NE62 . . . . .11 C6
Milcombe Cl SR3 . . . . .91 D6
Milcombe Cl SR3 . . . . .91 D6
Mildred St DH5. . . . . .90 E1
Milecastle Ct NE5 . . . . .36 D2
Milecastle Prim Sch NE5 .36 C2
Mile End Rd NE33 . . . . . . .42 C4
Milfield Ave
  Shiremoor NE27 . . . . .31 A3
  Wallsend NE28 . . . . .40 C4
Milford Gdns NE3 . . . . .28 B1
Milford Rd NE15 . . . . .54 C5
Military Rd
  Heddon-on-the-Wall NE15. .34 C3
  North Shields NE30 . . . . . .42 B6
Milkhope Ctr NE13. . . . . . .20 D5
Milk Market NE1. . . . . .99 C1
Milk Mkt NE1 . . . . .99 C1
Milkwell NE45 . . . . .47 A6
Milkwell La NE45 . . . . .47 A7
Millais Gdns NE34 . . . . .9 C2
Mill Bank SR5 . . . . .75 C4
Millbank Cres NE22 . . . . . .11 A1
Millbank Ind Est **3** NE33.42 C2
Millbank Rd
  Bedlington NE22 . . . . .11 B1
  Newcastle upon Tyne NE6. .57 A4
Millbank Terr NE21 . . . . . . .1 B2
Millbeck Gdns NE9 . . . . . . .71 B2
Millbeck Gr DH5. . . . . .94 D6
Millbrook
  Gateshead NE10 . . . . .71 E7
  North Shields NE29 . . . . . .41 E5
Millbrook Rd NE23 . . . . . . .16 D1
Millburn St SR4 . . . . .102 B3
Mill Cl
  North Shields NE29 . . . . . .41 E5
  Riding Mill NE44 . . . . .62 F7
Mill Cres
  Hebburn NE31 . . . . .57 C2
  Penshaw DH4 . . . . .90 B6
Millcroft Ct **4** NE24 . . . .17 F6
Mill Ct
  Bournmoor DH4. . . . . .89 E2
  Ellington NE61 . . . . .1 C4
  Hamsterley NE17 . . . . .77 B6
Milldale Ave NE24 . . . . . . .17 A7
Mill Dam NE33. . . . . .42 B2
Milldene Ave NE30 . . . . . . .42 C8
Mill Dene View NE32 . . . . .58 C5
Mill Dyke Cl NE25. . . . . . . .31 C6
Millennium Ct NE40 . . . . . .51 F1
Millennium Way SR5 . . . .102 C4
Millers Hill DH4 . . . . .90 C6
Miller's La NE16 . . . . .54 B1
Millers Rd NE6 . . . . .56 C7
Miller Terr SR3 . . . . .92 A8
Mill Farm NE61 . . . . .1 C4
Mill Farm Cl NE4 . . . . .98 B1
Mill Farm Rd NE39. . . . . . .78 A5
MILLFIELD 102 A3
Millfield
  Bedlington NE22 . . . . .16 A7
  Seaton Sluice NE26 . . . . . .24 D5
  Whickham NE16 . . . . .69 C7
Millfield Ct
  Chester le Street DH2. . . . .88 A1
  Newburn NE15 . . . . .52 F7
Millfield E
  Hexham NE46 . . . . .44 F5
  Seaton Sluice NE26 . . . . . .24 D5
  3 Whickham NE16 . . . . .69 C7
Millfield E NE12 . . . . .16 A7
Millfield Gdns
  Blyth NE22 . . . . .12 D1
  Gateshead NE10 . . . . .71 C8
  Tynemouth NE30 . . . . .42 C8
Millfield Gr NE30 . . . . .42 C8
Millfield La NE15 . . . . .52 F8
Millfield N NE22 . . . . .16 A8
Millfield Rd
  Riding Mill NE44 . . . . .62 F7
  Whickham NE16 . . . . .69 B6
Millfield S NE22 . . . . .16 A7
Millfield St SR4 . . . . .102 B3
Millfield Terr
  Hexham NE46 . . . . .44 F5
  Whitburn SR6. . . . . .60 F2
Millfield W NE22 . . . . .16 A8
Millford Cl NE10 . . . . .72 B6
Millford Ct NE10 . . . . .72 B6
Mill Gr
  South Shields NE34 . . . . . .60 B4

Mill Gr continued
Tynemouth NE30 . . . . .42 C8
Mill Grange NE44 . . . . .63 A8
Millgrove View NE3 . . . . . . .37 F3
MILL HILL 92 B6
Mill Hill DH5 . . . . .94 D6
Mill Hill Prim Sch 16 SR3 .92 A5
Mill Hill Rd
Newcastle upon Tyne NE5 . . .53 F8
Silksworth SR3 . . . . .92 A6
Mill Ho NE2 . . . . .98 B4
Milling Ct NE8 . . . . .100 C2
Mill La
Ebchester DH8 . . . . .76 E4
Hebburn NE10, NE31 . . . . . .57 E2
Heddon-on-the-Wall NE15 . . .34 F3
Newcastle upon Tyne NE4 . .100 A4
North Shields NE29 . . . . . . .42 B4
Seghill NE23 . . . . .22 D1
Sherburn DH6 . . . . .96 A1
Slaley NE44 . . . . .62 A1
Urpeth DH2 . . . . .81 D1
Whitburn SR6 . . . . .60 F2
Winlaton Mill NE21 . . . . .68 B7
Mill Lane Ind est NE4 . . . . .98 A1
Millne Ct NE22 . . . . .10 F1
Millom Pl NF9 . . . . .71 B4
Mill Pit DH4 . . . . .90 B6
Mill Race CI NE17 . . . . .77 B6
Mill Rd
Chopwell NE17 . . . . .77 B8
Gateshead NE8 . . . . .101 C4
Mill Rise NE3 . . . . .38 E4
Mills Gdns NE28 . . . . .40 B3
Millside 7 NE61 . . . . .8 F8
Mill St SR4 . . . . .102 B3
Mill Terr
Houghton-le-Spring DH5 . . . .94 D6
Shiney Row DH4 . . . . .90 B6
Millthorp CI SR2 . . . . .87 A1
Mill Vale NE15 . . . . .52 F8
Mill View
Gateshead NE10 . . . . .71 C7
West Boldon NE36 . . . . .74 A7
Mill View Ave SR6 . . . . .75 D3
Millview Dr NE30 . . . . .42 C8
Mill View Rise NE42 . . . . . . .50 D4
Millway
Gateshead NE8 . . . . .71 A7
Seaton Sluice NE26 . . . . . . .24 D5
Mill Way NE15, NE42 . . . . . .50 D7
Millway Gr NE26 . . . . .24 D5
Milner Cres NE21 . . . . .53 A1
Milner St NE33 . . . . .42 E2
Milne Way NE3 . . . . .37 F6
Milrig CI SR3 . . . . .91 E5
Milsted CI SR3 . . . . .91 D5
Milsted Ct NE15 . . . . .36 B2
Milton Ave
Hebburn NE31 . . . . .57 E6
Houghton-le-Spring DH5 . . . .94 F7
Milton CI NE2 . . . . .99 C3
Milton Gn NE2 . . . . .99 C3
Milton PI
Newcastle upon Tyne NE2 . . .99 C3
North Shields NE29 . . . . . . .41 F6
22 Springwell NE9 . . . . .71 F1
Milton Rd NE16 . . . . .69 B8
Milton Sq NE8 . . . . .56 A2
Milton St
Jarrow NE32 . . . . .58 B8
1 South Shields NE33 . . . . . .59 D8
Sunderland SR4 . . . . .102 A3
Milton Terr NE29 . . . . .41 F6
Milvain Ave NE4 . . . . .54 E6
Milvain CI NE8 . . . . .101 C1
Milvain St NE8 . . . . .101 C1
Milverton Ct NE3 . . . . .37 C6
Mimosa Dr NE31 . . . . .57 E3
Mimosa Pl NE4 . . . . .54 D8
Minden St NE1 . . . . .99 B1
Mindrum Terr
Newcastle upon Tyne NE6 . . .56 F5
North Shields NE29 . . . . . . .41 D4
Mindrum Way NE25 . . . . . . .23 D3
Minehead Gdns 9 SR3 . . . .92 A8
Miners Cotts NE15 . . . . .54 A7
Miner's Cotts NE16 . . . . . . .69 C6
Minerva CI NE5 . . . . .36 C4
Mingarry DH3 . . . . .82 E2
Mingary CI DH5 . . . . .94 C4
Minorca CI SR1 . . . . .103 C2
Minorca PI NE3 . . . . .37 F3
Minskip CI SR3 . . . . .91 E5
Minster Ct NE8 . . . . .101 C3
Minster Gr NE15 . . . . .36 B3
Minster Par NE32 . . . . .58 C7
Minting PI NE23 . . . . .22 A5
Minton Ct NE29 . . . . .41 F4
Minton La NE29 . . . . .41 F4
Minton Sq 4 SR4 . . . . .85 E7
Mirk La NE8 . . . . .101 B4
Mirlaw Rd NE23 . . . . .21 F5
Mistletoe Rd NE2 . . . . .38 E1
Mitcham Cres NE7 . . . . .39 B4
Mitchell Ave
Newcastle upon Tyne NE2 . . .38 E2
Whitley Bay NE25 . . . . .31 D4
Mitchell Dr NE63 . . . . .7 B3
Mitchell Gdns NE34 . . . . . . .59 F7
Mitchell's Bldgs NE34 . . . . .72 A1

Mitchell St
Birtley DH3 . . . . .82 C4
Crawcrook NE40 . . . . .51 E3
Newcastle upon Tyne NE6 . . .57 B5
Mitchell Terr DH9 . . . . .79 B2
MITFORD 8 A8
Mitford Ave
Blyth NE24 . . . . .17 C6
Pegswood NE61 . . . . .4 E4
Seaton Delaval NE25 . . . . . .23 C3
Mitford CI
Chester le Street DH3 . . . . . .88 D8
Washington NE38 . . . . .83 B4
Mitford Dr
Ashington NE63 . . . . .6 D2
Newcastle upon Tyne NE5 . . .36 E3
Sherburn DH6 . . . . .96 A2
Mitford Gdns
Dunston NE11 . . . . .70 A5
Stakeford NE62 . . . . .10 F8
Wallsend NE28 . . . . .40 F5
Wideopen NE13 . . . . .28 C6
Mitford PI NE3 . . . . .38 A6
Mitford Rd
Morpeth NE61 . . . . .3 E1
South Shields NE34 . . . . . . .59 E6
Mitford St
North Shields NE28 . . . . . . .41 C2
Sunderland SR5 . . . . .75 E4
Mitford Terr NE32 . . . . .58 B2
Mitford Way NE13 . . . . .27 B7
Mithras Gdns NE15 . . . . . . .34 E2
Mitre Ind Est NE33 . . . . . . .59 B7
Mitre PI NE33 . . . . .59 B7
Moat Gdns NE10 . . . . .72 C8
Modder St NE6 . . . . .56 F3
Model Dwellings 1 NE38 .83 E4
Model Terr DH4 . . . . .90 A8
Modigars La NE43 . . . . .64 F4
Moffat Ave NE32 . . . . .58 E4
Moffat CI NE29 . . . . .41 C8
Moine Gdns SR6 . . . . .75 E3
Moir Terr 15 SR2 . . . . .93 A6
Molesdon CI NE30 . . . . .32 A1
Molineux CI 8 NE6 . . . . .56 B6
Molineux Ct 3 NE6 . . . . .56 B6
Molineux St NE6 . . . . .56 B6
Mollyfair CI NE40 . . . . .52 A4
Monarch CI 6 NE12 . . . . . . .39 A6
Monarch Rd NE4 . . . . .100 A2
Monarch Terr NE21 . . . . .53 C2
Monarch Way SR3 . . . . .91 C5
Monastery Ct 11 NE32 . . . . .58 B7
Monday Cres NE4 . . . . .98 B2
Monday PI NE4 . . . . .98 B2
Monkchester Gn NE6 . . . . . .56 E5
Monkchester Rd NE6 . . . . . .56 E4
Monk Ct NE8 . . . . .101 C2
Monkdale Ave NE12 . . . . . . .17 A6
Monkhouse Ave NE3 . . . . . . .28 B2
Monkhouse Prim Sch
NE30 . . . . .32 B1
Monkridge
Newcastle upon Tyne
NE15 . . . . .36 B2
Whitley Bay NE26 . . . . .31 E7
Monkridge Gdns NE11 . . . . .70 A7
Monks Ave NE25 . . . . .31 D3
MONKSEATON 31 F5
Monkseaton Com High Sch
NE25 . . . . .31 E2
Monkseaton Dr NE25,
NE26 . . . . .31 E6
Monkseaton Mid Sch 1
NE25 . . . . .31 E4
Monkseaton Rd NE25 . . . . . .31 B5
Monkseaton Sta NE25 . . . . .31 F5
Monkseaton Terr NE63 . . . . . .6 E1
Monksfeld NE10 . . . . .71 E7
Monksfield CI 6 SR3 . . . . . .91 F5
Monkside
Cramlington NE23 . . . . .21 F5
Newcastle upon Tyne NE6 . . .56 D8
Monkside CI NE38 . . . . .83 A2
Monks Mdws NE46 . . . . .45 D4
Monkstone Ave NE30 . . . . . .42 C8
Monkstone CI NE30 . . . . . . .42 C8
Monkstone Cres NE30 . . . . . .32 C1
Monkstone Grange NE30 . .32 B1
Monksway NE32 . . . . .58 E6
Monks Way NE30 . . . . .32 C1
Monks Wood NE29 . . . . .41 F8
Monkswood Sq SR3 . . . . . . .92 B6
MONKTON 58 A4
Monkton Ave NE34 . . . . .59 A4
Monkton Bsns Park N
NE31 . . . . .57 F2
Monkton Bsns Park S
NE10 . . . . .57 F2
Monkton Hall NE32 . . . . .57 F4
Monkton Hall Hospl NE31 .57 F4
Monkton Inf Sch NE34 . . . . .59 A3
Monkton Jun Sch NE34 . . . .58 F4
Monkton La
Hebburn NE32 . . . . .57 F4
Jarrow NE31, NE32 . . . . . . .58 A4
Monkton Rd NE32 . . . . .58 B7
Monkton Stadium NE32 . . . .58 A4
Monkton Terr NE32 . . . . .58 C6

MONKWEARMOUTH 75 D1
Monkwearmouth Hospl
SR5 . . . . .75 C2
Monkwearmouth Sch Perf
Arts Coll SR6 . . . . .75 C5
Monkwearmouth Station
Mus* SR5 . . . . .103 A4
Monmouth Gdns NE28 . . . . .41 A4
Monroe PI NE5 . . . . .37 D2
Mons Ave NE31 . . . . .57 E6
Mons Cres DH4 . . . . .90 C6
Montagu Ct NE3 . . . . .38 A2
Montagu Ct NE3 . . . . .38 A2
Montague Ct NE9 . . . . .70 F8
Montague St
Newcastle upon Tyne
NE15 . . . . .53 D6
Sunderland SR6 . . . . .75 D3
Monterey
Silksworth SR3 . . . . .91 E5
Washington NE37 . . . . .72 D1
Montford CI SR3 . . . . .91 D5
Montgomerie Ct NE63 . . . . . .6 F4
Montpelier PI NE3 . . . . .37 F3
Montpellier Terr SR2 . . . . . . .86 E3
Montrose CI NE25 . . . . .23 D6
Montrose Cres NE9 . . . . . . .71 B7
Montrose Dr NE10 . . . . .72 C7
Montrose Gdns SR3 . . . . . . .86 A3
Monument Mall Sh Ctr
NE1 . . . . .99 A1
Monument Rd NE38 . . . . . . .84 B5
Monument Sta NE1 . . . . . . .99 A1
Monument Terr
11 Birtley DH3 . . . . .82 C4
Penshaw DH4 . . . . .90 A8
Monument View DH4 . . . . . .90 B8
Moonfield NE46 . . . . .45 B4
Moor CI
Sunderland SR1 . . . . .103 C3
Tynemouth NE30 . . . . .42 D8
Moor Cres NE3 . . . . .38 C3
Moor Crest Terr 2 NE29 . . .41 F8
Moor Croft NE61 . . . . .7 E5
Moorcroft CI NE15 . . . . .53 D7
Moorcroft Rd NE15 . . . . . . .53 E6
Moor Ct
Bournmoor DH4 . . . . .89 E3
Newcastle upon Tyne NE3 . . .38 B2
Whitburn SR6 . . . . .75 E8
Moordale Ave NE24 . . . . . . .17 A6
Moore Ave
Dunston NE11 . . . . .69 F8
South Shields NE34 . . . . . . .59 F6
Moore Cres DH3 . . . . .82 C6
Moore Crescent N DH5 . . . .94 E7
Moore Crescent S DH5 . . . .94 E7
Moore Ct NE15 . . . . .52 B7
Moor Edge Prim Sch
NE12 . . . . .29 C3
Moor Edge Rd NE27 . . . . . . .30 E4
Moore St NE8 . . . . .56 A1
MOOR FARM ESTATE 14 D8
Moorfield NE2 . . . . .38 D3
Moorfield Gdns SR6 . . . . . . .75 A8
Moorfields NE61 . . . . .9 A6
Moorfoot Ave DH2 . . . . .88 C2
Moorfoot Gdns NE11 . . . . . .70 A5
Moor Gdns NE29 . . . . .41 C8
Moor Grange NE42 . . . . .50 D1
Moorhead NE5 . . . . .37 E1
Moorhead Mews NE5 . . . . . .37 E1
Moorhill Ct SR2 . . . . .86 E2
Moor Ho NE4 . . . . .98 B2
Moorhouse CI NE34 . . . . . . .59 D5
Moorhouse Est 1 NE63 . . . . .6 E1
Moorhouse Gdns DH5 . . . . .95 B2
Moorhouse La NE63 . . . . .6 F3
Moorhouses Rd NE29 . . . . . .41 C7
Moorings The 8 NE6 . . . . . .56 C4
Moor La
Cleadon SR6 . . . . .75 A7
Newcastle upon Tyne NE5 . . .37 A4
Ponteland NE20 . . . . .25 C4
South Shields NE34 . . . . . . .59 D6
Stannington NE61 . . . . .14 C6
Whitburn SR6 . . . . .75 D8
Moorland Ave NE22 . . . . . . .11 E3
Moorland Cotts 6 NE22 . .11 D3
Moorland Cres
Bedlington NE22 . . . . .11 E3
Newcastle upon Tyne NE6 . . .56 B8
Moorland Ct NE22 . . . . .11 E3
Moorland Dr NE22 . . . . .11 E3
Moorland Ho NE5 . . . . .37 C2
Moorlands
Dipton DH9 . . . . .78 E1
Hedworth NE32 . . . . .58 D1
Prudhoe NE42 . . . . .50 E1
Moorland Sq SR4 . . . . .85 F8
Moorland View NE17 . . . . . . .77 B8
Moorland Villas NE22 . . . . .11 E3
Moorland Way NE23 . . . . . . .16 B2
Moor Lane E NE34 . . . . .59 F7
Moormill NE11 . . . . .81 D6
Moormill La NE11 . . . . .81 E6
Moor Park Ct NE29 . . . . . . .41 C7
Moor Park Rd NE29 . . . . . . .41 C7
Moor PI NE3 . . . . .38 C3
Moor Rd NE2 . . . . .60 E7
Moor Road N NE3 . . . . .38 D3
Moor Road S NE2, NE3 . . . .38 D3
Moorsburn Dr DH4 . . . . .90 C1
Moors CI DH4 . . . . .90 C1
Moorsfield DH4 . . . . .94 B8
MOORSIDE 91 D5
Moorside
Hedworth NE32 . . . . .58 C1

Moorside continued
Longbenton NE12 . . . . .29 B2
Washington NE37 . . . . .83 B7
Moorside Com Prim Sch
NE4 . . . . .98 A2
Moorside Ct NE5 . . . . .37 E1
Moorside Fst Sch NE64 . . . .7 D5
Moorside N NE4 . . . . .54 F8
Moorside PI NE4 . . . . .54 F8
Moorside Rd SR3 . . . . .91 D5
Moorside S NE4 . . . . .54 F7
Moorsley Rd DH5 . . . . .94 F2
Moor St SR1 . . . . .103 B3
Moor Terr SR1 . . . . .103 C3
Moorvale La NE5 . . . . .37 E2
Moor View
Newcastle upon Tyne NE40 . .52 A4
High Pittington DH6 . . . . . . .96 D4
Killingworth NE12 . . . . .29 C4
Newbeggin-by-the-Sea NE64 . .7 E5
Whitburn SR6 . . . . .75 E8
Moor View CI NE6 . . . . .4 E3
Moorview Cres NE5 . . . . . . .37 E2
Moor View Wlk NE12 . . . . . .29 C4
Moorway NE23 . . . . .83 B6
Moorway Dr NE15 . . . . .53 E7
Moot Hall* * NE8 . . . . .101 B4
Moot Hall Gall The 9
NE46 . . . . .45 B5
Moraine Cres NE17 . . . . . . .77 B6
Moralee CI NE7 . . . . .39 C3
Moran St SR6 . . . . .75 E2
Moray CI DH3 . . . . .82 D1
Moray St SR6 . . . . .75 D3
Morcott Gdns NE29 . . . . . . .41 F4
Morden St NE1 . . . . .99 A2
Mordey CI SR2 . . . . .103 B1
Morecambe Par NE31 . . . . . .58 A2
Moreland Rd NE34 . . . . .59 D3
Moreland St SR6 . . . . .75 D2
Moresby Rd NE23 . . . . .16 C2
Morgan Bsns Ctr NE12 . . . .29 B5
Morgan St SR5 . . . . .75 B2
Morgans Way NE21 . . . . . . .53 A2
Morgy Hill E 4 NE40 . . . . . .51 F3
Morgy Hill W 2 NE40 . . . . . .51 F3
Morinda CI DH4 . . . . .89 F5
Morland Ave NE38 . . . . .83 E4
Morland Gdns NE9 . . . . .71 B7
Morley Ave NE10 . . . . .57 B2
Morley Ct 6 NE6 . . . . .56 C7
Morley Hill Rd NE5 . . . . .53 F8
Morley PI NE27 . . . . .30 F4
Morley Terr
Fence Houses DH4 . . . . .90 A1
6 Gateshead NE10 . . . . .71 D8
Morningside NE38 . . . . .88 E8
Morningside Ct 5 DH3 . . . .88 C4
Mornington Ave NE3 . . . . . . .37 F3
MORPETH 9 A8
Morpeth All Saints CE Fst
Sch NE61 . . . . .3 D2
Morpeth Ave
Jarrow NE32 . . . . .58 B3
Pegswood NE61 . . . . .4 E4
South Shields NE34 . . . . . . .59 E7
Wideopen NE13 . . . . .28 C7
Morpeth Chantry Bagpipe
Mus* 3 NE61 . . . . .9 A8
Morpeth CI
Guide Post NE62 . . . . .10 E7
Washington NE38 . . . . .83 A4
Morpeth Clock Twr* NE61. .8 F8
Morpeth Cottage Hospl
NE61 . . . . .8 F6
Morpeth Ct NE61 . . . . .9 A8
Morpeth Cty Fst Sch 20
NE61 . . . . .9 A8
Morpeth Dr SR3 . . . . .91 D6
Morpeth Rd
Ashington NE61 . . . . .9 A8
Guide Post NE62 . . . . .10 E7
Morpeth Riverside Ctr
NE61 . . . . .8 F8
Morpeth Road Cty Fst Sch
NE24 . . . . .17 D8
Morpeth St NE2 . . . . .98 B4
Morpeth Sta NE61 . . . . .9 A7
Morpeth Terr NE29 . . . . .41 D4
Morris Ave NE34 . . . . .59 B3
Morris Cres NE35 . . . . .74 A8
Morris Ct NE23 . . . . .29 B8
Morris Gdns NE10 . . . . .72 D8
Morrison Rd NE61 . . . . .4 A1
Morrison St NE10 . . . . .100 C2
Morris Rd NE16 . . . . .69 B8
Morris St
Birtley DH3 . . . . .82 C4
Gateshead NE8 . . . . .70 C8
Washington NE37 . . . . .83 C8
Morriss Terr DH6 . . . . .94 F7
Morrit Ct NE7 . . . . .39 C5
Morston Dr NE15 . . . . .53 E6
Mortimer Ave
Newcastle upon Tyne NE5 . . .36 F3
North Shields NE29 . . . . . . .41 D6
Mortimer Chase NE23 . . . . .16 C3
Mortimer Comp Sch
NE33 . . . . .59 D7
Mortimer Prim Sch NE34 .59 D7
Mortimer Rd NE33, NE34 . . .59 D7
Mortimer St SR4 . . . . .85 F7
Mortimer Terr
Pegswood NE61 . . . . .4 F4
Seaton Delaval NE25 . . . . . .23 E2
Morton CI NE38 . . . . .83 D4
Morton Cres
Great Lumley DH4 . . . . .89 F1

Morton Cres continued
Woolsington NE5 . . . . .36 B6
Morton Grange Terr DH4 . .89 E1
Morton St
Newcastle upon Tyne NE6 . . .56 F6
1 South Shields NE33 . . . . . .42 D4
Newcastle upon Tyne NE6 . .56 F6
Morval CI SR3 . . . . .91 D5
Morven Dr NE10 . . . . .57 B1
Morven Lea NE21 . . . . .53 B2
Morven PI NE63 . . . . .6 B4
Morven Terr NE63 . . . . .6 B4
Morwick CI NE23 . . . . .22 A5
Morwick PI 3 NE5 . . . . .37 D1
Morwick Rd NE29 . . . . .41 D8
Mosley St NE1 . . . . .99 B1
Moss Bank NE9 . . . . .71 B3
Moss CI NE15 . . . . .53 C8
Moss Cres NE40 . . . . .52 A4
Mosspool NE21 . . . . .53 A2
Moss Side NE9 . . . . .71 C3
Mostyn Gn NE3 . . . . .37 F5
Motcombe Way NE23 . . . . . .16 D2
Moulton Ct NE5 . . . . .37 C2
Moulton PI NE5 . . . . .37 C2
Mountbatten Ave NE31 . . . . .57 E4
Mount CI
Killingworth NE12 . . . . .29 D4
Sunderland SR4 . . . . .85 B6
Whitley Bay NE25 . . . . .31 D3
Mount Ct
Birtley DH3 . . . . .82 D5
North Shield DH3 . . . . .82 D5
Mountfield Gdns NE3 . . . . . .37 E5
Mountfield Prim Sch NE3 .37 E5
Mountford Rd NE25 . . . . . . .23 D7
Mount Gr
Dunston NE11 . . . . .69 F7
Sunderland SR4 . . . . .86 A4
Mount La NE9 . . . . .82 E8
MOUNT PLEASANT 56 A1
Mount Pleasant
Birtley DH3 . . . . .82 C5
6 Blaydon NE21 . . . . .53 B1
Dipton DH9 . . . . .78 E1
Houghton-le-Spring DH5 . . . .94 F8
10 Newcastle upon Tyne
NE6 . . . . .56 C6
3 Newcastle upon Tyne NE6 . .56 C6
DH3 . . . . .82 C5
Mount Pleasant Bglws 4
DH3 . . . . .82 C5
Mount Pleasant Ct NE15 . .35 D2
Mount Pleasant Gdns
NE8 . . . . .56 A1
Mount Rd
Birtley DH3 . . . . .82 D5
Gateshead NE9 . . . . .82 E8
Sunderland SR4 . . . . .85 F4
Mount Ridge DH3 . . . . .82 D5
Mountsett CI DH9 . . . . .78 C2
Mountside Gdns NE11 . . . . .69 F7
Mount Terr NE33 . . . . .42 C2
Mount The
Ryton NE40 . . . . .52 C5
Throckley NE15 . . . . .35 C2
Mount View
17 Crawcrook NE40 . . . . . . .51 F3
Mount View Terr NE43 . . . . .64 A7
Mourne Gdns NE11 . . . . . . .70 A6
Mowbray CI SR2 . . . . .103 A1
Mowbray Ct NE62 . . . . .10 F7
Mowbray First School
NE62 . . . . .10 F7
Mowbray Gdns NE34 . . . . . .59 F5
Mowbray Mews NE33 . . . . . .42 E2
Mowbray Pk* SR1 . . . . . . .103 A2
Mowbray Rd
Longbenton NE12 . . . . .39 E8
North Shields NE29 . . . . . . .41 D6
South Shields NE33 . . . . . . .42 E1
Sunderland SR2 . . . . .103 B1
Mowbray St NE6 . . . . .56 A7
Mowbray Terr NE62 . . . . . . .10 F7
Mowbray Villas NE33 . . . . .42 F1
Moyle St NE16 . . . . .79 A4
Mozart St NE33 . . . . .59 C8
Muirfield
South Shields NE33 . . . . . . .42 F1
Whitley Bay NE25 . . . . .31 D5
Muirfield Dr
Gateshead NE10 . . . . .71 E6
Washington NE37 . . . . .72 C3
Muirfield Rd NE7 . . . . .39 C5
Mullen Ct NE4 . . . . .54 E4
Mulberry CI NE24 . . . . .17 D4
Mulberry Cres NE34 . . . . . . .59 F5
Mulberry Gdns NE10 . . . . . .56 F2
Mulberry Gr NE16 . . . . .79 A4
Mulberry Pk NE9 . . . . .70 F5
Mulberry PI NE4 . . . . .100 B3
Mulberry St NE10 . . . . .56 F2
Mulberry Trad Est NE10 . . .56 C1
Mulcaster Gdns NE28 . . . . .40 A3
Mulgrave Dr SR6 . . . . .75 E1
Mulgrave Terr NE8 . . . . .101 B3
Mulgrave Villas NE8 . . . . . .101 B2
Mullen Dr NE40 . . . . .52 D4
Mullen Gdns NE28 . . . . .40 A4
Mullen Rd NE28 . . . . .40 B4
Mull Gr NE32 . . . . .58 B3
Mundella Terr NE6 . . . . .56 B7
Mundle Ave NE21 . . . . .68 C6
Mundles La NE36 . . . . .74 D6
Municipal Terr NE38 . . . . . . .83 D6
Munslow Rd SR3 . . . . .91 DE
Murphy Gr SR2 . . . . .92 F2
Murray Ave DH4 . . . . .90 A1

Murray Ct DH2 . . . . .88 B3
Murrayfield NE23 . . . . .22 F2
Murrayfield Rd NE5 . . . . .37 D3
Murray Gdns 1 NE11 . . . . .70 A7
Murray PI DH2 . . . . .88 C3
Murray Rd
  Chester le Street DH2,
  DH3 . . . . .88 C3
  Wallsend NE28 . . . . .40 F3
Murray St NE21 . . . . .53 C3
Murston Ave NE23 . . . . .16 C2
MURTON. 31 B2
Murton La
  Easington Lane DH5 . . . . . . .95 D1
  Tynemouth NE27, NE29 . . . .31 B2
Murton St NE1 . . . . .103 B2
Muscott Gr NE15. . . . . .54 A6
Musgrave Prim Sch NE9 . .70 F6
Musgrave Rd NE9. . . . . .70 F6
Musgrave Terr
  Gateshead NE10 . . . . .57 A1
  Newcastle upon Tyne NE6 . .56 B8
  Washington NE38 . . . . .83 D6
Mus of Antiquities* NE1 . .99 A3
Muswell Hill NE15 . . . . .54 A5
Mutual St NE8 . . . . .40 B1
Mylord Cres NE12. . . . . .29 B5
Myrella Cres SR2 . . . . .86 C2
Myreside PI 3 NE12 . . . . . .39 B6
Myrtle Ave
  Dunston NE11 . . . . .69 F8
  Whitburn SR6. . . . . .60 F1
Myrtle Cres NE12 . . . . .29 D1
Myrtle Gr
  Burnopfield NE16. . . . . .78 F6
  Gateshead NE11 . . . . .70 F5
  Newcastle upon Tyne NE2 . .38 C2
  South Shields NE34 . . . . . . .59 F4
  Wallsend NE28 . . . . .40 B4
Myrtle Rd NE21 . . . . .53 C1
Myrtles DH2. . . . . .88 A3
Myrtle St NE63 . . . . .6 D4

N

Nafferton PI NE5 . . . . .54 C8
Nairn Cl
  Birtley DH3 . . . . .82 D2
  Sunderland SR4. . . . . .85 D4
  Washington NE37 . . . . .72 C2
Nairn Rd NE23 . . . . .22 B7
Nairn St NE32 . . . . .58 E3
Nansen Cl NE5. . . . . .36 F2
Napier Cl DH3 . . . . .88 D8
Napier Ct NE16. . . . . .69 B4
Napier Rd NE16. . . . . .54 A1
Napier St
  Jarrow NE32 . . . . .58 B7
  Newcastle upon Tyne NE2 . .99 C2
  South Shields NE33 . . . . . . .59 B6
Napier Way NE21 . . . . .53 E2
Napoleon Cl SR2 . . . . .92 F7
Narvik Way NE29 . . . . .41 A4
Nash Ave NE34 . . . . .59 D3
Naters St NE26 . . . . .24 B7
National Glass Ctr (Mus)*
  SR6 . . . . .103 B4
Natley Ave NE36 . . . . .74 E7
Navan Cl NE26 . . . . .11 D8
Navenby Cl
  Newcastle upon Tyne NE15 .38 D8
  Seaham SR7. . . . . .93 A1
Naworth Ave NE30 . . . . .32 A1
Naworth Dr NE5 . . . . .36 E3
Naworth Terr NE2. . . . . .58 D4
Nawton Ave NE5 . . . . .75 C2
Nayland Rd NE23 . . . . .22 A7
Naylor Ave NE21. . . . . .68 C6
Naylor Ct NE21 . . . . .53 E4
Naylor PI NE26 . . . . .24 B7
Neale St
  Prudhoe NE42 . . . . .50 D3
  Sunderland SR6. . . . . .75 E3
  Tantobie DH9 . . . . .79 B2
Neale Terr 1 DH3 . . . . .82 C4
Nearlane Cl NE13 . . . . .28 C8
Neasdon Cres NE30. . . . . . . .32 B1
Neasham Rd SR7 . . . . .93 A1
NEDDERTON 18 B8
Nedderton Cl NE5 . . . . .36 B4
Nedderton Colliery Old Rd
  NE22. . . . . .10 C2
Needham PI NE23. . . . . .22 B7
Neill Dr NE16 . . . . .69 B2
Neilson Rd NE10. . . . . .56 B3
Neil St DH5. . . . . .95 C1
Nellie Gormley House
  NE12 . . . . .29 B2
Nell Terr NE39 . . . . .67 C1
Nelson Ave
  Cramlington NE23 . . . . .21 F8
  Newcastle upon Tyne NE3 . .38 A5
  South Shields NE33 . . . . . . .42 E3
Nelson Cl
  Ashington NE63. . . . . .6 E2
  Sunderland SR3. . . . . .103 B1
Nelson Cres NE29. . . . . .41 D2
Nelson Dr NE23 . . . . .15 F1
Nelson House 14 NE30 . . . .42 D7
Nelson Ind Est NE23 . . . . . . .15 D1
Nelson Park Ind Est NE23 .15 E1
Nelson Park Network Ctr
  NE23 . . . . .15 D1
Nelson Park West NE23 . . .15 D1

Nelson Rd
  Cramlington NE23 . . . . .15 D1
  Earsdon NE25 . . . . .31 B5
  Newcastle upon Tyne NE6 . .57 B4
  Stakeford NE62 . . . . .11 A7
Nelson St
  Chester le Street DH3 . . . . . .88 C2
  Dunston NE11 . . . . .54 F2
  Gateshead NE8 . . . . .101 C3
  Greenside NE40. . . . . .51 F1
  Hetton-le-Hole DH5. . . . . . . .95 A3
  Newcastle upon Tyne NE1 . .99 A1
  1 South Shields NE33 . . . . .42 C3
  Sunderland SR2. . . . . .92 F7
  Washington NE38 . . . . .83 E4
Nelson Terr
  Chopwell NE17. . . . . .66 B1
  North Shields NE29 . . . . . . .41 D3
  Sherburn DH6. . . . . .96 A1
Nelson Way NE23 . . . . .15 E2
Nene Ct 11 NE37. . . . . .83 E8
Nent Gr NE46. . . . . .45 C4
Neptune Rd
  Newcastle upon Tyne, Denton
  Burn NE15 . . . . .53 E7
  Newcastle upon Tyne, Lemington
  NE15. . . . . .53 D6
  Wallsend NE28 . . . . .57 B8
Nesburn Rd SR4 . . . . .102 A1
Nesham PI DH5. . . . . .94 F8
Nesham Rd NE46 . . . . .100 A3
Nesham Terr SR1 . . . . .103 B3
Ness Ct NE21 . . . . .53 A2
Neston Ct NE5 . . . . .37 D3
Nest Rd NE10 . . . . .56 D2
Netherburn Rd SR5. . . . . .75 C2
Netherby Dr NE5 . . . . .54 C8
Netherdale NE22. . . . . .10 D1
Nether Farm Rd NE10. . . . . .56 F1
Nether Riggs NE22 . . . . .10 D1
Netherton NE12. . . . . .29 C4
Netherton Ave NE15 . . . . .53 E7
Netherton Gdns NE13 . . . . . .28 B6
Netherton Gr NE22. . . . . .41 D2
Netherton La NE22. . . . . .10 C1
Netherwitton Way NE3. . . . . .28 B1
Nettleham Rd SR5 . . . . .75 C2
Nettles La SR3. . . . . .92 B6
Network Bus Ctr NE63 . . . . . .6 E5
Neville Cres DH3 . . . . .82 C6
Neville Ct 3 NE37. . . . . .83 F8
Neville Rd
  Newcastle upon Tyne
  NE15. . . . . .53 E7
  Sunderland SR4. . . . . .85 F7
Neville's Cross Rd NE11. . . .57 F5
Neville Sq NE61. . . . . .2 A2
Neville St NE1 . . . . .101 A4
Nevill Rd NE43. . . . . .64 D7
Nevinson Ave NE34 . . . . .59 E3
Nevis Cl NE26 . . . . .31 E8
Nevis Ct NE26 . . . . .31 E8
Nevis Gr NE36. . . . . .74 B7
Nevis Way NE26 . . . . .31 E7
Newark Cl NE22 . . . . .10 D2
Newark Cres SR7. . . . . .93 A1
Newark Dr SR6. . . . . .75 F8
Newark Sq NE29. . . . . .41 F4
Newarth Cl NE15. . . . . .53 E7
Newbank Wlk NE21. . . . . .53 A1
NEWBIGGIN-BY-THE-SEA . .7 E3
Newbiggin Cty Mid Sch
  NE64 . . . . .7 C4
Newbiggin Hall NE15. . . . . . .37 A5
Newbiggin Rd NE63. . . . . .6 E1
Newbold Ave NE5 . . . . .75 C2
Newbolt Ct NE8. . . . . .56 D5
Newbolt Ct NE8. . . . . .56 A2
NEWBOTTLE 90 E3
Newbottle Prim Sch DH4 . .90 D3
Newbottle St DH4. . . . . .90 E3
Newbridge Ave SR5. . . . . .75 C2
Newbridge Bank DH3 . . . . . .88 F5
New Bridge St NE1 . . . . .99 C1
New Bridge Street W NE1,
  NE99. . . . . .99 B2
Newbrough Cres NE2 . . . . . . .38 E2
Newburgh Ave NE23 . . . . .23 D2
NEWBURN. 52 F7
Newburn Activity Ctr
  NE15. . . . . .52 E8
Newburn Ave SR5. . . . . .75 C2
Newburn Bridge Rd NE15,
  NE21. . . . . .52 E6
Newburn Cres DH4 . . . . .90 D1
Newburn Ct NE33 . . . . .42 D1
NEWBURN HAUGH 53 C4
Newburn Haugh Ind Est
  NE15. . . . . .53 C6
Newburn Ind Est NE21. . . . . .53 A6
Newburn Lane End NE15. . .35 D2
Newburn Manor Prim Sch
  NE15. . . . . .52 F8
Newburn Rd
  Newburn NE15. . . . . .52 F8
  Throckley NE15 . . . . .35 E1
Newburn Riverside Bus Pk
  NE15. . . . . .53 D4
Newbury Ave NE8. . . . . .70 D8
Newbury Cl NE15 . . . . .53 D7
Newbury St
  South Shields NE33 . . . . . . .59 D7
  Sunderland SR5. . . . . .75 D3
Newby Cl NE12 . . . . .11 C3
Newby La DH6. . . . . .96 C5
Newby PI NE9 . . . . .71 B4

Newcastle Arts Ctr*
  NE1. . . . . .101 A4
Newcastle Bank NE9. . . . . . .82 B7
Newcastle Bus Pk NE4 . .100 A3
Newcastle City Heliport
  NE4 . . . . .100 B3
Newcastle Coll (Rye Hill
  Campus) NE4 . . . . .100 B4
Newcastle Coll (Sandyford
  Campus) NE1 . . . . .99 B3
Newcastle General Hospl
  NE4 . . . . .54 F6
Newcastle Guildhall*
  NE1. . . . . .101 B4
Newcastle International
  Airport NE13 . . . . .26 D3
Newcastle Nuffield Hospl
  The NE2 . . . . .99 B4
Newcastle Preparatory Sch
  NE2 . . . . .99 B3
Newcastle Rd
  Birtley DH3 . . . . .82 C6
  Blyth NE24. . . . . .17 C4
  Chester le Street DH3 . . . . . .88 C5
  Corbridge NE45. . . . . .47 B5
  Sunderland SR5. . . . . .75 C3
  West Boldon NE10, NE36 . .73 C7
Newcastle Rd/Leam La
  NE34 . . . . .58 F5
Newcastle School for Boys
  (Junior Sch) NE3. . . . . . .38 B4
Newcastle School for Boys
  (Middle Sch) 5 NE3. . . .38 C4
Newcastle School for Boys
  (Senior Sch) NE3. . . . . . .38 A4
Newcastle St NE29. . . . . .42 A5
Newcastle Terr 5 NE30 . . .42 D7
Newcastle University NE1 .99 A3
Newcastle University (City
  Wal Bldg) NE1 . . . . .98 C1
Newcastle Univ (Paul
  O'Gorman Bldg) NE2 . . .98 C3
Newcastle Univ (The Dove
  Marine Laboratory)
  NE25 . . . . .32 C3
Newcastle Univ (The
  Facuaity of Medical
  Science) NE2 . . . . .98 C3
NEWCASTLE-UPON-
  TYNE. 98 C3
Newcastle Upon Tyne Sta
  NE1. . . . . .101 A4
New Cotts NE61 . . . . .3 A1
New Delaval NE24. . . . . .17 B3
New Delaval Fst Sch
  NE24 . . . . .17 B4
Newdene Wlk NE15 . . . . .53 D7
New Dr SR7 . . . . .93 B1
New Durham Rd SR2. . . . . . .102 C2
Newfield Wlk NE16 . . . . .69 A6
New Front St DH9 . . . . .79 F1
Newgate Sh Ctr NE1 . . . . . . .99 A1
Newgate St
  Morpeth NE61 . . . . .3 F1
  Newcastle upon Tyne NE1 . .99 A1
New George St NE33 . . . . . . .42 C1
New Green St NE33 . . . . .42 C1
Newham Ave NE13. . . . . .28 A4
NEW HARTLEY 23 D6
New Hartley Fst Sch
  NE25 . . . . .23 D6
Newhaven Ave SR5 . . . . .75 C2
NEW HERRINGTON 90 B6
New Herrington Ind Est
  DH4 . . . . .90 D6
New Horton Grange Cotts
  NE13 . . . . .19 F4
Newington Ct
  Sunderland SR5. . . . . .75 C1
  Washington NE37 . . . . .83 C1
Newington Dr NE29 . . . . .31 F1
Newington Rd NE6. . . . . .56 A6
Newker Prim Sch DH2. . . . . .88 B2
New King St NE64 . . . . .7 F5
NEW LAMBTON 89 F2
Newland Ct NE34 . . . . .59 C5
NEWLANDS. 76 D4
Newlands 2 NE30 . . . . .32 A2
Newlands Ave
  Blyth NE24. . . . . .17 D5
  Newcastle upon Tyne NE3 . .28 B1
  Sunderland SR3. . . . . .86 B3
  Whitley Bay NE25 . . . . .31 D1
Newlands PI NE24 . . . . .17 D5
Newlands Rd
  Blyth NE24. . . . . .17 D5
  Newcastle upon Tyne NE2 . .38 D3
Newlands Road W SR7 . . .93 A1
Newlyn Cres NE29 . . . . .41 E5
Newlyn Dr
  Cramlington NE23 . . . . .22 B8
  Jarrow NE32. . . . . .58 D6
Newlyn Rd NE3 . . . . .37 E5
Newman PI 10 NE8 . . . . . . .71 B4
Newman's Way 2 NE46. . . .45 B4
Newman Terr NE8 . . . . .71 A8
Newmarch St NE32 . . . . .58 A7
Newmarket Wlk 1 NE33 . .42 C1
New Mills NE4. . . . . .98 B2
New Mills Ho NE4 . . . . .98 B2
Newminster Cl DH4. . . . . .90 B2
Newminster Mid Sch NE3 .1 E1
Newminster Rd NE4 . . . . .54 D7
Newmin Way NE16 . . . . .68 F5
New Moor Cl NE63. . . . . .5 F4
New Penshaw Prim Sch
  DH4 . . . . .90 B8
New Phoenix Yd 1 NE61. . . .9 A8

Newport Gr 6 SR3 . . . . .92 A8
New Quay NE29. . . . . .42 B4
Newquay Gdns 4 NE9 . . . .71 A2
New Queen St NE4. . . . . .7 E5
New Rainton St DH4. . . . . . . .90 B8
New Rd
  Burnopfield NE16. . . . . .79 B7
  Dunston NE11 . . . . .70 B6
  Gateshead NE10 . . . . .72 C5
  Washington NE38 . . . . .89 C8
  West Boldon NE35. . . . . .74 B8
NEW RIDLEY. 64 B3
New Ridley Rd NE43 . . . . . . .64 D5
Newriggs NE38 . . . . .83 E4
New Sandridge NE46. . . . . . . .7 F2
New Seaham Prim Sch
  SR7. . . . . .92 F1
NEWSHAM. 17 B5
Newsham Ct SR3. . . . . .86 C4
Newsham Fst Sch NE24 . . .17 C5
Newsham Rd NE24 . . . . .17 D4
NEW SILKSWORTH 92 B8
New Silksworth Inf Sch
  SR3. . . . . .92 B7
New Silksworth Jun Sch
  SR3. . . . . .92 B7
New South Terr DH3. . . . . . . .82 C4
New St
  Sherburn DH6. . . . . .96 A1
  5 Sunderland SR4 . . . . . . .85 A6
Newstead Rd DH4 . . . . .90 C2
Newsteads Cl NE25 . . . . .31 D5
Newsteads Dr NE25 . . . . .31 D5
Newstead Sq SR3. . . . . .92 A6
NEWTON. 48 C6
Newton Ave
  Tynemouth NE30 . . . . .32 B3
  Wallsend NE28 . . . . .40 F3
Newton Cl NE15 . . . . .53 D7
Newton Gr NE34 . . . . .59 A5
Newton Ho NE4 . . . . .98 C2
Newton PI NE7 . . . . .39 B2
Newton Rd NE7. . . . . .39 B2
Newton St
  Dunston NE11 . . . . .54 F2
  Gateshead NE8 . . . . .70 D8
Newton Terr NE43. . . . . .49 E1
NEW TOWN
  Houghton-le-Spring. 94 F8
  West Boldon 73 B8
NEW YORK. 31 E4
New York Ind Pk NE27 . . . .41 A8
New York Prim Sch NE29 . .41 C8
New York Rd
  Shiremoor NE27 . . . . .30 E2
  Tynemouth NE29 . . . . .31 B1
New York Way NE27. . . . . . . .41 A8
Nicholas Ave NE3 . . . . .75 F8
Nicholas Dr NE45. . . . . .95 B5
Nichol Ct NE4. . . . . .54 D5
Nicholson Cl SR1 . . . . .103 B2
Nicholson Terr NE12 . . . . . . .29 E1
Nichol St NE4 . . . . .54 D5
Nidderdale Ave DH5 . . . . .94 F2
Nidderdale Cl NE24. . . . . .17 A8
Nidsdale Ave NE6 . . . . .57 A7
Nightingale Cl SR4. . . . . .85 B4
Nile Cl NE15. . . . . .53 C8
Nile St
  North Shields NE29 . . . . . . .42 A5
  South Shields NE33 . . . . . . .42 B3
  Sunderland SR1. . . . . .103 B3
Nilverton Ave SR2. . . . . .86 D3
Nimbus Ct 13 SR3. . . . . .92 A6
Nine Lands DH4 . . . . .94 C8
Ninth Ave
  Blyth NE24. . . . . .17 D6
  Chester le Street DH2. . . . . .88 B3
  Gateshead NE11 . . . . .70 D3
  Morpeth NE61 . . . . .9 B7
  Newcastle upon Tyne NE6 . .56 C8
Ninth Avenue E NE11 . . . . . .70 D3
Ninth Row NE65 . . . . .6 B4
Nissan Way SR5 . . . . .84 B7
Nithdale Cl NE6. . . . . .57 B8
Nixon St NE8 . . . . .56 A4
Nixon Terr NE24 . . . . .17 F6
Noble Gdns NE34 . . . . .59 B6
Noble's Bank Rd SR2 . . . . .103 C1
Noble St
  2 Gateshead NE10 . . . . . . .56 D1
  Newcastle upon Tyne NE4 . .54 F3
  Sunderland SR2. . . . . .103 C1
Noble Street Ind Est NE4 . .54 F3
Noble Terr
  10 Morpeth NE61 . . . . .9 A8
  Sunderland SR2. . . . . .103 C1
Noel Ave NE21. . . . . .68 C6
Noel Terr NE21. . . . . .68 C6
Noirmont Way SR3. . . . . .91 E6
Nolan Hall NE2 . . . . .58 B6
Nookside SR4 . . . . .85 C4
Nookside Ct SR4. . . . . .85 C4
Nook The
  North Shields NE29 . . . . . . .41 F5
  Whitley Bay NE25 . . . . .31 F4
Nora St
  South Shields NE34 . . . . . . .59 C5
  Sunderland SR4. . . . . .85 F4
Norbury Gr NE6. . . . . .56 D5
Nordale Ho NE24 . . . . .17 A8
Nordale Way NE24 . . . . .17 A8
Norfolk Ave
  Birtley DH3 . . . . .82 D1
  New Silksworth SR3 . . . . . . .91 F8

Norfolk Cl
  Ashington NE63. . . . . .6 A4
  Seaham SR7. . . . . .93 A1
Norfolk Ct 10 NE30. . . . . . . .42 B6
Norfolk Dr NE37 . . . . .72 D2
Norfolk Gdns NE28. . . . . .40 E4
Norfolk Mews 1 NE10 . . . .42 A6
Norfolk PI DH3 . . . . .82 D1
Norfolk Rd
  Gateshead NE8 . . . . .56 A4
  South Shields NE34 . . . . . . .60 C7
Norfolk Sq 11 NE6 . . . . .56 B6
Norfolk St
  Hetton-le-Hole DH5. . . . . . . .94 F4
  North Shields NE30 . . . . . . .42 B5
  Sunderland SR1. . . . . .103 A3
Norfolk Way NE15 . . . . .53 E7
Norham Avenue N NE34 . .60 A8
Norham Avenue S NE34 . . .60 A8
Norham Cl
  Blyth NE24. . . . . .17 C7
  Brunswick Village NE13. . . . .28 A5
Norham Com Tech Coll
  NE29 . . . . .41 D5
Norham Ct
  Bournmoor DH4. . . . . .89 D1
  Washington NE38 . . . . .83 B4
Norham Dr
  Morpeth NE61 . . . . .9 B5
  Newcastle upon Tyne NE5 . .36 E3
Norham Gdns NE62 . . . . .6 A1
Norham PI NE2 . . . . .38 E1
Norham Rd
  Ashington NE63. . . . . .6 D2
  Newcastle upon Tyne NE3 . .38 B6
  North Shields NE29 . . . . . . .41 C5
  Whitley Bay NE25, NE26 . . .31 F5
Norham Road N
  Shiremoor NE29 . . . . .41 B7
  Tynemouth NE29 . . . . .41 D0
Norham Terr NE32 . . . . .58 B3
Norhurst NE16. . . . . .68 E5
Norley Ave SR5 . . . . .75 C2
Norma Cres NE26. . . . . .32 C4
Norman Ave SR3. . . . . .92 B7
Normanby Cl SR7. . . . . .93 A1
Normanby St SR6. . . . . .75 F1
Normandy Cres DH5 . . . . . . .94 F8
Norman Rd NE39 . . . . .67 F1
Norman Terr
  High Pittington DH6. . . . . . . .96 C5
  Morpeth NE61 . . . . .9 A8
  Wallsend NE28 . . . . .41 B2
Normanton Terr NE4 . . . . . . .98 A1
Normount Ave 2 NE4. . . . . .54 E5
Normount Gdns 4 NE4 . . .54 E5
Normount Rd
  Dunston Hill NE11 . . . . .69 F7
  Newcastle upon Tyne NE4 . .54 E5
North App DH2 . . . . .88 B4
North Ave
  Guide Post NE62 . . . . .10 E7
  Newcastle upon Tyne, Gosforth
  NE3. . . . . .38 C4
  South Shields NE34 . . . . . . .59 F6
  Washington NE37 . . . . .72 C1
North Balkwell Farm Ind Est
  NE29 . . . . .41 B7
North Bank Ct 7 SR5. . . . . .75 B2
NORTH BIDDICK. 83 E2
NORTH BLYTH. 12 E1
Northbourne Ave NE61 . . . . .3 F2
Northbourne Ho NE9 . . . . . . .70 F5
Northbourne Rd NE31,
  NE32 . . . . .58 A6
Northbourne St
  Gateshead NE8 . . . . .70 F8
  Newcastle upon Tyne NE4 . .54 F4
North Bridge St SR5 . . . . . .103 A4
North Burns DH3 . . . . .88 C4
North Church St 2 NE30 . .42 B6
North Cl
  4 Newcastle upon Tyne
  NE6. . . . . .56 C7
  Ryton NE40 . . . . .52 C5
  South Shields NE34 . . . . . . .59 F6
Northcote Ave
  Newcastle upon Tyne NE5 . .36 C1
  Sunderland SR1. . . . . .103 B2
  Whitley Bay NE25 . . . . .31 D4
Northcote St
  Newcastle upon Tyne NE4 . .98 A1
  7 South Shields NE33 . . . .59 D8
North Croft NE12 . . . . .39 E7
North Cross St NE3. . . . . .38 C5
North Dene SR2. . . . . .82 C7
North Dr
  Chester le Street NE38 . . . . .88 E7
  Cleadon SR6 . . . . .59 F1
  Hebburn NE31 . . . . .57 C4
North Durham St SR1. . . . .103 B3
North East Aircraft Mus*
  SR5 . . . . .73 E3
North Eastern Ct NE16 . . . .69 E8
Northern Counties Sch
  NE2 . . . . .38 D1
Northern Gallery of
  Contemporary Art*
  SR1 . . . . .103 A2
Northern Stage* NE1. . . . . .99 A3

Northern Terr NE23 ....22 A1
Northern Way SR5 ....75 A2
North Farm NE22 ....15 A8
North Farm Ave NE8 .....85 B2
North Farm Ct NE15 ....35 C2
North Farm Rd NE31 ......57 D5
North Fawdon Prim Sch
NE3 ....37 F7
Northfield NE22 ....12 B4
Northfield Cl NE16 ....68 F5
Northfield Dr
Killingworth NE12 ....29 B2
Sunderland SR4 ....85 B2
Northfield Gdns NE34 ....59 F8
Northfield Rd
Newcastle upon Tyne NE3 ..38 B4
South Shields NE33 ....42 F1
Northfields Cl 2 NE6 ....56 C7
Northfields Ho 2 NE6 ....56 C7
Northgate NE12 ....29 D4
Northgate Hospl NE61 .....3 D4
North Gr
Ryton NE40 ....52 D5
Sunderland SR6 ....85 A4
North Grange NE20 ....25 E8
North Guards SR6 ....75 F8
North Hall Rd NE4 ....85 D4
North Hylton Rd SR5 ......74 E2
North Hylton Road Ind Est
SR5 ....74 D2
North Jesmond Ave NE2 ...38 C2
North King St NE30 ......42 B6
North La
East Boldon NE36 ....74 C7
Hetton-le-Hole DH5 ......95 E5
Northland Cl SR4 ....85 B2
Northlands
Blaydon NE21 ....53 B1
Chester le Street DH3 ....88 C5
Tynemouth NE30 ....32 B1
Northlands Rd NE61 ....3 F2
NORTHLEA 93 B1
Northlea NE15 ....53 E8
North Leech NE61 ....3 D2
North Leigh DH9 ....79 E2
North Lodge DH3 ....88 D7
North Lodge Apartments 11
NE21 ....53 B1
North Magdalene DH8 .....77 B1
North Main St NE33 ....42 E2
North Mason Lodge NE13 ..27 B8
North Mdws NE42 ....50 B5
North Milburn St SR4 ...102 B3
North Moor Ct SR3 ....85 E1
North Moor La SR3 ....91 E8
Northmoor Rd NE6 ....56 E8
North Moor Rd SR3 ....85 E1
North Nelson Ind Est
NE23 ....15 E2
Northolt Ave NE23 ....22 B7
North Par
Choppington NE62 ....10 E6
Whitley Bay NE26 ....32 B5
North Pl NE61 ....3 E1
North Ravensworth St
SR4 ....102 B3
North Rd
Boldon Colliery NE35 .....58 E1
Boldon Colliery, New Town NE35,
NE36 ....73 F7
Chester le Street DH3 ....88 C7
Dipton DH9 ....78 E2
East Boldon NE36 ....74 C7
Hetton-le-Hole DH5 ......94 E4
Houghton-le-Spring DH5 ..94 E4
Ponteland NE20 ....25 E8
Seaham SR7 ....93 D1
Slaley NE47 ....62 A4
Tynemouth NE29 ....42 A8
Wallsend NE28 ....40 B2
North Ridge
Bedlington NE22 ....10 D1
Bedlington NE22 ....10 E1
Whitley Bay NE25 ....31 C6
North Row NE42 ....54 A2
North Sands Bsns Ctr
SR6 ....103 B4
NORTH SEATON 11 B4
North Seaton Ind Est NE63 .6 F1
North Seaton Rd
Ashington NE63 ....6 D2
Newbiggin-by-the-Sea NE64 ..7 D3
NORTH SHIELDS 41 F4
North Shields Sta NE29 ..42 A5
Northside DH3 ....82 D6
NORTH SIDE 100 B2
North Side NE8 ....100 B2
Northside Pl NE25 ....23 E2
North St
Birtley DH3 ....82 E3
Blaydon NE21 ....53 A2
Cleadon SR6 ....60 A1
East Rainton DH5 ....94 D4
Jarrow NE32 ....58 D7
Newbottle DH4 ....90 D4
New Silksworth SR3 ......92 A8
South Shields NE33 ......42 C3
5 Sunderland SR5 ....75 C1
West Rainton DH4 ....94 A2
North Street E NE1 ......99 B2
North Terr
Chopwell NE17 ....66 B2
Hexham NE46 ....45 B4
Newcastle upon Tyne NE2 ..98 C3

North Terr *continued*
11 New Silksworth SR3 ...92 A8
1 Shiremoor NE27 ....30 E1
Wallsend NE28 ....40 E2
North Tyne Ind Est NE12 ..40 A8
North Tyneside General
Hospl NE29 ....31 E1
North View W NE39 ....41 C5
NE29 ....41 C5
Northumberland Aged
Mineworkers Homes
NE23 ....22 D5
Northumberland Ave
Bedlington NE22 ....10 E1
Longbenton NE12 ....39 D7
Newbiggin-by-the-Sea NE64 ..7 D4
Newcastle upon Tyne NE3 ..38 A3
Wallsend NE28 ....40 F2
Northumberland Bus Pk W
NE23 ....22 D5
Northumberland Cl NE63 ..6 A4
Northumberland Coll NE63 ..6 C2
Northumberland Ct
Hebburn NE31 ....57 D5
Prudhoe NE42 ....50 E4
Northumberland Dock Rd
NE28 ....41 C1
Northumberland Gdns
Newcastle upon Tyne, Jesmond
Vale NE2 ....56 A8
Newcastle upon Tyne NE5 ..36 B3
Northumberland Park Sta
NE27 ....30 D3
Northumberland Pl
Birtley DH3 ....82 D1
Newcastle upon Tyne NE1 ..99 A2
9 North Shields NE30 ....42 A6
Northumberland Rd
Newcastle upon Tyne,
Lemington NE15 ....53 C6
Newcastle upon Tyne NE1 ..99 B2
Ryton NE40 ....52 C6
Northumberland Sq
4 North Shields NE30 ....42 B6
3 Whitley Bay NE26 ......32 A5
Northumberland St
Gateshead NE8 ....100 C1
Newcastle upon Tyne NE1 ..99 A2
North Shields NE30 ......42 C6
Wallsend NE28 ....40 C2
Northumberland Terr
22 Newcastle upon Tyne
NE6 ....56 B6
Tynemouth NE30 ....42 D7
Wallsend NE28 ....40 F2
Northumberland Toy Mus*
NE63 ....6 C4
Northumberland Villas
NE28 ....40 E2
Northumberland Way
Washington, Columbia NE37,
NE38 ....83 F4
Washington, Usworth NE10,
NE37 ....72 D3
Northumbria Univ (City
Campus) NE1 ....99 B2
Northumbria Univ (Coach
Lane Campus) NE7 ....39 C3
Northumbria Wlk
Newcastle upon Tyne, East
Denton NE5 ....37 A2
Newcastle upon Tyne NE5 ..36 F1
North View
Ashington NE63 ....6 C4
7 Bedlington NE22 ......11 D3
Bournmoor DH4 ....89 E2
Cambois NE24 ....12 C6
Crawcrook NE40 ....51 E7
Dinnington NE13 ....27 B7
Easington Lane DH5 ......95 C1
Gateshead NE9 ....71 B3
Haswell DH6 ....97 F3
Hazlerigg NE13 ....28 A4
High Spen NE39 ....78 A4
Jarrow NE32 ....58 A6
4 Longbenton NE12 ....39 D8
Medomsley DH8 ....77 B1
Mickley Square NE43 .....49 E1
Newbiggin-by-the-Sea NE64 ..7 D3
Newcastle upon Tyne NE6 ..56 B7
Newcastle upon Tyne NE6 ..56 C7
Ouston DH2 ....81 F1
Rowlands Gill NE39 ......67 C2
Ryton NE40 ....52 A5
Sherburn Hill DH6 ....96 D1
South Shields NE34 ......59 F8
Stakeford NE62 ....11 C8
Sunderland, Castletown SR74 C1
Sunderland, Monkwearmouth
SR6 ....75 D3
18 Sunderland SR2 ....92 F6
Tynemouth NE29 ....41 F8
Wallsend NE28 ....40 C2
Washington NE37 ....83 D8
Whickham NE11 ....69 A7
Whitley Bay NE30 ....32 C4

North View *continued*
Wrekenton NE9 ....71 B3
North View Terr
Fence Houses DH4 ....94 B8
Gateshead NE8 ....56 C1
Prudhoe NE42 ....50 B2
Stocksfield NE43 ....64 C7
North View W NE39 ....67 C2
North Villas NE23 ....22 A1
NORTH WALBOTTLE 36 A3
North Walbottle Rd
Newcastle upon Tyne NE5 ..36 B4
Walbottle NE15 ....36 A2
North Way
Gateshead NE9 ....71 B7
Guide Post NE62 ....10 F7
Throckley NE15 ....35 D3
North West Side NE8 ...100 B2
Northwood Ct SR5 ....75 C2
North Wylam View NE42 ..50 A2
Norton Ave NE7 ....93 A1
Norton Cl 1 DH2 ....88 A1
Norton Rd SR5 ....75 A3
Norton Way NE15 ....53 E6
Norway Ave SR4 ....85 A4
Norwich Ave NE13 ....28 B5
Norwich Cl NE63 ....7 A5
Norwich Way
Cramlington NE23 ....22 A7
Hedworth NE32 ....58 B1
Norwood Ave
Newcastle upon Tyne, Brunton
Park NE3 ....28 C1
Newcastle upon Tyne, Heaton
NE6 ....39 B1
Norwood Cres NE39 ......67 F2
Norwood Ct
Gateshead NE9 ....71 C2
Longbenton NE12 ....39 D6
Norwood Gdns 4 NE9 ..71 A8
Norwood Nature Park Nature
Reserve* NE11 ....70 C7
Norwood Rd
Gateshead NE11 ....70 B7
Newcastle upon Tyne NE15 .53 D8
Nottingham NE22 ....10 D2
November Courtyard
NE8 ....100 B2
November Ctyd NE8 ......100 B2
Numbers Garth SR1 ....103 B3
Nuneaton Way NE5 ......36 B4
Nunn Gdns 12 NE16 ....69 A7
Nunn St DH4 ....90 A5
Nunnykirk Cl NE42 ......50 A4
Nuns La
Gateshead NE8 ....101 C3
Newcastle upon Tyne NE1 ..99 A1
Nuns Moor Cres NE4 .....54 E7
Nuns Moor Rd NE4 ....54 E7
Nun St NE1 ....99 A1
Nunthorpe Ave SR2 ......86 F1
Nunwick Gdns NE29 .....41 C6
Nunwick Way NE7 ....39 D4
Nursery Cl SR3 ....86 A2
Nursery Ct NE17 ....77 B6
Nursery Gdns NE5 ....54 B8
Nursery Grange NE46 ....44 F3
Nursery La
Cleadon SR6 ....60 A1
Gateshead NE10 ....71 C7
Nursery Mews NE61 ....9 A7
Nursery Pk NE63 ....6 E1
Nursery Rd SR3 ....86 A2
Nutley Pl NE15 ....54 A5
Nye Bevan Ho NE24 .....17 F6
Nye Dene SR5 ....74 B1

O

O2 Academy Newcastle*
NE1 ....99 A1
Oakapple Cl NE22 ....10 F1
Oak Ave
Dinnington NE13 ....27 C7
Dunston NE11 ....69 F7
5 Houghton-le-Spring DH4 .94 D8
South Shields NE34 ......60 A5
Oak Cl NE46 ....44 E3
Oak Cres SR6 ....61 A2
Oakdale NE22 ....15 B8
Oakdale Cl NE15 ....53 D6
Oakdale Terr DH3 ....82 C6
Oakenshaw NE15 ....53 E6
Oakey's Rd DH9 ....79 F1
Oakfield Ave NE16 ....69 B6
Oakfield Cl
Sunderland SR3 ....91 C6
Whickham NE16 ....69 B6
Oakfield Dr
Killingworth NE12 ....29 F3
Whickham NE16 ....69 B6
Oakfield Gdns
Newcastle upon Tyne
NE15 ....54 D5
Wallsend NE28 ....39 F3
Oakfield Grange NE13 ....27 B7
Oakfield Inf & Jun Schs
NE12 ....29 F3
Oakfield N NE42 ....50 B5
Oakfield Pk NE42 ....50 D2
Oakfield Rd
Dunston NE11 ....70 A6
Newcastle upon Tyne NE3 ..38 B3
Whickham NE16 ....69 B6
Oakfields NE16 ....79 B7

Oakfield Terr
Gateshead NE10 ....57 A1
Killingworth NE12 ....29 E1
Newcastle upon Tyne NE3 ..38 B4
Oakfield Way NE23 ....22 F1
Oak Gr
Longbenton NE12 ....39 D8
Wallsend NE28 ....40 D1
Oakham Ave NE16 ....68 F6
Oakham Gdns NE29 ......41 E5
Oakhurst Dr NE3 ....38 A3
Oakhurst Terr NE12 .....39 D7
Oakland Rd
Newcastle upon Tyne NE2 ..38 D2
Whitley Bay NE25 ....31 D4
Oaklands
Newcastle upon Tyne NE3 ..38 C3
Ponteland NE20 ....25 D4
Riding Mill NE44 ....43 A2
Whickham NE16 ....69 C8
Oaklands Ave NE3 ....38 C3
Oaklands Cres SR5 ......75 A2
Oaklands Ct NE3 ....38 C3
Oaklands Pl NE42 ....50 E2
Oaklands Rise NE44 .....62 F7
Oaklands SR4 ....102 A1
Oakland Terr
Ashington NE63 ....6 C3
Lynemouth NE61 ....2 A2
Oaklea
Chester le Street DH2 ...88 A5
Shiney Row DH4 ....89 F4
Oakleigh NE16 ....79 A6
Oakleigh Gdns SR6 .....60 A2
Oakley Cl NE23 ....29 B8
Oakley Dr NE23 ....22 D7
Oakley Gardens Sch SR4 ..60 B2
Oakmere Cl 2 DH4 .....90 B6
Oak Rd NE29 ....41 B7
Oakridge NE16 ....68 F6
Oak Sq NE8 ....101 C1
Oak St
Great Lumley DH4 ....89 E1
Jarrow NE32 ....58 A7
Mickley Square NE43 ....64 E8
Seaton Burn NE13 ....28 B8
Sunderland SR1 ....103 C2
1 Throckley NE15 ....35 D2
Washington NE38 ....83 F4
Oaks The
Greenside NE40 ....52 B1
Hexham NE46 ....44 F3
Penshaw DH4 ....90 B8
Sunderland SR2 ....103 B1
Oaks W The SR2 ....103 B1
Oak Terr
Blaydon NE21 ....53 C1
Burnopfield NE16 ....79 C6
Tantobie DH9 ....79 B2
Oaktree Ave NE6 ....40 A1
Oaktree Gdns NE25 .....31 E3
Oaktree Terr NE42 ......50 D2
Oakville NE63 ....7 A2
Oakwell Ct NE17 ....77 C5
Oakwellgate NE8 ....101 C4
Oakwell Terr NE10 ......50 D2
OAKWOOD 45 E8
Oakwood
Gateshead NE10 ....71 E5
Hebburn NE31 ....57 C7
Oakwood Ave
Gateshead NE9 ....71 A3
Newbiggin-by-the-Sea NE64 .7 D5
Wideopen NE13 ....28 C5
Oakwood Bank NE46 ....45 C4
Oakwood Cl NE9 ....71 F1
Oakwood Gdns NE11 ....70 B5
Oakwood Pl 2 NE5 ....37 C1
Oakwood SR2 ....102 B1
Oakwood Way NE63 ......7 B5
Oatens Bank NE15 ......33 A2
Oates St SR4 ....102 A2
Oatfield Cl NE63 ....6 B2
Oatlands Rd SR4 ....86 E8
Oban Ave NE28 ....40 F4
Oban Ct NE6 ....56 C5
Oban Gdns 8 NE6 .....56 C5
Oban St
Brockley Whins NE32 ....58 E3
Gateshead NE10 ....56 C1
Ocean Rd
South Shields NE33 .....42 D3
Sunderland SR2 ....86 F2
Ocean Road N 1 SR2 ..86 F2
Ocean Road S 7 SR2 ..86 F2
Ocean View
Newbiggin-by-the-Sea
NE64 ....7 E4
8 Sunderland SR2 ....93 A8
Whitley Bay NE26 ....32 C4
Ochiltree Cl NE26 ....24 D6
Octavia Cl NE22 ....10 E2
Octavia Ct NE28 ....40 F4
Octavian Way NE11 .....70 C3
October Ctyd NE8 ......100 B2
Odinel Ct NE42 ....50 D3
OFFERTON 84 F3
Offerton Cl 7 SR4 .....85 A6
Offerton La
Sunderland, Offerton SR4 ..84 F4
Sunderland, South Hylton
SR4 ....85 A5
Offerton St SR4 ....102 B2
Office Pl DH5 ....95 A3
Office Row
New Herrington DH4 .....90 E7
Washington NE38 ....83 A1
Off Quay Bldg The 1 NE6 56 A5

Ogden St SR4 ....102 B2
Ogle Ave
Hazlerigg NE13 ....28 A4
Morpeth NE61 ....8 E8
Ogle Dr NE24 ....17 C7
Ogle Gr NE32 ....58 A3
O'Hanlon Cres NE28 ....40 A4
Oil Mill Rd NE6 ....57 C7
Okehampton Ct 2 NE9 ..71 A2
Okehampton Dr NE9 ....71 A2
Okehampton Sq SR5 .....75 A3
Old Bakehouse Yd 11 NE61 ..8 E8
OLD BENWELL 54 B5
Old Brewery Sq NE42 ....49 C4
Old Brewery The 1 DH4 .94 E8
Old Coastguard Cotts
NE30 ....42 E7
Old Coronation St NE33 ..42 C2
Old Course Rd SR6 ......75 A8
Old Custom Ho NE29 ....42 B4
Old Durham Rd NE8, NE9 .71 B6
Old Farm Ct NE16 ....79 B7
Oldfield Rd NE6 ....56 E7
OLD FOLD 56 C1
Old Fold Rd NE10, NE8 ..56 C2
Old Forge The NE43 .....48 C5
Old Gaol The* NE46 ....45 B5
Oldgate NE61 ....8 F8
Oldgate Ct 1 NE61 .....8 F8
Old George Yd 6 NE1 ..99 A1
Old Main St NE47 ....51 E3
Old Mill Rd
Sunderland, Hendon SR2 ..103 C1
Sunderland SR5 ....75 A3
Old Orchard The NE44 ..63 A7
Old Rectory Cl DH9 .....79 D4
Old Sawmill NE61 ....8 A8
Old Station Cl NE20 ....25 C3
Oldstead Gdns SR4 .....85 C6
Old Vicarage Wlk 21 NE6 .56 C6
Old Well Ave NE21 ......53 B1
Old Well La NE21 ....53 B1
Olga Terr NE39 ....67 C1
Olive Gdns NE9 ....71 A6
Olive Pl NE4 ....54 D7
Oliver Ave NE4 ....54 E6
Oliver Cres DH3 ....82 C6
Olivers Mill 10 NE61 ...8 F8
Oliver St SR2 ....83 E4
Olive St
South Shields NE33 .....59 B6
Sunderland SR1 ....102 C2
Ollerton Dr NE15 ....35 B2
Ollerton Gdns NE10 ....71 C6
Olney Ct NE23 ....22 D7
Olwen Dr NE31 ....57 D6
Olympia Ave NE62 ......10 F7
Olympia Gdns NE61 ......4 A1
Olympia Hill NE61 ....3 F2
Ongar Way NE12 ....39 B7
Onslow Gdns NE9 ....70 F5
Onslow St SR4 ....85 E1
Open The NE1 ....99 A2
Open Univ The NE8 ....101 C4
Oram Ct NE11 ....9 B3
Orange Gr
Annitsford NE23 ....22 B1
Whickham NE16 ....69 C8
Orchard Ave NE39 ......67 D1
Orchard Cl
Killingworth NE12 ....29 F2
Morpeth NE61 ....9 B8
Prudhoe NE42 ....50 D1
Rowlands Gill NE39 .....78 D8
Orchard Cres NE45 .....47 A5
Orchard Ct
Greenside NE40 ....51 F1
Ryton NE40 ....52 C5
Tynemouth NE29 ....42 A8
Orchard Dene NE39 .....67 D1
Orchard Gdns
Chester le Street DH3 ...88 C1
Hexham NE46 ....71 A4
Wallsend NE28 ....40 A4
Whitburn SR6 ....75 E8
Orchard Gn NE5 ....37 D4
Orchard Hill NE42 ......50 D3
Orchard-Leigh NE15 ....53 E6
Orchard Mews 3 F1
Orchard Pk DH3 ....82 C4
Orchard Pl 2 NE2 .....38 F1
Orchard Rd
Rowlands Gill NE39 .....67 D1
Whickham NE16 ....69 C7
Orchard Rise NE15 .....53 B7
Orchard St
Birtley DH3 ....82 C4
Newcastle upon Tyne NE1 ..101 A4
Sunderland SR4 ....85 F7
Orchard Terr
Chester le Street DH3 ...88 C1
4 Hexham NE46 ....45 B5
Newcastle upon Tyne NE15 .53 C6
Rowlands Gill NE39 .....78 D8
8 Throckley NE15 ......35 D2
Orchard The
Chester le Street DH3 ...88 D4
East Boldon NE36 ....74 C7
Hepscott NE61 ....9 E5
4 North Shields NE29 ..42 A6
Whickham NE16 ....69 C7
Wylam NE41 ....51 A6
Orchard View
Corbridge NE45 ....46 F6
Linton NE61 ....1 B3

Orchid Cl
Ashington NE63 . . . . 6 C2
South Shields NE34 . . . . . . 59 B5
Orchid Gdns 1 NE34 . . . . . 59 F5
Ord Ct NE4 . . . . 54 D7
Orde Ave NE28 . . . . 40 A2
Ordley Cl NE15 . . . . 53 E6
Ord St NE4 . . . . 100 C3
Ord Terr NE62 . . . . 11 B8
Oriole Ho NE12 . . . . 39 D7
Orion Way NE29 . . . . 41 B5
Orkney Dr SR2 . . . . 92 D8
Orlando Rd NE29 . . . . 41 E6
Ormesby Rd NE6 . . . . 75 D3
Ormiscraig NE15 . . . . 53 E6
Ormiston NE15 . . . . 53 E6
Ormonde Ave NE15 . . . . . . 54 A6
Ormonde St
Jarrow NE32 . . . . 58 B7
Sunderland SR4 . . . . 102 A1
Ormsby Dr NE5 . . . . 54 A8
Ormskirk Cl NE15 . . . . 53 D6
Ormskirk Gr NE23 . . . . 22 C7
Ormston St NE23 . . . . 16 B3
Orpen Ave NE34 . . . . 59 C3
Orpine Cl NE4 . . . . 6 C2
Orpington Ave NE6 . . . . . . 56 E6
Orpington Rd NE23 . . . . . . 22 C7
Orr Ave SR3 . . . . 92 B6
Orton Cl NE4 . . . . 54 E4
Orwell Cl NE34 . . . . 59 E2
Orwell Gn NE3 . . . . 37 E3
Osbaldeston Gdns NE3 . . . 38 B3
Osborne Ave
Hexham NE46 . . . . 44 F5
Newcastle upon Tyne NE2 . 99 C4
South Shields NE33 . . . . . . 42 E1
Osborne Cl NE22 . . . . 11 C2
Osborne Ct NE2 . . . . 99 C4
Osborne Gdns
Tynemouth NE29 . . . . 42 A7
Whitley Bay NE26 . . . . 31 F5
Osborne House NE28 . . . . 40 E2
Osborne Pl NE12 . . . . 29 F1
Osborne St
South Shields NE33 . . . . . . 42 E2
Sunderland SR6 . . . . 75 D2
Osborne Terr
Cramlington NE23 . . . . 22 A7
Gateshead NE8 . . . . 101 A1
Newcastle upon Tyne NE2 . 99 B3
Osborne Villas NE2 . . . . . . 99 B4
Osier Ct NE62 . . . . 11 C7
Oslo Cl NE29 . . . . 41 B4
Osman Cl SR2 . . . . 103 B1
Osmund Terr 10 DH4 . . . . . 90 B6
Osprey Dr
Blyth NE24 . . . . 17 F5
Shiremoor NE28 . . . . 41 A6
Osprey House NE2 . . . . . . 38 E1
Osprey Way NE34 . . . . 59 B4
Oswald Rd
Hetton-le-Hole DH5 . . . . . 95 A5
Morpeth NE61 . . . . 4 A2
Newbeggin-by-the-Sea NE64 . 7 D5
Oswald St
Sunderland SR4 . . . . 102 A3
Whitelands NE34 . . . . 59 C3
Oswald Terr
Gateshead NE8 . . . . 101 A1
2 Sunderland, Grangetown
SR2 . . . . 86 F2
Sunderland SR5 . . . . 74 C1
Oswald Terrace S SR5 . . . . 74 C1
Oswald Wlk NE15 . . . . 38 E5
Oswestry Pl NE23 . . . . 22 C7
Oswin Ave NE12 . . . . 39 D8
Oswin Ct NE12 . . . . 29 E1
Oswin Rd NE12 . . . . 29 E1
Oswin Terr NE29 . . . . 41 D5
Otley Cl NE23 . . . . 22 D7
Otterburn Ave
Earsdon NE25 . . . . 31 B4
Newcastle upon Tyne NE3 . 38 A4
Otterburn Cl NE12 . . . . 39 F8
Otterburn Cres DH4 . . . . . . 90 C1
Otterburn Ct
Gateshead NE8 . . . . 101 A1
Whitley Bay NE25 . . . . 31 B4
Otterburn Dr NE63 . . . . 6 B1
Otterburn Gdns
Dunston NE11 . . . . 70 A7
Gateshead NE9 . . . . 70 E5
South Shields NE34 . . . . . . 59 E6
Whickham NE16 . . . . 69 B7
Otterburn Gr NE24 . . . . 17 B8
Otterburn Rd NE29 . . . . 41 F7
Otterburn Terr NE2 . . . . 38 E1
Otterburn Villas S NE2 . . . 99 B4
Otter Burn Way NE42 . . . . . 50 B1
Ottercap Cl NE15 . . . . 53 D6
Ottercops NE42 . . . . 50 B1
Otterington NE38 . . . . 84 B4
Ottershaw NE15 . . . . 53 D6
Otto Terr SR2 . . . . 102 B1
Ottovale Cres NE21 . . . . 53 A1
Ottringham Cl NE15 . . . . . . 53 D6
Otus Gr NE62 . . . . 10 F8
Oulton Cl
Cramlington NE23 . . . . 22 C7
Newcastle upon Tyne NE5 . 37 B4
Our Lady Queen of Peace RC
Prim Sch DH4 . . . . 90 A7

Our Lady & St Annes' Prim
Sch NE4 . . . . 100 C4
Ousby Ct NE3 . . . . 37 D7
Ouseburn Cl SR2 . . . . 92 F8
Ouseburn Rd
Newcastle upon Tyne, Jesmond
Vale NE2, NE6 . . . . 56 A8
Newcastle upon Tyne, St Ann's
NE1 . . . . 56 A6
Ouselaw NE11 . . . . 81 D6
Ouse St NE1 . . . . 56 A5
Ouslaw La NE11 . . . . 81 B6
OUSTON 81 F2
Ouston Cl NE10 . . . . 72 C7
Ouston Inf Sch DH2 . . . . . . 82 A1
Ouston Jun Sch DH2 . . . . . 81 F1
Ouston St NE15 . . . . 53 F5
Outram St DH5 . . . . 90 E1
Oval Park View NE10 . . . . . 71 D7
Oval The
Bedlington NE22 . . . . 11 C1
Blyth NE24 . . . . 17 B3
Houghton-le-Spring DH4 . . 90 D8
Longbenton NE12 . . . . 39 E6
Newcastle upon Tyne NE6 . 56 D4
Ouston DH2 . . . . 81 F7
4 Sunderland SR5 . . . . . . 75 B2
Washington NE37 . . . . 83 D8
Woolsington NE13 . . . . 36 F8
Overdale Ct NE62 . . . . 10 E6
Overdene NE15 . . . . 53 F7
Overfield Rd NE3 . . . . 37 F5
Overhill NE15 . . . . 34 E2
Overhill Terr NE8 . . . . 101 A1
Overstone Ave NE40 . . . . . 51 F2
Overstone Gdns NE46 . . . . 45 A3
Overton Cl NE15 . . . . 53 D6
Overton Rd NE29 . . . . 41 E8
Ovett Gdns NE8 . . . . 56 B2
OVINGHAM 50 B5
Ovingham CE Fst Sch
NE42 . . . . 50 A3
Ovingham Cl NE38 . . . . 83 F5
Ovingham Gdns NE13 . . . . 28 B6
Ovingham Mid Sch NE42 . . 50 A3
Ovingham Rd NE41 . . . . 51 A6
Ovingham Way NE25 . . . . . 23 C4
OVINGTON 49 C4
Ovington Gr NE16 10 . . . . . 54 D8
Ovington View NE42 . . . . . . 50 B1
Owen Brannigan Dr NE23 . 29 B7
Owen Ct NE2 . . . . 98 C3
Owen Dr NE35, NE36 . . . . . . 74 B8
Owen Terr
Chopwell NE17 . . . . 77 C8
Tantobie DH9 . . . . 79 A1
Owlet Cl NE21 . . . . 53 A1
Owlet Grange NE37 . . . . 77 E5
Oxberry Gdns NE10 . . . . . . 71 C7
Oxbridge St SR2 . . . . 86 F2
OXCLOSE 83 B5
Oxclose Com Sch NE38 . . . 83 A4
Oxclose Rd NE38 . . . . 83 E4
Oxclose Village Prim Sch
NE38 . . . . 83 A5
Oxford Ave
Cramlington NE23 . . . . 22 C7
5 South Shields NE33 . . . . 59 D8
Wallsend NE28 . . . . 40 A3
Washington NE37 . . . . 83 B8
Oxford Cl
2 Longbenton NE12 . . . . . 39 B6
New Silksworth SR3 . . . . . . 91 F8
Oxford Cres
Hebburn NE31 . . . . 57 F6
Hetton-le-Hole DH5 . . . . . . 94 F4
Oxford Pl DH3 . . . . 82 C1
Oxford Rd NE62 . . . . 11 A7
Oxford Sq SR4 . . . . 85 E7
Oxford St
Blyth NE24 . . . . 17 F7
Newcastle upon Tyne NE1 . 99 B2
South Shields NE33 . . . . . . 59 D8
Sunderland SR4 . . . . 85 E7
Tynemouth NE30 . . . . 42 D7
Whitley Bay NE26 . . . . 32 B5
Oxford Terr
Gateshead NE8 . . . . 101 B1
Shiney Row DH4 . . . . 90 A6
Oxford Way NE32 . . . . 58 B1
Oxley Mews 7 NE25 . . . . . . 58 E1
Oxnam Cres NE2 . . . . 98 A3
Oxted Cl NE23 . . . . 22 D7
Oxted Pl NE6 . . . . 56 E3
Oystershell La NE4 . . . . 98 C1
Oyston St SR3 . . . . 42 C2
Ozanan Cl NE23 . . . . 29 B7

P

Packham Rd SR4 . . . . 85 C5
Paddock Cl
Cleadon SR6 . . . . 59 E1
Prudhoe NE42 . . . . 50 E2
Shiney Row DH4 . . . . 89 F5
Paddock Hill NE20 . . . . 25 F7
Paddock La SR3 . . . . 92 C7
Paddock Mews NE46 . . . . . 12 C6
Paddock Rise NE63 . . . . 6 B2
Paddocks The NE12 . . . . . . 12 C7
Paddock The
Ashington NE63 . . . . 7 B2
Blyth NE24 . . . . 17 C7
East Cramlington NE23 . . . 22 D5
Gateshead NE10 . . . . 71 F6
New Herrington DH4 . . . . . 90 F7
Seaton Delaval NE25 . . . . . 23 E3

Paddock The continued
Stocksfield NE43 . . . . 64 C5
Walbottle NE15 . . . . 35 F1
Woolsington NE13 . . . . 36 F8
Padstow Rd NE42 . . . . 50 E2
Pader Cl NE13 . . . . 28 B5
Padgate Rd SR4 . . . . 85 C6
Padonhill 5 SR3 . . . . 91 E5
Padstow Cl 2 SR2 . . . . 92 F8
Padstow Gdns NE9 . . . . . . 70 F2
Padstow Rd NE29 . . . . 41 E4
Page Ave NE34 . . . . 59 E7
Page's Bldgs NE35 . . . . 73 E8
Page St NE31 . . . . 57 F7
Paignton Ave
Newcastle upon Tyne NE4 . 54 F5
Whitley Bay NE25 . . . . 31 E4
Paignton Sq SR3 . . . . 85 E2
PAINSHAWFIELD 64 C6
Painshawfield Rd NE43 . . . . 64 C6
Paisley Sq SR3 . . . . 85 E2
Palace Rd NE22 . . . . 11 D2
Palace St NE4 . . . . 100 B4
Palatine Pl NE11 . . . . 70 A8
Palatine View DH6 . . . . 96 C1
Palermo St SR4 . . . . 85 F8
Paley St SR1 . . . . 102 C3
Palgrove Rd SR4 . . . . 85 C5
Palgrove Sq SR4 . . . . 85 C5
Pallinsburn Ct NE5 . . . . 37 B3
PALLION 85 D7
Pallion Ind Est SR4 . . . . . . 85 F8
Pallion New Rd SR4 . . . . . . 85 F8
Pallion Pk SR4 . . . . 85 F7
Pallion Rd SR4 . . . . 85 F7
Pallion Ret Pk SR4 . . . . 85 E8
Pallion Sta SR4 . . . . 85 E8
Pallion Subway SR4 . . . . . . 85 F8
Pallion Trad Est SR4 . . . . . . 85 D8
Pallion West Ind Est SR4 . . 85 D7
Palm Ave
Newcastle upon Tyne NE4 . 54 D7
South Shields NE34 . . . . . . 60 A5
Palm Ct NE34 . . . . 29 F1
Palmer Community Hospl
NE32 . . . . 58 B7
Palmer Cres NE31 . . . . 57 F6
Palmer Gdns NE10 . . . . 72 C8
Palmer Rd DH9 . . . . 78 E1
Palmers Gn NE12 . . . . 29 E3
Palmers Hill Rd SR6 . . . . . 103 A4
Palmer's Hill Rd SR6 . . . . . 103 A4
Palmer St NE32 . . . . 58 A7
Palmerston Ave NE6 . . . . . 56 E7
Palmerston Rd SR4 . . . . . . 85 B3
Palmerston Sq SR4 . . . . . . 85 B3
Palmerston St NE33 . . . . . . 59 C8
Palmerston Wlk NE8 . . . . . 101 A2
PALMERSVILLE 30 A1
Palmersville SR4 . . . . 30 A1
Palmersville Sta NE12 . . . . 30 A1
Palmer Walk NE8 . . . . 58 B7
Palmstead Rd SR4 . . . . 85 C5
Palmstead Sq SR4 . . . . 85 C5
Pancras Rd SR3 . . . . 85 E2
Pandon NE1 . . . . 99 B1
Pandon Bank NE1 . . . . 99 B1
Pandon Ct NE2 . . . . 99 C2
Pandon Quays NE1 . . . . . . 99 C1
Panfield Terr DH4 . . . . 90 B5
Pangbourne Ct NE15 . . . . . 53 C8
Pankhurst Gdns NE10 . . . . 72 A8
Pann La SR1 . . . . 103 A3
Panns Bank SR1 . . . . 103 A3
Pantiles The NE37 . . . . 72 D2
Parade Cl NE6 . . . . 57 A5
Parade The
Chester le Street DH3 . . . . 88 D1
Newcastle upon Tyne NE6 . 57 A5
Sunderland SR2 . . . . 103 C1
Wallsend NE28 . . . . 40 D5
Washington NE38 . . . . 83 E4
Paradise Row NE23 . . . . . . 22 B6
Park Ave
Bedlington NE22 . . . . 11 E3
Blaydon, Bleach Green NE21 53 B2
Blaydon NE21 . . . . 53 C2
Dunston NE11 . . . . 69 E7
Hexham NE46 . . . . 44 F5
Newcastle upon Tyne, Gosforth
NE3 . . . . 37 F7
Newcastle upon Tyne, Gosforth
NE3 . . . . 38 B6
New Silksworth SR3 . . . . . . 92 B7
North Shields NE30 . . . . . . 42 C7
Prudhoe NE42 . . . . 50 E1
Shiremoor NE27 . . . . 31 A3
South Shields NE34 . . . . . . 59 F4
Sunderland SR6 . . . . 75 E4
Wallsend NE28 . . . . 40 B2
Washington NE37 . . . . 83 D8
Whitley Bay NE26 . . . . 32 A5
Park Chare NE38 . . . . 83 D5
Park Cl NE4 . . . . 100 A4
Park Cotts NE17 . . . . 77 B6
Park Cres
North Shields NE30 . . . . . . 42 B7
Shiremoor NE27 . . . . 30 F3
Park Crescent E NE30 . . . . 42 C7
Park Ct
Gateshead, Chowdene
NE11 . . . . 70 D3
Gateshead NE8 . . . . 101 C3
Wallsend NE28 . . . . 40 A1
Parkdale Rise NE16 . . . . . . 69 A7

Park Dr
Blyth NE24 . . . . 17 B4
Longbenton NE12 . . . . 39 E8
Morpeth NE61 . . . . 8 F7
Newcastle upon Tyne NE3 . 28 C1
Stannington NE61 . . . . 9 E1
Whickham NE16 . . . . 69 C8
Parker Ave NE3 . . . . 38 B3
Parker Ct NE11 . . . . 54 E2
PARK ESTATE 24 C6
Park Farm Villas NE24 . . . . 17 C2
Parkfield NE32 . . . . 58 C1
Park Field NE40 . . . . 52 C5
Park Field Terr NE26 . . . . . . 24 C6
Parkgate DH5 . . . . 95 C3
Park Gate SR6 . . . . 75 E3
Parkgate La NE21 . . . . 68 B8
Park Gdns NE26 . . . . 32 A5
Park Gr
Shiremoor NE27 . . . . 30 F3
Washington NE37 . . . . 72 D1
Park Hall SR2 . . . . 103 A1
Park Head Rd NE7 . . . . 39 A1
Parkhead Com Prim Sch
NE21 . . . . 68 C8
Parkhead Gdns NE21 . . . . . 68 B8
Park Head Rd NE7 . . . . 39 A1
Parkhead Sq NE21 . . . . 53 C1
Parkhouse Ave SR5 . . . . . . 85 B8
Park House Gdns DH6 . . . . 96 A2
Parkhurst Rd SR4 . . . . 85 C5
Parkin Gdns NE10 . . . . 71 E7
Park La
Blaydon NE21 . . . . 68 B8
Gateshead NE8 . . . . 56 A3
Prudhoe NE42 . . . . 50 D1
Shiremoor NE27 . . . . 30 F2
Sunderland SR1 . . . . 103 A2
Parkland
Longbenton NE12 . . . . 39 D6
Ryton NE21 . . . . 53 A4
Parkland Ave NE21 . . . . 68 B8
Parklands
Gateshead NE10 . . . . 72 C8
Hamsterley Mill NE39 . . . . 77 F5
Ponteland NE20 . . . . 25 B2
Parklands Ct NE10 . . . . 57 C1
Parklands Way NE10 . . . . . 72 C8
Park Lane Intc SR1 . . . . . . 103 A2
Park Lane Sta SR1 . . . . . . 103 A2
Parklea NE26 . . . . 24 C6
Park Lea SR3 . . . . 91 B6
Park Lea Rd SR4 . . . . 85 A3
Parkmore Rd SR4 . . . . 85 A3
Park Par
Sunderland SR6 . . . . 75 E2
Whitley Bay NE26 . . . . 32 A5
Park Pl DH3 . . . . 88 D5
Park Place E SR2 . . . . 103 A1
Park Place W SR2 . . . . 103 A1
Park Rd
Ashington NE63 . . . . 6 B3
Bedlington NE22 . . . . 16 A8
Blyth NE24 . . . . 17 F7
Gateshead NE10, NE8 . . . . 56 E1
Hebburn NE31 . . . . 57 E5
Jarrow NE32 . . . . 58 A6
Lynemouth NE61, NE63 . . . . 2 A2
Newburn NE15 . . . . 52 F8
Newcastle upon Tyne NE4 . 100 A3
Rowlands Gill NE39 . . . . . . 67 D2
Seaton Delaval NE25 . . . . . 23 C3
Shiremoor NE27 . . . . 30 F3
Sunderland SR6 . . . . 75 E4
Wallsend NE28 . . . . 40 C1
Whitley Bay NE26 . . . . 32 A6
Park Rise NE15 . . . . 53 C7
Park Road Central DH3 . . . 88 D3
Park Road East NE63 . . . . . . 6 C4
Park Road N DH3 . . . . 88 D1
Park Road S DH3 . . . . 88 D1
Park Row
3 Gateshead NE10 . . . . . . 71 D8
Sunderland SR5 . . . . 75 A1
Parkshiel NE34 . . . . 60 A4
PARKSIDE 22 B7
Parkside
Bedlington NE22 . . . . 11 E3
Dunston NE11 . . . . 54 D4
Sunderland SR3 . . . . 91 B6
Tanfield Lea DH9 . . . . 79 C1
Throckley NE15 . . . . 35 E1
Tynemouth NE30 . . . . 32 D1
Wallsend NE28 . . . . 40 D3
Park Side NE61 . . . . 9 F5
Parkside Ave
Blaydon NE21 . . . . 53 C2
Newcastle upon Tyne NE7 . 39 B5
Parkside Cotts DH9 . . . . . . 79 C1
Parkside Cres NE30 . . . . . . 42 D8
Parkside Ct
Ashington NE63 . . . . 6 C2
Chopwell NE17 . . . . 66 C1
Whitley Bay NE26 . . . . 31 F5
Widopen NE13 . . . . 28 C6
Parkside S SR3 . . . . 91 B6
Parkside Terr NE28 . . . . . . 40 A4
Parks The DH1 . . . . 57 D4
Parkstone Cl SR4 . . . . 85 A3
Park Street S SR5 . . . . 74 C1
Park Terr
Bedlington NE22 . . . . 11 D3
Blaydon NE21 . . . . 53 D2
Burnopfield NE16 . . . . 79 A6
Dunston NE11 . . . . 69 F8
Killingworth NE12 . . . . 29 B2

Park Terr continued
Newcastle upon Tyne NE1,
NE2 . . . . 99 A3
North Shields NE30 . . . . . . 42 C7
Sunderland SR5 . . . . 75 A2
Wallsend NE28 . . . . 40 B2
Washington NE37 . . . . 72 D1
Whickham NE16 . . . . 54 A1
Whitley Bay NE26 . . . . 32 A6
Park View
Ashington NE63 . . . . 6 B4
Blaydon NE21 . . . . 68 C8
Blyth NE24 . . . . 17 F7
Bournmoor DH3 . . . . 89 D4
Burnopfield NE16 . . . . 79 B6
Hetton-le-Hole DH5 . . . . . 95 A3
Jarrow NE32 . . . . 58 B4
Longbenton, Forest Hall
NE12 . . . . 39 D8
Longbenton NE12 . . . . 29 B2
Lynemouth NE61 . . . . 2 A2
Newcastle upon Tyne NE5 . 57 A5
Seaton Delaval NE25 . . . . . 23 D3
Shiney Row DH4 . . . . 90 B6
Wallsend NE28 . . . . 40 B2
Whitley Bay NE26 . . . . 32 A5
Widopen NE13 . . . . 28 C6
Park View Cl NE40 . . . . 52 D5
Park View Com Sch DH3 . . 88 D3
Park View 1 NE26 . . . . 32 A5
Park View NE40 . . . . 52 D5
Park View Sh Ctr 4 NE26 . 32 A5
Park Villas
Ashington NE63 . . . . 6 B4
Wallsend NE28 . . . . 40 B2
Parkville NE6 . . . . 56 A7
Park Wall Cnr SR3 . . . . 91 B6
Parkway
Guide Post NE62 . . . . 10 F8
Washington, Biddick NE38 . 83 C4
Washington, Washington Village
NE38 . . . . 83 D5
Whickham NE16 . . . . 68 E6
Parkwood Ave NE42 . . . . . . 50 F3
Parliament St NE31 . . . . . . 57 C7
Parmontley St NE15 . . . . . . 53 F5
Parnell St NE4 . . . . 94 B8
Parrish View NE1 . . . . 99 A1
Parry Dr SR6 . . . . 60 E1
Parson Rd NE41 . . . . 51 B6
Parson's Ave NE6 . . . . 56 F5
Parsons' Gdns 5 NE11 . . . . 54 F1
Parsons Ind Est NE37 . . . . 83 B8
Parsons Rd NE37 . . . . 83 A8
Parsons St 10 NE24 . . . . . . 17 E8
Partick Rd SR4 . . . . 85 B4
Partick Sq SR4 . . . . 85 C4
Partnership Ct SR7 . . . . 92 E2
Partridge Cl NE38 . . . . 82 F4
Pasteur Rd DH6 . . . . 97 F7
Paston Rd NE25 . . . . 23 D2
Pastures The
Morpeth NE61 . . . . 17 D4
East Boldon NE36 . . . . 94 D4
Morpeth NE61 . . . . 8 D7
Stocksfield NE43 . . . . 64 B8
PATH HEAD 53 B3
Pathside NE32 . . . . 58 C2
Path The 8 NE24 . . . . 70 F4
Patience Ave NE13 . . . . 28 C8
Patina Cl NE15 . . . . 53 B3
Paton Rd SR3 . . . . 85 F2
Paton Sq SR3 . . . . 85 F2
Patrick Cain Ho NE33 . . . . . 59 B8
Patrick Cres DH6 . . . . 97 E8
Patrick Terr NE23 . . . . 29 B7
Patterdale Cl NE36 . . . . 74 C7
Patterdale Gdns NE7 . . . . . 39 B4
Patterdale Gr SR5 . . . . 75 C4
Patterdale Ho NE17 . . . . . . 14 A8
Patterdale Rd NE24 . . . . . . 17 A8
Patterdale St DH5 . . . . 95 A2
Patterdale Terr NE8 . . . . . . 70 F8
Patterson St NE46 . . . . 44 E3
Patterson St NE21 . . . . 53 E4
Patterson Way 5 DH4 . . . . . 6 F5
Pattinson Gdns
Washington NE38 . . . . 84 B6
Washington, Swan NE38 . . . 83 F3
Pattinson Rd NE38 . . . . 84 B4
Patton Way NE61 . . . . 4 E3
Pauline Ave SR6 . . . . 75 D3
Pauline Gdns NE15 . . . . 54 A7
Pauls Gn DH5 . . . . 94 E5
Pauls Rd SR1 . . . . 103 B2
Paulsway NE32 . . . . 58 E6
Pavilion Mews NE2 . . . . 99 C4
Pavilion Terr DH5 . . . . 95 A3
Pavilion The NE16 . . . . 53 F1
Pavillion Ct SR1 . . . . 103 A2
Pawston Rd NE21, NE39 . . . 67 B5
Paxford Cl NE7 . . . . 39 A5
Peacehaven Ct NE37 . . . . . 72 C2
Peacock Ct NE11 . . . . 70 A3
Peacock Street W SR4 . . . . 85 F6
Pearth Edge 2 NE9 . . . . 71 F1
Peareth Gr SR6 . . . . 75 F3
Peareth Hall Rd NE37, NE9 . 72 A4
Peareth Rd SR6 . . . . 75 F4
Peareth Terr DH3 . . . . 82 C3

Pearey Ho NE29 . . . . .42 A7
Pearl Rd SR3 . . . . .85 F2
Pearson Pl
  Jarrow NE32 . . . . .58 C8
  North Shields NE30 . . . . . . .42 B6
Pearson St NE33 . . . . .42 D4
Pearson's Terr **1** NE46 . . . .45 A5
Peart Cl DH6 . . . . .96 A1
Peartree Bglws NE17 . . . . . .77 C6
Peartree Ct NE17 . . . . .77 C6
Peartree Gdns NE6 . . . . .40 A1
Peartree Mews **8** SR2 . . . .86 C4
Pear Tree Terr
  Chopwell NE17 . . . . .77 B8
  Great Lumley DH3 . . . . .89 B1
Peary Cl NE5 . . . . .36 F2
Pease Ave NE15 . . . . .54 C6
Peascmoor Rd SR4 . . . . .85 B5
Pebble Beach SR6 . . . . .75 F7
Pecket Cl NE24 . . . . .17 A5
Peddars Way NE34 . . . . .59 B5
Peebles Cl NE29 . . . . .41 C8
Peebles Rd SR3 . . . . .85 E2
Peel Cl NE13 . . . . .28 B8
Peel Ctr The NE37 . . . . .83 F7
Peel Gdns NE34 . . . . .58 E4
Peel La NE11 . . . . .100 C4
Peel Ret Pk NE37 . . . . .83 F7
Peel St
  Newcastle upon Tyne
  NE1 . . . . .100 C4
  Sunderland SR2 . . . . .103 B1
Peepy Cotts NE43 . . . . .48 D2
PEGSWOOD 4 F3
Pegswood Fst Sch NE61 . . . .4 F4
Pegswood Ho NE4 . . . . .98 B2
Pegswood Ind Est NE61 . . . . .4 F4
Pegswood Prec NE61 . . . . . . .4 F3
Pegswood Sta NE61 . . . . .4 F3
Pegswood Village NE61 . . . . .4 E4
Pegwood Rd SR4 . . . . .85 C5
PELAW 56 F1
Pelaw Ave
  Chester le Street DH2 . . . . .88 C5
  Newbeggin-by-the-Sea NE64 . .7 D5
Pelaw Bank DH3 . . . . .88 C4
Pelaw Cres DH2 . . . . .88 B5
Pelaw Grange Ct NE10 . . . . .88 C8
Pelaw Ind Est NE10 . . . . . . .72 A8
Pelaw Pl DH2 . . . . .88 C5
Pelaw Quarry Pond Nature
  Reserve* NE32 . . . . .57 D2
Pelaw Rd DH2 . . . . .88 C5
Pelaw Sq
  Chester le Street DH2 . . . . .88 B5
  Sunderland SR4 . . . . .85 C7
Pelaw Sta NE10 . . . . .57 A1
Pelaw Way NE10 . . . . .57 A1
Peldon Cl NE7 . . . . .38 F5
Pelham Ct NE3 . . . . .37 D7
Pelltoedale Ave NE24 . . . . . .17 A8
Pelton Fell Rd DH2 . . . . .88 B4
Pelton Dr DH2 . . . . .88 B5
Pelton Rd SR4 . . . . .85 C4
Pemberton Bank DH5 . . . . . .95 C1
Pemberton Cl **2** SR5 . . . . .75 B1
Pemberton Gdns **3** SR3 . .86 B3
Pemberton St DH5 . . . . .95 A4
Pembridge NE38 . . . . .83 A5
Pembroke Ave
  Birtley DH3 . . . . .82 D1
  Newcastle upon Tyne NE6 . . .56 F7
  Silksworth SR3 . . . . .92 A6
Pembroke Ct
  1 Blyth NE24 . . . . .17 F6
  Newbeggin-by-the-Sea NE64 . .7 E5
  Newcastle upon Tyne NE3 . . .37 D7
Pembroke Dr NE20 . . . . .25 B4
Pembroke Gdns
  Ashington NE63 . . . . .7 A1
  Wallsend NE28 . . . . .41 A4
Pembroke Terr NE33 . . . . . . .59 C7
Pendeford Ave NE24 . . . . . . .56 E7
Pendamor Ct NE61 . . . . .5 D8
Pendeford NE38 . . . . .84 A4
Pendle Cl NE38 . . . . .84 A3
Pendle Gn SR4 . . . . .102 A1
Pendleton Dr NE23 . . . . .16 B1
Pendower Way NE15 . . . . . . .54 C5
Penfold Cl NE7 . . . . .39 C4
Penhale Dr SR2 . . . . .92 F7
Penhill Cl DH2 . . . . .81 F1
Penine View DH6 . . . . .96 D1
Penistone Rd SR4 . . . . .85 A4
Penman Pl NE29 . . . . .42 A4
Penman Sq SR4 . . . . .85 C4
Penman St NE29 . . . . .42 A4
Pennant Sq SR4 . . . . .85 C6
Pennine Ave DH2 . . . . .88 B2
Pennine Ct **2** SR3 . . . . . . .91 F6
Pennine Dr NE63 . . . . .6 E1
Pennine Gdns NE11 . . . . .70 A6
Pennine Gr NE36 . . . . .74 B7
Pennine View NE17 . . . . .77 B8
Pennine Way NE12 . . . . .39 A6
Penn Sq SR4 . . . . .85 C6
Penn St NE4 . . . . .100 B3
Pennycross Rd SR4 . . . . .85 A4
Pennycross Sq SR4 . . . . .85 A5
Pennyfine Cl NE29 . . . . .42 A8
Pennyfine Rd NE16 . . . . .69 C2
Pennygate Sq SR4 . . . . .85 A5
Pennygreen Sq SR4 . . . . . . .85 A5
Penny La NE22 . . . . .15 D5
Pennymore Sq SR4 . . . . .85 A4

Pennywell 85 B4
Pennywell Bsns Ctr SR4 . . . .85 C5
Pennywell Ind Est SR4 . . . . .85 A3
Pennywell Rd SR4 . . . . .85 C4
Pennywell Sh Prec SR4 . . . . .85 C4
Penrith Ave NE30 . . . . .32 A2
Penrith Gdns NE9 . . . . .71 B4
Penrith Ct NE22 . . . . .10 D2
Penrith Gdns NE9 . . . . .71 B4
Penrith Gr NE9 . . . . .71 B4
Penrith Rd
  Hebburn NE31 . . . . .57 F4
  Sunderland SR5 . . . . .75 C4
Penrose Gn NE3 . . . . .37 F5
Penrose Rd SR4 . . . . .85 B4
Pensford Ct NE3 . . . . .37 C6
PENSHAW 90 C7
Penshaw Gn NE5 . . . . .37 D3
Penshaw La DH4 . . . . .90 B8
Penshaw Monument*
  SR4 . . . . .84 C1
Penshaw View
  Gateshead NE10 . . . . .72 C8
  Hebburn NE31 . . . . .57 E4
  Jarrow NE32 . . . . .58 B4
Penshaw Way
  Birtley DH3 . . . . .82 E4
  North Side DH3 . . . . .82 D6
Pensher St E NE10 . . . . .56 C1
Pensher St
  Gateshead NE10 . . . . .56 C1
  Sunderland SR4 . . . . .102 B2
Pensher View NE37 . . . . .72 E1
Pent Ct NE40 . . . . .52 A1
Pentland Cl
  Ashington NE63 . . . . .6 E1
  Cramlington NE23 . . . . .16 B1
  Tynemouth NE29 . . . . .31 F1
  Washington NE38 . . . . .83 B3
Pentland Ct **1** DH2 . . . . . .88 C4
Pentland Gr NE12 . . . . .70 A7
Pentland Gdns NE12 . . . . . . .29 B1
Pentridge Cl NE23 . . . . .22 C7
Penwood Rd SR4 . . . . .85 C5
Penyghent Way NE37 . . . . . .83 A6
Penzance Par NE31 . . . . .58 A2
Penzance Rd SR4 . . . . .85 B4
Peplow Sq SR4 . . . . .85 C7
Peppercorn Ct NE1 . . . . . . .101 B4
Percival St SR4 . . . . .85 F7
Percy Ave NE30 . . . . .32 C3
Percy Cl NE46 . . . . .44 F3
Percy Cotts NE25 . . . . .23 E2
Percy Cres NE29 . . . . .41 D3
Percy Ct NE29 . . . . .41 D3
Percy Gardens Cotts
  NE30 . . . . .42 D8
Percy Gdns
  Dunston NE11 . . . . .70 A7
  Longbenton NE12 . . . . .39 D8
  Stakeford NE62 . . . . .11 A8
  Tynemouth NE30 . . . . .42 E8
  Whitley Bay NE25 . . . . .32 A2
Percy Hedley Sch NE12 . . . . .39 D7
Percy Hedley Senior Sch The
  NE12 . . . . .39 D2
Percy Lonnen NE42 . . . . .50 D3
PERCY MAIN 41 D3
Percy Main Prim Sch
  NE29 . . . . .41 D3
Percy Main Sta NE29 . . . . . .41 D3
Percy Park Rd NE30 . . . . . . .42 D8
Percy Pk NE30 . . . . .42 D8
Percy Rd NE26 . . . . .32 B5
Percy St S NE24 . . . . .17 F7
Percy Scott St NE34 . . . . . . .59 C3
Percy St
  Ashington NE63 . . . . .6 E4
  Blyth NE24 . . . . .17 F8
  Cramlington NE23 . . . . .22 C5
  Hetton-le-Hole DH5 . . . . . . .95 B4
  Jarrow NE32 . . . . .58 C7
  Longbenton NE12 . . . . .29 F1
  Newcastle upon Tyne, Lemington
  NE15 . . . . .53 C6
  Newcastle upon Tyne NE1 . . .99 A2
  5 South Shields NE33 . . . .42 D2
  Tynemouth NE30 . . . . .42 E7
  Wallsend NE28 . . . . .40 C2
Percy Terr
  Newburn NE15 . . . . .52 F7
  Blyth NE24 . . . . .17 F8
  Penshaw DH4 . . . . .90 A8
  Sunderland SR2 . . . . .86 E4
  4 Whitburn SR6 . . . . . . .60 F1
  Whitley Bay NE25 . . . . .31 E5
Percy Terrace S SR2 . . . . . . .86 F3
Percy Way NE15 . . . . .36 A1
Peregrine Ct NE28 . . . . .41 F6
Peregrine Pl NE12 . . . . .39 A7
Perivale Rd SR4 . . . . .85 B4
Perrycrofts SR3 . . . . .92 A6
Perry St NE8 NE9 . . . . .70 F8
Perry Stone Mews NE22 . . . .16 A8
Perth Ave NE32, NE34 . . . . . .58 E3
Perth Cl
  Tynemouth NE29 . . . . .41 C8
  Wallsend NE28 . . . . .40 F4
Perth Ct
  Gateshead NE11 . . . . .70 E3
  Sunderland SR3 . . . . .91 F5
Perth Gdns NE28 . . . . .40 F4
Perth Rd SR3 . . . . .85 E2
Perth Sq SR3 . . . . .85 F2
Pescott Cl **7** NE46 . . . . . . .45 A4
Pesspool Ave DH6 . . . . .97 F3
Pesspool Bglws DH6 . . . . . . .97 F3
Pesspool La DH6 . . . . .97 F3
Pesspool Terr DH6 . . . . .97 F3

Peterborough Cl NE8 . . . . . .101 B2
Peterborough Way NE32 . . . .58 B1
Petersfield Rd SR4 . . . . .85 B4
Petersham Rd SR4 . . . . .85 B4
Peter Stracey Ho SR6 . . . . . .75 D4
Petherton Ct NE3 . . . . .37 C6
Pethgate Ct **10** NE61 . . . . .9 A8
Peth Gn DH5 . . . . .95 B1
Peth Head NE46 . . . . .45 C5
Peth La NE40 . . . . .52 D6
Petrel Cl **12** NE33 . . . . . . .42 C4
Petrel Way NE24 . . . . .17 F4
Petteril NE38 . . . . .83 A3
Petworth Cl NE33 . . . . .42 D3
Petworth Gdns NE61 . . . . . . .4 E4
Pevensey Cl NE29 . . . . .31 F1
Pexton Way NE5 . . . . .36 F3
Pheasantmoor **3** NE37 . . .83 A7
PHILADELPHIA 90 C5
Philadelphia Aged Miners
  Homes **6** DH4 . . . . .90 B6
Philadelphia Complex
  DH4 . . . . .90 D6
Philadelphia La DH4 . . . . . . .90 C4
Philiphaugh NE28 . . . . .57 B8
Philip Pl NE4 . . . . .98 A2
Philip's Ct **3** NE9 . . . . . . .71 B5
Philipson St NE6 . . . . .56 F6
Philip Sq SR3 . . . . .85 E2
Philip St NE4 . . . . .98 A2
Phillips Ave **1** NE16 . . . . .69 A8
Phillips Cl DH6 . . . . .97 E3
Phobe Grange Cotts
  NE42 . . . . .50 D2
Phoenix Chase NE29 . . . . . . .41 C8
Phoenix Ct
  6 Morpeth NE61 . . . . .8 F8
  Newcastle upon Tyne NE29 . .41 C8
Phoenix Rd
  Sunderland SR4 . . . . .85 C6
  Washington NE38 . . . . .82 E6
Phoenix St NE21 . . . . .17 B4
Phoenix Way DH4 . . . . .94 C7
Piccadilly SR3 . . . . .91 E8
Picherwell NE10 . . . . .71 D7
Pickard St SR4 . . . . .102 A3
Pickering Ct NE32 . . . . .58 A7
Pickering Dr NE21 . . . . .53 D2
Pickering Gn NE9 . . . . .71 B2
PICKERING NOOK 79 A4
Pickering Rd SR4 . . . . .85 B4
Pickering Sq SR4 . . . . .85 B4
Pickersgill Ho SR5 . . . . .74 C3
Pickhurst Rd SR4 . . . . .85 B3
Pickwick Cl SR4 . . . . .85 B3
PICKTREE 88 D7
Picktree Cotts **2** DH3 . . . .88 D4
Picktree Cotts **3** DH3 . . . .88 D7
Picktree Farm Cotts NE38 . . .88 E7
Picktree La
  Chester le Street DH3 . . . . .88 D4
  Chester le Street, Picktree DH3,
  NE38 . . . . .88 E7
Picktree Lodge
  Birtley NE35 . . . . .82 E1
  Chester le Street DH3 . . . . .88 D5
Picktree Mews **6** DH3 . . . .88 D4
Picktree Terr **1** DH3 . . . . .88 D7
Pier Par NE33 . . . . .42 E4
Pier Rd NE30 . . . . .42 E7
Pier View SR6 . . . . .75 F2
Pikestone Cl NE38 . . . . .83 A3
Pilgrim Cl SR5 . . . . .75 C1
Pilgrims Ct NE12 . . . . .99 B4
Pilgrim St
  Newcastle upon Tyne NE1 . .101 B4
  Newcastle upon Tyne NE1 . .101 B4
Pilgrimsway
  Gateshead NE9 . . . . .71 B7
  Jarrow NE32 . . . . .58 E6
Pilgrims Way NE61 . . . . .8 D7
Pilton Rd NE5 . . . . .36 F3
Pilton Wlk **1** NE5 . . . . . . .36 F3
Pimlico Ct NE10 . . . . .70 F4
Pimlico Rd
  Hetton-le-Hole DH5 . . . . . . .95 B1
  Sunderland SR4 . . . . .85 B4
Pinders Way DH6 . . . . .96 D1
Pine Ave
  Burnopfield NE16 . . . . .78 F6
  Chester le Street DH3 . . . . .27 C7
  Guide Post NE62 . . . . .11 A8
  3 Houghton-le-Spring DH4 .94 D8
  Newcastle upon Tyne NE3 . . .37 F2
  South Shields NE34 . . . . . . .60 A5
Pinedale Dr DH4 . . . . .97 F7
Pinegarth NE20 . . . . .25 C2
Pine Rd NE21 . . . . .53 C2
Pine St
  Birtley DH3 . . . . .82 C5
  4 Chester le Street DH3 . . .88 C1
  Greenside NE40 . . . . .52 B1
  Jarrow NE32 . . . . .58 A6
  Seaton Burn NE13 . . . . .28 C8
  Sunderland SR4 . . . . .85 E7
  Throckley NE15 . . . . .35 D3
Pines The
  Greenside NE40 . . . . .52 B1
  Newcastle upon Tyne NE4 . .100 A3
Pinesway SR3 . . . . .86 B3
Pinetree Gdns NE25 . . . . . . .31 E3
Pinetree Way NE11 . . . . .54 B2
Pinewood NE31 . . . . .57 C7
Pinewood Ave
  Cramlington NE23 . . . . .16 B1
  Washington NE38 . . . . .83 C1
  Widopen NE13 . . . . .28 C5

Pinewood Cl
  Newcastle upon Tyne, Kingston
  Park NE3 . . . . .37 B7
  Newcastle upon Tyne,
  Walkerville NE6 . . . . .39 F1
  Washington NE38 . . . . .83 F3
Pinewood Dr NE61 . . . . .3 D2
Pinewood Gdns NE11 . . . . . .70 A5
Pinewood Rd SR5 . . . . .74 F2
Pinewood Sq **8** SR5 . . . . .74 F2
Pinewood St DH4 . . . . .89 E1
Pinewood Villas NE34 . . . . . .60 A6
Pink La
  Newcastle upon Tyne
  NE1 . . . . .100 C4
  Newcastle upon Tyne NE1 . .101 A4
Pinner Pl NE6 . . . . .56 E4
Pinner Rd SR4 . . . . .85 C5
Pintail Ct **10** NE34 . . . . . . .59 A4
Pioneer Terr NE22 . . . . .11 C2
Piper Rd NE42 . . . . .50 B5
Pipershaw NE37 . . . . .82 F6
Pipe Track La NE4 . . . . .54 D4
Pipewellgate NE8 . . . . .101 B3
Pitcairn Rd SR4 . . . . .85 C5
Pit Row SR3 . . . . .91 F8
Pittington La DH6 . . . . .96 A6
Pittington Prim Sch DH6 . . . .96 B3
Pittington Rd DH5, DH6 . . . . .96 A7
Pitt St NE4 . . . . .98 C2
PLAINS FARM 85 F2
Plains Farm Prim Sch
  SR3 . . . . .85 F2
Plains Rd SR3 . . . . .85 F2
Plaistow Sq SR4 . . . . .85 C6
Plaistow Way NE23 . . . . .16 B1
Planesway NE10 . . . . .71 E5
Planet Ho SR1 . . . . .103 A3
Planet Pl NE12 . . . . .29 C2
Planetree Ave NE4 . . . . .54 D8
Plane Tree Ct SR3 . . . . .91 E6
Plantagenet Ave DH3 . . . . . .88 D2
Plantation Ave
  High Pittington DH6 . . . . . . .96 E3
  Whickham NE16 . . . . .69 A8
Plantation Ct NE40 . . . . .66 E8
Plantation Gr NE10 . . . . .57 A7
Plantation Rd SR4 . . . . .85 F7
Plantation Sq **2** SR4 . . . . .85 F7
Plantation St NE28 . . . . .57 B8
Plantation Wlk DH6 . . . . .97 F7
Plawsworth Gdns NE9 . . . . . .71 C3
Pleasant Pl **1** DH3 . . . . . .82 C5
Plenmeller Pl NE16 . . . . .69 A3
Plessey Ave NE24 . . . . .17 F6
Plessey Cres NE25 . . . . .32 B4
Plessey Ct **1** NE24 . . . . . .17 B4
Plessey Gdns NE29 . . . . .41 D5
Plessey Rd NE24 . . . . .17 D5
Plessey Road Fst Sch
  NE24 . . . . .17 F7
Plessey Road Workshops
  NE24 . . . . .17 B4
Plessey St NE23 . . . . .16 B3
Plessey Terr NE7 . . . . .39 B2
Plessey Woods Ctry Pk*
  NE22 . . . . .15 B4
Plough Rd SR3 . . . . .91 F5
Plover Cl
  Blyth NE24 . . . . .17 E4
  5 Washington NE38 . . . . .82 F3
Plover Dr NE16 . . . . .79 C5
Plover Ho NE12 . . . . .29 F4
Plover Lodge DH3 . . . . .82 C6
Plummer St NE4 . . . . .100 C3
Plunkett Rd DH9 . . . . .78 E1
Plymouth Sq SR3 . . . . .85 E2
Point Pleasant Ind Est
  NE28 . . . . .40 F1
Point Pleasant Terr NE28 . . . .40 E1
Polden Cres NE29 . . . . .31 F1
Polebrook Rd SR4 . . . . .85 C6
Pollard St NE33 . . . . .42 D3
Polmaise St NE21 . . . . .53 C2
Polmuir Rd SR3 . . . . .85 E2
Polmuir Sq SR3 . . . . .85 E2
Polpero Cl DH3 . . . . .82 D3
Polperro Cl **6** SR2 . . . . . . .92 F8
Polton Sq SR4 . . . . .85 C6
Polwarth Cres NE3 . . . . .38 C8
Polwarth Dr NE3 . . . . .28 C1
Polwarth Pl NE3 . . . . .38 C8
Polwarth Rd NE3 . . . . .28 C1
Polworth Sq SR3 . . . . .85 E2
Pontdyke NE10 . . . . .71 F4
Pontefract Rd **2** SR4 . . . . .85 B3
PONTELAND 25 D6
Ponteland Cl
  Tynemouth NE29 . . . . .41 C7
  Washington NE38 . . . . .82 F4
Ponteland Com High Sch
  NE20 . . . . .25 F5
Ponteland Fst Sch NE20 . . . .25 F7
Ponteland L Ctr NE20 . . . . . .25 F6
Ponteland Mid Sch NE20 . . . .25 F5
Ponteland Rd
  Newcastle upon Tyne, Blakelaw
  NE5 . . . . .37 D3
  Newcastle upon Tyne, Kenton
  Bankfoot NE3 . . . . .37 B6
  Newcastle upon Tyne, Spital
  Tongues NE2 . . . . .98 A3
Ponteland NE20 . . . . .26 A5
Throckley NE15 . . . . .35 D5
Woolsington NE13 . . . . .37 A7

Pont Haugh NE20 . . . . .25 F7
Pontop Sq SR4 . . . . .85 C7
Pontop St DH5 . . . . .94 C4
Pontop View NE39 . . . . .67 D2
Pont Pk NE20 . . . . .19 A2
Pont St NE63 . . . . .6 B3
Pont View NE20 . . . . .25 F7
Poole Cl NE23 . . . . .22 C7
Poole Rd SR4 . . . . .85 C6
Pooley Cl NE5 . . . . .37 B1
Pooley Rd NE5 . . . . .37 B1
Poplar Ave
  Blyth NE24 . . . . .12 D1
  Burnopfield NE16 . . . . .78 F6
  Dinnington NE13 . . . . .27 C7
  1 Houghton-le-Spring DH4 .94 D8
  Newcastle upon Tyne NE6 . . .39 F1
Poplar Cl NE31 . . . . .57 E3
Poplar Cres
  Birtley DH3 . . . . .82 B5
  Gateshead NE11 . . . . .69 F7
  Gateshead NE8 . . . . .101 B2
Poplar Dr SR6 . . . . .60 F1
Poplar Gr
  Bedlington NE22 . . . . .11 C1
  7 Sunderland SR2 . . . . . .92 E8
Poplar Pl **1** NE3 . . . . .38 C5
Poplar Rd NE21 . . . . .53 C1
Poplar St
  Ashington NE63 . . . . .6 D4
  3 Chester le Street DH3 . . .88 C3
  Throckley NE15 . . . . .35 D3
Poplars The
  Easington Lane DH5 . . . . . . .95 C1
  Newcastle upon Tyne, Elswick
  NE4 . . . . .100 A3
  Newcastle upon Tyne, Gosforth
  NE3 . . . . .38 C3
  Newcastle upon Tyne NE3 . . .90 B8
  1 Sunderland, South Hylton
  SR4 . . . . .84 C2
  Washington SR5 . . . . .74 F2
Poplar Terr DH3 . . . . .83 D4
Popplewell Gdns NE9 . . . . . .71 A4
Popplewell Terr NE29 . . . . . .42 A8
Popular Ct **3** DH3 . . . . . . .22 C7
Porchester Dr NE23 . . . . .22 C7
Porlock Ct NE23 . . . . .16 A1
Porlock Ho NE32 . . . . .58 D5
Porlock Rd NE32 . . . . .58 D5
Portadown Rd **1** SR4 . . . . .85 B3
Portberry St NE33 . . . . .42 B1
Portberry Street Ind Est
  NE33 . . . . .59 B8
Portberry Way NE33 . . . . . . .42 B1
Portchester Gr NE35 . . . . . . .73 F8
Portchester Rd SR4 . . . . .85 C4
Porthcawl Dr NE37 . . . . .72 C2
Portia St NE63 . . . . .6 D3
Portland Cl DH2 . . . . .88 A1
Portland Gdns
  Cramlington NE23 . . . . .22 C7
  1 Gateshead NE9 . . . . . . .70 F2
  Tynemouth NE30 . . . . .42 A7
Portland Ind Pk NE63 . . . . . . .5 F5
Portland Mews NE2 . . . . .99 C3
Portland Rd
  Newcastle upon Tyne NE2 . . .99 C2
  Sunderland SR3 . . . . .85 F3
  Throckley NE15 . . . . .35 C2
Portland Sch
  Silksworth SR3 . . . . .91 E5
  Sunderland SR3 . . . . .85 F3
Portland St
  1 Blyth NE24 . . . . .17 D8
  Gateshead NE10 . . . . .57 A1
  Newcastle upon Tyne NE4 . . .54 F4
Portland Terr
  Ashington NE63 . . . . .6 D4
  Hexham NE46 . . . . .44 F5
  Newcastle upon Tyne NE2 . . .99 C3
Portman Mews NE2 . . . . .56 E3
Portman Pl NE6 . . . . .56 E3
Portman Sq SR4 . . . . .85 C6
Portmarnock NE37 . . . . .72 B2
Portmeads Rd DH3 . . . . .82 D4
Portmeads Rise DH3 . . . . . . .82 D5
PORTOBELLO 82 E4
Portobello Ind Est DH3 . . . . .82 F4
Portobello La SR5, SR6 . . . . .75 D1
Portobello Prim Sch DH3 . . . .82 D2
Portobello Rd DH3 . . . . .82 D4
Portobello Terr DH3 . . . . .82 D4
Portobello Way DH3 . . . . . . .82 D4
Portree Cl DH3 . . . . .82 D3
Portree Sq SR3 . . . . .85 E2
Portrush Cl NE37 . . . . .72 C2
Portrush Rd SR4 . . . . .85 C4
Portrush Way NE7 . . . . .39 C5
Portslade Rd SR4 . . . . .85 C4
Portsmouth Rd
  North Shields NE29 . . . . . . .41 C5
  Sunderland SR4 . . . . .85 B5
Portsmouth Sq SR4 . . . . .85 B5
Portugal Ph NE28 . . . . .40 B1
Postern Cres NE61 . . . . .9 B7
Post Office La NE29 . . . . .42 A6
Post Office St **4** NE24 . . . .17 F8
Potland View NE61 . . . . .1 A2
Potteries The NE33 . . . . .42 E1
Potter Sq SR3 . . . . .85 F3
Potter St
  Jarrow NE32 . . . . .58 A7
  Wallsend NE28 . . . . .41 A3
Pottersway NE9 . . . . .71 B3

Pottery Bank
Morpeth NE61 . . . . 3 E2
Newcastle upon Tyne NE6 . . . . 56 F3
Pottery Bank Ct NE61 . . . . 3 E2
Pottery La
Newcastle upon Tyne
NE1 . . . . 100 C3
Sunderland SR4 . . . . 85 A7
Pottery Rd SR5 . . . . 75 A1
Pottery Yd DH4 . . . . 94 E8
Potts St NE6 . . . . 56 C6
Poulton Cl NE28 . . . . 89 B8
Poulton Cl DH2 . . . . 88 A1
Powburn Gdns NE4 . . . . 54 E8
Pow Dene Ct NE30 . . . . 42 C6
Powis Rd SR3 . . . . 85 F2
Powis Sq SR3 . . . . 85 F2
Powys Pl NE4 . . . . 98 B2
Poynings Cl NE5 . . . . 37 C5
Praetorian Dr NE28 . . . . 40 B1
Precinct The
Blaydon NE21 . . . . 53 D3
Sunderland, Hillview SR2 . . . . 86 C2
Sunderland SR2 . . . . 102 B2
Prefect Pl NE7 . . . . 71 A7
Premier Rd SR3 . . . . 85 F2
Prendwick Ave NE31 . . . . 57 D3
Prendwick Ct NE31 . . . . 57 D3
Prengarth Ave NE6 . . . . 75 D3
Prensgarth Way NE34 . . . . . . 58 F3
Prescot Rd SR4 . . . . 85 C6
Press La SR1 . . . . 103 A3
Prestbury Ave NE23 . . . . 16 A1
Prestbury Rd SR4 . . . . 85 A3
Prestdale Ave NE24 . . . . 17 A7
Presthope Rd SR4 . . . . 85 B4
Prestmede NE10 . . . . 71 E7
PRESTON 42 A8
Preston Ave NE30 . . . . 42 B7
Preston Ct NE29 . . . . 42 A8
Preston Gate NE29 . . . . 31 F1
Preston Grange Prim Sch
NE29 . . . . 31 E1
Prestonhill ⁊ SR3 . . . . 91 E5
Preston North Rd NE29 . . . . 31 F1
Preston Pk NE29 . . . . 42 A7
Preston Rd SR2 . . . . 86 F4
Preston Road North NE29,
NE30 . . . . 42 A7
Preston Terr
⁊ Shiremoor NE27 . . . . 30 E1
⁊ Tynemouth NE29 . . . . 41 F8
Preston Twrs NE29 . . . . 42 A7
Preston Wood NE30 . . . . 32 A1
PRESTWICK 26 C5
Prestwick NE10 . . . . 71 E5
Prestwick Ave NE4 . . . . 61 C6
Prestwick Carr Rd NE13 . . . 27 A8
Prestwick Cl NE27 . . . . 72 C2
Prestwick Dr NE10 . . . . 72 C7
Prestwick Gdns NE3 . . . . 37 F4
Prestwick Ho NE4 . . . . 98 B2
Prestwick Ind Est NE20 . . . 26 C3
Prestwick Terr NE20 . . . . . . 26 C5
Pretoria Ave NE6 . . . . 8 F8
Pretoria St NE15 . . . . 54 A5
Pretoria Sq SR3 . . . . 85 E2
Price St
Hebburn NE31 . . . . 57 C7
Morpeth NE61 . . . . 3 E1
Priestclose Cotts NE42 . . . . . 50 D2
Priestclose Rd NE42 . . . . 50 D2
Priestclose Wood Nature
Reserve* NE42 . . . . 50 E1
Priestfield Cl SR3 . . . . 91 F5
Priestfields NE10 . . . . 78 F6
Priestlands Ave ⁊⁊ NE46 . . . . 45 A5
Priestlands Cl NE46 . . . . 45 A4
Priestlands Cres NE46 . . . . . 45 A4
Priestlands Dr NE46 . . . . 45 A4
Priestlands Gdns NE46 . . . . . 45 A3
Priestlands La NE46 . . . . 45 A4
Priestlands Rd NE46 . . . . 45 A4
Priestley Ct NE34 . . . . 59 A3
Priestley Gdns NE10 . . . . 72 B7
Priestly Cres SR4 . . . . 102 B4
Priestman Ct SR4 . . . . 85 D6
Priestpopple NE46 . . . . 45 B4
Primary Gdns SR2 . . . . 103 C1
Primate Rd SR3 . . . . 85 E3
PRIMROSE 58 C3
Primrose Ave NE34 . . . . 59 B5
Primrose Cl NE23 . . . . 29 A8
Primrose Cres
Bournmoor DH4 . . . . 89 E3
Sunderland SR6 . . . . 75 D3
Primrose Ct NE63 . . . . 6 B1
Primrose Gdns
Hedgefield NE40, NE15 . . . . . 52 E5
Ouston DH2 . . . . 81 F2
Wallsend NE28 . . . . 40 A4
Primrose Hill NE9 . . . . 71 A5
Primrose Hill Terr NE32 . . . 58 C3
Primrose Nature Reserve*
NE32 . . . . 58 C4
Primrose Prec SR6 . . . . 75 D3
Primrose St ⁊ SR4 . . . . 85 A6
Primrose Terr NE32 . . . . 58 C4
Prince Albert Terr NE2 . . . . 99 C2
Prince Consort Ind Est
NE31 . . . . 57 D6
Prince Consort La NE31 . . . . 57 D6
Prince Consort Rd
Gateshead NE8 . . . . 101 C1
Hebburn NE31 . . . . 57 D6
Jarrow NE32 . . . . 58 C6

Prince Consort Way NE29 . . 42 A3
Prince Edward Ct NE34 . . . . . 60 A5
Prince Edward Gr NE34 . . . . . 60 C6
Prince Edward Rd NE34 . . . . 60 A5
Prince Edward Road E
NE34 . . . . 60 C6
Prince George Ave SR6 . . . . . 75 D3
Prince Georg Sq ⁊⁊ NE33 . . . . 42 D3
Prince of Wales Cl NE34 . . . . 59 E5
Prince Philip Cl NE15 . . . . . . 54 C5
Prince Rd NE28 . . . . 40 B3
Princes Ave
Newcastle upon Tyne NE3 . . . 38 B7
Sunderland SR6 . . . . 75 E5
Princes Cl NE3 . . . . 38 B8
Princes Gdns
Sunderland SR6 . . . . 75 E5
Whitley Bay NE26 . . . . 31 E5
Prince's Gdns NE24 . . . . 17 C8
Prince's Mdw NE3 . . . . 38 A5
Princes Pk
Dunston NE11 . . . . 70 B6
Gateshead NE8 . . . . 70 C5
Princes Rd NE3 . . . . 28 B1
Princess Ct NE42 . . . . 50 D4
Princess Dr NE8 . . . . 100 A1
Princess Gdns DH5 . . . . 95 A5
Princess Louise Rd NE23 . . 22 C7
Princess Mary Ct NE2 . . . . . 99 A4
Princess Sq NE1 . . . . 99 B2
Princess St
Gateshead NE10 . . . . 57 A1
Sunderland SR2 . . . . 102 C1
Sunniside NE16 . . . . 69 B2
Princess Way
Newcastle upon Tyne NE3 . . . 38 B8
Sunderland SR6 . . . . 75 E5
Prince St
Chopwell NE17 . . . . 66 B1
Sunderland SR1 . . . . 103 A3
Princesway NE11 . . . . 70 C5
Princesway Central NE11 . . . 70 C3
Princesway S NE11 . . . . 70 C3
Princetown Terr SR3 . . . . . . 85 E2
Princeway NE30 . . . . 42 D8
Prinn Pl NE16 . . . . 69 B8
Priors Grange DH6 . . . . 96 B5
Prior's Ho NE30 . . . . 42 E7
Prior's Terr NE30 . . . . 42 D7
Priors Way NE28 . . . . 40 E2
Priors Wlk NE61 . . . . 8 E7
Prior Terr
Corbridge NE45 . . . . 46 F6
Hexham NE46 . . . . 45 A6
Priory Ave NE25 . . . . 31 F4
Priory Ct
Gateshead NE8 . . . . 101 C3
Gateshead, Wardley NE10 . . 72 B8
South Shields NE33 . . . . 42 D5
Tynemouth NE30 . . . . 42 E8
Priory Gdns NE45 . . . . 46 F7
Priory Gn ⁊⁊ NE6 . . . . 56 B6
Priory Grange NE42 . . . . 50 D4
Priory Mews ⁊ NE30 . . . . 42 D7
Priory Pl
Brunswick Village NE13 . . . . 28 A5
Newcastle upon Tyne NE6 . . . 56 C5
Stakeford NE62 . . . . 11 A8
Priory Prim Sch NE30 . . . . . 42 D8
Priory Rd NE6 . . . . 58 C8
Priory Way NE5 . . . . 36 E1
Proctor Ct NE6 . . . . 57 A5
Proctor Sq SR3 . . . . 85 F2
Proctor St NE6 . . . . 57 A5
Promenade
Newbiggin-by-the-Sea
NE64 . . . . 7 E4
Seaham SR7 . . . . 93 D1
South Shields NE33 . . . . 42 F3
Sunderland SR2 . . . . 87 A3
Whitley Bay NE26 . . . . 32 B5
Promontory Terr NE26 . . . . . 32 C4
Promotion Cl ⁊ SR6 . . . . 75 E2
Property Rd SR4 . . . . 102 A4
Prospect Ave
Seaton Delaval NE25 . . . . 23 C3
Seaton Delaval NE25 . . . . 23 C4
Wallsend NE28 . . . . 40 B3
Prospect Avenue N NE29 . . . 41 E7
Prospect Cotts NE22 . . . . . . 11 C5
Prospect Cres DH5 . . . . 97 C8
Prospect Ct NE4 . . . . 98 A1
Prospect Gdns NE36 . . . . 74 A7
Prospect Pl
Newbiggin-by-the-Sea
NE64 . . . . 7 F5
Newcastle upon Tyne NE4 . . . 98 A1
Prospect Row SR1 . . . . 103 C3
Prospect St ⁊ DH3 . . . . 88 C4
Prospect Terr
⁊ Chester le Street DH3 . . . . 88 C4
East Boldon NE36 . . . . 74 C7
Ebchester DH8 . . . . 76 F4
Gateshead NE9 . . . . 71 B3
Kibblesworth NE11 . . . . 81 C6
North Shields NE30 . . . . 42 C6
Prudhoe NE42 . . . . 50 B2
Prospect Terr Ind Est
NE30 . . . . 42 C6
Providence Pl ⁊⁊ NE10 . . . . . 56 D1
Provident Terr NE28 . . . . 40 A2
Provost Gdns NE4 . . . . 54 D4
PRUDHOE 50 D1
Prudhoe Castle* NE42 . . . . . 50 C3

Prudhoe Chare NE1 . . . . 99 A2
Prudhoe Com High Sch
NE42 . . . . 50 D1
Prudhoe Ct NE3 . . . . 37 E7
Prudhoe Football & Sports
Ctr NE42 . . . . 50 D1
Prudhoe Gr NE32 . . . . 58 B3
Prudhoe Pl NE1 . . . . 99 A2
Prudhoe Sta NE42 . . . . 50 B4
Prudhoe Street Back ⁊⁊
NE29 . . . . 42 A5
Prudhoe Terr
⁊⁊ North Shields NE29 . . . . . . 42 A5
Tynemouth NE30 . . . . 42 D8
Prudhoe Waterworld
NE42 . . . . 50 C2
Prudhoe West Fst Sch
NE42 . . . . 50 C2
Pudding Chare NE1 . . . . 99 A1
Pudding Mews ⁊ NE46 . . . . . 45 B5
Puffin Cl NE24 . . . . 17 F3
Pullman Ct NE9 . . . . 70 E5
Purbeck Cl NE29 . . . . 31 F2
Purbeck Gdns NE23 . . . . 22 C7
Purbeck Rd NE12 . . . . 39 B6
Purdy's Ho NE61 . . . . 3 E1
Purley NE38 . . . . 88 A4
Purley Cl NE28 . . . . 40 F4
Purley Gdns NE3 . . . . 37 F4
Purley Rd SR3 . . . . 85 E2
Purley Sq SR3 . . . . 85 E2
Putney Sq SR4 . . . . 85 B4
Pykerley Mews NE25 . . . . . . 31 E4
Pykerley Rd NE25 . . . . 31 E5

Q

QE Metro Riverside Hospl
NE11 . . . . 54 D3
Quadrant The
North Shields NE29 . . . . 41 E5
Sunderland SR1 . . . . 103 C3
Quality Row NE6 . . . . 56 A5
Quality Row Rd NE16 . . . . . . 54 A1
Quantock Ave DH2 . . . . 88 A2
Quantock Cl NE29 . . . . 31 F2
Quarry Bank Ct NE4 . . . . 98 B1
Quarry Cotts NE63 . . . . 7 B6
Quarry Edge NE46 . . . . 45 C3
Quarryfield Rd NE8 . . . . 101 C4
Quarry House Gdns DH5 . . . 94 C4
Quarry House La DH5 . . . . . . 94 C4
Quarry La
South Shields NE34 . . . . 60 B5
South Shields NE34 . . . . 60 C5
Quarry Rd
Hebburn NE31 . . . . 57 C5
Newcastle upon Tyne NE15 . . 53 C6
New Silksworth SR3 . . . . 92 B7
Sunderland SR1 . . . . 56 D1
Quarry Row NE16 . . . . 56 D1
Quarry Sq DH9 . . . . 79 B2
Quarry St SR3 . . . . 92 A7
Quatre Bras NE46 . . . . 44 F5
Quay Corner Ave NE32 . . . . . 58 D8
Quay Rd NE24 . . . . 18 A7
Quaysgate NE8 . . . . 101 C4
Quayside
Blyth NE24 . . . . 17 F8
Newcastle upon Tyne NE1, NE6 . 101 B4
Newcastle upon Tyne, St
Lawrence NE1, NE6 . . . . . . 56 A5
Quayside Ct
⁊ Blyth NE24 . . . . 17 F8
North Shields NE30 . . . . 42 B5
Quayside Ho SR1 . . . . 103 B3
Quay View NE28 . . . . 41 A2
Queen Alexandra Mews
SR2 . . . . 86 D3
Queen Alexandra Rd
Sunderland SR2 . . . . 86 D3
Tynemouth NE30 . . . . 42 D8
Queen Alexandra Road W
NE29 . . . . 41 E7
Queen Ann Ct ⁊⁊ NE6 . . . . . . 56 C7
Queen Elizabeth Ave NE9 . . 71 B6
Queen Elizabeth Ct NE34 . . 58 F3
Queen Elizabeth Dr DH5 . . 97 D8
Queen Elizabeth High Sch
NE46 . . . . 44 E4
Queen Elizabeth Hospl
NE9 . . . . 71 B6
Queen Elizabeth II Ctry Pk*
. . . . 6 F5
Queens Ave SR6 . . . . 75 E5
Queensberry St SR4 . . . . . . 102 B3
Queensbridge NE12 . . . . 38 F7
Queensbury Dr NE15 . . . . . . 36 B2
Queensbury Gate NE12 . . . . 39 A6
Queen's Cres
Hebburn NE31 . . . . 57 D4
Sunderland SR4 . . . . 102 A1
Wallsend NE28 . . . . 40 B3
Queens Ct
Gateshead NE8 . . . . 100 C1
Newcastle upon Tyne, Brunton
Park NE3 . . . . 28 C2
Newcastle upon Tyne NE4 . . . 98 B2
Walbottle NE15 . . . . 36 A1
Queens Dr
Sunniside NE16 . . . . 69 B2
Whickham NE16 . . . . 69 C5

Queen's Dr NE26 . . . . 32 A5
Queens Gdns
Annitsford NE23 . . . . 22 B1
Longbenton NE12 . . . . 39 D6
Queen's Gdns
Blyth NE24 . . . . 17 C8
Morpeth NE61 . . . . 8 E7
Queens Hall Arts Ctr*
NE46 . . . . 45 A5
Queens La NE1 . . . . 101 A4
Queensland Ave NE34 . . . . . 58 F4
Queensmere DH3 . . . . 88 C7
Queen's Par DH5 . . . . 75 F5
Queen's Pk DH3 . . . . 88 D2
Queens Pl NE64 . . . . 7 E5
Queens Rd
Annitsford NE23 . . . . 22 B1
Newcastle upon Tyne NE5 . . . 37 A3
Seaton Sluice NE26 . . . . 24 D6
Walbottle NE15 . . . . 36 A1
Queen's Rd
Bedlington NE22 . . . . 11 D2
Newcastle upon Tyne NE2 . . . 38 F5
Sunderland SR5 . . . . 75 B1
Whitley Bay NE26 . . . . 31 F6
Queen St
Ashington NE63 . . . . 6 E4
Birtley DH3 . . . . 82 B4
Gateshead NE8 . . . . 70 C8
Hetton-le-Hole DH5 . . . . 95 A4
Lynemouth NE61 . . . . 1 E5
Morpeth NE61 . . . . 9 E5
Newbiggin-by-the-Sea NE64 . 7 E5
Newcastle upon Tyne NE1 . . 101 B4
North Shields NE30 . . . . 42 C6
South Shields NE33 . . . . 42 C3
Sunderland, Grangetown
SR2 . . . . 92 F8
Sunderland SR1 . . . . 103 A3
Queen's Terr NE28 . . . . 40 C3
Queen's Terr E NE7 . . . . 38 F1
Queen Street E SR1 . . . . . . 103 B3
Queensway
Houghton-le-Spring DH5 . . . 94 F8
Morpeth NE61 . . . . 8 D7
Newcastle upon Tyne, Fenham
NE4 . . . . 54 D8
Ponteland NE20 . . . . 25 D2
Tynemouth NE30 . . . . 42 D8
⁊ Washington NE38 . . . . 83 E4
Queens Way NE46 . . . . 44 E5
Queensway Ct NE11 . . . . 70 C6
Queensway N NE11 . . . . 70 C5
Queensway S NE11 . . . . 70 D4
Queen Victoria Rd NE1,
NE2 . . . . 99 A3
Queen Victoria St NE10 . . . . 57 A1
Quentin Ave NE3 . . . . 37 D5
Quicksilver Way NE27 . . . . . 30 E1
Quigley Terr DH3 . . . . 82 B6

R

Rabbit Banks Rd NE8 . . . . 101 A3
Raby Cl
Bedlington NE22 . . . . 10 D1
Prudhoe NE42 . . . . 90 A1
Raby Cres ⁊⁊ NE6 . . . . 56 C5
Raby Cross ⁊⁊ NE6 . . . . 56 C5
Raby Dr SR3 . . . . 91 C7
Rabygate ⁊ NE6 . . . . 56 C5
Raby Gdns
Burnopfield NE16 . . . . 78 E6
Jarrow NE32 . . . . 58 B4
Raby Rd NE38 . . . . 83 B5
Raby St
Gateshead NE8 . . . . 70 F8
⁊⁊ Newcastle upon Tyne, Byker
NE6 . . . . 56 B6
Newcastle upon Tyne, St
Lawrence NE6 . . . . 56 C5
Sunderland SR4 . . . . 102 B2
Raby Way NE6 . . . . 56 C5
Rachel Cl SR2 . . . . 92 C7
Rackly Way NE16 . . . . 69 B8
Radcliffe Cotts ⁊ NE15 . . . . . 35 D2
Radcliffe Pl ⁊ NE5 . . . . 37 D2
Radcliffe Rd
Hexham NE46 . . . . 45 C4
Sunderland SR5 . . . . 74 E2
Radcliffe St DH3 . . . . 82 C3
Radlett Rd SR5 . . . . 74 D2
Radnor Gdns NE28 . . . . 41 A3
Radnor St NE1 . . . . 99 B2
Radstock Pl NE12 . . . . 39 C7
Rae Ave NE28 . . . . 40 B5
Raeburn Ave NE38 . . . . 83 E4
Raeburn Gdns NE9 . . . . 71 B7
Raeburn Rd
Sunderland SR5 . . . . 74 C3
Whiteleas NE34 . . . . 59 D2
Raglan NE38 . . . . 83 A5
Raglan Ave SR2 . . . . 86 E3
Raglan Pl NE16 . . . . 79 B6
Raglan Row NE24 . . . . 17 D6
Raglan St NE32 . . . . 58 D7
Raich Carter Sp Ctr SR2 . . 86 F4
Railton Gdns NE9 . . . . 71 B6
Railway Arches NE1 . . . . 99 B1
Railway Cotts
Birtley DH3 . . . . 82 B4
Blyth, Bebside NE24 . . . . 16 E1
Blyth, South Newsham NE24 . 17 C2
Cleadon NE36 . . . . 59 D1
Penshaw DH4 . . . . 90 A8

Railway Cotts continued
Riding Mill NE44 . . . . 63 A8
Wylam NE41 . . . . 50 F5
Railway Mus* NE41 . . . . 51 B6
Railway Row SR1 . . . . 102 B3
Railway St
Dunston NE11 . . . . 54 F2
Dunston NE11 . . . . 100 A1
Hebburn NE31 . . . . 57 F7
Hetton-le-Hole DH5 . . . . 95 A4
Jarrow NE32 . . . . 58 A7
Newbottle DH4 . . . . 90 D2
Newcastle upon Tyne NE4 . . 100 B3
⁊⁊ North Shields NE29 . . . . . 42 A5
Sunderland SR1 . . . . 103 C2
Railway Terr
Blyth NE24 . . . . 17 D7
Newcastle upon Tyne NE4 . . 100 B3
New Herrington DH4 . . . . 90 D6
North Shields NE29 . . . . 42 A5
Penshaw DH4 . . . . 90 A8
⁊ Sunderland SR4 . . . . 85 A6
Wallsend NE28 . . . . 40 D1
Railway Terrace N DH4 . . . . 90 D7
Raine Gr SR1 . . . . 103 B2
Rainford Ave SR2 . . . . 86 E3
Rainhill Cl NE37 . . . . 72 F1
Rainhill Rd NE37 . . . . 72 F1
RAINTON BRIDGE 94 E6
Rainton Bridge Ind Est
DH4 . . . . 94 C7
Rainton Cl NE10 . . . . 72 C6
RAINTON GATE 94 A1
Rainton Gr DH5 . . . . 94 E6
Rainton Meadows (Nature
Reserve)* NE38 . . . . 94 B6
Rainton St
Penshaw DH4 . . . . 90 B8
Sunderland SR4 . . . . 102 A2
Rainton View DH4 . . . . 94 A2
Rake La NE29 . . . . 31 E1
Raleigh Cl NE33 . . . . 59 B8
Raleigh Rd SR5 . . . . 74 E2
Raleigh Sq SR5 . . . . 74 D2
Ralph Ave SR2 . . . . 92 C8
Ralph St NE31 . . . . 57 F7
Ramilies SR2 . . . . 92 D6
Ramillies Rd SR5 . . . . 74 C3
Ramillies Sq SR5 . . . . 74 C3
Ramparts The NE15 . . . . 53 F8
Ramsay Rd NE17 . . . . 66 B2
Ramsay Sq SR5 . . . . 74 E3
Ramsay St
Blaydon NE21 . . . . 53 B1
High Spen NE39 . . . . 67 A5
Ramsey St DH3 . . . . 88 C2
Ramsgate Rd SR5 . . . . 74 E3
Ramshaw Cl NE7 . . . . 39 E3
Randolph St NE32 . . . . 58 C7
Rangoon Rd SR5 . . . . 74 C3
Ranmere Rd NE15 . . . . 54 A5
Ranmore Cl NE23 . . . . 22 B7
Rannoch Ave DH2 . . . . 88 B1
Rannoch Cl NE10 . . . . 72 C8
Rannoch Ho NE2 . . . . 38 F2
Rannoch Rd SR5 . . . . 74 C3
Ranson Cres NE34 . . . . 58 F5
Ranson St SR4, SR2 . . . . 86 B4
Raphael Ave NE34 . . . . 59 C2
Rapperton Ct ⁊ NE5 . . . . 36 F3
Rathmore Gdns NE30 . . . . . . 42 A7
Ratho Ct NE10 . . . . 71 E6
Ravel Ct NE32 . . . . 58 C6
Ravelston Cl SR3 . . . . 92 A5
Ravenburn Gdns NE15 . . . . . 53 F6
Ravenna Rd SR5 . . . . 74 C3
Ravensbourne Ave NE36 . . . 74 D8
Ravensburn Wlk ⁊⁊ NE15 . . . 68 F5
Ravenscourt Pl NE8 . . . . . . 101 A1
Ravenscourt Rd SR5 . . . . 74 C3
Ravensdale Cres ⁊ NE9 . . . . 71 A4
Ravensdale Gr NE24 . . . . 17 A7
Ravens Hill Dr NE63 . . . . 6 A2
Ravenshill Rd NE5 . . . . 36 E1
Ravenside Rd NE4 . . . . 54 E8
Ravenside Terr NE17 . . . . . . 66 A1
Ravenstone NE37 . . . . 83 B7
Ravenswood ⁊⁊ NE3 . . . . 71 A6
Ravenswood Cl NE12 . . . . . . 39 E8
Ravenswood Gdns NE9 . . . . 70 F3
Ravenswood Prim Sch
NE6 . . . . 39 C1
Ravenswood Rd
Newcastle upon Tyne NE6 . . . 39 C1
Sunderland SR5 . . . . 74 C3
Ravenswood Sq SR5 . . . . 74 B3
Ravensworth SR2 . . . . 92 D6
Ravensworth Apartments ⁊⁊
NE11 . . . . 70 A8
Ravensworth Ave
Fence Houses DH4 . . . . 90 A1
Gateshead NE9 . . . . 71 C2
Ravensworth Cl NE28 . . . . . . 40 F2
Ravensworth Cres NE16 . . . 79 D8
Ravensworth Ct
Bedlington NE22 . . . . 11 D3
Dunston NE11 . . . . 100 A1
Dunston NE11 . . . . 37 D7
South Hetton DH6 . . . . 97 F1
Ravensworth Gdns NE61 . . . 1 D4
Ravensworth Rd
Birtley DH3 . . . . 82 B5
Dunston NE11 . . . . 100 A1
Fence Houses DH4 . . . . 89 F1

Ravensworth St
Bedlington NE22 . . . . .11 D3
2 Bedlington NE22. . . . . . . .11 D3
Sunderland SR4 . . . . .102 B3
Wallsend NE28 . . . . .40 F2
Ravensworth Terr
3 Bedlington NE22. . . . . . . .11 D3
Dunston NE11 . . . . .70 A8
Jarrow NE32 . . . . .58 B3
South Shields NE33 . . . . . . .59 C8
Sunniside NE16 . . . . .69 B2
Ravensworth Terrace Prim
Sch DH3 . . . . .82 C4
Raven Terr 7 DH3 . . . . . . .82 C5
Ravine Ct SR6 . . . . .75 F3
Ravine Terr SR6 . . . . .75 F3
Rawdon Rd SR5 . . . . .74 E3
Rawling Rd NE8 . . . . .70 D8
Rawlston Way NE5 . . . . .37 C3
Rawmarsh Rd SR5 . . . . .74 C3
Rayburn Ct NE24 . . . . .17 C3
Raydale SR5 . . . . .74 E3
Raydale Ave NE7 . . . . .83 B8
Raylees Gdns NE11 . . . . . . .70 A7
Rayleigh Dr NE13 . . . . .28 B7
Rayleigh Gr NE7 . . . . .70 D8
Raynes Cl NE61 . . . . .8 D7
Raynham Ct NE23 . . . . .21 F3
Raynham Ct 8 NE33 . . . . . .42 C2
Readhead Ave NE33 . . . . . . .42 C2
Readhead Dr NE6 . . . . .56 F4
Readhead Rd NE34 . . . . .59 F8
Reading Rd
South Shields NE33 . . . . . . .59 D7
Sunderland SR5 . . . . .74 D3
Reading Sq SR5 . . . . .74 D3
Reasby Gdns NE40 . . . . . . .52 B5
Reasby Villas NE40 . . . . . . .52 B5
Reavley Ave NE22 . . . . .11 E3
Reay Cres NE35 . . . . .74 B8
Reay Ct 4 DH2 . . . . .88 C2
Reay Gdns NE5 . . . . .37 A3
Reay Pl
Newcastle upon Tyne NE3 . . .38 A5
South Shields NE34 . . . . . . .59 B5
Reay St NE10 . . . . .57 B2
Rectory Ave NE3 . . . . .38 E4
Rectory Bank NE36 . . . . . . .74 A7
Rectory Ct 6 NE16 . . . . . . .69 B7
Rectory Dene NE61 . . . . .8 F7
Rectory Gr NE3 . . . . .38 E4
Rectory Gr NE36 . . . . .73 F7
Rectory Gr NE25 . . . . .38 D5
Rectory La
Blaydon NE21 . . . . .68 B8
Ebchester DH8 . . . . .76 E3
Whickham NE16 . . . . .69 B7
Rectory Pk NE61 . . . . .8 F7
Rectory Pl NE8 . . . . .101 A1
Rectory Rd
Gateshead, Carr Hill NE10 . .71 C7
Gateshead, Shipcote NE8,
NE9 . . . . .70 E8
Hetton-le-Hole DH5 . . . . . . .95 A3
Newcastle upon Tyne NE3 . . .38 D4
Rectory Road E NE10 . . . . . .71 D7
Rectory Terr NE3 . . . . .38 E4
Red Admiral Ct NE11 . . . . . .70 B7
Red Barns NE1 . . . . .101 C2
Redberry Way NE34 . . . . . . .59 B4
Red Bglws NE9 . . . . .71 E1
Redburn Cl DH4 . . . . .94 C8
REDBURN DENE 41 F2
Redburn Rd NE5 . . . . .36 F4
Redby Cl SR6 . . . . .75 D2
Redby Prim Sch SR6 . . . . . .75 D2
Redcar Rd
Newcastle upon Tyne NE6 . . .39 D1
Sunderland SR5 . . . . .74 E2
Wallsend NE28 . . . . .41 A3
Redcar Sq SR5 . . . . .74 E2
Redcliffe Way NE5 . . . . .37 B3
Redcroft Gn NE5 . . . . .37 B3
Redditch Sq SR5 . . . . .74 D3
Rede Ave
Hebburn NE31 . . . . .57 E6
Hexham NE46 . . . . .45 C4
Rede Ct NE61 . . . . .1 E5
Redemarsh NE10 . . . . .71 F6
Redesdale Ave
Blaydon NE21 . . . . .67 F8
Newcastle upon Tyne NE3 . . .38 A6
Redesdale Cl
Longbenton NE12 . . . . .39 C8
Newcastle upon Tyne NE15 . .53 F7
Redesdale Gdns NE11 . . . . .69 F7
Redesdale Gr NE29 . . . . .41 D6
Redesdale Pl NE24 . . . . .17 B7
Redesdale Prim Sch NE28 .39 F4
Redesdale Rd
Chester le Street DH3 . . . . . .88 A1
North Shields NE29 . . . . . . .41 D6
Sunderland SR5 . . . . .74 C3
Rede St
Gateshead NE11 . . . . .70 C5
Jarrow NE32 . . . . .58 A5
Rede Terr NE46 . . . . .45 C4
Redewater Gdns NE16 . . . . .69 A6
Redewater Rd NE4 . . . . .54 E8
Redewood Cl NE5 . . . . .37 A1
Redford Pl NE23 . . . . .29 C5
Red Hall Dr NE7 . . . . .39 D3

Redheugh Bridge Rd NE1,
NE4 . . . . .100 C3
Redheugh Ct NE8 . . . . .70 B8
Redheugh Rd NE25 . . . . .31 B5
Redhill SR6 . . . . .75 E8
Redhill Dr NE8 . . . . .68 E4
Redhill Rd SR5 . . . . .74 D3
Redhills Way DH5 . . . . .95 A2
Redhill Wlk NE23 . . . . .22 B7
Red House Dr NE25 . . . . .31 C6
Red House Farm NE22 . . . . .15 D8
Red House Rd NE31 . . . . .58 A6
Redland Ave NE3 . . . . .37 E6
Redlands DH4 . . . . .90 A7
Red Lion Bldgs NE10 . . . . . .71 D1
Red Lion La NE37 . . . . .72 C2
Redmayne Ct 1 NE10 . . . . .71 D8
Redmires Cl DH2 . . . . .81 E1
Redmond Rd SR5 . . . . .74 E3
Redmond Sq SR5 . . . . .74 E3
Rednam Pl NE5 . . . . .37 B2
Red Rose Prim Sch DH3 . . .88 D1
Red Rose Terr DH3 . . . . .88 D2
Red Row Ct NE22 . . . . .11 C4
Red Row Dr NE22 . . . . .11 C4
Redruth Gdns NE9 . . . . .70 F2
Redruth Sq SR5 . . . . .74 D3
Redshank Cl NE38 . . . . .82 F2
Redshank Dr NE24 . . . . .17 E4
Redstart Ct NE39 . . . . .67 D2
Redwell Ct
Prudhoe NE42 . . . . .50 D2
South Shields NE34 . . . . . . .60 C7
Redwell La NE34 . . . . .60 D7
Redwell Rd NE42 . . . . .50 D2
Redwing Cl NE38 . . . . .82 F3
Redwing Ct NE6 . . . . .56 E7
Red Wlk NE7 . . . . .39 A1
Redwood Cl
Hetton-le-Hole DH5 . . . . . . .94 F4
Killingworth NE12 . . . . .29 C4
Redwood Ct NE63 . . . . .6 E2
Redwood Gdns NE11 . . . . . .70 B5
Redwood Gr SR3 . . . . .92 B7
Reed Ave NE12 . . . . .29 C4
Reedham Ct NE5 . . . . .37 B4
Reedling Ct SR5 . . . . .74 C4
Reedside NE40 . . . . .52 D5
Reedsmouth Pl NE5 . . . . . . .54 B8
Reed St
North Shields NE30 . . . . .42 B6
South Shields NE33 . . . . . . .59 C8
Reedswood Cres NE23 . . . . .22 E5
Reestones Pl NE3 . . . . .37 D5
Reeth Rd SR5 . . . . .74 D2
Reeth Sq NE5 . . . . .35 L1
Reeth Way NE15 . . . . .35 C1
Regal Rd SR4 . . . . .102 A3
Regency Ct NE2 . . . . .99 C4
Regency Dr
New Silksworth SR3 . . . . . . .92 B8
Whickham NE16 . . . . .68 F6
Regency Gdns NE29 . . . . . . .41 E7
Regency Way NE20 . . . . .25 A5
Regent Ave NE3 . . . . .38 B5
Regent Centre Sta NE3 . . . .38 A5
Regent Ct
Blyth NE24 . . . . .17 D7
Gateshead NE8 . . . . .101 D7
Hebburn NE31 . . . . .57 D5
Longbenton NE12 . . . . .29 B2
South Hetton DH6 . . . . .97 F7
South Shields NE33 . . . . . . .42 C1
Regent Ctr The NE3 . . . . . . .38 C6
Regent Dr NE16 . . . . .68 F4
Regent Farm Ct NE3 . . . . . .38 C5
Regent Farm Fst Sch NE3 .38 A6
Regent Farm Rd NE3 . . . . . .38 B6
Regent Rd
Jarrow NE32 . . . . .58 C6
Newcastle upon Tyne NE3 . . .38 C5
Ryhope SR2 . . . . .93 A5
Wallsend NE28 . . . . .40 A3
Regent Road N NE3 . . . . . . .38 C5
Regents Cl SR6 . . . . .75 F8
Regents Ct NE28 . . . . .39 C4
Regents Dr
Prudhoe NE42 . . . . .50 E4
Tynemouth NE30 . . . . .32 C1
Regents Pk NE28 . . . . .39 C3
Regent St
Blyth NE24 . . . . .17 E8
Hetton-le-Hole DH5 . . . . . . .95 A5
Regent Terr
Gateshead NE8 . . . . .101 B2
North Shields NE29 . . . . .41 E6
Sunderland SR2 . . . . .86 F2
Reginald St
Boldon Colliery NE35 . . . . . .73 F8
Gateshead NE8 . . . . .56 B1
43 Sunderland SR4 . . . . . . .85 F7
Regina Sq SR5 . . . . .74 D3
Regrave Cl NE38 . . . . .56 B2
Reid Ave NE28 . . . . .40 B3
Reid Park Cl NE2 . . . . .38 F2
Reid Park Ct NE2 . . . . .38 F2
Reid Park Rd NE2 . . . . .38 F2
Reid's La NE23 . . . . .22 E6
Reid St NE61 . . . . .9 A8
Reigate Sq NE23 . . . . .22 B7
Reins Ct NE46 . . . . .44 E5
Reiverdale Rd NE63 . . . . .6 D4
Rekendyke Ind Est NE33 . . .42 B1
Rekendyke La NE33 . . . . .42 B1
Relton Ave NE6 . . . . .56 F6
Relton Cl DH4 . . . . .94 A7
Relton Ct NE25 . . . . .31 E5
Relton Pl NE25 . . . . .31 E5

Relton Terr
Chester le Street DH3 . . . . . .88 C2
Whitley Bay NE25 . . . . .31 E5
Rembrandt Ave NE34 . . . . . .59 C2
Remscheid Way NE63 . . . . . . .6 C1
Remus Ave NE15 . . . . .34 D2
Remus Cl NE13 . . . . .28 B5
Renaissance Point NE30 . . .42 C6
Rendel St NE11 . . . . .54 F1
Rendle Rd NE6 . . . . .57 B4
Renforth Cl NE8 . . . . .56 B2
Renforth St NE11 . . . . .69 F8
Renney Rd NE29 . . . . .41 C8
Renfrew Gn NE5 . . . . .37 B3
Renfrew Pl DH3 . . . . .82 D2
Renfrew Rd SR5 . . . . .74 D3
Rennie Rd SR5 . . . . .74 B3
Rennie Sq SR5 . . . . .74 B3
Rennington NE10 . . . . .72 A5
Rennington Ave NE30 . . . . . .32 C1
Rennington Cl
Newburn NE15 . . . . .9 B5
Tynemouth NE30 . . . . .32 C1
Rennington Pl 5 NE5 . . . . . .37 D2
Rennison Mews NE21 . . . . . .53 C1
Renoir Gdns NE34 . . . . .59 D2
Renwick Ave NE3 . . . . .37 E6
Renwick Ct NE8 . . . . .70 C8
Renwick Ho NE61 . . . . .8 F7
Renwick Rd NE24 . . . . .17 D7
Renwick St NE6 . . . . .56 D6
Renwick Wlk NE61 . . . . .8 E8
Rescue Station Cotts DH5 .94 F6
Resida Cl NE15 . . . . .53 C8
Retail World NE11 . . . . .70 C2
Retford Rd SR5 . . . . .74 D3
Retford Sq SR5 . . . . .74 D3
Retreat The
Newburn NE15 . . . . .52 F7
Sunderland SR2 . . . . .102 B2
Revell Terr NE5 . . . . .37 E1
Revelstoke Rd SR5 . . . . .74 C3
Revesby St NE33 . . . . .59 C6
Reynolds Ave
Killingworth NE12 . . . . .29 B2
Washington NE38 . . . . .83 E4
Whiteleas NE34 . . . . .59 D3
Reyrolle Ct NE31 . . . . .57 D5
Rheims Ct SR4 . . . . .85 D7
Rheydt Ave NE28 . . . . .39 F2
Rhoda Terr SR2 . . . . .86 F1
Rhodesia Rd SR5 . . . . .74 C3
Rhodes St NE6 . . . . .57 A5
Rhondda Rd SR5 . . . . .74 B3
Rhuddlan Ct NE5 . . . . .37 B4
Rhyl Par NE31 . . . . .57 E3
Rhyl Sq SR5 . . . . .74 E3
Ribbledale Gdns NE7 . . . . . .39 B3
Ribble Rd SR5 . . . . .74 C2
Ribblesdale
Penshaw DH4 . . . . .90 B7
Wallsend NE28 . . . . .39 F4
Ribblesdale Ave 1 NE24 . . .17 A8
Ribble Wlk NE32 . . . . .58 C2
Richard Avenue Prim Sch
SR4 . . . . .86 B4
Richard Browell Rd NE15 . .35 C1
Richard Coates CE Mid Sch
NE20 . . . . .24 E8
Richardson Ave 2 NE34 . . .58 F4
Richardson Dees Prim Sch
NE28 . . . . .40 C3
Richardson Rd NE2 . . . . .98 C3
Richardson's Bldgs NE62 . .10 E5
Richardson St
Ashington NE63 . . . . .6 E1
1 Newcastle upon Tyne
NE6 . . . . .56 C8
Wallsend NE28 . . . . .40 C2
Richardson Terr
Chopwell NE17 . . . . .66 B1
7 Ryhope SR2 . . . . .93 A6
7 Washington NE37 . . . . . . .83 D8
Richard St
Blyth NE24 . . . . .17 E7
Hetton-le-Hole DH5 . . . . . . .95 A3
Richard Stannard Ho 11
NE24 . . . . .17 E8
Richmond SR2 . . . . .92 D7
Richmond Ave
Gateshead NE10 . . . . .57 C2
Washington NE38 . . . . .83 D6
Whickham NE16 . . . . .54 B1
Richmond Cl NE22 . . . . .10 E2
Richmond Ct
1 Gateshead, Low Fell
NE9 . . . . .70 F4
Gateshead NE8 . . . . .101 C1
Jarrow NE32 . . . . .58 D7
Richmond Dr DH4 . . . . .89 D1
Richmond Fields NE20 . . . . .25 D4
Richmond Gdns NE28 . . . . . .40 E3
Richmond Gr NE29 . . . . .41 E5
Richmond Lodge NE38 . . . . .38 D4
Richmond Mews NE3 . . . . . .38 A1
Richmond Pk NE28 . . . . .39 E3
Richmond St NE33 . . . . .42 D3
Richmond St SR5 . . . . .102 C4
Richmond Terr
12 Gateshead, Felling
NE10 . . . . .71 D8
Gateshead NE8 . . . . .101 B1
Haswell DH6 . . . . .97 F3
Walbottle NE15 . . . . .35 F1
Whitley Bay NE26 . . . . .31 F7
Richmond Way
Cramlington NE23 . . . . .22 A3

Richmond Way *continued*
Ponteland NE20 . . . . .25 A5
Rickaby St SR1 . . . . .103 C4
Rickgarth NE10 . . . . .71 F5
RICKLETON 88 E7
Rickleton Ave DH3 . . . . .88 D5
Rickleton Prim Sch NE38. .88 F8
Rickleton Village Ctr
NE38 . . . . .88 F8
Rickleton Way NE38. . . . . . .83 A1
Riddell Ave NE15 . . . . .54 C5
Riddell Ct 7 DH2 . . . . .88 C2
Riddings Rd SR5 . . . . .74 D3
Riddings Sq SR5 . . . . .74 D3
Ridge Ct NE13 . . . . .28 B4
Ridgely Cl NE20 . . . . .26 A6
Ridgely Dr NE20 . . . . .26 A6
Ridge The NE40 . . . . .52 C4
Ridge Villas NE22 . . . . .10 E1
Ridgeway
Ashington NE63 . . . . .7 A2
Birtley DH3 . . . . .82 C6
Gateshead NE10 . . . . .72 B6
Ridgeway The
Newcastle upon Tyne NE4 . . .54 E8
Seaton Delaval NE25 . . . . . . .23 E1
Stakeford NE62 . . . . .11 A8
Ridgeway Cres SR3 . . . . . . .86 B3
Ridgeway Prim Sch NE34 . .59 F4
Ridgeway The NE34 . . . . . . .59 F4
Ridge Way The NE3 . . . . . . .37 F4
Ridgewood Cres NE3 . . . . . .38 F5
Ridgewood Gdns NE3 . . . . .38 E5
Ridgewood Villas NE3 . . . . .38 E5
Riding Barns Way NE16 . . . .69 A2
Riding Cl NE40 . . . . .51 E3
Riding Cotts NE46 . . . . .45 A8
Riding Dene NE43 . . . . .49 F1
Riding Grange NE44 . . . . . . .62 D8
Riding La DH2, NE11 . . . . . . .81 B4
RIDING LEA 62 D8
Riding Lea NE21 . . . . .53 A1
RIDING MILL 62 E8
Riding Mill Sta NE44 . . . . . .62 F8
Ridings Ct NE40 . . . . .51 E3
Ridings The NE25 . . . . .31 C6
Riding Terr NE43 . . . . .49 F1
Riding The NE3 . . . . .37 E3
Ridley Ave
Blyth NE24 . . . . .17 F7
Chester le Street DH2 . . . . . .88 B2
Sunderland SR2 . . . . .92 F7
Wallsend NE28 . . . . .41 B4
Ridley Cl
Hexham NE46 . . . . .44 F3
Morpeth NE61 . . . . .8 E8
Newcastle upon Tyne NE3 . . .37 F8
Ridley Gr NE34 . . . . .60 A7
Ridley Mill Cotts NE43 . . . . .64 B6
Ridley Mill Rd NE43 . . . . . . .64 B5
Ridley Pl NE1, NE99 . . . . . . .99 A2
Ridley St
Blyth NE24 . . . . .17 F8
Cramlington NE23 . . . . .22 C5
Gateshead NE8 . . . . .70 E8
Sunderland SR5 . . . . .75 B2
Ridley Terr
Cambois NE24 . . . . .12 D4
Gateshead NE10 . . . . .71 E8
Hexham NE46 . . . . .45 A6
Sunderland SR2 . . . . .103 C1
Ridsdale NE42 . . . . .50 B1
Ridsdale Ave NE15 . . . . .36 E1
Ridsdale Cl
Seaton Delaval NE25 . . . . . . .23 C3
Wallsend NE28 . . . . .40 C4
Ridsdale Ct NE8 . . . . .101 A1
Ridsdale Sq NE63 . . . . .6 C3
Rievaulx NE38 . . . . .83 C4
Riga Sq SR5 . . . . .74 C3
Riggs The
Corbridge NE45 . . . . .46 F7
Houghton-le-Spring DH5 . . . .94 F8
Rignall NE38 . . . . .84 A5
Riley St NE32 . . . . .58 C3
Riley Street Ind Est NE32 . .58 A7
Ringlet Cl NE11 . . . . .70 B7
Ringmore Ct SR2 . . . . .86 C2
Rington Ct 15 NE30 . . . . . . .42 D7
Ringway
Stakeford NE62 . . . . .6 A1
Sunderland SR5 . . . . .85 A8
Ringway Fst Sch NE62 . . . . .10 F8
Ringwood Dr NE23 . . . . .22 A3
Ringwood Gn NE12 . . . . .39 C7
Ringwood Rd SR5 . . . . .74 D3
Ringwood Sq SR5 . . . . .74 D3
Rink St NE24 . . . . .17 F8
Ripley Ave NE29 . . . . .41 E4
Ripley Cl NE23 . . . . .16 A1
Ripley Ct NE9 . . . . .71 B1
Ripley Dr NE23 . . . . .22 A3
Ripley Terr NE6 . . . . .56 E6
Ripon Ct NE23 . . . . .21 F3
Ripon Gdns
Newcastle upon Tyne NE2 . . .56 A8
Wallsend NE28 . . . . .40 E3
Ripon Sq NE32 . . . . .73 B8
Ripon St
Chester le Street DH3 . . . . . .88 C1
Gateshead NE8 . . . . .101 B1
Sunderland SR6 . . . . .75 E1
Rise The
Newcastle upon Tyne NE3 . . .37 E4
Ponteland NE20 . . . . .25 B2
Ryton NE21 . . . . .53 A4
Seaton Sluice NE26 . . . . .24 E4

Rishton Sq SR5 . . . . .74 C3
Rising Sun Cotts NE28 . . . . .40 B5
Rising Sun Ctry Pk*
NE28 . . . . .40 B6
Ritson Cl NE29 . . . . .41 E7
Ritson St SR6 . . . . .75 E4
River Bank NE62 . . . . .11 C8
River Bank E NE62 . . . . .11 C8
Riverbank Rd SR5 . . . . .74 D2
Riverdale SR5 . . . . .85 B8
River Dr NE33 . . . . .42 C4
River La NE40 . . . . .52 C6
Rivermead NE38 . . . . .83 E1
Rivermede NE20 . . . . .25 F7
Riverside NE17 . . . . .77 B6
Riverside Ave NE62 . . . . .11 A8
Riverside Ct
Newcastle upon Tyne
NE15 . . . . .53 C6
Stakeford NE62 . . . . .11 A7
Riverside Ho NE62 . . . . .11 A7
Riverside Terr SR2 . . . . .102 B1
Riverside Way NE15 . . . . . . .53 C6
Riverside
9 Morpeth NE61 . . . . .8 F8
Ponteland NE20 . . . . .25 E6
Riverside Ave NE62 . . . . .10 D7
Riverside Bsns Pk NE28 . . .41 A1
Riverside Ct
Dunston NE11 . . . . .100 A1
South Shields NE33 . . . . . . .42 B2
Riverside Lodge NE15 . . . . .52 E7
Riverside Pk SR4 . . . . .85 B7
Riverside Prim Sch NE21 . . .41 F4
Riverside Rd SR5 . . . . .74 E2
Riverside Sculpture Pk*
NE8 . . . . .101 A3
Riverside Sports Complex
DH3 . . . . .88 E1
Riverside The NE37 . . . . . . .57 C7
**Riverside The (Durham City
Cricket Gd)** DH3 . . . . .88 E2
Riverside Way
Rowlands Gill NE39 . . . . .78 D8
Whickham NE11, NE16 . . . . .54 C2
Riverslea NE34 . . . . .60 A6
River Terr 5 NE33 . . . . .88 D4
Riverview NE38 . . . . .89 D7
River View
Bebside NE22 . . . . .11 D1
Blackhall Mill NE17 . . . . .77 B1
Blaydon NE21 . . . . .53 B2
Lynemouth NE61 . . . . .2 A3
North Shields NE30 . . . . . . .42 C6
Ovingham NE42 . . . . .50 A4
Prudhoe NE42 . . . . .50 C2
Ryton NE40 . . . . .52 E5
River View Cl NE21 . . . . .11 D1
Riverview Lodge NE4 . . . . . .54 F4
Roachburn Rd NE5 . . . . .36 E2
Robert Allan Ct NE13 . . . . . .28 A6
Robert Owen Gdns NE10 . .71 C2
Robertson Ct DH3 . . . . .88 C2
Robertson Rd SR5 . . . . .74 B2
Robertson Sq SR5 . . . . .74 B2
Roberts St NE15 . . . . .54 A5
Robert St
Blyth NE24 . . . . .17 E2
New Silksworth SR3 . . . . . . .92 C8
South Shields NE33 . . . . . . .42 D3
Sunderland SR4 . . . . .102 A3
Roberts Terr NE32 . . . . .58 B5
Robert Terr NE39 . . . . .66 F4
Robert Terr Cotts NE39 . . . .66 F4
Robert Westall Way NE29 . .41 C6
Robin Ct DH5 . . . . .94 C1
Robin Gr SR5 . . . . .74 C1
Robin La
East Rainton DH4, DH5 . . . . .94 C4
West Rainton DH4, DH5 . . . . .94 C4
Robinson Gdns
Wallsend NE28 . . . . .41 A1
2 Whitburn SR6 . . . . .60 F7
Robinson Sq NE64 . . . . .7 E5
Robinson St
5 Newcastle upon Tyne
NE6 . . . . .56 C2
8 South Shields NE33 . . . . .42 D
Robinson Terr
Burnopfield NE16 . . . . .79 A
Sunderland SR2 . . . . .103 C
2 Washington NE38 . . . . . . .83 F
Robinswood 8 NE9 . . . . . . .70 F
Robsheugh Pl NE5 . . . . .54 C
Robson Dr NE46 . . . . .44 F
Robson Pl SR2 . . . . .93 A
Robson St
7 Gateshead NE9 . . . . .71 A
Newcastle upon Tyne NE6 . . .56 B
Robson Terr
High Spen NE39 . . . . .67 B
Tantobie DH9 . . . . .79 E
Rochdale Rd SR5 . . . . .74 D
Rochdale St
Hetton-le-Hole DH5 . . . . . . .95 A
Wallsend NE28 . . . . .40 A
Rochdale Way SR5 . . . . .74 D
Rochester Cl NE63 . . . . .6 B
Rochester Gdns NE11 . . . . . .70 A
Rochester Sq NE32 . . . . .73 B
Rochester Terr 1 NE10 . . . .71 E
Rochford Gr NE23 . . . . .22 B
Rochford Rd SR5 . . . . .74 C
Rockcliffe
South Shields NE33 . . . . . . .42 D

Rockcliffe continued
Whitley Bay NE26 . . . .**32** C5
Rockcliffe Ave NE26 . . . . . **32** C4
Rockcliffe Fst Sch NE26 . . . .**32** C4
Rockcliffe Gdns
Newcastle upon Tyne
NE15 . . . .**53** F7
Whitley Bay NE26 . . . .**32** C4
Rockcliffe St NE26 . . . .**32** C4
Rockcliffe Way NE9 . . . . . .**71** D1
Rocket Way NE12 . . . .**39** F8
Rock Gr 4 NE9 . . . .**70** F5
Rockhope NE38. . . . .**88** F8
Rockingham Cl 2 SR7 . . .**93** C1
Rockingham Rd SR5 . . . . . .**74** C3
Rockingham Sq SR5 . . . . . .**74** C3
Rock Lodge Gdns SR6 . . . .**75** F3
Rock Lodge Rd SR6. . . . . . .**75** F3
Rockmore Rd NE21 . . . .**53** C1
Rock Terr
Newcastle upon Tyne NE2 . .**99** C2
8 Washington NE37. . . . . . .**83** F8
Rockville SR6. . . . .**75** E4
Rockwood Gdns NE40 . . . . .**51** E1
Rockwood Hill Est NE40. . .**66** L8
Rockwood Hill Rd NE40 . . .**51** F1
Rockwood Terr NE40 . . . . . .**51** F1
Rodin Ave NE34. . . . .**59** D2
Rodney Cl
Ryhope SR2 . . . .**92** C6
Tynemouth NE30 . . . .**42** D7
Rodney Ct NE34. . . . .**31** D7
Rodney St NE6. . . . .**56** B5
Rodney Way NE26. . . . .**31** F7
Rodsley Ave NE8, NE9 . . . . .**70** F8
Roeburn Way NE3 . . . .**37** F3
Roedean Rd SR5. . . . .**74** E3
Roehedge NE10. . . . .**72** B6
Rogan Ave 6 NE37. . . . . . .**83** A6
Rogerson Terr NE5. . . . .**36** B6
Roger St NE6. . . . .**56** B6
Rogues La NE13 . . . .**67** A5
Rokeby Ave NE15 . . . .**53** D6
Rokeby Dr NE13 . . . .**37** F4
Rokeby St
Newcastle upon Tyne
NE15 . . . .**53** D6
Sunderland SR4. . . . .**102** B2
Rokeby Terr NE6 . . . .**39** C1
Rokeby View NE9 . . . .**71** A1
ROKER **75** F2
Roker Ave
Sunderland SR6. . . . .**75** E1
Whitley Bay NE25 . . . .**31** F3
Roker Baths Rd SR6. . . . . .**75** E2
Rokerby Ave NE16 . . . .**69** C6
Roker Park Cl 10 SR6 . . . . .**75** F2
Roker Park Rd SR6 . . . .**75** F3
Roker Park Terr SR6 . . . . . .**75** F2
Roker Terr SR6 . . . .**75** F3
Roland Rd NE28 . . . .**40** E2
Roland St NE8 . . . .**83** E4
Rollesby Ct NE5 . . . .**37** B4
Rolley Way NE42. . . . .**50** E3
Rolling Mill Rd NE32 . . . . . .**58** A8
Romaldskirk Cl SR4. . . . . . .**85** B5
Roman Ave
Chester le Street DH3 . . . . . .**88** D3
Newcastle upon Tyne NE6 . . .**56** E6
Roman Ct NE28 . . . .**40** E4
Roman Rd
Hedworth NE10. . . . .**72** E8
Primrose NE32 . . . .**58** C3
South Shields NE33 . . . .**42** D4
Wardley NE10 . . . .**72** E8
Roman Road N NE33. . . . . .**42** A5
Roman Road Prim Sch
NE10 . . . .**72** A5
Roman Way NE45 . . . .**46** F6
Roman Way The NE5 . . . . . .**53** D8
Romford Cl NE23 . . . .**22** A3
Romford Pl NE9 . . . .**71** A8
Romford St 4 SR4. . . . .**85** F6
Romilly Gr NE10. . . . .**72** D7
Romilly St NE33 . . . .**42** D2
Romney Ave
Sunderland SR2. . . . .**86** E3
Washington NE38 . . . .**83** E4
Whiteleas NE34 . . . .**59** D3
Romney Cl
Shiney Row DH4 . . . .**90** C5
Whitley Bay NE26 . . . .**32** C4
Romney Gdns NE9 . . . .**71** C1
Romney Villas 5 NE38 . . . .**83** E4
Romsey Cl NE23 . . . .**22** A3
Romsey Dr NE35. . . . .**73** E8
Romsey Gr NE15. . . . .**53** C8
Ronald Dr NE15. . . . .**54** A6
Ronald Gdns NE31 . . . .**57** D4
Ronaldsay Cl 4 SR2. . . . . . .**92** E6
Ronald St NE6 . . . .**75** D3
Ronan Mews NE44 . . . .**94** A2
Ronsdorf Ct NE32. . . . .**58** B6
Rookery Cl NE24 . . . .**17** B7
Rookery La NE16. . . . .**68** E4
Rookery The NE16. . . . .**78** F6
Rooksleigh 6 NE21. . . . . . .**53** B1
Rookwood Dr NE13 . . . .**28** C8
Rookwood Gdns NE39. . . . . .**67** E3
Rookwood Rd NE15 . . . .**53** C8
Rookwood Rd NE5 . . . .**54** A8
Ropery La
Bournmoor DH4 . . . .**88** F3
Chester le Street DH3 . . . . . .**88** D2
Hebburn NE31 . . . .**57** D6
Wallsend NE28 . . . .**40** F2
Ropery Rd
Gateshead NE8 . . . .**70** B8

Ropery Rd continued
Sunderland SR4. . . . .**102** B4
Ropery The NE6 . . . .**56** B4
Rosalie Terr SR2 . . . .**86** F4
Rosalind Ave NE22 . . . .**11** B1
Rosalind St
Ashington, Hirst NE63. . . . . . .**6** E3
Ashington NE63 . . . .**6** E4
Rosa Parks Ho NE24. . . . . . .**17** F7
Rosa St NE33 . . . .**42** D2
Rose Ave
Cramlington NE23 . . . .**21** F8
Fence Houses DH4 . . . .**89** F1
Whickham NE16. . . . .**69** B7
Rosebank Cl SR2 . . . .**92** E8
Rosebank Hall NE28 . . . .**40** F2
Roseberry Ct 12 NE37 . . . . .**83** E8
Roseberry Grange NE12. . . .**30** A1
Roseberry Pl NE2. . . . .**99** C4
Roseberry St 4 SR5 . . . . . .**75** D1
Roseborough Rd NE37 . . . . .**38** D8
Rosebud Cl 8 NE16. . . . .**54** A1
Rose Cotts NE41. . . . .**51** A6
Rose Cres
Bournmoor DH4. . . . .**89** D3
Whitburn SR6 . . . .**60** F2
Rose Ct NE31. . . . .**57** D5
Rosedale
Bedlington NE22 . . . .**10** E1
Wallsend NE28 . . . .**39** F4
Rosedale Ave SR6 . . . .**75** E6
Rosedale Cres DH4 . . . .**90** C2
Rosedale Ct NE5. . . . .**36** D2
Rosedale Rd NE40 . . . .**51** F3
Rosedale St
Hetton-le-Hole DH5 . . . .**94** E1
Sunderland SR1. . . . .**102** B2
Rosedale Terr
Newcastle upon Tyne NE2 . . .**99** C3
North Shields NE30 . . . .**42** B7
Sunderland SR6. . . . .**75** E4
Roseden Ct NE12 . . . .**29** C7
Rosedene Villas NE23 . . . . . .**22** D6
Rosefinch Lodge NE9 . . . . . .**70** F5
Rose Gdns
Kibblesworth NE11 . . . .**81** C6
Wallsend NE28 . . . .**40** B4
Rosegill NE37. . . . .**83** B6
ROSEHILL **40** E2
Rosehill Cl NE22 . . . .**10** F2
Rosehill Rd NE28 . . . .**40** F2
Rosehill Way NE5 . . . .**37** C1
Roselea NE32. . . . .**58** C1
Roselea Ave SR2 . . . .**92** F7
Rosella Pl NE29 . . . .**42** A6
Rosemary Gdns NE9 . . . .**71** D2
Rosemary Rd SR5 . . . .**74** D3
Rosemary Terr NE24 . . . .**17** F6
Rosemount
Haswell DH6. . . . .**97** F4
Morpeth NE61 . . . .**9** A7
Sunderland SR4. . . . .**85** A5
Rosemount Ave NE10 . . . . . .**72** B7
Rosemount Cl 1 NE37 . . . . .**72** C2
Rosemount Ct NE36. . . . .**74** B7
Rosemount Way
Newcastle upon Tyne NE7 . . .**39** C5
Whitley Bay NE25 . . . .**31** C5
Roseneath Ct NE63 . . . .**6** C3
Rose St
Gateshead NE8 . . . .**100** C2
Hebburn NE31 . . . .**57** D5
7 Houghton-le-Spring DH4 .**94** D8
Sunderland SR4. . . . .**102** B3
Rose Street E DH4 . . . .**90** B8
Rose Street W DH4 . . . .**90** B8
Rose Terr
Greenside NE40. . . . .**52** C2
Newcastle upon Tyne NE5 . . .**37** E1
Seaton Sluice NE26 . . . .**24** D4
Rose Villa La NE16 . . . .**69** B7
Roseville St SR4 . . . .**102** B1
Rosewell Pl NE16 . . . .**69** A4
Rosewood NE12 . . . .**29** F3
Rosewood Ave NE3 . . . .**38** E6
Rosewood Cres
Newcastle upon Tyne NE6 . . .**39** F1
Seaton Sluice NE26 . . . .**24** D4
Rosewood Gdns
Chester le Street DH2. . . . . . .**88** B5
Gateshead NE9 . . . .**71** B5
Newcastle upon Tyne NE3 . . .**37** F4
Rosewood Sq SR4 . . . .**85** A2
Rosewood Terr
Birtley DH3 . . . .**82** B5
Wallsend NE28 . . . .**41** A2
Rosewood Way NE3 . . . .**38** B8
Roseworth Ave NE3 . . . .**38** D3
Roseworth Cl NE3 . . . .**38** D4
Roseworth Cres NE3 . . . .**38** D3
Roseworth Terr
Newcastle upon Tyne NE3 . . .**38** C4
Sunderland SR6. . . . .**69** B7
Roslin Pk NE22 . . . .**11** C1
Roslin Way NE23 . . . .**22** A3
Ross
Ouston DH2 . . . .**81** F2
Ouston DH2 . . . .**82** A1
Ross Ave NE11. . . . .**54** F1
Rossdale DH4 . . . .**90** A5
Rosse Cl 1 NE40 . . . .**51** F3
Rosse Cl NE37 . . . .**83** B8

Rossendale Pl NE12. . . . .**38** F6
Ross Gr NE23 . . . .**21** F7
Ross Lea DH4. . . . .**90** A5
Rosslyn Ave
Gateshead NE9 . . . .**71** A6
Newcastle upon Tyne NE3 . . .**37** E5
Sunderland SR2 . . . .**92** F7
Rosslyn Mews SR4. . . . . . .**102** A2
Rosslyn Pl DH3 . . . .**82** D2
Rosslyn St SR4 . . . .**102** A2
Rosslyn Terr SR4. . . . .**102** A2
Ross St SR5 . . . .**75** C1
Ross Way
Newcastle upon Tyne NE3 . . .**37** F8
Whitley Bay NE26 . . . .**31** E7
Rosyth Rd SR5 . . . .**74** E3
Rosyth Sq SR5 . . . .**74** E3
Rotary Parkway NE63 . . . . . .**6** B4
Rotary Way
Blyth NE24 . . . .**17** F5
Hexham NE46 . . . .**45** C6
North Shields NE29 . . . .**41** E3
Ponteland NE20. . . . .**26** A4
Rothay Pl NE5 . . . .**37** C2
Rothbury SR2. . . . .**92** D6
Rothbury Ave
Blyth NE24 . . . .**17** B6
Gateshead NE10 . . . .**57** A1
Hebburn NE32 . . . .**58** A4
Newcastle upon Tyne NE3 . . .**38** B6
Rothbury Cl
Chester le Street DH2 . . . .**88** A1
Killingworth NE12 . . . .**29** C4
Rothbury Dr NE63. . . . .**5** F5
Rothbury Gdns
Dunston NE11 . . . .**70** A5
Sunderland SR5 . . . .**74** D2
Wallsend NE28 . . . .**40** F3
Wideopen NE13 . . . .**28** C6
Rothbury Rd SR5 . . . .**74** D3
Rothbury Terr
Newcastle upon Tyne NE6 . . .**56** C8
North Shields NE29 . . . .**41** D4
Newcastle upon Tyne NE6 . . .**56** C8
Rotherdale Ct NE6 . . . .**57** A7
Rotherfield Cl NE23. . . . .**22** B7
Rotherfield Gdns 8 NE9 .**71** A2
Rotherfield Rd SR5 . . . .**74** C3
Rotherfield Sq SR5. . . . .**74** C3
Rotherham Cl DH4 . . . .**94** D6
Rotherham Rd SR5 . . . .**74** C3
Rothesay DH2 . . . .**81** F1
Rothesay Terr NE22 . . . .**11** C2
Rothlea Gdns NE62 . . . .**11** A8
Rothley NE38 . . . .**83** F2
Rothley Ave
Ashington NE63 . . . .**6** D2
Newcastle upon Tyne NE5 . . .**54** C7
Rothley Cl
Killingworth NE12 . . . .**29** D3
Sunderland SR5 . . . .**74** F4
Rothley Gdns NE30. . . . .**32** B1
Rothley Gr NE25 . . . .**23** C3
Rothley Terr DH8 . . . .**77** B1
Rothley Way NE26 . . . .**31** E7
Rothsay Terr NE64 . . . .**7** D2
Rothwell Rd
Newcastle upon Tyne NE3 . . .**38** C5
Sunderland SR5 . . . .**74** C2
Roundhill NE32 . . . .**58** D1
Roundhill Ave NE5 . . . .**37** C2
Roundstone Cl NE7 . . . .**39** D4
Roundway The NE12 . . . .**39** B7
Rowan Ave NE38. . . . .**83** C1
Rowanberry Rd NE12. . . . . . .**39** B6
Rowan Cl
Bedlington NE22 . . . .**10** F2
Sunderland SR4. . . . .**85** B5
Rowan Ct
Blyth NE24. . . . .**17** D7
Burnopfield NE16 . . . .**79** B6
Longbenton NE12 . . . .**29** F1
South Shields NE34 . . . .**59** A4
Rowan Dr
Hetton-le-Hole DH5 . . . .**94** F4
Newcastle upon Tyne NE3 . . .**37** F6
Ponteland NE20. . . . .**25** E7
Rowan Gr
Cramlington NE23 . . . .**22** D5
Prudhoe NE42 . . . .**50** B2
Rowans The 3 NE9 . . . .**71** E2
Rowanwood Ho NE4 . . . .**40** A1
Rowanwood Gdns NE11. . . . .**70** B5
Rowedge Wlk NE5 . . . .**37** A2
Rowell Cl SR2 . . . .**92** C6
Rowes Mews NE6 . . . .**56** D4
Rowland Burn Way NE39 . . .**67** E2
ROWLANDS GILL **67** F3
Rowlands Gill Com Prim Sch
NE39 . . . .**67** F3
Rowlandson Terr NE10 . . . .**71** D8
9 Sunderland SR2 . . . .**86** E4
Rowley St NE24 . . . .**17** E7
Rowlington Terr NE63. . . . . . .**6** E3
Rowntree Way NE29 . . . .**42** A3
Rowsley Rd NE32 . . . .**58** C5
Row's Terr NE3 . . . .**38** B1
Roxburgh Cl NE21. . . . .**68** A8
Roxburgh House NE26 . . . . . .**32** A5
Roxburgh Pl 2 NE6. . . . .**56** B7
Roxburgh St SR6. . . . .**75** D3
Roxby Gdns NE29 . . . .**41** E5
Royal Arc NE1 . . . .**99** B1
Royal Cres NE4 . . . .**54** E8

Royal Gram Sch NE2. . . . . . .**99** B3
Royal Ind Est NE32. . . . .**57** F8
Royal Quays Outlet Shopping
NE28 . . . .**41** E2
Royalty The SR2 . . . .**102** E2
Royalty Theatre* SR2. . . . .**102** B2
Royal Victoria Infmy NE2 . . .**99** C3
Roydon Ave SR3 . . . .**91** E3
Royle St SR2 . . . .**86** F2
Royston Terr NE6 . . . .**57** A4
Ruabon Ct NE23 . . . .**22** A3
Rubens Ave NE34 . . . .**59** D3
Ruby St DH5. . . . .**90** D2
Rudby Cl NE3. . . . .**38** D8
Rudchester 1 NE5. . . . .**54** C8
Ruddock Sq 11 NE6 . . . .**56** C4
Rudyard Ave SR2 . . . .**86** E3
Rudyerd Ct NE29. . . . .**42** B5
Rudyerd St
13 North Shields NE29 . . . .**42** A5
North Shields NE29 . . . .**42** B5
Rugby Gdns
Gateshead NE9 . . . .**71** C3
Wallsend NE28 . . . .**40** E3
Rislip Pl NE73 . . . .**21** F3
Ruislip Rd SR4. . . . .**85** A5
Runciman Rd SR2 . . . .**92** C7
Runcorn Rd SR5. . . . .**74** C3
Runhead Est NE40 . . . .**52** D2
Runhead Gdns NE40 . . . .**52** D5
Runhead Sta NE40 . . . .**52** E5
Runnymede SR2 . . . .**92** D7
Runnymede Gdns NE17 . . . . .**77** B7
Runnymede Rd
Ponteland NE20. . . . .**25** C5
Sunderland SR5. . . . .**74** C2
Whickham NE16. . . . .**69** A6
Runnymede Way
Newcastle upon Tyne NE3 . . .**37** F4
Sunderland SR5. . . . .**74** D3
Runswick Ave NE12 . . . .**38** F6
Runswick Cl SR3. . . . .**92** C7
Runswick Dr SR7 . . . .**93** D1
Rupert Sq SR5 . . . .**74** E3
Rupert St NE6 . . . .**60** F1
Rupert Terr NE15 . . . .**52** F8
Rushall Pl NE12 . . . .**39** B6
Rushbury Ct NE27. . . . .**30** C5
Rushcliffe SR6 . . . .**75** D3
Rushford SR2 . . . .**92** D6
Rushie Ave NE15 . . . .**54** C5
Rushley Cres NE21. . . . .**53** C3
Rushmore Grange NE38. . . . .**83** E6
Rushsyde Cl NE16. . . . .**68** E5
Rushton Ave SR2 . . . .**86** E3
Rushyrig NE37 . . . .**83** A6
Ruskin Ave
Ashington NE63. . . . .**6** F2
7 Dunston NE11 . . . .**54** F1
Easington Lane DH5 . . . .**94** F8
Longbenton NE12 . . . .**29** D1
Ruskin Cres NE34 . . . .**59** B3
Ruskin Ct NE42 . . . .**50** B1
Ruskin Dr
Newcastle upon Tyne NE7 . . .**39** B5
West Boldon NE35 . . . .**74** A8
Ruskin Rd
Birtley DH3 . . . .**82** C4
Gateshead N10, NE9 . . . .**71** B7
Whickham NE16. . . . .**69** A6
4 Whickham NE16 . . . .**69** A8
Russel Cl NE37 . . . .**38** F2
Russell Ave NE34 . . . .**60** A6
Russell Ct NE8. . . . .**100** C1
Russell Ho NE1 . . . .**103** B3
Russell Sq NE13 . . . .**28** B8
Russell St
Jarrow NE32 . . . .**58** C7
8 North Shields NE29 . . . . .**42** A5
2 South Shields NE33 . . . . .**42** C3
Sunderland SR1. . . . .**103** B3
Washington NE37 . . . .**83** C8
Russell Terr
Bedlington NE22 . . . .**15** F8
Birtley DH3 . . . .**82** C4
Newcastle upon Tyne NE1,
NE2. . . . .**99** C2
Rustic Terr NE64 . . . .**7** E5
Ruswarp Dr SR3 . . . .**92** B6
Ruth Ave NE21 . . . .**53** C2
Rutherford Ave 4 SR7 . . . . .**92** F1
Rutherford Cl NE62 . . . .**10** E7
Rutherford Pl NE61 . . . .**9** A7
Rutherford Rd
Sunderland SR5. . . . .**74** B3
Washington NE37 . . . .**72** E2
Rutherford Sq SR5 . . . .**74** B3
Rutherford St
Blyth NE24. . . . .**17** D7
Newcastle upon Tyne NE1 . . .**98** C1
Wallsend NE28 . . . .**41** B3
Rutherglen Rd SR5. . . . .**74** D3
Ruthergien Sq SR5 . . . .**74** E3
Ruthven St NE7 . . . .**38** F2
Rutland Ave SR3 . . . .**91** F7
Rutland Pl NE37 . . . .**37** E2
Rutland Rd
North Shields NE29 . . . .**41** F6
Washington NE37 . . . .**72** E2
Rutland Sq NE24 . . . .**17** D7
Wallsend NE28 . . . .**40** A1
Rutland Sq NE21 . . . .**53** F3
Rutland St
Ashington NE63 . . . .**6** C3
Hetton-le-Hole DH5 . . . .**94** F4
Sunderland SR4. . . . .**85** F7
Rutland Terr DH6 . . . .**97** E4

Ryal Cl
Blyth NE24. . . . .**17** C7
Seaton Delaval NE25. . . . .**23** E3
Ryal Terr NE6 . . . .**56** F5
Ryal Wlk NE3. . . . .**37** D4
Rydal NE10 . . . .**72** A8
Rydal Ave
Easington Lane DH5 . . . .**97** C8
Newcastle upon Tyne NE30 . . .**32** A2
Rydal Cl
East Boldon NE36 . . . .**74** C8
Killingworth NE12 . . . .**29** F3
Rydal Cres NE21 . . . .**68** B8
Rydal Gdns NE34 . . . .**59** E6
Rydal Mount
Newbeggin-by-the-Sea
NE64. . . . .**7** C4
Sunderland, Castletown SR5 .**85** A8
Sunderland SR5. . . . .**75** C3
Rydal Rd
Chester le Street DH2. . . . . . .**88** C1
Newcastle upon Tyne, Gosforth
NE3. . . . .**38** D5
Newcastle upon Tyne, Lemington
NE15 . . . .**53** D8
Rydal St NE8 . . . .**101** B3
Rydal Terr NE13. . . . .**28** B4
Ryde Pl NE23 . . . .**22** B7
Ryde Terr NE11 . . . .**100** A1
Rye Cl NE15 . . . .**35** E1
Ryedale
Sunderland SR6. . . . .**75** F7
Wallsend NE28 . . . .**39** F5
Ryedale Cl NE63 . . . .**6** E2
Ryedale Ct 7 NE34 . . . .**59** A4
Ryedale Ho NE24 . . . .**16** F8
Ryehaugh NE20 . . . .**25** F6
Rye Hill
Newcastle upon Tyne
NE4. . . . .**100** B4
Newcastle upon Tyne NE4 . .**100** C4
Ryehill View DH5 . . . .**94** C5
Ryemount Rd SR2 . . . .**92** D7
Rye Terr NE46 . . . .**44** F5
Rye View SR2 . . . .**92** F7
RYHOPE **92** F6
RYHOPE COLLIERY **92** E5
RYHOPE ENGINES Mus*
SR2. . . . .**92** E5
Ryhope Gdns NE9 . . . .**71** D2
Ryhope General Hospl
SR2. . . . .**92** F5
Ryhope Grange Ct SR2. . . . .**86** F1
Ryhope Inf Sch SR2 . . . .**92** F7
Ryhope Jun Sch SR2. . . . . . .**92** F7
Ryhope Rd
Ryhope SR2 . . . .**93** A8
Sunderland SR2 . . . .**86** E3
Ryhope St Patricks Prim Sch
14 SR2. . . . .**92** F6
Ryhope St
Houghton-le-Spring DH5 . . . .**94** F4
Ryhope SR2 . . . .**92** F7
8 Sunderland SR2 . . . .**86** F2
Ryhope Street S SR2. . . . . . .**92** F7
RYTON **52** A5
Ryton Com Jun Sch NE40 . . .**52** A5
Ryton Comp Sch NE40 . . . . . .**52** B5
Ryton Ct NE33 . . . .**42** D1
Ryton Hall Dr NE40 . . . .**52** C6
Ryton Ind Est NE21 . . . .**53** A5
Ryton Inf Est NE21 . . . .**52** A5
Ryton Sq SR2 . . . .**92** C6
Ryton Terr
Newcastle upon Tyne NE6. . . .**56** F4
Shiremoor NE27 . . . .**30** D1
Ryton Willows Nature
Reserve* NE40. . . . .**52** D7
RYTON WOODSIDE **52** B2

S

Sackville Rd
Newcastle upon Tyne NE6. . . .**39** C1
Sunderland SR3. . . . .**85** E3
Sacred Heart High Sch
NE4 . . . .**54** D7
Sacred Heart Prim Sch
NE4 . . . .**54** D7
Sacriston Ave SR3 . . . .**85** F3
Sacriston Gdns NE9. . . . .**71** C2
Saddleback NE37 . . . .**83** B7
Saffron Pl NE6. . . . .**57** A5
Saga Cl NE6 . . . .**39** F1
Sage Cl NE15 . . . .**53** C8
Sage Gateshead The*
NE8 . . . .**101** C4
St Acca's CE Sch NE46 . . . . . .**44** F5
St Agnes' Gardens N NE40 **51** E4
St Agnes' Gardens W
NE40 . . . .**51** E4
St Agnes' Gdns NE40. . . . . . .**51** E4
St Agnes' Terr NE40. . . . .**51** E4
St Aidan's Ave
Sunderland SR2. . . . .**86** F2
Wallsend NE28 . . . .**30** C1
St Aidan's CE Prim Sch
NE8 . . . .**100** C1
St Aidan's St NE29 . . . .**41** D8
St Aidan's Cres NE61. . . . .**9** A6
St Aidans Ct DH4 . . . .**90** E6
St Aidan's Ct NE30. . . . .**42** C7

Saint Aidan's Ho NE29 ....41 D8
St Aidans RC Fst Sch NE63 6 D1
St Aidans RC Sch SR2....86 C4
St Aidan's Rd
  South Shields NE33........42 D4
  Wallsend NE28............40 A1
St Aidan's Sq NE12.........30 C1
St Aidan's St NE8..........101 A1
St Aidan's Terr DH4........90 E6
St Albans Cl NE63...........7 A2
St Albans Cl NE25.........31 A5
St Alban's Cres
  Gateshead NE10..........71 C7
  Newcastle upon Tyne NE6..39 D2
St Alban's Pl
  Gateshead NE10..........71 C7
  Tynemouth NE30..........42 D7
St Albans Prim Sch
  Gateshead NE10..........57 A1
  Newcastle upon Tyne NE6..86 F3
St Alban's St SR2..........86 A3
St Alban's Terr NE8.......101 C1
St Albans View NE27........30 F2
St Aldate's St SR4.........85 A2
St Aloysius RC Inf Sch
  NE31....................57 F7
St Aloysius RC Jun Sch
  NE31....................57 E7
St Aloysius View NE31....57 D6
St Andrews DH4............94 B8
St Andrews Ave NE7.......83 B8
St Andrews Church* SR6 .75 E3
St Andrews Cl NE25........31 C5
St Andrews Cl 4 NE29...41 F8
St Andrew's Ct NE7.......39 C5
St Andrew's Dr NE9........70 E3
St Andrew's La NE42......49 D4
St Andrews RC Fst Sch
  NE24....................17 C7
St Andrew's Rd
  Hexham NE46.............45 A4
  Kip Hill DH9............79 F1
St Andrew's St
  Hebburn NE31............57 C7
  Newcastle upon Tyne NE1..98 C1
St Andrew's Terr
  Ashington NE63...........6 E3
  Sunderland SR6..........75 E2
St Anne's Ct NE25.........31 E3
St Annes RC Prim Sch
  NE9.....................71 B2
St Anne's RC Prim Sch
  SR4....................85 B5
ST ANN'S..................56 A5
St Ann's Cl NE1..........56 A5
St Ann's Quay NE1.........99 C1
St Ann's St NE1...........99 C1
St Anselm Cres NE29......41 C7
St Anselm Rd NE29........41 C7
ST ANTHONY'S.............56 E3
St Anthonys CE Prim Sch
  NE6....................56 F3
St Anthony's Ct NE6......56 F6
St Anthony's Girls' Sch
  SR2...................102 C1
St Anthony's Ho NE6......56 F3
St Anthony's Rd NE6......56 F4
St Anthony's Wlk NE6.....56 F3
St Asaph Cl NE12.........39 D4
St Augustines RC Prim Sch
  NE10....................72 A6
St Austell Cl NE15........54 B2
St Austell Gdns NE9.......70 F2
St Barnabas DH4...........89 D3
St Barnabas Way SR2....103 C1
St Bartholomews CE Prim
  Sch NE12.................39 D5
St Bartholomews Cl NE61..2 A7
St Bede's Cl DH5.........95 A4
St Bede's Dr NE8........101 C2
St Bede's Ho NE42........45 A4
St Bedes Pl NE24.........17 B4
St Bedes RC Fst Sch NE22 15 E8
St Bede's RC Prim Sch
  Denton Burn NE15........53 F6
  2 Jarrow NE32..........58 C7
  South Shields NE33......42 D2
  Washington NE37.........72 D1
St Bedes Rd NE24.........17 B4
St Bedes Wlk NE27........30 C1
St Benedicts RC VA Mid Sch
  NE63.....................6 F3
St Benet Biscop VA High Sch
  NE22...................15 E8
St Benets RC Prim Sch
  SR6.....................75 D2
St Bernard's RC Prim Sch
  DH2....................81 F1
St Bernadettes RC Prim Sch
  NE28...................40 B5
St Buryan Cres NE5.......37 C4
St Catherine's Ct SR5....74 D1
St Catherines Gr NE2.....56 A7
St Catherines RC Prim Sch
  1 NE2..................56 A8
St Cecilia's Cl SR2......56 F4
St Chad's Cres SR3.......91 B7
St Chad's Rd SR3.........91 B7
St Chad's Villas 6 NE36..74 D2
St Charles RC Prim Sch
  NE3....................38 B6
St Christophers Cl 3 NE63. 6 F5
St Christopher's Ho NE61 . 8 E8
St Christopher's Rd SR3 ..86 A2

St Christopher Way NE29. .41 C2
St Clements Ct
  Ashington NE63...........7 A2
  3 Longbenton NE12......39 A6
  Newcastle upon Tyne NE3..37 F8
  Sunderland SR4..........85 D6
St Columba's Ct SR5......75 C2
St Columbas RC Prim Sch
  NE28...................40 A2
Saint Ct SR3.............92 A5
St Cuthbert Ave DH3......88 D3
St Cuthbert's Ave NE34...60 A8
St Cuthberts Cl
  Hexham NE46.............45 A4
  Prudhoe NE42............50 C2
  Wallsend NE27...........30 D1
St Cuthbert's Cl DH5.....95 A4
St Cuthberts Ct NE24.....17 F7
St Cuthbert's Ct
  Gateshead NE8..........101 A2
  Newcastle upon Tyne NE3..38 A5
St Cuthbert's Dr NE10....71 F7
St Cuthbert's Gn NE5.....54 C7
St Cuthbert's La NE46....45 A4
St Cuthbert's Pk NE8.....80 A8
St Cuthbert's Pl NE8....101 A1
St Cuthberts RC Lower Sch
  NE15...................54 C6
St Cuthberts RC Prim Sch
  1 Chester le Street DH3 ..88 D2
  Newcastle upon Tyne NE5..42 A5
  2 North Shields NE29....42 A5
  Sunderland SR4..........85 D3
  Walbottle NE15..........35 F2
St Cuthberts RC (Upper) Sch
  NE15...................54 B6
St Cuthbert's Rd
  Gateshead NE8..........101 A2
  Gateshead, Windmill Hills
  NE8....................101 B3
  Newcastle DH4...........90 D3
  Newcastle upon Tyne, Benwell
  NE5....................54 B7
  Newcastle upon Tyne, Fenham
  NE5....................54 C8
  New Herrington DH4......90 F7
  Sunniside NE16..........80 B7
  Wallsend, Holystone NE27..30 C1
  Wallsend NE28...........40 E3
St Cuthbert's Terr
  Bedlington NE22..........11 B1
  Hexham NE46.............45 A4
  Sunderland SR4.........102 B3
St Cuthberts Way
  Blaydon NE21............53 D3
  Wallsend NE27...........30 C1
St Cuthbert's Wlk DH3....88 C3
St David's Cl NE26........31 F8
St David's Way
  Hedworth NE32...........58 C1
  Whitley Bay NE26........31 F8
St Ebba's Way DH8........76 E3
St Edmund Campion RC Sch
  NE9....................71 B2
St Edmund's Ct NE8.......56 F2
St Edmund's Dr NE10.....71 F7
St Edmund's Rd NE8......101 C1
St Etienne Ct 12 NE10....56 D1
St Gabriel's Ave
  Newcastle upon Tyne NE6..39 B7
  Sunderland SR4..........85 F5
St George's Cl NE22.......38 E2
St Georges Cres NE35.....31 F4
St George's Cres NE29....41 F5
St Georges Ct NE10.......72 B7
St George's Est NE38.....83 C1
St George's Park Hospl
  NE61....................4 A2
St George's Pl NE15......53 E5
St Georges RC Prim Sch
  NE3....................53 D5
St George's Rd
  Hexham NE46.............45 A4
  Newcastle upon Tyne NE15..53 E5
  Tynemouth NE30..........32 C3
St George's Terr
  East Boldon NE36........74 D7
  Newcastle upon Tyne, Lemington
  NE15...................53 E5
  Newcastle upon Tyne, West
  Jesmond NE2............38 E2
  Sunderland SR6..........75 F2
St George's Way SR2....103 A1
St Godric's Dr DH4......94 A1
St Gregory's Ct NE34.....59 F5
St Gregorys RC JMI Sch
  NE34....................60 A7
St Helen's Cres NE9......70 F5
St Helen's La NE45.......47 A6
St Helen's St NE45.......46 F6
St Helens Terr NE15......70 F5
St Hilda Ind Est 4 NE33..42 C2
St Hilda's Ave NE28.......40 E3
St Hilda's Rd NE46.......45 A4
St Hilda St NE33.........42 C2
St Ignatius Cl SR2......103 B1
St Ives Way NE5..........37 C4
St James Bldg NE1, NE4 ..100 C4
St James Cl NE44.........62 F7
St James' Cres NE15......54 D4
St James Ct 15 NE8.......56 B1
St James' Gate NE1......100 C4
St James Gdns NE15......54 D5
St James Lodge 4 NE8....54 D5
St James' Mall NE31......58 D5

St James' Pk (Newcastle Utd
  FC) NE1.................98 C2
St James RC Prim Sch
  NE31...................57 F4
St James' Rd NE8.........56 A2
St James' Rd NE15........54 D5
St James Sq NE8..........56 A2
St James St
  Newcastle upon Tyne NE1..98 C2
  Newcastle upon Tyne NE3..38 E5
  Sunderland SR3 a NE1....98 C1
St James Terr
  7 Morpeth NE61...........3 F1
  Riding Mill NE44.........63 A7
St James' Terr NE31......41 D3
St John Bosco RC Prim Sch
  SR5....................74 A4
St John Boste RC Prim Sch
  NE38...................83 A5
St Johns SR1............103 C4
St John's Ave NE31.......57 D5
St John's Cl NE26........31 D3
St John's Cres NE22......11 D3
St John's Ct NE12........29 D1
St John's Ct
  Backworth NE27..........30 C4
  Newcastle upon Tyne NE4..54 E4
  North Shields NE29......41 D3
  South Shields NE33......42 D2
  Newcastle upon Tyne NE3..38 A5
St John's Mall NE31......57 D5
St Johns Pl NE10.........71 D8
St John's Pl
  Bedlington NE22.........11 D2
  Birtley DH3.............82 C4
  Whitley Bay NE26........31 F8
St Johns Prim Sch NE5....54 E4
St John's Rd NE46........45 A3
St John's Rd
  Bedlington NE22.........11 D2
  High Pittington DH6.....96 B5
  Newcastle upon Tyne NE4..54 E4
St John's St NE29........41 D3
St John St NE1...........99 A1
St John's Terr
  East Boldon NE36........74 E7
  Jarrow NE32.............58 B7
  Seaton Sluice NE26......31 D3
  7 Seaham SR7...........92 E1
St Johns Vale SR4........85 A4
St John's W NE22.........11 D2
St John's Wlk
  Hebburn NE31............57 E5
  Newcastle upon Tyne NE4..54 E4
  North Shields NE29......41 D3
St John the Baptists RC Prim
  Sch NE10................71 D8
St John Vianney RC Prim Sch
  NE5....................36 D1
St Joseph's Ct
  8 Birtley DH3..........82 C5
  Hebburn NE31............57 D3
St Joseph's RC Comp Sch
  NE31...................57 D2
St Josephs RC Inf Sch
  DH3....................82 C5
St Josephs RC Mid Sch 17
  NE46...................44 F4
St Josephs RC Prim Sch
  Rowlands Gill NE39......67 B2
  Washington NE38........83 D6
St Joseph's RC Prim Sch
  Blaydon NE21............53 B3
  Gateshead NE8..........101 C2
  Hedworth NE32...........58 B1
  Newcastle upon Tyne NE15..54 D4
  North Shields NE29......41 E4
  10 Sunderland SR4......85 F7
St Joseph's RC VA Prim Sch
  NE8....................101 C2
St Joseph's Way SR2......58 C1
St Jude's Terr NE33......59 C8
St Julien Gdns
  Newcastle upon Tyne NE7..39 D2
  Wallsend NE28...........41 B3
St Just Pl NE5...........37 C4
St Keverne Sq NE5........37 C4
St Kitt's Cl NE26........31 F8
St Laurences RC Prim Sch
  12 NE6.................56 C5
ST LAWRENCE.............56 B5
St Lawrence Cl DH6.......96 C5
St Lawrence Rd
  High Pittington DH6.....96 B5
  Newcastle upon Tyne NE6..56 C4
St Lawrence Sq NE6.......56 B5
St Leonard's La NE61......3 B2
St Leonards RC Prim Sch
  NE3....................92 B7
St Leonard St SR2........86 F4
St Leonard's Wlk NE61.....3 C2
St Lucia Cl
  Sunderland SR2.........103 B1
  Whitley Bay NE26........31 F8
St Lukes Cl NE31.........57 D4
St Lukes Rd NE46.........45 A4
St Luke's Rd
  North Shields NE29......41 D3
  Sunderland SR4..........85 C6
St Luke's Terr SR4.......85 F7
St Margarets Ave DH6.....96 D6
St Margaret's Ave SR5....74 A1
St Margaret's Ct SR5.....74 A1
St Margaret's Ct
  Dr DH9.................79 D4
St Margaret's Rd NE15....54 A4

St Mark's Cl 11 NE6.......56 C7
St Mark's Cres SR4......102 B2
St Marks Ct
  Backworth NE27..........30 E3
  Newcastle upon Tyne NE5..36 F4
St Mark's Ct NE29........41 D2
St Marks RC Prim Sch
  NE5....................36 F4
St Marks Rd NE46.........45 A3
St Mark's Rd SR4........102 B2
St Mark's Road N SR4 ...102 A2
St Mark's St
  Morpeth NE61............3 E1
  16 Newcastle upon Tyne
  NE6....................56 C7
  Sunderland SR4.........102 B2
St Mark's Terr SR4......102 B2
St Mark's Way NE31.......41 D3
St Martin's Cl NE26......31 F7
St Martin's Ct NE26......31 F7
St Martin's Way NE26.....31 F7
St Mary & St Thomas
  Aquinas Prim Sch NE21..53 A4
St Mary's Ave
  South Shields NE34......59 F6
  Whitley Bay NE26........31 F7
St Mary's Business &
  Enterprise Ctr NE4.....98 C1
St Marys Cath Comp Sch
  NE7....................39 A5
St Mary's Chare 6 NE46..45 B5
St Mary's Cl NE27........88 B1
St Mary's College Flats
  NE4....................54 E7
St Mary's Ct
  Gateshead NE8..........101 C2
  South Shields NE33......59 B7
St Mary's Dr
  Blyth NE24..............17 B6
  Seaton DH4..............94 A2
St Mary's Field NE61......8 F7
St Mary's Gn 4 NE16......69 B7
St Mary's Island Nature
  Reserve NE26...........24 G2
*St Mary's Lighthouse**
  NE26...................24 G2
St Mary's Lodge NE26.....31 F5
St Mary's Pl
  Newcastle upon Tyne NE1..99 A2
  Throckley NE15..........35 E2
St Mary's Place E NE1....99 A2
St Marys RC Fst Sch 10
  NE46...................45 A4
St Mary's RC Prim Sch
  Brockley Whins NE32.....58 D3
  1 Longbenton NE12......29 D1
  Sunderland SR2..........86 B6
  Tynemouth NE30..........32 A2
  Whickham NE16...........69 C7
St Mary's Sq NE8........101 C4
St Mary's St NE1.........99 C1
St Mary's Terr
  East Boldon NE36........74 E7
  Ryton NE40..............52 B5
St Mary's Way SR1.......103 A3
St Marys Whickham RC Prim
  Sch 8 NE16.............69 C7
St Mary's Wynd
  7 Hexham NE46..........45 B5
  Seaton Sluice NE26......24 E4
St Mathews La NE42.......50 D2
St Matthews Cath Fst Sch
  NE42...................50 C2
St Matthew's RC Prim Sch 8
  NE32...................58 A2
St Matthews Rd NE46.....44 F3
St Matthew's Terr DH4....90 D4
St Matthews View SR3.....92 A7
St Michaels DH4..........94 B8
St Michael's Ave
  New Hartley NE25........23 D6
  South Shields NE33......42 D1
St Michael's Avenue N
  NE33...................42 D1
St Michaels Cl NE45......45 A4
St Michael's Mount 3
  NE6....................56 C4
St Michaels RC Prim Sch
  Houghton-le-Spring DH5..94 D7
  Newcastle upon Tyne NE4..100 A3
St Michael's Rd NE6......56 B5
St Michael's Way NE11...102 C2
St Michael's Way NE11....54 C1
St Michaels Workshops 10
  NE6....................56 B5
St Nicholas Ave
  Newcastle upon Tyne, Gosforth
  NE3....................38 B4
  Newcastle upon Tyne, South
  Gosforth NE3............38 C4
  Sunderland SR3..........91 B3
St Nichola's Cath* NE1...99 B1
St Nicholas' Church Yd
  NE1....................99 A1
St Nicholas Cl NE63.......6 F5
St Nicholas Hospl NE3....38 A5
St Nicholas Rd
  Hexham NE46.............45 A4
  West Boldon NE36........74 A7
St Nicholas' Sq 7 NE1....99 A1
St Nicholas' St NE1......101 A4
St Nicholas View NE36....74 A7
St Omers Rd NE11........54 F2
St Oswald's Ave NE6......56 E6
St Oswalds CE Prim Sch
  NE42...................50 E3
St Oswalds Ct NE42......50 E3

St Oswald's Gn NE6........56 E7
St Oswalds RC Prim Sch
  Gateshead NE9..........71 C3
  Newcastle upon Tyne NE3..38 D7
  Whiteleas NE34.........59 D3
St Oswald's Rd
  Hebburn NE31............57 F7
  14 Hexham NE46.........45 A4
  Wallsend NE28...........40 E4
St Oswald's Terr 8 DH4..90 B6
St Oswin's Ave NE30......32 C3
St Oswin's Pl NE30.......42 D7
St Oswin's St NE33.......59 D7
St Patrick's Cl NE10.....71 D8
St Patrick's Terr SR2....92 F6
St Patrick's Wlk NE10....71 D8
St Pauls CE Prim Sch
  Newcastle upon Tyne
  NE4...................100 B4
  Ryhope SR2.............92 F6
St Pauls Ct NE63.........6 F5
St Pauls Ct NE8.........100 C1
St Pauls Dr DH4..........89 E8
St Paul's Gdns NE25......32 A4
*St Pauls Monastery**
  NE32...................58 D7
St Paul's Pl NE4.........98 A1
St Pauls RC Fst Sch NE33 22 B5
St Pauls Rd NE46.........44 F4
St Paul's Terr 6 SR2.....92 F6
St Peter & Paul RC Prim Sch
  1 NE33.................59 B6
ST PETER'S...............56 C4
St Peter's Ave NE34......59 F7
St Peter's Church* SR6..103 B4
St Peter's Ct NE6........56 C5
St Peter's Gate SR6......103 A4
St Peter's Quayside E
  NE6....................56 C4
St Peters Quayside W 9
  NE6....................56 C4
St Peters RC Mid Sch
  NE23...................22 B4
St Peters RC Prim Sch
  NE9....................71 A6
St Peter's Rd
  Newcastle upon Tyne NE6..56 C5
  Wallsend NE28...........40 D3
St Peter's Sixth Form Coll
  SR6...................103 A4
St Peter's Sta SR5......103 A4
St Peters' Way SR6.......103 A4
St Peter's Wharf NE6.....56 C4
St Philip Neri RC Prim Sch
  NE11...................70 A8
St Philips Cl NE4.........98 A1
St Philips Way NE4.......98 B1
St Robert of Newminster RC
  Sch NE38...............83 A3
St Roberts RC Fst Sch 11
  NE61...................2 B8
St Rollox St NE31........57 D5
St Ronan's Dr NE26......24 B7
St Ronan's Rd NE25......31 F4
St Ronans View NE9.......71 A2
St Simon St NE34.........59 A4
St Stephen's Cl NE25.....23 B3
St Stephens RC Prim Sch
  NE12...................39 B7
St Stephen's Way NE29 ...41 F3
St Stevens Cl DH4........89 E8
St Teresas RC Prim Sch
  NE34...................59 D6
St Thomas Cl NE42........50 D2
St Thomas' Cres NE1......99 A2
St Thomas Mews NE42.....50 D2
St Thomas More RC High Sch
  NE29...................41 D7
St Thomas More RC Sec Sch
  NE21...................53 B3
St Thomas' Sq NE1........99 A2
St Thomas St 6 NE9.......71 A5
St Thomas'
  Newcastle upon Tyne NE1..99 A2
  Sunderland SR1.........103 A3
St Thomas' Street Bsns Ctr
  NE1...................99 A2
St Thomas' Terr NE1......99 A2
St Vincent Cl NE34.......59 A1
St Vincents Cl NE15......53 E8
St Vincents Ho NE30......42 D7
St Vincent's Pl NE26.....31 F8
St Vincents RC Prim Sch
  NE34...................59 D6
St Vincent St
  Gateshead NE8..........56 A3
  South Shields NE33......42 E3
  Sunderland SR2.........103 B3
St Vincent's Way 1 NE26..31 F8
St Wilfrids Cl NE24......17 D2
St Wilfrid's Ct NE45.....47 A6
St Wilfrid's Cr 9 NE46...45 A4
St Wilfrids RC Comp Sch
  NE34...................59 D6
St Wilfrid's RC Prim Sch
  NE10...................56 E1
St Wilfrid's Rd NE46.....45 A4
Saker Pl 1 NE28..........40 B7
Salcombe Ave NE32.......58 B3
Salcombe Gdns NE9.......70 F7
Salem Hill SR2..........103 B3
Salem St
  Jarrow NE32.............58 C8
  South Shields NE33......42 C2

Salem St continued
Sunderland SR2 . . . . .103 B1
Salem Street S SR2 . . . . . . .103 B1
Salem Terr SR2 . . . . .103 B1
Salisbury Ave
10 Chester le Street DH3 . .88 C2
Tynemouth NE29 . . . . .42 A7
Salisbury Cl
7 Ashington NE63 . . . . 6 F2
Cramlington NE23 . . . . .21 E6
Salisbury Gdns NE2 . . . . . . .56 A8
Salisbury Ho NE6 . . . . .56 A6
Salisbury Pl NE33 . . . . .42 E3
Salisbury St
Blyth NE24 . . . . .17 D8
Gateshead NE10 . . . . .57 A1
Morpeth NE61 . . . . 9 B8
South Shields NE33 . . . . . . .42 D2
Sunderland, South Hylton
SR4 . . . . .85 A7
Sunderland SR1 . . . . .103 B2
Salisbury Way NE32 . . . . . . .58 B1
Salkeld Gdns NE9 . . . . .71 A8
Salkeld Rd NE9 . . . . .71 A6
Sallyport Cres NF1 . . . . .99 B1
Sallyport Ho NE1 . . . . .99 B1
Salmon St NE33 . . . . .42 D4
Saltburn Cl DH4 . . . . .90 C1
Saltburn Gdns NE28 . . . . . . .41 B3
Saltburn Rd NE3 . . . . .85 E3
Saltburn Sq SR3 . . . . .85 E3
Salterfen La SR2 . . . . .93 A8
Salterfen Rd
Ryhope SR2 . . . . .93 A8
8 Sunderland SR2 . . . . . .93 A8
Salters Ct NE3 . . . . .38 E6
Salters St NE3 . . . . .38 E6
Salter's La
Haswell DH6 . . . . .97 E6
Houghton-le-Spring SR3 . . . .91 E1
Salters' La NE3, NE12 . . . . . .38 F7
Salters' La SR7 . . . . .95 F6
Saltford Rd NE3 . . . . .71 A2
Saltford NE9 . . . . .71 A2
SALTMEADOWS 56 A4
Saltmeadows Ind Pk NE8 .56 B3
Saltmeadows Rd NE10,
NE8 . . . . .56 B4
SALTWELL 70 E7
Saltwell Pk* NE8/9 . . . . . . .70 E7
Saltwell Pl NE8 . . . . .70 D7
Saltwell Rd NE8 . . . . .70 D7
Saltwell Road S NE9 . . . . . .70 E4
Saltwell St NE8 . . . . .70 D6
Saltwell Towers Visitor Ctr*
NE9 . . . . .70 E6
Saltwell View NE8 . . . . .70 E7
SALTWICK 13 A4
Sams Ct NE23 . . . . .28 F8
Samson Cl NE12 . . . . .29 C2
Sancroft Dr DH5 . . . . .94 E7
Sandalwood NE4 . . . . .54 D5
Sandalwood Sq SR4 . . . . . . .85 B2
Sanderling Cl NE40 . . . . .52 D4
Sanderlings **3** NE28 . . . . .40 B1
Sanders Gdns DH3 . . . . .82 C5
Sanders' Memorial Homes
DH2 . . . . .88 A5
Sanderson Rd
Newcastle upon Tyne NE2 . . .38 C2
Whitley Bay NE26 . . . . .31 F5
Sanderson St NE4 . . . . .54 F3
Sanderson Villas NE8 . . . . . .56 B2
Sandfield Rd
Cambois NE22 . . . . .12 B4
Tynemouth NE30 . . . . .32 B3
Sandford Ave NE23 . . . . .16 B1
Sandford Ct SR2 . . . . .86 C3
Sandford Mews NE3 . . . . . . .28 A5
Sandgate NE1 . . . . .99 C1
Sandgrove SR6 . . . . .60 A1
Sandhill NE1 . . . . .99 B1
Sandhill View Sch SR3 . . . . .85 D2
Sandhoe Walk NE8 . . . . .41 A2
Sandholm Cl NE28 . . . . .40 F5
Sandhoe NE10 . . . . .32 C2
Sandiacres NE32 . . . . .58 C1
Sandison Ct NE13 . . . . .27 F6
Sandmartin Cl NE63 . . . . . . .11 E8
Sandmere Pl NE15 . . . . .54 A5
Sandmere Rd SR2 . . . . .86 D1
Sandoe Gdns NE15 . . . . .54 B5
Sandon Cl NE27 . . . . .30 C5
Sandown NE25 . . . . .31 D5
Sandown Cl NE23 . . . . .23 D2
Sandown Ct NE8 . . . . .41 A4
Sandown Gdns
Gateshead NE8 . . . . .70 D8
New Silksworth SR3 . . . . . . .91 F8
Wallsend NE28 . . . . .40 F4
Sandpiper Cl
Blyth NE24 . . . . .17 F4
Ryton NE40 . . . . .52 D4
Washington NE38 . . . . .82 F2
Sandpiper Ct NE30 . . . . .42 D8
Sandpiper Pl NE12 . . . . .39 A7
Sandpiper Way NE63 . . . . 6 E5
Sand Point Rd SR6 . . . . .75 F1
Sandray Cl DH3 . . . . .82 D1
Sandridge NE64 . . . . 7 F5
Sandringham Ave NE12 . . . .39 D6
Sandringham Cl NE25 . . . . . .31 B4
Sandringham Cres SR3 . . . . .91 C6
Sandringham Ct
6 Gateshead NE10 . . . . . .71 C8
Longbenton NE12 . . . . .39 A6
Sandringham Dr
Blyth NE24 . . . . .17 D3

Sandringham Dr continued
Whickham NE16 . . . . .69 A7
Whitley Bay NE25 . . . . .31 C4
Sandringham Gdns NE29 . .42 A7
Sandringham Meadows
NE24 . . . . .17 D3
Sandringham Mews **8**
NE28 . . . . .40 F4
Sandringham Rd
Newcastle upon Tyne, South
Gosforth NE3 . . . . .38 C4
Newcastle upon Tyne, West
Denton NE5 . . . . .53 E8
Sunderland SR6 . . . . .75 E2
Sandringham Terr SR6 . . . . .75 E2
Sandringham Way NE20 . . .25 C4
Sandsay Cl SR2 . . . . .92 D8
Sands Ind Est NE16 . . . . .54 A1
Sands Rd NE16 . . . . .54 A1
Sandstone Cl NE34 . . . . .58 F3
Sandwell Dr DH4 . . . . .89 F8
Sandwich Rd NE29 . . . . .31 F1
Sandwich St NE6 . . . . .56 F3
Sandy Bank NE44 . . . . .62 F7
Sandy Bay Cvn Pk NE63 . .12 C8
Sandy Chare SR6 . . . . .75 E8
Sandy Cres NE6 . . . . .56 C4
Sandyford Ave NE42 . . . . . . .50 F3
Sandyford Pk NE2 . . . . .99 C4
Sandyford Rd NE2 . . . . .99 B3
Sandygate Mews NE16 . . . . .69 B1
Sandy La
Ashington NE63 . . . . 7 B2
Brunswick Village NE13 . . . . .27 E6
Gateshead NE9 . . . . .71 D1
Melton Park NE3 . . . . .28 B3
Riding Mill NE44 . . . . .62 E8
Wideopen NE3, NE12 . . . . . .28 E4
Sandy Lane Ind Area NE3 .28 E4
Sandypath La NE16 . . . . .79 A7
Sandysykes NE42 . . . . .50 B2
Sans St S SR1 . . . . .103 B3
Sans St SR1 . . . . .103 B3
Sarabel Ave NE42 . . . . .10 E7
Sargent Ave NE34 . . . . .59 D2
Satley Gdns
Gateshead NE9 . . . . .71 C2
Sunderland SR3 . . . . .86 B2
Saunton Ct DH4 . . . . .90 C3
Saville Lodge **5** NE3 . . . .42 D3
Saville Pl
Newcastle upon Tyne NE1 . .99 B2
Sunderland SR1 . . . . .103 B2
Saville St
North Shields NE30 . . . . .42 B5
4 South Shields NE33 . . . .42 D3
Saville Street W NE29 . . . . . .42 A5
Savory Rd NE28 . . . . .40 F3
Sawmill Cotts DH9 . . . . .78 E1
Saxilby Dr NE3 . . . . .38 D8
Saxon Cl SR6 . . . . .75 B4
Saxon Cres SR3 . . . . .85 F3
Saxondale Rd NE3 . . . . .37 E5
Saxon St NE30 . . . . .32 C1
Saxon Way NE32 . . . . .58 C7
Saxton Gr NE7 . . . . .39 A4
Scafell DH3 . . . . .82 D1
Scafell Ct **22** SR3 . . . . . . .91 F6
Scafell Dr NE5 . . . . .37 D3
Scafell Gdns NE11 . . . . .70 A6
Scalby Cl NE3 . . . . .38 D8
Scales Cres NE11 . . . . .50 F2
Scarborough Ct
Cramlington NE23 . . . . .22 B5
Newcastle upon Tyne NE6 . .56 D6
Scarborough Par NE31 . . . . .58 A2
Scarborough Rd
Newcastle upon Tyne NE6 . .56 D6
New Silksworth SR3 . . . . . . .91 F8
Sceptre Cl NE4 . . . . .100 A4
Sceptre Pl NE4 . . . . .98 A1
Sceptre St NE4 . . . . .98 A1
Schalksmuhle Rd NE22 . . . .10 F1
Schimel St SR5 . . . . .75 B2
School App NE34 . . . . .60 A6
School Ave
Dunston NE11 . . . . .69 F8
Guide Post NE62 . . . . .10 F7
School Cl NE10 . . . . .71 D6
Schoolhouse La NE16 . . . . . .79 E7
School La
High Spen NE39 . . . . .67 A3
Whickham NE16 . . . . .69 A4
School Loaning **2** NE34 . .59 B5
School Rd
Bedlington NE22 . . . . .11 D3
East Rainton DH5 . . . . .94 C4
School Row
Hedley on the Hill NE43 . . . .64 F3
Prudhoe NE42 . . . . .50 E3
School St
Birtley DH3 . . . . .82 C4
Gateshead NE8 . . . . .101 A1
Hexham NE31 . . . . .57 F7
Whickham NE16 . . . . .69 A7
School Terr DH3 . . . . .89 E1
School View DH5 . . . . .97 D8
School Yd NE42 . . . . .50 F3
Scorer's La DH3 . . . . .89 B1
Scorton Cl NE29 . . . . .41 F5
Scotby Gdns NE9 . . . . .71 B3
Scotland Cl NE21 . . . . .53 A1
SCOTLAND GATE 10 F7
Scotland Head NE21 . . . . . . .68 A8
Scots Gr NE3 . . . . .93 A6
Scot's Ho NE36 . . . . .73 B6
SCOTSWOOD 54 D3
Scotswood Rd NE15, NE4 . .54 B4
Scotswood View NE11 . . . . . .54 C2

Scott Ave NE23 . . . . .21 F8
Scott Cl NE46 . . . . .44 F2
Scott Ct NE34 . . . . .59 A3
Scot Terr NE17 . . . . .66 B1
Scottish Life Ho NE2 . . . . . .99 B3
Scott's Ave **13** NE40 . . . . .51 F3
Scott's Ct NE10 . . . . .72 B6
Scott St
Cramlington NE23 . . . . .16 B3
East Hartford NE23 . . . . .16 B3
Houghton-le-Spring DH4 . . .94 D8
Scott's Terr DH5 . . . . .95 A4
Scoular Dr NE63 . . . . 7 A3
Scrogg Rd NE6 . . . . .56 F6
Scruton Ave SR3 . . . . .85 F3
Sea Banks NE30 . . . . .42 E8
SEABURN 75 F4
Seaburn Ave NE25 . . . . .23 D6
Seaburn Cl **1** SR6 . . . . . . .75 E4
Seaburn Dene Prim Sch
SR6 . . . . .75 D5
Seaburn Dr **1** DH4 . . . . . .94 C8
Seaburn Gdns
Gateshead NE9 . . . . .71 D3
Sunderland SR6 . . . . .75 E4
Seaburn Dr NE26 . . . . .24 C6
Seaburn Hill SR6 . . . . .75 D4
Seaburn Sta SR6 . . . . .75 C4
Seaburn Terr SR6 . . . . .75 F4
Seaburn View NE25 . . . . .23 D6
Seaburn Wellness Ctr
SR6 . . . . .75 D5
Seacombe Ave NE30 . . . . . . .32 C3
Seacrest Apartments
NE30 . . . . .32 C1
Seacrest Ave NE30 . . . . .32 C2
Sea Crest Rd NE64 . . . . 7 E6
Seafield Mews NE26 . . . . . . .24 B7
Seafield Rd NE26 . . . . .17 E5
Seafields SR6 . . . . .75 E5
Seafield View NE30 . . . . .42 D8
Seaforth Rd SR3 . . . . .86 A3
Seaforth St NE24 . . . . .17 E8
SEAHAM 93 C1
Seaham Cl NE34 . . . . .59 A4
Seaham Comp Sch Tech Coll
SR7 . . . . .93 A1
Seaham Gdns NE9 . . . . .71 C2
SEAHAM GRANGE 92 F2
Seaham Grange Ind Est
SR7 . . . . .92 E2
Seaham Rd
Houghton-le-Spring DH5 . . .95 A8
Ryhope SR2 . . . . .93 A6
Seaham St SR3 . . . . .92 A7
Sea La SR6 . . . . .75 E4
Sea Rd SR6 . . . . .75 E4
Seascale Pl NE9 . . . . .71 B4
Seasons Edge NE8 . . . . .100 B1
Seatoller Ct **3** SR3 . . . . . .91 F6
Seaton Ave
Annitsford NE23 . . . . .22 B1
Bedlington NE22 . . . . .11 B1
Blyth NE24 . . . . .17 C4
Houghton-le-Spring DH5 . . .95 A7
Newbiggin-by-the-Sea NE64 . 7 D4
SEATON BURN 21 B1
Seaton Burn Coll NE13 . . . .28 C8
Seaton Cl NE10 . . . . .72 B6
Seaton Cres
Holywell NE25 . . . . .23 F2
Seaham SR7 . . . . .92 A7
Whitley Bay NE25 . . . . .23 F2
Seaton Croft NE23 . . . . .29 C8
SEATON DELAVAL 23 C2
Seaton Delaval Fst Sch
NE25 . . . . .23 B3
Seaton Delaval Hall*
NE26 . . . . .24 A6
Seaton Gdns NE9 . . . . .71 C3
Seaton Hirst CE Mid Sch
NE63 . . . . 6 C2
Seaton La SR7 . . . . .92 E1
Seaton Pl
Brunswick Village NE13 . . . . .28 A6
Newcastle upon Tyne NE6 . .56 E3
Seaton Rd
Shiremoor NE27 . . . . .31 A4
Sunderland SR3 . . . . .85 D3
SEATON SLUICE 24 C5
Seaton Sluice Mid Sch
NE26 . . . . .24 B7
Seaton Sluice South Fst Sch
NE26 . . . . .24 D5
Seatonville Cres NE25 . . . . .31 E3
Seatonville Gr NE25 . . . . . . .31 E3
Seatonville Rd NE25 . . . . . . .31 E3
Sea View
Ashington NE63 . . . . .12 A8
Lynemouth NE61 . . . . 2 B3
Ryhope SR2 . . . . .93 A6
Windy Nook NE10 . . . . .71 C6
Sea View Gdns SR6 . . . . .75 E3
Sea View La NE26 . . . . 7 E5
Sea View Pk
Cramlington NE23 . . . . .22 D6
Whitburn SR6 . . . . .75 D8
Sea View Prim Sch NE34 . . .60 A8
Sea View Road W SR2 . . . . .86 F2
Sea View St SR2 . . . . .86 F2
Seaview Terr NE33 . . . . .42 F4
Sea View Villas NE25 . . . . . .22 D6
Sea Way NE33 . . . . .42 E5

Sea Winnings Way
South Shields NE33 . . . . .42 E2
South Shields NE33 . . . . .42 F2
Second Ave
Ashington NE63 . . . . 6 C4
Blyth NE24 . . . . .17 D6
Chester le Street, Canada
DH2 . . . . .88 B2
Chester le Street, South Pelaw
DH2 . . . . .88 B8
Dunston NE11 . . . . .70 B6
Morpeth NE61 . . . . 9 B7
Newcastle upon Tyne NE6 . .56 C7
North Shields NE29 . . . . .41 B4
Second Row
Ellington NE61 . . . . 1 E4
Linton NE61 . . . . 1 A3
Secretan Way NE33 . . . . .42 C2
Sedbergh Rd NE30 . . . . .32 B2
Sedgefield Ct NE12 . . . . .29 B8
SEDGELETCH 90 B2
Sedgeletch Ind Est DH4 . .90 A2
Sedgeletch Rd DH4 . . . . .90 A2
Sedgemoor NE12 . . . . .29 D4
Sedgewick Pl NE15 . . . . .54 A4
Sedgewick Pl NE8 . . . . .101 B1
Sedley Rd NE28 . . . . .40 E4
Sedling Rd NE38 . . . . .83 B2
Sefton Ave NE6 . . . . .39 C1
Sefton Ct NE23 . . . . .16 C1
Sefton Sq SR3 . . . . .86 A3
Segedunum Cres NE28 . . . . .40 E4
Segedunum Roman Fort
Baths & Mus* NE28 . . . . . .40 C1
Segedunum Sta NE28 . . . . . .40 B1
Seghill CE Prim Sch NE23 . .22 F1
Seghill Ind Est NE23 . . . . . . .22 E2
Seine Ct NE32 . . . . .58 C6
Selborne Ave NE9 . . . . .70 E4
Selborne Gdns NE2 . . . . .56 A8
Selbourne Cl NE35 . . . . .58 E1
Selbourne St
2 South Shields NE33 . . . .42 D2
Sunderland SR6 . . . . .75 D1
Selbourne Terr NE23 . . . . . . .12 D3
Selby Cl NE23 . . . . .16 B1
Selby Ct
2 Jarrow NE32 . . . . .58 F4
Newcastle upon Tyne NE6 . .56 F4
Selby Gdns
Newcastle upon Tyne NE6 . .56 F4
Wallsend NE28 . . . . .40 B3
Selby's Grave NE21 . . . . .67 F8
Selby Sq SR3 . . . . .85 E3
Sele Ct SR3 . . . . .85 F3
Sele Fst Sch The NE46 . . . . .45 A5
Selina Pl SR6 . . . . .103 B4
Selkirk Cres DH3 . . . . .82 C6
Selkirk Gr NE23 . . . . .16 C1
Selkirk Sq SR3 . . . . .58 E3
Selkirk St NE32 . . . . .58 E3
Selkirk Way NE29 . . . . .41 C8
Selsdon Ave SR4 . . . . .85 A2
Selsey Ct NE10 . . . . .71 D5
Selwood Ct NE34 . . . . .59 F5
Selwyn Ave NE25 . . . . .31 D3
Selwyn Cl NE5 . . . . .37 D4
Senet Enterprise Workshops
NE63 . . . . 6 C1
September Courtyard
NE8 . . . . .100 B1
Serin Ho NE5 . . . . .37 A3
Serlby Cl NE37 . . . . .72 F2
Seton Ave NE34 . . . . .58 F4
Seton Wlk NE34 . . . . .58 F3
Setting Stones NE38 . . . . . . .89 A8
Settlingstone Cl NE7 . . . . . . .39 E3
Sevenoaks Dr SR4 . . . . .85 A2
Seven Stories, The Centre
for Children's Books* **9**
NE1 . . . . .99 A6
Seventh Ave
Ashington NE63 . . . . 6 E2
Blyth NE24 . . . . .17 D6
Chester le Street DH2 . . . . . .88 B8
Gateshead NE11 . . . . .70 D4
Morpeth NE61 . . . . 9 B7
Newcastle upon Tyne NE6 . .56 C7
Seventh Row NE63 . . . . 6 B4
Severn Ave NE31 . . . . .57 E3
Severn Ct **8** SR3 . . . . .91 F6
Severn Dr NE32 . . . . .58 C2
Severn Gdns NE8 . . . . .71 A7
Severn Hos NH37 . . . . .83 A8
Severn St NE17 . . . . .66 C1
Severs Terr NE5 . . . . .36 B6
Severus Rd NE4 . . . . .54 E7
Sextant Ho **6** NE6 . . . . . . .56 A3
Seymour Ct
Ashington NE63 . . . . 7 B3
Dunston NE11 . . . . .100 A1
Seymour St
Dunston NE11 . . . . .100 A1
North Shields NE29 . . . . .42 A4
Seymour Terr
Hetton-le-Hole DH5 . . . . .95 B1
Ryton NE40 . . . . .52 A5
Sezze Bldg **8** NE24 . . . . . .17 F8
Shadfen Cres NE61 . . . . .4 F3
Shadfen Park Rd NE30 . . . . .32 A3
Shadon Way DH3 . . . . .82 D1
Shaftesbury Ave
Jarrow NE32 . . . . .58 E5
Ryhope SR2 . . . . .92 F7
Whitley Bay NE26 . . . . .31 F6

Sal–She 141

Shaftesbury Cres
Sunderland SR3 . . . . .85 F3
Tynemouth NE30 . . . . .32 A3
Shaftesbury Gr NE6 . . . . .56 B7
Shaftesbury Ho NE33 . . . . . .59 B6
Shaftesbury Wlk NE8 . . . . .100 C2
Shafto Ct NE15 . . . . .54 B5
Shaftoe Cl NE40 . . . . .51 F3
Shaftoe Cres NE46 . . . . .45 A5
Shaftoe Ct
Killingworth NE12 . . . . .29 D3
Newcastle upon Tyne NE3 . .38 A7
Shaftoe Leazes NE46 . . . . . .44 F4
Shaftoe Rd SR3 . . . . .85 D2
Shaftoe Sq SR3 . . . . .85 D2
Shaftoe Way NE13 . . . . .27 B7
Shafto St
Newcastle upon Tyne
NE15 . . . . .54 A5
Wallsend NE28 . . . . .40 F3
Shakespeare Ave NE31 . . . . .57 E6
Shakespeare St
Houghton-le-Spring DH5 . . .94 E7
Newcastle upon Tyne NE1 . .58 B8
Newcastle upon Tyne NE1 . .99 A1
18 South Shields NE33 . . .42 D1
Sunderland SR5 . . . . .75 B2
Wallsend NE28 . . . . .40 F3
Shakespeare Terr SR2 . . . . .102 C1
Shalcombe Cl NE23 . . . . .92 A6
Shallcross SR2 . . . . .86 B4
Shallon Cl NE63 . . . . 7 E1
Shalstone NE37 . . . . .72 F1
Shamrock Cl NE15 . . . . .53 C8
Shandon Way NE3 . . . . .37 E5
SHANKHOUSE 21 C4
Shanklea Fst Sch NE23 . . . .22 B7
Shanklin Pl NE23 . . . . .21 E6
Shannon Ct NE3 . . . . .74 A1
Shannon St NE33 . . . . .37 C7
Shap Cl NE23 . . . . .83 D3
Shap Ct **2** SR3 . . . . .91 F6
Shap Rd NE5 . . . . .37 A1
Shap Rd NE30 . . . . .32 A2
Sharnford Cl NE27 . . . . .30 D5
Sharon Cl NE12 . . . . .29 B2
Sharpendon St NE31 . . . . . . .57 E7
Sharperton Dr NE3 . . . . .28 A1
Sharpley Dr **8** SR7 . . . . . . .92 E1
Shaw Ave NE34 . . . . .59 B4
Shawbrow Cl NE7 . . . . .39 B4
Shaw Gdns NE10 . . . . .72 B8
Shaw La DH8, NE17 . . . . . . .76 F4
Shaws La
Hexham NE46 . . . . .44 D4
Shaws Pk NE46 . . . . .44 D5
Shearlegs Rd NE8 . . . . .56 A3
Shearwater NE4 . . . . .60 F3
Shearwater Cl NE5 . . . . .37 A4
Shearwater Way NE24 . . . . .17 F4
Sheelin Ave DH2 . . . . .88 C1
Sheen Cl DH4 . . . . .94 A2
Sheen Ct NE5 . . . . .37 B5
Sheepfolds N SR5 . . . . .103 A4
Sheepfolds Rd SR5 . . . . .103 A4
SHEEP HILL 79 B7
SHEEPWASH 10 E8
Sheepwash Bank NE62 . . . . .10 E7
Sheepwash Rd NE62 . . . . . . .10 F7
Shefton Mus of Greek Art &
Archaeology* NE1 . . . . . . .99 A2
Sheldon Ct NE12 . . . . .29 C1
Sheldon Gr
Cramlington NE23 . . . . .16 B1
Newcastle upon Tyne NE3 . .38 A3
Sheldon Rd NE34 . . . . .42 F1
Sheldon St NE32 . . . . .58 B7
Shelford Gdns NE15 . . . . . . .53 E7
Shellbark DH4 . . . . .89 F6
Shelley Ave
Easington Lane DH5 . . . . . . .97 D8
South Shields NE33 . . . . . . .60 B5
West Boldon NE35 . . . . .74 F1
Shelley Cres NE24 . . . . .17 C5
Shelley Dr NE8 . . . . .56 A2
Shelley Rd NE15 . . . . .53 A7
Shepherd's Quay NE29 . . . . .42 B4
Shepherd St SR4 . . . . .102 A3
Shepherds Way NE38 . . . . . .83 F2
Sheppey Ct SR3 . . . . .92 A6
Shepton Cotts NE16 . . . . . . .69 C3
Sheraton NE10 . . . . .72 A5
Sheraton St NE2 . . . . .98 C3
Sherborne Ave NE29 . . . . . . .41 D8
Sherborne Villas NE62 . . . . .10 F7
SHERBURN 96 C1
Sherburn Gn NE39 . . . . .67 F3
Sherburn Grange N NE32 . . .58 A5
Sherburn Grange S NE32 . . .58 A5
SHERBURN HILL 96 C1
Sherburn Hill Prim Sch
DH6 . . . . .96 D1
Sherburn Park Dr NE39 . . . .67 F3
Sherburn Terr
Gateshead NE10 . . . . .71 C2
Hamsterley NE17 . . . . .76 F5

Sherburn Village Prim Sch
DH6 . . . . .96 A2
Sherburn Way NE10 . . . . .72 C7
Sherfield Dr NE7 . . . . .39 D2
Sheridan Gn NE38 . . . . .83 A1
Sheridan Rd NE34 . . . . .59 A3
Sheridan St 5 SR4 . . . . .85 F7
SHERIFF HILL 71 B6
Sheriffs Cl NE10 . . . . .71 B8
Sheriffs Hall Villas 7
NE9 . . . . .71 A5
Sheriff's Highway NE9 . . . . . .71 A6
Sheriff's Moor Ave DH5 . . . . .97 C8
Sheringham Ave NE29 . . . . . .41 D7
Sheringham Ct SR3 . . . . .92 A4
Sheringham Dr NE23 . . . . .21 E6
Sheringham Gdns NE15 . . . . .35 B2
Sheringham Ho 6 NE38 . . . . .83 F4
Sherrington Ave NE3 . . . . .37 E4
Sherwood NE27 . . . . .31 B2
Sherwood Cl
Tynemouth NE27 . . . . .31 B2
Washington NE38 . . . . .83 D5
Sherwood Ct 8 SR3 . . . . .92 A6
Sherwood Pl NE3 . . . . .28 C2
Sherwood View NE28 . . . . . . .40 A4
Shetland Ct 1 SR3 . . . . .92 A6
Shibdon Bank NE21 . . . . .53 D2
Shibdon Bsns Pk NE21 . . . . . .53 E3
Shibdon Cres NE21 . . . . .53 D2
Shibdon Ct NE21 . . . . .53 C3
Shibdon Park View NE21 . . . .53 D2
Shibdon Pond Nature
Reserve* NE21 . . . . .53 E2
Shibdon Rd
Blaydon NE21 . . . . .53 D3
Blaydon NE21 . . . . .53 E2
Shibdon Way NE21 . . . . .53 F2
Shield Ave NE16 . . . . .54 B1
Shieldclose 2 NE37 . . . . .83 A6
Shield Ct
Hexham NE46 . . . . .45 B3
Newcastle upon Tyne NE2 . . . . .99 C3
SHIELDFIELD 99 C2
Shieldfield Gn NE2 . . . . .99 C2
Shieldfield Ho NE2 . . . . .99 C2
Shieldfield La NE2 . . . . .99 C2
Shield Gr NE3 . . . . .38 B6
Shield La 1 NE6 . . . . .56 C6
Shields Pl DH5 . . . . .90 E1
Shields Rd
Chester le Street DH3 . . . . .88 D5
Cleadon NE34 . . . . .60 A3
Cleadon SR6 . . . . .60 A2
Gateshead NE10 . . . . .71 F8
Morpeth NE61 . . . . .9 B7
Newcastle upon Tyne NE2 . . . . .99 B2
Newcastle upon Tyne NE6 . . . . .56 C7
Sunderland SR5, SR6 . . . . .75 B5
Whitley Bay NE25 . . . . .31 F3
Shields Road W 5 NE6 . . . . . .56 A6
Shield St NE2 . . . . .99 C2
Shiel Gdns NE23 . . . . .21 C6
Shillaw Pl NE23 . . . . .29 B5
Shilmore Rd NE3 . . . . .37 F5
Shilton Cl NE34 . . . . .60 B5
Shincliffe Ave NE34 . . . . .74 C2
Shincliffe Gdns NE9 . . . . .71 D3
SHINEY ROW 90 B5
Shiney Row Prim Sch
DH4 . . . . .90 B5
SHIPCOTE 70 E8
Shipcote La NE8 . . . . .70 F8
Shipcote Terr NE8 . . . . .70 E8
**Shipley Art Gallery* NE8 . . .70 F8
Shipley Ave
Newcastle upon Tyne NE4 . . . . .54 C6
Sunderland SR6 . . . . .75 E4
Shipley Ct NE8 . . . . .101 C1
Shipley Pl 18 NE6 . . . . .56 B6
Shipley Rd NE30 . . . . .42 C7
Shipley Rise 9 NE6 . . . . .56 C6
Shipley St NE15 . . . . .53 C6
Shipley Wlk 2 NE6 . . . . .56 B6
Shipton La NE5 . . . . .37 D3
Shire Farm Gr NE63 . . . . .6 A2
SHIREMOOR 30 F3
Shiremoor Prim Sch
NE27 . . . . .30 F3
Shiremoor Sta NE27 . . . . .30 F4
Shirlaw Cl NE15 . . . . .36 F4
Shirley Gdns SR3 . . . . .86 B3
Shirwood Ave NE16 . . . . .69 A5
Shop Row DH4 . . . . .90 C5
Shop Spouts NE21 . . . . .53 C3
Shoreham Ct NE3 . . . . .37 C7
Shoreham Sq SR3 . . . . .85 E3
Shore St SR6 . . . . .75 D1
Shorestone Ave NE30 . . . . . . .32 B3
Shoreswood Dr 3 SR3 . . . . . .92 B7
Shoreswood Way NE3 . . . . . . .37 D8
Shortridge St 1 NE33 . . . . . . .42 D3
Shortridge Terr NE2 . . . . .38 F1
Short Row NE4 . . . . .36 B6
Shot Factory La NE4 . . . . . . .100 C3
Shotley Ave SR5 . . . . .75 B3
Shotley Cl NE63 . . . . .7 A4
Shotley Gdns NE9 . . . . .71 A7
Shotley Gr NE36 . . . . .74 B7
SHOTTON 20 E8
Shotton Ave NE24 . . . . .17 E6
Shotton La
Cramlington NE23 . . . . .15 C2
Shotton NE61, NE13 . . . . .20 F8

Shotton St NE23 . . . . .16 B3
Shotton Way NE10 . . . . .72 E6
Shrewsbury Cl NE12 . . . . .39 D4
Shrewsbury Cres SR3 . . . . . . .85 F3
Shrewsbury Dr NE27 . . . . .30 C5
Shrewsbury St NE11 . . . . .69 F8
Shrewsbury Terr NE33 . . . . . .59 C7
Shrigley Cl NE38 . . . . .89 B8
Shrigley Gdns NE3 . . . . .37 F5
Shummard Cl DH4 . . . . .89 F5
Shunner Cl NE37 . . . . .83 A6
Sibthorpe St NE29 . . . . .42 B5
Side NE1 . . . . .101 B4
Side Cliff Rd SR6 . . . . .75 E3
Sidlaw Ave
Chester le Street DH2 . . . . .88 A2
Tynemouth NE29 . . . . .31 F1
Sidlaw Ct NE63 . . . . .6 E1
Sidmouth Cl DH4 . . . . .90 C4
Sidmouth Rd
Gateshead NE9 . . . . .70 F3
North Shields NE29 . . . . .41 C5
Sidney Gdns NE24 . . . . .16 F8
Sidney Gr
Gateshead NE8 . . . . .101 A1
Newcastle upon Tyne NE4 . . . . .98 A2
Sidney St
Blyth NE24 . . . . .17 D7
Boldon Colliery NE35 . . . . .73 F8
North Shields NE29 . . . . .42 A5
Silkey's La NE29 . . . . .41 F5
Silkstun Ct 8 SR3 . . . . .92 A7
SILKSWORTH 91 F7
Silksworth Cl SR3 . . . . .91 F8
Silksworth Gdns NE9 . . . . .71 C2
Silksworth Hall Dr SR3 . . . . . .91 F6
Silksworth La
New Silksworth SR3 . . . . .91 F7
1 New Silksworth SR3 . . . . . . .92 A8
Sunderland SR3 . . . . .86 A2
Silksworth Rd
New Silksworth SR3 . . . . .92 A7
Sunderland SR3 . . . . .91 C6
Silksworth Row SR1 . . . . .102 C3
Silksworth Sports Complex*
SR3 . . . . .85 F1
Silksworth Terr SR3 . . . . .92 A7
Silkwood Cl NE23 . . . . .16 B1
Silkworth Way SR3 . . . . .91 E6
Silloth Ave NE5 . . . . .54 A8
Silloth Dr NE37 . . . . .72 C2
Silloth Pl NE30 . . . . .32 B2
Silloth Rd SR3 . . . . .85 D2
Silvas Ct NE61 . . . . .4 A1
Silverbirch Ind Est NE12 . . . .29 B4
Silverbriar SR5 . . . . .74 F1
Silver Ct 3 NE9 . . . . .71 A8
Silverdale Ave SR3 . . . . .92 A4
Silverdale Ho NE10 . . . . .72 D8
Silverdale Dr NE11 . . . . .88 A3
Silverdale Rd NE23 . . . . .16 B1
Silverdale Sch NE38 . . . . .41 A5
Silverdale Terr NE8 . . . . .70 F8
Silverdale Way
Brockley Whins NE34 . . . . .58 F3
Whickham NE16 . . . . .68 F4
Silver Fox Way
Earsdon NE27 . . . . .31 A1
Wallsend NE27 . . . . .40 F8
Silverhill Dr NE5 . . . . .54 B7
Silverlink Biodiversity Nature
Reserve* NE27 . . . . .30 F1
Silverlink Bus Pk NE28 . . . . . .41 A6
Silverlink N The
Shiremoor NE27 . . . . .30 E1
Wallsend NE27 . . . . .40 F7
Silverlink Ret Pk NE28 . . . . . .41 A6
Silverlink The NE28 . . . . .40 F6
Silver Lonnen NE5 . . . . .54 B8
Silvermere Dr NE40 . . . . .52 D4
Silver St
Sunderland SR1 . . . . .103 C3
Tynemouth NE30 . . . . .42 D7
Silverstone NE12 . . . . .29 E3
Silverstone Rd NE37 . . . . .83 E8
Silverton Gdns NE40 . . . . .52 A1
Silvertop Terr NE40 . . . . .66 F8
Silverwood Gdns NE11 . . . . . .70 B5
Simonburn NE38 . . . . .82 F4
Simonburn Ave
Newcastle upon Tyne NE4 . . . . .54 B8
North Shields NE29 . . . . .41 C6
Simonburn La 2 NE63 . . . . . . .6 F2
Simon Pl NE11 . . . . .28 A5
SIMONSIDE 58 E5
Simonside
Prudhoe NE42 . . . . .50 B1
Seaton Sluice NE26 . . . . .24 D4
Simonside Ave
Stakeford NE62 . . . . .11 B8
Wallsend NE28 . . . . .40 F4
Simonside Cl
Morpeth NE61 . . . . .9 A8
Seaton Sluice NE26 . . . . .24 D4
Simonside Com Prim Sch
NE5 . . . . .36 F5
Simonside Hall NE34 . . . . .58 F5
Simonside Ind Est NE32 . . . . .58 E5
Simonside Pl 2 NE9 . . . . .71 B2
Simonside Prim Sch
NE32 . . . . .58 D4
Simonside Rd
Blaydon NE21 . . . . .53 C1
Sunderland SR5 . . . . .74 B1
Simonside Sta NE35 . . . . .58 F5
Simonside Terr
Newbiggin-by-the-Sea
NE64 . . . . .7 E4

Simonside Terr continued
Newcastle upon Tyne NE6 . . . .56 C8
Simonside View
Jarrow NE32 . . . . .58 C4
Ponteland NE20 . . . . .25 D7
18 Whickham NE16 . . . . .69 A7
Simonside Way NE12 . . . . .29 F4
Simonside Wlk NE11 . . . . .70 A5
Simpson Cl NE35 . . . . .73 E8
Simpson Ct NE21 . . . . .53 B2
Simpsons Memorial Homes
NE40 . . . . .52 A4
Simpson St
Blyth NE24 . . . . .17 E8
North Shields NE29 . . . . .41 E5
Sunderland SR4 . . . . .102 B4
Tynemouth NE30 . . . . .32 C4
Simpson Street Ind Est
SR4. . . . . .102 B4
Simpson Terr
Newcastle upon Tyne
NE2 . . . . .36 B1
Newcastle upon Tyne, Shieldfield
NE2 . . . . .99 B2
Sinclair Dr DH3 . . . . .88 D8
Sinclair Gdns NE25 . . . . .23 D3
Sinderby Cl NE3 . . . . .38 D8
Sir Charles Parsons Sch
NE6 . . . . .57 A7
Sir GB Hunter Memorial
Hospl NE28 . . . . .40 C2
Sir Godfrey Thomson Ct
NE10 . . . . .71 C8
Siskin Ho NE12 . . . . .39 E8
Sixth Ave
Ashington NE63 . . . . .6 E2
Blyth NE24 . . . . .17 D6
Chester le Street DH2 . . . . .88 B3
Gateshead NE11 . . . . .70 C4
Morpeth NE61 . . . . .9 B7
Newcastle upon Tyne NE6 . . . . .56 A6
Skaylock Dr NE38 . . . . .83 A3
Skegness Par NE31 . . . . .58 A2
Skeider Ave NE12 . . . . .39 B6
Skelton Ct NE3 . . . . .37 E8
Skendleby Dr NE3 . . . . .37 D3
Skiddaw Dr SR6 . . . . .75 C5
Skiddaw Pl NE9 . . . . .71 B4
Skinnerburn Rd NE1,
NE4 . . . . .100 C3
Skipper Cl NE11 . . . . .70 B7
Skipsea View SR2 . . . . .92 D7
Skipton Cl
Bedlington NE22 . . . . .10 D2
Cramlington NE23 . . . . .16 C1
Skipton Gn NE9 . . . . .71 B2
Skirlaw Cl NE38 . . . . .83 D4
Ski View SR3 . . . . .91 F8
Skye Ct 3 SR3 . . . . .92 A6
Skye Gr NE32 . . . . .58 E2
Slake Rd NE32 . . . . .58 D8
SLALEY .62 A2
Slaley NE38 . . . . .83 E1
Slaley Cl NE10 . . . . .72 C7
Slaley Ct
Bedlington NE22 . . . . .11 A1
4 Silksworth SR3 . . . . .92 A6
Slatyford La NE5 . . . . .54 A8
Sled La NE40, NE41 . . . . .51 D3
Sleekburn Ave NE22 . . . . .11 E3
Sleekburn Bsns Ctr NE22,
NE24 . . . . .12 A6
Sleekburn Ho NE22 . . . . .11 D2
Slingley Cl 4 SR7 . . . . .92 E1
Slingsby Gdns NE7 . . . . .39 D3
Sloane Ct NE2 . . . . .99 B3
Smailes La NE39 . . . . .67 C2
Smallholdings NE6 . . . . .7 C6
Smeaton Ct 5 NE28 . . . . .41 A1
Smeaton St 2 NE28 . . . . .41 A1
Smithburn Rd NE10 . . . . .71 E7
Smith Gr SR2 . . . . .92 E6
Smith St 5 SR2 . . . . .92 F6
Smith St
Ryhope SR2 . . . . .92 F6
South Shields NE33 . . . . .59 B8
Smith's Terr DH5 . . . . .95 B1
Smithyford NE9 . . . . .71 A1
Smithy La NE11, NE9 . . . . .70 F1
Smithy Sq NE33 . . . . .22 B6
Smithy St 2 NE33 . . . . .42 C3
Smyrna Pl SR1 . . . . .103 B2
Snipes Dene NE39 . . . . .67 E3
Snowberry Gr NE34 . . . . .59 F5
Snowdon Gdns NE11 . . . . .70 A6
Snowdon Gr NE36 . . . . .74 B7
Snowdon Terr NE39 . . . . .66 F5
Snowdrop Cl NE21 . . . . .53 A2
Soane Gdns NE34 . . . . .59 D3
Softley Pl NE15 . . . . .53 C7
Solar Ho SR1 . . . . .102 C2
Solingen Est NE24 . . . . .17 F5
Solway Ave NE30 . . . . .32 B2
Solway Rd NE31 . . . . .57 F4
Solway Sq SR3 . . . . .85 E3
Solway St NE6 . . . . .56 C4
Somerford NE9 . . . . .71 F2
Somersby Dr NE3 . . . . .37 E5
Somerset Cl NE63 . . . . .6 C2
Somerset Cotts 4 SR3 . . . . . .92 A8
Somerset Gdns NE28 . . . . . . .40 A3
Somerset Pl NE4 . . . . .98 A1
Somerset Rd
Hebburn NE31 . . . . .57 F3
Sunderland SR3 . . . . .85 D3

Somerset Sq SR3 . . . . .85 D3
Somerset St SR3 . . . . .92 A8
Somerton Ct NE3 . . . . .37 D6
Somervyl Ave NE12 . . . . .38 F6
Sophy St SR5 . . . . .75 B2
Sorley St SR4 . . . . .102 A2
Sorrel Cl NE63 . . . . .6 C2
Sorrel Gdns NE34 . . . . .59 C3
Sorrell Cl NE34 . . . . .54 D7
Soulby St NE3 . . . . .37 D8
Sourmilk Hill La NE9 . . . . .71 A6
Souter Dr SR7 . . . . .93 C1
**Souter Lighthouse* SR6 . . . .60 F5
Souter Rd NE3 . . . . .38 A5
Souter View SR6 . . . . .60 F2
South App DH2 . . . . .88 C2
South Ave
Ryton NE40 . . . . .52 C5
South Shields NE34 . . . . .59 F5
Washington NE37 . . . . .83 C8
Whickham NE16 . . . . .69 B5
South Beach Fst Sch
NE24 . . . . .17 E4
South Bend NE3 . . . . .28 B1
SOUTH BENTS 75 E7
South Bents Ave SR6 . . . . .75 F6
South Benwell Rd NE15 . . . . .54 C4
SOUTH BENWELL 54 D4
SOUTH BOLDON 74 B7
Southburn Cl DH4 . . . . .94 C8
South Burns DH3 . . . . .88 C4
South Burn Terr DH4 . . . . .90 C6
South Cl
Easington Lane DH5 . . . . .97 D8
Ryton NE40 . . . . .52 C4
South Shields NE34 . . . . .59 F5
Southcliff NE26 . . . . .32 C4
South Cliff SR6 . . . . .75 F2
Southcote NE16 . . . . .69 A5
South Cres
Boldon Colliery NE35 . . . . .73 F8
Great Lumley DH4 . . . . .89 F1
Washington NE38 . . . . .89 B8
Southcroft NE38 . . . . .83 D1
South Croft NE12 . . . . .39 E7
South Cross St NE3 . . . . .38 C5
South Dene NE34 . . . . .59 B6
Southdowns DH2 . . . . .88 C2
South Dr
Cleadon SR6 . . . . .59 F1
Hebburn NE31 . . . . .57 D4
Shotton NE13 . . . . .20 C6
Woolsington NE13 . . . . .37 A8
South Durham Ct SR1 . . . . . .103 B2
East East Farm NE15 . . . . .50 D8
South Eldon St NE33 . . . . .59 B8
South End
Cleadon SR6 . . . . .74 E8
High Pittington DH6 . . . . .96 C5
Southend Ave NE24 . . . . .17 C6
Southend Par NE31 . . . . .58 A2
Southend Rd
Gateshead NE9 . . . . .71 B5
Sunderland SR3 . . . . .85 C2
Southend Terr NE9 . . . . .71 B6
Southern Cl NE63 . . . . .7 B3
Southern Rd NE6 . . . . .56 F4
Southern Way NE40 . . . . .52 C4
Southey St NE33 . . . . .59 D8
South Farm
Nedderton NE22 . . . . .15 B8
5 Ryhope SR2 . . . . .93 A6
SOUTHFIELD 22 B3
Southfield Gdns NE16 . . . . . . .69 C6
Southfield Gn NE16 . . . . .69 C6
Southfield La NE39 . . . . .77 F3
Southfield Rd
Longbenton NE12 . . . . .39 D6
2 South Shields NE34 . . . . . . .60 A8
Whickham NE16 . . . . .69 C6
Southfields NE23 . . . . .29 A8
Southfields Ho 1 NE6 . . . . . . .56 B6
Southfield Terr
Newcastle upon Tyne NE6 . . . .57 A4
Whickham NE16 . . . . .69 C6
Southfork NE15 . . . . .53 C8
South Frederick St NE33 . . . .59 B7
South Front NE2 . . . . .99 B4
Southgarth East 2 NE33 . . . .59 E8
Southgate NE12 . . . . .29 D3
Southgate Ct NE12 . . . . .38 F6
Southgate Mews NE61 . . . . . . .9 A5
Southgate Wood
Morpeth NE61 . . . . .9 A5
Stobhill NE61 . . . . .9 A5
SOUTH GOSFORTH 38 E4
South Gosforth Fst Sch 11
NE3 . . . . .38 E4
South Gosforth Sta NE3 . . . . .38 E4
South Gr NE40 . . . . .52 D4
South Grange Pk SR7 . . . . . . .92 F2
South Hetton Ind Est DH6 . . .97 F7
South Hetton Prim Sch
DH6 . . . . .97 F7
South Hetton Rd DH5,
DH6 . . . . .97 D8
South Hill Cres SR2 . . . . .102 B1
Southhill Rd NE34 . . . . .60 A6
South Hill Rd NE8 . . . . .101 A1
SOUTH HYLTON 85 A6
South Hylton Prim Sch
SR4 . . . . .85 A6
South La
South Shields SR4 . . . . .85 B6
18 Springwell NE9 . . . . .71 F1
Southlands
Gateshead NE9 . . . . .71 C2
Hedworth NE32 . . . . .58 D1

Southlands continued
Hexham NE46 . . . . .44 D4
Newcastle upon Tyne NE7 . . . . .39 A2
Tynemouth NE30 . . . . .32 B1
Southlands Mid Sch NE32 . . .58 C3
Southlands Sch NE30 . . . . . . .32 A1
South Lea
Blaydon NE21 . . . . .53 C1
Horsley NE15 . . . . .50 C8
Southleigh NE26 . . . . .32 B5
South Leigh DH9 . . . . .79 D1
South Lodge Wood NE1 . . . . . .4 E3
South Magdalene DH8 . . . . . . .77 B1
South Market St DH5 . . . . .95 B4
Southmayne Rd SR4 . . . . .85 D4
Southmoor Com Sch SR2 . . . .86 E3
Southmoor Rd NE6 . . . . .56 F7
South Nelson Ind Est
NE23 . . . . .21 E8
South Nelson Rd NE23 . . . . . .21 E8
SOUTH NEWSHAM 17 D3
South Newsham Rd NE24 . . . .17 D3
South Par
Choppington NE62 . . . . .10 E6
Gateshead NE10 . . . . .57 B2
Stocksfield NE43 . . . . .64 A7
Whitley Bay NE26 . . . . .32 B5
SOUTH PELAW 88 B6
South Pelaw Inf Sch DH2 . . . .88 B5
South Pk NE46 . . . . .45 B3
Southport Par NE31 . . . . .58 A3
South Preston Gr 1 NE29 . . . .42 A3
South Preston Terr 2
NE29 . . . . .42 A3
South Rd
Chopwell NE17 . . . . .66 C1
Prudhoe NE42 . . . . .50 D2
South Ridge
Ashington NE63 . . . . .7 B6
Newcastle upon Tyne NE3 . . . . .38 B8
Southridge Fst Sch NE25 . . . .31 D6
South Riggs NE22 . . . . .15 F8
South Row NE8 . . . . .56 A4
South Sherburn NE39 . . . . . . .67 E1
SOUTH SHIELDS 42 E4
South Shields Com Sch
NE34 . . . . .59 D6
South Shields Mus & Art
Gall* NE33 . . . . .42 C3
South Shields Sta NE33 . . . . .42 C3
South Shore Rd
Gateshead, East Gateshead
NE8 . . . . .56 B3
Gateshead, Saltmeadows
NE8 . . . . .56 A4
South Side
Ashington NE63 . . . . .7 B2
Cresswell NE61 . . . . .2 D1
Southside Gdns SR4 . . . . .85 A5
South St
Chester le Street DH2 . . . . .88 B4
East Rainton DH5 . . . . .94 A8
9 Felling NE10 . . . . .56 C1
9 Froe Houses DH4 . . . . .94 A8
Gateshead NE8 . . . . .101 C1
Hebburn NE31 . . . . .57 F7
High Spen NE39 . . . . .66 F4
Newbottle DH4 . . . . .90 E3
Newcastle upon Tyne, Coxlodge
NE3 . . . . .38 A5
Newcastle upon Tyne NE1 . . . .101 A4
Sherburn DH6 . . . . .96 A1
Shiremoor NE27 . . . . .30 F4
Sunderland SR1 . . . . .103 A3
West Rainton DH4 . . . . .94 A2
South Street Com Prim Sch
NE8 . . . . .101 C1
South Terr
Chopwell NE17 . . . . .77 B8
Morpeth NE61 . . . . .7 F1
Sunderland SR5 . . . . .75 B1
Wallsend NE28 . . . . .40 C2
South Tyneside Coll
(Hebburn Ctr) NE31 . . . . .57 C2
South Tyneside Coll (Marine
Safety Training Ctr)
NE33 . . . . .42 E4
South Tyneside Coll (South
Shields Ctr) NE33 . . . . .59 E8
South Tyneside District
Hospl NE34 . . . . .59 D5
South View
Annitsford NE23 . . . . .22 B1
Ashington NE63 . . . . .9 A2
Birtley DH3 . . . . .82 D4
Blyth NE24 . . . . .17 C4
Cambois NE24 . . . . .12 C6
Chopwell NE17 . . . . .77 B8
Crawcrook, Clara Vale NE40 . . .51 F7
Crawcrook NE40 . . . . .51 F4
Easington Lane DH5 . . . . .97 D8
East Sleekburn NE22 . . . . .11 F3
10 Gateshead NE10 . . . . .71 C8
Guide Post NE62 . . . . .10 E7
Hazlerigg NE13 . . . . .28 A4
High Spen NE39 . . . . .66 F3
Jarrow NE32 . . . . .58 B2
Longbenton NE7 . . . . .39 C5
Mickley Square NE43 . . . . .49 E1
Newcastle upon Tyne NE5 . . . .53 E8
Pegswood NE61 . . . . .4 F3
Prudhoe NE42 . . . . .50 D2
Sherburn Hill DH6 . . . . .96 D1
Shiney Row DH4 . . . . .90 B6
10 Springwell NE9 . . . . .71 F1
Sunderland, South Hylton
SR4 . . . . .85 B5
Sunderland SR6 . . . . .75 D3

South View *continued*
Tantobie DH9 79 B2
Whitburn SR6 60 F3
South View E NE39 67 C2
South View Gdns NE46 45 A4
South View Pl NE23 22 B6
South View Rd SR4 85 B5
South View Terr
Fence Houses DH4 94 B8
Whickham NE16 69 B6
Whickham, Swalwell NE16 69 B8
South View W
Newcastle upon Tyne NE6 56 A6
Rowlands Gill NE39 67 C2
Southward NE26 24 D5
Southward Cl NE26 24 D5
Southward Way NE25 23 E1
Southway
Gateshead NE9 71 B6
Newcastle upon Tyne NE15 53 E7
SOUTH WELLFIELD 31 A5
South Wellfield Fst Sch NE25 31 B4
SOUTHWICK 75 A2
Southwick Ind Est SR5 74 F2
Southwick Prim Sch SR5 75 A2
Southwick Rd SR5 75 C1
Southwold Gdns SR3 91 F8
Southwold Pl NE23 21 E6
South Woodbine St 1 NE33 42 D2
Southwood Cres NE39 67 F2
Southwood Gdns NE3 37 F4
Sovereign Ct
Newcastle upon Tyne, Jesmond NE2 99 C4
Newcastle upon Tyne NE4 100 A4
Sovereign House 16 NE30 42 D7
Sovereign Pl NE4 100 A4
Spalding Cl NE7 39 C4
Sparkwell Cl DH4 90 C4
Spartylea NE38 83 F1
Spa Well Cl NE21 68 B8
Spa Well Dr SR5 74 C2
Spa Well Turn NE21 68 E7
Speculation Pl NE37 83 D8
Speedwell NE9 71 C5
Speedwell Ct NE63 6 B1
Spelter Works Rd SR2 86 F3
Spelvit La NE61 8 F7
Spen Burn NE39 67 A4
Spencer Ct
Blyth NE24 12 B1
Newburn NE15 52 F8
Spencer Dr NE61 4 E3
Spencer Gr NE16 69 A8
Spencer Rd NE24 12 B1
Spencers Bank 3 NE16 54 A1
Spencer St
Hebburn NE31 57 F7
Newcastle upon Tyne NE6 56 C8
20 North Shields NE29 42 A5
Spencer Terr NE15 36 B1
Spence Terr 1 NE29 41 F5
Spenfield Rd NE5 37 D3
Spen La
Greenside NE39, NE40 66 F7
High Spen NE39 67 B3
Spen Rd NE39 66 F5
Spenser St NE32 58 B8
Spenser Wlk NE34 59 A3
Spetchells 3 NE42 50 D3
Spetember Courtyard NE8 100 B1
Spinneyside Gdns NE11 69 F7
Spinney Terr NE6 56 F6
Spinney The
Annitsford NE23 22 C1
Killingworth NE12 29 E2
Morpeth NE61 9 A6
Newcastle upon Tyne NE7 39 B2
Washington NE38 83 D2
Spire Rd NE37 83 F7
Spires La NE6 56 C6
Spital Cres NE64 7 D3
Spital La NE46 44 F7
Spital Rd NE64 7 C3
Spital Terr NE3 38 D5
SPITAL TONGUES 98 B3
Spital Villas NE15 33 A3
Spittal Terr NE46 45 A5
Split Crow Rd NE10, NE8 71 B8
Spohr Terr NE33 42 D2
Spoors Cotts NE16 69 A6
Spoor St NE11 100 A1
Spout La
Washington, Concord NE37 83 D8
Washington NE37 83 D7
Washington, Washington Village NE38 83 D6
Spoutwell La NE45 47 A5
Springbank Ho NE2 56 A7
Springbank Rd
Newcastle upon Tyne NE2 56 A7
Sunderland SR3 85 D3
Springbank Sq SR3 85 D3
Spring Cl DH8 76 E2
Springfeld NE10 71 F4
Springfell DH3 82 D3
Springfield
5 North Shields NE29 42 A6
Ovington NE42 49 D4
Springfield Ave NE9 71 C1
Springfield Cl NE42 49 D4
Springfield Gdns
Chester le Street DH3 88 C5
Wallsend NE28 39 F3
Springfield Gr NE25 31 E3
Springfield Pl NE9 71 A6
Springfield Rd
Blaydon NE21 53 C1
Hexham NE46 45 C4
Newbottle DH4 90 D3
Newcastle upon Tyne NE5 37 D2
Springfield Terr 1 NE10 71 C7
Spring Garden Cl SR1 103 B3
Spring Garden La NE4 98 B2
Spring Gardens Ct 12 NE29 42 A6
Spring Gardens Prim Sch NE29 41 F6
Spring Gdns NE29 41 F5
Springhill Gdns NE15 54 D6
Springhill Wlk NE61 8 E7
Springhouse La DH8 76 E2
Spring St
Newcastle upon Tyne NE4 98 B2
Newcastle upon Tyne NE8 100 B1
Springs The DH3 82 E3
Springsyde Cl NE16 68 E5
Spring Terr NE29 42 A6
Spring Ville NE22 11 F4
SPRINGWELL
Sunderland 85 D3
Washington 71 F2
Springwell Ave
Gateshead NE9 71 C3
Jarrow NE32 58 C6
Newcastle upon Tyne NE6 56 E4
Springwell Cl NE21 53 D1
Springwell Dene Sch SR3 85 E3
Springwell Dr NE61 1 E4
Springwell Rd
Gateshead NE9 71 D3
Jarrow NE32 58 B5
Springwell NE9 71 F1
Sunderland SR3, SR4 85 D3
Springwell Sta* NE9 71 F3
Springwell Terr
Gateshead NE9 71 E3
Hetton-le-Hole DH5 95 A2
17 Springwell NE9 71 F1
Springwell Village Prim Sch NE9 71 F1
Springwood NE31 57 C7
Square Hos 4 NE10 71 C7
Square The
Fulwell SR6 75 B6
Guide Post NE62 10 F7
Ponteland NE20 26 C5
Riding Mill NE44 63 A8
3 Whickham NE16 69 B7
Squires Gdns NE10 71 D7
Stable Block NE45 47 C5
Stable Cl NE61 4 E7
Stable La NE3 37 F8
Stables The DH4 90 F7
Stadium Ind Pk NE10 56 B3
Stadium of Light Sta SR5 75 D1
Stadium of Light (Sunderland FC) SR5 102 C4
Stadium Rd NE10 56 B3
Stadium Villas NE28 40 C2
Stadium Way SR5 102 C4
Stafford Gr
Ryhope SR2 92 E6
Sunderland SR5 75 B2
Staffords La 3 SR6 75 F8
Stafford St
Hetton-le-Hole DH5 94 F4
Sunderland SR1 103 C4
Stafford Villas 19 NE9 71 F1
Stagshaw NE12 29 C5
Stagshaw Rd NE45 46 F6
Staindrop NE10 72 A5
Staines Rd NE6 56 D4
Stainthorpe Ct 1 NE46 45 B4
Stainton Dr NE10 71 D8
Stainton Gdns NE9 71 C2
Stainton Gr SR6 75 C5
Staithes Ave NE12 39 C6
Staithes Ct SR7 93 C1
Staithes La NE61 4 A1
Staithes Rd
Dunston NE11 100 A2
Penshaw NE38 84 A3
STAITHES SOUTH BANK 100 B2
Staithes St NE6 57 B6
Staith La NE21 53 A4
STAKEFORD 11 B7
Stakeford Cres NE62 11 B8
Stakeford Fst Sch NE62 11 C8
Stakeford La NE62 11 A7
Stakeford Rd NE22 11 C3
Stakeford Terr NE62 11 A7
Stalks Rd NE13 28 B6
Stamford NE12 29 D4
Stamford Ave
Seaton Delaval NE25 23 E1
Sunderland SR3 85 F3
Stamfordham Ave NE29 41 D5
Stamfordham Cl NE28 40 A2
Stamfordham Dr NE15 35 B8
Stamfordham Mews 7 NE5 37 D1
Stamfordham Rd
Newcastle upon Tyne NE5 36 C4
Ponteland NE15, NE5 35 D7
Stamp Exchange NE1 101 A4
Stampley Cl NE21 68 A8
Stamps La SR1 103 C3
Stancley Rd NE42 50 E2
Standfield Gdns NE10 72 C8
Stanelaw Way DH9 79 F1
Staneway NE10 71 E5
Stanfield Bsns Ctr SR2 103 C1
Stanfield Ct NE7 39 E3
Stang Wlk NE12 39 C7
Stanhope NE38 83 A5
Stanhope Cl DH4 94 D7
Stanhope Par 6 NE33 59 D8
Stanhope Prim Sch NE33 59 C7
Stanhope Rd
Jarrow NE32 58 D5
South Shields NE33 59 C7
Sunderland SR6 75 E4
Stanhope St
Greenside NE40 51 F1
Newcastle upon Tyne NE4 98 B2
South Shields NE33 42 C3
Stanhope Way NE4 98 B2
Stanley Cres
Prudhoe NE42 50 E3
9 Whitley Bay NE26 32 B4
Stanley Gdns
Gateshead NE9 71 C2
Seghill NE23 22 F1
Stanley Gr
Bedlington NE22 11 B1
Newcastle upon Tyne NE7 39 B3
Stanley St W NE29 42 A5
Stanley St
Blyth NE24 17 F7
Houghton-le-Spring DH5 90 E1
Jarrow NE32 58 C7
Newcastle upon Tyne NE4 54 F4
North Shields NE29 42 A5
South Shields NE34 59 B5
2 Sunderland SR5 74 B1
Wallsend NE28 40 F3
Stanley Terr
Chester le Street DH3 88 D2
4 Penshaw DH4 90 B6
Stanmore Rd NE6 39 C1
Stannerford Rd NE40 51 F6
STANNERS 53 A8
STANNINGTON 14 C4
Stannington Ave NE6 56 B7
Stannington Fst Sch NE61 14 B4
Stannington Gdns SR2 86 C2
Stannington Gr
5 Newcastle upon Tyne NE6 56 B7
Sunderland SR2 86 D2
Stannington Pl
1 Newcastle upon Tyne NE6 56 B7
Ponteland NE20 25 E8
Stannington Rd NE29 41 D5
Stannington St NE24 17 F7
Stannington Station Rd NE61 14 D8
Stannington Vale NE61 14 D1
Stansfield St SR6 75 E1
Stanstead Cl SR5 85 A8
Stanton Ave
Blyth NE24 17 B5
South Shields NE34 59 E7
Stanton Cl NE10 72 D7
Stanton Dr NE61 4 E3
Stanton Gr NE30 32 A1
Stanton Rd
Shiremoor NE27 30 E3
Tynemouth NE30 32 A1
Stanton St NE4 98 A2
Stanway Dr NE7 39 A3
Stanwick St NE30 42 D8
Stanwix 1 NE28 40 F4
Stapeley Ct 5 NE3 37 D5
Stapeley View NE3 37 D5
Stapleford Cl NE5 37 B1
Staple Rd NE32 58 C7
Stapylton Dr SR2 86 B4
Starbeck Ave NE2 99 C3
Starbeck Mews NE2 99 C3
Stardale Ave NE24 17 A6
STARGATE 52 E3
Stargate Gdns NE9 71 C2
Stargate Ind Est NE40 52 E3
Stargate La NE40 52 E4
Starlight Cres NE25 23 C3
Starling Wlk NE16 69 C2
Star of the Sea RC Prim Sch NE25 31 E2
Station App
Cleadon NE36 74 E8
Gateshead NE11, NE9 70 D3
Longbenton NE12 39 D6
1 South Shields NE33 42 C3
Station Ave DH5 95 A3
Station Avenue N DH4 89 F1
Station Avenue S DH4 90 A1
Station Bank
Mickley Square NE43 49 E2
Ryton NE40 52 C6
Station Burn Nature Reserve* NE35 58 F2
Station Cl NE44 62 F8
Station Cotts
Burnopfield NE39 78 C6
Longhirst NE61 5 B7
Morpeth NE61 9 A7
Ponteland NE20 25 E6
Seghill NE23 23 A1
Station Field Rd DH9 79 F1
Station Ind Est NE42 50 B3
Station La DH2, DH3 82 B4
Station Mews 10 NE30 42 D7
Station Rd
Ashington NE63 6 B4
Backworth NE27 30 D3
Bedlington NE22 11 C2
Station Rd *continued*
Boldon Colliery NE35 58 E2
Chester le Street DH3 88 C3
Corbridge NE45 46 F4
Cramlington NE23 22 A7
Crawcrook NE41 51 C5
Dudley NE23 28 F8
East Boldon NE36 74 D7
Gateshead, Bill Quay NE10 57 B2
Gateshead, Low Fell NE9 70 E5
Hebburn NE31 57 D6
Heddon-on-the-Wall NE15 35 A1
Hetton-le-Hole DH5 95 A3
Hexham NE46 45 C5
High Pittington DH6 96 A6
Houghton-le-Spring DH4 90 D1
Killingworth NE12 29 B3
Longbenton NE12 39 D7
Newburn NE15 52 F7
Newcastle upon Tyne, Kenton Bankfoot NE13 37 B6
Newcastle upon Tyne, South Gosforth NE3 38 E5
Newcastle upon Tyne, Wincomblee NE6 57 A5
North Shields NE29 41 D4
Penshaw DH4 89 E8
Prudhoe NE42 50 B3
Prudhoe NE42 50 C3
Rowlands Gill NE39 67 F1
Ryhope SR2 93 A6
Seghill NE23 23 A1
Shiney Row DH4 90 A6
South Shields NE33 42 C2
Sunderland SR5, SR6 75 D4
Tynemouth NE30 32 C3
Wallsend NE28 40 B2
Wallsend NE28 40 C1
Wallsend, Willington Quay NE28 41 A1
Washington, Columbia NE38 83 E4
Washington, Fatfield DH4, NE38 83 E1
Washington NE38 84 A4
Whitley Bay NE26 32 B4
Wylam NE41 51 B5
Station Road N
Hetton-le-Hole DH5 95 A3
Longbenton NE12 39 D8
Station Sq 1 NE26 32 B4
Station St
4 Bedlington NE22 11 D3
Blyth NE24 17 E8
Haswell DH6 97 F3
Jarrow NE32 58 B7
Sunderland SR1 103 A3
Station Terr
Choppington NE62 10 F3
East Boldon NE36 74 E7
Fence Houses DH4 89 F1
Tynemouth NE30 42 D7
10 Washington NE37 83 E8
Station View DH5 95 A3
Staveley Rd SR6 75 C5
Stavordale Terr NE9 71 A7
Staward Ave NE25 23 D2
Staward Terr NE6 56 F4
Staynebrigg NE10 72 A6
Steadings The
Ashington NE63 6 A2
Seaton Sluice NE26 24 E4
Stead La NE22 11 C1
Steadlands Sq NE22 11 C1
Stead Lane Fst Sch NE22 11 C1
Stead St NE28 41 A3
Steads The NE61 9 A6
Stedham Cl NE37 72 E2
Steenbergs 8 NE1 56 A6
Steep Hill SR3 91 C7
STELLA 53 A4
Stella Bank NE21 52 F5
Stella Hall Dr NE21 53 A4
Stella La NE21 53 A4
Stella Rd
Blaydon NE21 53 B4
Ryton NE21 53 B4
Stephen Ct NE32 58 C6
Stephenson Bldg NE2 99 C2
Stephenson Cl DH5 95 B4
Stephenson Ct
Bedlington NE22 11 A3
North Shields NE30 42 B5
Wylam NE41 51 C6
Stephenson Ho 15 NE46 45 A5
Stephenson Ind Est
Killingworth NE12 29 C2
Washington NE37 72 E2
Stephenson Meml Prim Sch NE28 41 A2
Stephenson Railway Mus* NE29 41 A7
Stephenson Rd
Newcastle upon Tyne NE7 39 B1
Washington NE37 72 E2
Stephenson's Dial Cottage* NE12 29 C1
Stephenson's La NE1 101 A4
Stephenson St
Gateshead NE8 70 D8
North Shields NE30 42 B5
1 Tynemouth NE30 42 D7
Wallsend NE28 41 B1
Stephenson Terr
Gateshead NE10 71 D8
Newcastle upon Tyne NE15 36 B1
Throckley NE15 35 D2
Wylam NE41 51 B6
Stephenson Way
Bedlington NE22 11 A4
Blaydon NE21 68 B8
Stephen St
Blyth NE24 17 E8
East Hartford NE23 16 B3
Newcastle upon Tyne NE6 56 A6
Stepney Bank NE1 56 A6
Stepney La NE1 99 C1
Stepney Rd 1 NE1, NE2 56 A6
Sterling Cotts NE10 71 C7
Sterling St SR4 102 A2
Stevenson St DH4 94 D8
Steward Cres NE34 60 B6
Stewart Ave SR2 92 E6
Stewart Dr NE36 74 B7
Stewartsfield NE39 67 D1
Stewart St
New Silksworth SR3 92 A7
Sunderland SR4 102 B1
Stileford NE10 72 A7
Stillington Cl 4 SR2 92 F5
Stirling Ave
Brockley Whins NE32 58 E4
Rowlands Gill NE39 67 E1
Stirling Cl
Springwell SR4 85 D3
Washington NE38 84 A4
Stirling Ct NE11 70 E2
Stirling Dr
Bedlington NE22 11 C2
Tynemouth NE29 41 C8
Stirling La NE39 67 F1
Stobart St SR5 102 C4
STOBHILL 9 A6
STOBHILLGATE 9 B7
Stobhillgate Cty Fst Sch NE61 9 C7
Stobhillgate Fst Sch NE61 9 B7
Stobhill Villas NE61 9 A7
Stockfold NE38 83 E2
Stockholm Cl NE29 41 B5
Stockley Ave SR5 74 C2
Stockley Rd NE38 83 F6
STOCKSFIELD 64 B7
Stocksfield Ave NE5 54 C7
Stocksfield Avenue Prim Sch NE5 54 B7
Stocksfield Gdns NE9 71 B2
Stocksfield Hall NE43 64 A8
Stocksfield Sta NE43 64 A7
Stockton Rd
North Shields NE29 41 F3
Ryhope SR2, SR7 92 F2
Sunderland SR2 103 A1
Stockton Terr 8 SR2 86 F2
Stockwell Gn NE6 56 F8
Stoddart Ho NE2 99 C2
Stoddart St
Newcastle upon Tyne NE1, NE2 99 C2
South Shields NE34 59 C6
Stoker Ave NE34 58 F4
Stoker Terr NE39 67 A3
Stokesley Gr NE7 39 A3
Stokoe Dr NE63 7 A3
Stone Cellar Rd NE37 72 C2
Stonechat Cl 3 NE38 82 F3
Stonechat Mount NE21 53 A4
Stonechat Pl NE12 39 A7
Stonecroft Gdns NE7 39 D3
Stonecrop NE9 71 C5
Stonecross NE63 6 C2
Stonefold Cl NE5 37 B3
Stonegate NE15 33 D1
Stonehaugh Way NE20 25 B2
STONELAW 22 A5
Stonelaw Mid Sch NE23 22 A4
Stoneleigh NE61 9 E4
Stoneleigh Ave NE12 39 A7
Stoneleigh Cl DH4 90 C2
Stoneleigh Pl 1 NE12 39 A6
Stonesdale DH4 89 E8
Stone St NE10 71 C6
Stonethwaite NE29 41 E3
Stoneycroft East NE12 29 E2
Stoneycroft Way 1 SR7 93 C1
Stoneycroft West NE12 29 E2
Stoneygate Cl NE10 56 E1
Stoneygate Gdns NE10 56 E1
Stoneygate La NE10 56 E1
Stoneyhurst Ave NE15 54 B5
Stoneyhurst Rd NE3 38 E4
Stoneyhurst Road W NE3 38 D4
Stoney La
Springwell NE9 71 F1
Sunderland SR5 75 A1
Stoneylea Cl NE40 51 E3
Stoneylea Rd NE5 53 F8
Stoneywaites NE40 66 E8
Stonybank Way NE43 64 E8
Stonycroft NE37 83 C7
Stonyflat Bank NE42 50 E2
Store Bldgs NE35 73 E8
Store Farm Rd NE64 7 C5
Store St
Blaydon NE21 53 B1
Newcastle upon Tyne NE15 53 C6
Store Terr DH5 95 B1
Storey Cres NE64 7 C5
Storey La NE21 53 A4
Storey St NE23 22 C5
Stormont Gn NE3 37 F3
Stormont St NE29 42 A5
Stothard St NE32 58 C7

Stott's Pasture DH4 . . . . .90 A4
Stotts Rd NE6 . . . . .57 A8
Stowe Gdns NE61 . . . . .4 E4
Stowell Sq NE1 . . . . .98 C1
Stowell St NE1 . . . . .98 C1
Stowell Terr NE10 . . . . .71 E8
Straker Dr NE46 . . . . .44 E3
Straker St NE32 . . . . .58 D6
Straker Terr NE34 . . . . .59 C5
Strand The SR3 . . . . .91 E8
Strangford Ave **2** DH2 . . . . . .88 B1
Stranton Terr SR6 . . . . .75 D2
Stratfield St SR4 . . . . .85 E7
Stratfield Ave SR2 . . . . .86 E3
Stratford Cl
　Cramlington NE23 . . . . .21 E7
　Killingworth NE12 . . . . .29 E3
Stratford Gdns NE9 . . . . .70 F6
Stratford Gr NE6 . . . . .56 A7
Stratford Grove Terr NE6 . .56 A7
Stratford Grove W NE6 . . . .56 A7
Stratford Rd
　Newcastle upon Tyne NE6 . .56 A7
　Washington NE38 . . . . .84 A3
Stratford Villas NE6 . . . . .56 A7
Strathaven Way NE3 . . . . .37 F7
Strathmore Ave NE39 . . . . .67 E1
Strathmore Cres
　Byermoor NE16 . . . . .79 D8
　Newcastle upon Tyne NE4 . .54 E6
Strathmore Cl NE29 . . . . .59 C4
Strathmore Rd
　Gateshead N10, NE9 . . . . . . .71 B7
　Newcastle upon Tyne NE5 . .38 C7
　Rowlands Gill NE39 . . . . .67 E1
　Sunderland SR3 . . . . .85 E2
Strathmore Sq SR3 . . . . .85 E2
Stratton Cl SR2 . . . . .93 A8
Stratus Ct **12** SR3 . . . . .92 C5
Strawberry Ave NE23 . . . . .29 C5
Strawberry Cotts NE62 . . . . . . .11 B8
Strawberry Gdns NE28 . . . . . . .40 A4
Strawberry La NE1 . . . . .98 C1
Strawberry Mews NE62 . . . . . .11 B8
Strawberry Pl NE1 . . . . .98 C2
Strawberry Terr NE13 . . . . .27 F4
STREET GATE 69 C3
Street Gate Pk NE16 . . . . .69 D3
Street The NE30 . . . . .82 B5
Stretford Ct NE9 . . . . .71 A1
Stretton Cl DH4 . . . . .94 A7
Stretton Way NE27 . . . . .30 C5
Stridingedge NE37 . . . . .83 B6
Stronsay Cl **2** SR2 . . . . .92 E8
Strothers Rd NE39 . . . . .66 F5
Strothers Terr NE39 . . . . .66 E4
Struan Terr NE36 . . . . .74 E7
Struddars Farm Ct NE21 . . .53 F2
Stuart Ct NE31 . . . . .37 C6
Stuart Gdns NE15 . . . . .35 D2
Stubbs Ave NE16 . . . . .69 A8
Studdon Wlk NE3 . . . . .37 D5
Studland Cl NE29 . . . . .31 F1
Studley Gdns
　2 Gateshead NE9 . . . . .70 F5
　Whitley Bay NE25 . . . . .32 A4
Studley Terr NE4 . . . . .98 A3
Studley Villas NE12 . . . . .39 E7
Sturdee Gdns NE2 . . . . .38 E3
Styan Ave NE26 . . . . .32 B5
Styford Gdns NE15 . . . . .53 E7
SUCCESS 90 C4
Success Rd DH4 . . . . .90 B4
Sudbury Way NE23 . . . . .21 E6
Suddick St **2** SR5 . . . . .75 B1
Suez St NE30 . . . . .42 B6
Suffolk Cl NE63 . . . . .6 A4
Suffolk Gdns
　South Shields NE34 . . . . .60 C7
　Wallsend NE28 . . . . .40 E4
Suffolk Pl
　Birtley DH3 . . . . .82 D1
　Gateshead NE8 . . . . .56 A4
Suffolk Rd NE31 . . . . .57 F3
Suffolk St
　Hetton-le-Hole DH5 . . . . .94 F4
　Jarrow NE32 . . . . .58 B6
　Sunderland SR2 . . . . .103 B1
Sugeley Dene Nature
　Reserve* NE15 . . . . .53 E7
Sugley Dr NE15 . . . . .53 D6
Sugley St NE15 . . . . .53 D6
Sugley Villas NE15 . . . . .53 D6
SULGRAVE 83 F8
Sulgrave Ind Est NE37 . . . .72 C1
Sulgrave Rd NE37 . . . . .72 F1
Sullivan Wlk NE31 . . . . .57 E5
Summerfield NE17 . . . . .77 A5
Summerfield Rd NE9 . . . . .70 F7
Summerhill
　Blaydon NE21 . . . . .53 B3
　Hedworth NE32 . . . . .58 D1
　Newcastle upon Tyne NE4 . .100 A4
　Sunderland, Middle Herrington
　SR3 . . . . .91 B7
　Sunderland SR2 . . . . .102 B2
Summerhill Ave NE3 . . . . .28 C1
Summerhill Gr NE4 . . . . .98 A1
Summerhill Rd NE34 . . . . .60 A7
Summerhill St NE4 . . . . .98 B1
Summerhill Terr NE1 . . . . .100 C4
Summerhouse Farm DH5 . .94 D5
Summerhouse La
　Ashington, North Seaton
　NE63 . . . . .7 B3

Summerhouse La continued
　Ashington, Woodbridge NE63 . .7 B4
Summerson St DH5 . . . . .95 B4
Summerson Way NE22 . . . . . .11 D2
Summers Pass NE8 . . . . .100 B1
Summers St **7** NE24 . . . . .17 E8
Summer St NE10 . . . . .56 D1
Sunbury Ave NE2 . . . . .38 E2
SUNDERLAND
　86 E6
　102 C3
Sunderland Aquatic Ctr
　SR5 . . . . .102 C4
Sunderland Empire SR1 . .102 C3
Sunderland Ent Pk SR5 . .85 B8
Sunderland Eye Infirmary
　SR2 . . . . .86 D3
Sunderland High Sch
　SR2 . . . . .103 A1
Sunderland Highway NE37,
　NE38 . . . . .83 C6
Sunderland Jun & High Sch
　SR2 . . . . .86 C3
Sunderland Minster*
　SR1 . . . . .102 C2
Sunderland Mus & Winter
　Gdns* SR1 . . . . .103 A2
Sunderland Rd
　Cleadon SR6 . . . . .75 B7
　East Boldon NE36, SR5 . . . .74 E6
　Gateshead, Felling NE10 . . . .71 E8
　Gateshead, Heworth NE10 . . .71 F8
　Gateshead, Wardley NE10 . . .72 C7
　Newbottle DH4 . . . . .90 C4
　South Shields, Harton NE34 . .59 F6
　South Shields NE33 . . . . .59 E8
　Sunderland SR5 . . . . .75 D1
Sunderland Ret Pk SR6 . . .75 D1
Sunderland Royal Hospl
　SR4 . . . . .102 A2
Sunderland St
　Houghton-le-Spring DH5 . . . .90 E1
　2 Houghton-le-Spring, New
　　Town DH4 . . . . .94 E8
　Newcastle upon Tyne NE1 . .100 C4
　Sunderland SR1 . . . . .103 B3
Sunderland Sta (BR & Metro)
　SR1 . . . . .103 A2
Sundew Rd NE9 . . . . .71 C4
Sundridge Dr NE10 . . . . .72 C7
Sunhill NE16 . . . . .69 B2
Sunholme Dr NE28 . . . . .40 A5
Sunlea Ave NE30 . . . . .32 C2
Sunnidale NE16 . . . . .68 E5
Sunnilaws NE34 . . . . .60 A3
Sunningdale
　South Shields NE33 . . . . .42 E1
　Whitley Bay NE25 . . . . .31 D5
Sunningdale Ave
　Newcastle upon Tyne NE6 . . .57 A6
　Wallsend NE28 . . . . .40 C2
Sunningdale Cl NE10 . . . . .71 D7
Sunningdale Dr NE37 . . . . .72 C2
Sunningdale Rd SR3 . . . . .85 E3
Sunningdale Sch SR3 . . . . . . .85 E3
Sunnirise NE34 . . . . .60 A4
SUNNISIDE 90 C2
Sunniside
　North Shields NE29 . . . . .41 E5
　Sunderland SR4 . . . . .85 D6
SUNNISIDE 69 A2
Sunniside Ct NE16 . . . . .69 B3
Sunniside Dr NE34 . . . . .60 A4
Sunniside Gdns
　Gateshead NE9 . . . . .71 C2
　Newcastle upon Tyne NE15 . .54 B6
Sunniside La NE34, SR6 . . . . .60 B2
Sunniside Rd NE16 . . . . .69 B3
Sunniside Sta* NE16 . . . . .69 B1
Sunniside Terr SR6 . . . . .60 B2
Sunnybank Ave NE15 . . . . .54 D5
Sunny Brae NE40 . . . . .46 F8
Sunnybrow SR3 . . . . .91 F8
Sunnycrest Ave NE6 . . . . .56 F6
Sunnycroft Ct **1** NE15 . . . . .53 F8
Sunnygill Terr NE40 . . . . .51 F2
Sunnyside NE23 . . . . .22 B6
Sunny Side S NE8 . . . . .100 B1
Sunnyway NE5 . . . . .36 D1
Sunrise Ent Pk SR5 . . . . .85 A8
Sunrise La **1** DH4 . . . . .90 C1
Sun St **3** NE38 . . . . .69 B2
Sun View Terr SR6 . . . . .59 E1
Surrey Ave SR3 . . . . .92 A6
Surrey Cl NE63 . . . . .6 A4
Surrey Pl
　Newcastle upon Tyne NE4 . . .98 A1
　Penshaw DH4 . . . . .90 C6
Surrey Rd
　Hebburn NE31 . . . . .57 F3
　North Shields NE29 . . . . .41 D6
Surrey St
　Hetton-le-Hole DH5 . . . . .94 F4
　Jarrow NE32 . . . . .58 A6
　Penshaw DH4 . . . . .90 C6
Surrey Terr DH3 . . . . .82 C1
Sussex Gdns NE28 . . . . .40 E3
Sussex Pl NE37 . . . . .72 C1
Sussex St
　2 Blyth NE24 . . . . .17 F8
　Jarrow NE32 . . . . .58 A6
　New Silksworth SR3 . . . . .92 A8
Sutherland Ave
　Newbiggin-by-the-Sea
　NE64 . . . . .7 D4
　Newcastle upon Tyne NE4 . . .54 F7
Sutherland Ct NE34 . . . . .59 D2
Sutherland Dr SR4 . . . . .85 D4

Sutherland Grange DH4 . . .90 D6
Sutherland St
　Gateshead NE8 . . . . .101 C1
　Seaham SR7 . . . . .93 B1
　Sunderland SR6 . . . . .75 D2
Sutton Cl DH4 . . . . .90 A6
Sutton Ct NE28 . . . . .39 F5
Sutton St NE6 . . . . .56 F7
Sutton Way NE34 . . . . .60 B5
Swainby Cl NE3 . . . . .38 D8
Swaledale
　Sunderland SR6 . . . . .75 F7
　Wallsend NE28 . . . . .39 F5
Swaledale Ave NE24 . . . . .17 A7
Swaledale Cl DH5 . . . . .94 F1
Swaledale Cres DH4 . . . . .90 A8
Swaledale Ct NE24 . . . . .17 A7
Swaledale Gdns
　Newcastle upon Tyne NE7 . . .39 B3
　Sunderland SR6 . . . . .85 F5
Swallow Cl NE63 . . . . .11 E8
Swallow Ct NE12 . . . . .29 C4
Swallow Pond & Plantation
　Nature Reserve** NE12 . .40 B7
Swallows The NE38 . . . . .84 A1
Swallow Tail Ct NE34 . . . . .59 B5
Swallow Tail Dr NE11 . . . . .70 B7
SWALWELL 54 B1
Swalwell Bank
　Fellside NE16 . . . . .68 F8
　Whickham NE16 . . . . .69 A8
Swalwell Cl NE42 . . . . .50 C2
Swalwell Prim Sch NE16 . .69 B8
SWAN 83 F3
Swan Ave NE28 . . . . .40 D3
Swan Cl NE11 . . . . .100 A1
Swan Dr NE11 . . . . .100 A1
Swan Ind Est NE38 . . . . .83 F4
Swan Ind Est (South)
　NE38 . . . . .83 F3
Swan Rd
　Newcastle upon Tyne NE6 . . .57 B4
　Washington NE38 . . . . .83 F3
Swan St
　Gateshead NE8 . . . . .101 C3
　Sunderland SR5 . . . . .75 C1
Swanton Cl NE5 . . . . .37 B4
Swanway NE9 . . . . .71 B7
Swards Rd NE10 . . . . .71 E7
Swarland Ave NE7 . . . . .39 B5
Swarland Rd NE25 . . . . .23 D2
Swarth Cl NE37 . . . . .83 A6
Sweetbriar NE61 . . . . .3 E2
Sweetbriar Way NE24 . . . . .17 C4
Sweethope Ave
　Newcastle upon Tyne NE6 . . .9 A6
　Blyth NE24 . . . . .17 D8
Sweethope Dene NE61 . . . . .9 A6
Swiftdale Cl NE22 . . . . .10 F1
Swinbourne Gdns NE26 . . .31 F6
Swinburne St NE32 . . . . .58 B3
Swinburne Pl
　Birtley DH3 . . . . .82 C3
　Gateshead NE8 . . . . .101 C3
　Newcastle upon Tyne NE4 . . .98 B2
Swinburne St
　Gateshead NE8 . . . . .101 B3
　3 Jarrow NE32 . . . . .58 E6
Swinburn Rd NE25 . . . . .23 D2
Swindale Cl NE10 . . . . .71 C8
Swindale Cotts NE41 . . . . .51 B6
Swindon Rd SR3 . . . . .85 D3
Swindon Sq SR3 . . . . .85 E3
Swindon Terr NE6 . . . . .39 B1
Swinhope NE38 . . . . .89 A8
Swinley Gdns NE15 . . . . .53 F6
Swinton Cl NE61 . . . . .9 B6
Swirle The NE1 . . . . .99 C1
Swirral Edge NE37 . . . . .83 C7
Swynnoft NE10 . . . . .72 B7
Sycamore DH2 . . . . .88 A5
Sycamore Ave
　Blyth NE24 . . . . .12 D1
　Dinnington NE13 . . . . .27 C7
　Guide Post NE62 . . . . .10 E7
　Ponteland NE20 . . . . .25 D4
　South Shields NE34 . . . . .59 F4
　Washington NE38 . . . . .83 B1
　Whitley Bay NE25 . . . . .31 F4
Sycamore Cl
　Newcastle upon Tyne NE2 . . .38 F2
　Rowlands Gill NE39 . . . . .67 D3
Sycamore Dr SR5 . . . . .75 B3
Sycamore Gr
　Gateshead NE10 . . . . .71 E8
　Prudhoe NE42 . . . . .50 A2
　Springwell NE9 . . . . .71 F1
Sycamore Pl NE12 . . . . .29 C4
Sycamore Rd
　Ashington NE63 . . . . .6 D3
　Throckley NE15 . . . . .35 C1
　Wallsend NE28 . . . . .40 C1
Sycamore St
　Ashington NE63 . . . . .6 D3
　Burnopfield NE16 . . . . .79 C5
　Guide Post NE62 . . . . .10 E7
　Newcastle upon Tyne NE4 . .100 A3
　Sunderland SR2 . . . . .86 E3
Sycamores The DH6 . . . . .97 F3
Sydenham Terr
　14 South Shields NE33 . . . .42 D3
　Sunderland SR4 . . . . .102 A1
Sydney Ct NE8 . . . . .101 B3

Sydney Gdns NE34 . . . . .58 F3
Sydney Gr NE28 . . . . .40 A5
Sydney St DH4 . . . . .89 E2
Syke Rd NE16 . . . . .78 F5
Sylvan Cl NE61 . . . . .8 D7
Sylverton Gdns NE33 . . . . .42 F1
Symington Gdns SR3 . . . . .91 F8
Symon Terr NE17 . . . . .77 B8
Synclen Ave NE45 . . . . .47 A6
Synclen Rd NE45 . . . . .47 A6
Synclen Terr NE45 . . . . .47 A6
Syon St NE30 . . . . .42 D8
Syron NE16 . . . . .68 F7
Syston Cl DH4 . . . . .94 A7

T

Taberna Cl NE15 . . . . .34 E2
Tadcaster Rd SR3 . . . . .85 C1
Tadema Rd NE33 . . . . .42 F2
Talbot Cl NE38 . . . . .83 D4
Talbot Cotts DH3 . . . . .82 C4
Talbot Gn NE5 . . . . .53 F8
Talbot Rd
　South Shields NE34 . . . . .59 C6
　Sunderland SR6 . . . . .75 E3
Talbot Terr **12** DH3 . . . . .82 C4
Talgarth NE38 . . . . .84 B5
Talisman View **6** NE9 . . . . . .71 A2
Talley Ct NE38 . . . . .83 C5
Tamar Cl NE29 . . . . .41 D8
Tamar Ct **2** SR3 . . . . .91 F6
Tamar Way NE9 . . . . .71 C5
Tamar St DH5 . . . . .97 C8
Tamerton Dr DH3 . . . . .82 D2
Tamerton St NE4 . . . . .85 F6
Tamworth Rd NE4 . . . . .98 A2
Tamworth Sq SR3 . . . . .85 C1
Tanbank DH4 . . . . .89 F6
TANFIELD 79 D3
Tanfield Gdns NE34 . . . . .60 B6
Tanfield Lea Com Prim Sch
　DH9 . . . . .79 D1
TANFIELD LEA 79 C1
Tanfield Lea Com Prim Sch
　DH9 . . . . .79 D1
Tanfield Lea Ind Est North
　DH9 . . . . .79 D2
Tanfield Lea Ind Est South
　DH9 . . . . .79 F1
Tanfield Pl NE9 . . . . .71 C2
Tanfield Rd
　Gateshead NE9 . . . . .71 C2
　Sunderland SR3 . . . . .85 D1
Tanfield Rly* NE16 . . . . .80 B6
Tanfield St NE4 . . . . .85 E7
Tangmere Cl NE23 . . . . .22 C7
Tankerville Pl **3** NE2 . . . . . . .38 E1
Tankerville Terr NE2 . . . . .38 E1
Tanners' Bank NE30 . . . . .42 C6
Tanners Row **1** NE46 . . . . . .45 A5
Tantallon DH3 . . . . .82 D2
Tantallon Ct DH4 . . . . .89 D1
TANTOBIE 79 A2
Tantobie Rd NE15 . . . . .54 A6
Tarlton Cres NE10 . . . . .71 C8
Tarn Dr SR2 . . . . .86 F1
Tarragon Way NE34 . . . . .59 C3
Tarrington Cl NE28 . . . . .40 B5
Tarset Dr NE42 . . . . .50 D2
Tarset Pl NE3 . . . . .38 A6
Tarset Rd NE25 . . . . .31 B5
Tarset St NE6 . . . . .56 A5
Tasmania Rd NE34 . . . . .58 F3
Tasman Rd SR3 . . . . .91 C8
Tate St **8** NE24 . . . . .17 F8
Tatham St SR1 . . . . .103 B2
Tatham Street Back SR1 . .103 B2
Tattershall SR2 . . . . .86 B4
Taunton Ave
　Jarrow NE32 . . . . .58 E5
　Tynemouth NE29 . . . . .31 D1
Taunton Cl NE28 . . . . .40 F5
Taunton Pl NE23 . . . . .22 B8
Taunton Rd SR3 . . . . .85 D2
Taunton Sq SR3 . . . . .85 D2
Taylor Ave
　Ashington NE63 . . . . .7 B3
　Widopen NE13 . . . . .28 C6
Taylor Gdns
　Gateshead NE10 . . . . .57 A1
　Seaton Sluice NE26 . . . . .24 D6
　10 Sunderland SR2 . . . . . .86 E4
Taylor's Bldgs NE22 . . . . .11 D2
Taylors Ct **4** NE1 . . . . .99 A1
Taylor St
　Blyth NE24 . . . . .17 A8
　South Shields NE33 . . . . .59 B8
Taylor Terr **8** NE27 . . . . .30 E1
Taynton Gr NE23 . . . . .22 F2
Tay Rd SR3, SR4 . . . . .85 C2
Tay St
　Chopwell NE17 . . . . .66 C1
　Easington Lane DH5 . . . . . . .97 D8
Teal Ave NE24 . . . . .17 F4
Teal Cl

Team St NE8 . . . . .100 B1
TEAM VALLEY 70 D5
Team Valley Bsns Ctr
　NE11 . . . . .70 D6
Team Valley Trad Est
　NE11 . . . . .70 C6
Teasdale Ho NE5 . . . . .37 A5
Teasdale St SR2 . . . . .103 C1
Tebay Dr NE5 . . . . .53 F8
Tedco Bsns Ctr NE32 . . . . . . .57 F8
Tedco Bsns Wks **1** NE33 . .42 C2
Teddington Cl NE3 . . . . .37 B7
Teddington Rd SR3 . . . . .85 C2
Teddington Sq SR3 . . . . .85 C2
Tedham Rd NE15 . . . . .53 C7
Tees Cl
　16 Silksworth SR3 . . . . . . .91 F6
　South Shields NE34 . . . . .59 C6
Teesdale Ave DH4 . . . . .90 A8
Teesdale Gdns NE7 . . . . .39 B3
Teesdale Gr NE12 . . . . .39 D8
Teesdale Pl **3** NE24 . . . . .16 F8
Tees Rd NE31 . . . . .57 E3
Tees St
　Chopwell NE17 . . . . .66 C1
　Easington Lane DH5 . . . . . . .97 D8
Tees Terr **9** NE37 . . . . .83 D8
Teignmouth Gdns NE9 . . . . . . .70 F4
Telford Cl NE27 . . . . .30 C5
Telford St
　Gateshead NE8 . . . . .70 D7
　North Shields NE28 . . . . .41 C2
Temperley Pl NE46 . . . . .45 A4
Temperly Pl **15** NE46 . . . . . . .45 A4
Tempest St NE21 . . . . .53 A4
Temple Ave NE24 . . . . .17 C7
Temple Bldgs **4** NE1 . . . . . . .98 C1
Temple Gn
　Gateshead NE8 . . . . .70 C8
　South Shields NE34 . . . . .59 C5
Temple Park Inf Sch
　NE34 . . . . .59 D3
Temple Park Jun Sch
　NE34 . . . . .59 D4
Temple Park L Ctr NE34 . . .59 D4
Temple Park Rd NE34 . . . . . . .59 D6
Temple St
　Gateshead NE8 . . . . .70 D7
　Newcastle upon Tyne NE1 . .100 C4
　South Shields NE33 . . . . .59 B7
Temple Street W NE33 . . . . . .59 B7
Temple Town NE33 . . . . .59 B8
Tenbury Cres
　Longbenton NE12 . . . . .39 C7
　Tynemouth NE29 . . . . .31 E1
Tenby Rd SR3 . . . . .91 C8
Tenby Sq NE23 . . . . .22 C8
Ten Fields DH5 . . . . .95 A3
Tennant St
　Hebburn NE31 . . . . .57 D5
　3 South Shields NE34 . . . .59 B8
Tennyson Ave
　Hebburn NE31 . . . . .57 F6
　West Boldon NE35 . . . . .74 B8
Tennyson Cres **2** NE16 . . . . .69 A8
Tennyson Ct
　Gateshead NE8 . . . . .56 A2
　Prudhoe NE42 . . . . .50 B1
Tennyson Gn NE3 . . . . .37 F3
Tennyson St
　1 South Shields NE33 . . . .42 D2
　Sunderland SR5 . . . . .75 B1
Tennyson Terr NE29 . . . . .42 B6
Tenter Garth NE15 . . . . .35 C2
Tenter Terr NE61 . . . . .9 A8
Tenth Ave
　Blyth NE24 . . . . .17 C6
　Chester le Street DH2 . . . . . .88 B3
　Gateshead NE11 . . . . .70 D2
　Morpeth NE61 . . . . .9 B6
Tenth Avenue W NE11 . . . . .70 D1
Tern Cl NE12 . . . . .29 C4
Terrace Pl NE1 . . . . .98 C2
Terraces The NE38 . . . . .83 E4
Terrace The
　6 Boldon Colliery NE35 . . .58 F3
　8 East Boldon NE36 . . . . .74 D2
　Longbenton NE12 . . . . .39 C6
　Ovingham NE42 . . . . .50 A4
Terrier Cl NE22 . . . . .11 C1
Tesla St DH4 . . . . .90 D4
Tetford Pl NE12 . . . . .39 C6
Teviot NE38 . . . . .83 A3
Teviotdale Gdns NE7 . . . . .39 B2
Teviot St
　Easington Lane DH5 . . . . . . .97 C8
　Gateshead NE8 . . . . .71 A8
Teviot Way NE32 . . . . .58 A3
Tewkesbury NE12 . . . . .29 D4
Tewkesbury Rd NE15 . . . . .53 C2
Thackeray Rd SR3 . . . . .85 D2
Thackeray St DH4 . . . . .94 D1
Thames Ave NE32 . . . . .58 A2
Thames Cres DH4 . . . . .94 A8
Thames Gdns NE28 . . . . .40 A3
Thames Rd
　Hebburn NE31 . . . . .57 F7
　Sunderland SR3 . . . . .91 C8
Thames St
　Chopwell NE17 . . . . .66 C1
　Easington Lane DH5 . . . . . . .97 C8
　Gateshead NE8 . . . . .56 A4

Thanet Rd SR3 . . . . .85 D1
Tharsis Rd NE31. . . . . .57 D5
Thatcher Cl NE16. . . . . . . .69 A5
THE ALLOTMENT. 30 E1
Theatre Pl 21 NE29. . . . . . .42 A5
Theatre Royal* NE1 . . . . . .99 A1
The Beacons NE25. . . . . . .23 C4
The Brambles NE25. . . . . .23 D5
The Bucca NE24 . . . . .12 C7
The Lairage NE20. . . . . . . .25 E6
THE LAWE 42 C4
The Limes NE12 . . . . .29 C1
Thelma St SR4. . . . . .102 B1
Theme Rd SR3. . . . . .91 C8
The Parkside NE42. . . . . . .50 E3
Theresa Russell Ho NE6. .56 C6
Theresa St NE21. . . . . .53 C3
Thetford NE38 . . . . .83 D4
The Willows NE22. . . . . . . .11 C4
Thieves Bank NE61 . . . . . . .5 E1
Third Ave
  Ashington NE63. . . . . .6 E3
  Blyth NE24. . . . . .17 D6
  Chester le Street, Canada
    DH2. . . . . .88 B3
  Chester le Street, South Pelaw
    DH2. . . . . .88 B7
  Gateshead NE10 . . . . . . .70 C6
  Morpeth NE61. . . . . .9 B7
  Newcastle upon Tyne NE6. .56 C7
  North Shields NE29. . . . . .41 B5
Third Row
  Ellington NE61. . . . . .1 E4
  Linton NE61. . . . . .1 A3
Third St NE28. . . . . .40 D1
Thirkeld Pl DH4. . . . . .90 A7
Thirlington Cl NE5 . . . . . . .37 B3
Thirlmere
  Birtley DH3 . . . . .82 E2
  Cleadon SR6 . . . . .60 A1
  Gateshead NE10 . . . . . . .72 A8
Thirlmere Ave
  [?] NE31. . . . . .58 B1
  Easington Lane DH5 . . . . .97 C8
  Tynemouth NE30 . . . . . . .32 A2
Thirlmere Cl NE12 . . . . . . .29 F3
Thirlmere Cres
  Blaydon NE21 . . . . .68 B8
  Penshaw DH4 . . . . .90 B6
Thirlmere Ct NE31. . . . . . .57 F4
Thirlmere Terr NE64 . . . . . .7 E4
Thirlmere Way
  Blyth NE24. . . . . .12 A1
  Newcastle upon Tyne NE5. .37 B1
Thirlmoor NE37. . . . . .83 A6
Thirlmoor Pl NE62. . . . . . .11 A8
Thirlwall Ct NE12 . . . . . . .38 F6
Thirlwell Gr NE32. . . . . . . .58 B3
Thirsk Rd NE8. . . . . .56 A3
Thirsk Rd SR3. . . . . .85 D2
Thirston Dr NE23 . . . . .22 C6
Thirston Pl NE29. . . . . . . .41 D7
Thirston Way NE3. . . . . . . .37 D5
Thistle Ave NE40. . . . . . . .52 C6
Thistlecroft DH5 . . . . .94 E7
Thistle Ct NE31. . . . . .57 F4
Thistledon Ave NE16. . . . . .68 F6
Thistle Ho SR3 . . . . .92 A5
Thistle Rd SR3. . . . . .85 C1
Thistley Cl NE6 . . . . .56 E8
Thistley Gn NE10 . . . . .57 B1
Thomas Bell Ho 8 NE34 .59 A4
Thomas Bewick Sch NE5. .36 C2
Thomas Bewick Sq NE1. 101 A4
Thomas Dr NE31. . . . . . . .57 D6
Thomas Ferguson Ct
  NE30. . . . . .42 C6
Thomas Hawksley Pk SR3 86 A3
Thomas Hepburn Com Sch
  The NE10. . . . . .71 A6
Thomas Horsley Ho NE15 .54 B5
Thomas St
  9 Chester le Street DH3 . .88 C2
  Gateshead NE10 . . . . . . .71 D1
  Hetton-le-Hole DH5. . . . .95 B5
  Newcastle upon Tyne NE5. .36 F2
  Ryhope SR2. . . . . .92 F6
  South Shields NE33. . . . .42 C3
  8 Washington NE37. . . . .83 E8
  Wickham NE16. . . . . . . .69 A7
Thomas Street N SR6 . 103 A4
Thomas Street S
  Ryhope SR2. . . . . .92 F6
  Sunderland SR5. . . . . . . .75 A1
Thomas Taylor Cotts
  NE27 . . . . .30 C5
Thomas Walling Prim Sch
  NE5 . . . . .37 C2
Thompson Ave NE12 . . . . .29 C4
Thompson Cres 7 SR5 .74 B1
Thompson Gdns NE28. . . .40 B2
Thompson Pl NE10. . . . . . .71 D8
Thompson Rd SR5 . . . . . . .75 B3
Thompson's Bldgs NE24. .90 C5
Thompson St
  9 Bedlington NE22. . . . . .11 D3
  Blyth NE24. . . . . .12 D1
  Blyth NE24. . . . . .12 E1
Thompson Terr 9 SR2 . .93 A6
Thorburn St SR6. . . . . .75 D4
Thornbank Cl SR3. . . . . . . .85 B2
Thornbeck Coll SR2. . . . . 102 C1
Thornborough Ho 16 NE6 .56 C6
Thornbridge NE38. . . . . . . .84 A5
Thornbury 8 NE21 . . . . . . .53 B1
Thornbury Ave NE23 . . . . .23 A2
Thornbury Cl
  Boldon Colliery NE35. . . .58 E1

Thornbury Cl continued
  Newcastle upon Tyne NE3 . .37 B5
Thornbury Dr NE15 . . . . . .31 C6
Thornbury St SR4. . . . . . . 102 A3
Thorn Cl NE13. . . . . .28 A5
Thorncliffe Pl NE29. . . . . . .41 E5
Thorndale Pl 2 NE24. . . . .17 A8
Thorndale Rd
  Newcastle upon Tyne
    NE15. . . . . .53 F5
  Sunderland SR3. . . . . . . .85 B1
Thorne Ave NE10 . . . . .72 B8
Thorne Brake NE10 . . . . . .72 A7
Thornehill Gdns NE62. . . . .11 A8
Thorne Rd SR3 . . . . .85 C1
Thorne Sq SR3. . . . . .85 C1
Thorne Terr NE6 . . . . .56 E7
Thorneyburn Ave NE25. . . .31 B5
Thorneyburn Cl DH4. . . . . .90 C2
Thorneyburn Way NE24 . . .17 C7
THORNEY CLOSE. 85 B2
Thorney Close Prim Sch
  SR3. . . . . .85 D1
Thorney Close Rd SR3 . . . .85 D1
Thorneyfield Dr NE12 . . . . .29 B2
Thorneyford Pl NE20. . . . . .25 E7
Thornfield Gr SR2 . . . . 8₆ E7
Thornfield Pl NE39. . . . . . .67 E3
Thornfield Rd NE3. . . . . . . .38 B4
Thorngill NE37. . . . . .83 A6
Thornhaugh Ave NE16 . . . .68 F6
Thornhill Cl
  Gateshead NE11. . . . . . . .70 A8
  Seaton Delaval NE25. . . . .23 D2
Thornhill Cres SR2. . . . . . 102 C2
Thornhill Gdns
  Burnopfield NE16. . . . . . .78 F5
  Sunderland SR2. . . . . . . 102 C1
Thornhill Pk
  Ponteland NE20. . . . . . . .25 E7
  Sunderland SR2. . . . . . . 102 C1
Thornhill Rd
  Longbenton NE12. . . . . . .39 D6
  Ponteland NE20. . . . . . . .25 E7
Thornhill St DH4. . . . . .94 D8
Thornhill St NE29. . . . . . . 102 C1
Thorn Ho SR3 . . . . .92 A5
Thornholme Ave NE34 . . . .60 B6
Thornholme Rd SR2 . . . . . 102 C2
Thornhope Cl NE38 . . . . . .83 F6
Thornlea NE61. . . . . .9 E4
Thornlea Gdns NE9 . . . . . .70 F6
Thornleigh Gdns SR6 . . . . .60 A3
Thornleigh Rd NE2. . . . . . .38 E1
Thornley Ave
  Cramlington NE23 . . . . . .22 C6
  Gateshead NE10 . . . . . . .71 B8
Thornley Cl NE16 . . . . .69 A4
Thornley La NE21, NE39. . .68 A6
Thornley Rd NE5. . . . . .53 F8
Thornley Terr NE62. . . . . . .11 C6
Thornley View NE39 . . . . . .67 D3
Thornley Wood* NE21. . . . .68 B6
Thornton Ave NE33 . . . . . .59 B7
Thornton Cl
  Cramlington NE23 . . . . . .22 C6
  Washington DH4. . . . . . . .90 B2
Thornton Cotts NE40. . . . . .52 C6
Thornton Cres NE13 . . . . . .23 C3
Thornton Ct NE38. . . . . . . .83 C5
Thornton Ho 10 NE1. . . . . .98 C1
Thornton St NE1. . . . . .98 C1
Thornton Terr NE12 . . . . . .30 A1
Thorntree Ave NE13. . . . . .21 E5
Thorntree Cl NE25. . . . . . . .31 B4
Thorntree Cotts NE13 . . . . .21 E1
Thorntree Ct NE12 . . . . . . .39 F8
Thorntree Dr
  Earsdon NE25. . . . . .31 A4
  Newcastle upon Tyne NE15. .54 A7
  Whitley Bay NE25 . . . . . .31 C4
Thorn Tree Dr NE22. . . . . .10 F2
Thorntree Gdns NE63. . . . . .7 A2
Thorntree Mews SR3 . . . . .85 C2
Thorntree Way NE24 . . . . .16 F7
Thorntree Wlk NE32 . . . . . .58 D2
Thornwood Gdns NE11 . . . .70 B6
Thornyford Ho NE4 . . . . . . .98 B2
Thornygarth NE10 . . . . . . .71 E7
Thoroton St NE24. . . . . . . .17 E8
Thorp Ave NE61. . . . . .4 A2
Thorp Cotts NE40 . . . . .52 A5
Thorp Cotts NE40. . . . . . . .52 A5
Thorpe Cl NE4. . . . . .98 A2
Thorpe Dr NE40. . . . . .52 E5
Thorpeness Rd SR3. . . . . . .85 C1
Thorpe St NE4 . . . . .98 A2
Threap Gdns NE28. . . . . . .40 E4
Three Mile Ct NE3 . . . . . . .38 C8
Three Rivers Ct NE36. . . . .74 A7
Threlkeld Gr SR6. . . . . .75 F3
Thrift St NE29 . . . . .42 A4
Thristley Gdns SR3 . . . . . . .86 C3
THROCKLEY. 35 D1
Throckley Prim Sch NE15 . .35 D2
Throckley & Walbottle Dene
  Nature Reserve* NE15 .35 E3
Throckley Way NE34. . . . . .59 B5
Thropton Ave
  Blyth NE24. . . . . .17 C5
  Newcastle upon Tyne NE7 .39 B5
Thropton Cl
  Chester le Street DH2. . . .88 A1
  Gateshead NE10 . . . . . . .72 C6
Thropton Cres NE3 . . . . . . .38 B6
Thropton Ct NE24. . . . . . . .17 C7

Thropton Pl NE29. . . . . . . .41 D7
Thropton Terr NE7 . . . . . . .39 B2
Thornton Ct 5 DH5. . . . . .94 F8
Thrush Gr 2 SR5. . . . . . . .74 C1
Thurleston DH4. . . . . .90 C4
Thurlow Way DH5. . . . . . . .94 D6
Thursby DH3 . . . . .82 E2
Thursby Ave NE30. . . . . . . .32 B2
Thursby Gdns NE9 . . . . . . .71 B3
Thurso Cl SR3. . . . . .85 B1
Tiberius Cl 6 NE28. . . . . . .40 B1
Tidings The NE10 . . . . .57 B2
Tilbeck Sq SR3. . . . . .92 A5
Tilbury Cl DH4. . . . . .90 C5
Tilbury Gdns SR3 . . . . .91 C8
Tilbury Gr NE30. . . . . .32 A3
Tilbury Rd SR3. . . . . .91 C8
Tileshed La NE36. . . . . . . .59 D1
Tileshed Nature Reserve*
  NE36. . . . . .59 D1
Till Ave NE21 . . . . .53 B2
Tilley Cres NE42 . . . . .50 D3
Tilley Rd NE38. . . . . .82 F5
Till Gr NE61. . . . . .1 C5
Tillmouth Ave NE25. . . . . . .23 E2
Tillmouth Gdns NE5 . . . . . .36 F1
Tillmouth Park Rd NE15. . . .35 D1
Till St 7 NE6. . . . . .56 C4
Tilson Way NE3 . . . . .37 F6
Timber Beach Rd SR5. . . . .74 D1
Times Sq NE1 . . . . 100 C4
Timlin Gdns NE28 . . . . . . .41 B3
Timothy Duff Ct NE30. . . . .42 F7
Tindal Cl NE4 . . . . .98 B1
Tindale Ave NE23 . . . . .22 C6
Tindale Dr NE16. . . . . .69 A6
Tindal St NE4. . . . . .98 B1
Tinkler's Bank NE45. . . . . .46 F3
Tinklers Yard NE45. . . . . . .46 F3
Tinkler Terr DH3 . . . . .89 B1
Tintagel Cl
  Cramlington NE23. . . . . . .22 D7
  Sunderland SR3. . . . . . . .85 B1
Tintern St NE28 . . . . .83 C3
Tintern Cl DH4 . . . . .90 C2
Tintern Cres
  Newcastle upon Tyne NE6. .56 B7
  Tynemouth NE29 . . . . . . .41 D8
Tintern St SR4. . . . . 102 B2
Tiree Ct SR3. . . . . .92 A6
Tirril Pl NE5 . . . . .36 F1
Titan Ho NE6 . . . . .57 A6
Titan Rd NE6 . . . . .57 A5
Titchfield Rd NE38. . . . . . .83 C4
Titchfield Terr
  Ashington NE63. . . . . .6 D2
  Pegswood NE61. . . . . .4 F4
Tithe Cotts NE20. . . . . . . .25 E7
Titlington Gr NE31. . . . . . . .57 D3
Tiverton Ave
  1 Newcastle upon Tyne
    NE4. . . . . .54 E5
  Tynemouth NE29 . . . . . . .31 C1
Tiverton Cl
  Newbottle NE28. . . . . . . .90 C4
  Wallsend NE28 . . . . .41 A5
Tiverton Gdns NE9 . . . . . . .70 F3
Tiverton Pl NE23. . . . . .22 B8
Tiverton Sq SR3. . . . . .85 C1
Tivoli Bldgs DH4. . . . . .90 C6
Toberty Gdns NE10. . . . . . .72 B8
Todd's Nook NE4 . . . . .98 B1
Togstone Pl 4 NE5. . . . . . .37 C1
Toll Bar Rd SR2. . . . . .93 A8
Toll Bar Rd SR2. . . . . .92 G8
Toll Bridge Rd NE21. . . . . .53 F3
Tollerton Dr SR5. . . . . .74 A1
Tollgate Rd NE39 . . . . .77 F5
Tolls Cl NE25 . . . . .31 C6
Tomlea Ave NE22 . . . . .11 D1
Tom Urwin Ho 11 SR3. . . .92 A7
Tonbridge Ave NE29 . . . . . .41 E4
Toner Ave NE31. . . . . .57 D3
Toner Avenue Prim Sch
  NE31. . . . . .57 D3
Topcliff SR6 . . . . 103 B4
Topcliffe Gn NE3 . . . . .71 B2
Toppings St NE35. . . . . . . .58 E1
Torcross Way NE23. . . . . . .22 B8
Tor Mere Cl NE37. . . . . . . .83 A6
Toronto Rd SR3. . . . . .85 D2
Toronto Sq SR3. . . . . .85 D2
Torquay Gdns NE9. . . . . . . .70 F3
Torquay Par NE31. . . . . . . .57 E3
Torquay Rd SR3. . . . . .85 D2
Torrance Cl NE63 . . . . .6 F4
Torrens Rd SR3. . . . . .85 D2
Torrington Cl DH4 . . . . .90 C4
Torver Cl NE13. . . . . .28 B5
Torver Cres SR6. . . . . .75 D5
Torver Pl NE9 . . . . .71 B4
Torver Way NE30. . . . . .31 F2
Torwood Cl NE23 . . . . .22 C6
Tosson Cl NE22 . . . . .11 B1
Tosson Pl
  Ashington NE63. . . . . .6 E3
  North Shields NE29 . . . . .41 D5
Tosson Terr NE6 . . . . .39 C1
Totnes Cl SR3. . . . . .85 B1
Totnes Dr NE23. . . . . .22 B8
Toward Rd
  Sunderland SR1, SR2. . . 103 A2
  Sunderland SR3. . . . . . . 103 B1
Tower Ct
  Dunston NE11. . . . . 100 A1
  Easington Lane DH5. . . . .95 C1
Tower Gdns NE40. . . . . . . .52 C5

Tower Ho NE1 . . . . .99 C1
Tower Pl 1 SR2. . . . . .86 E4
Tower Rd NE37 . . . . .83 E7
Towers Ave NE2. . . . . .38 E3
Towers Cl NE22. . . . . .16 A8
Towers Pl NE34. . . . . .58 E5
Tower St
  Newcastle upon Tyne NE1. .99 B1
  Sunderland SR2. . . . . . . 103 C1
Towers The SR1. . . . . .85 B5
Tower Street W SR2 . . . . 103 B1
Tower View NE15 . . . . .54 C6
TOWN CENTRE 83 C4
Towne Gate The NE15. . . . .34 E2
Towneley Cotts NE40. . . . . .52 A4
Towneley Ct NE42. . . . . . . .50 E3
Towneley Terr NE39. . . . . . .66 E4
Townend Ct NE34 . . . . .59 C5
TOWN END FARM 73 E4
Town End Prim Sch SR5 . . .73 F4
Town Farm Field NE45. . . . .46 F6
Townfield Gdns NE15 . . . . .52 F8
Townley Fields NE39 . . . . . .67 F2
Townley Rd NE39 . . . . .67 D2
Townsend Cres NE61. . . . . .8 D6
Townsend Rd SR3. . . . . . . .85 D1
Townsend Sq SR3. . . . . . . .91 C8
Townsville Ave NE25 . . . . . .23 D2
Towton NE12 . . . . .29 D4
Toynbee NE38 . . . . .84 A5
Tracey Ave NE36. . . . . .74 B8
Trafalgar House 17 NE30 .42 D7
Trafalgar Rd NE37. . . . . . . .72 F1
Trafalgar Sq SR1. . . . . . . 103 C3
Trafalgar St NE1. . . . . .99 B1
Trafford NE9. . . . . .71 A1
Trafford Rd SR5. . . . . .75 A1
Trafford Wlk NE5 . . . . .36 E3
Trajan Ave SR3. . . . . .42 D4
Trajan St NE33. . . . . .42 D4
Trajan Wlk NE15 . . . . .34 D2
Tranfield Ho NE[?]. 86 C1
TRANWELL. 8 C4
Tranwell Cl
  Newcastle upon Tyne NE3. .37 F8
  Pegswood NE61. . . . . .4 E3
Tranwell Cotts NE61 . . . . . .8 D4
Tranwell Ct NE61 . . . . .8 D4
Tranwell Dr NE25 . . . . .23 E2
Travers St SR4 . . . . .90 C6
Treby St SR4. . . . . 102 A3
Tredegar Cl NE5 . . . . .37 A4
Treecone Cl SR3 . . . . .92 A5
Tree Ct 25 SR3. . . . . .91 F6
Tree Top Mews 7 NE28 . . .40 E5
Treetops The NE32 . . . . . . .58 A4
Treherne Rd NE2 . . . . .38 D3
Trent Ave NE31. . . . . .57 E3
Trent Dr NE32 . . . . .55 D2
Trent Gdns NE8 . . . . .71 B8
Trentham Ave NE7. . . . . . . .39 B5
Trentham Gdns NE61. . . . . .4 F4
Trenton Ave NE38. . . . . . . .83 D6
Trent Rd SR3. . . . . .85 C1
Trent St
  Chopwell NE17. . . . . .66 C1
  Easington Lane DH5 . . . . .97 C8
Trevarren Dr SR2 . . . . .92 F7
Trevelyan Ave
  Bedlington NE22 . . . . . . .11 B1
  Blyth NE24. . . . . .17 C6
Trevelyan Cl SR3. . . . . .85 B1
Trevelyan Dr NE5. . . . . . . .37 A5
Trevethick St NE8. . . . . . . .70 D8
Trevone Pl NE23 . . . . .22 A2
Trevor Gr SR6 . . . . .75 A8
Trevor Terr NE30 . . . . .42 B7
Trewhitt Rd NE6. . . . . .56 C8
Trewit Rd NE26 . . . . .32 B5
Triangle Ho 5 NE1 . . . . . . .98 C1
Tribune Pl NE1 . . . . .71 B6
Trident Dr NE24. . . . . .17 F4
Trident Rd SR3 . . . . .92 A7
Trimdon Gr NE9 . . . . .71 D3
Trimdon St SR4. . . . . 102 B3
Trimdon Street W SR4 . . . 102 B3
Trinity Bldgs NE30 . . . . . . .42 C5
Trinity Cl 2 NE29. . . . . . . .42 A4
Trinity Ct
  Corbridge NE45. . . . . . . .46 F6
  Gateshead NE8 . . . . 101 C3
  9 North Shields NE29 . . .42 A4
Trinity Ctyd NE6 . . . . .56 C4
Trinity Gr NE23 . . . . .23 A2
Trinity House NE1. . . . . . . .99 B1
Trinity House* NE1. . . . . . 101 B4
Trinity Pk DH4. . . . . .90 B5
Trinity Pl NE29 . . . . .42 A4
Trinity Sch (Deneview Site)
  NE3 . . . . .38 F7
Trinity Sch (Kenton Lodge
  Site) NE3 . . . . .38 B2
Trinity Sch (Oakfield Coll)
  NE4 . . . . .54 D6
Trinity Sq SR1 . . . . 103 B3
Trinity St
  North Shields NE29 . . . . .42 A4
  Sunderland SR5. . . . . . . .74 F2
Trinity Terr
  Corbridge NE45. . . . . . . .46 F6
  9 North Shields NE29 . . .42 B1
Trojan Ave NE6 . . . . .56 E7
Tromso Cl NE29 . . . . .41 C5
Trool Cl SR3 . . . . .92 A5
Troon Cl NE37. . . . . .72 C2
Trotter Gr NE22 . . . . .11 C1
Trotter Terr SR2. . . . . .92 F6

Troutbeck Ave NE6. . . . . . .56 F5
Troutbeck Gdns NE9 . . . . .71 A3
Troutbeck Rd SR6. . . . . . . .75 C5
Troutbeck Way NE38 . . . . .58 F3
Troutdale Pl NE12. . . . . . . .38 F6
Trowan Cl NE4 . . . . .54 E4
Trowbridge Way NE31. . . . .37 F5
Truro Gr NE29. . . . . .41 D8
Truro Rd SR3 . . . . .85 D1
Truro Way NE32. . . . . .58 C1
Tuart St DH3 . . . . .88 C3
Tudor Ave NE29 . . . . .41 E6
Tudor Ct NE20. . . . . .25 C4
Tudor Dr DH3. . . . . .79 D3
Tudor Gr SR3. . . . . .85 F3
Tudor Rd
  Chester le Street DH3 . . . .88 D5
  South Shields NE33. . . . .42 C2
Tudor Way NE3 . . . . .37 B6
Tudor Wlk NE3 . . . . .37 C6
Tudor Wynd NE6. . . . . .39 D2
Tulip Cl NE21. . . . . .53 B2
Tulip St
  Gateshead NE8 . . . . .56 C1
  Prudhoe NE42 . . . . .50 B2
Tummel Ct SR3. . . . . .92 A6
Tumulus Ave NE6. . . . . . . .57 A8
Tunbridge Rd SR3. . . . . . . .85 D2
Tundry Way NE21. . . . . . . .53 F4
Tunis Rd SR3. . . . . .85 C2
TUNSTALL. 92 C7
Tunstall Ave
  Newcastle upon Tyne NE6. .56 D6
  South Shields NE34 . . . . .60 B6
Tunstall Bank SR2, SR3 . . .92 D7
Tunstall Hill Cl SR2. . . . . . .86 C2
Tunstall Hills Nature
  Reserve* SR3. . . . . .86 C1
Tunstall Hope Rd SR3. . . . .92 C8
Tunstall Pk SR2. . . . . .86 C2
Tunstall Rd SR3. . . . . .86 B2
Tunstall Terr
  New Silksworth SR2 . . . . .92 B7
  Ryhope SR2 . . . . .92 D7
  Sunderland SR2 . . . . . . 102 C2
Tunstall Terrace W SR2 . . 102 C2
Tunstall Vale SR2. . . . . . . .86 C4
Tunstall View NE3 . . . . . . .92 B8
Tunstall Village Gn SR3 . . .92 B7
Tunstall Village Rd SR3 . . .92 B7
Tunstall Villas SR3 . . . . . . .92 B7
Turbinia Gdns NE7. . . . . . .39 D2
Turfside
  Gateshead NE10 . . . . . . .72 B7
  Hedworth NE32 . . . . .58 D1
Turnberry
  Ouston DH2 . . . . .81 F2
  South Shields NE33 . . . . .42 E1
  Whitley Bay NE25 . . . . . .31 C5
Turnberry Cl NE37 . . . . . . .72 C2
Turnberry Ct NE10 . . . . . . .72 B7
Turnberry Way
  Cramlington NE23 . . . . . .22 C6
  Newcastle upon Tyne NE3. .38 E6
Turnbull Ho 8 SR5 . . . . . . .75 B1
Turnbull St NE1. . . . . 103 C4
Turnbull The NE1. . . . . . . 101 A4
Turner Ave NE34 . . . . .59 D2
Turner Cl NE40 . . . . .52 D4
Turner Cres NE3 . . . . .38 A5
Turner St NE27 . . . . .30 E1
Turners Way NE61. . . . . . . .3 D7
Turnham Rd SR3. . . . . .85 C1
Turnstile Mews 7 SR6 . . . .75 F2
Turnstone Dr NE38. . . . . . .82 F3
Turn The NE61. . . . . .8 F5
Turret Rd NE15 . . . . .53 F7
Tuscan Rd SR3 . . . . .91 C8
Tweed Av NE61 . . . . .1 E5
Tweed Cl SR2. . . . . .92 F8
Tweed Gr NE61 . . . . .9 E1
Tweed Gr NE15. . . . . .53 C7
Tweedmouth Ct 8 NE3 . . .38 E4
Tweed St
  Ashington NE63 . . . . .6 E4
  Chopwell NE17. . . . . .66 C1
  Easington Lane DH5 . . . . .97 C8
  Hebburn NE31. . . . . .57 E5
  Jarrow NE32 . . . . .58 A5
  Newcastle upon Tyne NE4. .98 A2
  Washington NE38 . . . . . .83 F4
Tweedy's Bldgs NE40. . . . .52 B2
Tweedy St NE24. . . . . .17 A8
Tweedy Terr NE6. . . . . .56 F6
Twelfth Ave
  Blyth NE24. . . . . .17 D6
  Chester le Street DH2. . . .88 B4
Twentyfifth Ave NE24. . . . .17 C5
Twentyfirst Ave NE24. . . . .17 C5
Twentysecond Ave NE24. . .17 C5
Twentysixth Ave NE24. . . . .17 C5
Twentythird Ave NE24. . . . .17 C5
Twickenham Ct SR3 . . . . . .85 C2
Twickenham Rd SR3. . . . . .85 C2
Twizell Ave NE21. . . . . .53 C3
Twizell Pl NE20. . . . . .25 E6
Twizell St NE24. . . . . .17 F6
Two Ball Lonnen NE4, NE5 .54 D8
Twyford Cl NE23 . . . . .22 B8
Tyldesley Sq SR3 . . . . .85 C1
Tyndal Gdns 4 NE11 . . . . .54 F1
Tyne App NE32 . . . . .58 A4
Tynebank NE21 . . . . .53 D2
Tyne Ct NE46. . . . . .45 A6

Tynedale Ave
Wallsend NE28 . . . . .40 B4
Whitley Bay NE26 . . . . .31 F6
Tynedale Cl
Heddon-on-the-Wall NE15 . .34 D1
Wylam NE41. . . . . .51 B6
Tynedale Cres DH4. . . . . .90 B7
Tynedale Dr NE24 . . . . .17 A7
Tynedale Gdns NE43 . . . . . . .64 D5
Tynedale Ho NE15 . . . . .54 B5
Tynedale Mews NE45. . . . . . .46 F5
Tynedale Rd
South Shields NE34 . . . . .59 F8
Sunderland SR3. . . . . .85 C1
Tynedale Ret Pk NE46. . . . . . .45 B5
Tynedale St DH5 . . . . .94 E1
Tynedale Terr
Hexham NE46 . . . . .44 F4
Newcastle upon Tyne NE12 . . .39 D6
Tyne Dock Sta NE33. . . . . . . .59 B6
Tyngate Office Precinct
NE8 . . . . .101 C2
Tyne Gdns
Ovingham NE42 . . . . .50 B4
Ryton NE40 . . . . .52 E4
Washington NE37 . . . . .72 D1
Tyne Green NE46 . . . . .45 A6
Tyne Green Ctry Pk*
NE46 . . . . .45 B6
Tyne Green Rd
Hexham NE46 . . . . .45 A6
Hexham NE46 . . . . .45 A6
Tyne Ho 20 SR3 . . . . .91 F6
Tynell Wlk NE3 . . . . .37 B5
Tyne Main Rd NE6, NE10 . . .56 C3
Tyne Metropolitan Coll
North Shields NE29 . . . . .41 F6
Wallsend NE28 . . . . .40 E5
Tyne Mills Ind Est NE46 . . . .45 C5
TYNEMOUTH. 42 B8
Tynemouth Castle* NE30. .42 E7
Tynemouth Cl 3 NE6 . . . . . .56 C7
Tynemouth Ct 7 NE6 . . . . . .56 C7
Tynemouth Gr 8 NE6 . . . . . .56 C7
Tynemouth Dr 6 NE30 . . . . .42 D7
Tynemouth Priory* NE30. .42 E7
Tynemouth Rd
Jarrow NE32 . . . . .58 B2
Newcastle upon Tyne NE6 . . .56 C7
North Shields NE30 . . . . .42 C6
Wallsend NE28 . . . . .41 A3
Tynemouth Sq SR3. . . . . .85 D1
Tynemouth Sta NE30 . . . . . .42 D7
Tynemouth St NE30 . . . . . . .42 D7
Tynemouth Watch House
(Mus)* NE30 . . . . .42 E7
Tynemouth Way 8 NE6 . . . .56 C7
Tyne Point Ind Est NE32 . . .58 E5
Tyne Riverside Ctry Pk*
Prudhoe NE42 . . . . .50 B3
Throckley NE15 . . . . .52 D8
Tyne Road E NE8 . . . . .100 C2
Tyneside Rd NE4 . . . . .100 B3
Tyne St
Ashington NE63 . . . . .6 E4
Blaydon NE21 . . . . .53 B1
Chopwell NE17 . . . . .66 B1
Easington Lane DH5 . . . . .97 C8
Gateshead, Bill Quay NE10 . .57 A2
Gateshead, Felling Shore
NE10 . . . . .56 E2
Gateshead, Pelaw NE10 . . . . .56 F2
Jarrow NE32 . . . . .58 B8
Newcastle upon Tyne NE1 . .56 A5
North Shields NE30 . . . . .42 B5
Tyne Terr NE34. . . . . .59 C5
Tyne Theatre & Opera
House* 1 NE1 . . . . .98 C1
Tyne Tunnel (Tynemouth)
Trad Est NE29 . . . . .41 B5
Tynevale Ave NE21 . . . . .53 C1
Tynevale Terr
Gateshead NE8 . . . . .100 C1
Newcastle upon Tyne NE15 . .53 C6
Tyne Valley Gdns NE40 . . . .52 A5
Tyne View
Blaydon NE21 . . . . .53 C1
Crawcrook NE40 . . . . .51 F7
Hebburn NE31. . . . . .57 C7
Newcastle upon Tyne NE15 . .53 D6
Wylam NE41. . . . . .51 B6
Tyne View Ave NE16 . . . . . . .69 C8
Tyne View Gdns NE10 . . . . .56 F1
Tyneview Park (DWP)*
NE12 . . . . .39 D5
Tyne View Pl NE8 . . . . .100 C1
Tyneview Prim Sch NE6. . . .57 A5
Tyneview Terr NE46 . . . . . . .45 C3
Tyne View Terr
North Shields NE28 . . . . .41 C1
Prudhoe NE42 . . . . .50 D3
Stocksfield NE43 . . . . .64 D7
Tyne Wlk NE15. . . . . .35 D1
Tynewold Cl NE18. . . . . .100 C1
Tyzack Cres SR6. . . . . .75 D2

U

Uldale Ct NE3 . . . . .37 E7
Ullswater Ave
Easington Lane DH5 . . . . .97 C8
Hedworth NE32. . . . . .58 D3
Ullswater Cl NE24. . . . . .16 E8

Ullswater Cres NE21 . . . . . . .68 B8
Ullswater Dr NE12 . . . . .29 F3
Ullswater Gdns NE34. . . . . . .59 D6
Ullswater Gr SR5 . . . . .75 C4
Ullswater Rd
Chester le Street DH2 . . . . .88 B1
Newbeggin-by-the-Sea NE64. .7 C3
Ullswater Terr NE6. . . . . .97 E8
Ullswater Way NE5. . . . . .54 B8
Ulverstone Terr NE6. . . . . . . .56 E7
Ulverston Gdns NE9. . . . . . . .71 B4
Umfraville Dene NE42. . . . . .50 D3
Underhill Dr NE62 . . . . .10 E6
Underhill Rd NE34 . . . . .59 F1
Underhill Terr NE9 . . . . .72 A4
Underwood NE10 . . . . .72 A6
Underwood Gr NE23 . . . . . . .16 A1
Underwood Rd NE44 . . . . . . .63 A7
Union Alley NE33. . . . . .42 C3
Union La SR1. . . . . .103 B3
Union Quay NE30 . . . . .42 C6
Union Rd
Newcastle upon Tyne NE6 . . .56 C6
North Shields NE30 . . . . .42 C6
Union St
Blyth NE24. . . . . .17 F7
Hetton-le-Hole DH5 . . . . .95 A4
Jarrow NE32 . . . . .58 B8
Newcastle upon Tyne NE2 . . .99 C2
South Shields NE33 . . . . .42 C3
South Shields NE33 . . . . .59 B6
Sunderland, South Hylton
SR4. . . . . .85 A6
Sunderland SR1 . . . . .103 A3
Wallsend NE28 . . . . .57 B8
Union Stairs NE30 . . . . .42 B5
Unity Hall NE33. . . . . .42 B2
Unity Terr
Cambois NE24 . . . . .12 D4
Tantobie DH9 . . . . .79 B2
University of Sunderland
Tech Pk SR2 . . . . .102 C2
University Sta SR1 . . . . .102 C2
Univ of Sunderland
(Ashburne House) SR2 . .86 D4
Univ of Sunderland (Bede
Tower) SR2 . . . . .103 A1
Univ of Sunderland (Sir Tom
Cowie Campus) SR6 . . . .103 B4
Univ of Sunderland (The City
Campus) SR1 . . . . .102 C2
Uplands NE25. . . . . .31 D5
Uplands The
Birtley DH3 . . . . .82 D5
Newcastle upon Tyne NE3 . . .37 F4
Uplands Way NE11 . . . . .71 F2
Upper Camden St 10
NE30 . . . . .42 A6
Upper Crone St NE27 . . . . . . .30 F4
Upper Elsdon St 6 NE29 . . . .42 A5
Upper Fenwick Gr NE61. . . . . .4 A2
Upper Norfolk St NE30 . . . . .42 B6
Upper Pearson St NE30 . . . . .42 B6
Upper Precinct The NE21. .53 D3
Upper Queen St NE30 . . . . . .42 B6
Upton St NE8 . . . . .100 C1
Urban Gdns NE37 . . . . .83 D7
Urfa Terr 4 NE33 . . . . .42 D4
URPETH 81 E2
Urswick Ct NE33. . . . . .37 B5
Urwin St DH5. . . . . .95 B3
Ushaw Rd NE31. . . . . .57 F6
Usher St 3 SR5 . . . . .75 B1
Usk Ave NE37. . . . . .83 A6
USWORTH 72 C1
Usworth Ave
Gateshead NE10 . . . . .71 C7
Longbenton NE12. . . . . .39 D7
Sunderland, Grangetown
SR2. . . . . .86 E2
Sunderland, South Hylton
SR4. . . . . .85 B6
Wallsend NE28 . . . . .40 B2
Whitley Bay NE26 . . . . .32 B5
Usworth Colliery Prim Sch
NE37 . . . . .72 E1
Usworth Cotts SR5. . . . . .73 D3
Usworth Grange Prim Sch
NE37 . . . . .72 F1
Usworth Hall NE37. . . . . .72 E2
Usworth Sixth Form Coll
NE37 . . . . .72 D2
Usworth Station Rd
4 Washington, Concord
NE37 . . . . .83 E8
Washington, Sulgrave NE37 . .83 F8
Uxbridge Terr 3 NE10 . . . . .56 D1

V

Valebrook NE46. . . . . .44 F4
Valebrook SR2. . . . . .102 C1
Valebrooke Ave SR2. . . . . . . .102 C1
Valebrooke Gdns SR2 . . . . . .102 C1
Valehead NE25. . . . . .31 D5
Vale Ho NE2. . . . . .56 A8
Valentia Ave NE6 . . . . .56 E7
Valeria Ct NE28. . . . . .40 A3
Valerian Ave NE15 . . . . .34 F2
Valerian Ct NE63. . . . . .6 B1
Valeshead Ho 10 NE28 . . . . .40 B2
Valeside NE15 . . . . .35 C2
Vale St
Easington Lane DH5 . . . . .97 B8
Sunderland SR4. . . . . .102 B1
Vale Street E SR4 . . . . .102 B1
Vale Wlk NE2 . . . . .56 A8
Valley Cres NE21. . . . . .53 A2
Valley Dene NE17. . . . . .77 B7
Valley Dr
Dunston NE11 . . . . .69 F7
Gateshead NE9 . . . . .70 F7
Whickham NE16. . . . . .69 A8

Valley Forge NE38 . . . . .83 D6
Valley Gardens Mid Sch
NE25 . . . . .31 D6
Valley Gdns
Gateshead NE9 . . . . .71 A7
Wallsend NE28 . . . . .40 D3
Whitley Bay NE26 . . . . .31 D5
Valley Gn NE40 . . . . .51 F2
Valley La NE34 . . . . .60 C6
Valley Rd NE25 . . . . .23 F2
Valley Road Com Prim Sch
SR2. . . . . .86 F4
Valley Shopping Village
NE11 . . . . .70 D4
Valley View
Birtley DH3 . . . . .82 B6
Burnopfield NE16. . . . . .78 F7
Hetton-le-Hole DH5 . . . . .94 D1
Hexham NE46 . . . . .45 C4
Jarrow NE32 . . . . .58 B4
Newcastle upon Tyne, Jesmond
NE2. . . . . .38 F1
Newcastle upon Tyne, Lemington
NE15 . . . . .35 D2
Prudhoe NE42 . . . . .50 E1
Rowlands Gill NE39 . . . . .67 D2
Washington NE38 . . . . .83 E1
Valley View Prim Sch
NE32 . . . . .58 B4
Vallum NE14 . . . . .98 B1
Vallum Pl NE9 . . . . .71 B6
Vallum Rd
Newcastle upon Tyne NE6 . . .56 E6
Throckley NE15 . . . . .35 E2
Vallum Way NE4 . . . . .98 B1
Vanborough Ct NE25 . . . . . . .23 D2
Vanburgh Gdns NE61. . . . . . . .8 D7
Vance Bsns Pk NE11 . . . . .70 B7
Vance Ct NE21. . . . . .53 E4
Vancouver Dr NE7 . . . . .39 D2
Vane St NE38 . . . . .92 A7
Vane Terr SR2 . . . . .103 C1
Vanguard Ct SR3. . . . . .91 F6
Vardy Terr NE38 . . . . .90 E6
Vauxhall Rd NE6. . . . . .57 A8
Vedra St 1 SR5 . . . . .75 B1
Velville Ct NE3. . . . . .37 B6
Venerable Bede CE Sec Sch
SR2. . . . . .92 F6
Ventnor Ave NE4 . . . . .54 F5
Ventnor Cres NE9 . . . . .70 E5
Ventnor Gdns
Gateshead NE9 . . . . .70 E6
Whitley Bay NE26 . . . . .32 A6
Vera St NE40 . . . . .66 F8
Verdun Ave NE31 . . . . .57 E6
Vermont NE37 . . . . .83 D8
Vermont Ho NE37. . . . . .83 E8
Verne Rd NE29. . . . . .41 D6
Vernon Cl NE23 . . . . .59 B8
Vernon Dr NE25 . . . . .31 E4
Vernon Pl NE64 . . . . .7 E5
Vernon St NE37 . . . . .83 D8
Veryan Gdns SR3 . . . . .86 B3
Vespasian Ave NE33. . . . . . . .42 D4
Vespasian St NE33 . . . . .42 D4
Viador DH3. . . . . .88 C4
Viaduct St NE28 . . . . .40 A4
Vicarage Cl SR3 . . . . .91 F7
Vicarage La SR4 . . . . .85 A6
Vicarage Rd SR3 . . . . .92 A7
Vicarage St NE29 . . . . .42 A4
Vicarage Terr NE22. . . . . .16 A8
Vicaridge Cl DH5 . . . . .95 A4
Vicarsholme Cl SR3 . . . . .91 E5
Vicars' La NE7 . . . . .39 A5
Vicars Ave
Gateshead NE10 . . . . .71 C7
Longbenton NE12. . . . . .39 D7
Sunderland, Grangetown
SR2. . . . . .86 E2
Sunderland, South Hylton
SR4. . . . . .85 B6
Wallsend NE28 . . . . .40 B2
Whitley Bay NE26 . . . . .32 B5
Victoria Avenue W SR2. . . . .86 E2
Victoria Bglws NE11 . . . . . . .100 A1
Victoria Bldgs SR1. . . . . .102 C2
Victoria Cres NE29 . . . . .23 D3
Victoria Cres
6 North Shields NE29 . . . . . .41 F5
Tynemouth NE30 . . . . .32 C3
Victoria Ct
Gateshead NE8 . . . . .100 C1
Hebburn NE31. . . . . .57 D5
Sunderland SR2. . . . . .102 C2
Washington NE37 . . . . .83 D8
Victoria Gr NE42. . . . . .50 E4
Victoria Ho
Blyth NE24. . . . . .17 D7
Newcastle upon Tyne NE2 . . .56 A8
Whickham NE16. . . . . .69 A7
Whitley Bay NE26 . . . . .32 B5
Victoria Pl
15 Chester le Street DH3 . . .88 C2
7 Washington NE37 . . . . .83 D8
Whitley Bay NE25 . . . . .31 E4
Victoria Rd
Gateshead NE8 . . . . .70 C8
South Shields NE33 . . . . .42 C1
Washington NE37 . . . . .83 D8
Victoria Road E NE31 . . . . . .57 F6
Victoria Road W NE31. . . . . .57 D4

Victoria Sq
4 Gateshead NE10 . . . . .71 D8
Newcastle upon Tyne NE2 . . .99 B3
Victoria St
Crawcrook NE40 . . . . .51 F4
Dunston NE11 . . . . .100 A1
Hebburn NE31. . . . . .57 C6
Hetton-le-Hole DH5 . . . . .95 A4
Newcastle upon Tyne NE4 . .100 B4
North Shields NE29 . . . . .42 A4
Victoria Terr
Bedlington NE22 . . . . .11 C1
East Boldon NE36 . . . . .74 C7
5 Gateshead, Felling NE10 . .71 D8
Gateshead, Wrekenton NE9 . .71 C3
Hamsterley NE17. . . . . .77 B6
Jarrow NE32 . . . . .58 B4
Newbeggin-by-the-Sea NE64. .7 E4
Penshaw DH4 . . . . .90 C8
Prudhoe NE42 . . . . .50 D2
Rowlands Gill NE39 . . . . .67 C1
14 Springwell NE9. . . . . .71 F1
3 Throckley NE15 . . . . .35 D2
Whitley Bay NE26 . . . . .32 B5
Victoria Villas NE11 . . . . .11 B1
Victor St
5 Chester le Street DH3 . . . .88 C3
6 Sunderland SR6 . . . . .75 E1
Victory Cotts NE23 . . . . .22 A1
Victory House 15 NE30 . . . . .42 D7
Victory St SR4 . . . . .85 E7
Victory Street E DH5 . . . . . . .95 B4
Victory Street W DH5. . . . . . .95 B4
Victory Way SR3 . . . . .91 C5
Viewforth Dr SR5 . . . . .75 C3
Viewforth Gn 1 NE5. . . . . . . .37 C1
Viewforth Rd SR2 . . . . .92 F5
Viewforth Terr SR5. . . . . .75 C3
Viewlands NE63. . . . . .6 D4
Vigodale DH3. . . . . .82 E1
Vigo La
Birtley DH3 . . . . .88 D8
Washington NE38 . . . . .83 A1
Washington NE38 . . . . .83 B1
Viking Ind Est NE32. . . . . . . .58 A8
Viking Precinct 8 NE32. . . . .58 B7
Villa Cl SR4. . . . . .85 F6
Village Ctr NE26 . . . . .31 F5
Village Ctr
Washington, Biddick NE38. .83 F4
Washington, Donwell NE37 . .72 B1
Washington, Glebe NE38. . .83 D5
Washington, Lambton NE38 .83 B3
Village East NE40 . . . . .52 D8
Village Farm NE15 . . . . .36 A1
Village Hts NE8. . . . . .101 B2
Village La NE38. . . . . .83 D6
Village Pl NE6 . . . . .56 D5
Village Rd NE23 . . . . .22 C6
Village The SR2. . . . . .93 A6
Villa Pl NE8 . . . . .101 B1
Villas The
Ryhope SR2 . . . . .92 F5
Stannington NE61 . . . . .13 C7
7 Sunderland SR5 . . . . .74 C1
Wideopen NE13 . . . . .28 C5
Village Terr NE9 . . . . .71 A6
Villette Brook St 6 SR2. . . . .86 E4
Villette Path SR2 . . . . .86 E4
Villette Rd SR2 . . . . .86 E4
Villiers Pl 3 DH3 . . . . .88 C4
Villiers St SR1. . . . . .103 B3
Villiers Street S SR1 . . . . . . .103 B2
Vimy Ave NE31. . . . . .57 E6
Vindolanda 2 NE25 . . . . .23 D2
Vindomora Road DH8, ...76 E4
Vine Cl NE8 . . . . .100 C1
Vine Ct NE46. . . . . .45 B4
Vine La NE1 . . . . .99 A2
Vine Pl
8 Houghton-le-Spring
DH4. . . . . .94 E8
Sunderland SR1. . . . . .102 C2
Vine St
South Shields NE33 . . . . .59 C6
Wallsend NE28 . . . . .40 C1
Vine Terr NE46 . . . . .45 A4
Viola Cres DH2 . . . . .81 F2
Viola St NE37. . . . . .83 D8
Viola Terr NE16 . . . . .69 B7
Violet Cl NE14. . . . . .54 D4
Violet St
8 Houghton-le-Spring
DH4. . . . . .94 D8
Sunderland, South Hylton
SR4. . . . . .85 A6
Sunderland SR4. . . . . .102 B3
Violet Terr DH4. . . . . .89 D3
Viscount Rd 4 SR2 . . . . .92 A7
Vivian Cres DH2 . . . . .81 E1
Volary Gr NE24 . . . . .17 F4
Voltage Terr DH4 . . . . .90 D4
Vulcan Pl
Bedlington NE22 . . . . .16 A8
Sunderland SR5. . . . . .75 D1
Vulcan Terr NE12 . . . . .29 E1

W

Wade Ave NE15 . . . . .33 A7
Wadham Ct SR2 . . . . .92 E7
Wadham Terr NE34. . . . . .59 B5
Wadsley Sq SR2 . . . . .86 E3
Waggonway The 1 NE42. .50 D3

Wagon Way NE28 . . . . .40 D1
Wagonway Rd NE31. . . . . .57 E7
Wagtail Cl NE21 . . . . .68 C8
Wakefield Ave NE34. . . . . .60 B5
WALBOTTLE. 35 E2
Walbottle Brickworks Nature
Reserve* NE15. . . . . .53 A8
Walbottle Campus Tech Coll
NE15 . . . . .35 F2
Walbottle Dene Nature
Reserve* NE15. . . . . .35 E2
Walbottle Hall Gdns NE15 .36 A1
Walbottle Prim Sch NE15 . .35 F1
Walbottle Rd
Newburn NE15. . . . . .52 F8
Newburn NE15. . . . . .35 F1
Walcher Gr 8 NE8. . . . . .56 B1
Walden Cl NE37 . . . . .81 D2
Waldo St NE29. . . . . .42 B5
Waldridge Cl NE37. . . . . .83 A6
Waldridge Gdns NE9 . . . . . . .71 D4
Waldridge La DH2 . . . . .88 A2
Waldridge Rd DH2 . . . . .88 B2
Waldron Sq SR2 . . . . .86 E3
WALKER 56 F6
Walkerburn NE23 . . . . .22 B3
Walker Gr 11 NE16 . . . . .69 A7
Walkerdene Ho NE6. . . . . . . .57 B8
WALKERGATE 56 E8
Walker Gate Ind Est NE6 . .56 E8
Walkergate Park Hospl
NE6 . . . . .56 E8
Walkergate Prim Sch NE6 .56 E8
Walkergate Sta NE6. . . . . . . .56 E8
Walker Gr NE6. . . . . .56 E7
Walker Park Cl NE6 . . . . .57 A4
Walker Park Gdns NE6 . . . . .57 A4
Walker Pl NE30 . . . . .42 C6
Walker Rd NE6 . . . . .56 E5
Walker Riverside Ind Pk
NE6 . . . . .57 B4
Walker Riverside Pk*
NE6 . . . . .56 F3
Walkers Bldgs 22 NE29 . . . .42 A5
Walker Tech Coll NE6 . . . . . .56 F6
Walker Terr NE8 . . . . .101 B3
Walker View NE10. . . . . .71 B8
WALKERVILLE 39 F1
Wallace Ave NE16. . . . . .69 C8
Wallace Gn NE16 . . . . .71 E3
Wallace St
Dunston NE11 . . . . .100 A1
Houghton-le-Spring DH4 . . . .94 D8
Newcastle upon Tyne NE2 . . .98 B4
Sunderland SR5. . . . . .75 C1
Wallace Terr NE40 . . . . .52 C6
Wall Cl NE3 . . . . .38 A5
Waller Terr DH5. . . . . .94 E7
Wallinfen NE10 . . . . .71 F5
Wallingford Ave SR2 . . . . . . .86 E2
Wallington Ave
Brunswick Village NE13. . . . . .28 A6
Tynemouth NE30 . . . . .32 A1
Wallington Cl
Bedlington NE22 . . . . .11 C2
Blaydon NE21 . . . . .53 C2
Wallington Ct
Killingworth NE12 . . . . .29 C3
Newcastle upon Tyne NE3 . . .37 D7
Seaton Delaval NE25. . . . . .23 D3
Tynemouth NE30 . . . . .32 B1
Wallington Dr NE15. . . . . .53 E8
Wallington Gr 9 NE33 . . . . . .42 D3
Wallington Rd NE63 . . . . .6 F2
Wallis St
Penshaw DH4 . . . . .90 B8
12 South Shields NE33 . . . . .42 C3
Wallridge Dr NE25 . . . . .23 E1
WALLSEND 40 D2
Wallsend CE Prim Sch
NE28 . . . . .40 D2
Wallsend Dene Nature
Reserve* NE28. . . . . .40 C3
Wallsend Jubilee Prim Sch
NE28 . . . . .40 A4
Wallsend Rd
North Shields NE29 . . . . .41 C3
North Shields NE29 . . . . .41 D4
Wall St NE3 . . . . .38 A5
Wallmer Terr NE9. . . . . .56 E7
Walmer Terr NE9. . . . . .71 D1
Walnut Gdns NE8 . . . . .70 C8
Walnut Pl NE3 . . . . .37 F3
Walpole Cl 1 SR4 . . . . .85 F6
Walpole St
Newcastle upon Tyne NE6 . . .56 E8
South Shields NE33 . . . . .59 D1
Walsham Cl NE24. . . . . .17 B5
Walsh Ave NE31 . . . . .57 E7
Walsingham NE38. . . . . .83 C4
Walter St
Brunswick Village NE13. . . . . .28 A6
Jarrow NE32 . . . . .58 B7
Walter Terr
Hetton-le-Hole DH5 . . . . .95 B1
Newcastle upon Tyne NE4 . . .54 C6
Walter Thomas St 3 SR5 . .74 F2
Waltham NE38. . . . . .83 D4
Waltham Cl NE28 . . . . .39 F3
Waltham Pl 4 NE5 . . . . .37 B2
Walton Ave
Blyth NE24. . . . . .17 C8
Tynemouth NE29 . . . . .41 F7
Walton Dr NE62. . . . . .10 F8
Walton La SR1. . . . . .103 B3
Walton Pk NE29 . . . . .41 F8

Walton Rd
  Newcastle upon Tyne NE5 . . . .37 A1
  Washington NE38 . . . . .84 B5
Walton Terr DH8 . . . . .76 E4
Walwick Ave NE29 . . . . .41 D6
Walwick Rd NE25 . . . . .31 B5
Walworth Ave NE34 . . . . .60 C6
Walworth Gr NE22 . . . . .58 B3
Wandsworth Rd NE6 . . . . .56 B7
Wanless La NE46 . . . . .45 B4
Wanley St NE24 . . . . .17 E8
Wanlock Cl NE23 . . . . .22 C3
Wanny Rd NE22 . . . . .11 B1
Wansbeck NE38 . . . . .83 A1
Wansbeck Ave
  Blyth NE24 . . . . .17 E5
  Stakeford NE62 . . . . .11 A8
  Tynemouth NE30 . . . . .32 C2
Wansbeck Bsns Pk NE63 . . . .6 B5
Wansbeck Cl
  Ellington NE61 . . . . .1 E5
  Sunniside NE16 . . . . .69 A3
Wansbeck Cres NE61 . . . . .4 E3
Wansbeck Ct
  Bedlington NE22 . . . . .16 A8
  16 Newcastle upon Tyne NE3 . .91 F6
Wansbeck Fst Sch NE63 . . . . .6 C4
Wansbeck General Hospl
  NE63 . . . . .6 F4
Wansbeck Gr NE25 . . . . .23 D6
Wansbeck Ho NE15 . . . . .53 C6
Wansbeck Mews
  Ashington NE63 . . . . .6 B4
  South Shields NE34 . . . . .59 C5
Wansbeck Pl NE61 . . . . .3 E1
Wansbeck Rd
  Ashington NE63 . . . . .6 B2
  Dudley NE23 . . . . .28 F8
  Jarrow NE32 . . . . .58 B5
  Newcastle upon Tyne NE3 . . .38 A6
Wansbeck Riverside Pk*
  NE63 . . . . .5 F1
Wansbeck Road S NE3 . . . . . .38 A6
Wansbeck Road Sta NE3 . . . . .6 C4
Wansbeck Sh Ctr NE63 . . . . . .6 C4
Wansbeck Sq NE63 . . . . .6 C4
Wansbeck St
  Ashington NE63 . . . . .12 A8
  Chopwell NE17 . . . . .66 C1
  Newcastle upon Tyne NE3 . . .9 A8
Wansbeck Terr NE62 . . . . .11 D7
Wansbeck View NE61 . . . . . . .11 B8
Wansdyke NE61 . . . . .3 D1
Wansfell Ave NE5 . . . . .37 D3
Wansford Ave NE5 . . . . .37 B1
Wansford Way
  Whickham NE16 . . . . .68 F5
  Whickham NE16 . . . . .69 A4
Wantage Ave NE29 . . . . .41 D6
Wantage St NE33 . . . . .59 D7
Wapping 1 NE24 . . . . .17 F8
Wapping St NE33 . . . . .42 B4
Warbeck Cl NE3 . . . . .37 B6
Warburton Cres NE9 . . . . .71 A8
Warcop Ct NE3 . . . . .37 E7
Ward Ct SR2 . . . . .103 B1
Warden Gr DH5 . . . . .94 F7
Wardenlaw NE10 . . . . .71 F5
Warden Law La SR3 . . . . .91 F6
Wardill Gdns NE9 . . . . .71 B7
Wardle Ave NE33 . . . . .42 E1
Wardle Dr NE23 . . . . .29 B8
Wardle Gdns NE10 . . . . .71 E7
Wardle St NE3 . . . . .38 E5
Wardle Terr NE40 . . . . .51 F4
WARDLEY 72 B8
Wardley Cl NE10 . . . . .72 D8
Wardley Dr NE10 . . . . .72 D7
Wardley La NE10, NE31 . . . . .57 C1
Wardley Prim Sch NE10 . . .72 B8
Wardroper Ho NE6 . . . . .57 A4
Warenford Cl NE23 . . . . .22 C4
Warenford Pl NE5 . . . . .54 C7
Warenmill Cl NE15 . . . . .53 B7
Warennes St 3 SR4 . . . . .85 C7
Warenton Pl NE29 . . . . .31 B1
Waring Ave NE26 . . . . .24 B7
Wark Ave
  North Shields NE29 . . . . .41 C6
  Shiremoor NE27 . . . . .30 F4
Wark Cres NE32 . . . . .58 B2
Wark Ct 9 NE3 . . . . .38 E4
Warkdale Ave NE24 . . . . .17 A6
Wark St DH3 . . . . .88 C1
Warkworth Ave
  Blyth NE24 . . . . .17 E5
  South Shields NE34 . . . . .60 B7
  Wallsend NE28 . . . . .40 C4
  Whitley Bay NE26 . . . . .32 A5
Warkworth Cl NE38 . . . . .83 B4
Warkworth Cres
  Ashington NE63 . . . . .6 C3
  Newcastle upon Tyne NE3 . . .38 B6
Warkworth Dr
  Chester le Street DH2 . . . . . .88 A1
  Ellington NE61 . . . . .1 A7
  Pegswood NE61 . . . . .4 F3
  Widdeopen NE13 . . . . .37 D4
Warkworth Gdns NE10 . . . . .71 C8
Warkworth La NE61 . . . . .1 C1
Warkworth St
  3 Newcastle upon Tyne, Byker
    NE6 .56 C6
  Newcastle upon Tyne, Lemington
    NE15 . . . . .53 C6
Warkworth Terr
  Jarrow NE32 . . . . .58 B3

  Tynemouth NE30 . . . . .42 D8
Warkworth Woods NE3 . . . .28 B2
Warnham Ave SR2 . . . . .86 E2
Warnhead Rd NE22 . . . . .11 B1
Warren Ave NE6 . . . . .57 A8
Warren Cl DH4 . . . . .90 C4
Warren Ct NE63 . . . . .6 C2
Warrenmoor NE10 . . . . .72 A7
Warren Sq SR1 . . . . .103 C4
Warrens Wlk NE21 . . . . .53 A1
Warrington Rd
  Newcastle upon Tyne, Elswick
    NE4 . . . . .100 A4
  Newcastle upon Tyne, Fawdon
    NE3 .37 B6
Warton Terr NE6 . . . . .56 C8
Warwick Ave NE16 . . . . .69 B5
Warwick Cl
  Seghill NE23 . . . . .22 E1
  Whickham NE16 . . . . .69 A5
Warwick Ct
  Gateshead NE8 . . . . .101 C2
  Newcastle upon Tyne NE3 . . .37 D7
Warwick Dr
  Houghton-le-Spring DH5 . . . .94 E7
  Sunderland SR3 . . . . .91 C7
  Washington NE37 . . . . .72 D2
  Whickham NE16 . . . . .69 B5
Warwick Gr NE22 . . . . .10 D1
Warwick Hall Wlk NE7 . . . .39 D3
Warwick Rd
  Hebburn NE31 . . . . .57 F3
  Newcastle upon Tyne NE5 . . .53 E8
  South Shields NE34 . . . . .59 D7
  Wallsend NE28 . . . . .40 B1
Warwick St
  Blyth NE24 . . . . .17 C4
  Gateshead NE8 . . . . .101 C2
  Newcastle upon Tyne NE6 . . .56 A7
  Sunderland SR5 . . . . .75 D1
Warwick Terr SR3 . . . . .92 A8
Warwick Terrace W SR3 . . . .92 A8
Wasdale Ct NE23 . . . . .22 C3
Wasdale Ct SR6 . . . . .75 C5
Wasdale Rd NE5 . . . . .54 B8
WASHINGTON 83 F7
Washington Arts Ctr
  NE38 .83 D2
Washington 'F' Pit Mus*
  NE37 .83 C7
Washington Gdns NE9 . . . . .71 C3
Washington Highway
  Penshaw DH4, NE38 . . . . . . .89 C8
  Washington NE37, NE38 . . . . .83 F1
Washington Hospl (BUPA)
  NE38 .88 E8
Washington Millennium Ctr
  NE37 .83 D8
Washington Old Hall*
  NE38 .83 E6
Washington Sch NE37 . . . . . . .74 B2
Washington Sch NE37 . . . . . . .83 D7
Washington St NE34 . . . . .85 F6
Washington Terr NE30 . . . . . .42 C7
WASHINGTON VILLAGE 83 F7
Washington Wetland Ctr*
  NE38 .84 C5
Washingwell Comm Prim Sch
  NE16 .69 C6
Washingwell La NE16 . . . . . .69 D6
Washingwell Pk NE16 . . . . . .69 C6
Waskdale Cres NE11 . . . . .68 B8
Waskerley Cl NE16 . . . . .69 B3
Waskerley Gdns 3 NE9 . . .71 D3
Waskerley Rd NE38 . . . . .83 B5
Watch House Cl NE29 . . . . . . .42 A3
Watcombe Cl NE37 . . . . .72 F2
Waterbeach Pl NE5 . . . . .37 B2
Waterbeck Cl NE23 . . . . .22 C3
Waterbury Cl SR5 . . . . .74 F3
Waterbury Rd NE3 . . . . .28 B1
Waterfield Rd NE22 . . . . .12 B4
Waterford Cl
  East Rainton DH5 . . . . .94 D4
  Seaton Sluice NE26 . . . . .24 D6
Waterford Cres 6 NE26 . . .32 B4
Waterford Green SR4 . . . . . . .85 B4
Waterford Pk NE13 . . . . .27 F6
Watergate NE1 . . . . .101 B4
Watergate Bank NE11 . . . . . .69 E4
Water La NE15 . . . . .50 C8
Waterloo Ct 6 NE37 . . . . . . .83 E8
Waterloo Pl
  North Shields NE29 . . . . .42 A6
  Sunderland SR1 . . . . 103 A2
Waterloo Rd
  Blyth NE24 . . . . .17 E7
  Earsdon NE25 . . . . .31 A5
  Washington NE37 . . . . .72 F3
  Washington, Sulgrave NE37 . .72 E1
Waterloo Sq
  Newcastle upon Tyne
    NE1 . . . . .100 C4
  10 South Shields NE33 . . . . .42 C3
Waterloo St
  Blaydon NE21 . . . . .53 A1
  Newcastle upon Tyne NE1 . .100 C4
Waterloo Vale 3 NE33 . . . . . .42 C3
Waterloo Wlk NE37 . . . . .83 E8
Waterlow Cl SR5 . . . . .74 F4
Watermark The NE11 . . . . . . .54 C3
Watermill NE46 . . . . .52 C5
Watermill La NE10 . . . . .71 E8
Watermill Pk NE10 . . . . .71 D7
Water Row NE15 . . . . .52 E7
Waterside 8 NE61 . . . . .8 F8

Waterside Dr NE11 . . . . .54 E2
Waterside Pk NE31 . . . . .57 C6
Water St NE4 . . . . .100 B3
Waterville Pl 16 NE29 . . . . . .42 A5
Waterville Prim Sch NE29 . .41 F4
Waterville Rd NE29 . . . . .41 E4
Waterville Terr 8 NE29 . . . .42 A5
Waterworks Rd
  Ryhope SR2 . . . . .92 F5
  Seaham Grange SR7 . . . . . . .92 F3
  Sunderland SR1 . . . . 102 C2
Waterworks The SR2 . . . . .92 E5
Watford Cl SR5 . . . . .74 F4
Watling Pl NE9 . . . . .71 B6
Watling St NE45 . . . . .46 F5
Watson Ave
  Dudley NE23 . . . . .29 A8
  South Shields NE34 . . . . .60 B5
Watson Gdns NE28 . . . . .41 A3
Watson Pl NE34 . . . . .60 B5
Watson St
  Burnopfield NE16 . . . . .79 B6
  Gateshead NE8 . . . . .100 C1
  High Spen NE39 . . . . .67 A5
  Jarrow NE32 . . . . .58 C8
Watson Terr
  Boldon Colliery NE35 . . . . . . .73 F7
  17 Morpeth NE61 . . . . .9 A8
Watt's La NE64 . . . . .7 E5
Watts Moses Ho SR1 . . . . . .103 C3
Watt's Rd NE26 . . . . .32 A6
Watt St NE8 . . . . .70 D7
Wavendon Cres SR4 . . . . .85 E4
Waverdale Ave NE6 . . . . .57 A7
Waverdale Way NE33 . . . . . . .59 B7
Waverley Ave
  Bedlington NE22 . . . . .11 B1
  Bedlington NE22 . . . . .11 C2
  Whitley Bay NE25 . . . . .31 C4
Waverley Bus Pk NE33 . . . . .42 C3
Waverley Cl NE15 . . . . .53 D7
Waverley Cres NE15 . . . . .53 D7
Waverley Ct NE22 . . . . .11 C1
Waverley Dr NE22 . . . . .11 C2
Waverley Lodge NE2 . . . . . . .99 C3
Waverley Pl NE4 . . . . .99 C3
Waverley Prim Sch NE15 . .53 E6
Waverley Rd
  Gateshead NE9 . . . . .71 B1
  Newcastle upon Tyne NE4 . .100 B4
Waverley Terr
  Dipton DH9 . . . . .78 E1
  Sunderland SR3 . . . . .92 A8
Waverly Dr NE22 . . . . .11 D2
Waverton Cl NE23 . . . . .22 A3
Wawn St NE33 . . . . .59 D8
Wayfarer Rd SR5 . . . . .75 A1
Wayland Sq SR2 . . . . .86 E1
Wayman St SR5 . . . . .75 C1
Wayside
  Newcastle upon Tyne
    NE15 . . . . .50 B6
  South Shields NE34 . . . . .60 B6
  Sunderland SR2 . . . . .86 B4
Wealcroft NE10 . . . . .71 F5
Wealcroft Ct NE10 . . . . .71 F5
Wealleans Cl NE63 . . . . .7 B3
Wear Ct NE34 . . . . .75 C5
Weardale Ave
  Blyth NE24 . . . . .17 A8
  Longbenton NE12 . . . . .39 D8
  Newcastle upon Tyne NE6 . . .57 A6
  Sunderland SR6 . . . . .75 C2
  Wallsend NE28 . . . . .40 B4
Weardale Cres DH4 . . . . .90 B7
Weardale St DH5 . . . . .94 E1
Weardale Terr DH3 . . . . .88 D2
Wearfield SR5 . . . . .74 F1
Wearhead Dr SR4 . . . . 102 B1
Wear Ind Est NE38 . . . . .83 B2
Wear Lodge DH3 . . . . .88 C7
Wearmouth Ave SR5 . . . . .75 D2
Wearmouth Dr SR5 . . . . .75 D2
Wearmouth St SR6 . . . . .75 D3
Wear Rd NE31 . . . . .57 E3
Wear St
  Chester le Street DH3 . . . . . .88 D2
  Chopwell NE17 . . . . .66 B1
  Fence Houses DH4 . . . . .94 A1
  Hetton-le-Hole DH5 . . . . .95 A3
  Jarrow NE32 . . . . .58 B7
  Sunderland, Deptford 103 C2
  Sunderland, Low Southwick
    SR5 .75 A1
  Sunderland, South Hylton
    SR4 .85 A7
Wear Terr NE38 . . . . .83 E4
Wear View SR4 . . . . .85 B7
Weathercock La NE9 . . . . .70 F5
Weatherside NE21 . . . . .53 B1
Webb Gdns NE10 . . . . .72 A8
Wedderburn Sq NE63 . . . . .6 C3
Wedder Law NE23 . . . . .22 B3
Wedgewood Cotts NE15 . . .53 D6
Wedmore Rd NE5 . . . . .36 D3
Weetman St NE33 . . . . .59 D8
Weetslade Cres NE23 . . . . . . .29 A7
Weetslade Ind Est NE23 . . . .28 F5
Weetslade Rd NE23 . . . . .29 A7
Weetslade Terr NE23 . . . . .29 B5
Weetwood Rd NE23 . . . . .22 C4
Weidner Rd NE15, NE4 . . . . . .54 D6
Welbeck Com Fst Sch
  NE63 . . . . .7 A2
Welbeck Gn NE6 . . . . .56 E5
Welbeck Prim Sch NE6 . . . .56 D5

Welbeck Rd
  Guide Post NE62 . . . . .10 E7
  Newcastle upon Tyne NE6 . . .56 E5
Welbeck Terr
  Ashington NE63 . . . . .6 D2
  Pegswood NE61 . . . . .4 F4
Welburn Cl NE42 . . . . .50 C5
Welbury Way NE23 . . . . .22 B3
Weldon Ave SR2 . . . . .86 E2
Weldon Cres NE7 . . . . .39 B2
Weldon Pl NE29 . . . . .41 D8
Weldon Rd
  East Cramlington NE23 . . . . .22 E5
  Longbenton NE12 . . . . .39 B6
Weldon Terr DH3 . . . . .88 D2
Weldon Way NE3 . . . . .38 B6
Welfare Cres
  Ashington NE63 . . . . .6 F3
  Newbeggin-by-the-Sea NE64 .7 C4
Welfare Rd DH5 . . . . .95 A4
Welford Ave NE3 . . . . .38 A5
Wellands Cl SR6 . . . . .60 E1
Wellands Ct SR6 . . . . .60 E1
Wellands Dr SR6 . . . . .60 E1
Wellands La SR6 . . . . .60 E1
Well Bank NE45 . . . . .46 F5
Well Bank Rd NE37 . . . . .72 B1
Wellburn Rd NE37 . . . . .72 B1
Well Close Wlk NE16 . . . . . . .69 A6
Well Dean NE42 . . . . .50 D3
Wellesley St NE32 . . . . .58 B5
Wellesley Terr NE4 . . . . .98 A1
WELLFIELD 37 C4
Wellfield Cl NE15 . . . . .35 C1
Wellfield Ct NE40 . . . . .51 E3
Wellfield La NE5 . . . . .37 B2
Wellfield Mews NE22 . . . . . . .11 D2
Wellfield Mid Sch NE25 . . .31 B4
Wellfield Rd
  Newcastle upon Tyne NE4 . . .54 D5
  Rowlands Gill NE39 . . . . .67 C2
Wellfield Terr
  3 Gateshead NE10 . . . . .71 C7
  Newcastle upon Tyne NE10 . .71 C8
  Ryhope SR2 . . . . .92 F6
Wellgarth Rd NE37 . . . . .72 B1
Wellhead Dean Rd NE62 . . . .5 F2
Wellhead Terr NE63 . . . . .6 A4
Wellhope NE38 . . . . .88 F8
Wellington Ave NE25 . . . . . . .31 A5
Wellington Ct
  6 Gateshead NE10 . . . . .71 C8
  6 Washington NE37 . . . . . . .83 E8
Wellington Dr NE33 . . . . .42 C4
Wellington La SR4 . . . . 102 B4
Wellington Pl 1 NE32 . . . . .58 C7
Wellington Rd
  Dunston NE11 . . . . .54 E1
  Dunston NE11 . . . . .54 F1
  Stakeford NE62 . . . . .11 A7
Wellington Row DH4 . . . . . . .90 C5
Wellington St
  Blyth NE24 . . . . .17 C4
  Gateshead, Felling NE10 . . . .71 C8
  Gateshead NE8 . . . . .101 B3
  Hebburn NE31 . . . . .57 D5
  High Pittington DH6 . . . . .96 B5
  Lemington NE15 . . . . .53 D6
Wellington Street E 10
  NE29 .17 F8
Wellington Street W 12
  NE29 .42 A5
Wellington Wlk 2 NE37 . . .83 F8
Well La
  Gateshead NE9 . . . . .70 F4
  Tynemouth NE27 . . . . .31 B2
  Tynemouth NE27 . . . . .31 C2
Wellmere Rd SR2 . . . . .86 F1
Well Rd NE43 . . . . .64 A5
Well Ridge Cl NE25 . . . . .31 C6
Well Ridge Pk NE25 . . . . .31 C7
Wells Cl NE12 . . . . .29 C4
Wells Gdns NE9 . . . . .70 F2
Wells Gr NE34 . . . . .60 A8
Wellshede NE10 . . . . .72 B7
Wells St NE35 . . . . .58 E1
Well St SR4 . . . . .85 F7
Wellsway 8 NE61 . . . . .3 F1
Wellwood Gdns NE61 . . . . . . .4 A1
Welton Cl NE43 . . . . .64 D6
Welworth Way SR1 . . . . .102 C3
Welwyn Ave NE22 . . . . .11 D3
Welwyn Cl
  Sunderland SR5 . . . . .85 A8
  Wallsend NE28 . . . . .39 F4
Wembley Ave NE25 . . . . .31 C6
Wembley Cl SR5 . . . . .74 F3
Wembley Gdns NE24 . . . . . . .12 B6
Wembley Rd SR5 . . . . .74 F3
Wembley Terr NE24 . . . . .12 C6
Wendover Cl SR5 . . . . .74 C4
Wendover Way SR5 . . . . .74 C4
Wenham Sq SR2 . . . . .86 B4
Wenlock NE38 . . . . .87 D8
Wenlock Dr NE29 . . . . .41 D6
Wenlock Pl 6 NE34 . . . . .59 A4
Wenlock Rd NE34 . . . . .59 A4
Wensley Cl
  Newcastle upon Tyne NE5 . . .37 C4
  Urpeth DH2 . . . . .81 C1
Wensleydale NE28 . . . . .39 F5

Wensleydale Ave
  Penshaw DH4 . . . . .90 A7
  Washington DH37 . . . . .83 C8
Wensleydale Dr NE12 . . . . . .39 D8
Wensleydale Mid Sch
  NE24 .17 F6
Wensleydale Terr NE24 . . . . .17 F6
Wensley Ho 2 SR3 . . . . .91 F5
Wensley Pl NE3 . . . . .42 E1
Wentworth Cl NE10 . . . . .71 D7
Wentworth Ct NE10 . . . . .25 C4
Wentworth Dr NE37 . . . . .72 C2
Wentworth Gdns NE25 . . . . .31 C4
Wentworth Grange NE33 . . .38 D4
Wentworth L Ctr NE46 . . . . .45 B5
Wentworth Pl
  Hexham NE46 . . . . .45 B5
  Newcastle upon Tyne NE4 . .100 B4
Wentworth Terr SR4 . . . . 102 B3
Werhale Gn NE10 . . . . .71 D8
Wesley Cl
  Blaydon NE21 . . . . .53 D3
  1 Gateshead, Felling NE10 . .71 C8
Wesley Dr NE12 . . . . .30 B1
Wesley Mount NE40 . . . . .51 E3
Wesley Sq NE11 . . . . .101 C4
Wesley St
  Gateshead, Low Fell NE9 . . .70 F5
  Newcastle upon Tyne NE2 . . .99 C2
  Prudhoe NE42 . . . . .50 D2
  15 South Shields NE33 . . . . .42 C3
Wesley Terr
  Chester le Street DH3 . . . . . .88 C3
  Dipton DH9 . . . . .78 D1
  Prudhoe NE42 . . . . .50 D2
  Sherburn Hill DH6 . . . . .96 C1
Wesley Way
  Longbenton NE12 . . . . .30 B1
  Throckley NE15 . . . . .35 D2
Wessex Cl SR5 . . . . .74 F4
Wessington Prim Sch
  NE38 .83 D5
Wessington Terr NE37 . . . . . .83 D7
Wessington Way
  Sunderland, Castletown
    SR5 .85 B8
  Sunderland SR5 . . . . .74 E1
Westacre Gdns NE9 . . . . .54 C7
West Acres
  Blaydon NE21 . . . . .53 D2
  Dinnington NE13 . . . . .27 B8
Westacres Ave NE16 . . . . .69 B5
Westacres Cres NE15 . . . . . . .54 C6
WEST ALLOTMENT 30 E1
West Ave
  Guide Post NE62 . . . . .10 D7
  Longbenton, Forest Hall
    NE12 . . . . .29 F1
  Longbenton NE12 . . . . .39 D6
  Newcastle upon Tyne, Gosforth
    NE3 .38 C4
  Newcastle upon Tyne NE3 . . .38 C4
  North Shields NE29 . . . . .41 D5
  Rowlands Gill NE39 . . . . .67 C1
  South Shields NE34 . . . . .59 E6
  Washington NE38 . . . . .83 B1
  Whitley Bay NE25 . . . . .31 C5
West Bailey NE12 . . . . .29 B3
West Boldon NE36 . . . . .74 A8
WEST BOLDON 74 A8
West Boldon Prim Sch
  NE36 .74 A7
Westbourne Ave
  Gateshead NE8 . . . . .70 E8
  Newcastle upon Tyne, Gosforth
    NE3 .38 C7
  3 Newcastle upon Tyne
    NE6 .57 A6
  Newcastle upon Tyne, Walker
    NE6 .56 F7
  Stakeford NE62 . . . . .6 A1
Westbourne Cotts 11 DH4 . .90 A1
Westbourne Gdns 2 NE6 . .57 A6
Westbourne Gr NE34 . . . . . . .44 . .75
Westbourne Rd SR1 . . . . 102 B2
Westbourne Terr
  Seaton Delaval NE25 . . . . . . .23 E3
  2 Shiney Row DH4 . . . . .90 A6
West Bridge St
  Cambois NE24 . . . . .12 D3
  Penshaw DH4 . . . . .89 E8
Westbrooke 2 SR2 . . . . .86 D4
West Brunton Farm Cotts
  NE13 .27 D2
Westburn Gdns NE28 . . . . . . .39 F4
Westburn Mews NE40 . . . . . .51 E3
Westbury Ave NE6 . . . . .57 A8
Westbury Ct NE25 . . . . .39 A5
Westbury Rd NE29 . . . . .41 F8
Westbury St SR4 . . . . 102 B3
WEST CHIRTON 41 C6
West Chirton Ind Est
  NE29 .41 C5
West Chirton North Ind Est
  NE29 .41 B7
West Chirton Trading Ind Est
  NE29 .41 B6
Westcliffe Rd SR6 . . . . .75 F4
Westcliffe Way NE34 . . . . .58 F3
West Clifton NE12 . . . . .29 C4
West Copperas NE15 . . . . . . .53 F7
Westcott Ave NE33 . . . . .42 E1

Westcott Rd NE34........59 C6
Westcott Terr DH4........90 C8
West Cres
  Chopwell NE17...........77 B7
  Gateshead NE10..........72 C8
Westcroft SR6............60 E1
Westcroft Rd NE12........39 E8
West Ct NE24.............17 C6
West Dene Dr NE30.......42 A2
WEST DENTON............36 D1
West Denton CI NE15......36 D1
West Denton Fst Sch NE5..36 D1
West Denton Rd NE15.....53 D8
West Denton Ret Pk NE5...37 A2
West Denton Way NE5.....36 E1
West Dr
  Blyth NE24...............17 C4
  Cleadon SR6.............74 E8
West End NE26............24 D4
West End Front St NE22...15 F8
West End Terr ② NE22...10 E1
Wester Ct ⑤ SR3........91 F5
Westerdale
  Penshaw DH4............89 E8
  Wallsend NE28...........39 F4
Westerdale Rd NE6........57 B6
Westerham CI SR5........74 F3
WESTERHOPE.............35 D2
Westerhope Gdns ⑪ NE5..37 D1
Westerhope Prim Sch
  NE5....................36 E3
Westerhope Rd NE38......83 F5
Westerhope Small Bus Pk
  NE5....................36 F3
Westerkirk NE23..........22 C3
Western App
  South Shields, High Shields
  NE33...................42 C1
  South Shields, Tyne Dock
  NE34...................59 A6
Western App Ind Est ⑦
  NE33...................42 C2
Western Ave
  Gateshead NE11..........70 C4
  Newcastle upon Tyne, Elswick
  NE4....................54 E5
  Newcastle upon Tyne NE5..36 D1
  Prudhoe NE42............50 B2
  Seaton Delaval NE25......23 C3
Western Com Prim Sch
  NE28...................40 A2
Western Ct ⑤ NE26......31 F8
Western Dr NE4...........54 F5
Western Highway NE38...83 B2
Western Hill
  Ryhope SR2..............92 E7
  Sunderland SR2..........102 B2
Westernmoor NE37........82 F6
Western Rd
  Jarrow NE32.............58 A7
  Wallsend NE28...........40 F2
Western Terr
  Dudley NE23.............28 F8
  Washington NE37........83 D7
  West Boldon NE36........74 B7
Western View NE9........71 C1
Western Way
  Blaydon NE21............53 E2
  Ponteland NE20..........25 A2
  Ryton NE40..............52 C4
  Whitley Bay NE26........31 F8
West Farm
  Burdon SR3..............92 B3
  Medomsley DH8..........77 C2
West Farm Ave NE12......39 A6
West Farm Ct
  Cramlington NE23........22 B7
  Killingworth NE12........29 E2
West Farm Grange DH8...77 C1
West Farm La DH8........77 C2
West Farm Rd
  Cleadon SR6.............75 B8
  Newcastle upon Tyne NE6..56 E7
  Wallsend NE28...........40 F3
West Farm Wynd NE12...38 F6
Westfield
  Dudley NE23.............28 E2
  Gateshead NE10..........71 E6
  Hedworth NE32..........58 C1
  Morpeth NE61...........8 E7
  Newcastle upon Tyne NE3..38 B2
Westfield Ave
  Brunswick Village NE13...28 A6
  Crawcrook NE40.........51 F3
  Newcastle upon Tyne NE3..38 C3
  Whitley Bay NE25........31 D4
Westfield CI NE46........44 F5
Westfield Cres
  Crawcrook NE40.........51 F3
  Newbeggin-by-the-Sea NE64..7 D4
  ⑳ Springwell NE9.......71 F1
Westfield Ct
  Jarrow NE32.............58 B6
  Sunderland SR4..........85 E4
  Wallsend NE28...........57 B8
Westfield Dr NE3.........38 C3
Westfield Gr
  Newcastle upon Tyne NE3..38 B3
  Sunderland SR4..........85 E4
Westfield La NE40........9 C2
Westfield Lodge NE16....70 E4
Westfield Pk
  Newcastle upon Tyne NE3..38 C3
  Wallsend NE28...........40 A2

Westfield Rd
  Gateshead NE8...........70 E8
  Newcastle upon Tyne NE15..54 C5
Westfield Sch NE3.........38 B3
Westfield School Junior
  House NE3...............38 B3
Westfield Terr
  Gateshead NE8...........70 E8
  Hexham NE46............44 F5
  ⑪ Springwell NE9.......71 E1
West Ford Rd NE62.......11 B8
Westgarth NE5...........36 F4
Westgarth Terr ⑦ NE37..83 D7
Westgate NE61...........8 D7
Westgate Ave SR3........92 A8
Westgate CI NE25........31 C6
Gate Gate Com Coll NE4..54 D6
Westgate Ct NE4.........98 B1
Westgate Gr SR3.........92 A8
Westgate Hill Prim Sch
  NE4....................98 A1
Westgate Hill Terr NE4...98 C1
Westgate Rd NE1, NE4...98 A1
West George Potts St ⑰
  NE33...................42 D1
West Gns SR1 NE61.......9 A8
West Gr SR4.............85 B5
West Grange SR5.........75 C3
Westgreen NE62..........10 F5
WEST HARTON...........59 B6
Westheath Ave SR2.......86 E1
WEST HERRINGTON.......90 F7
West Hextol NE46.........44 F4
West Hextol CI NE46......44 F4
West High Horse CI NE39..68 A4
West Hill
  Morpeth NE61............8 E7
  Sunderland SR4..........85 E4
Westhills CI NE39........79 A2
West Holborn NE33.......42 B1
Westholme Gdns NE15....54 D6
Westholme Terr ⑫ SR2...86 E1
WEST HOLYWELL.........30 D6
Westhope CI NE34........60 A7
Westhope Rd NE34.......60 A7
WEST JESMOND..........38 D2
West Jesmond Ave NE2...38 E2
West Jesmond Prim Sch
  NE2....................38 E1
West Jesmond Sta NE2...38 E2
West La
  Blaydon NE21............68 A8
  Byermoor NE16..........68 C1
  Chester le Street DH3.....88 C2
  Killingworth NE12........29 D2
  Medomsley NE17.........77 B4
Westlands
  Hedworth NE32..........58 D1
  Newcastle upon Tyne, High
  Heaton NE7.............39 A2
  Newcastle upon Tyne NE5..36 C1
  Seaton Sluice NE26......24 C6
  Sunderland SR4..........85 F5
  Tynemouth NE30........32 B1
West Lawn SR2..........86 C4
West Law Rd DH8........76 D1
West Lawrence St
  Sunderland SR1..........103 B2
  Sunderland SR1..........103 B2
Westlea NE22............15 D8
West Lea
  Blaydon NE21............68 C8
  New Herrington DH4......90 D6
Westleigh Rd DH4........90 C3
Westley Ave NE26........24 F1
Westley CI NE26..........24 F1
Westline Ind Est DH2.....82 B2
Westloch Rd NE23........22 B3
Westmacott St NE15......52 E8
West Market St NE61......2 B3
West Mdws NE5..........36 D4
West Meadows NE17......42 C7
West Meadows Dr SR6....75 A8
West Meadows Rd SR6....75 B8
WEST MICKLEY...........68 E8
Westminster Ave NE29....41 B8
Westminster CI NE26......32 C4
Westminster Cres NE31....57 E2
Westminster Dr NE11......69 F6
Westminster St NE8.......70 D8
Westminster Terr ④ NE8..70 D8
Westminster Way NE12...39 D4
West Moffett St ⑧ NE33..42 D1
WEST MONKSEATON......31 C4
West Monkseaton Sta
  NE25...................31 D4
WEST MOOR..............29 B1
West Moor Ct NE12.......29 B1
Westmoor Dr NE12........29 B1
West Moor Dr SR6........75 A7
Westmoor Prim Sch NE12.29 C2
Westmoor Rd SR6........75 A7
West Moor Terr ⑪ SR4...85 E7
Westmoreland St NE28....40 C2
Westmorland Rd
  Newcastle upon Tyne, Elswick
  NE1, NE4...............100 A4
  Newcastle upon Tyne NE4..100 C5
  Shiremoor NE29.........41 B7

Westmorland Rd continued
  South Shields NE34.......60 C7
Westmorland Ret Pk
  NE23...................21 F6
Westmorland Way NE23...22 A6
Westmorland Wlk NE4....54 F3
West Mount
  Killingworth NE12........29 C3
  Sunderland SR4..........85 E5
Westoe Ave SR3..........42 E1
Westoe Crown Prim Sch
  NE33...................42 E2
Westoe Dr NE33..........42 E1
Westoe Hall ⑪ NE33.....59 E8
Westoe Rd NE33..........42 D1
Westoe Village NE33......59 E8
Weston Ave NE16.........68 F5
Westover Gdns NE9.......70 F7
West Par
  Hebburn NE31...........57 D5
  Newcastle upon Tyne NE4..100 A4
WEST PARK..............59 C7
West Park Gdns NE21.....53 C1
West Park Rd
  Cleadon SR6.............60 A1
  Gateshead NE8...........70 E7
  South Shields NE33.......59 C7
West Park View NE23......28 F8
West Pastures
  Ashington NE63..........6 B2
  West Boldon NE36........73 C5
West Percy Rd NE29......41 F5
West Percy St NE29......42 A5
West Percy St ⑱ NE29...42 A6
West Pk
  Dunston NE11............54 F1
  Morpeth NE61...........8 E7
  Sunderland SR4..........91 B6
Westport CI SR5..........74 F4
West Quarter NE46.......44 F5
West Quay Rd SR5........74 F1
WEST RAINTON..........94 B2
Westray NE23............22 D7
Westray CI ⑤ SR2.......92 E8
West Rd
  Bedlington NE22.........11 D2
  Newcastle upon Tyne NE15,
  NE5....................54 C6
  Ponteland NE20.........25 E6
  Prudhoe NE42...........50 B2
  Tantobie DH9............79 A1
West Riggs NE22.........15 F8
West Rig The NE3.........37 E4
West Row DH3............82 E3
West Salisbury St ④
  NE24...................17 D8
WEST SLEEKBURN.......11 D7
West Sleekburn Ind Est
  NE62...................11 D7
West Sleekburn Mid Sch
  NE62...................11 D7
West Spencer Terr NE15..36 B1
West St
  ⑤ Birtley DH3..........82 C4
  Gateshead NE8..........101 B3
  Hebburn NE31...........57 F7
  High Spen NE39.........66 F4
  New Silksworth SR3......92 A8
  Shiremoor NE27.........30 D1
  Sunderland SR1.........102 C3
  Wallsend NE28..........40 A2
  Whickham NE16.........69 A7
West Stainton St ⑤ NE33.42 D1
West Stevenson St ⑦
  NE33...................42 D1
West Sunniside SR1......103 A3
West Vale NE46...........44 F5
West Terr
  Corbridge NE45..........46 F6
  Seaton Sluice NE26......24 D6
  Stakeford NE62..........11 C7
West Thorn Wlk NE16....69 A6
West Thorp NE5..........36 F5
Westvale NE15...........35 B2
West Vallum NE15........53 F7
West View
  Ashington NE63..........6 B2
  Bedlington NE22.........11 C3
  Blaydon NE21............53 C3
  Bournmoor DH4.........89 E3
  Burnopfield NE16........79 A6
  Cambois NE24...........12 C6
  Chester le Street DH3.....88 C4
  Crawcrook NE40.........51 E6
  Dudley NE23.............28 F8
  Earsdon NE25...........31 A5
  Gateshead NE9..........71 C4
  Kibblesworth NE11.......81 D6
  ⑤ Longbenton NE12....39 D8
  Morpeth NE61...........3 C5
  Newbeggin-by-the-Sea NE64..7 E5
  Newbottle DH4..........90 D4
  Newcastle upon Tyne, Lemington
  NE15...................53 C6
  Pegswood NE61..........4 E3
  Penshaw DH4............90 B8
  Ryhope SR2.............92 E6
  Seghill NE23.............22 F1
  Sherburn Hill DH6........96 C1
  Shiney Row DH4.........90 B4
  ⑥ Sunderland, Castletown
  SR5....................74 B1
  Sunderland, Monkwearmouth
  SR6....................75 D3
  Widopen NE13...........28 B7
  Wylam NE41.............51 B6

West View Bldgs NE30....32 C3
West View Terr NE46......45 C3
West Walker Prim Sch
  NE6....................57 A4
West Walls NE1...........98 C1
West Walpole St NE33....42 B1
Westward ⑪ NE5.........36 E3
Westward Gn NE25.......31 C4
Westward PI NE38.........83 B1
Westway
  Blaydon NE21............53 B2
  Throckley NE15..........35 E3
West Way
  Dunston NE11............70 A7
  South Shields NE33.......59 C7
  West Wear St SR1.......103 A3
Westwell Ct NE3..........38 F4
Westwood CI NE16........79 B7
Westwood Gdns
  Ashington NE62..........5 F1
  ⑥ Gateshead NE9.......71 D3
  Newcastle upon Tyne NE3..37 E4
Westwood La NE17........77 B5
Westwood Rd NE3.........28 C1
Westwood St SR4.........85 F6
Westwood View
  Chester le Street DH3.....88 C1
  Crawcrook NE40.........51 F3
WEST WYLAM...........50 E3
West Wylam Dr NE42.....50 E3
West Wynd NE12..........29 D4
Wetheral Gdns NE9.......71 A3
Wetheral Terr NE6........56 F4
Wetherby CI NE63.........6 C2
Wetherby Gr NE8.........70 D7
Wetherby Rd SR2.........87 A1
Wet n'Wild Water Pk*
  NE15...................81 F2
Wettondale Ave NE24....17 A7
Weybourne Lea NE37.....93 C1
Weybourne Sq SR2.......86 E2
Weyhill Ave NE29.........41 D4
Weymouth Dr DH4........89 F5
Weymouth Gdns NE9.....71 A2
Weymouth Rd SR3........91 E4
Whaggs La NE16..........69 B6
Whalebone La NE61......8 F8
Whalton Ave NE3........38 A6
Whalton Ct
  Gateshead NE10.........72 C7
  Morpeth NE61...........9 B5
  Sherburn DH6...........96 A1
Whalton Ct
  Newcastle upon Tyne NE38..38 A6
  South Shields NE34.......59 E6
Wharfdale PI NE6.........57 B7
Wharfedale
  Penshaw DH4............90 A8
  Wallsend NE28...........39 F5
Wharfedale Ave NE37.....83 C8
Wharfedale Dr NE33......59 C7
Wharfedale Gdns NE24...17 A8
Wharfedale Gn NE9.......71 B1
Wharlands Gr NE15.......53 F7
Wharncliffe St SR1.......102 B2
Wharrier St NE6..........56 F4
Wharrier Street Prim Sch
  NE6....................56 F4
Wharton CI DH5..........94 D4
Wharton St
  Blyth NE24..............17 C5
  South Shields NE33.......42 D2
Wheatall Dr SR6..........60 F2
Wheatear CI ⑪ NE38....82 F3
Wheatfield CI NE42.......50 B5
Wheatfield Gr NE12......29 C7
Wheatfield Rd NE5.......36 F3
Wheatfields NE25.........23 B4
Wheatley Gdns NE36......74 A7
Wheatridge NE25.........23 B4
Wheatsheaf Ct SR6.......75 F1
Wheler St ⑧ DH4........90 A4
Whernside CI ④ NE37....83 A6
Whernside Ct ② SR3.....91 F6
Whernside PI NE23.......22 B3
Whernside Wlk NE40.....52 D4
Whetstone Bridge Rd
  NE46...................44 F4
Whetstone Gn NE46......44 F4
Whickham Ind Est NE16...54 A4
Whickham La NE16.......69 C5
WHICKHAM..............69 B7
Whickham Ave ⑥ NE16..69 A7
Whickham Bank ⑥ NE16..69 A7
Whickham CE Prim Sch ⑪
  NE16...................68 F5
Whickham CI NE34........94 C8
Whickham Comp Sch
  NE16...................69 A6
WHICKHAM FELL.........69 A4
Whickham Highway NE11,
  NE16...................69 C6
Whickham Ind Est NE16...68 F8
Whickham Lodge NE16....69 C7
Whickham Lodge Rise
  NE16...................69 C7
Whickham PI NE6.........56 F4
Whickham Rd NE31.......57 E6
Whickham St SR6.........75 E1
Whickham Street E ⑤ SR6.75 E1
Whickham Thorns Outdoor
  Activity Ctr NE11........69 D8
Whickham View
  Gateshead NE9..........71 A4

Whickham View continued
  Newcastle upon Tyne NE15..54 A6
Whickhope NE38.........83 E2
Whinbank NE20...........25 D2
Whinbrooke NE10........72 A6
Whinbush PI NE15........54 A5
Whinchat Ho NE28.......40 D5
Whinfell NE37............83 B7
Whinfell CI NE23..........22 C3
Whinfell Ct ④ SR3.......91 F6
Whinfell Rd NE25.........25 D3
Whinfield Ind Est NE39....67 C1
Whinfield Terr NE39......67 D2
Whinfield Way NE39......67 C1
Whinham Way
  Morpeth NE61...........9 B5
  Stannington NE61.......14 C6
  Stobhilgate NE61........9 B5
Whinlatter Gdns NE9......71 A4
Whinlaw NE9.............71 C4
Whinmoor PI NE5.........36 F1
Whinney CI NE21.........68 A8
Whinneyfield Rd NE6.....56 F7
Whinny La
  Eachwick DH3...........76 E1
  Morpeth NE61...........3 A8
Whinshaw NE10..........71 C4
Whinstone Mews NE12...39 D6
Whinway NE37...........83 B7
Whistler Gdns NE34......59 D3
Whitbeck Ct NE5.........37 A1
Whitbeck Rd NE5.........54 A8
Whitbourne CI NE37......72 E2
WHITBURN..............60 E1
Whitburn Bents Rd SR6...75 F7
Whitburn CE Sch SR6....75 F8
Whitburn Coastal Pk*
  SR6....................61 A4
Whitburn Gdns NE9.......71 D3
Whitburn Hall SR6........75 F6
WHITBURN MOOR.......75 B6
Whitburn PI NE23.........22 B3
Whitburn Prim Nature
  Reserve* SR6...........61 A4
Whitburn Rd
  Cleadon SR6.............74 F8
  Sunderland SR6.........75 F4
Whitburn Road E SR6.....60 B1
Whitburn St SR6.........103 A4
Whitburn Terr
  East Boldon NE36........74 D7
  Sunderland SR6.........75 D4
Whitburn Village Prim Sch
  SR6....................75 E8
Whitby Ave
  Hexham NE46............44 F5
  Sunderland SR6.........75 F7
Whitby CI NE8...........101 C1
Whitby Cres NE12........39 C6
Whitby Dr NE38..........83 D3
Whitby St NE30..........42 B6
Whitchester Ho NE4......54 F4
Whitchurch CI
  Boldon Colliery NE35.....58 E1
  Sunderland SR5.........74 A4
Whitchurch Rd
  Sunderland SR5.........74 F4
  Sunderland SR5.........75 A4
Whitdale Ave NE24.......17 A6
Whiteacres NE61.........9 A7
Whitebeam PI NE4.......100 B3
Whitebridge CI NE3.......38 D7
Whitebridge Ct NE3.......38 C7
Whitebridge Parkway
  NE3....................38 D8
Whitebridge Pk NE3.......38 D8
Whitebridge Wlk NE3.....38 D8
Whiteburn NE42.........50 B2
Whitecliff CI NE29........41 F8
Whitecroft Rd NE12......29 B2
White Cross NE46........45 C4
Whitefield Cres
  Pegswood NE61.........4 E3
  Penshaw DH4...........90 A7
Whitefield Farm Cotts
  NE61...................5 A2
Whitefield Gdns NE40....66 F8
Whitefield Gr NE10.......71 D8
Whitefield Terr NE6.......39 D1
Whiteford PI NE23........23 A2
Whitefriars Way NE12....54 F2
White Gates Dr DH5......95 B2
Whitehall Rd
  Gateshead NE8.........101 B1
  Gateshead, Shipcote NE8..71 C7
  Walbottle NE15.........35 F2
Whitehall St NE33.........42 B2
Whitehall Terr ⑦ SR4....85 F6
Whitehead St
  South Shields NE33.......59 B7
  Shields, West Harton
  NE33...................59 B7
Whitehill NE10............71 F5
Whitehill Dr NE10........71 F5
Whitehill Hall Gdns DH2..88 A4
Whitehill Rd NE23........16 A1
White Hill Rd DH5........97 C8
WHITEHILLS.............60 C6
White Horse View NE14..60 C6
Whitehouse Cres NE9....71 C3
Whitehouse Farm Ctr*
  NE61...................13 E8
Whitehouse Ind Est NE15..54 C4
Whitehouse La
  Gateshead NE9..........71 C3

Whitehouse La continued
Tynemouth NE29 . . . . .41 D8
Whitehouse Mews NE28. . .40 C2
White House Pk SR2 . . . . .103 D2
Whitehouse Prim Sch
NE29 .41 E8
Whitehouse Rd
Newcastle upon Tyne, Delaval
NE15. . . . . .54 C4
Newcastle upon Tyne, Old
Benwell NE15. . . . . .54 B4
Sunderland SR2. . . . . .103 D2
White House Way NE10 . .71 E5
Whiteladies CI NE38 . . . . .83 D6
Whitelaw Pl NE23 . . . . . . .22 C4
WHITELEA 22 A5
WHITELEAS 59 D3
Whiteleas Way NE34 . . . . .59 C3
Whitelees CI NE3 . . . . .37 E7
WHITE-LE-HEAD 79 A1
White-le-Head Gdns DH9 .79 A1
Whiteley CI NE42 . . . . .52 A1
Whiteley Rd NE21 . . . . .53 E4
Whitemere CI SR2. . . . . . . .86 E1
White Mere Com Prim Sch
NE10 . . . . .72 C7
White Mere Gdns NE10. . . .72 C8
White Oaks NE10 . . . . .71 E5
White Rocks Gr SR6 . . . . . .60 F3
White Rose Way NE10. . . . .72 E5
Whites Gdns NE31 . . . . .57 D6
White Swan CI NE1 . . . . . . .29 D3
Whitethorn Cres NE5 . . . . .37 E2
Whitethroat CI 6 NE38 . . .82 F3
Whitewell CI NE40 . . . . .52 C5
Whitewell La NE40 . . . . .52 C5
Whitewell Rd NE40 . . . . . . .53 C2
Whitfield Dr NE12. . . . . .39 A6
Whitfield Rd
6 Longbenton NE12. . . . . . .39 D8
Newcastle upon Tyne NE15. .53 F3
Seaton Delaval NE25. . . . . . .23 D3
Whitfield Villas NE33 . . . . .59 B6
Whitgrave Rd NE5 . . . . .37 D3
Whithorn CI NE24. . . . . .17 C7
WHITLEY BAY 32 C6
Whitley Bay High Sch
NE26 . . . . .31 D8
Whitley Bay Sta NE25 . . . . .32 B4
Whitley CI 7 NE8 . . . . .71 F7
Whitley Lodge Fst Sch
NE26 . . . . .31 E8
Whitley Memorial CE Fst Sch
NE22 . . . . .16 A8
Whitley Pl NE25 . . . . .23 E2
Whitley Rd
Earsdon NE25 . . . . .31 A5
Longbenton NE12. . . . . .40 A8
Whitley Bay NE26 . . . . .32 B4
Whitley Terr
5 Bedlington NE22 . . . . . . .11 D3
Seaton Delaval NE25. . . . . . .23 C3
Whitmore Rd NE21. . . . . . . .53 C3
Whitsun Ave NE22. . . . . . . .11 A1
Whitsun Gdns NE22 . . . . . . .11 A1
Whitsun Gr NE22 . . . . .11 A1
Whittingham CI
Ashington NE63. . . . . .6 A2
Tynemouth NE30 . . . . .32 C2
Whittingham Rd
Newcastle upon Tyne NE5 . . .37 A4
Tynemouth NE30 . . . . .32 C1
Whittington Gr NE5 . . . . . . .54 C8
Whittleburn NE10 . . . . .71 F5
Whitton Ave NE24. . . . . .17 B5
Whitton Gdns NE29 . . . . . . .41 D7
Whitton Pl
Newcastle upon Tyne NE7 . . .39 B4
Seaton Delaval NE25. . . . . . .23 D3
Whittonstall NE38. . . . . .83 F1
Whittonstall Rd NE17 . . . . .66 A1
Whittonstall Terr NE17 . . .66 A1
Whitton Way NE3 . . . . .38 B6
Whitwell Terr NE40 . . . . . . .52 C6
Whitworth CI
Gateshead NE8 . . . . .70 D7
Newcastle upon Tyne NE6. . .57 A5
Whitworth Pl NE6. . . . . .57 A5
Whitworth Rd NE37. . . . . . .82 F7
Whorlton Grange Cotts
NE5 .36 E4
Whorlton La
Callerton NE5. . . . . .36 C6
Newcastle upon Tyne NE5. . .36 C6
Whorlton Pl 1 NE5. . . . . . .36 B3
Whorlton Terr NE5 . . . . . . .36 B4
Whorral Bank NE61 . . . . . . .4 B2
Whyndyke NE10. . . . . .71 F5
Whytrigg CI NE23 . . . . .23 B3
Whytrig Mid Sch NE25 . . . .23 C4
Wickets The NE3 . . . . .38 D4
Wicklow Ct NE62 . . . . .11 D8
Widdrington Ave NE34 . . . .60 B8
Widdrington Gdns NE13 . . .28 C6
Widdrington Rd NE21 . . . . .53 C2
Widdrington Terr
4 North Shields NE29 . . . . .42 A5
Ryton NE21 . . . . .53 A4
WIDEOPEN 28 C5
Widnes Pl NE12. . . . . .39 C7
Wigeon CI NE38 . . . . .83 A2
Wigham Terr NE16 . . . . .79 A4
Wigmore Ave NE6 . . . . .56 E4
Wilber Ct 8 SR4 . . . . .85 F7

Wilberforce St
Jarrow NE32 . . . . .58 C7
Wallsend NE28 . . . . .57 B8
Wilberforce Wlk NE8. . . . .100 C2
Wilber St SR4. . . . . .85 F6
Wilbury Pl NE5 . . . . .37 C2
Wildbriar NE38 . . . . .83 E2
Wilden Ct SR3. . . . . .86 B2
Wilden Rd NE38 . . . . .84 A3
Wildshaw CI NE23 . . . . .22 C3
Wilfred St
Boldon Colliery NE35. . . . . . .73 F8
Chester le Street DH3 . . . . . .88 C2
Newcastle upon Tyne NE6. . .56 A6
Sunderland SR4. . . . . .85 E7
Wilfrid St DH3. . . . . .82 C3
Wilkes CI NE5 . . . . .36 F2
Wilkinson Ave NE31. . . . . . .57 D3
Wilkinson Ct 4 NE32 . . . . .58 B7
Wilkinson Terr NE32. . . . . .92 E6
Wilkwood CI NE23 . . . . .22 C4
Willerby Dr NE3 . . . . .38 D8
William Allan Homes
NE22 . . . . .15 D8
William Armstrong Dr
NE4. .54 F3
William CI NE12 . . . . .40 A8
William Doxford Ctr SR3 . .91 F6
William Hopkinson Way
NE4 . . . . .54 F3
William IV Yd NE8 . . . . . . .101 B4
William Morris Ave NE10 . .71 F5
William Roberts Ct NE12 . .29 D1
Williamson Terr SR6 . . . . .103 A4
Williams Pk NE12. . . . . .39 C6
William St
Blyth NE24. . . . . .17 E6
Chester le Street DH3 . . . . . .88 C3
Chopwell NE17. . . . . .66 A6
Gateshead NE10 . . . . .56 D1
Hebburn NE31. . . . . .57 D7
Newcastle upon Tyne NE3 . . .38 E5
North Shields NE29 . . . . .42 A5
Pegswood NE61. . . . . .4 F3
6 South Shields NE33 . . . . .59 B8
8 Sunderland, South Hylton
SR4. . . . . .85 A6
Sunderland SR1 . . . . .103 A3
9 Whickham NE16 . . . . .69 A7
Williams Terr NE32 . . . . . . .92 E6
William Street W
Hebburn NE31. . . . . .57 D6
14 North Shields NE29 . . . . .42 A5
William Terr NE10 . . . . .71 F5
William Whiteley Homes
NE40 . . . . .52 A1
WILLINGTON 40 F4
WILLINGTON QUAY 41 B2
WILLINGTON SQUARE 40 E3
Willington Terr NE28 . . . . .40 E3
Willis St DH5 . . . . .95 A5
Willmore St SR4 . . . . .102 A2
Willoughby Dr NE29 . . . . . . .31 E7
Willoughby Rd NE29 . . . . . .41 E6
Willoughby Way NE26. . . . .31 E7
Willow Ave
Blyth NE24. . . . . .12 D1
Dunston NE11. . . . . .70 B8
Newcastle upon Tyne NE4. . .54 D8
Willowbank Gdns 10 NE2 . .38 E4
Willow Bank Rd SR2 . . . . . .86 C3
Willowbrook CI NE22. . . . . .11 C4
Willow CI
Morpeth NE61. . . . . .9 B8
Whickham NE16 . . . . .69 B6
Willow Cres
Blyth NE24. . . . . .17 C4
Easington Lane DH5 . . . . . . .95 D1
Willow Ct
Ryton NE40 . . . . .52 D6
Stakeford NE62 . . . . .11 E7
Willow Dene NE61 . . . . .8 F7
Willow Dyke NE45 . . . . .47 A6
Willowfield Ave NE3 . . . . . .37 F6
Willow Fields Com Prim Sch
SR5. .74 F4
Willow Gdns NE12 . . . . .29 C4
Willow Gn 7 SR2. . . . . .86 C4
Willow Gr
Gateshead NE10 . . . . .71 E8
South Shields NE34 . . . . .59 F5
Wallsend NE28 . . . . .40 D1
Willow Grange NE32 . . . . . .58 A7
Willow Pl NE20 . . . . .25 E4
Willow Rd
Blaydon NE21 . . . . .53 D2
Houghton-le-Spring DH4 . . . .94 C8
Newcastle upon Tyne NE15. .53 A6
Willows CI NE13 . . . . .28 A5
Willow's CI 1 NE38. . . . . . .83 F4
Willows The
Hebburn NE31. . . . . .57 E4
Hedworth NE32 . . . . .58 C1
Morpeth NE61. . . . . .9 A8
Newcastle upon Tyne NE4. . .100 A3
Seaton Burn NE13. . . . . .21 B1
Throckley NE15 . . . . .35 D1
Washington DH4. . . . . .88 A5
Willow Way NE20 . . . . .25 E3
Wills Mews NE7 . . . . .39 E2
Wills Oval NE7. . . . . .39 E2
Willow Ave NE3 . . . . .38 B3
Wilson Ave
Birtley DH3. . . . . .82 C5
Cambois NE22 . . . . .12 D4
Wilson Gdns NE3 . . . . .38 B3

Wilson's Ct 5 NE1. . . . . . . .99 A1
Wilson's La NE9 . . . . .70 F5
Wilson St
Dunston NE11. . . . . .69 F8
South Shields NE33 . . . . .42 C2
Sunderland SR4. . . . . .85 F6
Wallsend NE28 . . . . .56 F4
Wilson Street N SR5 . . . . .102 C4
Wilson Terr
1 Longbenton NE12. . . . . . .39 D8
New Silksworth SR3 . . . . . . .92 A8
Wilsway NE15 . . . . .35 C2
Wilton Ave NE6 . . . . .56 E4
Wilton CI
Cramlington NE23. . . . . .22 C3
Whitley Bay NE25 . . . . .31 C5
Wilton Cotts 5 NE35 . . . . .58 E1
Wilton Dr NE25. . . . . .31 B5
Wilton Gardens N NE35 . . .58 E1
Wilton Gardens S NE35 . . .58 E1
Wilton Manse NE25 . . . . . . .31 B4
Wilton Sq SR2. . . . . .86 E4
Wiltshire CI SR5. . . . . .74 E4
Wiltshire Dr NE28. . . . . .39 F4
Wiltshire Gdns NE28 . . . . . .39 F4
Wiltshire Pl NF37 . . . . .72 D2
Wiltshire Rd SR5 . . . . .74 E3
Wimbledon CI SR5. . . . . .74 F3
Wimborne CI NE35. . . . . . . .73 E8
Wimpole CI NE37 . . . . .72 E2
Wimslow CI NE23 . . . . .39 F3
Winalot Ave SR2. . . . . .86 E2
Wincanton Pl NE29 . . . . . . .21 E4
Winchcombe Pl NE7 . . . . . . .39 A3
Winchester Ave NE24 . . . . .17 E7
Winchester CI NE63 . . . . . . .6 F2
Winchester CI NE32. . . . . . .58 B1
Winchester St NE33 . . . . . .42 D3
Winchester Terr NE4 . . . . . .98 B1
Winchester Wlk NE13 . . . . .28 B6
WINCOMBLEE 57 B5
Wincomblee Rd NE6 . . . . . .57 B4
Windburgh Dr NE23. . . . . . .22 B3
Windermere
Birtley DH3. . . . . .82 D2
Cleadon SR6 . . . . .60 A1
Windermere Ave
Chester le Street DH2. . . . . . .88 C1
Easington Lane DH5 . . . . . . .97 C8
Gateshead NE10 . . . . .71 F8
Windermere CI
Cramlington NE23. . . . . .22 B3
7 Wallsend NE28 . . . . .40 A1
Windermere Cres
Blaydon NE21 . . . . .68 B8
Hebburn NE31. . . . . .57 E3
Hedworth NE32 . . . . .58 D3
Penshaw DH4 . . . . .90 C6
South Shields NE34 . . . . .59 E6
Windermere Dr NE12 . . . . . .29 C3
Windermere Gdns NE16 . . .69 C7
Windermere Rd
Newbeggin-by-the-Sea
NE64 .7 C3
Newcastle upon Tyne NE5. . .54 B8
Windermere St
Gateshead NE8 . . . . .101 B1
Sunderland SR2. . . . . .86 F2
Windermere Street W
NE8 . . . . .101 B1
Windermere Terr NE29 . . . .41 F6
Windhill Rd NE6 . . . . .56 F3
Winding The NE13 . . . . .27 B7
Windlass La NE37 . . . . .83 C7
Windlass La NE37 . . . . .83 C7
Windmill Ct NE2 . . . . .98 C4
Windmill Gr NE24 . . . . .17 A8
Windmill Hill
Ellington NE61 . . . . .1 E5
Hexham NE46 . . . . .45 A5
South Shields NE33 . . . . .42 B1
Windmill Hill CI NE61 . . . . . .1 E6
WINDMILL HILLS 101 B2
Windmill Hills Com Prim Sch
NE8 . . . . .101 B2
Windmill Hts NE61 . . . . .1 E6
Windmill Ind Est NE21 . . . .15 C2
Windmill Sq NE35 . . . . .75 C4
Windmill Way
Gateshead NE8 . . . . .101 A2
Hebburn NE31. . . . . .57 E8
Morpeth NE61. . . . . .9 B8
Windshields Wlk NE15 . . . . .35 C1
Windsor Ave
Gateshead NE8 . . . . .70 B8
Windsor CI
3 Newcastle upon Tyne
NE3 .38 E4
Whitley Bay NE26 . . . . .32 C4
Windsor CI
Wallsend NE28 . . . . .41 A4
Whickham NE16. . . . . .69 A4
Windsor Cotts NE28. . . . . . .41 A4
Windsor Cres
Hebburn NE31. . . . . .57 F6
Houghton-le-Spring DH4 . . . .94 F8
Newcastle upon Tyne NE5. . .37 A3
Ovingham NE42 . . . . .50 B5
Whitley Bay NE26 . . . . .32 C4
Windsor Ct
Bedlington NE22 . . . . .15 F8
Corbridge NE45. . . . . .47 A6
Cramlington NE23. . . . . .16 A1
7 Gateshead NE10. . . . . . . .71 C8
Newcastle upon Tyne, Kingston
Park NE3. . . . . .37 E7

Windsor Ct continued
Newcastle upon Tyne, South
Gosforth NE3 . . . . .38 E5
Rowlands Gill NE39 . . . . .67 F2
Windsor Dr
Blyth NE24. . . . . .17 D3
Cleadon SR6 . . . . .59 F1
Houghton-le-Spring DH5 . . . .94 E6
New Silksworth SR3 . . . . . . .92 A7
South Hetton DH6 . . . . .97 F8
Wallsend NE28 . . . . .41 A4
Windsor Fst Sch NE64 . . . . .7 C3
Windsor Gardens W NE26 .31 F6
Windsor Gdns
Bedlington NE22 . . . . .15 F8
Gateshead NE10 . . . . .71 C8
South Shields NE34 . . . . .59 E7
Tynemouth NE29 . . . . .42 A7
Whitley Bay NE26 . . . . .31 F6
Windsor Pk NE28 . . . . .41 A4
Windsor Pl
Longbenton NE27. . . . . .30 C1
Newcastle upon Tyne NE2. . .99 B3
Ponteland NE20. . . . . .25 B4
Windsor Rd
Birtley DH3. . . . . .82 B6
Newbeggin-by-the-Sea NE64 .7 A4
Springwell NE9 . . . . .71 F1
Whitley Bay NE25 . . . . .31 E5
Windsor Terr
Choppington NE62. . . . . .10 F4
Corbridge NE45. . . . . .47 A6
Crawcrook NE40 . . . . .52 A4
Haswell DH6 . . . . .97 F2
Hexham NE46 . . . . .44 F5
Newbeggin-by-the-Sea NE64 . .7 A4
Newcastle upon Tyne, South
Gosforth NE3 . . . . .38 E4
Newcastle upon Tyne, South
Gosforth NE3 . . . . .38 E4
1 Springwell NE9. . . . . .71 F1
Sunderland, East Herrington
SR3. . . . . .91 C6
3 Sunderland, Grangetown
SR2 . . . . .86 F2
Whitley Bay NE26 . . . . .32 C4
Windsor Villas NE62. . . . . . .11 A7
Windsor Way NE3 . . . . .37 D7
Windsor Wlk
Ashington NE63. . . . . .7 A2
Newcastle upon Tyne NE3 . . .37 D7
Windt St NE13 . . . . .28 A5
Windy Gyle NE63 . . . . .6 E1
WINDY NOOK 71 D6
Windy Nook Nature
Reserve* NE10. . . . . .71 C6
Windy Nook Prim Sch
NE10 . . . . .71 C6
Windy Nook Rd N10, NE9 . .71 B6
Windy Ridge NE10 . . . . .71 C7
Windy Ridge Villas NE10. . .71 C7
Wingate CI
Houghton-le-Spring DH4 . . . .94 D8
Newcastle upon Tyne NE15. .53 E6
Wingate Gdns NE9 . . . . .71 D3
Wingrove NE39 . . . . .67 C2
Wingrove Ave
Newcastle upon Tyne NE4. . .54 F6
Sunderland SR6 . . . . .75 E3
Wingrove Gdns NE4 . . . . . . .54 F7
Wingrove Ho NE33 . . . . .59 C6
Wingrove Prim Sch NE4. . . .54 F7
Wingrove Road N NE4 . . . . .54 F7
Wingrove Terr 11 NE9. . . . .71 F1
Winifred Gdns NE28 . . . . . . .40 C1
Winifred St SR6 . . . . .75 E3
Winifred Terr SR1. . . . . . . .103 B2
WINLATON 53 B1
WINLATON MILL 68 C6
Winlaton West Lane Prim
Sch NE21. . . . . .68 A8
Winlaton Ave 1 NE29. . . . . .31 F1
Winsford Ave NE29 . . . . . . .41 D5
Winship CI SR6 . . . . .59 C3
Winship St NE24 . . . . .17 B6
Winship Terr 15 NE6 . . . . . .56 C6
Winskell Rd NE34 . . . . .59 A4
Winslade CI SR3. . . . . .92 B8
Winslow CI
Boldon Colliery NE35. . . . . . .58 F2
Newcastle upon Tyne NE6. . .56 A6
Sunderland SR5. . . . . .74 F4
Winslow Gdns NE9 . . . . .70 E5
Winslow Pl NE6. . . . . .56 A6
Winster NE38 . . . . .83 A1
Winster Pl NE23 . . . . .22 B3
Winston Cres SR4. . . . . .85 E4
Winston Gn NE9. . . . . .71 F1
Winston Gn DH4 . . . . .89 F8
Winston CI NE34 . . . . .59 A3
Winton CI NE23 . . . . .23 A2
Winton Way NE3 . . . . .37 F1
Wirralshir NE10 . . . . .72 B8
Wiseton Ct NE7 . . . . .38 F5
Wishart Ho NE4. . . . . .54 D6
Wishart Terr NE39. . . . . .66 F4
Wishaw CI NE23 . . . . .23 A2
Wishaw Rise NE15 . . . . .53 E7
Witham Gn NE32. . . . . .58 D3
Witham Green NE32 . . . . . . .58 D3
Witham Rd NE31. . . . . .57 F3
Witherington CI NE7 . . . . . .39 A3
Withernsea Gr SR2 . . . . .92 D7
WITHERWACK 74 E4
Witney Ct SR5. . . . . .74 F4
Witney Way NE36 . . . . .74 A7
Witton Ave NE34 . . . . .60 A6
Witton Ct
Newcastle upon Tyne NE3 . . .37 E6

Witton Ct continued
Sunderland SR3. . . . . .86 B2
Washington NE38 . . . . .83 B4
Witton Gdns
1 Gateshead NE9 . . . . .71 D2
Jarrow NE32 . . . . .58 B3
Witton Gr DH4 . . . . .94 C7
Witton Rd
Hebburn NE31. . . . . .57 F8
Shiremoor NE27 . . . . .30 F3
Wittonstone Ho NE4 . . . . . .98 B2
Witty Ave NE31 . . . . .57 F5
Wivenhoe NE38. . . . . .83 D4
Woburn CI
Cramlington NE23 . . . . .16 A1
Wallsend NE28 . . . . .39 F3
Woburn Dr
Bedlington NE22 . . . . .11 C2
Sunderland SR3 . . . . .92 A6
Woburn Way NE5 . . . . .37 A2
Wolmer Rd NE24 . . . . .17 F5
Wolseley CI NE8 . . . . .100 C1
Wolseley Gdns NE2 . . . . . . .56 A8
Wolseley Terr SR4 . . . . . . .102 A1
Wolsey Ct NE34. . . . . .59 C6
Wolsingham Ct NE23 . . . . . .22 B3
Wolsingham Gdns 8 NE9 .71 D3
Wolsingham Rd NE3. . . . . . .38 B4
Wolsingham St NE4. . . . . . .100 A3
Wolsley Rd NE24 . . . . .17 C7
Wolveleigh Terr NE3 . . . . . .38 D5
Wolviston Gdns 4 NE9 . . . .71 D3
Woodbine Ave
Newcastle upon Tyne NE3. . .38 C4
Wallsend NE28 . . . . .40 B2
Woodbine CI NE4 . . . . .54 D7
Woodbine Cotts NE40 . . . . .52 B5
Woodbine Pl NE8 . . . . .101 B1
Woodbine Rd NE3 . . . . .38 C5
Woodbine St
Gateshead NE8 . . . . .101 B1
2 South Shields NE33 . . . . .42 D3
Sunderland SR1 . . . . .103 C3
Woodbine Terr
Birtley DH3. . . . . .82 D4
Blyth NE24. . . . . .17 F6
Corbridge NE45. . . . . .47 A6
Gateshead, Bensham NE8 .101 B1
Gateshead, Bill Quay NE10 . .57 A1
Gateshead, Felling NE10 . . . .71 B8
Hexham NE46 . . . . .44 F5
Sunderland SR4. . . . . .85 F8
Woodbine Villas NE8 . . . . . .71 B8
WOODBRIDGE 7 A4
Woodbrook Ave NE5 . . . . . .54 A8
Woodburn NE10 . . . . .71 E5
Woodburn Ave NE4 . . . . . . .54 E8
Woodburn Dr
Burnside DH4 . . . . .90 C1
Whitley Bay NE26 . . . . .31 E7
Woodburn Gdns NE11. . . . . .70 A6
Woodburn Sq NE15 . . . . . . .53 C7
Woodburn Terr NE42. . . . . .50 B2
Woodburn Way NE26. . . . . .31 E7
Woodchurch CI
NE12. . . . . .39 D4
Wallsend NE27 . . . . .39 D3
Woodcliff CI NE38 . . . . .83 E3
Woodcroft CI NE23. . . . . . . .22 B1
Woodcroft Rd NE41. . . . . . . .51 A6
Wooden Rd NE40 . . . . .20 C2
Woodend Way NE3 . . . . .37 D8
Wood Fields NE20 . . . . .25 C6
Woodford NE9 . . . . .70 F1
Woodford CI SR5 . . . . .74 F4
Woodgate Gdns NE10. . . . . .71 B7
Woodgate La NE10. . . . . . . .71 B7
Wood Gr NE15. . . . . .53 C7
Woodhall CI DH2. . . . . .81 E2
Woodhall Ct NE25 . . . . .23 C3
Woodhall Spa DH4. . . . . .90 A4
Woodhead Rd
Newcastle upon Tyne NE6. . .56 F8
Prudhoe NE42. . . . . .50 F3
Woodhill CI NE23 . . . . .22 C4
Woodhill Dr NE61 . . . . .8 E6
Wood Ho 3 SR3. . . . . .91 F5
WOODHORN 7 B6
Woodhorn Cotts 11 NE63 . . .6 F5
Woodhorn Cres NE64 . . . . . .7 F5
Woodhorn CI NE63 . . . . .6 F2
WOODHORN DEMESNE 7 C5
Woodhorn Dr NE62 . . . . .10 F8
Woodhorn Farm NE63. . . . . .7 B6
Woodhorn Gdns NE13. . . . . .28 A6
Woodhorn La NE63 . . . . .7 E5
Woodhorn Northumberland
Mus* NE63 . . . . .6 F5
Woodhorn Pk NE63 . . . . .6 E4
Woodhorn Rd
Ashington NE63. . . . . .6 E4
Newbeggin-by-the-Sea NE64. .7 C3
Woodhorn Villas NE63. . . . . .6 F5
Woodhouse La NE34 . . . . . .60 C7
Woodhouses La
Whickham, Fellside NE16 . . .68 E6
Whickham, Swalwell NE16 . .68 E6
Woodhurst Gr SR4 . . . . .85 A2
Woodkirk CI NE23 . . . . .22 C4
Wood La NE22. . . . . .11 B1

Woodland Cres NE15......**54** C4
Woodland Dr SR4......**85** E4
Woodland Grange DH4...**89** F1
Woodland Mews NE2....**38** F2
Woodland Rise SR3....**91** E6
Woodlands
  Burnopfield NE16..........**79** B6
  Chester le Street DH3.....**88** C4
  Great Lumley DH4..........**89** F1
  Hexham NE46..............**45** D4
  Newcastle upon Tyne NE3...**38** C3
  Ouston DH2...............**81** F2
  Ponteland NE20...........**25** D3
  Seaham SR7...............**93** A1
  Throckley NE15...........**35** C2
  Tynemouth NE29...........**42** A7
  Washington NE38.........**88** E8
Woodlands Cl
  Earsdon NE25.............**31** A5
  High Spen NE39...........**67** A3
Woodlands Ct
  Kibblesworth NE11........**81** D6
  Throckley NE15...........**35** C2
Woodlands Dr SR6.......**75** A8
Woodlands Grange NE12..**29** E1
Woodlands Ho NE24......**17** B8
Woodlands Park Dr NE21..**53** D2
Woodlands Park Villas
  NE13...................**28** C4
Woodlands Pk NE13......**28** C5
Woodlands Rd
  Ashington NE63............**7** A2
  Cleadon SR6..............**75** A8
  Newcastle upon Tyne NE15.**53** D7
  Rowlands Gill NE39.......**67** D2
Woodlands Terr
  Gateshead NE10...........**71** C8
  Longbenton NE12..........**29** E1
  5 South Shields NE33.....**42** D4
Woodlands The NE11.....**81** D6
Woodlands View SR6.....**75** A8
Woodland Terr
  Penshaw DH4..............**90** A8
  Washington NE37..........**83** E8
Woodland View DH4......**94** A1
Woodlawn Sch NE25.....**31** D3
Woodlea
  Longbenton NE12..........**29** D1
  Newbeggin-by-the-Sea NE64..**7** E5
Wood Lea DH5............**95** A7
Woodlea Cl DH5..........**95** A4
Woodlea Cres NE46......**45** C4
Woodlea Ct NE29.........**41** E3
Woodlea Gdns NE3........**38** B6
Woodlea Prim Sch DH4...**89** E1
Woodlea Rd NE39.........**67** B2
Woodlea Sq NE29.........**41** E3
Woodleigh Rd NE25......**31** E4
Woodleigh View NE5.....**37** E3
Woodman Cl NE61.........**8** E7
Woodman Rd NE63........**6** E4
Woodman St NE28........**41** B3
Woodmans Way NE16.....**68** F4
Woodpack Ave NE16.....**68** F6
Woods Gn NE10..........**57** C1

Woodside
  Bedlington NE22...........**11** C1
  Blyth NE24...............**17** F6
  Hexham NE46..............**45** D4
  Morpeth NE61..............**8** D7
  Ponteland NE20...........**25** C2
  Prudhoe NE42.............**50** F2
  Sunderland, East Herrington
    SR3..................**91** C6
  Sunderland SR2..........**102** C1
Woodside Ave
  Corbridge NE45...........**47** B6
  Newcastle upon Tyne NE6...**57** B7
  Seaton Delaval NE25......**23** D2
  Throckley NE15...........**35** E2
Woodside Cl
  Monkton NE32.............**58** A4
  Ryton NE40...............**52** C5
Woodside Cres NE12......**39** E8
Woodside Ct NE12........**39** E8
Woodside Gdns NE11......**69** F7
Woodside Gr
  Sunderland SR3...........**91** C6
  Tantobie DH9.............**79** C3
Woodside La
  Greenside NE40...........**52** B3
  Ryton NE40...............**52** B5
Woodside Rd NE40.......**52** B5
Woodside Terr
  Chopwell NE17............**77** RR
  Sunderland SR3...........**91** C6
Woodside Villas NE46....**45** D4
Woodside Way
  Ryton NE40...............**52** C5
  South Shields NE33.......**59** B7
Woodside Wlk NE39.......**67** C1
Wood St
  Burnopfield NE16.........**79** A6
  Dunston NE11.............**69** F8
  Sunderland SR4..........**102** A3
Woods Terr NE8.........**101** C1
Woodstock Ave SR2......**86** E2
Woodstock Rd
  Gateshead NE8............**71** B2
  Newcastle upon Tyne NE15.**54** A4
Woodstock Way NE35....**73** E7
Woodstone Terr DH4.....**89** D1
WOODSTONE VILLAGE...**89** D1
Wood Terr
  Gateshead NE10...........**57** B2
  High Spen NE39...........**67** A2
  Jarrow NE32..............**58** A4
  South Shields NE33.......**59** D8
  4 Washington NE37.......**83** D8
Woodthorne Rd NE2......**38** E3
Woodvale NE20..........**25** C2
Woodvale Dr NE31........**57** C4
Woodvale Gdns
  Gateshead NE9............**71** C6
  Newcastle upon Tyne NE15.**53** E7
  Wylam NE41...............**51** B6
Woodvale Rd
  Blaydon NE21.............**53** D2
  Killingworth NE12........**29** C4
Woodville Cres SR4......**85** E4
Woodville Ct SR4........**85** E4
Woodville Rd NE15.......**53** D8
Woodwynd NE10..........**71** F6
Wooler Ave NE29.........**41** D4

Wooler Cres NE8........**70** C8
Wooler Gn NE15.........**53** B7
Wooler Sq
  Sunderland SR2...........**86** E3
  Wideopen NE13............**28** C7
Woolerton Dr
  Gateshead N10, NE9.......**71** C6
  Gateshead NE9............**71** B6
  Newcastle upon Tyne NE15.**53** E7
Wooler Wlk NE32........**58** A4
Wooley St NE28.........**40** B1
Woolmer Ct NE7.........**39** E3
WOOLSINGTON...........**36** E8
Woolsington Ct NE22....**10** F1
Woolsington Gdns NE13..**36** F8
Woolsington Park S NE13.**36** F8
Woolsington Rd NE29....**41** C7
Woolwich Cl SR5........**74** F4
Woolwich Rd SR5........**74** F4
Wooperton Gdns NE5....**54** C7
Worcester Gn NE8......**101** B2
Worcester St SR2.......**102** C1
Worcester Terr SR2.....**102** C2
Worcester Way NE13....**28** C5
Wordsworth Ave
  Blyth NE24...............**17** C6
  Easington Lane DH5.......**97** D8
  Hebburn NE31.............**57** E6
  Whickham NE16............**69** B8
Wordsworth Avenue E
  DH5....................**94** E7
Wordsworth Avenue W
  DH5....................**94** E7
Wordsworth Cl NE46.....**45** A6
Wordsworth Cres NE9....**71** F1
Wordsworth St NE8......**56** A2
Worley Ave NE4.........**70** F4
Worley Cl NE4..........**98** B1
Worley Mews NE9........**70** F4
Worley St NE4..........**98** B1
Worley Terr DH9........**79** A1
Worm Hill Terr NE38....**83** E1
Worsdell St NE8........**101** B3
Worsdell St NE24........**12** E1
Worset La NE28.........**39** F4
Worswick St NE1........**99** B1
Worthing Cl NE28.......**39** F3
Worthington Ct NE2.....**99** C4
Wouldhave Ct NE33......**42** E3
Wouldhave St NE33......**42** E3
Wraith Terr SR2.........**92** E6
Wraysbury Ct NE3.......**37** D7
Wreay Wlk NE23.........**22** C3
Wreigh St NE31.........**57** D6
Wreken Gdns NE10.......**72** C8
WREKENTON............**71** C3
Wrekenton Row NE9.....**71** C2
Wrekenton Sta NE9......**71** D2
Wren Cl NE38...........**83** A3
Wren Gr **1** SR5........**74** C1
Wretham Pl NE2.........**99** C2
Wright Dr NE23.........**29** A7
Wrightson St NE23......**16** B3
Wright St NE24.........**17** D8
Wright Terr DH4........**90** A5
Wroxham Ct
  Newcastle upon Tyne NE5..**37** B4
  Sunderland SR2...........**86** E2
Wroxton NE38...........**83** C3

Wuppertal Ct NE32......**58** B6
Wychcroft Way NE5......**37** C2
Wych Elm Cl NE61........**1** D4
Wych Elm Cres NE7......**39** C3
Wycliffe Ave NE3........**37** F3
Wycliffe Rd SR4.........**85** F4
Wydon Pk NE46..........**45** A3
Wyedale Way NE6........**57** A7
Wye Ave NE32...........**58** C3
Wye Rd NE31............**57** E3
WYLAM.................**51** B6
Wylam Ave NE25.........**23** F2
Wylam Cl
  South Shields NE34.......**59** E5
  Washington NE37..........**72** E1
Wylam Fst Sch NE41.....**51** B6
Wylam Gdns NE28........**40** F4
Wylam Gr SR1..........**103** B2
Wylam Haughs Nature
  Reserve* NE41...........**51** A5
Wylam Mill NE41........**51** B6
Wylam Rd NE29..........**41** F3
Wylam St NE32..........**58** B7
Wylam Sta NE41.........**51** C5
Wylam View NE21.......**53** B2
Wynbury Rd NE9.........**71** A5
Wyncote Ct NE7.........**39** B2
Wynde The
  Ponteland NE20...........**25** D4
  South Shields NE34.......**59** D5
Wyndfall Way NE3.......**38** A3
Wyndham Ave NE3........**37** F3
Wyndham Prim Sch NE3..**38** A3
Wyndham Way NE29......**41** B8
Wynding The
  Annitsford NE23..........**22** B1
  Bedlington NE22..........**10** E1
Wyndley Cl NE16........**68** F5
Wyndley Ho NE3.........**37** F3
Wyndley Pl NE3.........**37** F3
Wyndrow Pl NE3.........**37** F3
Wyndsail Pl NE3.........**38** A3
Wynd The
  Longbenton NE12..........**29** F1
  Newcastle upon Tyne NE3..**38** A4
  Throckley NE15...........**35** D1
  Tynemouth NE30...........**42** A8
Wyndtop Pl NE3.........**38** A3
Wyndward Pl NE3........**38** A3
Wyndways Dr DH9........**78** E1
Wynn Gdns NE10.........**56** F1
Wynyard DH2............**88** A3
Wynyard Gdns NE9.......**71** C2
Wynyard Sq SR2.........**86** E2
Wynyard St
  Dunston NE11.............**69** F8
  Fence Houses DH4........**94** A8
  New Silksworth SR3.......**92** A7
Wythburn Pl NE9........**71** B4
Wyvern Sq SR2..........**86** E2

Y

Yardley Gr NE23........**22** A8
Yarmouth Dr NE23.......**22** A8
Yatesbury Ave NE5......**37** B3

Yeadon Ct NE3..........**37** C7
Yeavering Cl NE3........**38** B4
Yeldon Cl SR2...........**92** F5
Yellow Leas Farm NE36..**74** C7
Yelverton Cres NE6......**56** F3
Yelverton Ct NE23.......**22** A8
Yemeni Sch The NE33....**42** B1
Yeoman St NE29.........**42** B5
Yeovil Ct NE23..........**22** A8
Yetholm Ave DH2........**88** B2
Yetholm Pl NE5.........**37** A4
Yetholm Rd NE8.........**100** B1
Yetlington Dr NE3.......**38** A4
Yewburn Way NE12.......**39** C6
Yewcroft Ave NE15......**54** A6
Yewdale Gdns NE9.......**71** A4
Yewtree Ave SR5........**74** F2
Yew Tree Dr NE22.......**10** F2
Yewtree Gdns NE6.......**40** A1
Yewtrees NE10..........**71** E5
Yewvale Rd NE5.........**37** D1
York Ave NE32..........**58** B3
York Cl
  Cramlington NE23.........**22** A8
  Gateshead NE8............**70** C7
York Cres DH5...........**94** F4
York Ct
  Chester le Street DH3.....**88** D1
  9 Wallsend NE28.........**40** B1
Yorkdale Pl NE6.........**57** A6
York Dr NE28............**40** B1
York Gr NE22............**10** D2
York Ho SR5............**74** A4
York Rd
  Birtley DH3..............**82** C1
  Whitley Bay NE26.........**32** B5
York St
  Blyth NE24...............**17** E8
  Gateshead NE10...........**57** A1
  Hetton-le-Hole DH5.......**94** E1
  Jarrow NE32..............**58** A6
  Newcastle upon Tyne NE4..**98** B1
  New Silksworth SR3.......**92** A8
  Sunderland SR1..........**103** A3
York Terr
  Chester le Street DH3.....**88** D1
  Gateshead NE10...........**71** D8
  7 North Shields NE29....**42** A5
York Way NE34..........**60** A6
Yorkwood NE31..........**57** C7
Younghall Cl NE40.......**52** A1
Young Rd NE12..........**29** F1

Z

Zetland Dr NE25.........**31** F2
Zetland Sq **9** SR6......**75** E1
Zetland St SR6..........**75** E1
Zion St SR1............**103** B3
Zion Terr
  Blaydon NE21.............**53** B2
  Sunderland SR5...........**75** C3